Retail Management
TEXT AND CASES

Retail Management
TEXT AND CASES

U.C. Mathur
Director MDP
Integrated Academy of Management and Technology
Ghaziabad

ISBN: 978-93-89307-43-6

Edition: 2019

Printed at: Rekha Printers

Preface

In India and perhaps in the entire world, at least the next decade is going to belong to the Retail Management. With steady growth of surplus funds with middle and upper-class people, the habit of going out for making purchases has become a regular pastime with the market segment belonging to the Consumer Group. Some enterprising businesspersons have anticipated the retail boom and opened their retail outlets pre-empting the increasing demand for such stores.

To be successful the retailers need to learn the areas, among others, that are of great significance for their business in the present scenario as given below:

1. Buying behaviour, customer and market focus
2. Brand selection, staying flexible and responsive to market needs
3. Mean Time Between Purchase(MTBP)—depends on products, package sizes and economic level of the customers of the target market segment
4. Need to hold on to valuable professionals at all levels
5. Optimizing use of time

As the competition is intensifying information about customers' needs, competitor's capabilities, and the strengths of company's products and brand and services are essential and critical to retail company's success.

Market information takes a route to reach the decision-makers. It starts from the field salesperson's level and through the hierarchy goes to the top with unnecessary filters diluting the same. At times the relevant information does not reach the decision-makers as the field salespersons have rare access to the top management. It appears that the hierarchy is meant only to prevent the information flow to the top. The filters along the route create waste paper baskets to dump the information without realizing the importance it might have for the top decision-makers.

The best way, therefore is to make people at each level responsible for making strategy as then the companies can get out of the top management myopic syndrome where everything gets tuned and fine-tuned by them.

Flexibility of operations would provide sustainable competitive advantage to the retail outlets. With it the company can take full advantage of the market information gathered by the field salespersons. Since the strategic implementation has to be carried out at each level, its formulation at each level would make the field force participant in strategic formulation and its implementation. The workforce becomes more knowledgeable, loyal and committed to the company's goals.

Retailers have to realize that their major asset is the intellectual capital in the form of the valuable personnel. The new generation of knowledge workers want more control of their work lives and more say in company's operational plans. The knowledge workers are going to help build the company's competitive advantage and therefore must be cherished and motivated whenever possible.

Competitive advantage comes from dedicated approach to time management as with local field persons take crucial decisions on customer complaints, promotion plans without the approval of the top management the time factor helps in gaining customer approval and brand acceptance creating customer loyalty in the shortest possible time.

Townsfolks have been depending on the neighbourhood retailers for the daily needs. In the last five years, the entire retail business has undergone major metamorphosis with these retail shops facing competition from super marts, shopping malls which have sprung up like mushrooms in metro cities and they are seeping into the small towns with gusto and audacious thrust as they look at the proven success of such businesses in the metro cities. Some enterprising businesspersons have gone deep into the buyer psychology to provide the right ambience for a family outing rather than just a solo purchase mission. The next step for start of mega malls appears to be a natural corollary in the rural or semi-urban markets.

Middle-class Indians have been enjoying shopping expeditions for generations. Today, they plan outings not just for shopping but also for a movie and a meal with the family. The shopping malls/complexes have been designed to cater to these expeditions as the malls attract the customer through sheer magnitude of the visit experience. Retail management is going to get a boost in the business with international players joining hands with Indian counterparts to establish retail businesses here. These new business deals would bring about dramatic and yet more customer-friendly changes in the retail trade.

Some of the more important aspects of retail business are given below:

1. Purchasing: A good stock of saleable merchandise is a big plus factor for the retailers as it ensures that the customers will rarely go disappointed, without making purchases.
2. Merchandising and visual merchandising: The products need to be purchased correctly and to be on proper display to attract attention of the buyers who are, in many cases going to make impulse purchases of items they may not be needing at the time. Special offers, promotional programmes add that extra purchase incentive to the buyers.
3. Children's corner including a crèche: The retailers have realized the importance of making shopping not only a comfortable task but also make it a delightful experience. Family with small children finds a well laid out crèche an ideal place to keep their children for their safety and well-being as it goes shop hunting.
4. Movie halls: Going to movies is a regular pastime of the shoppers and when the well-groomed movie halls are located in the malls, it becomes an easy task to give in to the temptation to see a movie.

5. Food plazas and eateries: Families, couples, people going on dates find the eating joints exclusive, of high standard and yet within their budget. At times couples just sit and chat in the air-conditioned ambience of the malls without having to spend a rupee. As these couples become familiar with the malls they select these malls for shopping as well.
6. Live music, dance shows on special occasions: The malls organize such shows that attract large crowds and then it is left to the different shopkeepers to entice them into buying their wares.
7. Gaming stalls hold special attraction for the young at heart who love spending time and money there.
8. Festival programmes: Special interior decorations, promotion programmes and live performances are the highlights of malls celebrating Christmas, Deepawali, Durga Pooja, Eid and the like.
9. Discount stores: Such shops thrive on volume business as they offer low price of standard products, including exchange offers. They keep a limited variety of goods and have an eye on budget buyers, who accept even slightly odd products for low prices.
10. Easy travel, car parking, valet parking: These add to customer's comfort and are good for the entire shopping mall.
11. Point of purchase (PoP) advertising: The PoP advertising in such malls is designed to focus the customer's eyes on the products on display.
12. Interior decorations: Attractive interiors help in getting the customers inside the shops who otherwise were doing window-shopping only. Once inside the shop salespersons use all their expertise to sell at least something to the visitor.
13. Window displays: These form part of interiors of shops and create an urge to step in at least to have a better view of the window displays.
14. Banners and signage: These form the guide-factors for leading the buyers without actually pushing them.
15. Ingress and egress: Ease of entry and exit are essential elements of success of any retail outlet.

The book inter alia, covers these important aspects of retail business.

Certain products like medicines, automobiles, petrol, tyres and confectionary are sold through retail stores that are exclusively devoted to these products. India has witnessed in the last sixty years or more two major companies having their "company owned" retail outlets, Usha and Bata. Usha started retailing its own fans and sewing machines in their exclusive retail shops. Bata too put up a large number of shoe outlets all over the country for sale of their shoes. It was only after decades of having near monopoly situation in their product range that only in the last twenty years or so these companies thought of diversifying into related products. Usha started selling a large range of consumer durables, by making them or by just buying and selling to make optimum use of their prime location shops. Bata too has a range of personal wear materials like T-shirts, cardigans, tracksuits and their sales have strong synergy with sale of shoes. These companies realised that their shops all over were gold mines with a regular customer group coming to buy their main products.

Bata and Usha are classical examples of planning long-term customer brand recall, getting improved brand equity through standard merchandising practices. The shop outer looks; their façade and their interiors have been designed with such expertise and precision that the brand identity becomes obviously clear once one or more signs appear before the customers. The exteriors and interiors of shops are full of such signage. These companies have started selling other brands including international ones but their main focus remains on their own brands.

Retail management has become a multifaceted discipline with a large variety of products being retailed and a host of retail channels available for doing the same. The book attempts to converge on the basic nuances that integrate these disciplines as the student learns the retail business with live wire real-life examples and interactive sessions as well as selected corporate case studies. A class tested management game has been included in the book that starts from the end of the first chapter and runs through the entire book. The game is expected to motivate the students in learning the finer nuances of retail management through practical sessions.

I wish to place on record my thanks and gratitude to the publisher and to Ms. Punam Dayal, Mr. Sanjoy Mathur and Mr. Pankaj Mathur.

U. C. Mathur

Contents

CHAPTER

1

Introduction

Aims

Retail management has really come of age in the last decade of 20th century. Retail shops have grown from being mere storage depots of the first half of 20th century to the chain of supermarkets of today. In rural India there is usually a grocery shop, which sells a variety of products. The chapter introduces the vital aspects of retail management.

Outcomes

The students would learn the basic retail systems and understand their value in the context of retail thrust coming at staggering speed in the world.

India has a vibrant retail market, more especially in the organized sector that promises to reach 450 billion dollars in 2015, five years hence. The buoyancy in retail brings with it, besides opportunities, challenges for the retail trade. New development, innovations are going to be the key success areas. The demand pattern of retail buyers is too undergoing a sea change with the burgeoning consumer group and economic all-round growth of the country.

Businesses have to consider how they can leapfrog 20th century growth models and build sustainable social and economic growth in the Indian consumer markets, where new consumers are aspiring to lifestyles that are 10 times more resource intensive than the current average? It was suggested that diversification of product range, creation of value chain as per the consumer needs, and enhancement of communication with consumers, are possible ingredients of growing consumer markets in India. The need of developing the supply chain in general, and the cold chain in particular, together with improvement in agricultural efficiency and linkages to local markets are the key engines of growing consumer markets.

Indian consumer is highly ambitious. The major challenge before the retailers, therefore, is to match or change the expectations of the consumers with heavy promotional plans.

During recession the retailers could take two different approaches to deal with it in their home markets. They would switch their investments to emerging markets for growth or they could withdraw from the international markets where they are not doing well and bring back management to the home market.

It is believed that in the manufacturing sector the flow of information is one way, in retail it flows both ways. There has to be a sort of synergy between the home markets and the new markets. Often the innovations in the secondary markets are adopted in the home markets for efficiency of operations. During the last few years, there has been an increased sharing of market knowledge between two secondary markets. For example, innovations in retail in China have been adopted by the same retailer in the Japanese market without going through the home market in UK. The internationalization also has led to flexibility of operations in different markets. The retailers are no longer standardizing everything. There is localization of store, produce and suppliers. Systems and management operations are standardized. Retail formats of the general merchandise retailer have done well in the international markets.

It can be said without fear of contradiction that retailing has come of age in India. Retail industry is considered one of the fastest growing industries in world. According to ASSOCHEM the estimated growth of retail sector is 8% per annum and for organized retail it is 40% per annum. India is considered one of the most attractive retail destinations from amongst 30 emerging markets. India's vast middle class consumer and its almost untapped retail needs are main attractions for global retail giants wanting to enter newer markets. India's total retail market is valued at Rs. 912 crore, which is expected to grow at a rate of 30 per cent over the next five years. At present retail industry contributes 14 per cent to the Gross Domestic Product (GDP). It employs nearly 7 per cent of the total workforce which means 42 million (4.2 crore) people. Retail business is definitely one with immense growth potential from the Indian economy viewpoint.

When goods are sold directly to the consumer or the user for personal use or for their family it is retail selling. Purchase of cars, petrol, and food at restaurants are part of retail sales. Big Bazaar, Subhiksha are competing for the urban buyer's money by proclaiming as the "lowest price" sellers in retail. With the advent of international players entering the retail market more such claimants will come to the market making it even more interesting and profitable for the customers.

Retailers have been in existence for generations and yet the severity of competition today calls for carefully planned strategies, both long term and short term, besides the ability to change with the times to be a continuous success in retail field. The three models in retail have succeeded, one is the hyper-mart model, second is the convenience store format. The third model that has done well is the specialist retail model which largely involves retailers like Zara, Mango, H&M.

While China is an exciting market for international retailers, India too has become important. India has been a little bit protected from this new trend. Much of the retail here is home grown. International retailers might make their presence felt in the next decade. One of the main consequences of this international retail spread would be the development of agriculture and supply chains. Those who are working with international retailers are expected to have different relationships. The retailer's bring their own quality and standards to the new market which again have implications on restructuring of supply chain.

In India for decades retail has been stagnant with organized retail amounting to little more than a supermarket. That is starting to change as retail chains employ technology to deliver a smoother shopping experience. Take, for instance, the shopping carts with scanners that Shoppers Stop claims to have deployed. These let shoppers scan the goods they are purchasing before they reach the counter, saving time.

There are other such innovations being tested abroad and rest assured that they will land up in India, sooner rather than later. One such idea is Veggie Vision, a gadget from IBM that identifies fruit and vegetables using a camera doing away with the need to punch in a numeric code while weighing the produce. Something like this could let shoppers weigh their purchases on their own without waiting for shop floor assistants to do the needful. IBM also has the Everywhere Display, a sales tool that converts any old surface in a store into an interactive display.

One area where stores even in India have caught up with the technological curve is in surveillance. CCTV cameras are a fact of life at any chain store and these will eventually shift to IPcams as digitally storing and searching through recordings is a lot easier than hunting for the right tape.

At the back-end there's a significant presence of IT in Indian retail—be it CRM for loyalty programmes and personalized service or ERP to run a retail chain's operations.

There's a lot more that technology can contribute to making shopping a pleasurable experience and by encouraging shoppers to spend more and come back, boost the bottom line. It's all beginning now. CRM has got a big vote even in the retail market as retailers are into telemarketing, competitive games, scratch cards for gifts. With increased competition they are realizing that innovation in promotion is the name of the success in retail game.

Retailing in India is up for transition. It has broken the safe and claustrophobic space and rearing to grow into a giant that is already matching the retailing practices of the west.

For example, K. Raheja Corp are the pioneers in organized retail by taking a first giant step to successfully establish a retail store know as "Shopper's Stop". The group is expanding its retail chains across the country on the back of the vast experience it gathered from feedbacks and keen observance of people's taste keeping in tune with its culture, customs, traditions and income. Crossword, Inorbit Mall & Hyper City have set new benchmarks on the basis of information and adaptation of worldwide changes, innovations and new techniques in retailing practices.

Retail trade is having a major impact on the country's economy as can be seen in the next paragraph. Besides, retail offers career opportunities as never existed before. In the USA retail is almost one-third of the total economy. Manufacturers have understood the importance of retailing, as it is the last link in the distribution chain between them and the consumer. While the manufacturers want to promote their own brand the retailer keeps a large number of brands that helps in satisfying the needs of a large variety of customers with different brand needs. Distribution chain or channel, in its simplest form is given below:

Manufacturer – –> Distributor – – – –> Retailer – – – – –> Final customer

The retail industry is divided into organized and unorganized sectors. Indian organized sector was accounting for just 2 per cent of the trade in the last century but now the situation has changed a great deal. As per figures available from ASSOCHEM it could well be around 7 per cent of the trade, growing at the rate of 38% annually as per the Indian Retail Report of 2007. Retail employs more than a million people today. Unorganized retailing refers to the traditional formats of low-cost retailing such as the local kirana shops, owner-manned general stores, paan shops, convenience stores, handcart and pavement vendors, and employs about 40 million people. This sector is highly fragmented, with about 110 lakh outlets in the country.

As per the market figures, the organized sector is expected to grow from seven per cent of 2008 to twelve per cent by 2010. With the rise in consumer demand, high disposable incomes and increased awareness levels, the retail industry is undergoing a major transition. Various functional aspects of retailing industry are given below:

Retail Visual Merchandising & Category Management—a visual merchandiser's job is to ensure that the shop looks attractive with neat display of the product on sale.

Category Management: Its task is to concentrate on one product category like soap and develop the entire sales strategy for the entire brand range of soaps.

- Entertainment
- Retail Selling & Customer Service Management
- Store Operations
- HRM
- Logistics and Supply Chain Management
- Inventory management
- Pricing
- Visual Displays, Merchandising & Store Design
- Retail Marketing & Customer Management
- In-house shop entertainment, advertising POP.
- Some of the major players in the industry are:
- Usha shops
- Bata shops
- Shoppers Stop
- Westside stores
- Subhiksha
- Globus
- Planet M
- Titan
- Madura Garments
- Pantaloon's Big Bazaar and Food Bazaar

- Spencers and FoodWorld, and Metro Cash & Carry
- Ninety-nine rupee shops
- Besides, a large number of international and national players are planning to start operations in the country, like Wal-Mart in collaboration with the Indian telecom giant the Bharti group.

Retail Ethics

In India retailers are fast realizing the importance of the following ethical issues that normally confront them:

- Employing child labour
- Wage disparity between genders
- Unsafe working conditions
- Correct pricing
- Inflating prices before announcing SALE

Controllable variables that retailers have:

- Number of counters and people manning them
- Point of purchase advertising
- Retail prices, MRPs and bulk purchase discounts
- Sales promotions with or without manufacturers support, seasonal or normal
- Number of products and their brands, with brand inventories

Other variables like taxes, road traffic parking area are not in their control.

Retail Manpower Planning

It requires study of skills required for people of different work areas. A number of existing business schools have started training programmes in Retail Management, while some retail majors are starting their own training establishments like the Essel Group. Pantaloons, a major retail chain and Bharti (along with Wal-Mart of USA) are tying up with Business Schools for starting retail training programmes.

Indian population is undergoing major changes in its demographics. A large young working population, nuclear families in urban areas, along with increasing working women population and opportunities in the services sector are going to be the key drivers of the organized retail sector in India. And these would need a large number of persons trained in specialized skills to run these organizations as given below:

- Strategic retail management—strategising like brand selection pricing, targeting and positioning, marketing and site selection.
- Merchandise management—Vendor selection, inventory management, pricing.
- Store management—Layout, merchandising and display, customer relationship, and inventory management.
- Management—Administration, Human resources, finance, marketing.

Retail-counter service or self-service are the two options that the retailers can have, depending on the store area and the product range. In controlled drugs where medicines are sold on prescription only counter sales are possible. Service at the retail outlet makes the major difference in customer satisfaction and customer delight. The retailers must be proud of their merchandise, must deliver what they promise including and especially during their promotional phase, value their customers and their time without any discrimination and do convey their thanks to the customers for patronizing the shop.

Retailing today has become a pyramid industry and is not just restricted to malls, as most urbanites tend to believe. The industry offers ample opportunity and has room for everyone starting from entry level to senior management level in its present growth scenario.

While retailing provides employment to the largest section of the population across most industrialized nations, it is also an industry that promises a profitable growth path. The boom in the retail industry has brought with it many employment opportunities in this area. People with varied skills and talents are required in this fast emerging industry. A career in retailing is considered a challenging option with growth potential as can be seen from the following:

Service and Sales Positions

1. Salesperson like counter handler
2. Cashier-cum-salesperson
3. Store supervisor
4. Material handler, tester for quality, stocking, inventory manager.

These persons handle customers, get the sales, revenue, profits.

The sales-related retail career area includes positions like salesperson, cashier, store stock supervisor, and stock taker/receiver. These frontline positions bring retail's core business of serving the customer and generating sales. The obsession for working with a variety of people, flexibility in mindset, level-headedness, problem solving ability, and teamwork are critical for success in this area. These positions are typically entry points into retail careers. Commission-based sales areas like jewellery, appliances, are preferred sales jobs. Frontline sales experience is valued and many retailers promote from within.

Store Management

Retail professionals in the store operations career area cover overall store operations and profits. They include Head of Store Operations, Regional Manager, and District Manager, and responsibilities in this area may include functions like loss prevention and human resources.

The store manager and his team has responsibilities ranging from departmental to overall establishment. Managers at all levels supervise and assist sales and other employees. Additional responsibilities, depending upon store/company size and management level include opening and closing the store, staffing, administration, and financial functions. Promotions to management positions can be earned through experience, and the right qualifications like an MBA degree may afford direct entry to management.

Marketing and Advertising

Marketing functions may be centralized in one department, divided into different departments (like advertising, sales promotion, art and visual merchandising, and public relations), or group in various combinations. Marketing also conducts marketing research functions like focus groups and statistical analysis of customer buying patterns to develop strategies and plans that guide marketing components like stock quantities, ads, websites, store signage.

Supply Chain Management, Logistics and Distribution

This retail career area overseas movement and storage of saleable products. Responsibilities include management and facilitation of distribution centres, logistics, traffic management, trucking and other transportation operations, and may include import/export shipping and related duties.

Purchase Planning

Purchase professionals select the merchandise to be sold in the stores by sourcing vendors. They organize order follow-up, inventory flow through and allocation of merchandise to stores, attending to issues like flow quantities and timing. Statistical development and analysis are increasingly woven into this retail career area, where team members also coordinate gross margin planning and analysis responsibilities, develop distribution plans for merchandise categories and subclasses, and balance stock unit ratios by store on the basis of average sales in a given time frame.

E-Commerce and IT

Information Technology careers are numerous and varied in the retail industry. From web design to servers and network systems management, inventory systems and are growing in the retail industry. Since online retailing has become a reality in India even the real brick and mortar shops are making in roads into online retailing, like Big Bazaar is setting up Future Bazaar.

Financial and Accounting

Financial and accounting skills are equally important in retail as in other businesses; they offer career opportunities. The finance retail career area includes all accounting and treasury functions like accounting for income, paying expenses, compiling and maintaining financial records, money management and cash flow control, banking, investment, credit control, payment of the government taxes, audit and preparation of annual accounts and balance sheets.

Prevention of Losses

The loss prevention career area is responsible for safeguarding company assets and may include risk management issues, like customer and employee safety. Members of loss prevention teamwork together to prevent merchandise loss due to shoplifting, employee theft, paperwork errors, and vendor fraud. Physical security of store and company buildings is also a part of loss prevention.

HRM

Recruiting and hiring employees and responsibilities such as training, designing training programmes, overseeing compensation and benefits, and planning for and ensuring legal compliance in hiring and employment practices.

Entrepreneurship

The following qualities are essentially required in retail trade:

1. People skills
2. Zeal
3. Communication skills
4. Team spirit

The industry is set for a boom with the entry of big industrial corporations and international retailers making their entry into this sector. The industry constantly requires good, motivated personnel. It also promises a complete, enriching working experience with profitable inputs.

Definition of Retail as per the author

Retail comes from the French word *retaillier* which means "cutting off, chip and divide" in terms of tailoring (1365). It was first recorded as a noun with the meaning of a "sale in small quantities" in 1433.

Retailing is defined as to buy in larger quantities and sell on in smaller quantities. It is the sale of goods or merchandise, from a fixed location such as a departmental store or kiosk, in small or individual lots for direct consumption by the customer/purchaser or end-user. It arranges goods in their finished state to be sold to the customers who are prepared to pay for the pleasure of eating, wearing or experiencing particular product.

Retailing may include auxiliary services, such as packing and delivery. Purchasers may be individuals or businesses.

The term retailing applies not only to the selling of tangible product like loaves of bread or pairs of shoes, but also to the selling intangible service products. Companies who provide meals, haircuts sessions are all essentially retailers, as they sell to the final consumer, and yet customer does not take goods away from these retailers in a carrier bag. The consumption or use of the service product becomes the act of retailing.

Retail sales are mainly dependent on the following types of buyers:

- Impulse buyers, where the buyers respond to the stimulus provided by PoP, advertising or visual merchandising
- Regular purchasers, where buyers buy daily need products like food items or clothings. Buyers who plan save and then buy.
- Promotion assisted buyers, where sales promotion generates the desire in window shoppers to buy the products that are promoted.

Retail strategy is developed in the following sequence:

1. Defining retail business: full service, self-service, solo brand or multiple brand
2. Location, home delivery, e-business
3. Store's own brand image
4. Sales, profit and market share plans
5. Consumer behaviour of the target segment customers
6. Pricing, inventory management and merchandising
7. Evaluation of performance on regular basis

Retailers buy goods in large quantities from manufacturers or importers, either directly or through a wholesaler, and then sell smaller quantities to the end-user. For example, a convenience store would buy tins of coke in units of two-dozen boxes, but sell as single tin. However, a retailer is not the only business entity to **'break bulk'**. A wholesaler also buys in larger quantities and sells on to their customers, mostly retailers, in smaller quantities. It is the type of customer, rather than the activity, that distinguishes a retailer from other distributive traders; a retailer sells to final consumers, unlike a wholesaler who sells on to a retailer or other business organization.

A retail shop is an establishment that is engaged in selling merchandise to buyers for personal or household consumption and in rendering services required for the sale of goods.

There are, however, many businesses that carry out retailing activity that are not in themselves strictly classified as retailers; for example, a factory may engage in retailing activity by selling 'second'-quality goods in the shop attached to its manufacturing premises.

In UK a retailer is only classified as such for government reporting if the business gains over half of its income from selling to the final consumer.

Retail establishments are often called shops or stores. Retailers are at the end of the supply chain or the distribution channel. Manufacturers see the process of retailing as a part of their overall distribution strategy.

> **Retail trade or marketing:** It is also defined as "The sales made through a business location usually a store, in which the principal activity is the sale of merchandise and related services to the general public, for household or personal consumption".

An Overview of the Retailing Business

The pricing technique used by most retailers is cost plus pricing. This involves adding a mark up amount or a percentage to the retailers' cost. Another technique is retail pricing, which involves charging the amount suggested by the manufacturer and usually printed on the product by the manufacturer as Maximum Retail Price–the MRP.

There are three major types of retailing as given below:

- First is the **market**, a physical location where buyers and sellers converge. Usually this is located on town squares, sidewalks or designated streets and may involve the construction of temporary structures as market stalls.
- Second is **shop or store trading**. Some shops use counter-service, where goods are out of reach of buyers and must be obtained from seller. This type of retail is common for small expensive items, e.g. jewellery, and other controlled items like medicine and liquor. Self-service, where goods may be handled and examined prior to purchase, has become more common.
- Third form of retail is **virtual retail,** where products are purchased via mail, telephone or online without having been examined physically but seen in a catalogue, on television or on a website.
- Building for retail has changed considerably over time. From market halls in the middle ages, which were essentially just covered marketplaces to the departmental stores of 19th century, which were a street of several different shops, roofed over. One of the novelties of the departmental store was the introduction of fixed prices, making haggling unnecessary, and browsing more enjoyable. This is commonly considered the birth of consumerism. In cities, these were multi-storey buildings, which pioneered the escalator.

In the 1920s the first supermarket opened in the United States, starting a new era of retail including self-service. Around the same time the first shopping mall was constructed which incorporated elements from both the shop-rows and the departmental store. A mall consists of several departmental stores linked by arcades (many of whose shops are owned by the same firm under different names). All the stores rent their space from the mall owner. By mid-century, most of these were being developed as single enclosed, climate-controlled, projects in semi-urban and urban areas. The malls have had a considerable impact on the retail structure and urban development.

In addition to enclosed malls, there are also open malls, and in Britain they are called retail parks. These are often connected to supermarket stores. Also in high traffic areas, other businesses may lease space from the supermarket or store to sell their goods or services. A recent development is a very large shop called a superstore. These are sometimes located as stand-alone outlets, but more commonly are part of open mall or Retail Park.

Local shops known as Kirana shops in India and as brick and mortar stores in the United States. Many shops are part of a chain: a number of similar shops with the same ownership, name, selling the same products in different locations like Subhiksha chain. One company may own the shops, or there may be a company that has franchising agreements with the shop owners, including restaurant chains.

Some shops sell second-hand goods. Often the public can also sell goods to such shops, sometimes called "pawn" shops. In India jewellery and at times furniture is sold in these shops. In other cases, especially in the case of a non-profit shop, the public donates goods to the shop to be sold. There are also consignment shops, where a person can place an item in a store, and if it sells the person gives the shop owner a percentage of the sale price. The advantage of selling an item this way is that the established shop gives the item exposure to more potential buyers.

The term retailer is also applied where a service provider services the need of a large number of individuals, such as with a telephone or electric power.

Retailer and E-tailing

The word E-tailing is derived from Internet retailing or electronic retailing. E-tailing is emerging as an attractive alternative to the traditional kirana or brick-and-mortar retailing. Chances are that they will coexist profitably. Sometimes, a key question arises i.e. to retail or to e-tail?

Retailing as an attractive business was slowly emerging out of the shadows. Quite a few corporate houses began looking at retailing as one way to corporate salvation. Notable among them are: the R.P. Goenka Group, the Tatas, the S. Kumars, the Raheja group and the Piramal Group. And many more are still in the process of finalizing their forays into retailing. Even as loose ends of retailing plans are being tied up, e-tailing has begun catching the attention of many entrepreneurs. Suddenly, buyers started hearing e-tailing names such as Rediff.com, Jaldi.com, Fabmart.com, Tsnshop.com and Satyamonline.com. This could well be the beginning of an e-tail revolution. How large is the retailing industry? Is e-tailing large enough to take on so many players? e-tailing are still new and growing. One estimate is that the organized retailing sector should be as large as Rs. 5,000 crore and e-tailing in India should be just about Rs. 12 crore. The growth potential for both retailing and e-tailing is tremendous.

However, while detailing of retailing and e-tailing, the differences in the way business is conducted in both the areas becomes clear as given below:

While a retailer is confined to his shop or at best as a home delivery vendor, to his locality, the e-tailer can target large areas, practically the whole world. E-tailer does not require any physical real estate, which is a must for a retailer and which can account for upto fifty per cent of retail initial investment. E-tailer has to make attractive websites to convert prospective browsers into buyers, while the retailer, as the last point of distribution chain has to ensure that the visiting propective customers goes back happy after making a purchase. E-tailer has to spend huge amount on advertising to lure the prospects to its website and customer retention takes major efforts in time and money, which more than offsets the benefits gained in real estate and inventory. Retailer needs to furnish his shop, stock it with saleable brands and maintain proper inventory. Displays of product wares, visual merchandising play an important part in retailers' selling efforts. Retailers can use CRM to make strong customer loyalty while e-tailers have little leaverage in that direction and retention is an expensive task. E-tailers can offer a large variety of goods counting upto millions as no physical stocks are needed at low prices as they do not have major overheads. Stockouts in e-tailing is not possible. The despatch of orders takes place from godowns or at times from their suppliers' place directly. Retailers can carry limited stocks may be upto about

10,000 vareities only. This is normally as per the needs of the target segment. Net offers easy and comfortably obtained information as a major advantage that shopping on the Net offers. In the retail shops valuable time is lost. Shopping on the Internet for 15 minutes, could save a two-hour trip to the mall. Traditional retailing in contrast has the consumer searching, running up and down, grilling a poorly trained store assistant who is unable to help him out. In the bargain, time is lost. Consumers prefer to save time so that they can devote more time for their professional and domestic activities. However, the opportunities for personal attention available to the retail client are much more than those enjoyed by the Internet buyers.

After all that advertising spending, will the customer remain loyal to the e-tailing site? The Internet customer's buying behaviour is hard to predict and is different from the normal customer. Retaining him is not so simple. While a retailer can expect strong loyalty, such a loyalty on the Net is difficult to obtain. A customer may shift from the Internet if someone else offers him a better deal, could be to a better e-tailing site or even to a regular brick and mortar shop.

A case in point is Jaldi.com which will be using a mix of marketing tools such as public relations, advertising, promotions, direct marketing and Internet advertising to spread awareness among its target audience. Jaldi.com has gone a step ahead. Its offline promotions started with a successful consumer launch held at Priya PVR theatre in New Delhi where 3,600 free *Phir Bhi Dil Hai Hindustani* tickets were given to every customer who logged on and registered at the site Jaldi.com.

Customer retention is the toughest thing on the web. It is difficult to get a consumer come to your site. After he comes in, the task is to retain him and get him frequently visit you. Once he is confident about you, he will use his credit card to make his purchases at your site. Hence, retaining an e-tail customer is certainly a costly affair. If you offer some free gifts, a customer may keep on coming to your site, with the expectation every time that there would be some freebies out there. The moment you stop freebies, you could simply lose the customer and managing e-tailing promotion through freebies could be a self-defeating affair. The first time a person shops on the Net is always a special occasion. If anyone has to try this new medium of shopping, there should be overwhelming reasons for doing so. The benefits must go beyond mere convenience. For one, the consumer will certainly be interested if he gets things cheaper on the Net. The Net being a new medium, it has to convince people to use this new medium to buy. For convincing a customer to use the Internet one has to offer an incentive to buy on the Net. Otherwise, it would be very difficult to get a customer to shop. Therefore, easier and faster shopping are the reasons for shopping on the Net. On the other hand, as people love to go out for shopping getting a few things cheaper and easier is possible on a retail outlet, since their overheads are low as compared to e-tailers advertising expenses. One can go to a kirana or the 'stand-alone' retailer who could offer you 10,000 items in his store. Chances are that he might be out of stock. On the other hand, the Internet offers millions of products with no chances of an out-of-stock situation. Easy and comfortably-obtained information is another advantage that shopping on the Net offers. On the Internet, product information is just a few clicks away, all accessed in the comfort of a home. Simply put, shopping on the Internet for, say 15 minutes, could save a two-hour trip to the mall. Consumers who prefer to save time. However, the element of outdoor picnic is lost while the customers search the web.

The Indian scenario is quite different from that of the West. For good reasons, Indians have always been great shoppers and enjoy shopping anywhere in the world. The lady would love to feel the silk of the dress physically rather than by viewing it on the Internet. It would be only possible with a great deal of experience from the product purchase of the brand from normal stores that the buyers would venture to buy the same on the Net. There are hurdles in India for any successful e-tail project. Growth in e-tail will come not from well-designed websites or web-marketing only but also from deeper penetration of the Internet.

A case has been made out for increasing broadband Internet connections which are faster than the dial-up connections, as can be seen below:

One estimate is that India has some lakh Internet users, mostly concentrated in the metros. Web analysts feel that in many areas of retailing and commerce, Internet is unlikely to get a sizable slice of the market, for several years to come. This is true, especially in businesses where margins are thin. Consider fast moving consumer goods, the FMCG sector. In the Indian FMCG business, margins are as low as 10 per cent. Hence, e-tailing in such areas will catch on with growth of fast broadband connections on the Net.

Two, despite a higher Internet penetration, cities like Mumbai or New Delhi might not be haven for an e-tailer. For things like grocery, there is a shop at every nook and corner. All that an individual has to do is just make a phone call and the goods are delivered at his doorstep. Thrown in along with free home delivery is a month's credit. In case of perishables such as fruits and vegetables, the Indian buyers prefer them farm-fresh. While returning from work, they drop in at the vegetable market and complete their purchases.

Three, cheap labour. Thanks to easy availability of domestics at an affordable wage bill, quite a few of the rich customers hire them for doing domestic chores which include shopping. Indians have an aversion to use credit cards. Thanks to low penetration of credit cards and the lack of popularity of debit cards, e-tailing might find it an uphill task to catch on. Also elder citizens are averse to using even the computer. However, they are at ease while using the remote control of a television set. That brings up an interesting solution. Accessing the Internet through a television in the near future might be something that an individual should be offered if e-tailing is to grow faster.

An important hurdle to the growth of the e-tailing industry is the efficient management of logistics. Here the role of a courier company is extremely important. Most portals offering e-commerce have tied up with courier companies. Jaldi.com has tied up with Gati for taking care of their delivery logistics. There are other examples too. Blue Dart plans to enter the household shipment business in a big way to serve the needs of the online community in India. Blue Dart is targeting a 80 per cent annual jump in its business, mostly from the shipment requirements of its online customers. For this purpose, Blue Dart has already invested Rs. 40 crore to tune up its existing infrastructure and interface it with e-commerce potential. Blue Dart is upgrading its intranet facility, linking 1,300 terminals with over 2,000 people at 70 locations to meet the e-commerce requirements. This means that e-shoppers in these locations can log on to Bluedart.com and ask for the shipment of ordered goods from these e-shops. Also, Blue Dart has aligned with leading portals and e-shops like Rediff.com and Fabmart.com to meet their distribution needs. The kind of retailing model is going to deliver the goods in the India is the cost advantage of e-tailing comes from elimination of intermediaries and economical distribution. For example, book e-tailing means dispensing with big shops replete with slow-moving stock. Consider the case of Amazon.com, where the orders go straight to the wholesaler. That means the working capital costs are cut down drastically. Not just that, an e-tailer is paid before he pays his distributor and needs lower working capital. One has to compare these gains against certain Internet-related costs. Running a website and servicing it to ensure that it is reliable is not easy. Logistics and distribution are of importance and that is where many e-tailers are known to have gone wrong. Many e-tailers have been able to cut costs as they have lost large sums of money in the process of offering goods at low prices. A few of them who have made profits have ploughed them back for financing customer acquisition or retention.

Therefore, it can be seen that traditional retailing is not going to die. E-tailing will have to coexist with traditional retailing. For music and books, a whole new market will be created. This will increase the demand manifold. E-tailers will have to work in combination with traditional retailers. Even the known e-tailers in the business such as Amazon.com have realised this and are setting up distribution warehouses for the same.

As the combination of retailing and e-tailing set to deliver the goods, the trend of using the Internet as another service medium will gradually catch up. E-tailers like Jaldi.com have already set up kiosks in various cities which have been successful. Tsnshop.com makes use of its teleshopping network franchisees in various cities for selling its products. It helps in gaining customers fast as individuals have the option of returning the goods purchased if they do not like it. They can just go across to the shop. This gives them a certain level of comfort and confidence. Such a comfort and confidence-level is a must for a successful e-tailing venture.

What is being witnessed at the moment is certainly a tip of the iceberg. Such is the growth potential in the e-tailing industry that it is not possible to put a figure for the industry's size or growth. There are pluses and minuses in the case of retailing and e-tailing. With so many hurdles around for e-tailing, it would be sometime before e-tailing really catches up as the trend has begun. The model which will work in such an Indian context is a peaceful and complementary coexistence of retailing and e-tailing. The new technological capabilities, the Internet, makes possible huge shrinking in the cost of access to customers that brings an additional threat to retailers in the form of disintermediation. Disintermediation is the direct selling of goods by manufacturers to consumers avoiding retailers. For example, Compaq sold its computers through retailers, whereas Dell computers grew rapidly by selling online. Established store-based retailers begin to doubt their future as more business goes into direct online marketing. They fear, being disintermediated and losing out on retailing by the new e-tailers. While the prospect of disintermediation appears attractive, its implementation may be problematic for manufacturers. Majority of manufacturers are unwilling to sell online because of the nature of their product, and because of potential channel conflict. Disintermediation also requires heavy investment in the new channel that is unlikely to be profitable in the short term. The additional investment is not just in the Internet/electronic interface, but also requires infrastructural investments in the delivery of small orders. Such a strategy is risky as it assumes that a significant proportion of customers are prepared to switch channels, which may not be the case. But disintermediation was only the half story. Although some middlemen lost their business, new middlemen sprang up to supply Internet services to both businesses and consumers. Reintermediation took place on grand scale. As for the traditional 'physical store' firms-Compaq, dragged their feet hoping that the assault of "pure click" firms would falter or disappear. Then they started their own online sales channel, becoming "brick and click" competitors. They had to do this carefully in order to retain the loyalty of retailers, brokers, and agents. The irony is twofold. First, many brick-and-click competitors became stronger contenders than the pure-click firms, since they had a larger pool of resources to work with and well-established brand names. At the same time, many other pure-click dot-coms are surviving and even prospering in today's marketplace.

Retail Power

Earlier the producers of FMCG products, like Procter and Gamble, used to dominate their retailers, but the growing importance of mass distribution have transformed the power of retailers and now retailers tend to dominate the producers. Retailers can now choose among an ever increasing number of products. Producers compete in order to obtain the shelf space for their products, and in the process confer a stronger bargaining power to retailers, who can threaten to take their products away from their shelves to obtain more profitable retail conditions. Shelf space has become the bargaining power and manufacturers are offering cash incentives for better and more prominent shelf space at the retail outlets and even rentals for decent shelf space for their products.

The reasons for the development of retail power are given below:

- Sales of most grocery items, drugs, and merchandising chains, have not been increasing at rapid rates. As the retailers need to grow, they must take sales at par with their competitors rather than waiting for overall demand to expand. This has created enormous pressure on retailers to perform, given that most chains tend to carry the same products. The type of competition tends to be price oriented. In other words, better prices coupled with prime locations, appealing stores, top-rate service have been the major routes to survival and success in this area. The chain retailers have increasingly begun to pressurize suppliers for price concessions and improved business terms like credit facility, increase in advertising expenditure. The power of producers with respect to customer contacts is diminished internationally by traditional retail chains of the west such as Wal-Mart, K-Mart.
- In the competitive environment, the nature of supplier-retailer relationship in the grocery area have changed significantly. Retailers are concerned with improving their productivity. While it is almost impossible for them to raise prices, it is not possible to find ways to lower costs for increasing profitability. This can be achieved by achieving economies of scale, along with providing convenience of one stop

shopping. They can build larger stores, increasing their fixed costs. creating higher break-even points, forcing supermarkets and mass-merchandisers, discount stores to place even greater emphasis on generating larger sales volume. The resulting competition leads to consolidation, where stores tend to keep their dominant position by holding on to their tested strategies including penetrating pricing, advertising and promotion plans.

- There is increased pressure on employees of the retail companies. Earlier they focused on purchasing and maintaining balanced inventories. Now, they are profit centres that are also responsible for capital management, service levels, turnover, retail margins and pricing, quality control, competitiveness and variety, operating costs, shelf space and position, and vendor selection and terms of purchase from them. In order to help the companies make money, they look for suppliers to give them price discounts and merchandising support, and they become upset when these discounts and support are not forthcoming.
- Retailers have many new categories of products; they have to choose from them, what to stock on their shelves. The store sizes have not increased significantly. Therefore, retailers are likely to choose products to stock on their shelves with a goal of making themselves profitable and viable and not the manufacturers. The manufacturer's bargaining position is weakened further because most new products do not succeed, by any reasonable definition of success. Proctor and Gamble has responded to this challenge by decreasing the number of product offerings it sells to retailers. In addition, manufacturers have engaged in many new product price and promotional allowances as a way of forcing their way onto retailer's shelves. These activities play into the hands of already powerful retailers.
- Information technology has spread throughout retailing to such an extent that virtually all of the major retailers can capture item-by-item data, via scanning devices, at their electronic point-of-sale terminals. The universal product code is used to help track the movement of product at retail and reduce both stockouts and supply cycle time. The knowledge gained from market information has permitted retailers to calculate the Direct Product Profitability of individual items, track what moves and what does not move well in their stores, engage in forward investment buying, and leverage suppliers. The retailers use this data for their benefit and to coordinate the channel. For example, supermarket retailers can now plan promotional offers to their loyalty card shoppers that link directly to their past buying behaviour, rather than needing to offer the same deal to all consumers.

The Retail Marketing functions are given below:

- The primary focus is upon the major issues and strategies of retail management, including selection of merchandise, purchase, inventories, merchandising, product pricing and point of purchase advertising.
- Formulating retail strategy on sales promotion, advertising as a joint exercise along with the manufacturers based upon understanding of customer needs and buying motives.

- Evaluate and apply multi-attribute analysis given below, and other decision models to customers' brand choices, and choices of suppliers and merchandise.
- Organize basic concepts of economics notably demand elasticity and diminishing marginal returns, to pricing, space allocation, service.
- Evaluate retail marketing performance through a range of quantitative and qualitative consumer research techniques, including focus groups, spot evaluation through questionnaire method.
- Analysis of Retail Markets –Segmentation of retail markets; consumer motives for selecting stores and centres; consumer images of retail companies and stores; target marketing and positioning.
- Retail Location and Planning – Identification of optimum locations and the assessment of specific sites; catchment area analysis and models of retail location; issues and framework of town planning; the internationalization of retail companies and store formats.
- Marketing Mix Strategies – Retail pricing strategies, category management and buying, product range development and private labels, retail promotion and advertising, merchandising, space allocation and display, retail design and atmospherics, role and techniques of personal selling.
- Technology and Retailing – Ways in which technology has impacted upon and helped to shape retail structure, for example, e-commerce, retail strategy like relationship management and retail operations.

Customer Behaviour

Take a simple **Customer Behaviour** pattern. It includes the following elements of internal information processing, guided by external information and stimuli.

- Belief: It is the customer's conviction and firm opinion of a product/brand.
- Perception: It comes from a customer's product recognition as a desirable product based on his intuition and information gathered on sensory plane.
- Attitude: It is the customer's way of thinking about the product, his firm's opinion about it.
- Preference: Out of his belief, perception and attitude the customer makes his preference of one product over other products, and tries to buy it.

Thus, we can define the Multi-attribute Decision-Making process as, "based on concepts of beliefs, attitudes, perceptions and preferences" which is the notion that objects in a choice set can lead to external behaviour. Each object in the set has a value on each attribute used to define the choice set.

Let us take an example to illustrate the point. The purchase of a car in a family is a major event and decision-making process is a multi-dimensional one. While film stars buy the car as a status symbol, middle-class persons buy it as a means of transport only. Let us take four cars in the economy segment and plot their benefits to the customer. (The figures given in the table are only arbitrary and not conclusive.)

Benefits	Zen	Santro	Matiz
Comfort	7.5	8	8.5
Economy	4	5	6
Safety	3.8	4.5	5
Brand equity	4	7	6
Service facilities	9	6	5

The figures are based on a scale from 0-10.

On a different plane another matrix can be made with benefits on one axis and decision-making concepts for each car separately, before the final decision is taken as follows:

Decision concepts/ Benefits	Comfort	Economy	Safety	Brand equity
Beliefs				
Attitudes				
Perceptions				
Preferences				

The two tables given above would help the decision-makers.

The following steps can be taken for the purpose:

1. Which attributes are used to define the product? (For example, for a car it could be its brand name, comfort or economy. For a house it could be its location, its construction and area.)
2. What is the possession level of the attributes in the product? (Is the car running very economical as compared to another car in the same category?) This is really the value of the attribute, its perception in the customer's mind. Another example could be of an airline, where the passenger safety is of prime concern. However, the airlines never talk about the safety aspect as all airlines are supposed to be safe. They prefer to talk about, a) ease of getting their tickets b) food c) in-flight service and entertainment and d) easy check-ins. And the customers form attitudes on the basis of these attributes.
3. What is the relative importance of each attribute in the overall product performance? In airline business is in-flight service more important than easy of getting tickets?
4. Do the customers weigh each of the attributes to reinforce their perceptions of overall product performance? How much weightage is given to each of the attributes and does it differ from customer to customer, or is product specific?

Note: At this stage the students should do a Attributes-Perception study for different products to find out how the customer's perceptions and preferences are formed.

It will be found that different customers have separate yardsticks for looking at the attributes. They trade off one against the other while making the purchase decisions as can be seen from the following example:

(a) Some people buy car only for its brand name, e.g. Mercedes
(b) Some buy car for its speed and power.
(c) Yet others buy the car for its mileage only.

Some look for several of the attributes in some descending order of their importance. This is called the **Dictionary Rule.**

Dictionary Rule: If a customer finds two products having the first or the most important attribute to be equally present in both the products, and then they look for disparity in the next level attribute. They keep doing so till they arrive at the attribute where there is a difference in the two products. (In dictionary when you look for a word you go with its first alphabet and then to the next, so on, till you find the exact word).

Buying a car, would the customer prefer lower price or better mileage? Can the seller charge one hundred thousand rupees more if the car gives 8 km per litre more?

Multi-attribute analysis helps sellers understand customers who represent identifiable segments in terms of their perceptions and preferences.

Let us consider the levels of competition, or competitor's hierarchy. A competitor can be defined as the seller who compete for the same customer rupee as the widest competition level.

Narrowing it down the competitors are those who sell same products from the same industry.

Further narrow definition of competitors would be the market segment competitors.

To clarify the above, let us take the banking business.

First level would be the banking system, which would include banks, financial institutions, non-banking financial institutions, merchant bankers and moneylenders.

Second level would be a bank who caters to the customers with a few of the banking products.

Third level is the bank in the same town or the same street.

Competition is becoming diversified as can be seen from the following:

1. Banking services have competition from software companies now, as a lot of online Internet banking is being done with the help of relevant software.
2. Used cars compete with the new cars.

It is therefore possible to define competition by analyzing customer's data. It can be tried as given below:

- Define a product.
- Let the prospective customers decide the possible uses and benefits, as many as they can imagine the product possesses. Can they think of other ways of getting the same benefits? This way the firms can get Differential Competitive Analysis from the customer's viewpoint.
- The customers should determine the products, which satisfy with their usage, and the benefits, which accrue to the customers from their use.
- The data thus obtained can be listed with priority as given by the customers.

The data thus obtained will provide the firm the information on the Competitors for each product in their range.

In summary, it can be said that—

"Competitors analysis requires the prudent use of secondary and primary information to determine current and likely strategies. Customers can be employed to classify uses and benefits of products and to rank the competitors".

Let us see the assets and skills grid for competitors. These can be divided into two parts as follows:

1. Primary: Product development, product quality, product manufacturing cost, product differentiation, customer satisfaction and market share.
2. Secondary: Flexi-production, financial muscle, sales force, distribution network, brand image/equity, advertising and promotion, quality of service and growth of the market for the product.

Student's discussion points:

- Explain the principle of multi-attribute analysis
- Broad and narrow definition of competition
- How can a customer help in competitor's analysis?
- Define unmet needs of the customers with examples.

Role of Strategic Planning in Retailing

Retailing is one of the key elements of a marketing strategy; it facilitates the market targeting process, making sure that a product reaches particular groups of consumers, the selected market segment. Retailing is important in a marketing strategy because it is concerned with matching the area in which a product is purchased to the benefits and characteristics of the product itself and its price as per customer's orientation. Retailers provide a collection of service benefits to their customers such as being located in convenient places, editing product ranges according to shopping tasks, and selling goods in quantities that match personal consumption levels. Ensuring that this process runs smoothly presents a host of managerial challenges. Retailing is therefore a deceptively simple management process, yet fascinatingly complex in its detail, as the purchase motivation of buyers get more and more complex. The retailers need to have updated buyers behaviour pattern through a process of continuous monitoring and research. The strategic plans are created with the following areas of concern:

Defining the business policy and mission, and corporate objectives.

The strategic planning process starts by identifying the firm's mission or purpose for its existence. A mission statement needs to identify the products and services to be offered and the customers to be served. It also needs to indicate how the resources and capabilities of the firm will be used to create customer satisfaction and how the firm intends to compete in its chosen markets. The mission also indicates the firm's philosophy for the way it intends to conduct its business.

Situation Analysis

The purpose of situation analysis (also referred to as situation audit) is to determine where the organization is at present and to forecast where it will be if existing strategies are pursued. The difference between the two is called the planning or strategic gap. The purpose of strategic management is to bridge this gap. Situational analysis can be divided into two broad components, namely external or environmental analysis and internal analysis. The purpose of external analysis is to identify opportunities and threats in the environment, and that of internal analysis to identify the key strengths and weaknesses of the organization.

The major components of external analysis are the macro-environment and the task or operating environment. The macro-environment consists of economic, political and legal, sociocultural and technological forces that affect retailers and over which they have very little control. The task environment, on the other hand, can be influenced directly by a retailer's own strategies and includes competitors, suppliers and customers.

While understanding competitive environment, it is useful to use Michael Porter's five-force model. In good old days, competition meant only the players in the field. The five-force model makes a comprehensive statement on what constitutes competition. The model is explained below:

	New Entrants threat	
Suppliers bargaining power	**Present competitors**	Buyer bargaining power
	Substitutes	

Five-Force Model

New Entrants

They pose a disguised threat as their entry time and manner is not known till the very last moment. Each business area has some entry barriers and exit barriers. If entry barrier is high and exit barrier low, then it is the best place to be, because new firms will not enter and low performing firms will quit instead of trying to undersell and make every one lose profits. Entry barriers are one or more from the following list:

1. Government regulations like licences
2. Inhospitable terrain, bad roads, poor infrastructure
3. High project costs
4. Technology difficult to obtain
5. Market in maturity or decline stage
6. Paucity of needed raw materials
7. Non-availability of channel members
8. Difficult to get the right managerial talent

More players in the field mean excess production capacity; lower profit margins for the players.

Substitute Products

They need to be watched carefully as with innovation, new technology they can pose a major threat. Home interior walls can be covered by lime wash (*choona*), emulsion paints, wallpaper or wood panels. Each has its own pricing formula, plus and minus points. In rural India, *gobar* (cow dung) is being used for covering the outside of the huts and *gobar* gas is also used for cooking and lighting purposes.

Suppliers

Suppliers to the firm play a key role in product costs. If the buyers are few and suppliers several, then buyers will enjoy the power to bargain. In case there are only a handful of suppliers and several buyers, suppliers hold advantage. Suppliers in rural India face problems of transportation, communication links, power and water supply both for manufacturing and for drinking. There is the imminent need of improving the rural infrastructure at the grass-roots level for bringing businesses and industry to the countryside.

Buyers

Buyers of the firm are always the most important part in the game of marketing. With large number of buyers and few suppliers, the buyers can be at the supplier's mercy. In rural markets too, the buyers play a vital role with increasing number of competitive players opting to get into the rural markets.

Competitors

Need to be analyzed, are they strong, large in number and aggressive, or the firm can lead the pack of competitors.

How to locate the competitors is a vital question for the firm. Pepsi knows that Coke is its biggest competitor, and yet they cannot neglect minor competitors. In the area of TVs in India, Sony, Samsung, Philips, are the known competitors and yet there are several small assemblers in each major centre and they account for nearly twenty-five per cent of total sale of TVs. Same thing is true for many industries including the computer industry. For this purpose the firm should arrange regular feedback from its marketing or field sales force, so that the real picture of competition, its business terms, and prices can be known. Otherwise the firm is fighting a battle with ghosts.

The purpose of internal analysis or an internal audit is to assess the strategic capabilities of the retailer by examining the quality and quantity of resources available, how effectively they are used and the extent to which they are unique and difficult to imitate by competitors. Resources can be grouped into physical assets, human resources, financial resources, and intangible resources. Intangible resources include goodwill embodied in the retailer's own brands and the retailer's image.

Competitive Strategies

For long-term survival, retailers need to build sustainable competitive advantage (SCA) over their rivals in the market. Major methods of creating SCA include convenient locations, building customer loyalty, close relationships with suppliers, efficient logistics and supply-chain management, good information systems (including customer database management), exclusive merchandise (including own brands), buying economies of scale, superior customer service, and a knowledgeable and motivated sales force.

Evaluation of Strategic Opportunities

The retailer should be able to identify its key strengths and weaknesses and the major opportunities and threats that it faces by organizing SWOT analysis—Strengths, Weaknesses, Opportunities and Threats. It is also sometimes referred to as TOWS analysis emphasizing that analysis of the external environment, threats and opportunities should take place before internal analysis, strengths and weaknesses.

After conducting the situation analysis the retailer needs to decide on the strategic direction for the organization as given below:

- Retail productivity strategies aim to improve earnings and increase the efficiency of current resource allocation through cost reductions, higher turnover and margins through an improved assortment of goods and higher prices.
- Strategies for improving efficiency include increasing inventory turnover by utilizing store space more effectively by better merchandising, reducing costs of labour, credit, logistics and other operating costs. Usha and Singer along with Bata have realized the importance of shop space usage.
- Consolidation would require specific changes in the way the company operates. Recovering lost market share in the mature market is difficult. In mature markets retailers need to consolidate their position by increasing emphasis on building customer loyalty through promotion programmes, improving service quality, increasing marketing activity of advertising, promotion, publicity and increasing emphasis on worker productivity improvements, through training programmes.

Alternative Retailing Strategies

Having delineated the strategic options available, the retailer needs to decide on specific strategic action. This requires the evaluation of the strategies in terms of how they help to bridge the strategic gap between planned and actual profitability, risk and the ability of the organization to undertake the particular strategy of penetrating or skimming prices. One useful method of doing this is to compare the attractiveness of the market opportunities with the competitive advantages of the retailer with the help of BCG matrix given below:

Boston Consultancy Group

Resources can be defined as finance, human, technology, and information and managerial. So far the discussion has been on getting the competitive advantage for individual product. However, in case of a multi-product firm, emphasis should be on managing the products together and not separately. For making an analysis of firm's strength the Boston Consultancy Group, BCG, have developed a matrix as given below:

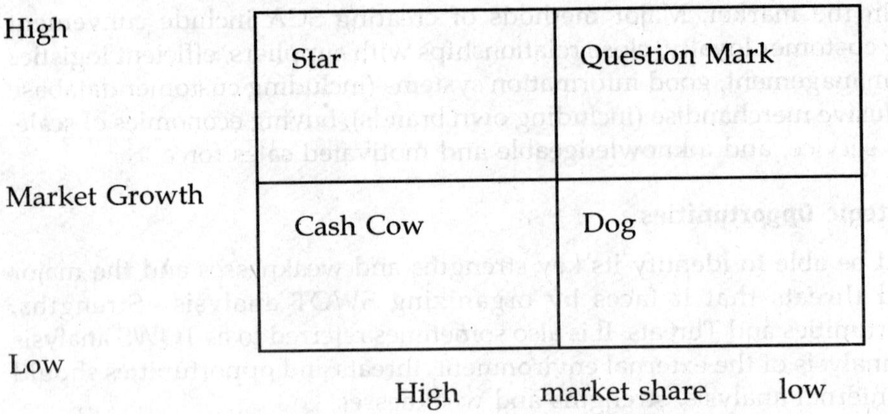

In BCG Matrix, the horizontal axis shows the market share of the product and the vertical axis shows the market growth.

Let us see the position of products in different quadrants.

Quadrant Star: In this quadrant the market growth of the product is high and the firm's product enjoys high market share. It is characterized by the following:

- The firm's product enjoys a strong market position that of the leader.
- The market growth of the product is high and attractive.
- Competitor's better technology and superior market acceptance can make the firm's business risky, even if enjoys leadership position.
- Low profits, as the leader has to spend large amount on marketing advertising to maintain the leadership.
- High expenditure required for marketing mix factors.

Strategic options in Star Quadrant are as follows:

1. Increase share: Invest in anticipation of higher market growth. Put entry barriers for newcomers through pricing, innovative distribution and advertising.
2. Maintain share: Have good market intelligence to be able to counter their actions. Invest in marketing mix selectively

Quadrant Question mark: In this quadrant, the market share is low although the growth of the market is high. The position of the product is as follows:

- The product is in growth stage while the firm's product is having low market share.
- The firm has the opportunity to increase its market share by investing in advertising and promotion.
- It is often a new entrant. It could be that all players are new or one could have assumed leadership in the market.
- Risks are high, technology and basic product acceptance in the market is not fully established.
- Negative profits and huge expenses in marketing for either concept selling or for increasing market share.
- Needs long-term and strong commitment of the management for the product's growth to attain star position.

- The firm must decide to how many of its products are in this quadrant and how many of them it can support on long-range basis.
- The firm could get into some niche market segment
- If the firm has several products in this quadrant, and you keep all you are in a strategic trap, because it cannot place proper resources for them and is in danger of losing all.

Quadrant-Cash Cow is where the firm has high market share but the market growth is low. The firm can reduce its marketing expenses as it is already in dominant marketing position and can become low cost supplier. The firm can have the following market situations:

- Dominant market position
- Slow market growth
- Low cost supplier
- Good profit and cash generation
- Low market risk

Strategies for Cash Cow Quadrant are as given below:

1. Manage for cash, maintain market share
2. Requires cautious investment in market as growth is low
3. Cash generation can be used for products in question mark quadrant
4. Harvest: Go for niche market if future prospects are low
5. Divest if product demand is going down at a rapid pace, because of new technology products have come into the market, or because the customer's tastes have been changing.

Quadrant Dog: In this quadrant, the market growth is weak and the firm has low market share. The market situation can be described as given below:

- Weak market position.
- Slow market growth.
- High cost supplier.
- Poor or no profit and cash generation. However, by managing it carefully, using the niche market route it can be profitable too.
- Several times the product could be based on management ego as once it was a star product.
- High management turnover, as the product is not doing well, "customers know us because of this product."
- The product takes a lot of management time in planning its strategies for hardly any gain.

Strategies for Dog Quadrant are given below:

1. Maintain market share for whatever cash the product generates
2. Plan for changing or adding some market segments
3. Stop all new investment in the product
4. Divest: Sell and use the funds for other products in question mark stage

5. Keep the product for any goodwill it may have or there are strong exit barriers
6. Turn around: By innovating, product differentiation, down sizing
7. Get into niche market

Investment Cycle for the BCG Matrix, therefore is as given below.

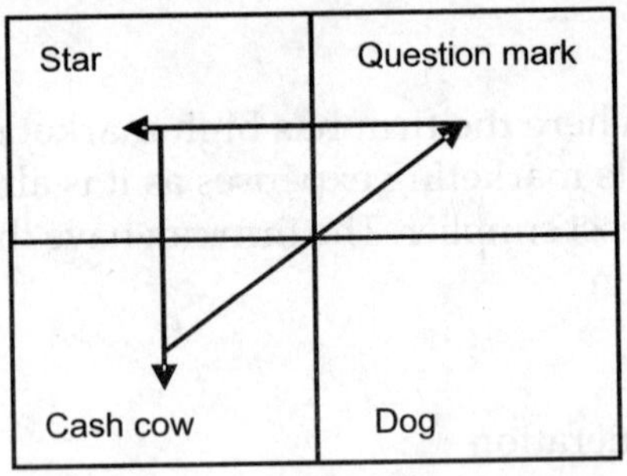

The extra cash generated in cash cow stage is invested in the question mark stage to bring the product into star stage. Over time the market growth of star product goes down when it reaches the maturity stage of its life cycle, and it starts having extra cash, which is invested in question mark stage to complete the cycle.

GE Model

Matrix has been fine-tuned by the GE Model, which can be used to define markets and products position as follows:

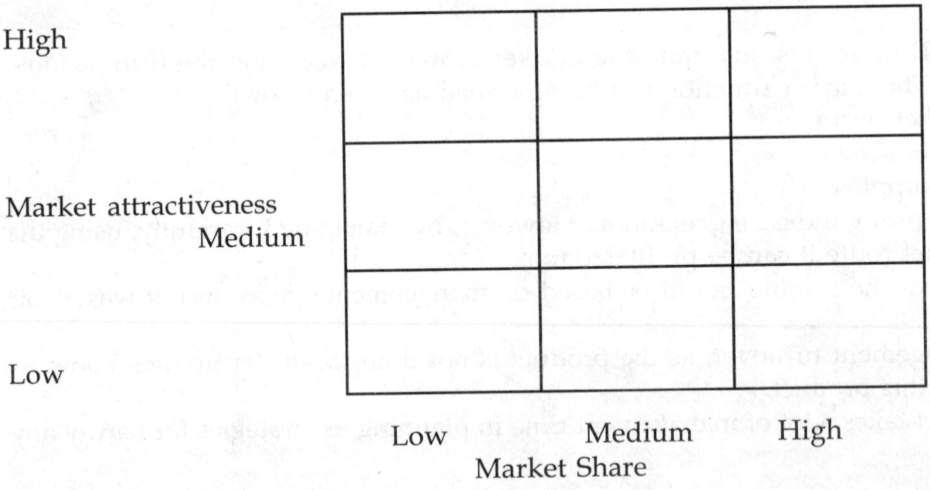

In the GE Matrix the market attractiveness and firm's market share for a product can be ranked as high, medium and low, thus enabling the firm to understand the position more accurately and plan its strategies accordingly.

Market attractiveness can be measured as given below:

- Market size and growth
- Degree of market concentration, is it localized or is it spread out
- Industry profitability
- Price sensitivity of demand
- Exit and entry barriers
- Strength of channel members
- Rate of obsolescence or technology change

Firm's market share and its competitive position can be seen from the following:

- Market share
- Profit margins
- Brand loyalty
- Degree of product differentiation
- Proprietary technology

The technique suggests that the highest amount of resources should be invested in opportunities where the retailer has the strongest competitive advantage. For instance, a retailer targeting a new segment would evaluate the attractiveness of market opportunity in terms of:

a. Market size.
b. Market growth rate.
c. Level of competition.
d. Profitability of the segment.
e. Technology requirement bar codes, computerized inventory and billing.
f. Legal and regulatory issues.
g. Human resource requirements.
h. Environmental issues.

This information must be compared with the retailer's strengths relative to that of competition on factors such as:

- Current market share.
- Merchandising skills.
- Buying strength.
- Supply-chain management and supplier relations.
- New product development.
- Own-label reputation.
- Financial resources.
- Sales force.
- Managerial competence.
- Fit with current retaiier image in terms of breadth and depth of product lines, quality and reliability, customer service.

Development of Marketing and Positioning Strategies

Once the retailer has set objectives and analyzed a number of opportunities it needs to decide on a specific direction for the organization and the opportunities it wishes to take advantage of. For each of the opportunities chosen the retailer now needs to set specific objectives and allocate resources to achieve the objectives. In order to achieve the set objectives, marketing strategies have to be devised. These are normally developed for specific market segments rather than the market as a whole, as this makes more effective use of resources. After selecting the target markets a positioning strategy must be developed.

Retail Positioning

This positioning is a relative concept and understanding customers' viewpoint and perceptions is the key to effective positioning in the market. Positioning is an attempt to differentiate from the rest of the market, an attempt to be as close as possible to the shopper's view of an ideal retailer in a market segment.

A positioning strategy is a plan of action for how the retailer will communicate with his customers and prospects and compete in the targeted markets and how he will differentiate itself from competitors in those markets. Retail positioning is the process of creating and maintaining a distinctive brand image of the retailer in the target customer's mind relative to its competitors. The positioning should be either merchandise or service-led. The basis for positioning strategies is to distinguish between symbolic and functional merchandise, and whether it attracts high or low margins. The reason is that people are motivated to buy the two categories and shop for them in different ways. The three main positioning strategies, are product differentiation, service and personality augmentation, and price leadership.

Product differentiation is achieved through unique or exclusive products or brands, own-branded products, and unusual merchandise assortments. Service and personality augmentation can be achieved in many different ways, including high levels of personal service, convenient locations, long opening hours, generous returns policy, home delivery. Price leadership can be established through offering low or discounted pricing and good value or price promotions on key items.

Positioning is a continuous process. Because of changes in the market environment of consumers and the competitors, the positioning may need to be adjusted. Repositioning needs to be considered where there is a big discrepancy between consumers' perceptions and management perceptions. This is usually reflected in poor performance and declining market share. Repositioning can also be used to target a new set of customers.

The Retail Mix

The retail marketing and positioning strategy is put into effect by the retail mix—the set of controllable variables that the retailer can use to satisfy customers' needs and to influence their buying behaviour and compete effectively in the market. To implement a specific retailing strategy, managers must decide the best combination of retail-mix variables and coordinate the activities of the different elements of the mix such as given below:

- Merchandise assortment.
- Location.
- Price.
- Visual merchandising.
- Store atmosphere, ambience.
- Customer service.
- Advertising.
- Promotions.
- Personal selling.

Positioning is regarded as planning of the four main areas of the retailing marketing mix; namely,

1. Trading style/format strategy
2. Merchandise strategy, which products, brands to stock and display
3. Customer service
4. Customer communications strategy

Plan Implementation and Control

Without effective implementation, strategies are of not much use. Effective implementation requires that appropriate resources be allocated to required tasks, which requires budgeting in respect of specific elements of the retailing mix, personnel, shelf and floor space and merchandising. Effective implementation also requires scheduling and coordination of retailing activities. It needs the translation of retailing strategies into tactics. Functional strategies lead to the establishment of long-term objectives that must be focused into day-to-day operational decisions. For instance, when to advertise, what media to use, and the length of promotion campaigns are tactical decisions influenced by the competitive environment and the communication strategy.

The implementation of retailing strategies inevitably requires changes in working methods and responsibilities which can lead to resistance from employees, and organizations need to develop strategies to reduce this resistance to a minimum and better still to totally convert them into believing in the new strategy as the management actively sells the new strategies to their employees. It is possible by the following method:

- Transparent communication of strategic changes being planned
- Equitable distribution of workload amongst the team members, taking the work specialization, load bearing capacity, and fairness.
- Training of the team for helping them adjust to the changes planned
- Possibility of upward movement with the change for the dedicated personnel.

In order to assess how effectively strategies are being implemented and how far the strategic objectives are being achieved, control procedures need to be established. These control plans help to determine whether the objectives set are being achieved in the specified time periods. Such procedures allow unsatisfactory performance to be identified at an early stage, and remedial action or the reevaluation of retailing strategies and objectives to be instituted. Periodic reporting systems help the management in comparing the actual performance with set targets.

Emergent Strategy versus Planned Strategy

In practice, it is more than likely that the realized strategies are combinations of planned and action taken. However, the planning approach has the advantage that it suggests that retail managers should be proactive in formulating retailing strategies rather than waiting for strategies to evolve. In the fast moving retailing environment, proactive strategic management is indispensable for long-term survival. It calls for understanding of the retail business environment including area demographics, social and cultural milieu, economic standards, government regulations of shop and establishment act and competitive environment of existing competitors, bargaining power of vendors and buyers, threat of new entrants and substitute retailing like e-tailing, pavement shops and street hawkers.

Challenges & Opportunities in Retail Marketing

The retail movement in India has become the Sunrise area and the Retail Management or the Last Mile Management, (so called by the manufacturers as Retail is the last distribution link between them and their final consumer) has the potential of emerging a clear winner. It offers tremendous opportunities for enterpreneurs and the employees alike.

Retail over the past decade has changed the definition of retail as manufacturers can no longer depend on sales taking place with inventory push alone. Retailing has gone beyond the realm of merchandising into Strategic Planning by creating a success story with the customer taking the centrestage as the retailers understand the aspirations, desires of the customers that help them in bonding lasting relationships with them. The knowledgeable customers of today expect much more than mere product when they make as purchase. They want more information about the usage, benefits and its life and resale value after they have finished with it. Retailers need to sell ideas, hopes and courtesy before they sell the product. Only then will retailers get repeat customers, loyal customers.

Customer Relationship in Retail

Customer value can be the yardstick as value for money product purchase. Value perception could be different for different customers—a rich buyer may consider the brand itself as value while a middle income buyer may consider economy of use as value for money. Pricing strategy is soon going to be a thing of the past as buyers can view the prevailing prices of different retailers on the net before making the purchases. Therefore, retail needs to differentiate itself not to be placed in the same category as other run-of-the mill retailers. Retail value comes with the benefits offered by the retailer and include retail's location, parking self or valet, service, brands stored, stocks of each brand and its reputation. Buyers look for the ultimate in benefits they obtain and not the process through which these benefits are bestowed on them. Home delivery in the neighbouring areas is becoming one of the most important benefit being offered by the retailers. Window displays, shopping hours, sales personnel, credit cards usage, shopping carts help the retailers in establishing the benefits being part of the shopping experience at the retail outlet. Besides the stores' ambience, air-conditioning, cleanliness, toilets, food courts, cinema halls create added value for the buyers. Value-price equation needs to be developed with participation of the buyers.

With different modes of retail outlets finding a place in the market, customer retention has become the prime concern. Gaining and retaining customer's needs, building relationships with the loyal customer by offering unique experience that cannot be copied easily. Retailers watch out for their customer base (some retailers keep customer data base like a master list of customers that can be generated on the computer with the billing activity and a few questions asked casually during customer visits).

Customer Service Plan

The following are a few customer service and add-on services: Free home delivery, free replacement on even a minor complaint, return acceptance on gift items. Initial extra warranty, free token gifts, gift wrapping facility, toilet attendents, valet parking are some add-ons that are becoming commonplace that retailers have to keep looking at others taking the buyers' needs into account, using a retail survey. Retailers can, certainly charge for these add-on services and yet for retailers needing to establish themselves these should be free optionals. Customer service is to be tailor-made giving individual customer service as per his requirements. Five-star hotels keep a data bank of their regular clients and therefore are able to offer the suite favoured by a client, welcome drink as per his choice, the entire service is planned on clients previous visits data. Retailers have to understand the relative cost and value to the customer with respect to the service being provided by them. If the service provided is high cost and it gives high degree of satisfaction to the customers, they would become loyal to the retailers in most cases. Credit sales, gift as promotional plan, speedy transaction would lead to the loyalty factor. With such service the customers do not become loyal, the reason could be mismatch between customer requirements and retail delivery. Home delivery in the absence of any householder is a good example of such failures. Service could become effective like courtesy, right customer councelling regarding product selection. The opposite could be true as well with low cost service customers could feel disappointed with the retailer and may not become loyal customers. Free parking, in store attendants are examples of such service.

Service providers the emerging opportunities in urban markets are in capturing and delivering better value to the customers. The last point connect seems to be increasingly lively with the customer taking the centrestage. Service providers face an exploding rural market, only marginally tapped due to difficulties in rural retailing. Innovative concepts and models are needed to survive and thrive in rural markets, because of the following reasons:

1. Poor infrastructure
2. Low income level of buyers with high mean time between purchase

3. Lack of retail shops
4. Lack of product knowledge

Service providers will increasingly face a host of specialist retailers, who use modern management techniques, backed with seemingly unlimited financial resources. Organized retail appears inevitable. Organized retail too faces innumerable opportunities and challenges in terms of product categories that it can profitably offer. Scale of organized retail demands the use of IT and sophisticated techniques to manage the supply chain and customers. For the organized retail, resources in these areas seem scarce. To conclude, every player in the arena, be it the manufacturer or service provider or the organized retailer, faces opportunities and challenges that can be met with flexible yet detailed strategic planning on issues like purchasing, merchandising and service to the customers.

For the last several years, the local retailer has been at a major disadvantage due to the following reasons:

- Widespread emergence of discount stores
- Internet as e-tailing has got the boost with high level proliferation of computers and the Internet.

On the plus side a retailer is his own boss and can decide on extra promotion, discounts on his own.

All businesses start with a laudable intent, including retail business. It is therefore, important to understand the business intents of retail entrepreneurs at this point, as different disciplines of retail have to interact with each other.

However, given below are a few examples of these interactions:

- Finance with shares—company secretary
- Sales with accounts
- Personnel with finance
- Materials with logistics

No management discipline can operate as an island, on its own. The coordination of all the disciplines, as also of different stakeholders of the firm for generating continuous profitable results and growth firms need to strategize their operations, else they are likely to go down into oblivion in no time. This brings in the holistic planning in a firm covering the entire gamut of activities and thought process. Even TQM, which was considered applicable only in manufacturing, has become an all-pervasive tool, which affects the entire organization today. It is, however, unfortunate that in practice several firms do just lip service to TQM and naturally when it does not bring about the desired change the firm is quick to blame the TQM. Strategy word comes to business from the armed forces, where during a war, strategies of defeating the enemy are formed. In peace time, the forces are kept at strategic places to ensure quick deployment when war is declared. Facing enemy, the commander of the forces needs information on the strength of the enemy forces, number of tanks, armoured vehicles, foot soldiers, aircraft are with the enemy and their exact deployment locations as also the contour of the terrain.

To find this out soldiers are sent on a reconnaissance trip who go behind the enemy lines to gather the information, at the risk of their lives.

In business parlance, it amounts to getting information on competition, business environment of the country and the trade practices followed. Ultimately, the business prospers when the firm surges ahead of competition. This can be achieved by creating Sustainable Competitive Advantage in the firm, which can be done in the following steps:

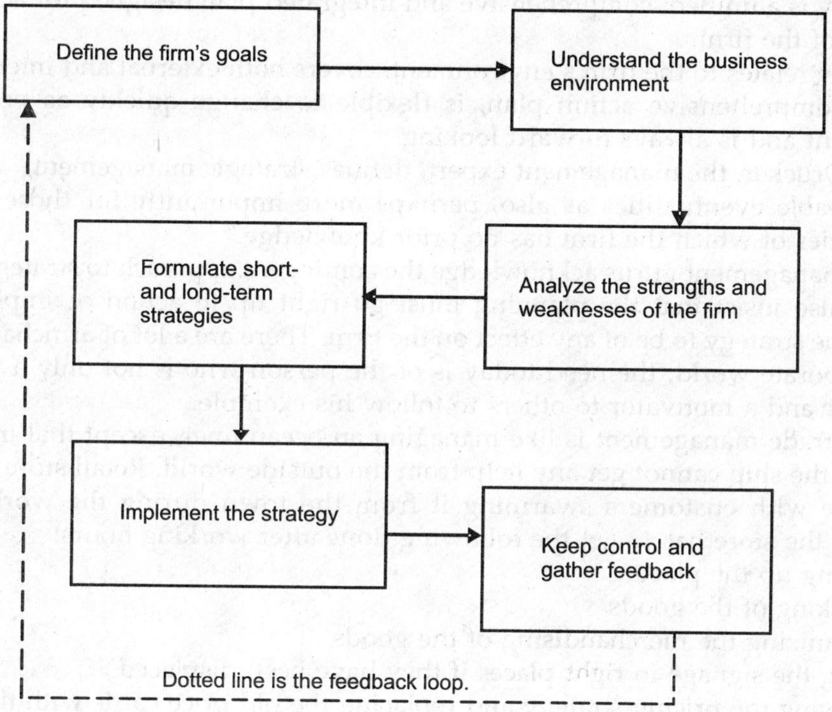

While setting up new retail projects, the project cost takes into account the fund required for any contingencies, which may arise, like increase in cost of the land, building, equipment from the time the project costs were finalized till actual purchase. In a running business contingencies are more of the law rather than exception; hence the need for planning to not only dealing with the contingencies but avoiding them by remaining proactive towards the environmental changes as also changes in the fortunes of the firm.

This above chart is the framework around which the book is being planned for benefiting readers, the students and others planning retail business strategies.

Retail Business Strategy

Business strategy of a firm includes the plans, policies and their implementation in a given time frame. Plans and policies are converted into action or activities where tasks are assigned to individuals or to teams for achieving specific targets.

Strategy can be defined as follows:

Strategy is a set of goals and objectives and the firm's policies and plans for achieving the same, correlating with the defined purpose of the firm.

Strategy is the way a firm reacts to its business environment, deploying its resources and marshalling its efforts for achieving its goals.

Strategy is the defining of long-and short-term goals of the firm and adopting action plans and resource deployment for achieving the same.

Strategy is a unified, comprehensive and integrated plan designed for achieving the objectives of the firm.

Strategy relates to the firm's environment, covers both external and internal factors, covers a comprehensive action plan, is flexible to change quickly as per changing environment and is always forward looking.

Peter Drucker, the management expert, defines strategic management," as planning for foreseeable eventualities as also, perhaps more importantly for those impossible contingencies of which the firm has no prior knowledge."

Most management gurus acknowledge the contingent approach to strategic planning but they also insist that the planning must go right up to action or implementation stage for the strategy to be of any effect on the firm. There are a lot of armchair managers in the corporate world; the need today is of the person who is not only a planner but also a doer and a motivator to others to follow his example.

Retail trade management is like managing an ocean liner, except that in a liner the captain of the ship cannot get any help from the outside world. Retail store is usually a busy place with customers swarming it from the town during the working hours. Therefore, the store has to get the following done after working hours:

1. Cleaning up the place
2. Restocking of the goods
3. Reorganizing the merchandising of the goods
4. Placing the signage in right places if they have been displaced
5. Reviewing the pricing strategy and replacing the old price cards with the new ones wherever required. The price change can be made even during the day, for example, some retailers may lower the price by the evening to clear the stocks, especially of perishable goods.
6. Allotment of duties for the next day for the team members
7. Planning for training of the salespersons at lean hours
8. Planning for getting new staff, if required
9. Checking the daily balance sheet, sales, sales returns, cash accruals and sales made on credit. It is necessary to know the reduction in credit with outstanding dues getting paid.
10. Going in-depth study of the customer complaints, if any, not just to find out the guilty person but to get into the real cause of the complaint to ensure that it does not recur in the future.

In the retail business of the 21st century the Stores Managers need to have a lot of imagination, inspiration and emotional bonding with their staff, customers, suppliers, in fact with all their stakeholders to be effective, successful and respected.

The store manager must be able to segregate different job profiles then train persons for each profile, besides a few more to allow and facilitate the members of the team in doing multi-tasking. For this purpose, the manager needs to have a good idea of the potential of each person with him. Knowledge about his team will enable the manager to fully and properly utilize the team.

The success of retail comes from its USP—the Unique Selling Preposition. The uniqueness and innovation are the main areas of retail success. The manager has to look into the following for remaining successful:

1. Never oversell to the customer: If the product can be delivered in two weeks time, ask for three weeks and deliver before the promised date to delight the customer. This is vital for building customer relations.
2. Never oversell even within the organization, to the owner, or even the salesperson.
3. Know your customers, at least the regulars and call them by their names as you respectfully address them.
4. Surprise your regular customers with something extra once in a while to keep them in good humour always. "Sir, this tie goes well with the shirt you just purchased and it is yours from our side."
5. Direct all your actions only towards achieving your sales and profit targets. This would help the retailers in remaining focussed on their main tasks.
6. Coordinate the sales and service actions for each customer by monitoring the actions of the team members.
7. Keep innovation by the team members as a healthy competition where the best innovator gets recognition as well as some awards.
8. Get the latest low-down on competition with the help of customers, your sales steam and competitors sales team.
9. Measure the results regularly with profits, sales volumes, quality and quantity as the yardsticks.

Questions for Discussion

1. Discuss the importance of retail in FMCG markets.
2. Is product selection of major concern in retail? Discuss.

Management Game 1

The faculty should divide the class into teams, each consisting of 4 to 5 students. The teams should select a product from the list of FMCG, Consumer Durables and locate a company dealing with it where they have access. Otherwise, they can form an imaginary company. Next they should select a name for the company, one product they will like to sell, its features and the customer benefits. They should define their target market segment for the product. Next, the students should decide the best way of reaching out to the consumers, the way they want to retail their product, stand-alone single shop, chain stores or shopping malls.

Select a product from either FMCG or Consumer Durable range, select the market coverage area and then decide about the right market segment that the team wants to do business with. Plan marketing strategies and make P&L Statement for first five years of operations, including sales on yearly basis, profit picture.

Discuss the yearly advertising plan, select the right media, get their rates, try your hand at creating an advertising campaign. Prepare an yearly advertising plan along with its budget.

Retail Basics for the Shopping Centres (places other than stand alone retail shops):

The urgency and significance of developing retail concepts, to achieve strong branding, deeper market penetration and higher consumer satisfaction is increasingly being realized by both retailers and brand managers. Since retail expansion is a complex and expensive process, it can best be achieved through partnerships. However, identifying the right partners is a difficult task, especially in as disparate a market terrain as India there is a need of top-notch professionals from the retail and allied support service industries, to offer innovative retail concepts the best modes of expanding and profiting through the right partners, who offer support in areas like advertising, visual merchandising and inventory management the areas that are the backbones of retail success. The retail industry has been facing a number of issues: stagnant sales, high vacancy rates, and intense competition. While their are many causes for the problems facing shopping centres, shopping centre owners and developers still need ways to address the nagging issues and improve performance.

There are many shopping centres that have responded well to adversity and are thriving, and there are many others in a state of decline. What many of the successful centre developers have done is to reinvent their centres, by such means as extensive repositioning/redevelopment strategies. For developers seeking growth strategies in this competitive market, there has been the creation of new formats. This issue of the strategic solution takes an in-depth look at regional shopping centres and how they have adapted to an ever-changing retail environment. Reviving the centre takes a look at how declining centres can be reinvigorated through renovations or if necessary, total reconfigurations. reinventing the centre takes a look at the recent growth of a new format, the value regional centre, and how it has been developed as a response to consumer preferences and adapts some of the best characteristics of existing formats. While retail area has increased physically, changing consumer habits has contributed to some difficult times for shopping centres. The problems have multiplied by the aging of many centres. As a response to these problems, many shopping centre owners and developers have implemented repositioning strategies to reverse the decline of their centres. Many of these strategies begin by gaining a better understanding of the consumer and market, and finish with significant physical alterations to the centre with the goal of improving its attraction and ultimately its performance. Shopping centres have undertaken research studies to detail exactly what trends are occurring within a market. Information about the consumer, via surveys and consumer research, has been critical in providing information about who shops at the centre, where they come from, and how much they spend. An understanding of the consumer has provided the framework upon which shopping centre owners and developers base decisions about how a centre should be altered to better meet the needs of current and potential customers.

Understanding Competition

Understanding competition provides information regarding such factors as which shopping centres have the greatest impact on the centre, what type of retail opportunity exists, and how a centre can differentiate itself from existing centres in the market. Competitive information is often acquired through field work. In addition, consumer surveys can provide insight into how consumers perceive various shopping opportunities in a market. Combined with the consumer data, competitive information is a powerful tool in making decisions about the future of a shopping centre. Shopping centre owners and developers have been turning their market information into dynamic repositioning activities in hope of strengthening weak centres and completely revitalizing distressed centres. The majority of large scale repositioning strategies have been focused around three areas: renovation, and reconfiguring. More often than not, the strategy typically used involves a combination renovating in some cases, complete reconfigurations, along with renovating takes place. These strategies have been implemented to re-energize centres by creating a "new" and exciting shopping environment, with the ultimate goal of improved productivity.

Renovations are required to the centres that have a worn look to take care of problems present in older centres including a lack of vibrant lighting, extensive use of drab colours, absence of food courts, and dilapidated bathrooms. The visual impact of a centre upon shoppers' perceptions has been well documented, particularly when the impact is negative. Correcting physical problems has been effective in communicating an image that a centre is a clean, safe, and fun place to shop. Reviving a centre visually, and often at the same time functionally, has been an important move for many centres to provide a "modern" feel and match newer centres on an aesthetic level. Renovations are often combined with an expansion of retail space, providing an even greater opportunity to add new and exciting tenants, as well as increase the overall attraction of a centre. The renovation strategy has worked best with regional centres that were once dominant, have faltered slightly, but not drastically. As part of the renovation strategy, many malls are also expanding. These malls have been able to renovate largely because they have retained their competitive positions in the market. In addition, these centres are located in markets with large numbers of affluent shoppers. While the initial costs of renovation and expansion may be expensive, good locations and strong markets can provide the financial pay-back.

Market demographics, competition, and logistics of the stores have led many distressed retail centres into adopting aggressive repositioning strategies. These strategies have been successful in increasing consumer traffic and ultimately the sales of the centre. As markets continue to be saturated, and centres continue to age, the opportunities for centre repositioning and redevelopment will continue to grow. It is up to the shopping centre owners, developers, and mangers to recognize these changes and adapt accordingly.

Value for Money

Value can be generalized as the perception of receiving a quality product at a good price. A good "bargain" price, as perceived by majority of buyers would typically be defined as a cost lower than full price, whether achieved through a sale, markdown (lowering the price), or via an discount outlet. Much to the dismay of many traditional retailers, many shoppers will no longer buy merchandise unless it is "on sale." While this discount strategy has increased sales for many retailers, it has also taught consumers to expect constant "sales". Few retailers have escaped the impact of the discount philosophy, even past stalwarts of margin protection, traditional departmental stores have resorted to significant sale events to promote the value aspect of their products. To satisfy consumers' demand for "value for money" in retail, some developers have ventured into the factory outlet mall arena. Between 1988 and 1996, square footage in factory outlet centres grew from approximately 14 million square feet to over 50 million square feet. While factory outlets represent a small percentage of total retail square feet, the growth rate indicates a clear response on the part of developers to changing consumer demands. However, these outlets are also facing some problematic issues, primarily the maturing of the industry and ever-changing consumer preferences. Consumers who are increasingly short on time may find an outlet centre too distant, or simply lacking in the conveniences offered by many regional centres, particularly food and entertainment. As a response to consumers' ever-changing needs, and the shortcomings of factory outlet centres and other retail formats, a new concept has emerged, the value regional mall.The value mall is not so much a new concept as it is a combination of several existing retail formats. The value mall combines concepts and ideas from outlet centres, traditional regional malls and entertainment complexes. By combining previously associated concepts that are isolated, developers have created a unique blend of retail choices and entertainment opportunities. The value mall concept has been driven not only by consumers' demand for "value," but also an exciting shopping environment with entertainment possibilities. Value regional centres differ from outlet and traditional centres in terms of composition, consumer base, and location strategy. However, there will always remain customers who do not bargain and want to pay the stated MRP of the product and this way they remain happy that they have not been cheated by the bargain offer where the lowest level remains a secret.

Hotels are a perfect source of referrals for hair salons, spas, nail boutiques, and other personal care services. Yet, when asked at the front desk of hotels, most do not know the names of any. Had the owner of the manicure store regularly dropped off business cards to the major hotels, perhaps even given some of the staff free manicures, they would have known the company's name. One should figure out who could send business your way and keep in touch.

- **Be visible.** Customers have to find you. Some of the most effective ways to be seen include having a well-trafficked location, good signage, an advertisement in the Yellow Pages, and a regular advertisement in the local newspaper.
- **Develop a mailing list (Master list of customers and prospects).** With a mailing list, retailers could have sent a reminder card to any customer they hadn't seen in a while, let customers know of special promotions, and if they ever changed locations, tell customers how to find them. One of the big mistakes companies make is failing to stay in touch with customers.

- **Give reminders of possible cross selling and repeat sales.** Most of the salon's customers come in for over an hour a week for manicures. But they don't get reminded of other ways to spend their money. The owners could have easily prompted customers with small signs saying things like "Looking for a gift? We sell gift certificates." "Treat yourself right – try a pedicure." "Take your color home – we sell nail polish."

In most businesses, you want to keep your customers around as long as possible. The longer they linger, the more they will usually spend. (Not always, of course; some companies, where traffic is heavy, want to get customers in and out quickly.) In any case, you want the customer to enjoy coming to you. While it is clean, the smell of acrylic is overpowering, and sales are good, the owners make no attempt to decorate. Look around at most small establishments; you will be amazed at how a few have bothered to provide a visually interesting or inviting space as part of merchandising. It would surprise many that inviting premises would enhance the traffic manifold.

A few of the retail strategies methods and tools are:

1. Vendor Managed Inventory
2. Enterprise Resource Planning (ERP) and Supply Chain Management (SCM)

Several Indian companies have already come up with either an indigenous ERP or SCM model or they use packages from well-established firms. There is a need for a strategic collaboration of the internal process with the business process of the suppliers and customers.

The face of the Indian retail industry is changing. India is passing through a retail boom today. A number of changes have taken place on the Indian retail front such as increasing availability of international brands, increasing number of malls and hypermarkets and easy availability of retail space. With the Indian government having opened up the doors for Foreign Direct Investment, the entry of foreign retailers into the country has become easier. India has come a long way from the traditional Kirana stores, (which will in any case remain in existence) and is on its way to becoming a 'mall country'. The emphasis has shifted from reasonable pricing to convenience, efficiency and ambience.

The major factors fuelling this change are the increase in disposable income of the people, improving lifestyles, increasing international exposure and increasing awareness among the customers. India has a large middle class as well as youth population, which has contributed greatly to the retail phenomenon. The middle class is considered to be a major potential customer group. The youth are perceived as trend setters and decision-makers. Tourist spending in India is increasing, which has also accelerated the retail boom.

Food and grocery are the two categories in the Indian retail sector which offer the most promising opportunities. Apart from this, the other areas where there are vast possibilities for Indian retailers are jewellery, apparel and consumer durables. Indian retailers are also trying to create a niche for themselves in areas such as books, gifts and music.

The long-term future is promising, but the next few years will remain challenging. While speaking about the current mall culture in India, it is believed that the malls as places to congregate and spend time for shopping and other activities have been well accepted. This concept will certainly grow stronger once new generations of malls are offering consumers/visitors an atmosphere of international standards, including trouble-free parking.

Liberalization of FDI norms in any form of retail are needed because they will not hurt traditional business. They bring to the retail additional funds, cutting edge supply chain solutions and process know how. The latter is needed to professionalize the retail sector, for improving efficiencies for retailer profits, as well as best services and best prices for the Indian consumer.

There have been several Indian manufacturers who sell their wares through their own retail outlets (for example, the well-known manufacturers of clothing, Raymond and Bombay Dyeing, jewellery manufacturers such as InterGold, Orra, Tanishq and watch manufacturers such as Timex, Titan besides, Usha, Singer and Bata). Most of these manufacturers have registrations of their brands in respect of goods but seldom register their brands for retail services rendered under that brand.

Manufacturers own retail brands registration is necessary if they want to have own shops. Such non-registration can cause serious difficulties. For example, in one case pertaining to Raymond, an unauthorized retail shop was selling several brands of clothing, including Raymond textiles. This shop had put up a 'Raymond' signboard at the entrance suggesting that it was an outlet authorized by Raymond. Raymond was not able to prevent such use—the court ruled that the retail shop owner was entitled to use 'Raymond' on its signboard as he was selling genuine Raymond clothing too. If Raymond had a retail brand registration, i.e. registration for Raymond for rendering retail services in respect of clothing, then it is likely that it may have been able to prevent use of its mark on the signboard on the basis of infringement of its service mark registration.

Until the beginning of 2006, the government policy prohibited foreign investments in the retail trade sector, the effect of which was that major international retailers were prohibited from setting up their retail operations in India. A recent liberalization measure with regard to foreign direct investment in the retail trade sector is directly linked with trademarks. Now, with government approval, foreign direct investment up to 51 per cent is permitted in retail trade of a 'single brand' product.

The retail trade operations in ventures having foreign investment up to 51 per cent are required to sell products under a single brand only and the same brand should be in use internationally. Further, the product categories should be approved by the government. Finally, the products should be branded during the manufacturing process.

But the term 'single brand' is not defined. Probably, retailers such as Wal-Mart and Tesco whose products carry different brand names of various manufacturers will not qualify as single brand retailers. On the other hand, companies like Levis, and the manufacturers of Rolex, Omega, Parker, Mont Blanc and Chanel, which want to set up retail operations in India would qualify for a licence for foreign direct investment. Also, it should be noted that foreign retail companies which purchase products from various manufacturers and then brand such purchased products (on selection basis) would not qualify for a licence for establishing retail operations as their products would not be branded during the manufacturing process. However, these policies are liable to change with time.

The retailers need to plan store layout, ambience, and create eye-catching visual merchandising displays, floor plans and interesting retail store designs. They need to learn how to select and care for store fixtures, use of special lighting techniques to focus on products.

A well-planned retail store layout allows a retailer to maximize the sales for each square foot of the allocated selling space within the store without clutter that causes problems in customer movements in the stores.

Store layout plans generally show the size and location of each department, any permanent structures, fixture locations and customer traffic patterns.

Each floor plan and store layout will depend on the type of products sold, the building location and how much capital the retailer can afford to put into the overall store design.

Basic Retail Floor Plans

Straight floor plan

The plan is meant for stores where the floor space is confined to narrow lanes and traffic can move only in one direction.

Diagonal store

The diagonal floor plan is a good store layout for self-service types of retail stores. It offers excellent visibility for cashiers and customers. The diagonal floor plan invites movement and traffic flow to the retail store without any hindrance.

Mixed floor plan

The mixed floor plan incorporates the straight, diagonal and angular floor plans to create the most functional store design. The layout moves traffic towards the walls and back of the store.

Geometric floor plan

The geometric floor plan is a suitable store design for clothing and apparel shops. It uses racks and fixtures to create an interesting and out-of-the-ordinary type of store design without a high cost.

Angular floor plan

The angular floor plan is best used for high-end specialty stores. The curves and angles of fixtures and walls make for a more expensive store design. However, the soft angles create better traffic flow throughout the retail store.

Store layout and visual merchandising are factors that contribute to the uniqueness of a store. The exterior and interior of a store convey several messages about the store to the consumers. The building that houses retail store (whether new or old) and the exterior design of the store are important aspects of the design of the store. Marquees, walkways, entrances, doors, display windows, the height and size of the building, colours and materials used, and theft prevention are some of the key factors to be kept in mind while developing a store's exterior.

Managing space is the first concern of retailers, when it comes to designing the store's interior. Space is always an expensive and scarce resource. Retailers always try to maximize the return on sales per square foot. Planning a layout for the store's interior is the first step in designing the store's interior.

One other plan has three kinds of layouts—grid layout, racetrack layout and freeform layout. Allocation of space can be based on many factors, like historical sales, gross margins, industry averages and strategic objectives. Apart from allocating space to various merchandise categories, space has to be allocated for carrying out some essential functions. Such space includes the back room for receiving the inventories and sorting them out, office and other functional spaces, aisles and customer service desks, floor space and wall space. The interior of a store influences the purchasing behaviour of the customers to a great extent. Designing the interior of a store in such a way as to influence customer behaviour is referred to as visual merchandising. It includes optimum and appropriate use of fixtures, displays, colour, lighting, music, scent, ceilings and floor, and designing all of these properly. Merchandise presentation is the most significant aspect of store design, because it helps attract customers' attention. A retailer can resort to many forms of presentation such as idea-oriented presentation, item-oriented presentation, price lining, colour presentation, vertical merchandising, and frontal presentation.

Prevention of losses due to merchandise pilferage is a major cause of concern for all retailers. This issue should be addressed at the initial stage of store design. The retailer can use many electronic security systems like CCTV for the prevention of such losses.

Merchandise Plans, Philosophy and Strategies

Merchandising plans need to take into account the buying formats and processes. These include forecasting, brand selections, purchase timing, store space allocation along with product category selections. Activities involved in acquiring particular goods and/or services and making them available at the places, times, and prices and in the quantity that enable a retailer to reach its goals. Merchandising philosophy should be concerned with the following areas:

1. Target market requirements
2. Retailer's type, stand-alone shop, chain store or shopping mall
3. Market positioning
4. Value chain
5. Supplier capabilities
6. Costs

7. Competitors
8. Product trends

Merchandising functions include:

1. Buying and selling
2. Brand selection
3. Pricing, display
4. Finally, sales to the customers.

At times the function may be confined to buying only. Retailers carry complementary goods and services to encourage shoppers to buy more, known as cross-merchandising. Some products complement each other like shoes and socks, cameras and films. Buying and selling functions in merchandising include multi-brand selections, pricing, advertising and promotion, POP displays, personal selling techniques and employee deployments.

Product-wise, item-wise, and for multiple stores chain store-wise forecasts are made of expected retail sales over a given period.

Types of Merchandise: These can be assorted type, fashion, seasonal, fad or staple type. Staple products are those that are regular with the retailer, like grocery store examples: milk, bread, canned food.

Basic stock lists specify inventory level, colour, brand, style, category, size and package.

With respect to certain merchandise like apparel, furniture, auto the retailer must carry a variety of products, several brands in order to give customers a proper selection.

Some stores keep fashion and seasonal merchandise as given below:

- Fashion Merchandise: which have a relatively small life.
- Seasonal Merchandise: Products that sell well over certain time period.

Purposive Planning

1. Remove old non-selling goods
2. Remove low or no profit goods
3. Be selective in buying mechandise
4. Ensure that you maintain high image/brand equity of the store

Planning Merchandise Quality

1. Number of competitors and their quality standards
2. Store location
3. Relate merchandise quality directly to the perception that customers have of the retailer
4. Retailer's image
5. Target market

Problems include:

1. An item is out of stock
2. Dissatisfaction with a current product or service
3. Consumer needs and wants not met
4. Related products/purchases not upto the mark
5. Marketer-induced or competition related problems
6. New products introduction can be problematic
7. Personal experience could be lacking in the people running the store

The relevant internal psychological process that is associated with information search is perception. Perception is defined as 'the process by which an individual receives, selects, organizes, and interprets information to create a meaningful picture of the world'.

The selective perception process—stage description selective exposure—consumers select which promotional messages they will expose themselves to. Selective attention consumers select which promotional messages they will pay attention to. Selective comprehension consumers interpret messages in line with their beliefs, attitudes, motives and experience. Selective retention consumers remember messages that are more meaningful or important to them.

Sometimes purchase intention does not result in an actual purchase. The marketing organization must facilitate the consumer to act on their purchase intention. The provision of credit or payment terms may encourage purchase, or a sales promotion such as the opportunity to receive a premium or enter a competition may provide an incentive to buy now. The relevant internal psychological process that is associated with purchase decision is integration.

Retail Site Selection

Before taking the final location decision it is necessary to scan the area thoroughly. Local newspapers and local retailers are good source of information. Demography of the area, especially the income levels, lifestyles and professions are good indicators of buying power and buying habits of the local population. Site for the retail store should be in close proximity of the buying population.

Accessibility, visibility and traffic flow should be easy and smooth on the adjacent road. The size of the traffic should not be taken as the size of the customers visiting the store. Yet, the retail space should have the following:

1. Customers should be able to drive or walk easily
2. There should be public transport facility passing through
3. Delivery vans should have easy access to the stocking areas
4. There should be enough parking place for customer vehicles like 10 parking slots to 1000 sq. metre of retail space.

Customers' viewpoint needs to be taken into account for visibility consideration. Store should be visible from main flow of traffic. Good visibility itself becomes an advertising point for the store. It is a good idea to understand the laws relating to retail shops from the local municipal corporation. There could be rules regarding signages, garbage disposal and in-house eateries. Other businesses in the area like factories, shopping malls or office complexes could help or destroy your business.

Other costs besides rental need to be seen are given below:

1. Cost of building maintenance, utilities, security, garden maintenance
2. Cost of air-conditioning maintenance
3. For remote location the travel time for the customers
4. Power, water charges
5. Painting of interiors
6. Off-day planning
7. Building as per municipal laws
8. Area crime rate
9. Special lights, fixtures

Retailers must consider the personal factors like their own travelling time from home to store and at times the restrictions placed on the tenant by the landlord or the community that can cause problems to the retailer.

Customer Relationship Management in Retail

Customer relationship programme has the role of increasing retailer's return on marketing investment and maximizing lifetime customer value. They need to learn how to choose the right kind of retail loyalty programme for business.

Retailers concentrate on wooing new customers and do not do enough to gain the loyalty and increased patronage of their current customers. Customer relationship management (CRM) helps to do just that. Its solutions need to cover key retail areas: merchandising, supply chain management, inventory management, sales audit, in-store operations, multi-channel retailing, and customer relationship management.

The researchers analyzed the business implications of CRM. Research has indicated that there is an increase in sales due to loyalty programmes. An added advantage is collating customer data, which should be used by marketers to customize data and reach clients.

While researching loyalty programmes in brand relationship implications researchers found that loyalty programmes do affect customer behaviour and the relationship a customer has with a store brand.

International customer loyalty programmes need to provide marketing services for airline, automotive, financial services, hotel, information technology (IT), luxury brand, creative showcase, and retail sectors worldwide. Customer profitability and lifetime value analysis, customer relationship management (CRM) strategy, data audit and analysis, database design, loyalty/relationship marketing software evaluation, loyalty marketing strategy and propositions, loyalty programme audit, loyalty programme business case/feasibility study, loyalty programme business requirements, loyalty programmes are major areas that need constant improvement.

Customer relationship management is the new mantra in media. What exactly does this mean to a common man? The simple answer to it is a way of differentiation between customers to provide greater value to more valuable customers. The meaning of more valuable would be in terms of the monetary spending received from the customer along with frequency of visit. Retail in India is at the crossroads. But because of the heavy initial investments required, break-even is difficult to achieve and many of these players have not tasted success so far. However, the future is promising; the market is growing, government policies are becoming more favourable and emerging technologies are facilitating operations. The whole concept of shopping has altered in terms of format and consumer buying behaviour, ushering in a retail revolution. Modern retail has entered India as seen in sprawling shopping centres, multi-storied malls and huge complexes offer shopping, entertainment and food all under one roof. He buys products from that marketer. Every retailer today is aiming at an attempt to make a casual customer into a loyal customer who develops a bond with the retail store he/she visits.

EXAMPLES

Pantaloons

Known as the 'Green Card' it is divided hierarchically into One star, Three star and Five star. Every point generated at all the levels is equivalent to Rs. 1

Criteria for points generation are:
Upto 399 points – One Star – 1 point for Rs. 50
400 or more additional points – Three star – 1 point for Rs. 40
800 or more additional points – Five star – 1 point for Rs. 25

It also stays in touch with its loyal customers through mailers, SMSes E-mails and telephone informing them about the developments and promotions.

Shoppers Stop

Known as the 'First Citizen Card'
Classic Moments – Earn 1 reward point for every Rs. 100 purchased.
Silver Edge – Earn 1 reward point for every Rs. 50 purchased.
Golden Glow – Earn 1 reward point for every Rs. 34 purchased.
Every point generated at all the levels is equivalent to Re. 1

It has a special scheme wherein it offers private label reward points to its silver edge and golden glow members.

Lifestyle

Known as the 'The Inner Circle'
For every Rs. 50 spent at any of the stores, 1 point is earned.
For every 100 points earned, gift voucher of Rs. 100 is received

Westside

Known as 'Club West'
It offers Classic and Gold membership
Offers 25 and 50 as the bonus points to Classic and Gold members

Classic – For every Rs. 50 spent at any of the stores, 1 point is earned.

Gold – For every Rs. 40 spent at any of the stores, 1 point is earned.

Piramyd Megastore

Known as the 'Piramyd Power Club'

It offers Silver, Gold and Platinum cards.

There are discount % which is offered on both Piramyd Store and its supermarket. As one moves from Silver to Gold the discount per cent also increases.

Piramyd Power Points are offered on all purchases. Silver, Gold and Platinum are awarded 1 point on every Rs. 80/-, Rs. 60/- and Rs. 40/- spent respectively.

Globus

Known as the Privilege Club card

An enhanced version with larger offerings is the 'Gold Card'

The monetary benefits which it offers is a holiday package depending upon the amount spent. The larger the spending the higher the value of the gift.

Tangible and Intangible Benefits

What is so special in CRM programmes which drive the customer back to the store?

It can be better understood from 2 perspectives:

Tangible benefit + Intangible benefit = Loyalty to Brand

The Tangible Value

Discounts, Offers, Promotions, Payback

There are regular discounts offered by a store either as a special scheme, yearly sale discount, mark down discount, etc. Over and above such schemes when a store offers additional offer to certain customers selected on certain specific criteria that would become a part of a CRM initiative. Such offers would be any new scheme which is being launched for any particular product or a group of products. For example, offer can be a product bundling wherein two products together are clubbed at a special price.

Promotion would indicate stress on any or a group of products for its maximum sale. These are footfall drivers to the store and store keeps on launching some or the other promotion schemes from time to time.

Payback can be linked to the parking fee. There are some stores and malls which charge a token fee for vehicle parking, however, the same is reimbursed against any purchase (as specified) at the store.

Loyalty point redemption system

The loyalty points earned by the customers can be reimbursed any time after the customer generates minimum specific points.

Exclusive offers

These are offers either designed for the loyal customers to make them come back or may even be designed for all to showcase and differentiate their offerings from that of the competitors.

Card upgradation

The loyal customers are generally automatically upgraded as per the purchase habits and number of points generated.

Exclusive invites to get-togethers and events

These are invitations meant for loyal customers to make them feel special. Lot of times customers are invited when any celebrity comes to the store for any new launch at the store. Or there may be invitations sent to customers for any event happening in their city or town.

Differentiated offers (linked to behaviour)

These are offers, which are linked to the behaviour of any particular set of customers depending upon a mix of their demographics and previous purchase habits. Lot of times product bundling is done as per the area where the store is located since it catches a specific area.

The customers are invited to provide their suggestions and recommendations for improvement of their shopping experience.

This would mean a retail store offering another discount coupon or some freebie, which is connected to a different brand. Pantaloons store are offering a discount to any merchandise purchased from Liberty.

Free home delivery of altered merchandise

This would be an add-on service to loyal customers by delivering their altered clothes as per their convenient time.

Offering them space for car parking is like inviting people with arms wide open. The reason for this is the increasing inconvenience customers face to shop on weekends due to non-availability of parking when the stores are huge crowd pullers.

To facilitate and serve the loyal customers better, stores designate special counters both for cash and customer service so that the premium customers can be attended with ease. To make the customer feel special the stores send greetings and special customized offers to these customers.

Special movie shows are organized and customers are sent passes from time to time.

This implies the homeliness aspect which the customer feels for the time he/she spends inside the store. It is the inner feeling, which they develop for the store. The reasons for visiting may not always be purchase, however if emotional connect is developed with the store then as and when need arises the stores enjoy top of the mind recall from the customers. The emotional connect coupled with strong functional value creates a long lasting relationship with the customer. At the grocer's the customer has to be clear with the requirements and there is little scope for too many questions. However, at a supermarket, the customer is at ease to choose products without any limited time frame.

With the fast changing retail scenario in the country, the role, which the entire CRM team plays, has changed dramatically. It is quite often also linked to strategy.

The reason for linking the CRM to the overall strategy is to:

- Build dynamic relationship with the customer
- To make CRM the key element to building customer loyalty to a store brand
- To build a significant competitive advantage

A shopper always wants to feel that he is an important person and more so when he enters a known retail outlet with his guests or relatives. Here CRM plays a major role in meeting customers' expectations.

Discussion Question

Discuss the retail concept and CRM role in retail.

CHAPTER

2

Retail Operating Plan

Aims and Outcome

The students will learn the retail operations, types of retail structures in India and a few other places and will be able to appreciate the similarities and differences of the retail operations.

Retail operations need to be structured and streamlined to avoid human errors. The plan should take into account the following parameters for this purpose.

Consider the store size, location of different shelfs and sales volumes for different products in parallel shelfs. Match the employees' competency to the product technology, sale volume and the needed sales talk. Managing product inventory becomes extremely important to avoid excess stocks with overflowing godowns, with heavy burden of increased current assets or stock outs endangering sales loss.

Safety of shoppers, employees is of great significance and firefighting equipment, fire drills are useful in this direction. Store level insurance, security, both electronic and human sentry based, are essential for the store.

Credit sales bring in large volume of business and while these need to be encouraged. Proper safeguards against fraudulent buyers are necessary.

Taking a restaurant service factors the following gives a bird's-eye view of the physical attributes that define the product venue while the service provided gives the entire operating plans.

Restaurant Concept Statement

Overview:

- Start to set the stage or tell the " story" about the guest experience
- A quick verbal tour through the restaurant or bar.
- Include brief descriptions of the menu, interior design, style of service.

The tour will take the reader through the restaurant, commenting on the important structural and design elements, colour, finishes and overall style that makes the outlet unique.

Use words to describe the positioning of the outlet such as casual, fine dining, upscale, family-friendly, etc.

Describing the style of service can give one a feeling for the energy level in the outlet. Include any special service pieces and uniquely presented

Beverages, bread, platters

Name, logo and tag line

Outlet Name

The guests form the first impression

- It can be positive (familiar, humorous, interesting) or it can be negative (confusing, unrelated)
- Search for names that relate to local history or geography
- Words associated with that style of cuisine, the restaurant/hotel's address or whimsical names may be appropriate

Personnel Utilization

Labour costs in India have been low but gradually they are increasing of late. Wages and benefits may account for one-third of the operating costs. Employees' turnover requires recruitment all the time, with cost of recruitment, training and supervision. Incorrect selection could cause loss of sales, irate customers because of incompetent service. While technology could compensate for poor worker activity and yet in India most stores are having labour intensive activity. The labour demand keeps changing with business surges and business downs. Moreover, in stores with unions the problem gets complicated since there is less of flexibility in utilization of workforce. Unions want strict timetables, overtime wages, seniority rights.

Hiring process needs careful screening of candidates, which will ensure low rate of attrition.

Work forecasts—for each time zone, season number and type of employees required need to be assessed.

Standardization of tasks and job rotation help in work simplification and multi-tasking by the workers when required. Cross-training helps in keeping workers motivated avoiding boredom and related disinterest in work.

Workers' performance assessment need to be made transparent with the workers knowing their tasks, goals and targets. The yardstick for judgment needs to be conveyed to the concerned workers.

Wages and extras, promotions, pension schemes keep the workers motivated.

Ushers and self-service stores ushers job is to take the buyers to the correct address where particular products are stored. They greet the customers as they arrive at the store and after knowing their buying plan take them to the right locations.

Seniority in service needs to be encouraged, as the senior persons are more productive if they are kept motivated throughout.

Stores need to be maintained like a ship, with continuous cleansing schedules, replenishment of stocks, merchandising. Periodic renovation, energy saving devices and refresher course training for employees form the bedrock of the retail operations.

Outsourcing of certain activities like consumer surveys, the stores can consider focusing on inventory management. Computerization has become a vital component with common bar codes, billing and inventory updates are early organized with the help of computers.

Service Provision at Retail Outlets

Based on the location and clientele retail outlets provide different types of services to the customers as given in the box below.

S. No.	Service type	Service plan
1.	Self-service	Customers pick and choose their required products with the help of price tags, location signages, carry them in trolleys or baskets to the payment counters
2.	Assisted self-service	Customers are provided information and details like specifications, guarantees of the products for help in decision-making process.
3.	Limited assistance	Customers can avail of credit or hire-purchase facilities at such outlets, get the products gift-wrapped if required.
4.	Full service	Salespersons assist in locating, comparing and selection process of the products. These types of outlets normally handle the following types: a. Affluent customers who can afford the prices at such outlets because of high cost of service persons. b. Speciality product shops like medical shops, jewellery shops. c. Outlets where rentals, hire-purchase are common factors in constant use.

Franchise Operations

> Retail trade has got a boost when companies with trademark and brand equity started giving franchise to other companies interested in starting same type of business. The operations are carried out in the following manner:
>
> The franchisee pays for being a business associate of the franchiser as follows:
>
> (a) Licence fee
>
> (b) Start up cost like rental, lease equipment and fixtures
>
> The franchiser offers, technology, management techniques, purchase modalities and a list of approved vendors for purchase of materials. The franchisee's business is add-on to the retail throughput to the franchisers business without any investment on their part. The franchisees gain as they do not have any business insecurities with well-established franchisers.

Crises Management /Loss Prevention

Retail stores can encounter a variety of crisis situations that must be diffused before they can do major damage to the organization.

The retail outlets should have contingency plans to avert disasters by nipping them in the bud. The following actions need to be taken:

- Get insurance covering for fire, thefts, natural disasters
- Place backup generators to cover power failures
- Prepare management succession plan
- Have firefighting equipment at suitable locations always in readiness, keep organizing fire drills or mock fire control exercises.
- Prepare emergency operation manuals, keep them at convenient location and go through their action sequence periodically to be used during emergencies.
- Display of emergency telephone numbers like fire station, police at prominent places is mandatory and can prove to be a veritable boon in crisis.
- Chain of command, the head of emergency need to be clearly specified in no uncertain terms

Retail Type Selection

Retail stores in India are of the following types:

1. Stand-alone multi-product shops like the locality grocers.
2. Stand-alone speciality shops catering to only one type of products like the shoe shops, pharmacies.
3. Retail store chains that are spread across the length and breadth of the country. These include discount stores like Subhiksha chain.
4. Retail multi-discipline malls that include a large variety of shops, eating places, movies halls.
5. Super marts.
6. Catalogue selling outlets.
7. Virtual marts that cater to customer demand only through internet shopping.

Grocers have been providing excellent community service by offering products of daily necessity at reasonable rates as they operate in competitive environment. From the last ten years in metro cities at least, they are facing tough competition from the store chains, malls and the virtual stores. They have tried to ward off competition by providing free home delivery to their patrons. However, the time has come when they need to have a serious thought on their future with the increase in shopping malls in practically all the neighbourhoods. They would do well to set up their outlet in a mall either as an additional outlet or as a replacement to their existing shop.

As business grows the single outlets become chain stores. These stores can plan on getting products made in their own brand, either by their own manufacturing unit or by outsourcing to some other manufacturer.

Strategies of inventory management, purchasing, logistics, merchandising apply to these grocers in equal measure as for other outlet described above. It is the better-managed outlet that will have better chances of survival and success.

Advertising, promotion and PR: The stand-alone shops have the following options left with them:

- Advertising in the local press: English language or local language press depending on the clientele to be served.
- Advertising in local TV channel, or cable TV.
- Distribute Leaflets, pamphlets in the vicinity
- Point of Purchase (PoP): Using danglers, posters, window displays, in-house TV programmes including advertisements of products sold along with entertainment films.
- Gifts like key chains for the customers containing the shop's advertising messages.

Stand-alone shops need to have dedicated, committed salespersons who enjoy their work and have been trained in the art of selling. The salespersons should have knowledge about the different products being sold, their exact location, price and possible discounts. The salespersons should be able to guide the customers through the shop to show the merchandise in the best possible manner and light.

Stand-alone speciality shop chains that are not part of a shopping mall.

These shops cater to only a narrow selection of products like the shoe shops of Bata. However, with severity of competition catching them up they have organized horizontal diversification by adding product range to the product portfolio. Bata has stared selling a large variety of garments, besides shoes making them more profitable than ever before.

Retail Store Chains

The chain store phenomenon is the product of the USA.

Therefore, a study of the American chains is considered most useful and is given below:

A retail chain differs from other industries by nature of its number of locations. A conventional manufacturing industry has a production at a limited number of locations and sales being handled from a few more. However, a retail industry has sales from a large number of locations. If it is in the food and beverage business, you could say that its production is also being done at all locations. This means that material handling, production, sales and distribution as well as finance transactions are being conducted at all their stores. Each store requires an inventory control system, a point of sales system and an accounting system (access to a production system).

Major procurement is conducted at the head office, material receipt is done at the stores and bill passing and bank payments conducted at the head office. Some extent of local procurement is also sometimes being done at the stores. Sales are an activity, which is being done completely at the stores. Most of these activities are handled through a point of sales system. However, while a point of sales system handles sales satisfactorily, it is generally not geared up to manage inventory, consumption or requisitions for material.

Caselet Wal-Mart

Wal-mart, the retail giant in the world wants to be known as a welcome and positive community partner. They want to explore ongoing commitments to being a better neighbour. They know what is needed by the customers in their own backyards; they do most of their business upto 90% at the local level. They believe community membership is a privilege. They believe that listening and learning from their stakeholders leads to a better Wal-Mart and a better local society. The company is coming to India in collaboration with the Bharti Enterprise.

Social Citizen

They try to help wherever possible in those locations affected and believe in using their resources to help make a positive difference in people's lives. The Wal-Mart Foundation is a not-for-profit organization dedicated to giving and doing whatever they can to help improve the quality of life for their customers, address environmental issues and promote education.

As the students understand the Wal-Mart supply chain and see how they are taking their first steps towards sustainability now, with an eye on the future of the planet, they will come to know the company better.

Their motto—Take care, Listen, Connect: Helping Families During Military Deployment in the USA. "Our associates around the world are committed to supporting their local communities. They post video clips about company culture, community involvement and more. They help students and kids to become responsible towards the environment by reducing waste."

Task for the Students

Wal-Mart takes good care of its stakeholders. Discuss.

Requirements of a Retail Chain Organization Operations

1. Reconciling goods receipts at multiple locations with supplier invoice
2. Reconciliation of cash and daily sales at each store
3. Stock position at each store
4. List of slow/fast/non-moving items
5. Requisitions for items
6. Daily sales figures at each outlet
7. Sales v/s consumption at each outlet (for retail food industry)
8. Cash position at each outlet

9. Daily/weekly/monthly expenses at each store
10. Tax details at each outlet
11. Multiple pricing based on location
12. Tracking of sales returns
13. Implementation of special discounts and promotion schemes
14. Shelf life/expiry date of perishable goods
15. Inventory planning based on reorder level
16. Multiple units of measurement

Computer provides a practical mix of online and offline connectivity and synchronization of databases. It ensures that local invoicing is managed offline while all goods receipts; financial transactions at each store are conducted onto the central database. Being a multi-company enterprise solution, computer treats each store as a separate unit and storage location and can provide profitability and even independent profit and loss statements for each store. Computer's retail application integrates seamlessly with the main central application-ensuring end of shift/end of day synchronization of data. A powerful definition system allows a central control over all codes across all stores as well as all other master data. In addition you can define new promotion schemes or new discount schemes in the central system and these would be automatically applicable at each store. Powerful analytical tools and MIS reports assist in assessing store performance and profitability.

Chain store proliferation has weakened local economies, eroded community character, and impoverished civic and cultural life. Moreover, consolidation has reduced competition and may harm consumers over the long-term. Contrary to conventional wisdom, the decline of independent businesses is not inevitable, nor is it simply the result of free market forces. Rather, public policy has played a major role, particularly through tax incentives and other development subsidies that give national chains a significant advantage. Meanwhile, a growing number of communities are taking a different approach. They are adopting land use rules that deter chain stores and actively encourage local ownership.

> Jane Jacobs wrote in her book, *The Death and Life of Great American Cities*, about the relationship between locally owned businesses and community. Community is one of those words so overused that we rarely pause to consider its meaning. For Jacobs, what constitutes community is not any one particular thing, but rather the many small interactions that occur in our everyday lives.
>
> "It grows," she writes, out of people stopping by the bar for a beer, getting advice from the grocer and giving advice to the newsstand man, comparing opinions with other customers at the bakery and nodding hello to the two boys drinking pop on the stoop, hearing about a job from the hardware man and borrowing a dollar from the druggist.
>
> "Most of it is ostensibly utterly trivial, but the sum is not trivial at all. The sum of such casual, public contact at the local level, most of it fortuitous, most of it associated with errands, is a feeling for the public identity of people, a web of public respect and trust, and a resource in time of personal or neighbourhood need. The absence of this trust is a disaster to a city street."

What Jacobs describes here could be an urban neighbourhood or a small town. Its defining feature and indeed the very foundation of this close-knit community is a vibrant local retail economy. It is a place of small stores and sidewalks; a place where public and private space overlaps; and a place where we buy goods and services from businesses owned by our neighbours.

Such places are increasingly rare. Small-scale, pedestrian streets are giving way to massive, impersonal shopping centres. Street life has suffered, as our daily errands revolve increasingly around stores accessible only by car. Locally owned businesses are disappearing, displaced by national chains that have limited ties and no long-term commitment to the community.

The loss of locally owned stores and the pace of retail consolidation is staggering. 11,000 independent pharmacies have closed since 1990. Independent bookstores have fallen from 58 per cent of book sales in 1972 to just 17 per cent today. Local hardware dealers are on the decline, while two companies have captured 30 per cent of the market. Five firms control one-third of the grocery market, up from 19 per cent just five years ago. A single firm, Wal-Mart, now accounts for seven per cent of all consumers' spending. If the current trends continue, independent retailers might soon be a thing of the past. But, in the midst of this unprecedented expansion by national retail corporations, another trend is underway: a growing number of communities are rejecting chain stores. Last summer, residents of Ashland, Virginia mounted a spirited campaign to block a proposed Wal-Mart. In October, the Planning Commission voted unanimously to reject the store. In Chelsea, Michigan, residents organized a picnic to protest plans for a Rite Aid drugstore. The event drew a crowd of 1100 people. Rite Aid quickly backed down. Similar events are occurring across the country.

Over the past two years, dozens, or perhaps hundreds, of neighbourhood groups have sprung up to protect their homegrown businesses. In Lake Placid, New York, a group known as the Residents for Responsible Growth is working with neighbouring towns to form a regional response to chain store expansion. In Flagstaff, Arizona, it was the arrival of a Barnes & Noble and a Home Depot that prompted residents to form the Friends of Flagstaff's Future. In Northfield, Minnesota, the Citizens for Responsible Development is working to defend the town's historic Main Street and local shops. The debate over chain stores is often characterized as a struggle between our hearts and wallets. We may feel sad at the loss of the corner drugstore, a fixture in the neighbourhood for three generations, or the local independent bookstore, but ultimately we believe that, as consumers, we are better off. We tend to take as self-evident the chain stores' claims that they bring us lower prices and wider selection.

Over the long-term, however, consumers are best served when there are numerous competitors in the market. The big retail corporations, like Home Depot, Toys R Us, and Best Buy, are known in the industry as "category killers." The name is significant. These businesses do not intend to compete with local stores; they aim to be the only players in town.

Typically, a chain store will enter a new market sporting discounts. Many chains employ loss leaders to attract customers. Wal-Mart has been known to sell gallons of milk for 25 cents or to price entire departments below its acquisition costs. This sets up a battle that local merchants cannot win. If they don't match the chain's prices, they risk losing customers. If they do match the chain's prices, they will lose money on every sale. While a chain can afford to operate a new outlet at a loss indefinitely, it's only a matter of time before the local business will be forced to close.

Once the chain has eliminated the local competition, prices tend to rise. In Virginia, a survey of several Wal-Mart stores statewide found prices varied by as much as 25 per cent. The researchers concluded that prices rose in markets where the retailer faced little competition. A similar conclusion was reached in a survey of Home Depot. Prices were as much as 10 per cent higher in Atlanta compared to the more competitive market in Greensboro, North Carolina.

As for wider selection, consumers should be especially wary of the claims made by chain stores. Independent merchants are usually the first to sell products made by small companies. By contrast, most national chains refuse to do business with small and mid-sized companies. They prefer to deal only with large manufacturers. The result is that small manufacturers even those that make innovative products, publish great books, or distribute ground-breaking films, are having an increasingly difficult time reaching consumers. Consider the impact of this on book publishing. Borders Books and Barnes & Noble certainly stock a large number of titles under one roof, but these are virtually the same titles found in each of their 2,000 stores. Although local bookstores tend to be smaller, collectively they stock and promote far more titles than either of the chains. They take risks on unknown authors and small publishers. A number of best-selling author's, including Barbara Kingsolver and Amy Tan, contends that, without independent booksellers, their first books would have gone quietly out of print.

Even if chain stores do save us a few dollars now and again, it comes at a great cost. Chain stores contribute far less to the local economy than independent businesses. Developers often present new chain store developments as major additions to the local economy. They note the growth in retail sales and shopping options. They tally up the number of new jobs and the added tax revenue that the development will bring.

We overlook the other side of the balance sheet. Unlike new manufacturing facilities, which create real economic growth, new retail stores simply shift consumer spending from one area of town to another. A new big store can only be successful at the expense of existing businesses.

A study in Iowa, found that new Wal-Mart stores derive on an average of 84 per cent of their sales from existing businesses within the community. Similar conclusions have been reached in studies of development in Massachusetts, Maine, Vermont, New York, California, and Virginia.

While the consumers benefit with better ambience, brand selection the studies suggest that only a fraction of the sales generated by a new retail store represent new retail spending. Instead these developments simply shift economic activity from one part of town to another. The end result is not economic development, but rather economic displacement.

Trading locally owned businesses for chain stores also entails the loss of significant secondary economic benefits. Local stores keep profits circulating within the local economy. They also support a variety of other local businesses. They create opportunities for service providers, like accountants and printers. They do business with the community bank. They advertise through independent radio stations and other local media outlets. They purchase goods from local or regional distributors. In this way, a dollar spent at a locally owned businesses sends a ripple of economic benefits through the community.

However, chain stores centralize these functions at their head offices. They keep local investment and spending to a minimum. They bank with big national banks. They bypass local radio stations in favour of national advertising. In this way, much of a dollar spent at a chain store leaves the community immediately. Small, independent stores also create economic diversity and stability. Because they are locally owned, these stores are firmly rooted in the community. They are unlikely to move and will do their best to weather economic hard times.

Independent stores tend to be located in humanly accessed, pedestrian-oriented shopping districts, as opposed to the sprawling, isolated experience of a chain store parking lot. The local stores create a sense of place and community identity. They reflect the local culture. They give neighbourhoods their distinct flavor. They are often a source of community pride and an attraction to visitors. Independent businesses strengthen community through their contributions to civic and cultural life. Local merchants are more than providers of goods and services. They often take a leadership role in community affairs. Many chair neighborhood organizations, host cultural events, or organize local festivals. Because they live in the places where they do business, local merchants tend to be far more committed to the community's well-being and long-term stability than distant corporations. This awareness is getting strengthened with the big stride being made by the big chain stores. This commitment manifests itself in a variety of ways. Finally, the shift from local to absentee-owned stores means that business decisions are no longer made locally by members of the community. Who decides whether to close a store in a distressed neighbourhood, stock a controversial book, sell produce from local farms, pay a living wage, or contribute to a local charity? In the case of chain stores, these decisions occur in distant boardrooms, where the values of the local community carry little or no weight.

There are interests that believe that public policy should have no role in shaping the retail economy. This is, after all, a free market. But public policy is never neutral, and has, in fact, played a major role in the expansion of national chain stores. In many ways, public policy has undermined local retailers by giving large retail corporations unfair advantages. Under these circumstances, even the most competitive, efficient, and popular independent businesses are struggling to stay afloat.

Shopping Malls

Shopping malls have sprung up in the metro India almost like mushrooms. These can be seen across the country's landscape and more are promising to come up. These malls are located in one building or at times, in a number of buildings with connected paths. Visitors to these malls can easily move from one area or building to the other because of adequate walking space and signages located at strategic positions. These paths are generally covered for the customers' sake to save them from inclement weather.

Historically the origin of the malls can be traced from the 10th century when such indoor retail markets existed in Iran, Turkey, UK, Italy and from 1828 in the USA. 20th century malls as they can be seen today are the creation of the automobile culture in the USA where customers enjoyed outings in cars for shopping which had become a good pastime for the families, especially the ladies.

In many cases, regional and super-regional malls exist as parts of large superstructures which often also include office space, residential space, amusement parks and movie halls. This trend can be seen in the construction and design of many modern supermalls even in India.

One controversial aspect of malls has been their effective displacement of traditional main streets. Many consumers prefer malls, with their spacious parking garages, well-maintained walkways, and private security guards, over public streets, which often suffer from limited parking, poor maintenance, and limited police coverage. Malls in Saket, Noida are perfect examples.

Catalogue Retailing

Several companies have been distributing or selling their well made catalogues to the customers in the right market segment in the hope that the catalogues will give a good view of the products they sell and the customers will on their own place orders on them. This type of retailing totally obviates the need for a shop as the sales are affected from the warehouses direct to the customers, reducing the selling costs to a large extent. However, with the increased use of Internet marketing the virtual marts have taken over the catalogue business in a large measure.

Critical Success Factors—CSF in Retail

The entrepreneurs need to understand that any effort made half-heartedly is going to produce less than mediocre results. From the days of industrial revolution and from the assembly line mass-producing techniques the business has deduced that standardization and impersonal approach is the best for success in the mass market of the consumers. Unfortunately, today only the reverse is true. Like-minded persons working in stereotype fashion almost like robots are hardly able to have innovation and personalized product and service as their new mantra. Followers try to change only to become like their boss or the leader. Since the days of independence innovation and breaking the old system has been looked upon with disdain. And the surprise situation is that even the customers, at least most of them, feel satisfied and happy with the typical retail trade handouts. However, the time has come that the retailers realize the importance of innovation, personalization and speed with which the product delivery is required by the busy customers of today.

The following caselet gives a bird's-eye view of shoppers' mindset over the years:

Caselet women shoppers over the years

1960- A housewife plans a shopping trip. Mrs. Rita Sinha is married with two teenage kids; husband a Manager in a private firm. Sinhas are upper middle class family. After sending husband to work and children to school, Rita takes off her apron, puts on lipstick, picks up her shopping list and carry bag and is off to the nearby market. She makes the shopping list once a week, which includes grocery, toiletry, washing powder and occasional chocolates for the kids. She walks the half a kilometre distance to the market. (On return journey she will take a rickshaw, as she would be carrying her shopping too).

At the market she goes to her favourite shops, orders the items, waits for the shop assistant to get her things with impatience, then she moves to the next shop. She is keen to react to any price variations and would haggle over the price even with a threat of changing shops. Getting a lower price gives her great satisfaction. She does care about the product quality, but rationalizing her cheaper purchase by saving money is easy.

The big day comes once a year, when she wants to buy things for the larger family, in-laws, cousins friends, when she forces her husband to accompany her and the children on a shopping expedition. Normally, they end up buying things for children and going to a restaurant on being pressurized by the young ones.

The shopkeepers and shop assistants know her needs, whims and fancies and they try to humour her to the extent possible within the time constraint, both for her as also for the shopkeepers.

On coming home she tries to figure out how and where she over spent, as the next pay cheque comes much later and day to day expense have to be met.

Women shoppers 21st Century

Working Women – They plan shopping well in advance. Holidays are meant for shopping, house cleaning and visiting friends. Today, Mrs. Reena Verma is planning a shopping expedition. She calls her friends Prema and Kimi on her cell phone in conference mode. They decide to meet at 11 am at the Shoppers Stop. Let us do some window shop at first and then we can decide to go for the real thing. They enter the cosmetic area and get busy trying out different shades of lipsticks, eye shadows, and nail polishes. Prema buys some items and flashes her credit card to make the purchase. Next they are in store for ready to wear dresses. Here Reena wants to buy a dress to wear at the next kitty party. Dress is selected after she has tried out a dozen dresses. Next, she must get matching shoes and accessories, which are luckily all available in the same shop at different counters. Time for a coffee break, McDonald's is the next stop. In the air-conditioned shopping mall the friends have forgotten that it is time they reach home to be with their kids at least on their holiday. Not to worry, the maidservant is there to give food to the kids.

Questions

1. Discuss the change in consumer behaviour and needs over the years.
2. What socio-cultural changes have occurred as per the case?
3. How have the marketers met the situation?

The third world countries are developing economies ready to grab the new product offerings as there the customers are becoming knowledgeable, economically better off. The customers look forward to better newer products, specialized and personalized service to suit the individual needs for retaining customers and building loyalty.

Retailers have been deriving competitive advantage from their location so far. Manufacturers had competitive advantage from the easy availability of raw materials, trained manpower, and nearness of the markets and are being able to obtain low cost finance as compared to competition. With easy distribution of materials, improved supply chains, location advantage started vanishing. For retailer as well, while for stand-alone shops location remains advantageous for shopping malls, it does not affect the customer a lot. Customers love to move to the mall areas where the ambience is attractive and offerings are a plenty. The shopping expeditions involve investment in time, money for the family and naturally they want to extract the best out of both. Retailers that have innovative selling techniques, latest technology products and recourse to financing for customers who require the products on hire-purchase basis are going to have the sustainable competitive advantage. The competitive advantage so far has been based on new research products. Today with copied products, licence purchases, such advantages are short-lived. Innovation becomes commonplace occurrence with "me too" products in shorter time than can be imagined.

The thinking therefore moved to innovations like JIT –Just-in-Time purchasing for lowest possible current assets, Business Process Reengineering for obtaining the optimized operating advantage, outsourcing for reducing unnecessary overheads, downsizing for keeping a lean organization. In the area of retailing thrust came on to the salespersons that could deliver by unique selling techniques and yet human angle with respect to the customers remained un-thought of. The time has come when retailers start looking at the service function as perhaps the most important one at the present time. The customer wants to be pampered with the best of service as the service has entered selling in a big way. The only innovation that cannot be easily copied is in the service delivery and this comes from the following areas:

- Product customization
- Customer communication—personal selling, advertising, promotion, publicity, PR
- Personalization in service with a smile, smiles are not easy to copy in any case.

Internet sales, auctions have posed different type of problems for the innovators with better designing of the websites more attractive offer statements. The winning e-tailer will be the one with the most outstanding site. In this area innovation must reflect an omnibus type of scheme to relate to customers worldwide.

In the final analysis people buy products not so much as they need them, especially a particular brand but because of some emotional bond, or heart string that tugs and makes the purchase decisions for them. That is the reason companies put great efforts in building brand equity and then in doing all in their power to keep strengthening the same. Most purchases are made on emotional level and it is soul searching that is required by the retailers for providing their customers of that emotional pulls relevant in today's hectic competitive actions, promotions and merchandising. When the customers of the day get like products in terms of price, quality and performance the selection becomes not only difficult but also confusing. Any good TV, vacuum cleaner, microwave oven, washing machine will give the same value for money with little to differentiate them. Deals in these circumstances are made with extras that are added like guarantee periods, free services, some accessories, like making price reduction in the real sense. It is all to the good, except when it comes to getting buyers emotionally attached to some brands. Once the brand takes hold of emotions and in a buyer's imagination, the purchases are more inspired than mundane. Some retailers are so obsessed with certain brands that have been their breadwinners that they will never give them up and they keep swearing by their power as leaders even much after they have lost their sheen. Such emotional ties can bind the retailers eternally to the "has been a product" forever. A good retailer would keep reviewing his product portfolio to keep only the winners and future winners and would shed the dead woods as fast as possible.

Given below is a case study of portfolio analysis that will help the students in understanding the concept.

Caselet Portfolio Management

Activity Base Corporation (ABC) is a multi-product firm with all India sales networks. While the firm has been growing at the market rate of growth, its profit picture has been rather dismal. The management has appointed a firm of consultants to recommend to them the action they should be taking to improve their bottom line. Some details of the firm are given below for student's perusal.

- Annual sales — Rs. 145 crore
- Raw material cost — Rs. 50 crore
- Fixed costs — Rs. 15 crore
- Available revenue — Rs. 80 crore
- Product costs — Rs. 65.5 crore
- Profit before tax — Rs. 14.5 crore
- Total — Rs. 80 crore

The next table gives the product-wise picture of revenue generation, share of cost, net revenue value, cost to profit coefficient.

S. No.	Rev. value	Rev. % of total	Cost value	Cost % of total	Net revenue value	%of net revenue value	Cost-profit coeff.	Remarks
1.	19	24	18.2	28	0.8	5	0.25	
2.	14	17.5	16.7	25.5	-2.7	-12	Loss	
3.	14	17.5	7.2	11	6.7	4.7	3.3	
4.	11	14	5.2	7.5	5.8	40	3.8	
5.	7	9	5.4	8	10.6	11	1.5	
6.	4	5	3.4	5	0.6	4	1.0	
7.	4	5	3.6	5	0.4	3	0.75	
8.	3.5	4.5	3.3	5	0.2	1.5	0.5	
9.	2	2.5	1.85	2.5	0.15	1	0.5	
10.	1	1	1.5	2	-0.5	-0.5	Loss	

The next table gives the management support as it exists for each product. Students can use the table to diagnose the problem in each product and plan strategies accordingly.

S.No.	Revenue	Working capital	Management support	Technical support	Sales service support	Remarks
1.	19	15	Very high	Very good	Very good	
2.	14	4.5	Very high	Very good	Very good	
3.	14	5	Very high	Low	Medium	
4.	11	3	High	Low	Medium	
5.	12	0.5	Nil	Low	High demand	
6,	4	Nil	High	High	Best	
7.	4	Nil	High	High	Best	
8.	3.5	15	Spl.task force	Very good	High pressure	
9.	2	5	Low	Low	Low in sale high for old products	
10.	1	Nil	High	High	Nil	

Tasks for the students: Formulate strategies for each product taking its position in the BCG Matrix considering revenue generation and support given and needed. Working capital needs give you a clue to the monetary support provided to each product. Can you find out which products are in the star, cash cow, question mark and dog stages of the BCG Matrix?

Companies have been experimenting with the idea of lateral thinking as they handle issues like quality, information and ethics from the viewpoint of organizational hierarchy, delegating the subjects to people who are considered most fit for the job. The hands-on leadership does not look over the team member's shoulders and yet provides for underhand stability even as the members are bust multi-tasking in the company. Imagine a scene in a retail shop at busy hour where there are more customers than it can usually handle. Any manager would like to have extra hands to cope with the rush hour and yet no one can recruit personnel on the basis of peak time. How about keeping the HR, Finance, Purchasing people on the alert to take over the extra burden with sufficient knowledge and training of the sales functions? Such learning organizations are the one's that are going to outlast and be more successful than the others. Persons who are seeped into their traditional trades have no value in today's business, more especially in the retail. It becomes the basic task of the leader to plan rotational assignments for the team members for creating a learning organization. This provides for releasing the total potential of the team as the members belonging to different disciplines come on a common platform with only one desire and that of delivering the goods and achieving the targets. Such an evolved team will have such cohesive force that will bring even the customers and suppliers into their ambit that would make them virtual partners of the company.

These success factors of the retail firm are derived from the following:

1. Industry factors, whether it is growing, if yes at what rate
2. Its position in the market life cycle
3. Business general environment factors
4. Technology updates
5. Competition

Critical Success Factors—CSF for a "stand-alone" grocer shop have to be carefully examined because with the onslaught of MNCs stepping in the retail race with big international brands, shopping malls and retail chain stores these grocer shops are facing extinction in foreseeable future. The following are the CSF for such shops:

1. Location of the shop
2. Ease of entry and exit
3. Façade, attractive building
4. Parking space and ease of parking, valet parking service
5. Merchandise offered
6. Pleasant ambience
7. Helpful, caring sales team
8. Displays and visual merchandising
9. Home delivery in the vicinity
10. Credit facility
11. Additional facilities like assistance in payment of electricity, water and phone bills
12. Acceptance of payment by credit cards
13. Personalized service

Location of the shop: The location selection should depend on the following factors:

Customer profile of the neighbourhood residential areas: Do they belong to the market segment that fits in the sellers product group?

1. Are shops available at reasonable rate for buying or for rental?
2. Are the shops having enough space inside for merchandise to be sold with provision for expansion?
3. Is the shop visible from a reasonable distance to attract customers with attractive signages?
4. Is there enough parking place?
5. Are there other shops in the neighbourhood selling similar wares? If yes what level of sales they have throughout the year?
6. What is the reputation of these shops among the customers visiting them? Is there a niche segment yet uncovered by the existing shops?

Normally the stand-alone shops should be near the residential areas. The ideal way for such shopkeepers to prosper is to build strong relationships with their customers by being helpful, courteous and ethical in dealings always.

Shop's entrance is of vital importance as it either invites or dissuades the customers from entering the shop. The shop should have attractive and proper signage on the approach areas near the shop that directs the customers into the shop without any problem. The road taking the customers should as traffic free as possible and with enough parking space for vehicles. Since such shops are small the point of purchase advertising materials like posters, danglers, in-house closed circuit TV should be placed strategically to offer customers product knowledge, buying incentives and floor plan to guide the customer to the right place where the product of their interest is on display. The salespersons should be well trained to be able to offer right suggestions or for clarifying customer's doubts without sounding superior and without becoming obtrusive like an intruder while they want to make purchases in peace and without any interference from any one. The salespersons should be like unnoticed observers who cross the buyers' path only when they need them.

The shop building can itself become its advertiser with its unique façade and friendly approach. Shop signs, decorative panels help in augmenting the "friendly neighbourhood" shop tag, and the customers can be almost forced into coming to the shop.

The shops should offer products that have a demand in the area, like grocery, ready-made garments, toiletries, cosmetics and gift items. An area selling confectionery is a useful addition in middle and upper middle-class market segment. The uncluttered look shop with neat product displays, courteous staff are the best success factors for the stand-alone shops. With shopping malls, chain stores coming up in the vicinity these shops need to become more assertive, helpful and customer oriented to survive and thrive. Shops own credit cards, valet parking, freebies and celebrations during festival time are great ways of creating that strong bond with the customers making them loyal as also making shopping more of a habit, a pleasant experience for the shoppers rather than a drudgery and a chore that is unpalatable, boring and therefore saps the customer's energy. Given below are certain basic rules of creating customer relationship that fosters continuous interaction between the buyers and the shop.

1. Place a notice board for the customers to put their messages, suggestions and give prizes to the best notices.
2. Publish a monthly newsletter giving news about the shop and of the community at large.
3. Sponsor neighbourhood school functions.
4. Sponsor local Rotary Club, Lions Club functions.
5. Arrange to pay customers electricity, telephone bills at no extra costs to them.
6. Remember birthdays, anniversaries of customers and send cards, flowers, small gifts on due dates.
7. Personalize the relationship by addressing the customers by their names, putting tags on their purchase container bags with their names like a card saying, "Especially selected oranges for Mr. Gupta".
8. Keep a stock of candies as giveaways for the customer's children, single roses for the lady customers (to be given on certain special occasions like Christmas, Diwali, Eid).
9. Have trained gift wrappers for arranging gift-wrapping for the customers buying gifts.

10. Keep a stock of greeting cards with envelopes, stamps especially during festive season and offer to get the post delivered at the post office.
11. Organise seasonal festivities with contests with gifts for the winners.
12. Organize sales promotion plans with giveaways for the visitors even if they do not buy anything during that visit. (In several promotion plans the shop can get sponsorships of companies who would be interested in promoting their own products. The shop needs to locate companies that are not competing with it and then let their banners, posters be displayed during the promotion in shop's prominent locations. These sponsors should be asked to donate some of their products to be given as gifts for the contest winners during the promotional campaign period.) Before starting the promotional campaign the shop must ensure the following:
    (a) There are enough stocks of products placed on promotional plans and more stocks will be available on request.
    (b) The shop undergoes thorough "spring cleaning" before the campaign.
    (c) The product displays, merchandising are reworked to give the best effect
    (d) Audio-visual advertising, unobtrusive soft music create a festive ambience during the campaign.
    (e) Train the salespersons anew in handling customers, providing courteous service and more importantly handling complaints deftly and with speed. They should be trained to avoid any form of gossip, idle talk, and discussion on politics or even on competitors to keep controversies away.
    (f) Salespersons should fully know the promotional details for educating the customers on the same. Several times half baked information makes customers cynical about sales promotion schemes as it has been found that the retailers often sell the product to the customer without the gift given for the purpose. Such incidents tarnish the retailers' image and it can take decades before it can be brought back to its original level.

Sustainable Competitive Advantage

Retail the small traders need to counter the upsurge of shopping malls to protect their interests and stay in the market with profit. It can be achieved in the following manner:

Differentiation: The retailers need to organize differentiations in all the 4 Ps-product, price, placement and promotion. Product differentiation can be in the shape of new packaging, retailer's own brand along with the major brands. Retailers can plan product bundling by offering two products that have similar or coordinated uses like soap and soap box, shoe and shoe polish with brush. Differentiation in price is possible with such bundling. Besides different packages like cartons, polythene bags can be used to pack items like sugar spices with different pricing for catering specific market segments. Retailers can resort to home delivery as differentiated placement of goods while in-house audio-visual advertising can be used for differentiating the promotion.

Cost benefits: These can be achieved if the retailer plans on volume trade with penetrating prices that will attract large number of customers and take them away from the shopping malls. Since retailers' overheads are not as large as compared to the malls, it is easier for them to work on low margins and yet make good money. In retail trade the inventory turnover is essential as it helps in building sales as also in keeping products factory fresh always.

Quick response to customer needs: It is an essential part of retail trade to anticipate the product demand by keeping close contact with the customer psyche and availability of new products that are about to be launched. Customer relationship can be fully exploited to understand the future product requirements and the retailer that starts selling them gains upper hand to start with. Later on, when others start offering the same product the wise retailer seeks fresh products that have anticipated demand.

In order to optimize their efforts the retail shops should define the market segment they are usually catering to. Once they understand the segment they can know the best possible 4Ps for the segment. The retail needs to price the products as acceptable to the segment customers. The retailers should find out the price sensitivity of the product before finalizing the price. The advertising and promotional plan needs to be dovetailed to directly relate to the segment customers. Such focus will ensure that the customers will get attracted to the shop and soon become its loyal customers.

Technological excellence in the products will surely help the retailers get the techno-savvy customers. It is therefore important to stock only those products that have been technically approved and accepted by the customers while the new accepted technology has not raised the price level to unacceptable heights.

Core competencies of retailers are given below:

(a) Materials management-purchase and logistics
(b) Visual merchandising including window displays
(c) Trained personnel in providing service, information, assistance in gift wrapping of purchased goods
(d) Finance to organize timely purchases of products as per their demand.
(e) CRM with the local customers
(f) Home delivery of products ordered
(g) Easy of entry and exit and adequate parking place

To be successful retailers need to have at least four of the above in good measure. Customer relationship is one of the most important areas that define the business volumes for any retailer. The following are the methods of building the relationships:

1. Courteous service
2. Correct advice or suggestions needed by the customers in selecting products
3. Help in any way required

Given below is an example of how retailers can grab any opportunity coming their way for building the relationship.

Example

A lady shopper dropped the bottle of tomato sauce just outside the retail shop. The shopkeeper replaced the bottle at no cost although since the bottle had broken after the purchase and outside the shop, the shop had no liability for the breakage. The shopkeeper, in the process got a customer for life.

Critical Success Factors for Retail Chain Stores

The main advantage of retail chain stores is uniformity of quality of goods and services at all the locations. To maintain the standards the chain owners need to have the following systems:

Common purchasing as far as possible, will help in maintaining the quality standards as the same products and brands will be available at the shops everywhere. C&A Stores, Marks and Spenser are two examples that have kept the same high standards in their stores around the world.

Common stores façade, signage that define the stores anywhere. Aesthetics, ambience and interior décor give the stores their individuality as they distinguish the store from others in the same area.

Same superior service given in the stores everywhere would provide a sense of comfort to shoppers who travel a lot and can be seen buying products from known store chains always.

Closing and opening hours, lunch breaks need to be coordinated even considering the different time zones in the world.

Even if the size of the store is small it should follow the same pattern while keeping the entire product and brand range albeit in smaller numbers.

In certain cases going by the local requirements the stores can add or subtract from the product portfolio and get into domestic market scene for better customer acceptance.

Seasonal changes, changes on account of festivals, holidays need to be made on local basis to remain in touch with the market needs. Continuous marketing research in each of the locales must be correlated to optimise the selling efforts and having a holistic marketing programme.

Retailers having international chains need to plan their presence in the following manner:

Global: For certain products like high value cars including Mercedes, the retailing strategy need not be altered and the same global marketing plans will work.

Multi-domestic: In case of other products the local demands in specifications, quality standards and quantity are required. Even brand names packages need to altered and the retailers need to address themselves on these matters.

Hybrid strategies help in planning taking both the global perspective as well as the domestic scenario that will give the retailers an edge on the purely global or multi-domestic stores.

At times retail chains keep a separate enclosure meant for goods belonging to the "seconds" standards. These enclosures offer products at discounts and therefore attract custom on the strength of lower prices, enabling the shopkeepers in meeting the demands of a larger variety of customers.

International retail chain brands help the tourists in shopping with confidence in these stores with the knowledge that they will get the same uniform quality and would not be cheated at all. It must be understood (and most regular international travellers are aware of it too) that in almost each of the countries there are retail sharks ready to cheat foreigners with the knowledge that these people are unaware of the local market scene and more importantly do not have the time to complain if they get to know that they have been cheated. In order to avoid any unpleasant situation seasoned travellers prefer to shop from international retail chains.

The following skill areas cover the areas of interest for the salespersons:

Skills Areas

The first skill area is that of communication, be it writing or verbal communication. The clarity of ideas, lucidity or flow of thoughts expressed in simple easily understood language always conveys more than communication with verbose styling using big words whose meaning even the writer may not be fully aware of. Salespersons should make the words their friends before using them.

1. It is better to go direct to the main point instead of meandering around trifling matters. Be direct. The readers normally have just a few minutes to read any document. It is better to place the biggest ideas and the best writing effort up front.
2. The ideas should be organized by starting with the big picture as the details are filled in to support the main idea. The question that needs to be answered is—what the writer is trying to convey and the readers reactions that are expected.
3. The writer should be having a good knowledge of the readers of the message, what they want to hear, what interests them. The writing should be in the language best understood by the readers. Technical terms or jargons unfamiliar to the readers are strictly prohibited.
4. Sales writing should be done in subdued form of advertising. The writings are in competition with hundreds of other documents. Hence, the advertising language would definitely catch their attention. Research the readership and aim the main point directly to their needs. As they are hit by the biggest idea in the first sentence or paragraph they would like to read the entire communication. The communiqué should be kept as short as possible in consideration with the time needed for reading the same.
5. The writing should be formatted in a fifteen second reading schedule that lets the readers gain the knowledge of the main point in fifteen seconds at a glance. They can read the entire message if they like the main idea.
6. Editing the communication is essential to cut the length and improve its focus. Any redundancy noticed should be assiduously deleted. Confusing sentences should be modified. When the writer has any doubt it is best to make the statement short.

7. Any criticism on the writing should be carefully analyzed and not brushed aside. A notebook covering the criticism should be maintained and gone through before the next document is written; this would prevent errors from creeping into the writings.
8. A dictionary, thesaurus is handy aids for writing messages.

Verbal communications should present ideas clearly as given below:

1. The speakers should avoid use of technical terms acronyms to persons outside of their sphere of activities. The speakers should remain direct, using simple straightforward language as they keep their comments to the point avoiding unnecessary details.
2. As the speaker organizes his ideas he needs to start with the big picture or the main theme while details are offered to support the main ideas. He must decide what he has to say and what reaction he would get from the audience.
3. The speaker must know his audience, one or even hundred, what the wants to hear, know their level of technical knowledge and expertise, know their interests. Try to put yourself in their shoes to realize what they want to hear.
4. Make a marketing pitch by selling the ideas to the audience. Dovetail the talk to their interests and use their interests as a vehicle to convey the ideas.
5. The speaker must ensure that the audience is listening. Ask them question to confirm their participation. The speaker should try to get one listener to sum up the talk given. The question answer session is a good indicator of the audience interest.
6. It is a good idea to practise the talk before a mirror and use a recorder to tape your voice and if possible record audience reaction also for analyzing the same later on. Make sure your voice does not drop or goes overboard as you end a sentence.
7. Body language is an important area for audience reaction. The speaker must keep his faculties open to non-verbal cues. If the speaker finds the audience confused or distracted, he should stop his speech and make sure that the communication comes back on track.

Successful planning of retail management:

1. Define goals and objectives of the retail project. Establish the key areas that would benefit the organization
2. Divide the project into sub-projects with their own time schedules. Plan to have one small part finished every week.
3. Communicate the goals and the objectives to the team members. Ensure that each member of the team knows the project intents and its time plans. The team members must know how the project will benefit the organization and each member of the team individually. Give task priorities.
4. Get cooperation of key persons. Talk to the people who will be affected by the project, as their help may be required at a later date. The project should be discussed with cross-functional teams for a cross-section of views.
5. The feedback loop must be put in place just as the project gets started. Discussion with knowledge people gives quality and a cutting edge to the project. Objectivity of advisors help in avoidance of problems as well as optimum utilization of resources and saving of time.

> Indian Oil in Rural Retail Marketing
> April 2007-04-20
>
> During the last financial year company commissioned more than 1300 new retail outlets out of which 748 low cost outlets were in rural markets with Kisan Seva Kendras. Out of the total 12964 outlets 1330 are in rural areas. Company is planning to improve its quality and quantity supply in rural and retail sectors by the following methods this year:
>
> 1. Automation at the retail outlets
> 2. Satellite-based tracking system for oil tank trucks.
>
> Company's automation plan will eventually cover over 2000 outlets. The company plans to fully automate all outlets selling more than 200 kilolitres of motor fuels a month in a phased manner.

Problem Solving

As the first problem becomes visible, it is not wise to jump to solutions; it is better to look for the larger problem that may be lurking underneath. Otherwise problem solving for small problems would become perpetual problems.

1. Retail problems often appear as symptoms. It is better to locate the problem. For example, if a salesperson is leaving for home early every day, it could be a symptom of some larger problem. He may be untrained for the job, bored with it.
2. Define the goals set for problem solving. In previous case, the goal could be retrain the employee and not just shouting at him to stay for longer hours.
3. It is better to make a list of possible causes of the symptoms observed. Next, cross-check the causes to eliminate those not contributing to the problem. With the list as guide experiments should be made till success is achieved.
4. If required second opinion from experts should be taken for defining the problem.
5. It is important to prioritise the problems and select the ones not worth the trouble and can be just dropped. At times problems bog down people to the extent that they forget their real tasks, while trifling problems unnecessarily take their time. Some problems can be given to others for solving and some can be just dumped.

Problem Solving: Alternative Solutions

1. The best way is to write down the possible solutions before evaluating them.
2. Personal experience, opinion helps in offering alternative innovative solutions for recurring problem. It is better not to assume that the solution that worked earlier would be right every time. The ideas, even novel ones should be written down for verification and debate.
3. Opinion leaders, technical experts should be consulted. People of different disciplines, background can offer their unique perspectives on the same problem. Outside contacts outside of immediate work group or bossiness can be a big help.
4. Get someone to play the devil's advocate. Get the worst-case scenario. Get to know both internal and external factors that would derail your solution.

5. It is advisable to have a contingency plan ready to handle most likely potential problems that have been identified. Such contingency plans can remain in outline form till their use becomes imminent; otherwise a lot of time gets wasted fighting ghosts.
6. Plans and contingency plans should be thoroughly discussed with the team that would implement them or be affected by them get their opinions, criticism and suggestions to refine the plans to make them more realistic.
7. Try to combine alternative solutions to integrate the benefits of each solution, at the least the most important ones they have on offer.

Strengthening Team Efforts

1. Managing teams calls for finding common ground with several points of agreement, common interest, common skills, especially when there is someone with a discordant note. The criticism should be made a part of the common points to avoid discord and confrontational situation.
2. Sharp dissonance should be avoided, as the person giving strong objection should be given acknowledgement for the effort even if the ideas are not accepted. The focus should be on specifics as any response is made to severe criticism.
3. Personal ideas should be shared, discussed by dovetailing them to the listeners' interest areas. This is important as even one discordant person can influence several others to block even legitimate solutions.
4. As the ideas are pushed the respect for other ideas should not be ignored. As the ideas are discussed with enthusiasm it is better not to criticize ideas placed by others. These should be acknowledged along with the plans put forward by others. Rational analysis of different ideas works better. If possible, it is best to integrate two or more opinions to obtain the best of these approaches.
5. Investment in building relationships with the teams pays and hence it is useful for the leader to be generous with time, patience in assisting people in the group or even just outside. Reputation as a team person is essential as it would provide the required help for success.

CHAPTER 3

Locating New Customers

Aims and Objectives

Marketers have to keep locating new retailers as they need to be added all the time as the retailers are not exclusively selling company's products. This exercise can be termed prospecting. In prospecting the salesperson has to identify and qualify new retailers, as this is one of the most important ways of creatively getting new business. The next step is to set up an objective for calls on the customers as well as on prospects. The sales person must know how to gather essential information about the prospect before making call plans. Next the call tactics need to be formulated.

The salesperson needs to have the right attitude before the call and this attitude can be developed. The salesperson should ensure that he gets the prospect interested in his proposition quickly enough. It is always useful to verify the efficacy of the call plans.

The salesperson must be fully aware of the features of the product or the service he has to sell. He must be able to distinguish between the features and the derived benefits from the features of the product. This will help him in putting together an effective presentation while maintaining the prospect's interest and believability in the presentation. Most prospective retailers will offer objections to change in their buying patterns (as they are perhaps buying from competition). The salesperson must be able to distinguish between valid and superficial objections. The most important plan of sales calls is the way calls should be closed with the retailer's purchase orders in hand.

Finally, salespersons need to know how to arrange a post call analysis to learn the gains of the plans as well as its shortcomings.

Prospecting

Prospecting can be divided into four parts, the advantages of having a skilled salesperson in the technique of prospecting, learning the methods and sources for identifying and locating the worthwhile prospects, qualifying the prospects by understanding the more desirable prospects from the less desirable ones, the relationship between prospecting and creative selling.

Every salesperson has to find new customer—the retailers as prospects. Customers, the present retailers are the existing buyers while prospects are likely buyers. Prospects can be considered potential buyers of the company's products. Prospecting can be defined as identifying and qualifying potential retailers/customers or prospects" salespersons need to learn the prospecting of potential retailers as customers to enable them to replace lost retailers as customers due to organizational changes, relocation, competitive activities. A skilled salesperson will be able to prioritize calls on prospects more likely to become their retailer/customers, making the sales calls more productive. Such salesperson will be able to broad base his retailer/customer list and increase the total number of his customers. He will reduce the number of unproductive calls in the process.

Prospect Identification

In several product groups it is easy to identify the prospects, like the cotton supplier will know the textile mills as his prospects, the airlines would identify the travel agents as the prospects. However, for products with a large number of possible customers like insurance, office supplies it is more difficult to locate the prospects. In such cases companies develop ingenious techniques for identifying the prospects. One insurance company's sales manual has a list of 140 different sources of prospects of life insurance. Published data, lists, telephone directories are good source of potential customers. Today's telemarketers use these lists for calling on the prospects to know their interest in the product being sold. Salespersons use referrals extensively for locating prospects. Company's existing customers are known to recommend another possible buyer to the salesperson. This can happen on the buyer's own volition or on salesperson's request. At times even prospects can give referrals of other prospects and the salesperson can use the endless chain of prospecting potential customers. Besides, influential business leaders, community leaders can become source of prospecting for customers. These influential persons are found at the centrestage of power. Even bankers, lawyers, educators can be used as such sources.

One major area that brings about prospects is the enquiries, (that could have been generated because of companies advertising efforts or sales promotion) which the company receives from prospects. These enquiries are passed on to the salespersons as business leads.

Salespersons should always be on the alert for locating new customers—the companies' prospects. It is a good idea to develop a data bank that is kept updated for the prospects by adding the prospects from all the possible sources.

Once the salesperson has got the name of the prospect his task actually starts. The salesperson must find out in the prospects organization the right person who should be met for business. Ideally the entire purchase decision hierarchy should be understood along with other particulars like phone, address, and email address. A study confirms that 60% of sales calls are made on wrong persons and are therefore ineffective. Sales calls are expensive as a lot of time is spent on planning and executing the calls. It is necessary that the time and effort are wisely invested. Salespersons should therefore, start with making calls on the best prospects, those whose chances of getting converted into customers are the most.

Qualifying the Customer–For a manufacturer, retailer is an important customer.

Qualifying helps the salesperson in selecting the best prospects on whom to call. The following three questions are used for qualifying the prospects:

1. Does the prospect meet with the company's policies?
2. Does the product fulfil a need of the prospect?
3. What is the current and future value of the prospect to the company?

In the case of company policy the salesperson should understand the prospects requirements on the following terms of business and the company's standards on the same:

1. Pricing and discounts
2. Credit as a sales tool
3. Cash discounts
4. Delivery needs
5. Order size
6. Servicing requirements

Prospects with odd or abnormal requirements that the company cannot comply with is not a good prospect as against the prospect who requires only the standard terms of business. Such prospects are likely to offer long-term business association to the company. The other, even more important question is, do company's product and service, including delivery periods fill the prospects needs? Prospects with urgent needs that can be met by the company have the best chance of becoming company's customers. However, in majority of cases the prospects do not see any need for the company's products in immediate future or even in the distant future. At such times it is the job of the salesperson to find out a way in which the company's product can satisfy some need of the prospect. It must be understood clearly that even if the prospect does not see any need of the company's product but the salesperson does see a need then the prospect is worth working on. A company modernizing its plant will have need of a bigger, more powerful air-conditioning system even if the company does not realize at the moment. It would be prudent for the salesperson to introduce his company's latest energy saving powerful air-conditioning system when the buyer is in the right frame of mind to listen.

Retail salespersons also make sales calls on customers. A salesperson read in a magazine that one industrial laboratory had many delicate instruments that needed soft lint free cloth to wipe off dust from the instruments. While the purchase person of the laboratory may never have thought of buying napkins for the purpose, the alert salesperson saw the need and now that and similar several other laboratories are using the napkins. Therefore, the salesperson should not get worried even if the prospect shows no interest in the product, and try to locate even hidden needs of which even the prospect is not aware.

The next level is to find out the present and future value of the prospect to the company/retailers. The prospects capacity is one yardstick for measuring the value. The biggest buyer gets to be the best prospect. Big value frequent orders from the prospect make him most valuable. However, even a small buyer with future growth possibilities can never be ignored. Besides, the prospects reputation is a major factor in considering its value. A small buyer who is a community leader and much respected should be rated high on value even against the bigger volume buyers who may be poorly regarded in the business circles.

Summarizing, the good prospect can be defined as the one that meets the business policy and terms of business of the company, has a definite need of the company's products and has a high present or future value for the company, or if the prospect enjoys leadership position in the industry or in the community.

So far a variety of techniques of prospecting have been studied. It is obvious that the prospecting techniques will differ greatly among the salespersons depending on the kind of selling job they are performing, the product. Prospecting for customers requires creative ability on the part of the salesperson. Salespersons creativity is perhaps the only limiting factor for developing prospecting plans for future customers. At the same time the creative salesperson can determine newer ways of product usage by the potential customers.

Planning Sales Calls

It should be assumed that the customer is a busy person and when he gives an appointment for a sales call, it is important that the salesman makes the best use of the time given, and hence the need for careful planning for each such call.

Planning sales calls should be done using the following steps:

- Study the customer's file; remember the name (with correct pronunciation), designation, level and authority of the person to be met. Review of any complaint from the customer, whether it has been attended to, satisfactorily so far or not. Is there any pending matter from the last call, which must be resolved before the call is made, or else the salesman may not be even welcome at the customer's premises? For example, if the salesman had promised replacement of defective product and it has not taken place so far, the sales call would end up in bitter criticism from the customer and undue justification from the salesman. No concrete result can come from such a situation.
- Plan the sales call objectives, both major and minor ones. It is better to write them down at least in first few calls.
- Carry the following in the briefcase to be used at the customer's place.
  - (a) Visiting cards
  - (b) Customer's file
  - (c) Product literature, especially of new products being introduced
  - (d) Testimonials from other customers
  - (e) Firms letterheads
  - (f) Price lists
  - (g) Terms of business

(h) Pen, pencils, erasers, carbon paper, stapler with staples
(i) Products benefits for the customer along with the benefits offered by competition (make sure your benefits always outscore the competitive benefits) the benefits should be written in sequence of their priority for the customer and it may be wise to alter the sequence for different levels of customers hierarchy.

The salesman should be smartly dressed and well groomed. In most cases, it is essential to take prior appointment from the customer. It is useful to reach customer's office a few minutes early (while waiting the salesman can compose himself, revise the file papers, plan his opening sentences, use the toilet to feel fresh, comb his hair).

In case of meeting a new customer, or one who has been mostly buying from competition dialogue plan, which has been found useful as at several steps the salesman is likely to find objections to his benefit story is given below. Of course, the salesman must keep his wits about him to modify it as the sales call progresses.

The main objective of sales calls is getting the purchase order from the customer. Salesmen usually plan a canned talk to persuade the customer to place the order on the salesman's firm. However, the salesman mostly, encounters resistance from the buyer due to the following reasons, one or all:

- The buyer is friendly to the competitor's salesperson.
- Competitive product gives better value for money in the eyes of the buyer.
- Competition provides better after-sales service as per the buyer.
- The users in the customer's side do not want a change, to avoid problems of duplicated inventories and confusion from unskilled/illiterate workers about a new product.
- The competition is providing some unspecified incentive, overtly or covertly to the buyer.

Following are the steps needed in guiding the buyer in deciding in favour of placing the order on the firm. It is called the **Decision Triangle** (when more than one buying decision person is involved then the triangle could take the shape of **Decision Pyramid**.)

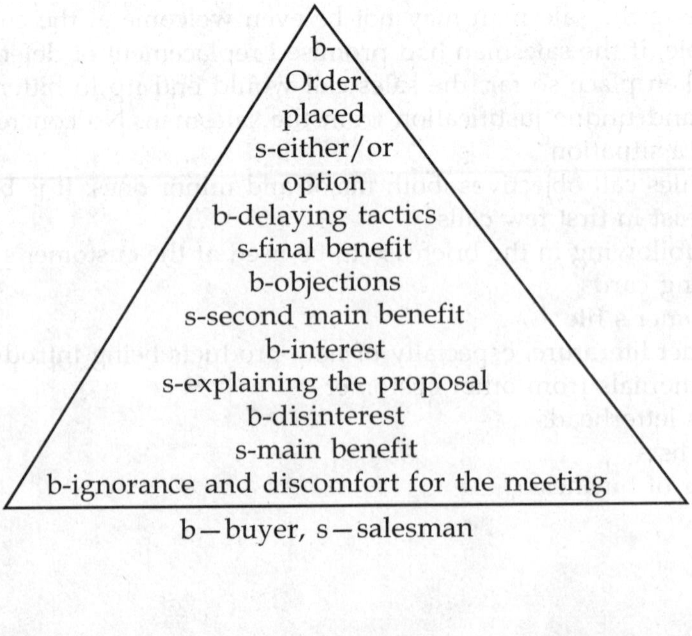

b—buyer, s—salesman

As can be seen in the beginning of the interview, the salesman is at a disadvantage as the customer is ignorant of his proposal. At this juncture it is best to give the most important benefit, which would attract the attention of the buyer. If the benefit could be translated into savings in rupees, it will click well with the CEOs, finance managers; time saving will go well with production managers. Even after the main benefit, the salesman need not feel complacent as the competitive strengths are still working to defuse their effort. At this stage the salesman must explain the proposal and if the buyer wants he can call other members of decision-making team to join him. It will save time for both seller and the buyer. Otherwise, similar dialogue will have to be carried out with other members separately. After some interest is generated, the salesman would do well to seize the opportunity by adding the other benefits till the buyer reaches the stage of purchase decision. At times there is a last hurdle, which is basically a delaying tactic on the part of the buyer, like I have to consult my father (who may not be even involved in the business at all). This can be surmounted by offering an option to the buyer, "Would you want us to provide the transit insurance or you would cover it yourself?" if the customer says, "we will take the insurance cover ourselves" your deal is finalized. Once the salesman gets the purchase order, he must make sure to thank the buyer and leave his office without delay. It has been known that if the salesman stays long enough he may lose the order, "Could you just give me that order back for a minute, I want it to be checked once more by our auditors." You hand over the order and can wish it goodbye as the next day the competitors salesman would walk in, get the benefit of your sales talk which has brought the buyer into buying mood, and he will walk away with *your order*.

In case there is buying committee to take decisions the salesman can act as a liaison man by getting the following to meet and put across the benefit story as per the mindset and need of the member of the committee, thus the decision triangle becomes decision pyramid:

- Firm's CEO with buyers CEO: This could perhaps be the last meeting unless of course the two CEOs know each other well.
- Technical manager/R&D manager with the buyers R&D manager
- Systems manager with buyers Production manager
- Logistics manager with buyers Materials manager
- Finance manager with buyers Finance manager

These meetings could be on one-to-one basis or altogether.

Detailed Call Planning

Note: In the following paragraphs the words used—Customer and prospect are interchangeable.

Salespersons need to learn in detail the various aspects of call planning before a call is made on a customer or a prospect. Sales calls are costly and time-consuming both for the salesperson and the buyer; it is essential that the calls are planned in advance and thoroughly. Some salespersons feel that playing by the ear will take them through a successful sales call. However, experience shows that such calls usually end in disaster. Planning needs to be first perceived in the mind only. Planning process takes the salesperson through what will be done in future well in advance. The sales calls are important assignments and the risk of lack of preparedness must be avoided at all cost. A successful call could generate business worth millions of rupees as the reverse is equally true. Call planning needs to be done in the following steps:

1. Establish the call objective
2. Gather the essential information
3. Select appropriate strategies or tactics

Establishing the Call Objectives

The call objective is what the salesperson hopes to achieve when he meets the customer or the prospect face to face. The objective must be set before the call is made. Finally, the objective that any salesperson has is to obtain an order from the customer or the prospect. The objective may quantify the order value for the call. However, more often than not, it takes several calls before an order can be obtained. Therefore, each call may have a different objective, while the major objective of obtaining the order is always at the back of the salesperson's mind. The immediate objective could be to find out changes in buying patterns with the change of purchase team of the customer. Other objective is to persuade the customer or prospect to see a product demonstration. One objective could be to obtain permission to supply samples for trial purposes. There can be a variety of objectives of sales calls and the calls can be considered fruitful if the objective for the call has been met. In any case since the final objective is getting the order, the other minor objectives should bring the main objective a little closer to the company. The objectives of preliminary calls should be used like the steps of an escalator that lead to the final destination, the order. The number of steps, or calls leading to the order would depend on the type of selling as also it will vary from customer to customer. Setting up objectives helps the salesperson in keeping calls on track of achieving the main objective. For example, if the salesperson wants to introduce a new type of denim cloth to the manufacturer of ready-made garments, the following route can be taken:

1. First objective: To get the agreement of the buyer about need of the denim
2. Second objective: Demonstrate the new denim to key individuals
3. Convince the buyer that the price and other terms of business are right and get the order.

As can be seen the intermediate objectives were in line with the major objective of getting the order. The objectives must follow a sequence in ascending order like an escalator, as it will help the salesperson in getting the order rather quickly.

Gathering the Essential Information

Once the objective has been defined the next step is gathering essential information about the customer or the prospect. During the prospecting stage the salesperson has obtained some information. However, the more information he has, the better chances of his success from the sales calls. While information gathering is time-consuming it is important to collect the essential information.

The salesperson has to determine what constitutes the essential information on the prospect. It is the objective of the call that defines the information need of the salesperson. It is useful to prepare a checklist of information needs in order to avoid overlooking any necessary information item. Given below is a dedicated checklist, which should be altered by the salesperson to suit individual requirements.

Business Information Checklist

1. Name
2. Address
3. Telephone numbers, Fax
4. Annual sales volume in rupees and units
5. Ownership
6. Management philosophy
7. Organizational structure
8. Key decision-makers
9. Reputation
10. Competition details
11. Credit rating
12. Number of employees
13. Current problems faced by the company
14. Products/services sold
15. Markets targeted—segments
16. Key customers
17. Plans and policies on purchasing
18. Budget policy
19. Frequency of purchase
20. Seasonal factors
21. Key suppliers
22. Attitude towards price, quality, product innovations
23. Raw material used
24. Components made/bought
25. Manufacturing process
26. Administrative process
27. Machine and equipment used
28. Schedule of maintenance
29. Volume potential for sales by the salesperson in rupees and in numbers
30. Previous experience with the salesperson's company
31. Salesperson's competition

The checklist of personal information

1. Name with correct spelling and pronunciation
2. Address

3. Age with date of birth
4. Position-title, responsibility, authority, line of communication, basis of evaluation by superiors
5. Length of time with the company
6. Business background
7. Education
8. Business or professional affiliations
9. Social affiliations
10. Marital status, family background and number of children
11. Other interests other than the job
12. Personal aspirations
13. Personal peculiarities
14. Best time to visit

While several of the items listed may not be considered essential, it is a good idea to go through the checklist to ensure nothing of vital importance is left out.

Salesperson need to know the sources from where they can gather the information. Information on existing customers is usually available with the salesperson's company. Besides, customers or prospects who give the business leads are another source of information—trade partners, the channel members, trade publications. Business calls should be used to gain information that help in adding onto the already available information. Prospects annual reports, balance sheets reveal important details on their financial standing, plans and new product launches. Prospects product literature, advertisements offer information that can be of use to the salesperson. The salesperson should use all possible means to get the information and keep it updated all the time.

Strategies and Tactics

Salespersons must plan their strategies for the sales calls to attain their call objectives. The calls normally follow the following pattern:

1. Approach
2. Presentation
3. Objections
4. Closing the call

Due to the importance of sales calls, call planning must become an essential part of the salesperson's activities and it should become a work habit with the salesperson. Planning being a mental activity should be carried out at a place where there are no distractions. Salesperson should concentrate on the three elements of call planning, establishing the objective, gathering the essential information and selecting the appropriate tactics. The planning can be done mentally. However, it is recommended that for important call the plan must be written down. Given below is a standard form for planning sales calls:

Call Planner

- Company
- Address
- Phone, fax
- Name of the customer/prospect
- Call objective
- Essential information on the company—on the individual

Call planner–continued

Tactics to use
(a) Approach
(b) Presentation
(c) Objections
(d) Closing

Approach

Once the call planning is complete, the salesperson starts the necessary arrangements to make the presentation before the customer or the prospect. This process is called approach that includes the purpose of approach and its definition. Besides the techniques of getting to see the prospect or the customer has to be learnt. The approach can be defined as the activity of the salesperson that begins with making arrangements to see the customer or the prospect and ends with the start of the presentation. The approach has three basic purposes:

1. To get to see the prospect or the customer
2. To put him in the right frame of mind for the presentation
3. To confirm the call plan

The first activity is to make an appointment for visiting the customer or the prospect. These appointments are made on telephone or through letters depending on time available between call and the appointment. In certain cases where the salesperson has become familiar with the customer and knows his routine, he may not make an appointment. For major business deals appointments must be considered essential. The timing of the call should be to the customer or prospect's convenience. If no appointment has been made, then the time the customer is usually free or the time he has kept for such meetings must be kept in mind. Many business deals have been lost due to wrong timing of the sales call.

For the meeting the salesperson must be decently dressed and polite in demeanour. He will, in all probability meet the receptionist, or the secretary of the person he has to meet and the first impression on these buffers must be perfect. These buffers usually screen the salesperson before he is allowed to meet the main person. Decent dress, courteous behaviour would do wonders in such cases. In case an appointment has not been taken these buffers can blackball the salesperson. In such cases, the best way to gain the appointment is to use the reference of some important person known to the customer or the prospect. Visiting cards, brochures or other mailed material to the prospect can also be used to gain the appointment. At times when the visiting card is given to the buffer the salesperson can write a small note on it to improve his chances for the meeting. These buffers or intermediaries play an important role in the salesperson getting the appointment. These are the virtual gatekeepers and it is best to keep them on the salesperson own side. The fact that the competitors are also doing the same thing should spur the salesperson into making friends of the buffers. Sending greeting cards to them, thank you notes and small gifts during festive periods will be of great help.

Most of the time the salesperson has to wait to meet the right person. The waiting time should be properly utilized by revising the presentation plans. The salesperson can try to obtain the essential information during the waiting time. The buffer may become a good source of such information. If none of these is possible, the salesperson should keep some trade publications or other reading material to fully utilize the waiting time.

Presentation Ready

When the salesperson comes face to face with the customer, the first few minutes make the vital impact on whatever happens afterwards. The presentation success would largely depend on the frame of mind of the customer or the prospect. Following possibilities would prove the point:

1. The prospect has been extremely busy and is meeting the salesperson just out of courtesy.
2. The prospects company is passing through a minor crisis situation.
3. The prospect has to rush out to meet some VIP.
4. The prospect has to meet a deadline and he is already late.

The salesperson needs to keep a positive outlook in all such times and he can gradually convert the negative frame of mind into positive approach of the prospect. The salesperson should ensure that prospect does not consider himself obliged under some duress into meeting him. The prospect should be ready and willing to meet and this happens when the salesperson is ready to help, and remains positive during the meeting. The sincerity and helpful nature are the prerequisites of success in the meeting. A negative behaviour from the salesperson would surely evoke similar response from the prospect. At times the history of earlier calls comes as a barrier of positive outlook of the salesperson and brings in a feeling of inadequacy. Conversely a successful earlier call could make the salesperson overconfident and aggressive. Salesperson's own business results can seriously affect his behaviour during the meeting. The maturity of the salesperson is in throwing off or ignoring these factors that tend to influence his behaviour.

The salesperson has to take each call as a fresh experience. The vital matter is of attitude the salesperson must have, and that should be positive and helpful towards the prospect. The attitude will help the salesperson in getting the prospect into transitional mode where the buyer's mind is gently moved from whatever he had been doing prior to the salesperson's meeting to an enthusiastic willingness to hear the presentation. The salesperson needs to build a good rapport with the prospect. Rapport is defined as a "harmonious relationship". The rapport can be built by even small things like knowing the title, and the correct pronunciation of his name. Small talk, talk about his hobbies, sports or other non-business subjects in which the prospect is genuinely interested will contribute to the rapport building exercise. However, the small talk bit must be kept small since the prospect would not want to waste his valuable time. The salesperson should also make the best usage of the meeting time. Once the rapport has been established the salesperson has to bridge the gap between the social conversation and the specific business of the call. A variety of techniques are used for bridging the gap as given below:

1. At times a question is asked for the purpose. "If I can show you how to reduce maintenance cost by 5%, would it be of interest to you?" is such a question.
2. The other method could be of offering assistance, "I would like to check your air-conditioning system for the coming summer. Of course, there will be no charge."
3. Announcing a significant fact can be used to bridge the gap like, "You will be happy to learn that since last December the electricity supply company is saving rupees fifty lacs."
4. Each year with the use of computerized billing system supplied by us."
5. Sometimes the product like a miniature cell phone needs to be shown for bridging the gap.

The salesperson should always avoid such trite questions," how is business" or "how do things look". Such questions are likely to get a negative response leading to the entire presentation becoming negative from the prospect viewpoint. The other failed technique is, "I was in the neighbourhood and thought I would drop in". Summarizing after the rapport has been built the salesperson needs to have a technique of bridging the gap between the social conversation and serious business talk.

Call Plan Verification

Call planning involves the three steps, establishing the objective, gathering essential information and selecting the right tactics. The salesperson believes that his objectives are attainable, information sufficient and tactics appropriate. However, it is a good idea to verify the plan if the opportunity for doing so presents itself. The verification becomes easy if the prospect is given full rein to talk fully and openly. Salesperson needs to ask a well-worded question after the gap has been bridged between the small talk and serious business talk leading to the presentation. Questions like, "Your new plant installation plan?" Or "Your maintenance plan for the machinery" would let the prospect hold the fort and he would enjoy talking about his ideas. The salesperson could ask, "Which part of the machinery is difficult to maintain?" or "Which is the most time-consuming manual operation that you want transferred to a computer?" The purpose of these questions is to have the prospect talk about his needs. The talks should be carried on till the call plan has been verified by the salesperson. The questions should be broad based to allow a general response. The salesperson should keep showing his interest by interjecting with, "This is interesting, tell me more". Attentive listening will help the salesperson in his verification process of the call plan. If the salesperson feels he can modify the plan as he goes along. He can decide if the original objective is still attainable or should he modify it to an extent. He would also realize if he has sufficient essential information or he should let the prospect keep talking. He can also understand if his tactics will work or do they need to be altered too. Can he use the tactics in handling the objections and in closing the presentation? The verification is the last step before the salesperson begins the presentation. As he is verifying his information base, the salesperson should help the prospect in redefining his needs from being generic to the needs of salesperson products through persuasive communication.

Sales Presentation

The salesperson has by now understood that unless he has a defined objective, has obtained the essential information and planned the right tactics he should not even attempt the call on the prospect. The start of the call is when the salesperson, through his persuasive communication gets the prospect change his generic needs to specific needs of the salespersons products. Let us discuss the persuasive communication in some detail.

The salesperson's products have some inherent unique qualities that can be defined as Product Features. Features need not be restricted to product physical qualities alone. They could well be part of the company policy, product availability, and related service. Countrywide advertising campaign would be part of company marketing policy. When the salesperson helps the distributor in managing the inventory, the service offered is unique and personal. Each company has to provide proper training to its salesperson in understanding its product's unique qualities including the service and the marketing policy. Salespersons must keep themselves abreast on these counts.

The salesperson must understand that the customers buy a product only for the benefits it offers to them. Benefits can be defined as the satisfaction the product provides to the buyers. The prospects are going to buy a product only if it provides the needed benefit to them. Youngsters do not buy motor-cycles; they buy the thrill they provide on high speeds. Women do not buy cosmetics; they buy the benefit of becoming alluring by using the same. However, different people are looking for different types of benefits from a product.

The salesperson therefore needs to list down the benefits different persons are looking from their product. Such a list needs to be continuously updated for each group of customers as the customer group keeps changing; market segment keeps changing with time. In early 1960s, the transistor radio was the craze with the elite of the society and today they would feel ashamed if found near a transistor set. The benefits could include reduced cost of labour, reduced maintenance cost, better quality control and increased worker safety. For retail traders the benefits could be better protection from competitive actions, increased stock turnover, higher margins, less customer returns and complaints.

A description of the product features would appear like a technical manual only. Likewise if the salesperson talks only about the benefits it would sound like parrot repeating what he has been taught. Persuasive communication should combine the two, with salesperson talking about the benefits along with the features from where the benefits are derived. Automatic transmission is a feature of some cars while convenience is the benefit to the car driver. Hence, if the salesperson tells the customer that with automatic transmission of our cars, you would find driving convenient and pleasurable, he is tying a feature with a benefit. For excelling in this type of communication the salesperson should prepare a Feature-Benefit worksheet, as given below:

Feature Benefit Worksheet

For–product–customer

Feature 1	Benefit 1	Benefit 2	Benefit 3	Benefit 4
Feature 2	Benefit 1	Benefit 2	Benefit 3	Benefit 4
Feature 3	Benefit 1	Benefit 2	Benefit 3	Benefit 4
Feature 4	Benefit 1	Benefit 2	Benefit 3	Benefit 4

Maslow's Hierarchy of needs gives a clear definition of different types of human needs and the salesperson would do well in relating the benefits to the needs, like physiological needs, need for safety, social acceptance need, need for recognition and respect and finally need for self-actualization, when the customer has attained the heights he had planned to achieve. It is assumed that in the worksheet given below that each feature will have multiple benefits.

Given below is a Feature Benefit Worksheet for a car:

Features	Benefits
Big seats	Comfort and lifestyle
Leg room, head clearance	Comfort and lifestyle
Large boot	Family luxury car
Power steering	Lifestyle
Plush finish	Self-actualized owner
Countrywide service facility	Peace of mind – comfort
Easy payment plan	Economical
Exchange facility	Easy on budget, economical
Test drive possible	Reconfirmation of quality, lifestyle
Service pickup and delivery	Comfort
50 years experience	Peace of mind, lifestyle

Before the salesperson starts his presentation, he should have developed the feature benefit worksheet. The features should be first listed and then the benefits added to the worksheet. In case of a car, the benefits can be listed as given below:

1. Comfort
2. Economy

3. Prestige enhancing lifestyle
4. Convenience
5. Safety

The salesperson should develop the Benefit Story using the possible benefits and writing down a paragraph for each benefit that will help him during the presentation, as given below.

Benefit Paragraph

Comfort

It is a comfortable car. The body is welded. The ride is so smooth that you can pour tea or coffee from the jug and it will not spill. The large seats will take a well-fed family of six and the leg room ensures comfortable seating for the long-legged teenagers.

The large boot is much bigger than several cars with big boots. You can really load it up without damage to your luggage or to the car.

It is a comfortable car for you, your family and your luggage.

Economy

The car costs less to run. The engine is newly designed for maximum efficiency. It is made out of aluminium to save weight. As a result you get up to 20 kilometres per litre. It is a real miser with petrol.

You can see the engine is uncluttered. It results in time saving for quick adjustments.

The body is welded, which means no rattle repairs. Its rustproof too, it will stand up to all weather.

The aluminium silencer will last twice as long as the ordinary one. The finish stays shiny so you save on waxing the car.

If you have a car to trade in, we will give a fair trade-in allowance, through our used car department.

You just cannot beat the economy of this model.

Prestige Enhancer—Lifestyle Product

It is a modern car. The new engine-101 horsepower will let you climb hills as though they were not there. Cruising speed in this model will leave you with plenty to spare for passing on motorways. You will not find a welded body like this even in the best imports of sports cars and the design and the gleaming finish makes it unusually attractive. Of course you get power steering, power breaks and automatic transmission to give the ride you will enjoy.

Convenience

The car makes driving easier and its uncluttered engine makes maintenance simpler too. It is, as can be seen 184 inch long and can be parked in places smaller than ever before for other cars. The car provides spare space in the garage.

The boot will easily hold enough luggage for the long trips planned in the new car. The finish is a cinch to keep glistening clean; only a cold water wash does it quickly.

For ease of driving, parking and safety the car has power steering, power brakes and automatic transmission.

For periodic maintenance checkups and adjustments, there is complete modern service department at your disposal. If you like, you can call me and will personally make arrangements for your service appointments. Should you need servicing in out of town locations in the country, we have provided with a list of our numerous authorized service stations in the country along with a route map so that you can never miss them. We have an easy payment plan so that you can keep your savings in the bank.

"I would like to take you out on a test drive to show you how easy the car is to drive, first hand".

Safety

It is a solid car. These are real doors and the engine is placed upfront for balance and greater control. You see the engine is V form and it gives a lower bonnet for battery visibility. The welded body gives you a substantial and strong car that takes all kinds of road punishments. Seat belts in rear seats are big safety plus in this car. You can rely on us to stand by the car. I have been selling cars for this dealer for the last fifteen years and hope to be here for another fifteen years.

As can be seen from the benefit paragraphs that all the benefits from different features on comfort have been listed at one place. Similarly, the other list of benefits is used to form sentences in the proper sequence for highlighting the benefits. Once the benefit story has been developed the next step is to find techniques for maintaining interest of the prospect.

Maintaining Interest

Salesperson's presentations are in many ways like telling a story. An interesting story is easy to listen while the same is not true for a boring story. Therefore, the next element of persuasive communication is maintaining the interest of the prospect. There are a number of techniques of maintaining the prospects interest as given below.

Customizing or Individualizing the Benefits

This means that the salesperson directs everything he says towards the needs of the prospect he is facing. This is important because each prospect wants to know how the product will satisfy his specific needs. Such individualization of benefits will ensure that prospect's interest is maintained. It must be understood that two prospects buying identical products may be motivated by different benefits. Car buyers may have different motivations as one may buy a car for its economy and the other for its convenience. Individualizing the needs and benefits means selecting those benefits that would satisfy the need of a particular prospect. Hence, the salesperson would have to scan the benefit paragraphs that are ideally suited to the prospects requirements. In other words, the salesperson must develop a storehouse of all possible features/benefit stories to be able to build instant rapport and continued interest in the presentation by the prospect. The right selection of the benefit paragraph could mean success of the presentation and in obtaining the objective of the call.

Using Descriptive Language

The other method of maintaining the prospect's interest is using descriptive language. For example, the car salesperson while using the comfort paragraph, does not just say that the car ride will be smooth, he says, "the ride will be so smooth that you can pour coffee" the vivid language helps in maintaining the prospect's interest. In the economy paragraph, the salesperson says "the car is a real miser on petrol" he is using the descriptive language to hold interest of the prospect. A good salesperson is ready with descriptive language that he has developed with practice and he uses it to good advantage to keep the interest of the prospect.

Participation

The salesperson can keep the interest of the prospect alive if he, instead of relating his benefit story even when the prospect is getting bored with it. Participation means getting him involved in the act. This can be done in the following ways:

Ask the prospect a question, which will ensure his active participation in the presentation. The salesperson can ask, "Do you recall the trouble you had during your last trip in your car?"

Have the prospect do some calculating or figuring out, which would involve him in the presentation. The prospect can be asked to calculate the kilometres per litre the car will give by giving him some documented figures.

For communicating persuasively the salesperson has to ensure that the prospect remains interested in the presentation, which he can do by individualizing the benefits for prospects need's, keep his language descriptive, and ensure prospect's participation.

Believability

The fifth element of persuasive communication is its believability. Unless the prospect believes in the salesperson the call can never be successful. One basic technique used by salesperson for ensuring the believability factor with the prospect is the use of testimonials. Testimonials are stories of satisfied customers that are most helpful for new products or when you are calling on a prospect. A testimonial issued by a reputed and respected company or person in the same field, helps in convincing the prospect of the desirability of the product. Salespersons with thorough knowledge of product features and the benefits sought by the prospect can also make a believable presentation. His knowledge should be so extensive and exhaustive that he is able to politely answer all the questions asked by the prospect and give his benefit story convincingly. In the event, the salesperson does not know the answer to a question it is best to admit it and confirm that in a day or two he will give the answer, instead of bluffing his way. Any wrong statement is going to have a snowballing effect and the chances are that the prospect will soon become disillusioned with the salesperson and his presentation. The third technique for creating believability in the prospect results from the demeanour of the salesperson. It is easy to believe a sincere person. The salesperson should try to take the role of a personal counsellor to the prospect. He needs to under claim and over achieve the key points of his presentation. This way he will achieve the believability factor of the prospect.

There are three methods of achieving believability of the prospect, use of testimonials, having a thorough knowledge of product features and benefits and the salesperson's sincerity towards the prospect

Demonstration

At times words are just not enough for achieving the call objective as the words appeal only to the prospect's sense of hearing. The other four senses are therefore neglected. We come to the sixth element of persuasive communication—demonstration. Demonstration means appealing to prospect's other sense to make the verbal presentation more persuasive. Demonstration in selling is basic. It is better for the buyer to enjoy chocolate slab rather than some one telling him how good it tastes. The housewife would rather feel the sari fabric than have a TV commercial describe how it feels.

Selling to the channel member, the retailer, if the salesperson does not describe the new advertising campaign but actually shows him the print copy.

A computer buyer would like to have hands on experience on the new model rather than only descriptive eulogy on the same. Buyers of air-conditioning plant would be happy to visit an existing installation of the salespersons company and see for themselves the efficacy of the plant.

Salesperson has to decide what needs to be demonstrated and what need not be demonstrated. This requires a careful study of the Benefit Paragraphs. Statements that can be strengthened through an appeal to the other four senses should be carefully considered. Demonstrations make the features and benefits more believable. With some originality, zest and excitement can be added with the demonstration making the presentation more interesting.

Sellers of stainless steel products offer a key chain to the buyer as a proof of its rust-proofing feature to increase the believability of the presentation.

Pictures of beautifully constructed villas can add the believability factor for the real estate salesperson.

With the huge dispersion of TV network in the country demonstration has become easy. Functions of an air compressor, farm equipment, dumpers, can be easily demonstrated on TV. In rural markets, the advertising vans help in demonstrating the products with the use of audio-visual equipment.

Demonstration that can involve the prospect's active participation will help in maintaining his interest. You must have noticed the detergent advertisements where the group of housewives are asked to join in the actual process of using the detergent. It is a good idea to indirectly demonstrate the service facilities the company has, by showing their pictures and a map where dotted locations of the facilities have been marked.

Demonstrations make features and benefits more understandable and believable. If they are original they make presentation more interesting. If the demonstration requires the use of physical materials like, OHP, LCD projector, charts the salesperson must ensure that the materials and the equipment are in good working order and that the salesperson has personally used it several times. If the salesperson was to fumble through the demonstration, the prospect will lose confidence. Therefore, all the equipment must be thoroughly checked before each call. Smooth demonstration would increase the believability of the presentation.

Planning Presentations for Specific Calls

Salesperson should list down the key elements of the presentation, the product features, benefits to stress, the technique of maintaining interest and achieving believability. Appeals to the other four senses that the salesperson plans to use must also be noted. The features and the benefits must be individualized for the prospect on each call. The demonstration planned must also be tailor-made for each prospect. The laptop computer salesperson gave a hands on demonstration to the users of the prospect's company, talked about the economies in usage with the prospect's Finance Director and gave the benefit story highlighting the latest features to the CEO. A good presentation converts the need to desire through persuasive communication. Individualized demonstration makes the presentation more effective.

Handling Objections

As the salesperson makes his presentation towards achieving his call objectives, the prospect is likely to make statements detrimental to the achievement of objectives. These statements can be defined as objections. The salesperson must realize that these are normal parts of every sales call and should not be discouraged by them. In fact, they may reveal new information that will help you to adjust your tactics. Realistically, therefore, objections should be considered as not deterrents in achievement of objectives but they may serve to help you in readjusting your sales tactics.

The following five steps need to be considered for handling objections.

The first step is listening to the prospect. The salesperson must train himself in the art of listening carefully to the objections raised by the prospects. Salespersons have a tendency to talk rather than to listen. A quiet and patient listener may find the prospect himself talking out of the objection. The prospect must be encouraged to speak uninterruptedly and the salesperson may get to know some additional information that he reveals, which could be of help to the salesperson. The prospect's manner of expressing the objection may confirm his personal negative feelings. The salesperson should not just listen to the words being spoken but also note the manner in which they are expressed. This way he will understand if the prospect has negative feelings as well as he may get some new information.

The second step is classifying the objections. Objections can be classified as valid or invalid. Let us consider the invalid objections. An objection is considered invalid when there is a concealed reason for it. Actually the prospect covers up how he feels by saying something else and hence should not be taken literally. A reluctance to make purchase decision could be the concealed or underlying reason behind the stated invalid objection. If the prospect says, "I cannot afford it just now, see me in a month", there may be an invalid objection as the prospect cannot say he is unable to decide at present. The other concealed reason for an invalid objection could be an aversion to change on the part of the prospect. "Regarding your product I will have to talk to my partner" the prospect may be concealing his reason for buying your product since he has been buying from his present supplier for the past seven years. A prospect may raise an invalid objection if the salesperson has said something or done something to antagonize him. Hard selling on the part of salesperson may offend some prospects. A flippant or derogatory remarks made unwittingly by the salesperson on some favourite project of the prospect could antagonize him.

An invalid objection is only a subtle front for a concealed, underlying reason for the prospect's objection. As the invalid objections are now understood, let us study the valid objections. A valid objection can be taken literally, as the prospect means exactly what he says. For example, if the prospect does not understand a technical point made by the salesperson he may raise a valid objection. "The new product is made of 16 gauge steel rather than 18 gauge" if the prospect does not know that the lower the gauge the thicker the steel, he may say, "I do not want something that is flimsy in construction". A valid objection may also be raised if the salesperson fails to stress the feature or the benefit of primary interest to the prospect. In case the buyer is especially interested in the construction of the product and the salesperson keeps emphasizing on low price, he is stressing the wrong benefit.

Valid objections occur most frequently during the presentation.

Handling Objections Details

After the first part is over, that of listening and understanding valid and invalid objection, the next step is disarming. As you meet an objection you are faced with a disagreement. It is best to show consideration for the other person's viewpoint as follows:

1. One popular and effective method is, "yes but" method and it is meant to show consideration to the other person's point of view.
2. Other way of showing consideration is "that is an interesting observation".
3. Or "I am glad you brought it up".
4. And yet again, " yes I know how you feel, but".

As you show consideration for the prospect's viewpoint, you are in fact avoiding confrontation and arguments. Disarming prevents objections from developing into arguments between the prospect and the salesperson.

Once the salesperson has understood the techniques of listening, classifying and disarming it is time to understand the subject of answering the prospect's objections. Let us take the invalid objections first. For invalid objections the salespersons can use a number of answers like giving a token answer. For example, if the prospect says, "I am too busy right now" the salesperson can say disarmingly, "yes sir, everybody is busy these days but let me tell you...."

The other way of handling invalid objection is to ignore it completely by pausing and then continuing. The salesperson can divert the prospect's attention from the objection by bringing up some other interesting fact instead of handling the invalid objection directly. If the classification of the objection as invalid is correct it will not recur. If the prospect says, "business is terrible", disarmingly the salesperson can reply, "things are pretty tough, but a few moments ago we agreed that our new machine would...."

While answering valid objections it was agreed that they need to be taken on their face value. One other technique is, "denial" that may be used to answer valid objections. The best time to use denial is when the objections are based on misunderstanding or misinterpretation of the salesperson's facts. Suppose the prospect says, "I am not interested in the sweaters as they are made of reconditioned wool" knowing that the label clearly shows that the product is 100% virgin wool, disarming the salesperson can say, "Yes sir, I am glad you brought it up; the quality of wool is most important, but all our sweaters are made of 100% virgin wool. Let me show you how we clearly mark the fact on our label."

Another example is, when the prospect says, "I am not buying now, times are too uncertain" the answer given disarmingly can be, "Yes sir, but, among the certainties is a steady rise in cost of living and prices generally. You should protect yourself to a reasonable degree."

Next, the valid objections can be handled using the YIELD technique. It is used most frequently to overcome objections based on an existing advantage offered by the competitor. The success of yield technique depends on the salesperson's ability to offset the existing benefit offered by the competitor. For example, if a doctor says, "your capsules are larger than those supplied by your competitor." The salesperson's response should be, "yes doctor, our capsule is larger but, it is especially designed for ease of swallowing."

In case you are uncertain if the objection is valid or not, the best way out is to ask, "why?" The why question will give the salesperson the necessary information to decide whether to classify the objection as valid or as invalid. For example, if the prospect says, "I want to look into some other offers". The salesperson can say, disarmingly," yes, but why would you want to look into other deals now?" the answer should help the salesperson determine if the objection is valid or not.

So far the discussion on answering objections has been on, listening, classifying, disarming and yielding. The last manner of answering the objections is that of continuing the presentation. After answering the prospects objection, you should continue with the presentation. Otherwise, the prospect will feel he has to raise another objection. The direction of the presentation will depend on what the salesperson has learnt from the objection. Suppose the prospect revealed a particular concern about his company's service, the salesperson should stress on those special features of his company's service that were left out in the answers to the objection.

Summarizing, the salesperson well versed with the storehouse of benefit paragraphs will be able to adept his presentation in response to the reactions of the prospect. The salesperson must continue his presentation as he reinforces the answers to the objection. It will prevent the objection from recurring later in the call.

Price Objection

After understanding the five ways of dealing with valid objections, let us consider a special case of valid objection, the price objection. The price objection is being handled separately because it is the one that plagues the salesperson most and is most difficult to handle. The price objections are of two types, "I cannot afford it" or "I can get it for less."

The first type of price objection, "I cannot afford it" can be said as, "your price is too high", or "I cannot spend that much" or yet another, "I am looking for a cheaper product."

The salesperson's response in such cases can be, "yes sir, money is important, but, in the long run your savings will far outweigh this additional expenditure."

Normally the price objection is raised when the prospect knows that he can get the same product for a different price. If the salesperson knows that his product has higher price than the competitive product it is best to use the yield technique. Disarmingly the salesperson can say, "Yes our price is Rs. 150 and competitive price is Rs. 125, but, the difference of Rs. 25 is eliminated by the one year free service we are offering that the competitor does not. You will agree that one year fee service is definitely more than Rs. 25. It is best to talk about the small difference and justify it rather than talk about the main price amount.

Call Closing

Call closing can be defined as a direct attempt on the part of the salesperson to attain the objective of the call. Let us, therefore, discuss the techniques the salesperson can use to obtain his call objective. At this point you may be wondering if the salesperson knows his objective, makes a good approach, gives an effective presentation, and handles objections skilfully, it should be sufficient to attain the call objectives. The problem arises because most persons are reluctant to take decisions especially if they involve spending money. Salesperson's good approach, effective presentation, skilful handling of objections normally moves the prospect to the verge of agreement with the objective. However, the reluctance may still remain. Closing techniques are, therefore, direct attempts by the salesperson to nudge the fully persuaded prospect to make a favourable decision.

The first closing technique can be called assumptive. The assumptive technique is used when the salesperson senses that the buyer is almost at the point of making a decision in favour of the objective and has met with little resistance. When the salesperson is using the assumptive technique he does nothing more than act as though a favourable decision has been made with respect to the call objective. A machine tool salesperson, whose call objective was to arrange for the buyer to visit nearby plant in order to see the machine in operation, uses the assumptive technique. Sensing the favourable decision, he says, "let me use your phone to tell them, we will be over there this afternoon" the salesperson has assumed that the favourable decision has been taken.

Another closing technique is of giving choice to the prospect. The technique is used when the salesperson senses that the buyer is close to agreement with his call objective but there still remains some resistance. The choice technique is a direct way of asking the prospect to make a favourable decision. In using the technique, the salesperson gives the prospect a choice between two buying alternatives. The prospect does not have to select between order or no order, he has a choice between something and another thing. A shirt salesperson saying, "Would you buy the green shirt" leaves the option of saying no and walking out. Once the salesperson knows that the prospect is nearly ready to decide in favour of his objective, he could say, "which one should I pack, the green or the light blue one?" the moment the prospect says the blue one, you have achieved your objective. In B-to-B sales, the question that can be asked just before the final decision could be, "you would like us to arrange for transit insurance or would you like to organize it?"

In another situation where installation and commissioning of a plant is involved, the salesperson can nudge the prospect into decision by saying," should I send my installation team next week or would you prefer earlier."

Suppose the salesperson is selling room air-conditioners and for nudging the prospect into action says, "so it is the two tonne one you will buy" he may get an answer, 'NO'. after sensing that the decision is near in his favour he should say, "1.5 tonne or 2 tonne, which one", and the chances are he will get the order for one of them.

The choice technique should be used when the salesperson has sensed that the decision in his favour is almost reached to help the prospect feel happier as he gets the last word and psychologically mastery over the salesperson. Anyway, you have achieved the call objective.

The third closing technique is the summary technique. This technique is used in conjunction with the choice technique after several features and benefits have been emphasized. The salesperson should summarize using those features and benefits that have stimulated the greatest desire in prospect's mind. In this technique, the salesperson uses the summary as he reviews the features and benefits putting them in a capsule form." Your interest in economy and convenience will be fully realized by our low rate contract, our quality maintenance service and our low cost spare parts. The summary technique is best used along with the choice technique.

The fourth closing technique is known as the Special Feature Technique. The features of a product have been defined earlier as unique qualities of the product. Sometimes, one of the features of the product may be used as closing technique to bring about favourable decision. If a product is in limited supply, it becomes its special feature. "These imported hoses do not come for the next six months. Shall I book hundred for you?" Prospects take favourable decision because they do not want to lose out on anything.

The favourable feature technique should be used only when the salesperson is sure of his facts and should be used with utmost care. Dishonest or short-sighted approach is absolutely not recommended.

Timing

As the salesperson learns about the closing techniques where a nudge is required to gain the call objective, it is a good idea to learn how to sense the right time when the prospect has been persuaded enough and his desire to buy has reached the peak. The timing gives the salesperson the clue when to use the closing technique. If the salesperson delays too long before using the closing technique, the prospect may make a favourable decision on his own. This may be all right except too much time has gone into the presentation. If the closing technique is used prematurely he may cause an objection to be raised. When the prospect is not fully convinced he needs a nudge to help him take a favourable decision. Therefore, proper timing will help the salesperson to attain his call objective quickly as well as to avoid objections. Prospects indicate through various means that their interest and desire are at a peak and they are ready for a favourable decision. The salesperson must be alert to the cues or the signs that tell that the right time to use the closing technique has come.

Sometimes the cues are obvious like the prospect asking, how soon can he get the samples? The salesperson should know that this is the right time to use the closing technique. The salesperson should reply, "In two days, shall I deliver it to you or have them mailed?" The salesperson is using the choice technique of call closing.

Another example of obvious clue is when the prospect says, "Can the survey be done after working hours?" The salesperson reply should be, "Certainly, I will have our engineer in at 5 p.m. tomorrow" once the clues are seen the salesperson should move quickly to close the call.

However, the clues normally are not so obvious. The salesperson should be alert to recognize the subtle clues like a smile of agreement or a nod other mention of a specific feature or benefit. Understanding the subtle clue the salesperson should use the losing technique. Prospect may start examining the sales aid and start some figure work, examine his stock he is on the verge of a favourable decision and the time is ripe for using the closing technique.

Summarizing, the salesperson should be alert to understand the obvious and also the subtle clues given by the prospect and that is the time for the use of closing technique.

Departure

The next step of the call is the departure and there are a few rules for an effective departure. At the end of the call, either the salesperson has attained his objective or he has not achieved it. In either case he must make an effective departure.

In case the objective has been achieved the salesperson should reassure the prospect that he has made a wise decision. Most people want such a reassurance. "Your decision to renew your service contract with us was an intelligent one that will mean continuous economies for your organization." Once the reassurance has been given it is best to leave quickly. Lingering on is not business like. Thank for the order and leave quickly is a golden rule. If a good rapport has been built a referral can be obtained before leaving.

However, if the objective has not been achieved remember the minor objective that keeps the door open and at least achieve it. The minor objectives should all be in line with the major call objectives, like, "when do you think it would be appropriate for me to contact you again". Or "we are organizing a seminar/an exhibition and I would like to personally invite you for the same." As he gains the minor objective his feeling of disappointment will vanish and he will be ready for the next call in a positive frame of mind. The minor objective may ultimately lead the salesperson in achieving the major objective sooner than the salesperson can imagine. It is difficult to realize that the customer would get disillusioned with his existing supplier and that would be the time he will think of you if you have left a good favourable impression on him.

The salesperson should appreciate that while the main objective has not been attained, the minor objective has been achieved, as well as more information has been gathered about the prospect's company as well as about the prospect himself, that will be useful in future calls.

Post-Call Analysis

After completing the call it is necessary to analyze the call just completed. The analysis starts with comparing the result of the call with the established call objective. The comparison will help the salesperson plan his next call on this prospect. If the sales objective of the call has been achieved the salesperson can consider the manner in which to plan the next call to escalate the prospect up towards some long range goal. If the objective was not attained, the salesperson should critically review to determine the cause of failure, starting from the formulation of the call objective, was it too ambitious, too broad or, perhaps too specific. The salesperson should take a look at the essential information gathered before making the call. Were there gaps in the information, and how serious were they?

Next he should analyze the tactics used. Were the techniques used either in approach, presentation, handling of objections or closing inadequate? Were they the cause of his failure to attain the objective of the call?

Summarizing the salesperson should review the three steps the salesperson had taken in planning the call as follows:

- Establish the call objective
- Gather the essential information
- Select appropriate tactics

Only after such a critical review should the salesperson plan his next call on the same prospect.

Post-call analysis serves a primary purpose of providing a sound basis for planning the next call on the prospect. Post-call analysis can serve a secondary, broader purpose of helping the salesperson in his personal development. In other words, post-call analysis should point out some of the strengths and weaknesses in the salesperson's overall performance which should go beyond this one call. The salesperson must accept the primary responsibility for the call failure and use the post-call analysis for improving on his call planning. For example, did the post-call review reveal a growing deficiency in some aspects of product knowledge, or weakness in a special skill such as group presentation? Did the call analysis, instead prove the existence of some new found strengths in handling people or in thinking creatively?

Summarizing, post-call analysis and personal development go hand in hand. The salesperson who uses each call experience for the purpose of personal improvement will move more rapidly towards a higher level of effective sales performance.

Defining Sales Obstacles

Following are the major obstacles that a salesperson faces during making a sale:

Habit: The customer is in the habit of using competitive product or service and finds it difficult to change.

Fear: The customer fears the unknown and has unwarranted feeling of impending trouble of risk or of loss that confuses his thinking and causes him to evade opportunities that help him to maximize his capabilities.

Price: The customer fails to see the benefits that outweigh their money value.

Complaint: The customer voices or feels dissatisfaction on the company's product or service.

Detail: The customer believes that the trouble that he has to take in buying the product is not worth the effort.

Lack of information: Sales progress gets impeded when the salesperson has not informed the customer either due to his own lack of knowledge on the same or when the customer lacks the technical skills to understand the sales talk. At times the customer could be lacking in imagination to visualize the benefits of the product or even when the salesperson's expressions are unclear and confusing.

Competition: The customer believes that the competitive benefits would be more suited to him.

It must be understood that at times companies face competition from dissimilar things like a housewife may choose a new cooking range over a new washing machine.

Friendship-Competition: The customer likes or respects competitive sales or other personnel or when the customer or the prospect believes that the competitive product will produce equal or greater amount of benefits to him.

Difficult personality: The prospect lacks emotional control and he allows the difference of opinion to degenerate or he indulges in temper, rudeness or other unwarranted behaviour that retards progress towards sales.

Time: Customer feels that the company's product does not merit the time to be spent on its purchase, or if the sales call is made too late and yet any further postponement would cause failure of the talks or if the delivery requirements of the customer are urgent and cannot be met.

Release: The prospect wants a release from further discussion of the subject.

Divided release: The prospect wants release as he sincerely or insincerely says he has to discuss the matter with someone not present.

Negative mood or manner: Salesperson's talk is creating through his frame of mind, manner of speaking and acting unfavourable reaction in the prospects mind causing dislike and lack of respect.

Poor judgement: When the salesperson does not care for the following:

- Prevailing conditions
- Comparing and separating right ways of doing things from wrong ways

- Planning the sales call—when to call, what to say and what to do.
- Deciding how to use the product benefits in the talk from the customers' viewpoint.
- Noting the effect on the customer on what is said or done.
- Keeping control of emotions.
- Using knowledge of human nature and practical selling methods secured through study, analysis and experience.

Countering the Obstacles

Benefit: Describe any good result the customer will get from putting a good quality of the product to use.

Good quality: Describe clearly the inherent trait or characteristic of the product or proposition or specific parts that make it possible to produce benefits when put to use.

Poor quality: Clearly but tactfully describe traits and characteristics of an alternative product (competitive) that make it produce losses when put to use.

Loss: Describe the losses poor quality will bring ever so subtly.

Proposition: Inform the prospect the salesperson's name, company's name, brand, price, terms of business, delivery time.

Prestige: Clearly describe the reputation and achievements of his company, its personnel, its products, services, and the customers, endorsers who lend their support.

Personal Prestige: Inform the prospect of the salesperson's accomplishments, experience and good reputation that creates a feeling of respect and confidence in the prospect.

Pride: Inform the prospect of the respect he enjoys with the salesperson by stating his achievements, his company's accomplishments, or by asking his advice on some matter that he can comment on.

Assurance: Use any combination of words to qualify the above stated counters with tactful directness or that has power to calm or reassure the prospect.

Story: Give an account of an event that indirectly informs the prospect of reasons, emotions or both that help him in deciding in the salesperson's favour.

Good turn: Salesperson should perform or offer to perform any good turn that has power to build liking and respect and which places the prospect under no obligation.

Contact: Classify the business or personal friendship between the salesperson and the prospect and mention friends, hobbies, other activities that establish common interests.

Explanation: Make the meaning of technical terms used by classifying words and use similes, demonstrations, charts, presentations, photographs to clarify details of an operation.

Mood and manner: Salesperson's frame of mind, manner of speaking and actions should help create liking and respect for him in the prospect's mind.

Question: Salesperson should ask questions indirectly as autosuggestion to reconfirm the sales story has become effective. The question could also be to elicit information in the form of investigation question.

Progress signal: The salesperson should look out for signals from the prospect in the form of comment or action to confirm that the salesperson has fully answered Prospect Viewpoint Questions adequately to keep things moving.

Good judgement: Classifies mindset operation where multiple analysis does the ways of doing and saying things for producing maximum benefits.

Command: Any command used directly or with other counters that effectively produce desired result from the prospect.

First benefit is the first result produced when a good quality is put to use.

Major Interest Benefit: Expresses a result that is one of the prospect's objectives.

Favourable condition is when the prospect's industry, company, group, or personal life from where he draws benefits or will benefit in future, and that is brought to his attention to prepare him to visualize that he has an opportunity to benefit still further through the salesperson's proposition. The favourable conditions also appeal to pride elements and give him still greater power to help him see and appreciate his opportunity.

Unfavourable Conditions: Any situation that creates losses for the prospect, for which the prospect, the salesperson or his company are not responsible and which brought to his attention discretely would help him see the need for the benefits of the salesperson's proposition.

Spar: Salesperson can use spar as a special action for mood and manner, assurance, and question, to meet the obstacles in a serene and considerate manner so that the objector's mind is reopened to reason.

The Twenty-first Century Challenge

With the multitudes of competitive companies, national, international and multinational in the fray, the salespersons are facing probably the greatest challenge ever encountered by any salesperson before. They are required to call on to the full, all their personal resources to meet the challenge. Some salespersons with years of experience have acquired a name for themselves in the market. Now they are required to compete with highly respected and internationally known brands by retaining the existing business and adding new channel members to cater to some hitherto virtually unknown markets.

One major area of retail interest in gaining sustainable competitive advantage has been the Store Design. For example, in Bangalore stores in Indiranagar have airline collages on walls, trunks in trial rooms, and the sailors knots and nautical miles have taken over the Brigade Road stores. It is the designer store that seems to be the theme of the 21st century stores. In Chandigarh, the art gallery theme has become prominent for stores, with vivid colours splashed all over.

The store managers assert that while it is not possible to have a unique theme for each store, store design has become an important focus point for stores. Stores want to create an experience for shoppers and these themes aim at making the stores destination points for customers. The retail boom has brought about designing retail space into focus which has assumed a great urgent need. The retailers are setting aside 20 to 30 per cent on designing stores. These amounts are diverted from advertising and marketing budget for retail design and merchandising. Retail spaces are integral parts of brand personality and they act as silent salespersons by motivating customers to buy. Retailers are therefore, customizing their spaces to suit the market segment customers. A sports retailer can use cricket bats, balls and wickets as design theme.

The country has been inundated with international brands that are busy retaining their global brand equity. This has further forced the Indian retailers to put their money in the theme design of the stores. Retail design combines overall look and stores functioning. Customers need to have a view of the products on sale without the inevitable clutter. Cash counters are placed centrally near fitting rooms, if possible. Colour schemes need to reflect the merchandise personality. Product stories need to be emphasized like, "the watch worn by Amitabh Bachhan in Sholay." Such innovative designs can increase the store revenue by, on an average by 25 per cent.

A word of caution is required on the issue of store design. Going overboard with fancy looks can make the stores overbearing and intimidating leaving customers overawed. The idea should be to fit the theme of the store design to the market segment customers.

Retail business faces challenges from the multinational companies that offer a cultural ambivalence to suit the generation next. This new mode of product offerings at once fascinate the buyers and unsettle the existing players who have been dominating the market so far. It will be creative genius of the individual retailers that will help them innovate and survive. With a little extra effort they can even upstage the new entrants, irrespective of their size, brand image worldwide and business acumen because the Indian retailer is rooted in the market psyche for long. They need to do the following:

1. Fight competition on mental level rather than just physical
2. Work your plan to gain small successes as a start
3. Make innovation the company's success mantra
4. Have patience and persevere in the ruthless pursuit of your success plan
5. Remain a learning organization as only the constant flow of information will help in modifying plans for continued success

Companies need to organize the planning process to cover the lowest level of hierarchy for it to be a sustained effort. If the workers are trained properly they will prevent disasters from happening by preventive measures. Today's worker is knowledgeable and is looking forward to opportunities to prove his worth, given a chance. By remaining proactive numerous firefighting situations can be avoided, where the senior members have to spend huge amount of time when they could be doing something constructive like planning, training.

The customers in the 21st century are demanding the best products possible, with unique features, outstanding service and the retailer who is able to provide these is going to be winner-making profits as well. Such a product-service delivery will enhance the sales traffic and even at competitive pricing the turnover profits would have a snowballing effect. Better technology, product and service delivery are going to be keystones for success.

The challenge is great and yet there are ways and means of countering it and coming out a winner. The salesperson with fortified skills, and with coordinated advertising campaigns would be amply confident of meeting the challenges.

Challenges always bring opportunities and by effectively meeting the new competitive environment, the salesperson can develop self-pride as the salespersons grow in stature in the eyes of the management, channel members and the customers. The main objectives of learning about the 21st century challenges are the following:

1. To empower the salespersons to meet the challenges with new skills, as their job becomes more rewarding and satisfying with new ideas and methods for achieving profitable results that will give you pride
2. To improve the confidence level of the channel members in the company as the salespersons with skills and ability would provide help the channel members in solving difficult problems.
3. To help the salespersons in effectively meeting the competition and with success, their stature and value in the eyes of the company and the customers will increase. Salespersons should develop better personal resources for achieving the kind of sales and profits results that will enhance their prestige and importance in their company and with the channel members.

For analyzing present knowledge base, the following needs to be understood:

1. Describe what is considered the basic goals or objectives of a salesperson's job.
2. Describe the critical success factors for any company from the customer's, channel member's and the company's viewpoint.
3. Describe the type of relationship the salespersons should have with the channel members in the present highly competitive age.
4. Pick up a well-known product and list down all possible benefit that would accrue to the customer by its use.
5. Describe what is considered important for fighting competition.

A company's selling efforts are as good as its sale team. It is the people who are the most valuable assets of any organization. They can make or break any organization. The other assets like technology, finance are poor substitutes as success barometers. Companies need to evaluate the benefit ratio of their team members as compared to the investment made in selecting and deploying talent. The amount of creative work, innovations, process improvements the team generates are the basic parameters of their success. Successful companies attract talent, nurture it, manage it and identify the talented persons from among their staff. The retail company most likely to gain competitive advantage is the one that keeps on innovating their operations, product range, merchandising, logistics and it keeps surprising the customers with dynamic promotional thrusts. The team leader needs to be the role model for others to emulate.

Retail Team Leader

The team leader has to be a good learner from the past successes, mistakes and even misadventures. He needs to be see who can visualize the future market and the position of the retailer in the market. The leader must be able to demonstrate his skills as an innovator, communicator, role model, negotiator and trouble-shooter.

Retail business involves a number of vital functions like purchasing, logistics, merchandising and while the objective of each remains the store's benefit there are areas of conflict that make each functional head consider themselves as supreme and irreplaceable.

Retail stores are giving way to chain stores and the shopping malls. The retail business is getting more complex with ERP solutions helping solve the difficult problems of coordination and optimum utilization of available resources that may be located anywhere in the organization. In such trying circumstances the company operating as a well oiled team will outshine others. Teams operating in retail business are directly dealing with the customers. They need to operate with the unknown member of their team, the buyer and the sooner they can make him part of their team the faster the team can start winning. The leader needs to spend time with his team members in order to keep them energized all the time.

Understanding People and Dealing with them Effectively

Given below is sales analysis chart

As effective sellers the entire approach to sales has to be customer oriented to be of any use. Hence, the first analysis is from the customer or the prospects viewpoint as follows:

1. Attention: Do I like and respect the salesperson?
2. Interest: What can his proposition do for me?
3. Desire: Can he support his claim?
4. Decision: Is it the best thing to-do now?
5. Sale or Action: I will buy or act

Given below are the emotion movers that persuade the buyer into favourable action:

1. Mood and Manner
2. Personal Prestige
3. Good Turn
4. Contact
5. Assurance
6. Question
7. Command

Reason Movers

1. Benefit
2. Good Quality
3. Poor Quality (negative for competition)
4. Loss
5. Proposition
6. Prestige
7. Explanation
8. Story
9. Good Judgement

The sale calls face the following obstacles:

1. Habit
2. Fear
3. Price
4. Complaint
5. Detail
6. Lack of Information
7. Competition
8. Friendship Competition
9. Difficult Personality
10. Time
11. Release
12. Divided Release
13. Negative Mood and Manner
14. Poor Judgement

As is noticed that there are favourable and unfavourable conditions when the salesperson has to use or perceive the following:

- Use test question
- Perceive Signal

Obstacles can be handled by using spar or practice or solution efforts.

Scene 1

A benefit mover describes clearly good result that a prospect will get from putting to use a good quality.

Material benefits:

1. Save thirty thousand rupees
2. Reduce switching costs by 10%
3. Bring in more customers at lunch time
4. Enable you to finish your work in half the time
5. Improve the strength of the foundation

Physical benefits:

1. Make you more comfortable
2. Save you that heavy lifting
3. Prevent foot, leg, back pain
4. You can work in a more upright position
5. Keep the dust out of your nose/lungs

Mental benefits:

1. You get more satisfaction out of your work
2. It will take a load out of your mind

3. Dealing with the company will be pleasant
4. The children will be perfectly safe
5. It may please the big boss

The benefit movers have certain powers and some limitations too as given below.

Powers

The benefit movers enable the salesperson to predict for his prospect listener, the **interesting** and **desirable** results of doing what he has proposed. It appeals to the listener's basic motive for taking action in favour of the company. It answers the Prospects Viewpoint Question, "What good will your plan do?" and therefore noblest salesperson to talk from the prospect's viewpoint and best interest.

Limitations

The benefit movers lacks the power to support itself. It cannot answer the Prospect Viewpoint Question, "Can you support your claim" and therefore, unsupported, cannot give the prospect reason to believe benefit predictions or claims.

Scene 2

Good Quality Movers

A good quality mover describes the inherent trait or characteristic of a proposition or a specific part that makes it possible to produce benefits when put to use.

Good Quality in Products

- Fine workmanship
- Improved design
- Mounted on live rubber
- Top grain cowhide
- Spring steel coils
- Three-ply construction

Good Quality in Service

- Our servicemen are well trained and experienced
- Company is sound in finance
- We have carefully planned direct mail campaign
- We take hourly meter readings
- We apply heat evenly
- Our methodology is well tested in the field
- It is the practical way

Good Qualities in Persons

- Honest and steady
- Skilled and experienced
- Intelligent
- Alert and enterprising
- Good natured
- Full of common sense
- Tactful
- Physically strong

The powers and limitations of the good quality mover are.

Powers

The good quality mover enables salesperson to tell his prospect what makes possible the beneficial results of using the product he is offering. It has power to support the benefit claim and get them believed.

Limitations

The good quality mover lacks the power to create interest and desire since it cannot describe the basic reason for buying, which is to obtain the benefit.

Analyzing a Talk for its Movers

The students need to identify the benefit or the good quality mover as the analysis is made.

Example 1

A bank equipment salesperson sees in a bank that the bus carrying bank money was being bumped against the walls, scratching and marring the walls. He got an idea and he expressed himself as follows in his talk with the bank personnel.

Salesperson: You could easily protect your walls and decorations by placing a continuous rubber bumper at the bottom of each bus. That would eliminate the scratches and the marks the buses make and save a lot of repair and maintenance costs.

Prospect: What are the bumpers like?

The talk has started revolving around the salesperson's objective.

Example 2

An engineer wants his prospect to appreciate the benefits that can be gained by the use of an automatic oil pump.

Engineer: Machine shutdowns will be reduced to a minimum because this positive gear oil pump will automatically keep every bearing coated with oil.

Example 3

Salesperson: You always wanted to guard your workers' health, I have just the practical way to protect their lungs. Got the time to hear about it?

Prospect: I will make time. What is it?

Benefits are possible because of the good qualities of the product.

Example 4

The shirt will be comfortable and long wearing because it is carefully tailored using terry silk material. It stays fresh, resists soiling all day long.

Analyzing Product for Sale Movers

Salesperson needs to understand the sequencing of his thought process as he builds the benefit, good quality mover's story. The analysis studies different kinds of reasons, as given below:

Product–Chest of drawers, extension arms.

Benefits	Good Quality
1. File drawer can be rolled in and out of the cabinet rapidly with least effort	Sturdy, steel extension arms using giant size ball bearings
2. Saves operator's energy	
3. Reduces errors due to fatigue	
4. Gets the desired correspondence quicker	
5. Time and expense saved	

Analysis of a proposition having both product and service parts

	Benefits	Good Qualities
Market Analysis		
Copy writing	1. First benefit-make a study of problems for which advertising is required 2. Write the copy then perfect it 3. Create copy that will get read 4. Bring inquiries	5. Trained and skilled copy writers, directed by experience and able supervisors
Art work		
Printing		
Papers		

Analysing a faulty situation for correction—machine operation

The correct plan		The situation	
Benefits	Right way	Wrong way	Losses
1. Keeps wrists for touching the bar 2. Machine will space perfectly	3. By holding wrists in arched position	4. Machine operator wrists sag slightly at times	5.Cuffs and wrists touch space bars that causes machine to space at wrong time.

The Correction Talk

Salesperson (in a pleasant manner): The easy way to make the machine space perfectly is by holding the wrists higher than usual that keeps cuffs and wrists from even the lightest touch of the space bar. You get perfect results.

The 4 Column Situation and Correction Analysis

Wrong actions:

1. Kitchen utensils stored where they cause the cook to take extra steps, not justified
2. Lawn mowing done in a shaggy way
3. Child strews things in a room which looks dirty

Select a situation and analyze using the analysis sequence.

Write short talk on correction of the situation, using the presentation sequence stating only the benefits which the right way of doing things will provide.

The thinking sequence starts with the wrong way and related losses and next come the right way and the benefits.

However, the presentation sequence starts by presenting the benefits of the right way. The salesperson can mention the wrong and the losses only after pointing out the right way benefits.

Examples of Poor Quality and Loss Movers

Poor quality movers clearly but tactfully describe the inherent traits and characteristics of a proposition, a situation or alternative product and plans that make it probable that it will produce looses when put to use. It is recommended for highlighting the competitive products.

Loss mover clearly but tactfully describes an undesirable result of putting poor quality product to use.

Examples

1. Steel corners of the truck carrying money will mar metal work and plaster walls that will cause considerable repair expense.

2. Engineers have found that reinforcement of steel bars less than 0.25 inch thick are too light and will fail to support even a slight overload.
3. Untested methods might prove unworkable.
4. Men lacking in experience can cause road accidents.

Power and Limitations of Poor Quality and Loss Movers

Powers

Help listeners to make wise choice when used after the benefit and good quality movers.

Limitations

When used alone, they often sound threatening, one-sided and arouse opposition.

Conclusion

Benefit and good quality movers are compared with poor quality and loss movers to help prospect reach the right decision.

Salesperson: In cold climate kota stone will stand up well because its square edges will hold mortar better during summer when the snow would melt. Slate has slanting tin edges which often fail to hold mortar when snow is melting and the sun is hot. Kota stone is cheaper to remain and hold appearance longer I would recommend it.

(Students should analyze the sentence by segregating the benefits, good quality, loss and bad quality).

The material salesperson should arrange the 4 column analysis of sale movers as given below:

Kota stone	Kota stone	Slate	Slate
Good qualities	Benefits	Poor quality	Losses
1. Kota stone has thick, strong slabs, with square edges	2. Will hold mortar well in freezing and melting weather. Retain looks and appearance for years and is cheaper to maintain	3. Slate has razor edge thin slanting edges	4. Mortar will split away from edges during melting season, requiring expensive repairs

Multiple Analyses of Products

The analysis covers the benefits and losses of different products, including competitive products as it helps in making a comparative study on the product having more benefits and less loss in comparison to the competitive product.

Kota stone

Benefits	Qualities	Losses
Hold mortar well under cool conditions or hot weather. Retain good appearance for years at low upkeep cost. Save on extra labour cost in a few years.	Large sawn slabs having square edges one inch thick.	More labour required to handle and to set. Costs about Rs. 10,000 more in labour to install.

Slate

Provides delicate beauty in pattern and colour Easier and faster to handle and save about Rs. 10,000 on labour of installing.	Has a variety of colours and scalloped edged shapes. Edges thin and sharp.	Mortar splits away from edges during snow melting season, beauty is marred, repair expense estimate at Rs. 5,000 annually over ten-year period.

Analysis can be made in such a manner that only the benefits are highlighted as the losses are listed down by underplaying them. This gives the salesperson a better idea on how to manage prospect's questions on competitive product. The best course ultimately is to lay stress on his own product's good qualities and benefits that accrue through its use rather than decry competition where the chances of going wrong with incorrect statements.

Multiple Analysis of a Situation

The salesperson should make an effort to find the true interests of competitors with most benefits and fewest losses will be found.

Galvanized Conduit

Benefits	Problem	Losses
1. Initial cost less to consumer, it will help the dealer procure the order and a quick sure profit will be made by the dealer	2. Can the galvanized conduit be sold for use where acid fumes are present	3. Acid will get through the conduit. Corrosion, stoppages will occur. Dealer's reputation will be damaged

Benefits	Problem	Losses
1. Consumer will find it will stand acid for years.	2. Will there be stress on the buyer to buy zinc	3. Purchase will cost 40% more.

Will save more than its cost by avoiding a single breakdown. 2. More profit for the dealer. 3. Effort to sell the right product will get respect of the buyers.	conduit with sealed surface?	4. Buyer may place order on someone else as his opposition may increase.

In order to understand the above stated analyses the following dialogue gives real life situations that will take the students as close to corporate world as possible.

Reasoning process in a multi-comparison form.

Salesperson: (approaches his dealer, greets him pleasantly, shows appreciation for a new vehicle the dealer has purchased. Takes care of routine business and says calmly) I talked to my office and was told you and one of your contractors were working on a major wiring job with the Singh Corporation (pauses, waits for reply).

Dealer (says sadly): Yes, Ramesh, you know , the contractor is and he tells me that a young assistant to the Works Manager is deaf to everything but low price.

Salesperson (slowly and thoughtfully): I see, well, he can make sure, quick profit that way.

Dealer: I guess that the young fellow is really tough. He is trying for a shrewd bargain. Just a wise guy.

Salesperson: Yes, I see, how much does the company need protection? How corrosive is the acid?

Dealer: Plenty. That is what worries me.

Salesperson: I can see how you feel but as a guess, how soon the corrosion might develop into power failures and production stoppages, if these stocks are used?

Dealer: Well, it will take some time, may be months. But a price-chiseller usually gets what he pays for. And some contractors go for low bids and quote these stocks.

Salesperson: It is a tough situation. I see that. There is a big profit if zinc conduits are used for all of us. But what will happen if the stocks are used when wire failure starts? Will this young fellow convince his boss that the contractor and us are to be blamed and we will get a black eye with the local business.

Dealer: It could hurt the contractor. But people ought to know that a dealer only fills a contractor's orders.

Salesperson: They should know that. Do you think it would put the contractor in right with the customers Works Manager if he went to him and helped him to see the years of protection he will get by using zinc conduits?

Dealer: Well maybe. Making a big issue of protecting each day's production might even make a big change in the young fellow's thinking and make it unnecessary to go up. But as you know these contractors often make low bids and do not fight for zinc conduits. But if he had your kind of backing he would feel strong. So how about going to the customer with him? I think I can fix a meeting just now.

Salesperson: It is a deal. I will try to make the young fellow or his boss see how much more good the zinc conduit will do. Make sure that the contractor understands that win or lose we insist on zinc conduits.

Dealer: Right boss. (picks the phone).

Prospect's Basic Needs and Desires

Most people have certain common basic needs and desires as given below:

Security: People need protection from loss of what they have, protection to health, income, skills, and mental powers, their company assets that are connected to their security and survival and of others whose welfare they have at heart.

Progress: People want to improve their personal and their team or group conditions, want to learn more, to do things better, besides they want the following:

- To earn more
- To live better
- To give better things and opportunities to their families
- To do work that increases in importance and responsibility
- To help their company so that in turn they get more opportunities

Respect: People want the respect of customers, peers, employees, bosses, families and neighbours.

Satisfaction and Enjoyment from Work and Life: People want a sense of achievement, peace of mind, happy associations, a sense of belonging, a feeling that their work is important and beneficial, besides they want the happiness of doing more than just for money.

Example 1

The salesperson is talking to a road-building contractor whose company security often depends upon making a profit in closely bid jobs. Hence, that becomes his job objective and a major interest area.

Salesperson (for road grader is talking to road contractor whom he knows well): To help our road contractor customers make a profit, our company makes a constant study of problems. The study goes right back to our designers. Take a tough problem of making a profit on closely bid jibs. One thing done, to help cut costs, to equip the controls of our new road grader with an improved hydraulic dumper. It eases pressure surges and eliminates the shock of starting and stopping the cutting blade. An operator can now place the blade faster and make more accurate cuts and yet do 20% more work per hour.

Example 2

The salesperson talks to the supervisor of the above stated road-contracting company. He has learnt that this prospect has had trouble in keeping good operators because of many rural road jobs.

Road grader salesperson: To help keep good persons on the job when they are long way from home, our designers have equipped the controls of the new model with improved hydraulic dumper. It eases pressure surges and eliminates shocks of starting and stopping the blade. With less effort, the operator can place the blade faster, make more accurate cuts, and do 20 per cent more work. The workmen love the machine and they actually stay on the job longer.

The talk continues.

The Bridge of Understanding

The first benefit expresses the first helpful thing a good quality will do for ANY user.

A major interest benefit expresses a final result that is one of the prospect's objectives.

The Mood and Manner Mover

A person's frame of mind and manner of speaking and acting that help to create liking and respect is a mood and manner mover.

When a listener/prospect sees a salesperson exhibit such mood and manner as the following, his emotions are favourable influenced:

1. Consideration and respect
2. Business-like intent
3. Friendliness
4. Enthusiasm
5. Confidence
6. Tactfulness
7. Emotional control
8. Patience

Besides the above, when a listener/prospect sees a salesperson exhibit such moods and manners as follows his emotions are favourably influenced:

1. Earnestness
2. Seriousness
3. Due concern
4. Sympathy
5. Thoughtfulness
6. Alertness
7. Self-respect
8. Resolution

The inviting appearance of a shop, displays, product, brochure, person on the counter, that create a favourable impression and help to create liking and respect are also classified under mood and manner movers.

Negative Mood and Manner

On the other hand, there are negative mood and manner that work as obstacles as given below:

A salesperson's frame of mind and manner of speaking and acting that impresses a listener/prospect unfavourably and that create dislike and lack of respect form negative mood and manner obstacle.

When a salesperson shows the following to the prospect through looks and actions his (prospects) emotions are affected unfavourably:

1. Selfishness
2. Arrogance
3. Impatience
4. Slyness
5. Overconfidence
6. Brittle temper
7. Insincerity
8. Superiority
9. Dislike

When appearance of a shop, display, brochure is uninviting and creates an atmosphere that puts the prospect in a negative mood the negative mood and manner is active.

Is negative mood and manner an obstacle?

Do the negative moods and manners, shown in these examples, place a negative influence over all that is said and therefore weaken or ruin their reasoning power?

Example 1

Supervisor: Do you want to stay out of trouble with the inspectors? If so, watch these edges better. You are getting careless.

Example 2

Salesperson: Listen, pack the glass right hereafter. That is the only way to save us from this kind of trouble.

Emotion Moves Used to Present Reason Movers

Example 1

An assurance mover is any combination used to present other movers with tactful directness, or that has power to calm or reassure the prospect.

The Question Mover

A question used by the salesperson to present other movers indirectly is a Suggestion Question.

A command mover is any command used by itself or in conjunction with some other movers that effectively produce a desired action from the prospect.

A story mover is an account of an occurrence that indirectly informs the prospect of reason movers, emotion movers or both.

An assurance mover, used to present benefit ideas positively.

Example 1

Machinery Salesperson: Yes, Mr. Gupta, your men will have even more protection than they have now.

The question mover, used to present benefits respectfully and open the door to more positive tactics

Example 2

Salesperson to experienced retailer: What would you think of this idea for getting faster turnover on storage cabinets? (Shows window display plans)

Retailer Prospect: Why do you have household items rather than office items in two of these cabinets?

Salesperson: I think it will catch the eye of many of the women who pass the shop and bring some of them in to buy cabinets or some other items.

(Talk continues)

The command mover, used to present reason movers.

Example 1

Salesperson (to retailer): Take the lower profit, faster turnover plan!

The story mover, used to present reason movers indirectly.

Example 2

Salesperson: Over in Kolkata last week I saw how Hindustan Motors is making their big reduction in rejects. First of all, they are practically eliminating paint fading by (story continues).

Food for Thought

It is interesting to understand that conclusions that are made are the product of a person's own mind and they become the basis on which he plans and acts. See how well you agree with the following:

1. The basic motive in taking any action is to benefit. A prospect can become interested only when he sees benefits available.
2. A prospect is a person or group that can be benefited to a desirable degree and who has the money or credit or is able to take the action proposed.
3. Effective planning of a sale begins with the finding of benefits that will be of interest to each prospect, Benefits for himself and others whose interest he has at heart.
4. The benefit mover has the power to create interest by answering the prospect-viewpoint question, "What GOOD will your plan do?"

5. The benefit, good quality, poor quality and loss movers have power to develop interest into desire to take action since they answer the prospect-viewpoint question, "Can you support your (benefit) claim?"

Three forms in which the prospects reason, when they make it clear that their purpose is to benefit are as given below:

1. The Benefit and Good Quality Form
2. The Comparison Form
3. The Conclusion Form

Any form of reasoning can be in assurance style, question style, command or story style, or in a mixture of these styles. The assurance and command styles are direct, the question and story styles are indirect.

Styles of presenting reason movers appeal mainly to the emotions and have power to open the listening mind to the reception of speaker's reasoning.

The mood and manner mover is an essential part of all presentation styles. It is the emotion mover that goes to work first in creating "liking and respect" and in answering the prospect-viewpoint question, "Do I like and respect you"

Tact is practiced by avoiding the expression of negative impulse judgements.

The recognition of forms of reasoning and styles of presenting reason movers will provide a guide for practising to-the-point reasoning of reason movers: Such practice provides a background to present ideas effectively without conscious effort.

It is not expected that facing his prospect the salesperson will pause and say to himself, "Now I will use the conclusion form and present my ideas in assurance style" any more than he will pause and think, "Now I will use a noun, a verb and an adverb."

The Personal Prestige Mover

A personal prestige mover clearly describes the good reputation or achievement of the salesperson's company, its personnel, its products, its services or customers, endorsers who lend prestige. It provides the prospect with evidence that benefit claims can be believed.

Example 1

Purchase manager to the purchase committee – The most experienced and reliable person in the paper business is Raghav Gupta.

Example 2

Prospect - on phone: Mr. Mathur told me of the clerical time and expense you have saved him. I would be happy if you come over to see me.

The examples show that good reputation built previously is active. In the next example, the speaker tries to build his prestige.

Example 1

Salesperson: During the two years I was at the factory, a problem in electronic controls crept up and we could solve it in no time.

Example 2

Manager to worker: Sure, I know this machine, Verma. I operated it for four years.

Personal prestige can be built by action.

Example

Salesperson dismantles part of the machine he is selling and then puts it together.

Limitation

The power of the personal prestige mover gets weak if the listener gets the impression that the speaker is trying to brag or is talking mainly to build his own confidence.

The Appeal to Pride Mover

An appeal to pride mover confirms the salesperson's respect for the prospect by stating the achievements of the prospect, his company or by asking for advice.

Example 1

Salesperson to his dealer: As I came in I heard some persons saying some nice things about the excellent job done on your display windows. You are making quite a success with you, is it not?

Example 2

Salesperson to another non-competitive salesperson: We are working on the colour scheme of our carton. Since you have done pioneering job in this area, we would welcome any advice you would kindly give.

Example 3

Salesperson: Our engineers thought that a reduction in maintenance costs would be one of the main things an engineer of your special experience would demand.

Example 4

Service engineer: The engineers in our head office will understand how you feel. They know you have always been fair-minded; so I am sure I can have this corrected in a day or two.

Example 5

Service manager: Our Delhi manager wrote to me about how well you planned the increase in sales of your engines in the North India.

Example 6

Salesperson: I really like the hardwood shop floors, they look nice and long lasting.

Misuse of Compliments

Example 1

Salesperson: You have a really well appointed office. It looks great.

The prospect has heard such a remark often over the past six years and further, he knows his office is nice but nothing unusual. On the day of the compliment it was rather dirty.

Example 2

Salesperson: You have made one of the best displays in the windows that I have seen. However, the way the special products are displayed really look shabby from the street.

If you soft paddle your criticism with a compliment the listener will always expect criticism whenever you offer a compliment.

Example 3

Salesperson of Bank Equipment to Bank teller: You sure can count money fast.

Teller: I ought to, I have been doing it for twenty years.

A prospect may not get any pleasure or satisfaction from a compliment on a task he performs as routine. On the other hand, a compliment put in a question style like, "in counting these brand new notes how do you keep a few from sticking together?" can appeal to pride power.

The Good Turn Mover

A good turn mover is a favour or free service performed or offered by the salesperson that has the power to build liking and respect and that places the prospect under no obligation.

Example 1

Salesperson: You can have my copy of the Planning Commission's Report on the five-year plan.

Example 2

Salesperson to the prospect: Your supplier is in Rampur, is it not. I am going there tomorrow on business. Suppose I drop in at the supplier's place and see if I speed up things a little.

Example 3

Salesperson to prospect: I just heard you are planning to go to Jaipur next Monday. I too have plans of going there by car. You are most welcome to come with me and I will drop you in Jaipur wherever you want.

Example 4

Salesperson for retail prospect: I have time on hand, if you want I can count the stock just arrived for you.

Example 5

An experienced engineer solved his prospect's problem unconnected to his own business. In this way, he did a good turn and later, the prospect said to another person in his company, "that fellow really knows his business" (personal prestige is earned through doing a good turn).

The Contact Mover

A contact mover is defined as classifying the business or personal friendship developed between a salesperson and a customer or the mention of common friends, hobbies, and other outside interest activities that help establish common interests.

When a prospect likes and treats a salesperson with more consideration because he is impressed by his mood and manner, a contact has begun. When a prospect is favourably impressed on finding that the salesperson is having a common friend or a person he respects, a degree of contact is formed. When a prospect and the salesperson love to talk about a practice the same hobby of contact is active. The strongest type of contact comes about when the customer appreciates the benefits that the salesperson has enabled him to enjoy.

Examples of Contact Mover in action

Example 1

Salesperson: I am Ramesh from Colgate company. Your friend Mr. Kapil suggested I drop in and introduce myself.

Prospect: Oh yes, Kapil phoned me about you.

Example 2

Salesperson: I may have a solution to your leaks problem. Can I call you tomorrow, I want half an hour of your time.

Prospect: How about nine thirty?

Common Uses of the Command, Question and Assurance Movers

The student must understand that the command, question and assurance movers are not used only to present reason movers. The following examples:

Example 1

Command Mover: Command used for routine directions

Salesperson to associate: Look at the second paragraph son.

Example 2

Command used to calm the customer.

Salesperson on phone: Do not worry it will do your job.

Mrs. Raj: It will do the cleaning easily.

Example 1

Question mover used to elicit needed information.

Salesperson: At your Rampur plant how many barrels of oil you use daily?

Example 1

Assurance mover used to calm.

Salesperson: I know how you feel. I understand, you can rely on the delivery date.

Assurance used to calm help prepare the prospect to listen to reason

Assurance mover used to instill trust and confidence and to help prepare prospect to open his mind to reason.

Example

Salesperson: There are four models Mr. Roy. All are built differently. The one that will do your work best is model 3 (follow with the benefit mover).

The first two assurances used in the example have power to build confidence in the prospect and they therefore help prepare him to open his mind to the reception of benefit ideas.

The purpose of emotion movers is to place the listener in a mood that will open his psyche to reason. The effective use of emotion movers, which is so much part of effective personality, is made possible by sales analysis. Such analysis often enables a salesperson to make specific improvements in his use of emotion movers. The foundation of instinctive or conscious utilization of such movers is the conviction that the listener can be benefited to a degree that will outweigh the cost.

Getting the Sales Talks Started

Example 1

Salesperson: I am Ramesh of Shiv Papers and since I am new to the area I came in to introduce myself.

Prospect: Glad you did. Have a chair.

Salesperson: Thank you. For the past five years I have worked out of Jaipur. By the way before I left Mr. Gopal said to say hello for him.

Prospect: Gopal? I saw him at the Mumbai convention last month. Good man.

Salesperson: Yes that he is. During the past three years he has taught me a lot about producing low cost frozen food boxes.

Secretary: Sorry for interrupting Mr. Verma is here to see you.

Prospect: All right. Ask him to come in.

Salesperson (rising): Thanks for letting me call on you without appointment. I sure am glad to have met you.

Prospect: Yes, call me up in a week or so. I want to hear about the low cost box experience.

Example 2

Salesperson is making a repeat call on a customer who has benefited a lot from the salesperson's company in the past. Personal prestige and contact are therefore established, plus a reasonable degree of liking and respect. On his last call he created interest in plan he proposed, was stopped by a problem and now he starts in a friendly and pleasant manner.

Salesperson: How are you Mr. Verma?

Prospect: Fine. Thanks. Have a seat. I will be right back. (leaves and comes back shortly) been to movies lately?

Salesperson: Have not had a chance. I was called back to the head office. And while I was there I think we found the solution to your colour draining problem.

Prospect: Is that so?

Salesperson: (continues his story).

Example 3-INQUIRY

Prospect (enters the office and asks): Is your salesperson's named Sinha?

Salesperson (who is in): How do you do sir?

Prospect: My name is P.K. Agarwal of the Planet Publishing House. I have seen your desk top publishing unit with BB and Company in working status. I thought I would come in and see the new model 55 you advertise.

Salesperson: Good. Come with me Mr. Agarwal and I will show you the model. It is in the demonstration room down the hall. (Pause) I appreciate your coming I to see us and I am glad I happened to be here too. (Pause) Do you have a problem something like what they had at the BB?

Prospect: No, we send out about ten thousand notices per month and they are printed as you can see. Raja of BB Company thinks your process might save us considerable money and I want to find that out.

Salesperson (decides that the sale has moved into desire zone for him and as he demonstrates the model he will carry on using rupees savings as his Major-Interest Benefit-says): I think we will find that Mr. Raja is right.

Types of Calls and Objectives of the Calls

The completely creative call exists when the prospect has no intention of buying and when motion has to be created from the start.

Various objectives of the completely creative call are given below:

1. To get acquainted, build personal prestige, make a contact and secure essential information for future use
2. To get permission to make a survey or a demonstration or to get the prospect to try or test a product
3. To start and move the sale to interest, desire or decision.

Partly Created Sales

The Inquiry: When the prospect has been moved to interest or desire to buy by means of advertising, satisfied customers, articles in magazines, and make an inquiry, one type of partly created sales exists.

Objectives in dealing with an inquiry: To build liking and respect for self, to find out how far the sale has progressed, to pick the sale up at whatever point it has reached and move it forward as far as possible by use of emotion and reason movers.

The favourable-attention call: When on his first call the salesperson finds that his company or product or plan is already known and respected to the extent that favourable attention is easily secured, or when someone has built Personal Prestige for him or when a user has created interest for him.

The problem for the salesperson is to capitalize upon the help secured and to use emotion and reason movers to develop the sale further.

The follow-up call exists when the salesperson has gained attention on a previous call or created interest and develop it into desire to buy.

The objective is to maintain favourable attention by means of emotion movers and to move the sale forward by use of emotion and reason movers.

The service call exists when the purpose of the visit is to give service or find out if service is needed or to clear up misunderstandings or errors.

The main purpose of these classifications of the types of calls is to make it clear that wherever progress has already been made, it is not necessary to start back from the beginning but to use movers to take it from there and carry on from the progress point that exists.

The Prestige Movers

When the good reputation of a company, its personnel, product or service or its customers and endorsers provides the prospect with evidence that benefit claim can be believed, the prestige mover is active.

Examples of Prestige Movers in Action

User Prestige

1. The Delhi plant of Smart ACs has been using the system for the past ten years
2. The Parliament house, the President's house and the PM's house have all been renovated by our company
3. Jayant Enterprises have been using our accounting software for the last six years

Company and personnel prestige

1. The new monitoring software is one of the greatest achievements of our research laboratories
2. Each one of our GMs has received national commendation for their efforts
3. Our company has been the pioneer in seamless tubing, a fact that makes us proud
4. We are responsible of at least 70% of production of artificial rubber in the country
5. We are the largest and oldest company in the business and also the most respected one
6. We hold the record of 100% zero defect production

Product or service prestige

1. More of these painting machines are employed in the automobile industry than any other
2. It was the first cooker in the market and has remained the market leader ever since
3. The TV manufacturers of the country have taken our standards as their norms
4. Yes, this road paving machine is used in every state of the country

Prestige of process, plan, idea, policy

1. The plan has been recognized by the Government recognized Railway Reconstruction Authority
2. The formula has worked in managing the mines in Bihar
3. Our MD has approved of the idea to merge the two production units
4. Problems in the use of the prestige mover.

Example A

Systems salesperson (After introducing himself, and having been invited to have a chair, thanks the prospect and says easily)—

From your recent magazine article I learnt of your interest in reducing the cost of operating records as well as machines. Since a practical and economically operated system for inventory control record has been developed by our company I hoped you would like to see it. I have come with an invitation for you to visit our factory to give you a demonstration. Could you give me about ten minutes now.

Prospect (smiles)–Let us hear it.

Example B

Systems Salesperson (After introducing himself and having been invited to have a seat, thanks the prospect and says proudly)—

My company is the oldest and largest in the field. We serve the Brass Group of companies. As an example of the advantage there is, in dealing with us , here is the inventory control system we produce for that group.

The Story Mover

A story mover is an account of an occurrence that indirectly informs the prospect of the reason movers, emotion movers or both.

Example 1

A salesperson whose products are industrial motors had, three weeks before, been told by a customer that cutting operating costs was his major problem. Now he returns and on his follow-up call, is told by a secretary that the prospect is about to leave for a trip through one of the company plants. Here is how he uses emotion and benefit movers to answer the first two prospect-view questions and thereafter uses the story to provide evidence that his claim can be believed.

Salesperson: How are you Mr. Singh?

Prospect: Very good, thanks.

Salesperson: Do you remember that last month you had told me cost cutting was a major problem?

Prospect: It still is. I am about to leave for the plant and that is one thing on my mind.

Salesperson: Good. I think I have an idea that can save them about 20% on finishing bases.

Prospect: That so? What is it?

Salesperson: By using a 10 hp motor instead of a smaller one and by using carbide cutters a smooth finish can be made with one fast cut. The reason I am sure of this is that I have seen it done at the Bengaluru plant of HMT. As they stated, chips fall like gravel deep and smooth cuts are made and their cost reduction has come to more than 25%.

Prospect: But what about the chatter?

Salesperson: I am glad you thought of that. They control it by (talk continues).

Example 2

Salesperson (to customer who has just taken delivery of 10 drums of transformer oil): I dropped in to thank you for your lube oil order and to make sure you have received in tact. Your stores manager tells me that he is planning to move it into the closed store area this afternoon which is a good news as this will ensure that the oil is protected from moisture and hold its dielectric strength. The reason I am concerned is that two years ago a customer in Mumbai insisted upon taking delivery of 50 drums of the same oil, while they did not have storage room for the same. When I checked it had not been stored yet but they promised to get it under cover. However, it stayed outside through out the monsoon. When they wanted to use it they found that its dielectric strength was affected so much by the moisture that it had to be condemned and they lost the entire investment.

The stories are given in some detail to show the various reason movers they contain.

Examples of some stories that have been used.

Story that contains appeal to pride, personal prestige, contact movers, used to build liking and respect.

Story that presents benefit and other movers indirectly. Used to answer prospect's viewpoint questions.

Story of a company achievement in developing products, services or plans that increased benefits to users. Used to support benefit claims.

Stories telling endorsements won from doctors, scientists, associations used to support benefit claims.

Story that presents poor quality and loss movers indirectly, following the direct use of benefit and good quality movers.

Research

Some examples of the use of prestige movers to research the need of company's products.

Example 1

Salesperson: I heard about your big increase in sales in Gujarat, your dealers must be full of praise of your products and their lasting quality.

Prospect: We are proud of our record there, and all trough the area for that matter.

Salesperson: The reason I came today to see you was on the problem of increasing the lifer of your cutting tools.

Example 2

Salesperson: The last time I had called on you I was told about how you started out small and built this big business empire. The most interesting thing was how you made all the rich people of the town your customers.

It made me think that with such a fine trade, you are in a special positing to make a nice profit on high quality storage cabinets.

Favourable Condition

A favourable condition is a situation in a prospect's industry, company, group or personal life that he is already benefiting or will benefit and that, when brought to his attention helps prepare him to see he has an opportunity to benefit still further through the salesperson's proposition.

When the efforts of the prospect or his company have created the favourable condition it has appeal to pride elements and still greater power to help him see and appreciate his opportunity.

Appeal to Pride on Favourable Conditions

Example 1

Salesperson to distributor: You have built a fine team of salespersons, Ram. You can trust them to solve problems for your prospects and customers on your regular line. Hence, it seems to me you are set to make some nice extra profit by taking on small motors (talk continues).

Example 2

Research Officer to Management: The survey shows that the area has grown steadily for the last twenty years. It gives indication of continuous growth. Its per capita income is above the country's average. Its farms are highly productive and its manufacture diversified. While details are ready to be given, the general view is that it is a safe, profitable location for a storage depot.

Example 3

Salesperson: How large is the payroll estimated for your new plant?

Prospect: Around Rs. 100 lac.

Salesperson: So much! Well you must be bringing some top mechanical engineers too?

Prospect: Yes, several, in fact.

Salesperson: What an opportunity for a housing complex, like this for instance (shows some layouts of such complexes his company has built in the past.

Unfavourable Conditions

An unfavourable condition is any situation creating losses for the prospect, for which the prospect, the salesperson or their companies are not responsible, and which brought to the attention of the prospect, tactfully will help him see his need for the benefits of the salesperson's proposition.

Part of the talk illustrating use of unfavourable conditions.

Sales Engineer: As long as the coal is loaded in open cars in monsoon time, it will be full of moisture. When this coal is pulverised it packs like putty and causes sparkles in the furnace, that quickly lowers the efficiency of the furnace.

The one way to solve the problem of getting full efficiency from such fuel is, of course, to have a pulverize equipped with a properly designed hot plate.

Salesperson now shows illustrations and tells how the hot plate in his product dries coal and makes it as efficient as coal from the mine in proper condition.

The Difference Between Unfavourable Conditions and Poor Quality and Loss Movers

The usefulness of separating poor quality and loss movers from unfavourable conditions for the prospect is that it reminds that unfavourable condition idea can usually be mentioned before benefits without arousing resentment while poor quality and loss movers are effective when used after benefit and good quality movers.

Example 1

Use of unfavourable conditions.

Salesperson: Is the monsoon giving your bus drivers the same schedule troubles I hear so much about?

Prospect: It sure is. We are having our troubles.

Salesperson: To help solve the schedule problems our engineers are doing a lot of careful research on wheel bearing protection.

Last winter, for example BEST in Mumbai made tests which, their records show make it possible to practically eliminate bearing failures (develops the story).

Example 2

Use of poor quality and loss mover.

Salesperson: I know you are having a lot of wheel bearing failures, due to the grease you are using and...

Prospect: Where did you get the idea we are having a lot of failures? (relations can get strained).

Unfavourable and favourable conditions used to prepare prospect to appreciate his need and opportunity to benefit.

Example 1

Salesperson (has built personal prestige and contact): How is the new raise in shipping rates going to affect your Kerala market?

Prospect: Well, the southern competition will have the advantage in price. That is the picture.

Salesperson: What about this idea? With the dealers, there, getting such good prices and demand for your product, could you hold up your sales and profits if I could get you a big supply of rare raw materials at old prices?

Prospect: How big a supply are you thinking of?

The Proposition Mover

The name of the company and its salesperson, the product, service or plan and the price, terms of business, delivery are classified as the proposition movers.

Example 1

The Capital Cabinet Manufacturing Company will furnish two model cabinets at Rs. 35,000 each for Delhi net. The payment terms are 30 days from dispatch and shipment will be made within six weeks of receipt of the order.

Example 2

These direct mail folders will cost Rs. 25 each for a minimum order of 10,000 numbers.

Example 3

The Singh Corporation offers this annual maintenance contract for your air-conditioners.

Example 4

I am Mitra from the Krone Crane Company.

Forms of Closing the Sale

The Benefit Sum-up and Close (Assurance Form)

Salesperson-to sum up, Mr. Roy, this cable will give you complete protection from breakdown. Your workmen will be protected from accidents due to the cutting of the cover. You will always be glad you chose it.

The Benefit Sum up and Close (Question Form).

Salesperson: Now, are there any questions I can answer about protection from breakdowns, or protection from accidents or time saving? Would you want it all sent to this mining area?

The Split-Decision Form of Close

1. How would you want it to be sent, by truck or by train?
2. Which colour would you prefer, white or blue?
3. Would you prefer a May delivery more than June?

The Question Form of Close

1. What is your idea on your quantity requirement?
2. How soon would you want it installed?

The Assurance Form of Close

1. You will do well to take this office Mr. Gupta
2. Ramesh, I will order fast if I were you.

The Command Form of Close

1. Order the purchase now, do not delay
2. Do what is recommended Mr. Seth

Combination Closes

1. Do that Ram. You will be glad you did.
2. You will need it for monsoon will you not? If so, order should be laced now.

The Explanation Mover

Works used to make clear the meaning of a technical term or details of an operation, are explanation movers. Demonstrations, photographs, blueprints, when used to make details clear are also known as explanation movers.

Example 1

The system should work well for us. The schedule is well planned. In this area, the metres are ready on Tuesday. The billing machine operators prepare the bills on Thursday and they are sent to the customers on Friday.

Example 2

It will reduce the amount of power required because it works on sound gravity principle shown here.

Example 3

Salesperson (about a poisonous matter sold as powder): You will find the material safe to handle and easy to measure as it is compressed into uniform tablets, looking like mini moth balls.

Example 4

Salesperson: You place the sheets of paper on paper on the transfer surface like this and pull the lever.

Example 5

To get perfect results you place the paper sheets accurately on the transfer plate like this. Next you pull down the lever like this, slowly and evenly.

Example 6

This is the delicious pure custard, we advertised in the *India Today*. Please taste it.

The usefulness of technical equipment is made easy and clear by demonstration and trial run.

Progress Signals and the Progress Test Questions.

Progress signals are comments and actions of a prospect that indicate that prospect viewpoint questions have been or are being answered adequately enough to keep them moving.

A question asked by the salesperson to test the progress being made in a talk is a progress test question.

Example 1

Salesperson: Your workers will be fully protected from shock-accidents since the tough tellurium cover has been placed on the cable. It will protect the men even if they hit it with a pick axe.

Prospect: Will it not cut?

Salesperson: It not only will cut that way, it stays whole even if one of your switch engines accidentally runs over it. Does it surprise you?

Prospect: Well it is a welcome surprise.

Salesperson: Over at the Mayurbhanj mines the workers have not only been protected from such accidents, but there has not been a production breakdown, due to cable cutting in two years.

Example 2

Salesperson: How does that look to you Mr. Prospect?

Example 3

Salesperson: Have I made that clear to you Mr. Prospect?
Prospect: Yes I understand,
Salesperson: (continues his talk).

Example 4

Salesperson: Would it be safe to say that the time of at least two workers could be saved?
Prospect: Well, I would say so.
Salesperson: In that case the system would pay for itself in just one year as its total cost is–

Example 5

Salesperson (after covering certain benefit and several important good quality movers): That is sound construction, is it not Mr. Jai?
Prospect: Good. Well thought out.

Types of Progress Signals

1. Prospect listens carefully.
2. Prospect nods and says "very interesting".
3. Prospect says, "I understand. That is clear.
4. Prospect asks, "Sounds good but I do not quite see how the oil can do that? (Wants more information on good quality).

Test Question Types

(Sometimes they can be combined with other movers)
1. Is that clear Mr. Ghosh?
2. Did I make it clear why anchoring the motor like this reduces the noise?
3. Is the saving desirable?
4. Are you happy with the safety part of the investment?

Timely Placement of the Test Question

Success of the test question depends on keeping it in line with the prospect viewpoint question being answered and by not asking the question that goes beyond the information given to the prospect.

Examples

Salesperson: Is there a problem of that type in your industry?

Salesperson selling financial deals regarding security features of an investment—that is the most important thing for you, is it not?

Salesperson: Have we offered a satisfactory solution to your quality improvement problem?

Prospect: Yes I think you have.

Salesperson: Good. The next problem then is, can operating costs be reduced to a decent level (talks carry on).

Limitations of the Test Question

The listener cannot answer in a manner that indicates progress if the question relates to something on which he has not yet been educated.

The question that ties back into a difference of opinion in a way that is embarrassing to the prospect is a non-use of the test. For example, "do you see how wrong you have been?"

Obstacle Descriptors

Habit

The habit obstacle is active when a person has been perform a task in a particular way for a long time and just by the force of habit would not like to change even if there is a much better way of performing the task. Such people become immune to change of ideas and create a strong resistance to the progress of sale.

Fear

The fear obstacle operates when a person has a justified fear of impending problems, of risk and consequent loss that overtakes his rational thinking. It causes him to by-pass the opportunity and keep performing below his potential with the help of new ideas.

Price

The price obstacle is active when the prospect does not realize the benefits offered would outweigh their money value.

Complaint

The complaint obstacle is active when the prospect shows his dissatisfaction through words or actions.

Detail

The detail obstacle operates when the prospect is of the opinion that the proposed plan is not worth the effort it will require to obtain and put it to use.

Lack of Information

The lack of information obstacle operates when the progress of sales gets hampered because the salesperson has not yet fully informed the prospect or he lacks the information. At times the prospect may not have the technical knowledge to understand the proposal. Prospect may not be able to get the full significance of the benefits that will be enjoyed. It can also happen if the salesperson's talk is unclear or confusing to the prospect.

Competition

The competition obstacle is active when the prospect compares the benefits or good qualities of the plan with another competitives plan and believe the later offers better benefits than the proposed plan.

(At times competition can be in dissimilar things like microwave oven and washing machine).

Friendship

The friendship-competition obstacle works when a competitive salesperson or his company personnel has the liking and respect of the prospect and when the prospect believes that competitive product would produce similar or even better benefits.

Difficult Personality

The difficult personality obstacle is active when a prospect lacks emotional control when he allows a difference of opinion to deteriorate into a personal attack or when he bursts out in anger, in rudeness, in deceit or other uncalled for behaviour which retards the progress.

Time

The time obstacle is active when the prospect thinks that the product or the plan under consideration is not worth the time it will need or it is late for making any changes. On the positive side, the time obstacle can be used to convey to the prospect that any delay in decision will endanger success.

Release

The release obstacle is operative when the prospect wants to be released from further consideration of the plan.

The Divided Release

The divided release obstacle is active when the prospect sincerely or insincerely seeks to end the interview by saying that he will take up the matter with a person not present.

Negative Mood and Manner

The negative mood and manner obstacle is active when a salesperson's frame of mind and manner of speaking and acting impresses the prospect unfavourably and creates dislike and lack of confidence.

Poor Judgement

The poor judgement obstacle is created by the salesperson's lack of consideration in looking at the ground realities, in separating the right ways of doing things from wrong, in planning the sales call, in deciding how to use the benefit story from the prospect's viewpoint. At times the salesperson can show disregard for the prospects reactions as the talks progress. The worst happens when the salesperson loses control of his emotions and forgets his knowledge of human nature and the practical selling techniques of study, analysis, planning and experience.

Examples of Obstacles

Prospect: Your proposal is likely to upset our work. We would not be interested.

Prospect: It is too much money. There is no point in talking about it.

Financier: If we have to choose between air compressor you offer and the new furniture; one thing is sure our budget cannot stand both.

Prospect: If you had called even a week ago, we would have been glad to have you in on the deal.

Prospect: We would need to keep our office force working overtime for weeks to install such a system.

Prospect: Frankly we buy all our supplies from X Tone Company. Swami of that company is very well liked around here.

Prospect: How do you people expect to be believed with your kind of delivery performance?

The Spar

The Spar is a special use of emotion movers, frequently mood and manners, assurance and question, to meet obstacles in a calming and considerate manner so the objector's mind is reopened to reason. Conditions are also used a Spar at times.

The Spar in action

Example 1

Prospect: What are you trying to get away with? This new machine looks hard to operate to me.

Salesperson: It does? Well, I guess it would look that way to anybody, yet you will be running it like feather touch only as an expert in just two hours. I mean it.

Prospect: Right, that suits me!

Example 2

Lady Prospect: Do not try to talk me into that? My husband would become mad if I bought the sofa of that colour.

Salesperson: He would? Well I can understand that—would this colour please him?

Example 3

Prospect: Ram, we have been using riveted joints in our castings for years and our customers have been perfectly satisfied.

Salesperson: That is right Sir. It was the cost cutting angle I have been thinking of (continues).

Note: The Spar may take just a second or two or it might be quite long.

How the movers in the Spar have been expressed?

Assurance

1. I know how you feel ...
2. I understand...
3. That is how it struck me at first...
4. I am glad you told me...

Question

1. Is that so?
2. It has?
3. You did?

Mood and Manner

1. Calmly
2. Sincerely
3. Earnestly
4. Politely
5. Sympathetically
6. Surprised

Meeting the Obstacles

Obstacle

Prospect: Why we have to keep records for twenty years? Our work is quite satisfactory. Is it not?

Example 1: The Spar

We know your work has been satisfactory. You have been doing great job. The idea now is to make your job more satisfactory to you, to lighten your rush hour burden.

And with the modern visible record system, you will find it easy to keep posting up to the minute....

Example 2: The Dominating Method

Calm down. Listen to me. This is being done for your own good, to make it easier for you to keep your work and you better appreciate it....

Checklist for Situations

Does the company have a need for my proposition? Can the money be secured? Have I got a prospect?

Are things being done, used or planned by this company that are causing or will cause loss?

Are the laws, economic environment, operating conditions or acts of others causing unfavourable conditions that create a need for my product, service or plan?

Do favourable conditions exist that provide the prospect with an opportunity to benefit through my proposition?

What major benefits can I use to answer the second Prospect-viewpoint question and create Interest?

How can I best expand and support my major benefit claims? Shall I rely on benefit, good quality, prestige and story movers or poor quality and loss movers essential to understanding and appreciation of the benefits?

Of all the possible obstacles which are the most likely to be active?

How can I use major benefits to avoid or weaken such obstacles? Am I prepared to Spar effectively and make a good and sound solution–effort if obstacles are voiced?

What company official should I see? What do I know about him? Is personal prestige or contact active? How can I use emotion movers to build or maintain liking and respect? What style shall I use to present my major benefit?

After studying the situation can I say that I have faith in my plan? Do I feel that I can help the prospect reach worthwhile objectives and do I look forward to seeing him?

If satisfactory answers to all the above questions cannot be found before the sales call, tactful use of the investigative question will be needed during the call.

Prospects Situation

Started Day-Night Medical Shop

24-hour operation by medical shop in the heart of the city centre
Yes
Do you gain late and early hours business
Yes
City laws permit 24 hours operation by medical shops
Extra sales and profits
Earlier there was fear, lack of information and the force of habit inhibiting the prospect
Extra profit outweighs extra expenses

Sales Talk Outline

24-hours operation

Night service also friendly earnest and sincere

Business build plans to be worked out

Build friendship

Good operation, good staff, better service to customers

Good location

Extra sales, extra profits over extra expense

Night person hiring who can take care of details—send direct mail, post records in the computer, keep the shop clean

Prospect: Worth a trial, certainly!

Note: Benefit of the night person doing detailing work proved to be desirable to the prospect.

CHAPTER

4

Retail Brand Management

Aims and Objectives

Retail stores depend heavily on the brand equity and strength for promoting product sales. However, most retailers' market multi-brand products, the brand that gives maximum revenue and profits gets retailers priority in pushing sales. The chapter provides for a comprehensive coverage of retail brand management and at the end of the students should become fully conversant with the concepts of retail marketing and usages of brands in retail sales.

National brands and international brands are mainly controlled and managed by the manufacturers and retailers have little to contribute to the brand value. Coke, Gillette, Kodak, Honda are some of the international brands that sell by themselves. In retail stores Harrods of London leads the way as can be seen from the box given below:

Harrods

Harrods is the most prestigious of superstores in the world. Following gives an idea of its various activities:

Menu

Services at Harrods

1. History
2. Restaurants
3. Recruitment
4. Harrods Card
5. By Appointment
6. Harrods Casino

7. Harrods Estates
8. Harrods Bank
9. Harrods Aviation
10. Air Harrods
11. Harrods Corporate Services

The following menu gives an idea of what to find in the store.

Hampers

£15 - £100£100 - £500 Complete Range

Sale

BeautyJewelleryWomensMensHomeWines & SpiritsHarrods Signature

Gifts

Gifts For HerGifts For HimGifts For PetsMy First ChristmasLuxury GiftsSignature GiftsHarrods StationeryFood GiftsChampagne GiftsWine GiftsDecorationsBearsHarrods Gift BoxesWrapology Gift WrappingClothing & AccessoriesBeautyDecorative Homeware

Certain large retailers organize private brands of their own. Spencers are one such big retailers that has its own brand besides it sells other brands as well. Big Bazaar has started its own brand too.

Sales Push

It comes from heavy loading of inventory by the vendors as then the retailer has no option but to get rid of the stocks by selling even at minimum profit margins, at times even at a loss, especially if his storage space is getting cramped.

Sales Pull

It comes from vendor or retailer's advertising efforts when the customers come in numbers asking for the brand. Advertising is organized by the vendors, manufacturers and retailers and at times it can be a cooperative venture between the manufacturer and the retailers.

Several large retailers have used their strength in retailing by marketing their own brands. They get the manufacturers to supply products that carry their, the retailer's brand. Such retailers try to persuade the buyers into buying their own brands unless they show a marked preference for a particular brand.

It is therefore important to understand the value of the brand as a positive asset to the company, be it as retail one or manufacturing company.

When companies introduce a new product, they start with an initial unique selling preposition, the USP, which gives the product the required boost in the marketplace. However, over a period of time, other competitive firms catch on the USP, and depending on the market size, profit margins, ease of obtaining the manufacturing technology and the requisite finance, place their own products in the market. Thus, the USP of the company's product is lost as there are other products, in the market, the **"me too"** products with perhaps better USPs. In such an event, which is an almost daily occurrence, the thing, which keeps the company's product on the top, is the brand. The brand, if projected well in the right market segment will carve a niche for itself in the mindset of the buyers with its emotional appeal.

Brands can become effective tools for differentiating products as they keep creating goodwill and become company's assets. A good brand price fixation becomes easier as higher price can be charged over the price of competitive products.

There are, however, discount stores with self-service facilities where the customers buy products at low costs and price is the main criteria with the customers. In such stores brand ceases to have a major selling point. Most retail shops sell several brands of any product. In such shops it is either the advertising pull, inventory push that makes the shop salesperson promote the sale of a particular brand or it could be the extra discount offered by one company or its distributor to the shop.

Brands have given a major fillip to customer buying habits. Customers are known to love some brands and are ready to swear by them. These customers take on themselves the role of brand advertisers or even brand ambassadors.

Brand can be defined as **"A unique name for a product of a particular manufacturer**." This unique name gives a large number of attributes to the product and the company marketing it. As such, along with the market share, brand equity is considered the most valuable possessions of a company. Considering this aspect of brand, several top retailers are going in for their own brand as well.

Brand, its uniqueness, its value or equity, brand building, have become extremely important areas that need constant attention of the top management of the firms. Brand building is an evolutionary process as it takes a lot of time before a company can have strong brand equity.

In case of most products, after the initial sales starts declining due to fading of its novelty, it is its emotional appeal that helps it sell. This emotional appeal or bonding comes from the appreciation of the brand by the buyers. Therefore, brand, its value or equity and its attraction for the buyers are perhaps the most valued properties, or assets of a company. There are a number of ways of promoting the brand's emotional appeal among the buyers and these will be discussed in detail in the coming chapters.

Brand is the most valued possession of a company. Take Maruti from the car and what have you got? Brand gives a product its separate identity, taking it away from other run-of-the-mill products. Companies increase their market share and profits on the basis and on the strength of the brand, brand image or brand equity. It helps companies as once the buyers establish the brands through the quality acceptance. The brand equity is further strengthened with continued advertising efforts.

Jaishree Sunder of Lintas says, "At the end of the day, brands are but promises packaged with emotion. The stronger the emotional bonding, the greater the probability a brand will have of accessing additional revenue streams."

It can therefore be summarized that as the products get branded, they get the emotional appeal, in most cases and the advertiser does well to use the emotional appeal while advertising the product with its brand.

Giving brand management the importance it deserves, companies have stated modifying their marketing department's structure as given below:

First Level Structure

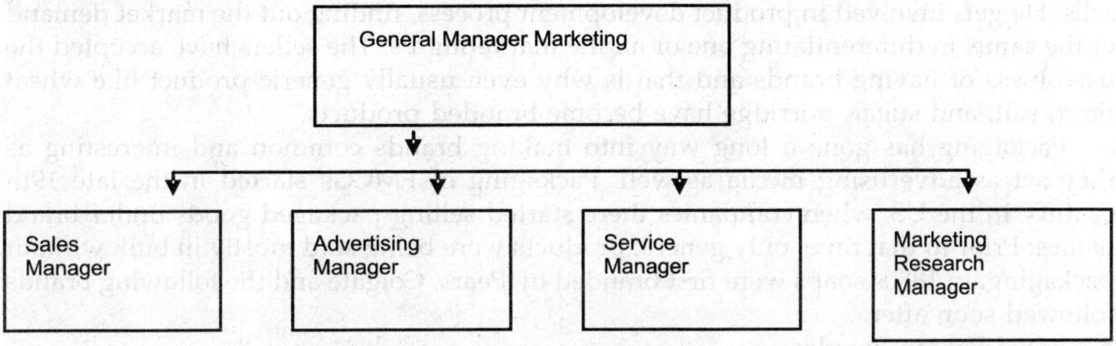

In the structure given above, the task of managing the brand is left to the Advertising Manager. With the growing importance of brand management, the structure has been modified in several companies as given below as second level structure.

Second Level Structure

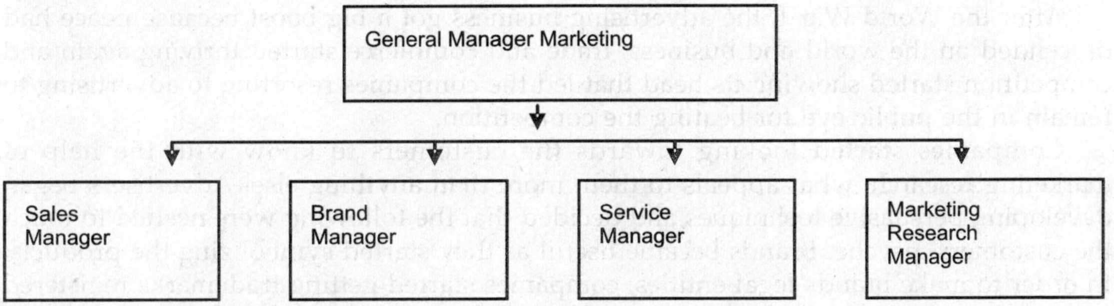

In certain companies there are several brands of one product like the Lever Brothers, or Hindustan Lever in India. There would be about eight brands of soaps, three of tea and hence, they have category managers looking after the category of soaps, tea, while they have brand managers working with them who look after individual brands as can be seen in the chart given be below:

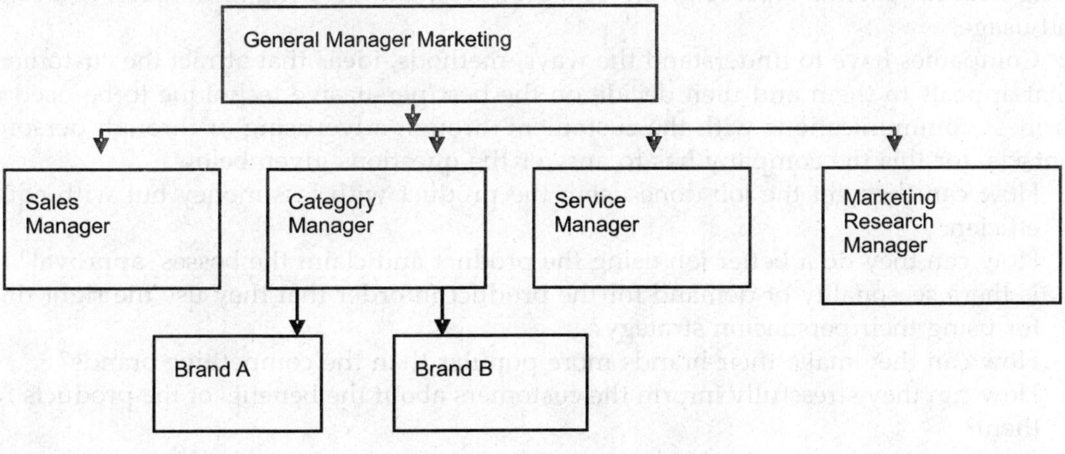

Brand manager in some companies operates like the virtual CEO for the brand he sells. He gets involved in product development process, finding out the market demand of the same, in differentiating one or all the marketing Ps. The sellers have accepted the usefulness of having brands and that is why even usually generic product like wheat flour, salt, and sugar, porridge have become branded products.

Packaging has gone a long way into making brands common and interesting as they act as advertising media as well. Packaging of FMCGs started in the late 19th century in the US, when companies there started selling packaged goods under brand names. Prior to that time, only generic products were being sold mostly in bulk without packaging. In 1880s soaps were first branded by Pears, Colgate and the following brands followed soon after:

- Royal Baking Powder
- Quaker Oats
- Regal shoes
- Waterman pens
- Coca Cola

After the World War I, the advertising business got a big boost because peace had descended on the world and business, trade and commerce started thriving again and competition started showing its head that led the companies resorting to advertising to remain in the public eye for beating the competition.

Companies started looking towards the customers to know with the help of marketing research, what appeals to them more than anything else. Advertisers began developing persuasive techniques and decided that the following were needed to touch the customers' psyche. Brands became useful as they started symbolizing the products. In order to make brands legal entities, companies started getting trademarks registered with their government bodies for protection against competitors stealing the brands. Trademarks are projected through words, symbols and styles used for placing these together on the product for easy identification as well as for in-built advertising effect the brands and the trademarks have.

Incidentally, the economic value of intellectual properties are also protected by law along with the patents that are given for a product manufacturing techniques, its design and usage.

Companies have to understand the ways, methods, ideas that attract the customers; what appeals to them and then decide on the best persuasive technique to be used in business communications with the customers through advertising or through personal contacts, for this the company has to answer the questions given below:

1. How can they get the job done using the product with less money but with equal efficiency?
2. How can they do a better job using the product and claim the bosses' approval?
3. Is there seasonality of demand for the product in order that they use the right time for using their persuasion strategy?
4. How can they make their brands more popular than the competitive brands?
5. How can they stressfully inform the customers about the benefits of the products for them?

6. Does the product help the customers in increasing their comfort levels; improve their appearance or their health so that emphasis can be made on these points in the advertising campaigns.

Maslow's Hierarchy of Needs

In this connection Maslow brought his hierarchy of needs theory given below:

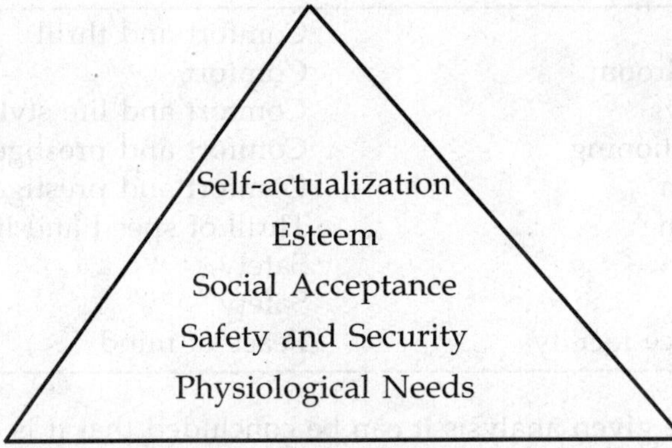

1. As companies try to persuade their buyers into purchasing their products, they have to understand consumer behaviour of the customers of their designated market segment. One basic method of understanding the consumer behaviour is through Maslow's hierarchy of needs, which deals with the human urges and requirements.

   The first basic need of people is physiological, that of food, clothing, shelter and human relationship. Next, people look for a safe and secure life. After that they need to have a place in the society leading to respect in the society. Finally, people expect a place in the top echelon; want to be known as achievers. Products should therefore support people's mindsets and should focus towards their needs. They can achieve this focus better with the help of a solid well-established brand.

   As the seller understands the hierarchy of human needs, he can plan the product communication according to the level of hierarchy he wants to satisfy with his product. For example, a basic food seller would talk about its nutritional value, calorie count for the weight conscious people. Cosmetic sellers would convey to his customer group about the beauty, allure and hope the products can provide to the users. Car sellers would give the concept of lifestyle associated with the car, besides the comfort, excitement, thrill it would provide rather than just talking about its use as a mode of transport.

The Benefit Story

The sellers must understand that nobody buys a product; people buy the benefits the products provide to them. For example, a shirt seller knows that the shirts are made of terry-silk and are available in a number of pastel shades. However, if he conveys to the customer the manner in which the shirt cloth would just flow on the buyer's body and that the shades, at least some of them would go well with the buyers complexion and physique. Given below is a table that corresponds with the Honda City features as they could be conveyed to the buyers.

Honda City Car

Feature	Benefits
Powerful engine	Comfort and thrill
Good leg and headroom	Comfort
Automatic windows	Comfort and life style
Powerful air-conditioning	Comfort and prestige
Good music system	Comfort and prestige
Aerodynamic styling	Thrill of speed and lifestyle
Strong body	Safety
Seat belts	Safety
Countrywide service facility	Peace of mind

From the above given analysis it can be concluded that it is a luxurious family car. The car advertisement showing the birthday episode uses this sequence of thinking as the advertisement is planned.

For creating a benefit story, the following areas need to be understood:

1. Creativity of minds
2. Standards of decency
3. Limits of the media that would carry the message
4. Legal restrictions
5. Reputation of the company

In the game of advertisement, brand plays a major role as it denotes the following:

1. Standards of product quality
2. Reliability of the product, the sellers
3. Value for money being spent by the customer for buying the product
4. Trademark that conveys the authenticity of the product

> Historically branding was carried out with the help of a hot ion on cattle as a proof of ownership in the 2000 BC in Egypt. Greeks and Romans branded their prisoners up till much later.

In the first half of the 20th century, firms in India depended on their goodwill, which gave them an edge over their competitors. As the number of competitors was low, the goodwill earned the firm the desired clientele. However, over the years, competition has increased manifold leading to dilution of goodwill value. Maybe the association of the word goodwill has ceased to excite the buyers leading to the emphasis on brand and its value for the buyers.

Brand power gets converted into economic value and it begins and ends with a focus on brands as corporate assets. Companies that outperform their peers and competitors in brand value creation understand this well and proactively manage their brands as they would other key strategic assets of the company as a way of securing long-term shareholder value.

Modern-day branding started in the 19th century when some US firms started selling packaged goods under a brand name.

In India, till a few years back most of the common products like flour, sugar, milk, candles and pickles were sold in bulk unbranded. Only of late these products have found brands and these sell in packages with distinctive brands, which differentiate almost similar products being sold by competing companies.

Historically, brands have been in vogue since 2000 BC, when tribes were branding their cattle in Egypt. In the 19th century BC Greeks and Romans were branding their prisoners and slaves as punishment.

After the World War I, advertising industry started to grow rapidly. With mass production techniques, assembly line operations, availability of products started exceeding the demand for the same, needing the use of persuasion techniques to sell products and each seller wanted his products to outdo others. This became the core of the branding base by the companies, where they could promote their brands by giving the factors that appeal to the buyers. Brands were on their way to becoming the biggest assets of the firms. Therefore, there is a close bonding between brand management and advertising management.

Companies have become aware that people needing a product are really looking for satisfaction of one or more of their needs. Cosmetics sell because people want to look good, beautiful, handsome, alluring may be better than others. One cosmetics seller advertised that he really sells hope; hope that his cosmetics will make people look so good that their mates would come running to them. Similarly, car makers provide, prestige, comfort, besides excitement to their buyers. Cars are used to transport people from location one to location two. However, luxury cars have given a new meaning to travel by car, as these have become status symbols as well.

Therefore, it can be surmised that the seller who can provide the required benefits to the buyers of his designated market segment will win the race. This requires two basic ingredients, a good product and a proper method of communicating with the target market segment. Let us assume that the product is good. For evolving the most appropriate communication the following channels are used by the sellers:

- Personal meetings, as in a retail shop, where the salesman directly interacts with the buyers
- Advertising where the contact is non-personal through mass media like TV, radio, the press
- Publicity where the firm draws attention of the buyers through either word of mouth communication between buyers and prospective buyers, or through free editorial contents given in the press, may be as the press notes given by sellers or suo-motto information given by the press on their own volition.

Most people, who are also buyers, look for the following:

- Ways of increasing their income
- Better paid jobs with improvement in prestige levels both in the company and in the society
- Job security as well as security of the family from ailments, thefts and other calamities
- Popularity in the company as well in the social circles
- Praise when due from seniors
- A comfortable life style for self and the family
- A good personality that attracts friends
- Good health

A brand gets established in the customer's mindset, through its qualities for providing benefits. However, the product idea, especially for a brand sets in through advertising efforts. Repeat exposure of brand to the customers help in getting the brand into the subliminal consciousness of the mind and at the time of purchase it gets into the conscious state. The benefit story that deals with the special features of the product binds the brand to the product. However, over-exposure can make a highly developed brand a generic brand like the case of Dalda and Mobil Oil, Dalda has become almost synonymous with cooking oil and Mobil Oil with car's engine oil.

In rural markets brands get established through endorsements of the village leaders, the Sarpanch and his team. With the spread of TV, villagers are getting acquainted with movie and sports stars and their endorsements too have affect on the villagers' psyche.

Product merchandising, with the help of its brand, provides effective product exposure through availability at a place convenient to the buyer, at time, price quantity as required by the buyers for profitable sales. Merchandising helps the sellers in product placement in retail, which helps in selecting the package size, shape, colour preferred by the trade and finally the customers. The package should lend itself to proper shelf display, demanding the right noticeable size and location of the shelf. The brand plays a pivotal role in grabbing the right shelf space.

Brand has the remarkable ability of differentiating the product from its competitors. It can therefore be asserted that the brand is **an asset** of the firm (like the goodwill of the years gone by). However, brand awareness, and brand loyalty have not yet penetrated into the village mindset because of their inability to buy high cost branded goods.

Branded products normally have fixed prices and bargaining is not a common phenomenon for branded products. Brands with high equity can claim high price as the quality assurance gets built into the brand. From the same yardstick, brands sell more and relatively with ease in retail stores selling several brands of the same product.

However, seeing the power of brands many retail stores or store chains sell their own brands, either in addition to others or exclusively. Then there are single brand stores along with speciality stores, which stock only one type of products in several brands. Brands have given rise to increase in consumer awareness of products.

Given below are the functions brands perform in the marketplace:

- Rural customers start loving the brands due to their trust in the brand, brand reliability for known results from the product usage and brands perception of its ability to provide desired satisfaction levels. Brand affordability adds to the brand loyalty amongst the rural customers
- Investors believe that brands get them higher dividends and increased share value
- Brand provides the sellers promise of product quality in the form of guaranty
- Brand (like Escorts tractors) get into hearts and minds of the customers
- Brand like the goodwill becomes an economic asset of the firm
- Brand helps in building a relationship between the seller and the buyer, both the trade partners and the actual consumers
- Brand results in buyer seller collaboration in brand promotion. A satisfied, happy customer will promote the brand in his business and home circles.

Advertising media that supports brands through exposing them in the market, consider a good brand as an assets as it generates good advertising revenue for them. Coke would not have any problem while buying media for advertising. Brand links media with the customers. "Yes, I saw the advertisement on Star Plus channel."

Brand develops an identity of its own, which supports and focuses the product on to the customers. Brands start living in the customer's minds. Ask any Coke addict, he would proclaim from the housetop why Coke is better than any other soft drink.

There are several types of brands as given below:

1. Unknown brand: The one that has been introduced and has not yet been promoted
2. Available brand: The one which can be purchased without any problem
3. Switchable brand: In which it is easy to change the brand due to low cost like the FMCG products. You can change the brand of toothpaste every month, while it may not be convenient to change the brand of your car or even refrigerator
4. Buy brands, the ones purchase regularly
5. Never tried brands: The ones just offered in the market, or even brands not advertised enough
6. Tried and rejected brands: The ones not accepted by the market
7. Orphan brands are those, which have no takers in the market as perhaps they were introduced in the market without proper market study
8. Substitute brands: That are available in the market and are bought in the event of non-availability of the preferred brand.

Brand Functions

Brands perform several functions in the marketplace, some for the buyers and others for the sellers.

Brand functions for the buyers are given below:

1. Brands make the choice of the product easier for the buyers
2. Brands reduce the cost of product search for the buyers
3. Brands reduce the time for product search

4. Brands reduce the risk factor for the buyers, in terms of quality, quantity, guarantee, resale price, after sales service.
5. Brands add to the identity and status of the buyers—he drives a Mercedes car!

Brands help the sellers as given below:

1. Sellers cost of sales reduces as brands almost pre-sale the products
2. Reduce their advertising and promotion costs
3. Reduce the cost of training of sales staff
4. Sellers can charge premium or skimming prices
5. Sellers can sell the entire brand line at the skimming price
6. Brands provide an entry barrier for firms planning to enter the market with the same product
7. Brands help in increasing the firm's share value
8. Brands provide an automatic product differentiation
9. Brands help in providing the promotional plans a market focus
10. Brands help in making the advertising messages simple as the brand itself conveys most to the buyers
11. Brands help in improved market focus in the advertising media
12. Brands help sell the entire product range under one brand

Branded products are pre-sold since the customers are aware of the benefits they can derive out of the products, as the brands become synonymous with the benefits. Maruti brand of cars signifies reliable cars with widespread service network in the country. Lux toilet soap brand itself proclaims its quality. There can be innumerable examples of the popularity of brands that helps the product sales with relative ease.

Information about products is communicated through advertising campaigns. Promotions lead to faster decisions by the customers for buying the products as the seller offers some extra benefit during the promotion period. However, when the brand gets customers' acceptance then the need for advertising and promotion reduces to that extent.

With high brand equity, the customers want to buy the product and they ask for it by its brand name and that releases the selling pressure from the retail salesperson. The companies can reduce expenses on training of the salespersons except for the customers new to the brand.

Pricing of branded products and brand lines becomes easy as with growing demand sellers can keep prices at relatively high level, or can charge skimming prices. It is only when competition catches up with similarly well known and accepted brand that the company has to look at reducing the price and going in for penetrating prices.

When a company has a brand that is well accepted and even admired by the buyers, other possible entrants in the market with same product would have to have serious consideration before they take any decision for entering the market as the good brand becomes an entry barrier for other companies planning their entry with same products, at least till someone can bring in a highly differentiated product with better benefits and yet reasonably priced.

A well-accepted brand requires less efforts in increasing the company's market share for the product as with the word of mouth publicity large number of non-customers start buying the product.

A good brand is at times enough to differentiate the product from other products in the market in the same category. This differentiation further helps in increasing the product sales, helps the company to achieve economies of scale, further reducing the production costs making the product more saleable.

Brand becomes the advertising media in retail stores and therefore it can significantly reduce the required impact of advertising and promotion for the product.

A good brand that becomes the umbrella brand helps sell the entire range of products sold under the umbrella.

CHAPTER

5

Strategic Human Resource Management in Retail

Aims and Outcomes

With the added significance of retailing in the 21st century, retailers are looking for the best available talent in their field of activity. The chapter reveals the importance of HR in retail as the retail outlets are becoming more and more sophisticated for the customers of the 21st century.

In retail the following questions need to be answered:

1. Availability of trained manpower for meeting consumer satisfaction
2. Are they trained for providing efficient and courteous service
3. Are the facilities well located and maintained
4. Are the signages adequate and well placed
5. Are the common areas well maintained, clean and uncluttered
6. Are the changing needs of the consumers being taken care of.

The employees working at the retail outlets need to know if their jobs are satisfying, chellanging enough. Are their promotional, increment plans in place? Is there transparency in decision-making with clearly laid out authority and responsibility and hierarchy?

The managers need to understand the value of competent staff, with well-defined personnel policies, proper hierarchy and reporting system, are the employees motivated and the strategies for keeping them motivated.

The tasks that need to be performed in retail context are as follows:

1. Purchase of goods from manufacturers or distributors
2. Shipping goods to retailer's godown
3. Receipt of goods, quality check on the goods, storage and inventory control
4. Pricing

5. Merchandising for visual effect
6. Maintenance, cleaning schedules
7. Consumer research
8. Customer communication through advertisement, personal selling, ushers/ salespersons
9. Ease of billing and payment through numerous counters
10. Speedy complaint handling
11. Repair of goods
12. Credit and its control
13. Personnel handling
14. Gift wrapping of goods
15. Sales forecasting and budgeting

For each of the tasks, retailers need trained personnel as given below:

1. Salesperson: Merchandising displays including shop window dressing, customer contact, gift wrapping, follow-up
2. Cashier: Invoicing, handling cash, credit purchases, entering transaction data
3. Display specialists: Window dressing, interior displays, mobile displays, audio-visual displays through CCTVs
4. Inventory personnel: Receiving, quality testing materials, marking goods, inventory storage, returning goods to suppliers if not up to the mark
5. Customer service personnel: Repairs, alterations to goods as required, or replacement, handling customer complaints
6. Janitor: Cleaning the store
7. Management: Personnel management, sales forecasting, budgeting, pricing and coordinating different activities.

Organization chart for a small store is given below:

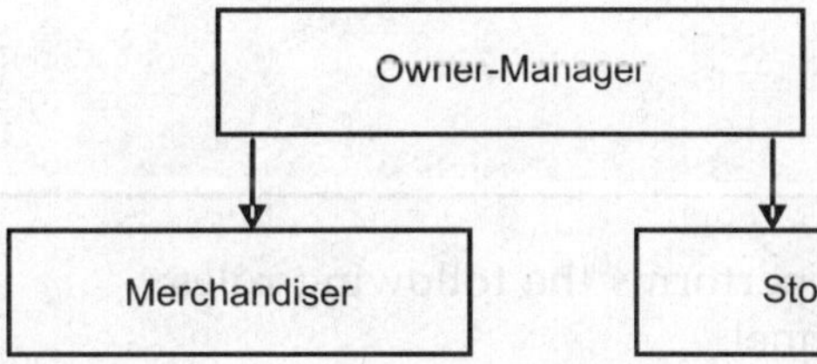

Organisation chart for a furniture company:

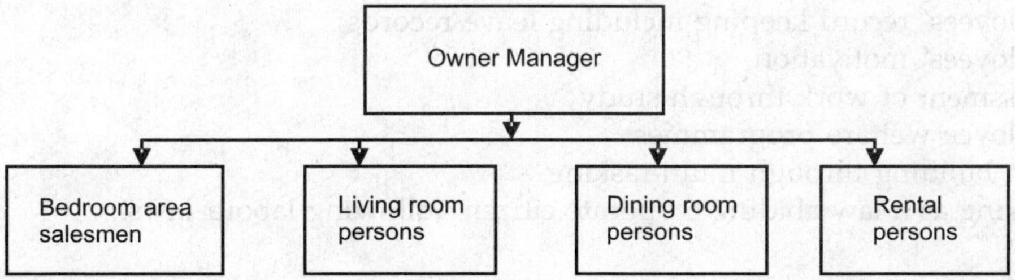

Functional chart for a retail organization:

		President		
Personnel Manager	Sales Promotion Manager	Merchandiser/ Visual merchandiser	Store Operations Manager	Credit Controller

Product based retail organization:

Stores Manager

Location based organization:

President			
Store Manager Delhi	Store Manager Jaipur	Store Manager Chandigarh	Store Manager Lucknow

Matrix organization

		President			
GM Stores	Sales Manager	Merchandiser	HR Manager	Purchaser and Inventory Controller	Credit Controller
Delhi Store Mumbai Store Kolkata Store Chennai Store					

The HR department in retail performs the following roles:

1. Recruiting, hiring new personnel
2. Training through classroom and on the job initiatives
3. Salary, wage administration
4. Employees' record keeping including leave records
5. Employees' motivation
6. Assessment of work through study
7. Employee welfare programmes
8. Team building through multi-tasking
9. Working as a law abiding corporate citizen, following labour laws

Certain problem keep coming up to the HR department that need to be resolved as given below:

1. Lack of motivation in employees
2. Conflict amongst employees especially gender based problems
3. Seniority based problems
4. Distinction between full-time and part-time employees
5. Lack of promotional opportunities
6. Compensation packet inequalities
7. Labour law transgressions

The best solution for the problems is transparency in decision-making that are taken without bias and prejudice.

HR department's training schedules need to include the following:

1. Lecture sessions by experts as one way indoctrination of retail theme
2. Demonstrations of various activities by experts
3. Audio-visual presentations of activities
4. Tailor-made instructions in structured manner with built-in feedback from the trainees.
5. Training conferences, as group activity for reinforcing the training imparted
6. Case study method gives the right real-life exposure to the trainees
7. Role play by trainees showcasing real situations
8. Hands on training or on the job training where the trainees work independently under close observation of their seniors

Normally, retail business requires the following types of personnel:

1. Store manager, who in small setups could also be the owner of the store.
2. Salespersons are the people who help the customers in selecting the products they aim to buy, brand, package and quantity.
3. Purchasers
4. Merchandisers
5. Logistics Managers
6. Storekeepers
7. Packaging Managers
8. Housekeeping personnel
9. Parking lot attendants
10. Security personnel
11. Delivery personnel
12. Accounts Managers
13. Cashiers
14. Complaint handlers

Store manager is the person who is overall responsible for the running of the store, its profitability, stock selection and inventory, hiring and firing of staff. He needs to be a person with a vision who can demonstrate leadership qualities and be a role model for the employees. He is the ultimate disturbance handler and therefore needs to keep his wits about him in times of crisis.

Salespersons in store are of two types as given below:

Ushers and helpers to customers as guides for them to reach the right place where the products they require are displayed. They also act as salespersons when the customers need to take decisions and they are finding it difficult to do so.

Salespersons who are all the time displaying product selections to the prospective buyers and persuading them to make the purchase.

Purchasers for retail outlets are the persons responsible for selecting vendors of the products the outlet wants to store, negotiating prices and other terms of business like credit and then finally placing orders on the vendors, checking both quantity and quality of products received from the vendors and getting them in the warehouse before they are needed in the retail store.

Merchandisers are the people responsible for the proper display of products in the stores where the customers can easily locate them. Merchandising aids in product advertising through product packaging, display in racks or panels or in shop windows. For example, merchandisers use mannequines in windows wrapped in dresses to attract the window shoppers and walkers on the street as well.

Logistics Managers are the persons responsible for getting the products in the stores at the right time in most economic and efficient manner. They arrange transportation, loading/unloading of goods and proper stacking in the storehouse.

Storekeepers hold the stocks in the storehouse till they are required in the shop for sales. They maintain inventories, give advice on when to order what product and report shortages, unsuitable products, damaged products to the store manager.

Packaging personnel are required for packing products sold in unpacked condition or when multiple product purchase has taken place and the buyer would like to carry only one bag. If the shop sells gift items, then gift wrapping becomes essential and is a specialized job for which experts are required.

Housekeeping persons job is to ensure that the shop is always clean with products in racks neatly stored and that there is no clutter on the pathways, the aisles in the shop.

Parking lot attendants should be able to get the customer's car parked properly so that there is no problem in parking and in taking it away from the parking lot. In some shops these attendants also double as valet parking attendants who drive away the car to the parking lot as the shoppers enter the shop in a carefree mind.

Security personnel are required to ensure the safety of the merchandise, shoppers' belongings, their cars and generally they have to see that no unwanted person enters the premises and there is no danger of theft or pilferage in the shop. However, a number of electronic security devices are available in the market including CCTV cameras that help curb pilferage.

Delivery personnel are required in shops that give added service to their customers of getting their purchases delivered to their homes or offices. Such purchases can be made over the phone without even visiting the shop. The delivery persons must be well trained in communication skills and courteous service.

Accounts managers look after the billing section both, for bills receivables and payables and they have to ensure that billing and payments are as per agreed terms only. They maintain shop records for preparing P&L Accounts, Balance Sheets and for declaring dividends and profits.

Cashier's job is to prepare bills after checking the product, brand, quantity and its price and they use the bar code system for the purpose, described in the price chapter. They also receive cash from the customers, get credit card payments and keep the cash counter in proper order.

While the retail gurus emphasize the richness of human resource practices among retailers, it rarely coordinates between the practices and the interest for establishing retailers' brands. Simultaneously, while the retail branding literature increasingly emphasizes the central role of human resource practices for retail branding, it rarely explains how retailers should carry out such practices.

New research should explore whether and how retailers create synergies between human resource and marketing functions to sustain their brand image. If the adoption of business practices by retailers is often discussed, this highlights that retailers could usefully transfer human resource best practices from leading retailers to develop their retail brand.

HRM strategies become most effective when they are synchronized with strategic goals of the organization. It will also make retailers more high performance workplaces and add creative talents to the retail industry.

Managing Retail Force

The theory that the way firms manage their labour forces should be consistent with their organization's strategy might seem both obvious and non-controversial. What this means in practice in a turbulent industry such as consumer financial service, however, is by no means obvious. Human resource management practices in banks are changing under pressure from an increasingly intense competitive environment.

The nature of these changes remains unclear, and questions centre around what forms the changes will take and around the effects of those changes. This draws on early interviews in a multi-year project on productivity in financial services firms. While the data are not sufficient to answer the question, it is believed that they provide clear directions to take in conceptualizing and further investigating the issues. It can only describe the issues involved with strategy, human resources and performance in retail banking. It can talk about the challenges associated with applying a model relating strategy to human resource decisions and suggest some considerations for the field of human resource management drawing on a capability-based approach. It can conclude with suggestions regarding further research in the study of strategic human resources in retail financial services.

In retail banking, uncertainty lies both in understanding the potential value of particular business strategies and in seeing what sort of outcomes different human resource management systems will produce. The few of the aspects of the set of human resource performance practices that are referred to in the literature as high performance workplace practises have been embraced by retail banks. What is not known is whether these practices can deliver valuable outcomes, or whether banks have simply failed to realize their potential. They suggest that corporate strategic issues may influence the ability of the retail bank to meet its strategic goals, and they may influence the time zones available to retail banks. They suggest that in a less turbulent climate, there might be more investment in human resources. Current pressure to contain costs in the immediate short run leaves retail banks in a difficult position.

Case—Banking Retail

Banking has remained a well-controlled and protected industry so far. However, with international competition the Government of India has realized that only the induction of new technology like IT, will help the banking sector realize its full potential as a service industry. With the MNC banks entering the market the government banks need to carefully assess their offerings and the associated service to their clients. Today, with the support of IT, banks are able to offer, ATM access across the country, banking on the Internet, and tele-banking.

Banks face reduction in profit margin with increasing competition. Banks are therefore, increasingly involved in streamlining their operations and cutting costs wherever possible. With governmental support of deregulation several financial institutions like HDFC, ICICI and UTI have ventured into the banking sector.

With the entry of private players into retail banking and with multinationals focusing on the individual consumer in a big way, the banking system underwent a phenomenal change. Multi-channel banking gained prominence. For the first time consumers got the choice of conducting transactions either the traditional way (through the bank branch), through ATMs, the telephone or through the Net. Technology played a key role in providing this multi-service platform.

The entry of private players combined with new RBI guidelines forced nationalized banks to redefine their core banking strategy and technology was central to this change.

Pressing issues

Today, banks have to look much beyond just providing a multi-channel service platform for its customers. There are other pressing issues that banks need to address in order to chalk-out a roadmap for the future. Here are the top three concerns in the mind of every bank's CEO.

Customer retention: Customer retention is one of the main priorities for banks today. With the entry of new players and multiple channels, customers have become more discerning and less 'loyal' to banks. Given the various options, it is now possible to open a new account within minutes. Or for that matter shift accounts within a couple of hours. This makes it imperative that banks provide best levels of service to ensure customer satisfaction.

Cost pressures: Cost pressures come into play when banks are not able to afford the cost of a certain service or initiative although they want to or need to have it in place. This is primarily because the cost structure at the backend is not efficient enough to offer that kind of service to the marketplace.

As Gunit Chadha, MD & CEO, IDBI Bank puts it, "In today's world of narrowing margins, a serious !ook at costs is definitely an imperative."

Increased competition: The entry of new players into the banking space is leading to increased competition. A recent example would be of Kotak Mahindra Finance Limited (KMFL)—a financial services company focused on investment consulting, auto finance, insurance, etc.—morphing into Kotak Bank. Many other such players are waiting on the sidelines.

Technology makes it easier for any company with the right channel infrastructure and money reserves to get into banking. This has been one of the major reasons behind this kind of competition from players who do not have a banking background. Kotak Bank overcame the initial costs of setting up its own ATM network by getting into a sharing agreement with UTI bank.

New entrants with strategies such as these make the banking game tougher.

Redefining objectives

To cope with cost pressures and increased competition as well as to retain existing customers, banks have started venturing into newer territories.

This is one of the main reasons why banks are focused on retail banking in a big way. The main advantage of getting into retail banking is that the risks involved are lesser in this segment. There are lower Non-Performing Assets (NPAs) in retail banking. This is one of the reasons why loans such as those for housing, automotive, etc. are being touted by banks like never before. Credit cards and debit cards are another focus area for banks.

With this banks have redefined their business priorities. They are now focused on:

- Cost reduction
- Product differentiation
- Customer-centric services

Although the ways in which banks implement these vary, the underlying objectives remain the same.

Cost reductions

Reduced costs basically translate to higher profit margins. If banks can reduce costs, it can go a long way in increasing profits.

The focus is on increasing the profit margins by cutting costs where it matters, on the operations side. Banks have woken up to the fact that they need to get into shape fast in order to handle competition.

"Banks have been increasingly facing sliding margins and fierce competition. It is imperative for them to increase the volumes and reduce the cost of operations," says K.P. Padmakumar, Chairman, Federal Bank.

Differentiation

The customer is interested in how he/she can benefit from the bank and its products. That's why it becomes necessary for a bank to differentiate its products from the others. Some of the ways in which differentiation can be introduced are through specialization, new products, and increasing the added value.

Specialization basically means that the bank gets involved only in selected areas. For example, the bank might be getting involved only in housing finance. Or, it could be limiting its services just for corporate banking clients. Another way to specialize could be by handling just specific sets of portfolios.

Banks can differentiate themselves by adding new products to their range of services. This will provide the bank with better yields per contact. Increasing the added value of products is another way of differentiation for banks. Operational excellence is also a key factor in effective differentiation from the competition.

Customer-centric model

Indian banks have realized that it no longer pays to have a 'transaction-based' operating model. This has led to the development of a relationship oriented model of operations focusing on customer-centric services.

While banks have to ensure product superiority and operational excellence, the biggest challenge today is to establish customer intimacy without which the other two are meaningless.

"In the financial world, product superiority does not last long as it is relatively easy to copy products. So, the real strength comes from operational excellence and understanding the customer and developing rapport with him," says Gunit Chadha.

In this context, it is very important that banks identify and understand customer needs. This will help banks in tailoring their products according to customer needs. It also helps in new business opportunities like cross-selling and 'upselling,' which takes cues from customer aspirations and transaction patterns.

Customer relationships have to be managed in the best possible manner. This will ensure that the customer comes back to the bank. In addition to good customer retention rates, it will also provide better income generation capability. This is because a major chunk of income of most banks comes from existing customers, rather than from new customers.

IT is central to banking. This is one of the major reasons why new private and multi-national banks have been able to survive, thrive, and adapt in an increasingly competitive space.

These banks were able to leverage on low-cost channels such as ATMs and Net banking to the optimum levels contributing to reduced operating costs.

Banks have realized that shifting customer access to lower cost channels can help bring down operating costs.

"These channels are used not only to improve customer service but also to divert traffic from the branches. It is a fact that the cost of transactions over these channels is lower than doing this through the branches," says Rangesh Nayar, Country Manager-Financial Services Sector, IBM.

"The cost of transactions over channels like ATMs and the Internet are lower than doing it through the branches"—Rangesh Nayar, Country Manager, Financial Services Sector, IBM.

But this does not mean that branch banking is obsolete. Rather, banks are reinventing their business models to offer new financial services through its branches.

Evolving IT

Banks are looking at newer ways to make a customer's banking experience more convenient, efficient, and effective. They are using new technology tools and techniques to identify customer needs and are offering tailor-made products to match them.

Centralized operations and process automation using core banking applications and IP-based networks improve efficiency and productivity levels tremendously. Core banking applications help a bank to shift from 'branch banking' to 'bank banking.' This basically means that a customer will be treated as a bank's customer than just the customer of a particular branch which was the case earlier. Also, IP-based networks lets a bank offer multiple services over the same network, resulting in costs savings.

CRM solutions, if implemented and integrated correctly, can help significantly in improving customer satisfaction levels. Data warehousing can help in providing better transaction experiences for customers over different transaction channels. This is made possible because data warehousing helps bring all the transactions coming from different channels under a common roof. Data mining helps banks analyze and measure customer transaction patterns and behaviour. This can help a lot in improving service levels and finding new business opportunities.

Risk assessment is another area where technology can play a major role. "Using technology, banks are able to better assess risks like interest risks, liquidity risks, FOREX risks, etc. The other driver for using IT is that banks can reduce costs and reduce the time to market," says Rangesh Nair, Country Manager, Financial Services Sector, IBM.

Is traditional branch banking dead?

The extent to which new regulatory policies and technology have transformed the banking industry brings us to one moot question: Is traditional branch banking dead?

With the emergence of various channels for (retail) banking, pundits all over have been predicting the end of traditional branch banking, at least in the metros and other upwardly urban areas.

But despite the benefits offered by other technologies in terms of lower costs or better reach, it looks like branch banking is very much here to stay.

The reason: Branch banking itself is undergoing a transformation. Traditionally, banks used their retail outlets to provide services to the individual customer. Now with ATMs, Net banking, and Tele-banking replacing traditional service channels, banks are more focused on enhancing customer value through branches. They are using their existing network of branches to advise on and sell new financial instruments like consumer loans, mutual funds, etc.

They are also using branches to inform and educate customers about other, more efficient channels to conduct common transactions like cash withdrawal or balance checks.

As Naresh Wadhwa, Vice President–West, Cisco Systems (India) says, "It is very interesting to observe that no channel has replaced any of the others. Rather, they are complementing each other. The customer remains one, but over the years, there are multiple channels being developed like ATMs, call centres, online banking, mail/fax, WAP, etc. The interesting trend is that customers are using all the available channels instead of settling for just one."

'The biggest challenge is to establish customer intimacy.'

Gunit Chadha, MD & CEO of IDBI Bank spoke to Network Magazine about the business issues in banking and how technology can be utilized to address these.

What are the main issues besides increased competition or lowering of costs that banks need to deal with?

These issues have always been there and all banks have to cope with these. In today's world of narrowing margins, a serious look at costs definitely is an imperative. One obviously has to ensure product superiority and operational excellence. However, to my mind, the biggest challenge today is to establish a customer intimacy without which the other two are meaningless. In the financial world, product superiority does not last for long as it is relatively easy to copy products. So, the real strength comes from operational excellence and understanding the customer and developing rapport with him.

What are the techniques used to ensure that consumer satisfaction and lower costs are achieved?

Notwithstanding what banks may feel about their products, customers utilize these products only for a few minutes. The key lies in making those few minutes convenient, efficient and effective. There are multiple ways to achieve these objectives. For instance, we introduced welcome kits wherein, a customer who comes in to open an account with our bank walks out with a fully enabled account, debit card, chequebook, Net Banking account, and phone banking account—in a matter of minutes.

Another key area that I can immediately think of is integration of services. Why should a customer receive multiple mailers from the bank when he can instead receive integrated financial statements? Why should a customer have multiple login IDs for different electronic channels?

These measures not only lead to customer convenience, they also help the banks save on cost. Identifying customer needs and tailoring products to match these needs is another area where a lot can be done. For example, we recently launched a 110 per cent Housing Loan to address other needs of a customer when he goes for a housing loan.

To what extent are the CEO and CFO involved in the decision for purchasing/ upgrading a bank's infrastructure? What's the process flow?

We have a well-established Discretion Policy wherein for budgeted items executives have discretion available to commit expenditure. However, for key and large expenses, the respective business head and CFO get involved in the decision process.

For larger expenditure amounts the CEO also participates in the decision process. Expenditure requests invariably originate from the respective businesses.

What factors are taken into account when planning IT infrastructure budgets every year?

IT infrastructure budgets take a medium term (18 to 24 months) view of the requirements. While cost optimization plays an important role, the key considerations are on high-availability, scalability and optimal level redundancy of the infrastructure. The key lies in making this infrastructure transparent to the end user.

What are the mistakes that banks have made in the past in terms of over investment in IT, underutilization of resources and so on?

I do not think Indian banks have at any stage done over-investment in technology. Expenditure has been right or perhaps less than what has been the need of the hour. However, expecting tangible and time-bound returns is today's minimum expectation from the investments in technology.

Mistakes can be that there was a lot of emphasis on doing things in-house and an improper alignment of technology with business requirements. Another issue is that of proper synchronization of tech innovations with businesses processes and rollouts. Without this, however, good a product or service may be, sales do not result. At the end of the day, anything that does not result in sales is not meaningful.

What are the main points to keep in mind when investing in IT?

The main points to be kept in mind while investing in IT are:

- A well-defined Return on Technology investment
- A visible addition to customer value
- Improvement of operational efficiencies leading to customer convenience and cost savings

HRM must also be considered in relationship not only to corporate and business strategy, but also to technology and the design of process. Do certain kinds of HRM suit different technologies? HRM practices do not function solely to serve strategic goals. Choices of particular HRM practices may reflect organizational power and politics and institutionalized norms of best practices as much as they reflect strategic goals or performance imperatives. While the U.S. retail banking sector has not been organized into unions, the industry may see more workers beginning to push for at least some of the high performance workplace practices regardless of strategic concerns of banks, should the current period of relative labour surplus prove to be transient.

The proposition that the way firms manage their labour forces should be consistent with their organization strategy might seem both obvious and non-controversial. What this means in practice in a turbulent industry such as consumer financial service, however, is by no means obvious. Human resource management practices in banks are changing under pressures from an increasingly intense competitive environment. The nature of these changes remains unclear, and questions centre around what forms the changes will take and around the effects of those changes. While the data are not sufficient to answer the question, it is believed they provide clear indications of directions to take in conceptualizing and further investigating the issues. The study describes the issues involved with strategy, human resources and performance in retail banking. It then describes the challenges associated with applying a model relating strategy to human resource decisions and suggests some considerations for the emergent field of strategic human resource management drawing on a capability-based approach. It concludes with suggestions regarding further research in the study of strategic human resources in financial services.

In retail banking, uncertainty lies both in understanding the potential value of particular business strategies and in seeing what sort of outcomes different human resource management systems will produce. Few of the aspects of the set of human resource performance practices that are referred to in the literature as high performance workplace practices have been embraced by retail banks. What is not known is whether these practices can deliver valuable outcomes, or whether banks have simply failed to realize their potential. The corporate strategic issues may influence the ability of the retail bank to meet its strategic goals, and they may influence the time horizon available to retail banks. In a less turbulent climate, there might be more investment in human resources. Current pressure to contain costs in the immediate short run, leaves retail banks in a difficult position.

Human Resource Management's role in the company's success increases each day. Human Resource Management is a vital function in organizations. It is becoming more important than ever. Line managers are getting involved in HRM, and human resource managers are becoming members of the management team. Also, everyone in the organization can make a contribution to the management of people and the success of the organization at the same time. Human resource management includes a variety of activities, such as the following:

1. What staffing needs to have and whether to use independent contractors or hire employees to fill these needs
2. Recruiting and training the best employees, ensuring they are high performers
3. Dealing with performance issues and ensuring its personnel and management practices conform to various regulations.

The following topics need to be discussed in detail:

(a) The special Human Resource Environment of retailing
(b) The process of Human Resource Management in Retailing Human Resource Planning
(c) Recruitment & Selection Training & Development Performance Management
(d) The Special Human Resource Environment of Retailing.

Staffs are a major resource in any business. This is particularly true in retail industry, which has a very large amount of employees and which provides a range of services to its customers. The retail human resource environment has its special features: a large number of inexperienced workers, long hours, highly visible employees, many part-time workers, and variations in customer demand.

The following features also create difficulties to retailers:

First of all, a large number of inexperienced workers and part-time staffs in a retail business may lead high employee turnover, poor performance, lateness and absenteeism. This is due to several seasons. One is that inexperienced workers can apply retail positions, such as check-out clerks, wrappers, stock clerks and some types of sales personnel, which doesn't require high education, training and skill. The other one is those employees who work in retailing companies likely live near the retailing stores. In addition, for part-time staffs it very easy to quit their jobs.

Secondly, long working hours may result that retailers need to consider two shifts of employees. As the trend of longer store hours (evening and weekend), retailers need to consider employing staff for evening and weekend use.

Thirdly, high visible employees mean that retailers have to monitor employees very closely. As consumers nowadays play a very important role in retail industry and employees are highly visible to the consumers, retailers must select and train employees carefully, especially care about their manners and appearance.

Finally, variations in customer demand may create difficulty to retailers to predict exactly how many employees are required. Retailers need to have the knowledge about what season, what number of employees is needed; and what day, what number of employees is needed; and which period of a day, what number of employees is needed.

The Process of Human Resource Management in Retailing

The four main activities of the process of Human Resource Management are Planning, Recruitment and Selection, Training and Performance. When retailers are applying the Human Resource Management process, the labour laws, diversity and employee's privacy has to be considered.

Planning

By analyzing the current workforce will allow the company to evaluate the department performance and helps to realize what kind of staff are required in order to form the skills which they needed. Retailers need to employ the right number of staff in order to make the workforce more efficient. Too many employees will increase costs, and too few will not able to carry out its work. Therefore, retailers have to analyze both current human resources within the retailing organizations, and future plans or strategies of the organization and the effect on human resource.

Meanwhile, because of the special human resource environment in the retail industry, the effects of the labour market factors have to be considered for their human resources planning. Due to the development of Information Technology, companies may not be able to find the employees who have the skills they required. In addition, internal staffing factors such as labour turnover, sickness or accident rates also have to be considered. However, planning has to be thought out carefully, and updated when other factors have changed. Take boots as an example, they evaluate the local market trend and qualification of local population, etc and seek to the staff that need to form the skills they lack.

This process takes time to operate. However, it is less expensive than the recruitment and selection process. Meanwhile, it will be helpful to find the employees who already have the skills that the retailers require.

Recruitment & Selection-Recruitment is the process of identifying the need for a new employee, defining the job and the appropriate person for it, attracting a number of suitable candidates, then selecting the one best suited to the job.

When a company is looking for new employees, they tend to use different channels in order to find the most suitable personnel. The channels could be educational institution, TV/magazine advertising, agency or any other channels which is the best way to find the right personnel. For example, in a retail company, when they are looking for a entry level sales personnel, they tend to reply on educational institutions, advertisements and employee recommendations. Moreover, when a retail company is looking for middle-management positions, they are likely to use employment agencies, competitors, advertisements and current employees. The recruitment process can be costly. It takes a great deal of time to set up an effective recruitment process. Therefore, the company has to carry out this job in a systematic way.

The next job is to select new employees from among those the company has recruited. The main objective in the selection process is to match the character of potential employees with the requirements of the jobs to be filled. The process of selection includes job analysis and description, the application blank, interviewing, testing, references and a physical examination. These processes should be followed in an integrated manner. However, the selection process can be very costly because the company has to pay for the postage of sending out application forms to candidates and they may also have to pay for the travel expenses for candidates' journey to interview.

Strategic Retail Management has been defined as the firm's plans and policies and the action, which is taken on their basis.

Some examples of plans are given below:

- We will increase our business in the southern states of Karnataka and Kerala to increase our sales by three per cent next year by starting new stores there.
- We will introduce a cheaper package to cater to the lower income areas.
- We will reduce paper work by thirty per cent and increase efficiency and speed in decision-making, especially in handling customer complaints.
- We will increase our advertising budget by thirty per cent to help meet our sales targets.

Examples of policies are given below:

- We will maintain price parity in the market
- We will not use unlawful means to achieve our legitimate goals
- We will give top priority to customer service and complaint redresses

Local retailers start business on the assumption that they can share the joy of supplying the products they love with their customers while making profits out of the sales. However, a more rational method would be to have a clearer idea of the success of their venture before starting the same.

1. Business study
2. Marketing plan
3. Feasibility study
4. Marketing research

Small retailers consider marketing research as a rich sellers domain. However, the research can be made easy by starting exploratory research in the following manner:

Asking several persons in the area about the place they go for shopping. Are they getting the right products at reasonable prices? The retailers can then select a few answers and expand the research to cover their target customer group in the right market segment.

These prospects can be asked questions regarding the following:

1. Products and brands required and preferred
2. Acceptable prices
3. Location most suited and yet within the range of practicality

At times the use of Focus Groups is advisable where the following questions can be discussed:

1. Where do you buy your needs?
2. Is there something you want and is not available there?
3. Price range acceptable to you?

Small retailers need to capitalize on their size rather than capitulate to the big players in the following manner:

1. Personalized service-calling customers by their names, knowing their preferred brands, quantities they buy and how they usually pay.
2. Home delivery facility at least in selected arras
3. Accepting payment, either on monthly basis or with every delivery through cheques
4. Going out of the way to meet a few unusual demands of certain selected customers (one retailer used to buy cinema tickets for certain important customers on no service charge basis)
5. Bulking and un-bulking packages to suit the customers
6. Providing instant relief in case of goods rejected by the customers

A new competitive phenomenon has appeared on the horizon—the factory outlet malls that are built in modular fashion with the flexibility of expanding when required. These are located on highways and while they compete with the local grocers they are purposely kept out of the trading areas of the local grocers to avoid direct competition, which might kill the small grocer. The malls depend on the impulse buying of the highway travellers who get attracted to the well-designed mall facades. These malls start by selling the companies first grade products. Later on, however, they can resort to selling seconds products as well.

Retailers in the developing countries have the following characteristics:

1. Mainly they are small-scale retailers
2. They could be the street vendors or pavement vendors
3. There are weekly markets as well
4. They could be door-to-door sellers—carpets, textiles, bread and butter (besides a host of other products) are sold in this manner
5. Pushcarts, wheelbarrows and cycle-rickshaws are quite popular as retail vendors

The retailing of products is of utmost importance since that is the final bridge between the manufacturer and the customer. However, it is only in this decade of the 21st century that retailing has assumed the significance it deserves.

The mega malls of the west are slowly but surely making in-roads in the Indian marketplace and yet the importance of individual stand-alone retail shop is not likely to disappear in a hurry, especially if the retailers take adequate precautions.

Given below are some suggestions that will help the retailers to keep their business intact.

Service in a retail store tells a story that should be appreciated by the customers and the prospects alike. The retail selling team should be like the actors on the stage that create an ambience and an aura that makes the storytelling effective, interesting and informative. The customer should be encouraged to become one of the actors playing his role for getting the best from him, the dialogue that each salesperson wants to hear—"please pack it, I will take it". The factors that contribute to the success of the play are given below:

1. Know your customer, build relationship with him, sending greeting cards, inviting on your anniversaries are just a few of the examples.
2. Know your own team, their individual strengths and weaknesses, where will they fit the best, what training they require.
3. Monitor, coordinate service activities.
4. Be unique in distribution, provide crèche for customer's small children, gaming area for teenagers.
5. Never oversell, deliver what you promise.
6. Honesty still remains the best policy in business.
7. Target your efforts towards your goals.
8. Be innovative, create profitable situations.

Sellers need to measure both the quantity and the quality being supplied to the customers. It is better to be self-judgemental rather than sorry. It is good to know your own core competencies, strengths and weaknesses, besides you must keep reminding yourself the reason you got into the business in the first place.

Sellers should be asking the following questions to know their own inclinations

1. Why am I in this business?
2. What are our USPs?
3. What are their delivery arrangements for telephonic orders?
4. Review consumer research, changing pattern of their needs, consumer bahaviour and paying habits.
5. Organize the answers to the questions given above and pick up the best three answers. Let three best answers be discussed in the Focus Group.

It can be said without fear of contradiction that retailing has come of age in India. Retail industry is considered one of the fastest growing industries in India. As per a survey, India is considered the second most attractive retail destination from amongst 30 emerging markets. India's vast middle class and its almost untapped retail industry are main attractions for global retail giants wanting to enter newer markets. India's total retail market is valued at approx. Rs. 912 crore, which is expected to grow at a rate of 30 per cent over the next five years. At present retail industry contributes 14 per cent to the national Gross Domestic Product (GDP). It employs nearly 7 per cent of the total workforce which means 42 million (4.2 crore) people. The retail industry is definitely one of the mainstays of the Indian economy.

The retail industry is divided into organized and unorganized sectors. Indian organized sector accounts for just 2 per cent of the trade and employs just 500,000 people. Unorganized retailing refers to the traditional formats of low-cost retailing such as the local kirana shops, owner-manned general stores, paan shops, convenience stores, handcart and pavement vendors, and employs over 40 million people. This sector is highly fragmented, with about 110 lakh outlets in the country.

As per the market figures the organized sector is expected to grow by about ten per cent by 2010. With the rise in consumer demand, high disposable incomes and increased awareness levels, the retail industry is undergoing a major transition. Various functional aspects of retailing industry are:

- Retail merchandising & category management
- Fashion & Apparel
- Food
- Jewellery
- Lifestyle accessories
- Entertainment

Besides the retailers need to strategize the following activities:

- Retail selling & customer service management
- Store operations
- Visual displays, merchandising & store design
- Retail marketing & customer management
- In-house shop entertainment, advertising PoP.

Some of the major players in the industry are:

- Usha shops
- Bata shops
- Shoppers Stop
- Westside stores
- Subhiksha
- Globus
- Planet M
- Titan
- Madura Garments
- Pantaloon's Big Bazaar and Food Bazaar
- RPG group's Giant and FoodWorld, and Metro Cash & Carry

The Indian population is witnessing a significant change in its demographics. A large young working population with median age of 24 years, nuclear families in urban areas, along with increasing working women population and emerging opportunities in the services sector are going to be the key growth drivers of the organized retail sector in India.

Need for Qualified and Trained Manpower

Qualified and trained manpower is of utmost importance in retail. The need for specialized skills is increasingly felt in the areas of:

- Strategic management: Strategizing, targeting and positioning, marketing and site selection
- Merchandise management: Vendor selection, inventory management, pricing
- Store management: Layout, display, customer relationship, and inventory management
- Administrative management: Human resources, finance, marketing

Retailing falls under a vertical industry and is not just restricted to malls, as most tend to believe. This industry offers ample opportunity and has room for everyone starting from entry level to senior management level.

Retailing provides employment to the largest section of the population across most industrialized nations. It is an industry that promises a profitable road. The boom in the retail industry has brought with it many employment opportunities in this arena. People with varied skills and talents are required in this fast emerging industry. A career in retailing is considered a challenging option with growth potential.

Sales and Sales-Related Jobs

The sales and sales-related retail career area includes positions like sales associate, cashier, store stock associate, and stock receiver. These frontline positions bring retail's core business of serving the customer and generating sales. The passion for working with all varieties of people, flexibility, level-headedness, problem solving, and teamwork are critical for success in this area. These positions are typically entry points into retail careers. High-end commission-based sales areas like jewellery, appliances, are highly preferred sales jobs. Frontline sales experience is highly valued and many retailers promote from within.

Store Operations

Retail professionals in the store operations career area oversee overall store operations and profits. They include Head of Store Operations, Regional Manager, and District Manager, and responsibilities in this area may include managing staff functions like loss prevention and/or human resources. Stores operation basically include the following areas:

1. Stores storage system
2. Material handling system
3. Issue of materials from stores
4. Packing in some cases
5. Transport
6. Stock verification
7. Scrap and surplus material disposal
8. Safety and security
9. Inventory control
10. Stores accounting

Store Management

The store manager or management team has responsibility ranging from departmental to overall establishment. Managers at all levels supervise and assist sales and other employees. Additional responsibilities, depending upon store/company size and management level include opening and closing the store, staffing, administration, and financial functions. Promotions to management positions can be earned through experience, or an MBA degree may afford direct entry to management. Stores management includes the following areas:

1. Building design
2. Storage facilities
3. Logistics chain
4. Materials management, including material identification system, receiving and inspection and storage system
5. Stores organization management
6. Site selection
7. Setting up the procedured for the stores

Marketing/Advertising

Depending upon company size, marketing functions may be centralized in one department, divided into different departments (like advertising, sales promotion, art and visual merchandising, and public/press relations), or group in various combinations. Marketing also conducts focus groups and statistical analysis of customer buying patterns to develop strategies and plans that guide marketing components like ads, websites, store signage, etc.

Distribution, Logistics, Supply Chain Management

This retail career area oversees movement and storage of consumer products. Responsibilities include management and facilitation of distribution centres, logistics traffic management, trucking and other transportation operations, and may include import/export shipping and related duties.

Merchandise Buying/Planning

These retail professionals select the merchandise to be sold in the stores by sourcing vendors. They facilitate order follow-up, inventory flow through and allocation of merchandise to stores, attending to issues like flow quantities and timing. Statistical development and analysis are increasingly woven into this retail career area, where team members also coordinate gross margin planning/analysis responsibilities, develop distribution plans for merchandise categories and subclasses, and balance stock unit ratios by store.

IT and E-Commerce

Technology careers are numerous and varied in the retail industry. From web design to servers and network systems management, inventory systems, etc. technology careers are growing in the retail industry.

Finance

Financial and accounting skills are more than a game in retail; they can be your career! The finance retail career area includes all accounting and treasury functions like accounting for income, paying expenses, compiling and maintaining financial records, money management and cash flow control, banking, investment, and credit lines. Auditory responsibilities also fall into retail career area.

Loss Prevention

The loss prevention career area is responsible for safeguarding company assets and may include risk management issues, like customer and employee safety. Members of loss prevention team work together to prevent and handle merchandise loss due to shoplifting, employee theft, paperwork errors, and vendor fraud. Physical security of store and company buildings is also a part of loss prevention.

Human Resources

Recruiting and hiring employees are the most obvious parts. But retail careers in human resources also include a wealth of other responsibilities such as training, designing training programmes, overseeing compensation and benefits, and planning for and ensuring legal compliance in hiring and employment practises.

Entrepreneurship

Many retail career areas and positions offer lots of opportunities to be entrepreneurial, without the ultimate responsibility of business ownership.

Moreover, single, independent, and privately-owned retail businesses account for 98% of the retail industry in India.

So, whether you are a plain graduate or an MBA or an IT or Finance graduate, if you have the following qualities, you are sure to conquer one of the fastest growing industries in the world:

1. People skills
2. Zeal
3. Communication skills
4. Team spirit

The industry is set for a boom with the entry of big industrial corporations and international retailers marking their entry into this sector. This industry constantly requires good, motivated personnel. It also promises a complete, enriching working experience with profitable inputs.

An example of China retail business is given below:

1. Execute, track and evaluate end user and retail marketing programmes
2. Develop consumer communication tools, key messages, advertising, PR release, POPs and merchandising materials to support retail business generation
3. Integrate consumer and brand programmes into sales and customer programmes as holistic approaches
4. Assist line manager to control and manage channel & retail marketing budget in cost efficiency
5. Work closely with OEM, Windows/Office, and so on internal teams

6. Develops and maintains relations with product marketing and channel marketing teams in China central marketing
7. Reports retail marketing programme monthly to line manager, task teams
8. Working closely with authorized marketing agencies, including lead retail outlet coverage programme and vendor management
9. Lead training programme as well as train internal staff

Key Result Areas

- Facilitate, develop and motivate channel and retail marketing function in both internally and externally
- Retail marketing programme in key customers and thematic marketing campaign in each quarter
- Marketing budget by programme
- Toolkits for each programme
- By programme post-programme analysis
- Monthly report first Monday of month

Historically, retailing started as sales by vendors who used pushcarts for carrying products of daily use. The cart puller was also the salesman who vended the product in residential areas. In the morning the housewife found the bread and butter seller at her doorstep. These salesmen, on earnings saved, hired or purchased shops in the same localities where they were selling on the carts. While they lost on mobility, they gained in larger product range, bigger clientele. Some shops became almost like morning clubs where friends would meet for making purchases and exchanging gossip and news. Despite the entry of supermarket chains, these shops have survived as they do provide a service to the local customers. In fact, even handcarts have also remained as retail links and a large variety of products are still sold on the carts like vegetables.

The home-to-home wandering salespersons are still carrying their wares like carpets; saris and daily need items including bread, butter, milk and eggs.

Retail sales has not lost its importance, even one bit. In fact, there have been maximum innovations in the retail business as given below:

- Supermarkets: The one-stop shops. These shops are really multiple shops in one with a large variety of products, sometimes complementary and sometimes totally dissimilar in nature and use. The common factor in all shops remains the type of customer who visits the shops. Now, the shoe shops sell sports wear, woollens, leather garments besides shoes. Gasoline stations have general merchandise shops from where patrons who come for filling their cars can purchase gift items, food products, and novelties to name a few products. Service centres have restaurants where the persons coming to get their car serviced can spend their time having a meal or snacks. Big departmental stores too keep a small eating areas and toilets for the shoppers. They have also added children centres for the kids to have a good time while their parents do the shopping.
- Discount stores are coming up for several manufacturers. Products, which have some small defect is sold at a discount at these shops. Manufacturers use these stores to

fight competition. While heavy discounts can be offered on practically good products, no price war can be started on this basis.

- Boutiques have sprung up in most cities to cater to the elite of the town. These shops keep the latest fashion garments and other accessories. The products are high priced, as the customers are not price conscious, they are looking for something unique as status symbols.
- Superstore chains have come up to provide same range of products, at the same prices and similar selling techniques. Normally, the customer has one such store near his house and he does not have to travel long distance to his supermarket for shopping. Marks and Spencer C &A in the UK are such chains. Now Delhi too has its own Marks and Spencer shop. With large volume business they offer competitive prices to the customers. The small shopkeeper with low volumes finds it difficult to compete with these giants. These chain stores dictate their terms to manufacturers as they hold large volume business. They at times, get the manufacturers to supply the product in their own brand name, rather selling the product with manufacturers brand.
- Shop-less shops: These sell products to customers through television shops, computer advertising and telephone marketing. Television has time slots during which products are shown and their use is demonstrated. The customer is then requested to place his order on telephone for delivery to his for cash payment. Internet too is used to give product demonstration and orders are solicited through Internet only, with payment to be made via credit cards. Telephone calls are used by tele-marketers, who give their sales pitch on telephone to carefully selected, likely customers. These calls are followed by visit of salesman to procure the order on the basis of telephone calls, which have, to an extent conveniences the customer into buying the products. With low overheads these sellers can offer low prices and one wonders if the days of supermarkets are numbered.
- Retailers are now using the latest electronic products like computers for billing, inventory control, building customer database, and electronic anti-theft and surveillance devices. Bank retailing has gone to the extent of salesman less sales through Automatic Teller Machines the ubiquitous ATMs.
- Manufacturers' own shops: Thus retail several manufacturers in India, like Usha, Bata and Singer, have tried system. These shops have the advantage of providing the genuine products at company prices. Customers can get the entire range of products, the full variety. However, if the manufacturers range of product is not large enough, the shop will not be a success as the customers visit shops for a range of products where they get to see the full variety. A manufacturer of only toothpaste, handkerchief or boot polish cannot sustain to run a shop just for a single product. For this reason only, Usha, Bata and Singer have all started to sell a complete range of products even on buy-sell basis. Shops diversify their product range by adding similar products/products which go as accessories with their main products to take the synergic benefit of add-on products.
- Eureka Forbes like retailing that is carried out as Direct Marketing or Personal Selling. There are no shops carrying their products. The sale is conducted by salespersons personally visiting the households for product demonstration and sales.

In several product groups and markets, with the help of direct selling catalogue and Internet sales the middlemen have been eliminated. They are supposed to be, by a section of society and business community, only money making bodies that do not perform any worthwhile task. "The distribution chain adds to the costs of sale, which, ultimately the customer has to bear. As most middlemen do not perform any value addition function these could be reduced if not totally eliminated."

However, it must be understood that to remain in competitive market, the middlemen have learnt to provide value-added services to the customers, like leasing, hire-purchase options, product servicing. Thus, they give the manufacturer chance of concentrating on production, product development and innovation, advertising and sales promotion.

It is therefore important for each manufacturer to weigh each of his concerns and then opt for a particular method of reaching his product to the people for whom they are meant and are produced in the first place, the customers-retailing or e-tailing.

Manufacturers like Eureka Forbes have eliminated the middlemen altogether, while others with the similar product ranges are still using the time-tested methods. Personal selling like what is done by Eureka Forbes helps in building relationships, but it calls for huge investments in manpower, their training and area coverage.

Leasing and Hire Purchase

Twenty-first century has seen great revolution in television and information technology in India. This has led to much greater awareness of consumer products among the people. They are thinking of buying high cost products, which they may not be able to afford. Consumerism, keeping up with the neighbours is the trend today. Manufacturers and sellers both not only encourage the trend as it helps them sell more, they also facilitate the buyers by giving them deferred payment options. For financing purchase by customers, the sellers are taking the help of finance leasing firms. Now buyers can buy cars, houses and other luxuries without having ready cash for the purchase. They can get the money from the leasing firms, on interest. The advantages of lease purchase are given below:

- As no money is to be paid, or only a token amount is to be paid, the buyer tends to buy more, many times he buys things, which he really does not want.
- The buyer buys larger quantity than what he needs.
- Buyer can possess items much beyond his capacity to purchase and feel good.
- Buyer can make payments for the purchase as per his capacity to pay on a monthly basis.
- Products with low brand awareness get sold.

The disadvantages of lease purchase are given below:

- Buyer buys products he does not want/Cannot afford
- Monthly payments can become a big dent in buyer's pocket
- Sellers may sell to a buyer who does not have the money to pay or may not have intentions of making the payments. In such a case, the seller has to run after the buyer and he may have to resort to legal action to claim the amount, which is not good for business of the seller.

As in the west, especially in America leasing and hire purchase has become a norm, it is expected to take further roots in India also.

Firms who have selected sales through channels rather than by their own salesperson face the following situations:

1. Dealer/distributor should be selling only their products exclusively. In such an event the dealers are not allowed to sell competitive products. These dealers therefore expect the seller to be also totally loyal to them and not sell their products through any other dealer or channel. The dealer expects the seller to remain competitive in the market and for this purpose he wants matching prices, discounts and other terms of business as compared to what the competitors are offering to their dealers. The seller has to remain vigilant in such situations as mostly the dealer tries to exaggerate the terms of competition for the better, which may not always be true. Seller needs to verify these statements from independent sources too.
2. Exclusive areas: Dealers want the sellers to offer the products only to them in their designated area. The dealer also gets bound to sell the products in his area only. In case the seller finds the dealer is not selling as per his expectations, he has to either cancel the dealership as per the agreed terms or consider appointing other persons to sell in the same area. To avoid any conflict the dealership agreement should have a clause, which allows the seller to appoint more dealers.
3. Product bundling: Many sellers try to sell their less selling products together with the fast moving ones. They sell the package deal or bundled products (popular name for computer software combinations). The dealers can object to such deals.

Monopolies and Restrictive Trade Practices Act, MRTP, as it is popularly known forbids the sellers to have such agreements and dealers can take recourse against any such practice by writing to MRTP. However, in practice, most such deals are done in full cooperation of the dealers and dealer agreements have only an unwritten clause for such activities.

We can summarize the activities of distributors/wholesalers as follows:

- Give large volume business to the manufacturers; operate through dealers and retailers to cover the geographic area assigned to them. Sell small number of items only. Sell to the second level of the distribution chain, the dealer or the retailer as also to bulk industrial buyers.
- Purchase goods for resale from manufacturers in India or through imports.
- Some have their own retail outlets also.
- Have technical knowledge required to sell the product. Can provide product service to the customers.
- Make profits on large turnover even with low margins.

Similarly, the activities of retailers can be summed up as given below:

- Sell a large variety of multi-brand products
- Sell in low volumes for each product as compared to the distributor of the product, who handles a large number of retailers.
- Sell to customers/consumers

- Purchase goods from wholesalers
- Location of retail shop, its façade, inner displays, window displays, salespersons and shop ambience are extremely important for the success of the shop.
- Profit margins for each product are higher than those of distributor
- Product mix, product shelf-life are major considerations

With Internet marketing, telemarketing and teleshopping networks, which sell through television the established channel of distribution, may be threatened in the near future.

Critical Success Factors in Retail Trade

Success in retail management comes from a variety of factors dependent on the nature of retailing, product, business environment and the market segment being catered to.

Product Related Analysis

It is important to know the product on offer fully, its detailed specifications—both static and dynamic as also the following:

- Who are the users of the product, why do they buy it, where do they buy it, how do they buy it and for how much?
- How do the customers use the product? Does it have a single use or multiple usages? How often do they use it?
- What are the benefits the customers are looking for in the product? Manufacturers may have a view of these benefits while the customers may have an entirely different notion of what they want. The sellers of washing powder are all talking of the whiteness of the wash, where the customers never talk about the whiteness as the reason for their buying a particular detergent powder. The best way to find out about the benefits the customers are wanting in the product is to arrange a market research in the desired market segment.
- Product pricing is an important aspect of marketing strategy. When a new product is launched and there is no competition, sellers go for skimming price, in other words they keep the price high to get the maximum profits before the competition starts and they are forced by it to reduce the prices. If the sellers are looking for increasing market share they put penetrating prices, low prices to attract large customer groups. It is important to know if the sales are affected by changes in price, i.e., price sensitivity of the product must be known by research.
- Knowledge about competition is needed on a continuous basis as regularly new competition keeps increasing and the existing competition keeps changing their plans and policies. It is necessary to know competitors 4 Ps with the knowledge updated regularly.
- Brand loyalty/equity of products, the firms and those of competitors should be well, assessed, as it is this single most important factor, responsible for market share.
- Market survey is required to find out the distribution of product need in different market segments. Which segment has the highest percent demand of the product

and which segments follow the demand pattern. Sub-segments, niche segments and crossover segment demand must be assessed. Only after this knowledge can the seller decide about the segment/s the firm should enter or should it plan for sale in a niche market only.

The airline industry has found that they have basically two types of customers as given below:

1. Business-customers of this class want an air service which is, reliable, on schedule, with wide body aircraft, easy to use airports with comfortable lounges, frequent flier programmes, telephone check-ins, variety of connections and in-flight entertainment. Possible upgrades from business class to first class.
2. Tourists look for low price travel, required schedules and several stopovers. For the sake of low price they do not mind night travels also. They look for package deals in which air tickets and hotel accommodations are all included.

Such details can only be found out by getting proper market research done.
The following gives a pattern in which the new products are introduced:

- Upgrade the old product
- Similar product or lateral diversification
- New product for the firm
- New product in the market
- New invention, or new product in the world
- Old products in newer markets

Upgrade the Old Product

Once the product has reached the maturity or decline stage of its life, firm's R&D can do innovations on the product, either technically or aesthetically to enable the product appear as a new product and get into the introductory stage of the life cycle. Selecting the right market segment for the now new product can tell the firm about its saleability in the market. This is usually done for products, which have had a good run in the market in their introductory, growth and maturity stages. Innovations should not render the product too expensive, out of the reach of the customers. However, the new products should appear different, should give extra benefits and still be **value for money**.

Similar Product or Lateral Diversification

Firms selling shoes can take up sandals, boots leather garments. These help the firm to establish their markets as they have already got the raw material sources and marketing channels. The following will give an idea of what firms can introduce in the market:

- Bakery can sell butter, yogurt, baked vegetables in cans, other canned food
- Car dealer can sell tyres batteries, accessories for the car
- Ready-made garment seller can sell upholstery material
- Banks can sell credit cards
- Business schools can sell business books
- Ice-cream vendor can bring out new flavours

New Product for the Firm

A firm making radios starts making television sets then it would be considered horizontal diversification. Such product extensions are cost-effective as they use the same distribution channels, have several common components and similar technology. Ultimately, it could prove that the new product overtakes the old ones in sales in no time.

New Product in the Market

Technological developments elsewhere take time to reach India. In the sixties and the seventies of the 20th century it took five to six years. Today, many technological advances are available to India almost in real time, i.e., as soon as they are in the market in the country of their origin. Computer software is a classic example. In fact, there is a big overseas trade in the development of software from India.

New Inventions or New Product in the World

A few years back cell phones or mobile phones were introduced in the market. These had come to India after the invention of these phones and they caught up with the rest of the world pretty fast.

Old Product in New Markets

Geographic diversification helps the firm in increasing sales and market share. Exporting can be one of the methods as well. Firms can also plan to diversify into different market segments, with minor changes in product offerings if required.

Reasons for Failure

Let us discuss why out of the several products launched each year only a few survive and the rest just fade out. The reasons of product failure are listed below:

- Product quality is substandard. Unless the product can provide some tangible or intangible benefit to the customer it will not succeed. A poor quality product cannot satisfy any need of the customer. Quality of a product can be defined as, "Conformance to the firm's static and dynamic standard specifications meant for the product, which have been devised by taking into account the customers' viewpoint or better still after doing a customer/consumer research about the product."
- **Lack of knowledge of the market:** Several car manufacturers set up large manufacturing bases in India with huge investments, like Daewoo Motors and came out with their Ceilo car which was not accepted in the market as per Daewoo's plans and it was only Matiz the smaller car which brought some business to it. Therefore, marketing research becomes extremely important in the fast changing business environment in India and the world over.
- **Incorrect selection of market segment:** Innovative products, the first time introduced products, which are in the introductory stage of product life cycle, are bought by the early birds or the innovative buyers. Later on only the people of the market segment

are the main buyers. Therefore, correct market segment helps in planning the right appropriate distribution channels and customer communications through advertising or personal contacts. Expensive watches are sold through the jewellers' shops, designer dresses through upmarket boutiques only. Proper product positioning is a must for the product to, succeed in the market.

- **Competitors resort to penetrating pricing:** When it comes to losing market share competitor's plan price reductions, promotions, and heavy advertising campaigns to ensure that the new entrant does not get a foothold in the market. Only a good brand image can ensure the success of the product despite competitive actions.
- **High overheads:** The product price becomes high if the overheads are higher than most competitors. This results in high pricing and loss of customers.
- **Government controls:** Some countries may have entry barriers which indirectly hinder the progress of the sale. It could be by way of extra high levies on imports, government insistence for allowing only local firms have majority share holding.

Product: There are the following types of products in the market for which different firms look for markets:

- Consumer durables
- Fast moving consumer goods: FMCGs
- Industrial capital goods
- Industrial raw materials and components
- Industrial consumables
- Service
- Events
- People
- Properties
- Firms
- Information
- Research outputs

Out of the list given above only the following are sold in retail:

1. Consumer durables
2. FMCG
3. Service

As the three product groups are basically different from the customers' perspective their retailing also needs specific and different methods, which will be taken up in separate chapters. The difference comes from mean time between Purchase, purchase investments needs, utility value of the purchase for the customer. With GDP going up and product purchase in practically every product also increasing the retailers have to maintain a firm grip on the market otherwise the rate of sales slippage is fast.

CHAPTER

6

Retail Specifics

Retailing is defined as given below:

Sale of goods or merchandise, from a fixed location such as a departmental store or kiosk, in small or individual lots for direct consumption by the purchaser. Retailing may include services, such as product delivery. Buyers may be individuals or businesses, a retailer buys goods or products in large quantities from manufacturers or importers, either directly or through a wholesaler, and then sells in smaller quantities or lots to the end-users or consumers. Retailers are the end links of the supply chain as an important part of manufacturing/marketer overall distribution strategy. Retail outlets may be on residential streets, or in shopping streets with few or no houses, or in a shopping centre or mall, could be located in the central business district.

Shopping is the act of locating, selecting and then buying products. Sometimes this is done to obtain necessities such as food and clothing; sometimes it is done as a recreational activity. Recreational shopping often involves window shopping and browsing and may result in a purchase. Most retail employees are learning merchandising like placing the goods in front of the customers even during product scarcity times. These are the tools used to create the look of a perfectly-stocked store.The pricing technique used by most retailers is cost-plus pricing unless there is a MRP – the maximum retail price declared by the manufacturers. This involves adding a markup amount or percentage to the retailer's cost. Another technique is suggested retail pricing. This simply involves charging the amount suggested by the manufacturer and usually printed on the product by the manufacturer. MRP should include all duties and taxes as applicable by country's law. MRP can be decided with a psychological angle like Rs. 99 and not Rs. 100.

Prices are fixed and displayed on package/labels. Alternatively, the retailer can have price discrimination for a variety of reasons. A retailer can charge higher prices to some customers and lower prices to others. For example, a customer may have to pay more if the seller determines that he or she is willing to pay, or is buying on credit. The retailer may conclude this due to the customer's wealth, carelessness, lack of knowledge, eagerness to buy or if the buyer is in possession of credit cards. Price discrimination can lead to a bargaining situation often called haggling, negotiations on the price. Economists theorise this as determining how the transaction's total surplus will be divided into consumer and producer surplus. Neither party has a clear advantage, because the threat of no sale exists, and the surplus vanishes for both. Retailers who are overstocked, or need to raise cash to renew stocks may resort to "sales", where prices are "marked down", often by advertised percentages – "50% off" for example. "Sales" are often held at fixed times of the year, for example, January sales, or end-of-season sales, or festive season sales. At times these sales coincide with the time companies pay bonus to their employees, who have extra cash for making purchases.

Major types of retailing:

1. A physical location where buyers and sellers meet. Usually this is done on shopping centres, sidewalks or designated streets and may involve the construction of temporary structures—stalls.
2. Next is shop or store trading. Some shops use counter-service, where goods are out of reach of buyers, and must be obtained from the salesperson. This type of retail is common for small expensive items like watches, jewellery and controlled items like medicine and liquor. Self-service, where goods may be handled and examined prior to purchase, has become more common.
3. A form of retail is virtual retail, where products are ordered via mail, telephone or online without having been examined physically but instead seen in a catalogue, on television or on a website.

Retail Buildings

Market halls were constructed in the Middle Ages, which were essentially just covered marketplaces. The first shops in the modern sense used to deal with just one type of article, and usually adjoined the producer (baker, tailor, cobbler) in the 19th century.

In the 1920s the first supermarket was opened in the United States, heralding in a new era of retail: self-service. A mall consists of several departmental stores linked by arcades—many of whose shops are owned by the same firm under different names. All the stores rent their space from the mall owner. By mid-century, most of these were being developed as single enclosed, climate-controlled, projects in suburban areas. The mall has had a considerable impact on the retail structure and urban economic development. Local shops are known as brick and mortar stores in the United States. Many shops are part of a chain: a number of similar shops with the same name selling the same products in different locations, Subhiksha is a fine example of the same. The shops may be owned by one company, or there may be a franchising company that has agreements with the shop owners some shops sell second-hand goods. Often the public can also sell goods to such shops, sometimes called 'pawn' shops. There are also 'consignment' shops, which is where a person can place an item in a store, and if it sells the person gives the shop owner a percentage of the sale price. The advantage of selling an item this way is that the established shop gives the item exposure to more potential buyers.

A store manager is ultimately responsible for the day-to-day operations of a retail store or supermarket. All employees working in the store report to the store manager. A store manager typically reports to a district or area manager, but in smaller businesses, may report directly to the store's owner. In some stores a store manager may be called a general manager or store director.

Store manager Job Profile

- Human resources, specifically: recruiting, training and development, performance management, payroll, and workplace scheduling;
- Store business operations, including managing profit and loss, facility management, safety and security, loss prevention and banking;
- Product management, including ordering, receiving, price changes, and handling damaged products;
- Logistics management including obtaining products from the vendors via transport carriers, storage, inventory management and issue to the retail counters.

The store manager is required to meet monthly, quarterly, or annual sales goals, depending on the company's fiscal cycle. This may be achieved by setting individual sales targets, holding contests for employees, or offering sales promotions. The salesperson may also receive a monetary incentive or bonus tied to the financial performance of the store over a specific time period. This incentive may be based on net sales, profitability, or both. Thus, the store manager may be forced to reduce payroll expenditures by decreasing employees' hours, or using other methods of reducing costs associated with operating the business.

The store manager has to personally see to ensure top class service to the customers. The manager receives solicited or unsolicited feedback from customers, and may be asked to intervene in confrontations between customers and employees. The store manager may also make exceptions to store policies, but in most cases is required to enforce policies set by the company that owns the store. Through effective training, managers can accept employees' best judgement in handling customer service situations.

The store manager may be called to the store before, during, or after business hours in the event of an emergency. The manager is also responsible for the safety of all customers and employees on store premises. Store managers may be required to hold safety meetings. A store manager may have several persons within the hierarchy of the store to whom he or she can delegate management-level responsibilities. These employees are sometimes called assistant managers, supervisors, keyholders, shift leaders or leaders. The store manager is responsible for the hiring, training, and developing employees. The manager must ensure that adequate staffing levels exist in order to effectively operate the store, and ensure that employees receive the training for employees to perform their job responsibilities independently.

> Store managers have to ensure that visual merchandising of the store is consistent with customers' expectations of the brand.
>
> In retail locations, store managers are responsible for visual merchandising. Many companies train the managers in how to merchandise their stores using directions to indicate product placement. This aspect is of great importance in case of chain stores where similarty of merchandising helps touring customers in locating their favourite stores with ease. Some merchandising need to include the colour schemes of the store's exteriors as well as interior designing of the stores. For managers, it is important to ensure that stores are IN LINE with the company's image. A supermarket is a departmentalized self-service offering a wide variety of household merchandise. It is larger in size and has a wide selection.

The supermarket products comprise meat, vegetable produce, and baked goods departments along with shelf space reserved for canned and packaged goods as well as for various non-food items such as household cleaners, pharmacy products, and pet supplies. Most supermarkets also sell a variety of other household products that are consumed regularly, such as alcohol (where permitted), household cleaning products, clothes, and some sell a wide range of non-food products. The supermarket occupies a large floor space on a single level and is situated near a residential area in order to be convenient to consumers. Its basic appeal is the availability of a wide selection of goods under a single roof at relatively low prices. Other advantages include ease of parking, valet parking at places and, frequently, the convenience of shopping hours that extend far into the evening. Supermarkets make outlays for advertising and present elaborate in-store displays of products. Supermarkets are often part of a chain that owns or controls (sometimes by franchise) other supermarkets located in the same or other towns; this increases the opportunities for economies of scale.

In the early days of retailing, products had to be fetched by an assistant from shelves on one side of a counter while the customers stood on the other side. Also, many items did not come in the individually wrapped consumer-size packages taken for granted today, so an assistant had to measure out the precise amount desired by the consumer. These practices were obviously labour-intensive and therefore expensive. The shopping process was slow, as the number of customers who could be attended at one time was limited by the number of clerks employed in the store. In India, these retail methods are still prevalant as labour is low cost in the country.

Most supermarkets are similar in design and layout due to trends in retail sales. Most products tend to be near the entrance of the store. Milk, bread, and other essential items may be located in the rear or other out of the way places. This is purposely done to ensure maximum time spent in the store, strolling past other items for promoting impulse buying. The store can be named for the price of the merchandise sold in the store. The names vary by area and time, as each country has a different currency, and the nominative price of the goods has increased over time due to inflation. In India a number of Rs. 99 stores have come up.

Products

Variety store products include:
1. Cooking supplies
2. Small tools
3. Personal hygiene supplies
4. Kitchen supplies
5. Organizational supplies
6. Small office supplies
7. Holiday decorations
8. Electronics supplies
9. Gardening supplies
10. Home decor novelties
11. Food products
12. Automotive supplies

There are the following reasons a 99 store is able to sell merchandise at such a low price:
1. The product is generic or lesser known brand, often specially manufactured for such stores.
2. The product was manufactured cheaply for a market and was then imported by an unauthorized distributor.
3. The product is purchased from another retail store or distributor as overstock, closeout merchandise, or seasonal merchandise at the end of the season.
4. The items were manufactured to coincide with the promotion of a motion picture, television show or special event.

Such stores are known as 49/99 shops in India. Typical price range in these shops are between 49/99 Indian rupees. 49 rupees was approximately equal to one US dollar when these started, also 49 and 99 are near rounds of 50 and 100 respectively to draw the shoppers. Items are generally cheap gift articles, toys, watches, office stationery and crockery. Most merchandise in these stores is imported cheaply from foreign countries. Usually, merchandise is imported by a general merchandise importer/ wholesaler, then sold to the stores at a wholesale rate. India's with a large population of middle class and its almost untapped retail potential are key attractions for global retail giants wanting to enter new markets. Driven by changing lifestyles, strong income growth and favourable demographic patterns, Indian retail is expected to grow 25 per cent annually.

Organized retail in India could be worth US$ 175-200 billion by 2016. With the economy booming, competition in the marketplace is fierce. Rising incomes, increasing consumerism in urban areas and an upswing in rural consumption will fuel this growth to around 7-8 per cent. Retailers in India are the most aggressive in

Asia in expanding their businesses, thus creating a huge demand for real estate. Their preferred means of expansion is to increase the number of their outlets in a city, and also expand to other regions. Food dominates the shopping basket in India. The US$ 6.1 billion Indian foods industry, which forms 44 per cent of the entire FMCG sales, is growing at 9 per cent and has set the growth agenda for modern trade formats. Since nearly 60 per cent of the average Indian grocery basket comprises non-branded items, the branded food industry is homing in on converting Indian consumers to branded food.

When it comes to Indian children, retailers are busy building their brands to bond with the children of the right market segment with targeted promotion plans for bonding with them.

- Monalisa, the Versace of kids is coming to India.
- Global lifestyle brand Nautica is bringing Nautica Kids.
- International brand Zapp tied up with Raymond to foray into kids' apparel.
- Disney launched exclusive chains, which stock character-based stationery.
- Pantaloon's joint venture with Gini & Jony will set up a retail chain to market kids' apparel.
- Swiss kidswear brand Milou is collaborating with Tirupur-based Sreeja Hosieries.
- Turner International India Pvt. Ltd. will launch Cartoon Network Townsville and Planet POGO—two theme parks designed around its channels—in the National Capital Region.
- Sahara One Television has also signed a Memorandum of Understanding to source content from Spacetoon Media Group, Middle East's largest kids' entertainment brand for animation and "live" action content.

Leading the kids' retail revolution is the apparel business, which accounts for almost 80 per cent of the revenue, with kids' clothing in India following international fashion trends. Industry experts say kids' retailing will touch annual growth of 30-35 per cent. Toys, stationery, sportswear, outerwear, tailored clothing, eyewear, watches, fragrance, footwear, theme parks, TV channels, the segment is growing rapidly at 10 per cent per annum. Margins are in the range of 20-25 per cent (for dealers and distributors), while companies enjoy an average gross margin of about 10 per cent.

Agriculture across India is heralding the country's second Green Revolution. 14 states, including Maharashtra, Punjab, Andhra Pradesh and Rajasthan amended the Agricultural Produce Marketing Committee (APMC) act this year, along the lines of the Model APMC Act, '02, which allows farmers to sell their produce directly to buyers offering them the best price. Agricultural sectors such as horticulture, floriculture, development of seeds, animal husbandry, pisciculture, aqua culture, cultivation of vegetables, mushroom under cultivated conditions and services related to agro and allied sectors are open to 100 per cent FDI through the automatic route.

For its e-Choupal scheme, ITC built Internet kiosks in rural villages so that farmers can access latest information on weather, current market prices.

1. Foods-in-demand,
2. With a US$ 5.6 billion, multi-year investment in agriculture and retail, Reliance Retail will establish links with farms on several thousand acres in Punjab, West Bengal and Maharashtra.
3. FieldFresh, planning to become India's first large-scale exporter of produce, will annually pay farmers over US$ 30,000 to lease land for vegetables, to hire tractors and to pay their workers.
4. Besides a five-year programme with the Punjab government to provide several hundred farmers with four million sweet-orange trees for its Tropicana juices by 2008, Pepsi Co—with agriculture exports worth US$ 40 million—also introduced farmers to high-yielding basmati rice, mangoes, potatoes, chilies, peanuts, and barley for its Frito-Lay snacks.
5. Export potential and a rapidly growing domestic demand for reliable produce from new supermarket chains is driving change. With 77 per cent of India's population relying on agriculture for a living, improved efficiency and new markets can benefit a large number of people.

The largest-ever 150-member British business delegation in India committed investments in the areas of food processing, agri retail and manufacturing. It is also likely to press for the liberalization of sectors like financial and legal services and retail.

- US-based home delivery and logistics company, Specialized Transportation Inc, will enter the Indian market through a strategic alliance with Patel Retail, a subsidiary of Patel Integrated Logistics.
- Among other big international players, Wal-Mart has announced its plans for India in partnership with Bharti, Tesco is sure to try again, and Carrefour too might finally find the right partner.

The government regulations allow 100 per cent FDI in cash and carry through automatic route and 51 per cent in single brand. Besides, the franchise route is available for big operators. Now, the Government also proposes further liberalization in the retail sector allowing 51 per cent FDI in consumer electronics and sports goods.

India is currently the ninth largest retail market in the world. And it is names of small towns like Dehradun, Vijayawada, Lucknow and Nasik that will up India's rankings soon.

Customer Demand Planning

Customers have become much more demanding in recent years, forcing retailers both large and small to operate quickly and efficiently. Thus customer demand planning is one of the key areas of operations for a retailer's business. There are immense benefits in managing your demand well, prime as given below:

Forecast: Provides all departments with a common forecast to drive the retail enterprise.

Inventory control for the following benefits:

1. Lowering current assets
2. Ensuring proper stock levels during regular price situations and promotions to avoid lost sales due to out of stock situations.
3. Reducing overstocks with correct forecasting on performance of a product or promotion
4. Improving efficiency: Streamlines the forecasting process, highlights potential problems and allows you to process large amounts of data quickly.

Profits are the direct result of accurate forecasting of demand.

> HCL, the computer company has worked with leading retailers in understanding their customers, sales patterns, and products they sell and promotions they run. They possess rich experience in advanced retail planning, Customer analytics, and promotions planning to name a few. Their solutions and services help accurately forecast sales using advanced algorithms on retail sales data, past trends and industry patterns.

Product Mix

Getting the right mix of product, which is store specific across the organization is a combination of customer knowledge, resource allocation and assortment techniques.The benefits of merchandise planning include reduced unplanned discounts and promotions, properly utilised floor space, low level store transfers, and increased turns throughout the chain helping retail bottom line.

Retail Plans

1. Merchandise Replenishment
2. Merchandise Analytics
3. Planning and Forecasting
4. Order generation, scheduling, and processing

Retail Pricing

Retailers are now implementing flexible pricing systems as given below:

(a) Manage permanent and promotional markup and markdown
(b) Price zone and price priority management
(c) Price books and derivative pricing
(d) Competitor pricing and corporate pricing strategies
(e) Multiple pricing methods and best price algorithms to maximize margins
(f) Price event performance analysis

Promotion Planning

Retailers start promotion planning with answers to questions like—when, what, and how to promote?

(a) Responsive promotion and price survey management
(b) Promotion performance forecasting including sales, volumes, margins, and profitability
(c) Promotional analytics for deciding promotion types
(d) Buying income and vendor funded promotions
(e) Product concept and event management and performance analysis
(f) Creation of catalogues and buying baskets at central level to negotiate price for volume

Inventory checks through the supply chain enables faster inventory response and ensures a balance between inventory cost efficiencies and customer service levels.

Improved inventory tracking combined with robust ordering, transfer, replenishment and integrated allocation functionality provides greater control over products and inventories resulting in fewer markdowns.

Strategic purchasing and efficient inventory movement with integration of daily activities provides greater gross margin efficiencies.

Business information across the enterprise reduces error potential and data redundancy and the user interface enhances productivity and provides a quick learning curve that results in decreased training time and expenses.

Merchandising and display are an important part of the marketing plan, and should have a reasonable budget allocated, even for a small retailer. Everyone is competing for the customers' rupee. There are more choices for consumers than ever before. With all these choices, what will grab the consumer's attention? Retailers have invested the money to get that expensive, high traffic location, but how will they keep the customers from walking right by the door? How will a retailer encourage them to return? What is unique about the store? After investing money on the important priorities such as merchandise, great location, part-time staff, insurance, accountant, advertising, carefully budgeted money can be lost if the store doesn't measure up to the customers' expectations. Posters covering the door and windows, hand lettered signs, lack of lighting and untidy displays send the message that the business isn't serious. Merchandising is more than simply the arrangement of products on the shelf. It is an integral component of the business image. It should be considered when designing the logo, business cards, brochures, letterhead, packaging, and product mix. Merchandising is also about understanding the way customers shop. By using this knowledge, retailer can position the merchandise to increase sales.

An ambience that attracts the customer who is comfortable to shop, and encourages the customer to return is needed.

1. Are the storefront and windows attractive and inviting?
2. Is all signage clear, professional and legible?
3. Is the store interior welcoming and comfortable?
4. Is merchandise presentation appealing?
5. Are seasonal and high-margin merchandise placed in high profile locations?
6. Overall, is the store appearance professional?

If the store is on a budget, it needs to start small, but it should make sure it includes a plan for growth. One of the exciting things about retail is that it is dynamic. If it does not grow and change, customers assume it has nothing new to offer them. It does not have to overhaul the entire store, but rotate merchandise, change displays, and change signage to make the customer feel that there is always something new for them to see or experience. Retail merchandising is such a part of everyday life people often take it for granted, but it is one of the fastest changing, most dynamic industries in the world today.

A new model for merchandising and supply chain management is emerging; it is about to transform the way in which retailers do business and deliver the customer experience. Many retailers see the supply chain simply as a means of moving goods from one place to another. In fact, a fully integrated merchandising-supply network can help companies achieve greater, sustainable growth by becoming more innovative and differentiating themselves in the marketplace. New market forces and internal constraints explain why most retailers still struggle to manage their merchandising and supply chain functions very effectively. But, if they are to satisfy their target customers, they must make fundamental changes. They must build networks in which the various merchandising and supply chain functions are fully integrated and supported by systematic business intelligence, including a much more detailed understanding of the customers they serve. They must also tailor their operations to suit different products, customer segments, markets and timeframes. It is the complete integration and optimization of the merchandising-supply network that makes it one of the key levers in delivering a customer-centric shopping experience.

Management Game

The faculty should divide the class into teams, each consisting of 4 to 5 students. The teams should select a product from the list of FMCG, Consumer Durables and locate a company dealing with it where they have access. Otherwise they can form an imaginary company. Next they should select a name for the company, one product they will like to sell, its features and the customer benefits. They should define their target market segment for the product. Next the students should decide the best way of reaching out to the consumers, the way they want to retail their product, stand-alone single shop, chain stores or shopping malls.

The students can play the game either individually or in teams, as per class consensus or as per the teaching faculty's choice. If in teams, the best way is to divide the class in teams each team consisting of 4 to 5 members as stated above. Once the teams have been formed the faculty can introduce the game to them as follows:

Select a product from either FMCG or consumer durable range, select the market coverage area and then decide about the right market segment that the team wants to do business with. Plan marketing strategies and make P&L statement for first five years of operations, including sales on yearly basis, profit picture.

Discuss the yearly advertising plan, select the right media, get their rates, and try your hand at creating an advertising campaign. Prepare a yearly advertising plan along with its budget.

Management Game 2

Merchandising

The teams should plan merchandising of the same product. Select the right shop and define your merchandising goals. Define your method of selecting merchandising. Prepare your plan for retailing giving the thoughts to the 4 Ps. Do you have a known brand product or will it need to be modified to suit the target segment customers. Plan visual merchandising inside the stores.

CHAPTER 7

External Business Environment

Aims and Outcomes

In India during the period 1950 to 1970 firms were making decisions on what to sell, how to sell at what price and how to advertise only by gut feeling. Today, the firms must realize that the performance of their business can be enhanced through proper alignment between the firm's strategy and its business environment, which is always changing.

Marketers find business opportunities to succeed, make profits and grow. These opportunities appear outside of the firm, in the marketplace for which constant vigil is required. Marketer cannot just afford to wait for changes in marketplace to take place. He has to be closely associated with the changes; at times he can be instrumental, to an extent in making the changes. Even if he cannot mould the changes to his benefit, he should certainly monitor the same to get the maximum mileage from the changes.

In the 21st century, the following can be highlighted as predominant changes in the business environment and prominent happenings in India.

- Market globalization and its effect on Indian economy
- Market recession
- Larger number of women in urban workforce including in positions of strength.
- Large production capacities, mostly idle
- Emergence of IT sector and its decline
- Growth of Management Schools
- Strong satellite television base with hundreds of channels giving jobs to millions of Indians.
- Invasion of Chinese products in various fields.
- Political problems including internal and external threats to country's suzerainty.
- Religious fundamentalism

- Privatization of government owned firms
- Genetic engineering and its effect of farm produce
- Rampant misuse of public funds

Business General Environment

The following need to be studied, assessed, screened and monitored in the context of the country for correct planning of marketing strategies.

- Demographic Factors: These are brought out in the census of the country, factors like, population dispersion in towns, villages, income levels for families, sex ratios, religious numbers. Shifts of population from villages to towns, from small towns to metro towns provide business opportunities, which no marketer can afford to miss. For a start low cost housing, clothing, transportation, eateries are needed.
- Social Factors: Like increase of working women in towns at all levels of income. It has given rise to a big boost in demand for time saving equipment like, washing machines, vacuum cleaners, microwave ovens, precooked foods. As women are coming out of homes, better dresses, cosmetics, health gyms are required. With double family income leisure time activities products, holiday outings, travels are looking up.
- Cultural Factors: India is a land of rich cultural heritage. Its culture is rich and diverse. Marketers and advertisers take full advantage of knowing the buying season in different parts of the country. During Deepavali, Hindus buy new clothes, household articles and exchange gifts. Muslims do it on Eid, Christians on Christmas. The cultural ethos provides innumerable themes for promoting sales. India is a vast country, with twenty languages spoken, several religions and varied cultures and subcultures. For example, in Punjab, there is the Punjabi culture and within there is the Sikh subculture. Karnataka has the Kannad culture and then its district; Coorg has its own subculture.
- Political Factors: It was the political will of the then government, which led to LPG, (Liberalization, Privatization and Globalization), in 1991. The influx of foreign capital, setting up manufacturing bases, joint ventures all sprung up from then onwards. Changes in Cash Reserve Ratio, taxation rates, duties are the political factors which have a major impact on business.
- Legal Factors: Supreme Courts directives have made car manufacture change the emission standards to Euro II. Diesel buses are on their way out in Delhi for the same reason. Ignoring the law of the lands can be detrimental to the interests of the firms operating in the country.
- Macroeconomics Factors: The interest rates, taxes and duties, balance of payment situation with the countries the firm wants to do business with, foreign currency rate fluctuations have major impacts on business and they must be well understood by the firm.
- Technology Factors: In the past decade, information technology, telecom, biotechnology, genetic engineering have revolutionized the business scene in the world as also Indian business scene.
- Global Factors: From the last decade, breaking of the Berlin wall with reunification of Germanys, breaking up of the USSR, and more recent attack on the World Trade

Tower in the New York, on the Indian parliament, liberation of Afghanistan have affected business worldwide and most countries are trying to recover the lost ground. On the brighter side the development in the area of medicine, agriculture and farming cloning of the sheep have helped in the giant strides the world is taking towards a better future for its children. Following are the major elements in globalized economy:

(i) World becoming smaller due to faster movement through supersonic jets, faster world communications through Internet.
(ii) Strong trade zones like European Union, NAFTA, ASEAN
(iii) Market economy in Russia
(iv) Multinational, transnational firms
(v) International strategic alliances
(vi) Global brands in foods like Kellogg's and cars

Indian retail business irrespective of its size cannot remain unaffected by the onslaught of globalization. Small firms, which were protected by government laws, are now facing severe competition from well-known international brands, and unless they have been able to sign up with a reputed international technology they are getting left out in the race. Surviving in the market jungle today can be defined by the criticality of the firm's marketing strength only.

Competitive Business Environment

Let us discuss the **Competitive Business** environment with the help of Michael Porter's 5 Force Model.

- Rivalry among the existing players: The most important factor must deal with the existing competition, which over the past decade has increased several fold. In most products in India the marketers were enjoying virtual oligopoly situation till the epoch making year 1991, when the Government of India opened up the country's economy for the foreign players. Severity of competition is manifest in the innovations in the marketing mix factors by most firms. Foreign players have brought with them the latest technology, well-known brands and management skills. And yet they lack the basic information about Indian buyers, their culture and mindsets. Indian firms can therefore gauge this intrinsic weakness from among the foreign players and gain advantage over them.
- Bargaining power of suppliers: Suppliers to a firm belong to one of the following types:
  (i) When there are several suppliers of undifferentiated product and a few buyer firms, like suppliers of nuts and bolts. In such cases, the buyers have the bargaining power and the large volume buyer gets the better price as quantity discount.
  (ii) When the suppliers are limited and there are several buyers, the bargaining power shifts to the suppliers as then the suppliers can pick and choose their buyers on the basis of their purchase value, proximity and adherence to payment schedules.

(iii) When the suppliers may be limited but they are making unique products for a particular firm, like car seat manufacturers. In such cases the buyers have the power to the extent that the supplier has to conform to the standards and delivery norms. As there are no other buyers for the product they can acquire bargaining power by cornering the firm into a tight supply position and the firm will accept any terms of business as long as it can keep its production going.

(iv) When the supplier is apart of the firms own group, as then the bargaining power is decided by the head of the group who has to have profit distribution among the various members of the group.

- Bargaining power of the buyers of the firm: The customers gets his power to bargain when there are several firms supplying the same product and the customer gets his choice of buying from any one of the sellers.
- Threat of new entrants: When the product demand is in the growth stage of the product life cycle, and the entry barriers are few, like high investment costs or government restrictions then newcomers find it difficult to start business in that area and in that product.
- Threats of substitute product: Paint manufacturers find Chuna makers, wallpaper, cement, wood panelling as the substitute competitive product.

In order to effectively counter the problems faced by firms on account of changes in business general environment factors and competitive environment factors, the firm must keep market research/scan continuously providing accurate market information all the time.

Cultural Revolution

Countries undergo Cultural Revolution, which affect the business. India has seen the teen revolution, the emergence of POP Music; DVDs, Discos. These changes bring about major shifts in demand patterns of certain products. In many areas meat eating and cooking is prohibited and in some, beef eating is taboo. Health awareness in urban areas has brought about huge business potential for health foods, gyms, exercising equipment and dieticians. The increase in the population of teenagers and of senior citizens (those above sixty-five years of age) provides unique opportunities to marketers while the disco culture is emerging with the youth of the country, the return to the roots with yoga, meditation is also happening. While the marketers may not be involved in bringing about the cultural changes, they can certainly take advantage of the changes. Plethora of goods to meet the demand comes to the market. As the customer is fickle, he keeps looking for new brands. The result is that the old brands are being refurbished with cosmetic changes. The desire for possessing something unique also spurs innovators, R&D engineers, designers, and artists to bring newness to the products.

India has the distinction of having twenty-one official languages, cultural diversities, climatic differences, area specialty in foods, which is at once an opportunity and a challenge to the marketing fraternity of the country and the foreign firms.

Summarizing it can be concluded that study of external environment is important ingredient of strategy planning. External forces have an impact on the firm and this must be understood clearly. Factors of external environment, demographic, socio-cultural, political-legal, macroeconomics, technology and global must be considered, as also factors of competitive environment, rivalry amongst existing players, threat of new entrants, threat of substitute products, bargaining power of buyers and bargaining power of suppliers. Firms should focus analysis on strategic industry only and should not dissipate its efforts on broad industry profile. At times it may be prudent to cooperate with competition in areas like research and development, international marketing. The power of environment of business of the firm must be taken into account while finalizing strategies.

Task for the students: Discuss the advantages of understanding external environment while building strategies for a firm.

Market Segmentation

Retailers need to understand their market segment right from the time they plan the store location. Markets are such a heterogeneous place that unless we get to understand each part of it we remain ignorant of the market. There are people buying Mercedes cars and in the market people are buying low cost bicycles as means of transportation. Marketers of Mercedes communicate with the rich elitist class to sell their product. These people reside in certain sections of the town; visit one club or the other, read a few business magazines like *Business India, Business Today*, and *India Today*. The cycle buyers go to cinema halls for low cost entertainment. Cycle sellers can show film advertising clips and slides to communicate to the segment. Both elite class and lower class would get the right message without too much clutter and in a language understood by them. Therefore, market segmentation helps both, the buyers and sellers.

Market segmentation is done on the following lines:

1. Geographic factors
2. Demographic factors
3. Psychological factors
4. Socio-cultural factors
5. Use related
6. Benefit segment
7. Combination of some of the above mentioned factors

In India Tanishq watches have the following segment:

As the price starts from Rs. 20,000 to Rs. 125,000 high income, elite life style persons living in fashionable localities, form the segment. Market research for the product can be conducted within the segment for accurate findings.

Changing nature of goals and needs: When a particular goal or need cannot be fulfilled, a substitute goal emerges. Similarly, after fulfilment a new goal or need arises.

In any case, needs can never be fully satisfied. When a person becomes Vice President of a firm, he changes his goal to becoming the President. Product updates, newer technologies help the firms to use this **urge** as a springboard for launching innovative products.

Once the basic needs are fulfilled, people want to achieve higher goals. After getting a good house to live people would like to be community leaders.

As the saying goes, "Nothing succeeds like success", success gives extra fillip to people for going to higher level goals. Failure, on the other hand make people redefine their goals, by either lowering the standard or taking a different road altogether.

Goal substitution occurs on non-attainment of goal. If you cannot buy Honda City car, buy a Maruti 800. Some people go into a dream world devoid of reality. .

Behaviour is oriented towards achieving personal goals. People have general types of goals and then they have product-oriented goals. *We will travel to the hills once I purchase my Ford IKON CAR* becomes a product and action oriented goal. We can see that everyone has rational and emotional motivations, with purely objective or subjective criteria. Personality is the sum total of individual traits of character, bearing and behaviour. Retailers need to understand the customer's psychology and personality types of their customers.

Personality Theory of People: Unlike Freud, other social scientists felt that motives cannot be confined to basic and sexual instincts. Social interaction and life style too gives motivation to people to act.

There are four types of personalities as follows:

a. Thinking and sensing types are rational, logical, objective and fast decision-makers
b. Feeling and sensing types believe in their ownselves, are subjective and they consult others in decision-making
c. Thinking and intuiting types take broad view, look for wider range of options and take decisions for long range of time
d. Feeling and intuiting types take broad view, are people oriented, take subjective decisions for long time zones

People can also be classified in three personality types:

1. Compliant types who seek company, want love and appreciation
2. Aggressive types go against others and try to excel to gain admiration
3. Detached types who remain away, want independence from interference and are keen to be solo winners

Let us discuss consumer materialism and compulsive buying. Materialistic people enjoy buying valuable goods and showing them off, which makes them egocentric and self-centred. They believe that their possessions would project their life style and yet no possession gives them real satisfaction because the more you have the more you want and there is no end to wanting. "My Swiss villa proves that I am a successful person."

Compulsive buying behaviour makes people buy things, which either they do not need or cannot afford. Sale offers, mail order people, catch those people who are on a buying spree.

Consumers get an image of the product on their mental screen. Marketers have to position their products in the right market segment to ensure that positive mental image is formed and that it stays. Repetition of advertisements is meant to fix the product on the mind's screen.

Pepsi has been positioned as a drink for the youth and to counter it (as youth remains the biggest segment Coke is positioned there too). Maruti 800 is positioned as the common man's car while Honda City has the slot of upper class car. Raymond Suiting is in the top position for the elite while Mayur Suiting is for the middle class.

Perceived price can be, high, low or fair. Then there is differential pricing like lower air ticket for senior citizens. There are sale prices when heavy discounts are offered, like save up to 50%, buy more at less price. Such offers can be deceptive, as the correct picture is not given to the consumers. While people feel happy at making purchases and acquiring products, if the price is the same as imagined by the buyer, then it does not give any pleasure. However, if the perceived price turns out to be more then the actual price then the transaction becomes interesting to the buyer. For example, buying a 200-litre refrigerator would cost the buyer Rs. 14,000, and it costs him as much then there is no joy. In case the purchase price is Rs. 13,500 only it gives mental satisfaction and pleasure to the buyer.

Most often, especially for consumer goods price and quality of a product get associated with each other and reduction in price can create doubts about the reduction in quality of the product. Similarly product, country, quality and price are perceived by the customers as a package, as can be seen from below:

1. Made in the USA best quality high price
2. Made in Germany, solid in technology medium price
3. Made in Japan, elegant, not sturdy, price quite high
4. Made in Korea, almost as good as from Japan lower in price
5. Made in India, low labour cost, low price, inconsistent quality. (This perception is not correct any more but Brand India needs to be strengthened to overcome this perception)

Price, quality and service relationship takes into account that each product has some service attached to it.

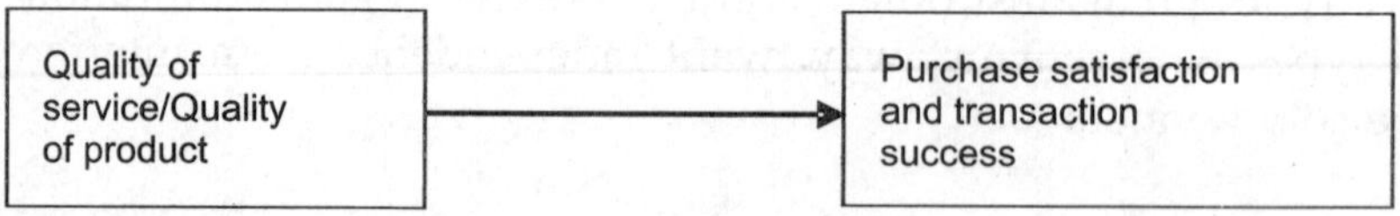

There are different types of consumers with unique personalities. There are consumers ready to experiment and they buy products in the introductory stage of product life cycle. Computer notepads, palmtop computers find a good market among this type of personality, who is always ready to innovate and experiment.

Dogmatic types have rigid behaviour pattern. When this type buys a new product it is contrary to their belief. Therefore, they have to be on the defensive and are uncomfortable with such purchases. They can be persuaded by authoritative, dramatic and dynamic advertisements, which help them, overcome their basic negative attitude.

Open-minded consumers take to new products easily.

Social "type sets"-self-centred persons look for answers within themselves while extroverts are ready and at times eager to find out what their peers and seniors have to say, (who says what becomes important and a significant purchase decision tool).

Stimulation levels are important guides for consumer behavior study. Some consumers lead a sedate life and minimum level of curiosity arousal is enough for them to become interested in the product. There are hard-core consumers who look for being shaken out of their slumber and for them heavy dosage of stimulation is needed. These persons can practically psyche themselves into the purchase mood.

Attitudes are predisposition levels people have towards a product or an idea. These positive or negative attitudes are based on, earlier experience, odd remark heard from a known or even unknown person, from persons like salesmen connected to the product, the environment or mood in which the message about the product was given to the consumer.

Attitudes are normally consistent for a particular product. If a thing is not liked then it is not to be purchased. Housewives may not even think of purchasing a twin drum-washing machine with the known benefits of single drum machines. At times attitudes change for reasons like, "let us economize" or non-availability of favorites brand in the shop visited and imminence of need. "Let us buy Godrej soap as Lux is not in stock." Such decisions for FMCG purchases are taken easily as the cost of replacement/ or repurchase is not heavy, unlike a consumer durable product like a car or TV, which cannot be purchased, everyday.

In communications the credibility of source, or who is saying it, matters a lot. Firm's brand equity can authenticate what is being put in the advertisements. Most firms use endorsers to talk about their products, which make the target segment believe in the product. Wrong endorsers can cause harm to the product or can have no impact rendering the advertisement useless. A top heroine endorsing washing powder may not have any impact as people know that she does not wash her clothes at all. When she endorses a beauty cream people believe her.

Sender or source's credibility is important as it defines how or how much the receiver is going to believe it. **"Let us take it with a pinch of salt."** Such negative impressions come with unreliable senders of information. Use of endorsers becomes necessary in such cases. Source or the sender has its own need for sending the message. How right is that need? For example, many firms resort to having **yearly sale** of their products. People want to know if it is a genuine sale, and if yes, why the firm is selling good products at heavily discounted prices? Is it that they have odd size unsold products, heavy inventory as their export order got cancelled, or, is it that the discounted prices are in fact the same as original? The firm increased the prices first and then declared the Sale. Increase of prices was of 20% and discount offered is 17%. Such types of sales lose their impact in no time and bring bad name to the sale and to the seller.

It is important to discuss the following areas with respect to Retail Management.

- Definition of Retail Marketing.
- An introduction and overview of the Retailing Business.
- Retailer vs E-tailing.
- Hurdles in the functioning of E-tailing in the Indian context
- Strategies to work out retailing model under Indian scenario
- Disintermediation and Re-intermediation
- Development of the Retail Power
- The Retail Marketing function
- Role of strategic planning in retailing
- Challenges and Opportunities in retail marketing

Definition of Retail Marketing

Retailing can be defined as selling gods to customers usually in small quantities and not for resale.

Retail comes from the French word *retaillier* which was used to denote the acts of "cutting off, chip and divide" regarding tailoring way back in 1365. It first was used as a noun with the meaning of a "sale in small quantities" in 1433.

Retailing can therefore be defined as "buying in larger quantities and selling in smaller quantities." It is the sale of goods or merchandise, from a fixed or moving location such as a departmental store or kiosk or a push cart in small or individual lots for consumption by the purchaser or end-user. It is concerned with getting saleable goods into the hands of customers who are prepared to pay for the pleasure of using (like eating, wearing or experiencing) the products.

Retailing may include subordinated services, such as delivery. Purchasers may be individuals or businesses.

The term retailing applies not only to the selling of tangible product, like loaves of bread *or* pairs of shoes, but also to the selling of service products. Companies who provide meals, haircuts and aromatherapy sessions are all essentially retailers, as they sell to the final consumer, and yet customers do not take goods away from these retailers. The consumption or usage of the service is part of retailing activities.

In trade, a **retailer** buys goods or products in large quantities from manufacturers or importers, either directly or through a wholesaler, and then sells smaller quantities to the end-user. For example, a convenience store would buy tins *of* coke in units of two-dozen boxes, but sell in single-tin units.

The un-bulking activity starts at the distributor's or the wholesaler's place. A wholesaler also buys in larger quantities and sells on to their customers, the down stream members in smaller quantities. It is the type of customer, rather than the activity, that distinguishes a retailer from other distributive traders; that distinction being that a retailer sells to final consumers, unlike a wholesaler who sells on to a retailer *or* other business organization.

One definition of a retailer can be given as 'any establishment engaged in selling merchandise for personal or household consumption and rendering services incidental to the sale of such goods'.

There are many businesses that carry out retailing activity in addition to their normal functions; for example, a factory may engage in retailing activity by selling goods in the shop attached to its manufacturing premises. In the UK, however, a retailer is only classified as such for government reporting if the business gains over half of its income from selling to the final consumer.

Retail establishments are often called shops or stores. Retailers are at the end of the supply chain. Manufacturing marketers see the process of retailing as a necessary part of their overall distribution strategies. In some companies there are depots carrying out retailing operations.

Retail trade can also be defined as "the aggregate sales made through a business location (usually a store or shop) in which the principal activity is the sale of merchandise and related services to the general public, for household or personal consumption."

The pricing technique used by most retailers is usually cost plus pricing. This involves adding a mark-up amount (or percentage) to the retailers cost. Another common technique is retail pricing. This simply involves charging the amount suggested by the manufacturer and usually printed on the product by the manufacturer as Maximum Retail Price (MRP). There are three major types of retailing:

- First, is the **market**, a physical location where buyers and sellers converge? Usually this is done on town squares, sidewalks or designed streets and may involve the construction of temporary structures (market stalls).
- Second, shop or store trading process? Some shops use counter-service, where goods are out of reach of buyers. And must be obtained from seller. This type of retail is common for small but expensive items (e.g., jewellery) and controlled items like medicine and liquor. Self-service, where goods may be handled and examined prior to purchase, has become more common since the second half of the 20th century.
- Third form of retail is **virtual retail,** where products are sold via mail, telephone or online without having been examined physically. Instead a catalogue, television or a website informs the customers about the products for selling. Sometimes this type of retailing replicates existing retail types such as online shops or virtual marketplaces such as eBay.

Buildings for retail trade have changed considerably over time. From **market halls** in the middle ages, which were essentially just covered marketplaces to the **departmental stores** of 19th century, which were a street of several different shops with one roof. One of the novelties of the departmental store was the introduction of fixed prices, making price negotiations unnecessary, and browsing on displayed merchandise more enjoyable. This is commonly considered the birth of consumerism, (consumerism can be defined as giving primacy in the buying-selling process to the consumer). In cities, these were multi-storey buildings with lifts and elevators for the benefit of the customers.

In the 1920s the first **supermarket** was opened in the United States, heralding in a new era of retail: self-service. Around the same time the first shopping mall was constructed which incorporated elements from both the mall and the departmental store. A mall consists of several departmental stores linked by arcades (many of their shops are owned by the same firm under different names). All the stores rent their space from the mall owner. By middle of the last century, most of these were being developed as single enclosed, climate-controlled, projects in suburban areas. The mall has had a considerable impact on the retail structure.

In addition to enclosed malls, there are also **strip malls—malls operating from open areas** which are 'outside" malls (in Britain they are called retail parks). These are often connected to supermarkets or big box stores. Also in high traffic areas, other businesses may lease space from the supermarket or big box store to sell their goods or services from. A recent development is a very large shop called a superstore. These are sometimes located as stand-alone outlets, but more commonly are part of strip mall or Retail Park.

Local shops may be known as **brick or mortar stores** in the United States. Many shops are part of a chain—a number of similar shops with the same name selling the same products in different locations. One company may own the shops, or there may be a franchising company that has franchising agreements with the shop owners (for example, McDonald's restaurant chains).

Some shops sell second-hand goods. Often the public can also sell goods to such shops, sometimes called "pawn" shops. In other cases, especially in the case of a non-profit shop, the public donates goods to the shop to be sold. In give-away shops goods can be taken for free.

There are also **consignment shops**, where a person can place an item in a store, and if it sells the person gives the shop owner a percentage of the sale price. The advantage of selling an item this way is that the established shops give the item exposure to more potential buyers.

The term retailer is also applied where a service provider services the need of a large number of individuals, such as with a **telephone** or electric power.

Retailer vs E-tailing

The word E-tailing is derived from Internet retailing or electronic retailing. With the spread of computers and Internet, **e-tailing is emerging as an attractive alternative to the traditional brick-and-mortar retaining. Chances are that they will coexist profitably**. Sometimes, a key question arises, i.e., to retail or to e-tail? The answer must be found in the number of potential customers belonging to the market segment having computers and Internet, who would be interested in purchasing the products on e-tailing, virtual shops.

The e-tail revolution: It all began a couple of years ago. Retailing as an attractive business was slowly emerging out of the shadows. Quite a few corporate houses began looking at retailing as one way to corporate salvation. Notable among them are: the R.P. Goenka group, the Tatas, the S Kumars, the Rajan Raheja group and the Ajay Piramal group. And many more are still in the process of finalizing their forays into retailing. Even as loose ends of retailing plans are being tied up, e-tailing has begun catching the attention of many entrepreneurs. Suddenly, you started hearing e-tailing names such as Rediff.com, Jaldi.com, Fabmart.com, Tsnshop.com and Satyamonline.com. This could well be the beginning of an e-tail revolution.

The e-tail arena: The questions that need to be addressed before venturing into e-tailing are:

- How large is the retailing industry?
- Is e-tailing large enough to take on so many players?

Both retailing and e-tailing are still in the nascent stage and growing. One estimate by consultants KSA Technopak is that the organised retailing sector should be as large as Rs. 5,000 crore and e-tailing in India should be just about Rs. 12 crore. Says K Vaitheeswaran, vice-president (marketing) of the Bangalore-based Fabmart: "But then the growth potential for both retailing and e-tailing is tremendous."

Once a detailed analysis is made the differences in the way business is conducted in retailing and e-tailing becomes clear as can be seen in the table given below:

E-tailing	**Retailing**
1. An e-tailer can go global.	1. Retailing is location driven.
2. Web-driven retailing, an e-tailer has no hassles of acquiring real estate.	2. In retailing, 50 per cent of the initial investment could go towards acquiring real estate.
3. The primary aim of every e-tailer is to attract a prospective customer to his e-tail site.	3. The primary aim of retailer is to maintain the continuity of distribution channel with continuous flow of customers to its outlet/shop.
4. e-tailer has to spend considerable time, effort and money for a large ad spend. Ad-spends by dot.com companies are so huge that whatever savings achieved in the areas of real estate and inventory is more than offset.	4. Post-acquisition of real estate, a retailer has to spend considerable time, effort and money in setting up his shop, stocking inventory and creating display patterns, merchandising and point of purchase advertising with banners, danglers, posters, window displays.
5. Customer retention is the toughest thing on the web and is a costly affair.	5. A retailer expects strong customer loyalty, because of factors like built relations over the years, location advantage, excellence in service and product quality.
6. Getting things is cheaper, easier and faster on the Net.	6. Getting things is cheaper and easier on the retail outlet.
7. The Internet offers millions of products with little chance of stock-outs.	7. Brick mortar retailers could sell thousands of items from his shop, of a large variety of brands.
8. Information is obtained easily and in comfort on the Net. In the bargain, valuable time is gained. Shopping on the Internet for, say	8. Traditional retailing stands out in stark contrast: the consumer searches frantically, runs up and down, grills a poorly trained store assistant who is

Table Contd.

E-tailing	Retailing
15 minutes, could save a two-hour trip to the mall. Consumers prefer to save this time so that they can devote more time for their professional and domestic priorities.	unable to help him out. In the bargain, valuable time is lost.
9. The opportunities for personal attention available to the brick-and-mortar client are incomparably greater than those enjoyed by the Internet consumer.	9. The opportunities for personal attention available to the Internet consumer are incomparably smaller than those enjoyed by the brick-and-mortar client.
10. Started/initiated/begun by the R.P. Goenka group, the Tatas, the S. Kumars, the Rajan Raheja group and the Ajay Piramal group.	10. e-tailing names such as Rediff.com, Jaldi.com, Fabmart.com, Tsnshop.com and Satyamonline.com. This could well be the beginning of an e-tail revolution.

1. A retailer is restricted to a particular location—retailing is location-driven. But, an e-tailer can go global. Being local in nature, a brick-and-mortar retailer has to identify a good location for his operations and wait for customers. A physical store caters only to a particular locality. On the other hand, an e-tailer has to virtually attract a customer to his site and offer him exemplary services going for a bigger and wider audience and still be in touch with individual preferences. In fact, location is no longer the key to success if e-tailing is what we are talking about. Thus, while the target customer remains the same both in retailing and e-tailing, the mode of conducting business is changing dramatically.
2. There is another distinct feature of e-tailing that is challenging. In retailing, as much as 50 per cent of the initial investment could go towards acquiring real estate. Post-acquisition of real estate, a retailer has to spend considerable time, effort and money in setting up his shop, stocking inventory and creating display patterns. Thanks to web-driven retailing, an e-tailer has no such hassles. But, there is a challenge before him: retaining a customer who has shopped through his site.
3. That is more than just a challenge. The primary aim of every e-tailer is to attract a prospective customer to his e-tail site. On the other hand, the primary aim of a retailer is to maintain the continuity of distribution channel along with customer satisfaction.
4. Attracting prospective customers calls for a large ad spend. e-tailer has to spend considerable time, effort and money for a large ad spend. Ad-spends by dot.com companies are so huge that whatever savings achieved in the areas of real estate and inventory is more than offset. On the other hand, post-acquisition of real estate, a retailer has to spend considerable time, effort and money in setting up his shop, stocking inventory and creating display patterns.
5. After all that ad-spend, will the customer remain loyal to the e-tailing site? "The Internet customer is very hard to predict and is different from the normal customer.

Retaining him is not so simple. While a retailer expects strong loyalty, such a loyalty on the Net is difficult to obtain. A customer may shift from the Internet if someone else offers him a better deal."

Example: That is why Jaldi.com will be using a mix of marketing tools such as public relations, advertising, promotions, direct marketing and Internet advertising to spread awareness among its target audience. Jaldi.com went a step ahead. Its offline promotions started with a successful consumer launch held at Priya PVR I theatre in New Delhi where 3,600 free *Phir Bhi Dil Hai Hindustani* movie tickets were given to every customer who logged on and registered at the site Jaldi.com.

It must, however be understood that customer retention is the toughest thing on the web. First of all, it is difficult to get a consumer come to your site. After he comes in, the task is to retain him and get him frequently. Once he is confident about you, he will use his credit card to make his purchases at the site." On the other hand, a retailer expects strong customer loyalty.

Summarizing, it can be stated that, retaining an e-tail customer is certainly a costly and difficult affair.

6. "If you offer some freebies, a customer may keep on coming to your site, with the expectation every time that there would be some freebies out there. The moment you stop freebies, you could simply lose the customer." So, managing e-tailing promotion through freebies could be a tricky affair.

   "The first time a person shops on the Net is always a special occasion. "If anyone has to try this new medium of shopping, there should be overwhelming reasons for doing so. The benefits must go beyond mere convenience. For one, the consumer will certainly be interested if he gets things cheaper on the net. "The Net being a new medium and channel for distribution of goods it is necessary to convince people to use this new medium to buy." "For convincing a customer to use this new medium, one has to offer an incentive to buy on the Net. Otherwise, it would be difficult to get a customer to shop with you." Therefore, easier and faster shopping are the reasons for shopping on the Net. On the other hand, buying products can be cheaper and easier on a retail outlet. These retail outlets provide their customers a reason for coming out of their houses and for buying while enjoying a picnic like outing with friends and relatives.

7. You can go to a brick-and-mortar retailer who could offer you 10,000 items in his store. Chances are that he might be 10 per cent out of stock. On the other hand, the Internet offers millions of products with no chances of an out-of-stock situation.
8. Easy and comfortably-obtained info is another advantage that shopping on the Net offers. On the Internet, product information is just a few clicks away, all accessed in the comfort of a home. Traditional retailing stands out in stark contrast: the consumer searches frantically, runs up and down, grills a poorly trained store assistant who is unable to help him out. In the bargain, valuable time is lost. Simply put, shopping on the Internet for, say 15 minutes, could save a two-hour trip to the mall. Consumers prefer to save this time so that they can devote more time for their professional and domestic priorities.

Hurdles in the functioning of E-tailing in the Indian context. The Indian scenario is quite different from that of the West. For good reasons, Indians have always been great shoppers and enjoy shopping anywhere in the world. There are hurdles in India for any successful e-commerce project. Consider: **growth in e-commerce** will come not from well-designed websites or web marketing but from deeper penetration of the Internet. That is why a case has been made out for increasing **broadband Internet connections, which** are faster than **the dial-up connections.**

- One estimate is that India has a mere 20 lakh Internet users, mostly concentrated in the metros. Web analysts feel that in many areas of retailing and commerce, Internet is unlikely to **garner a sizable slice of the market**. And that could be for several years to come. This is true, especially in businesses where margins are thin. Consider fast moving consumer goods, the FMCG sector. "In the Indian FMCG business, margins are as low as 10 per cent. Hence, e-tailing in such areas might not catch on."
- Two, despite a higher Internet penetration, cities like Mumbai or New Delhi might not be a haven for an e-tailer. Reason: for things like grocery, there is a **shop at every nook and corner.** All that an individual has to do is just make a phone call and the goods are delivered at his doorstep. Thrown in along with free home delivery is a month's credit. In case of perishables such as fruits and vegetables, the Indian buyer prefers them farm-fresh. What does he do? While returning from work, he drops in at the vegetable market and purchases.
- Three, cheap labour. Thanks to easy availability of domestics at an affordable wage bill, quite a few of the rich customers hire them for doing domestic chores, which include shopping.
- Four, the usual Indian **aversion to use credit cards.** Thanks to low penetration of credit cards and the lack of popularity of debit cards, e tailing might find it an uphill task to catch on. Also "Elder citizens are averse to using even the computer." However, they are at ease while using the remote control of a television set. That throws up an interesting solution. Accessing the Internet through a television in the near future might be something that an individual should be offered if e-tailing is to grow faster.
- The last and the most important hurdle to the growth of the e-tailing industry is the efficient management of logistics. Here the role of a courier company is extremely important. Most portals offering e-commerce have tied up with courier companies. For instance, Jaldi.com has tied up with Gati for taking care of their delivery logistics.

There are other examples too. Blue Dart plans to enter the household shipment business in a big way to serve the needs of the online community in India. Looking at the coming e-commerce boom, Blue Dart is targeting a 80 per cent annual jump in its business, mostly from the shipment requirements of its online customers. For this purpose, Blue Dart has already invested Rs. 40 crore to tune up its existing infrastructure and interface it with e-commerce potential.

On the technological front, Blue Dart is upgrading its intranet facility, linking 1,300 terminals with over 2,000 people at 70 locations to meet the e-commerce requirements. This means that e-shoppers in these locations can log on to Bluedart.com and ask for the shipment of ordered goods from these e-shops. Also, Blue Dart has aligned with leading portals and e-shops like Rediff.com and Fabmart.com to meet their distribution needs.

Strategies to work out retailing model under Indian scenario: The most important question now is this: what kind of retailing model is going to deliver the goods in the Indian scenario?

- The most important cost advantage of e-tailing comes from elimination of intermediaries and economical distribution. For example, book e-tailing means dispensing with big shops replete with slow-moving stock. Consider the case of Amazon.Com, where the orders go straight to the wholesaler. That means the working capital costs are cut down drastically. Not just that, an e-tailer is paid before he pays his distributor. The implication: need for lower working capital.
- However, one has to compare these gains against certain web-related costs. Running a website and servicing it to ensure that it is cent per cent reliable is not easy. Logistics and distribution are of utmost importance and that is where many e-tailers are known to have gone wrong. While it is true that many e-tailers have been able to cut costs, they have lost large sums of money in the process of offering goods at low prices. A few of them who have made profits have ploughed them back for financing customer acquisition or retention.

All these do not mean an end to traditional retailing. **E-tailing will have to co-exist with traditional retailing.** "For things such as music and books, a whole new market will be created. This will increase the market manifold." E-tailers will have to work in combination with traditional retailers. Even the biggies in the business such as Amazon.com have realized this and are setting up distribution warehouses for the same.

As the combination of retailing and e-tailing set to deliver the goods, the trend of using the Internet as another service medium will gradually catch up. E-tailers like Jaldi.com have already set up kiosks in various cities, which have been successful. Tsnshop.com makes use of its tele-shopping network franchisees in various cities for selling its products." It helps in gaining customers fast as individuals have the option of returning the goods purchased if they do not like it. They can just go across to the shop. This gives them a certain level of comfort and confidence." Such a comfort and confidence-level is a must for a successful e-tailing venture.

On balance, what we are witnessing at the moment is certainly a tip of the iceberg. Such is the growth potential in the e-tailing industry that it is not possible to put a figure against the industry's size or growth. So, there are pluses and minuses in the case of retailing and e-tailing. With so many hurdles around for e-tailing, it would be long time before e-tailing really catches up. But, the trend has begun. The model, which will work in such an Indian context, is this: a peaceful and complementary coexistence of retailing and e-tailing.

Disintermediation and Re-intermediation

The new technological capabilities – the Internet, makes possible huge shrinking in the cost of access to customers that brings an additional threat to retailers in the form of disintermediation. Disintermediation is the direct selling of goods by manufacturers to consumers (that is, avoiding retailers). For example, Compaq sold its computers through retailers, whereas Dell computers grew rapidly by selling online. Established store-based retailers began to doubt their future as more business went into direct online marketing. They feared, being disintermediated by the new e-tailers. While the prospect of disintermediation appears attractive, its implementation may be problematic for manufacturers. Majority of manufacturers (57%) are unwilling to sell online because of the nature of their product, and/or because of potential channel conflict. Disintermediation also requires additional heavy investment in the new channel that is unlikely to be profitable in the short term. The additional investment is not just in the internet/electronic interface, but also requires infrastructural investments in the delivery of small orders. Such a strategy is risky in that it assumes that a significant proportion of customers are prepared to switch channels, which may well not be the case.

But disintermediation was only the half story. Although some middlemen lost their business, new middlemen sprang up to supply internet services to both businesses and consumers. Re-intermediation took place on grand scale. As for the traditional 'brick-only" firms like Compaq, dragged their feet, hoping that the assault of "pure click" firms would flatten or disappear. Then they started their own online sales channel, becoming "brick and click" competitors. They had to do this carefully in order to retain the loyalty of retailers, brokers, and agents. The irony is twofold. First, many brick-and-click competitors became stronger contenders than the pure-click firms, since they had a larger pool of resources to work with and well-established brand names. And second, many formidable pure-click dot-corns started to falter as investors sensed a bubble, and began to disinvest, dropping the value of dot-com stocks, causing mass staff layoffs, and sending many such as Pets.com, Mothernature.com, Boo.com, Garden.com, Eve.com into bankruptcy. At the same time, many other pure-click dot-corns are surviving and even prospering in today's marketplace.

Development of the Retail Power

Earlier the producers of companies (like Procter and Gamble) used to dominate retailers, but the growing importance of mass distribution has transformed the power of retailers, now retailers tend to dominate them. In recent years, the number of products sold by grocery stores has grown faster than shelf life at the retail level. Retailers can now choose among an ever-increasing number of products. Producers compete in order to obtain the listing of their products, and in the process confer a stronger bargaining power to retailers, who can threaten to pull out their products to obtain more profitable retail conditions.

The reasons for the development of retail power are:

- Sales of most grocery items, drugs, and merchandising chains, have not been increasing at rapid rates. So if the retailers are to grow, they must take sales at par with their competitors rather than waiting for overall demand to expand. This has created enormous pressure on retailers to perform, given that most chains tend to carry the same products. The type of competition tends to be price oriented. In other words, better prices coupled with excellent locations, appealing stores, reasonable service have been the major routes to survival and success in this arena. The chain retailers have increasingly begun to pressurize suppliers for price concessions. The power of producers is diminished by traditional retailers such as Wal-Mart, k-mart. Consequently, new entrants are diminishing their power.

- In the competitive environment, the nature of supplier–retailer relations in the grocery arena have changed significantly. Retailers are concerned with improving their productivity. Although it is virtually impossible for them to raise prices, but it is not possible to find ways to lower costs. This can be achieved by high economies of scale, simultaneously providing convenience of one stop shopping, consequently they can build larger stores, thereby increasing their fixed costs. Creating higher break even points, forcing supermarkets and mass-merchandisers (discount stores) to place even greater emphasis on generating enormous sales volume. The resulting competition has led to consolidation.
- There is increased pressure on employees of the retail companies. Earlier they focused on purchasing and maintaining balanced inventories. Now, they are profit centres that are also responsible for capital management, service levels, turnover, retail margins and pricing, quality control, competitiveness and variety, operating costs, shelf space and position, and vendor float and terms. In order to help their companies make money, they look for suppliers to give them price breaks and merchandising support, and they become very upset when those price breaks and support are not forthcoming.
- Retailers have many new categories of products; they have to choose from them, what to stock on their shelves. As store sizes have not increased significantly, therefore, retailers are likely to choose products to stock on their shelves with a goal of making themselves (not the manufacturers). Hence, the manufacturer's bargaining position is weakened further because most new products do not succeed, by any reasonable definition of success. Procter and Gamble has responded to this challenge by decreasing the number of product offerings it sells to retailers. In addition, manufacturers have engaged in many new-product price and promotional allowances as a way of "bribing" their way onto retailer's shelves. These activities play in the hands of already powerful buyers.
- Information technology has diffused throughout retailing to such an extent that virtually all of the major retailers can capture item-by-item data, via scanning devices, at their electronic point-of-sale terminals. The Universal Product Code (UPC) is used to help track the movement of product at retail and reduce both stock-outs and supply cycle time.

The knowledge gained from this information has permitted retailers to calculate the Direct Product Profitability (DPP) of individual items, track what moves and what does not move well in their stores, engage in forward investment buying, and leverage suppliers. The retailers use this data for their own benefit more than to coordinate the channel.

For example, supermarket retailers can now tailor promotional offers to their loyalty card shoppers that link directly to their past buying behaviour, rather than needing to offer the same deal to all consumers. In one instance, retailers like American Stores and Grand Union installed kiosks inside their store, accessible with a consumer's loyalty card, that distribute coupons related to shoppers prior purchases.

The Retail Marketing Function

- The primary focus is upon the major **issues and strategies of retail management.**
- **Formulating retail strategy** based upon a clear understanding of customer needs and motives.
- **Evaluate and apply** multi-attribute and other **decision models** to customers' choices, and buyers' choices of suppliers and merchandise.
- Organize basic **concepts of economics,** notably elasticity and diminishing marginal returns, to pricing, space allocation, service and other retail decision areas.
- Evaluate retail-marketing performance through a range of quantitative and qualitative consumer **research techniques**.
- **Analysis of Retail Markets** – Identification and segmentation of retail markets; consumer motives for selecting stores and centres; consumer images of retail companies and stores; target marketing and positioning.
- **Retail Location and Planning** – Identification of optimum locations and the assessment of specific sites; catchments area analysis and models of retail location; issues and framework of town planning; the internationalization of retail companies and formats.
- **Marketing Mix Strategies** – Retail pricing strategies, category management and buying, product range development and private labels, retail promotion and advertising, merchandising, space allocation and display, retail design and atmospherics, role and techniques of personal selling.
- **Technology and Retailing** – Ways in which technology has impacted upon and helped to shape
- Retail structure (e.g., e-commerce),
- Retail strategy (e.g., relationship management)
- Retail operations **Role of strategic planning in retailing**
- Locating and focusing on the Critical Success Factors in Retail Management

Retailing is one of the key elements of a marketing strategy; it facilitates the targeting process, making sure that a product reaches particular groups of consumers. It is important in a marketing strategy because it is concerned with matching the arena in which a product is purchased to the benefits and characteristics of the product itself and its price. Retailers provide a collection of service benefits to their customers such as being located in convenient places, editing product ranges according to shopping tasks, and selling goods in quantities that match personal consumption levels. Ensuring that this process runs smoothly presents a host of managerial challenges. Retailing is therefore a deceptively simple management process yet fascinatingly complex in its detail.

Competitive Advantage and Competitive Strategies

For long-term survival, retailers need to build sustainable competitive advantage (SCA) over their rivals in the market. Major methods of creating SCA include convenient locations, building customer loyalty, building close relationships with suppliers, efficient logistics and supply-chain management, good information systems (including customer database management), exclusive merchandise (including own brands), buying economies of scale, superior customer service, and a knowledgeable and motivated sales force. The study of competitive environment is done with the help of **Michael Porter's 5-force model.**

Evaluating Alternative Retailing Strategies

Having delineated the strategic options available, the retailer needs to decide on specific strategic action. This requires the evaluation of the strategies in terms of how they help to bridge the strategic gap, profitability, risk and the ability of the organization to undertake the particular strategy. One useful method of doing this is to compare the attractiveness of the market opportunities with the possible competitive advantages of the retailer. The technique suggests that the highest amount of resources should be invested in opportunities where the retailer has the strongest competitive advantage. For instance, a retailer targeting a new segment would evaluate the attractiveness of market opportunity in terms of:

- Market size.
- Market growth rate.
- Degree of competition and competitive structure.
- Profitability of the segment.
- Technology requirements.
- Legal and regulatory issues.
- Human-resource requirements.
- Environmental issues.

This information must be compared with the retailer's strengths relative to that of competition on factors such as:

- Current market share.
- Merchandising skills.
- Buying strength.
- Supply-chain management and supplier relations.
- New product development.
- Own-label reputation.
- Financial resources.
- Sales force.
- Managerial competence.
- Fit with current retailer image in terms of breadth and depth of product lines, quality and reliability, customer service.

Development of Marketing and Positioning Strategies

By this stage the retailer has set general objectives and analyzed a number of opportunities and decided on a specific direction for the organization and the opportunities it wishes to take advantage of. For each of the opportunities chosen the retailer now needs to set specific objectives and allocate resources to achieve the objectives. In order to achieve the set objectives, marketing strategies have to be devised. These are normally developed for specific market segments rather than the market as a whole, as this makes more effective use of resources. After selecting the target markets a positioning strategy must be developed.

Retail Positioning

A positioning strategy is a plan of action for how the retailer will compete in the targeted markets and how it will differentiate itself from competitors in those markets. Retail positioning is the process of creating and maintaining a distinctive and valued image of the retailer in the target customer's mind relative to its competitors. This emphasizes the fact that positioning is a relative concept and understanding consumers' perceptions is the key to effective positioning in the market. Positioning can be a deliberate attempt to differentiate from the rest of the market (for instance Harrods), or an attempt to be as close as possible to the average shopper's view of the attributes of an ideal retailer in a particular market segment.

Positioning involves the following activities:

1. Selecting the right market segment/s
2. Selecting the four Ps of marketing to get a perfect fit in the segment

Positioning should be either merchandise-led or service-led. Another basis for positioning strategies is to distinguish between symbolic and functional merchandise, and whether it attracts high or low margins. People are motivated to buy the two categories and shop for them in different ways. Three main positioning strategies are:

(a) Product differentiation,
(b) Service and personality augmentation,
(c) Price leadership.

Product differentiation is achieved through unique or exclusive products or brands, own-branded products, and unusually broad or deep merchandise assortments.

Service and personality augmentation can be achieved in many different ways, including high levels of personal service, convenient locations, long opening hours, generous returns policy, home delivery and so forth.

Price leadership can be established through offering low or discounted pricing and good value or price promotions on key items.

Positioning is not a once-and-for-all decision. Because of changes in the market (consumers and the competitors) the positioning may need to be adjusted. Repositioning needs to be considered where there is a big discrepancy between consumers' perceptions and management perceptions. This is usually reflected in poor performance and declining market share. Repositioning can also be used to target a new set of customers.

The Retail Mix

The retail marketing and positioning strategy is put into effect by the retail mix—the set of controllable variables that the retailer can use to satisfy customers' needs and to influence their buying behaviour and compete effectively in the market. To implement a specific retailing strategy, managers must decide the best combination of retail-mix variables and coordinate the activities of the different elements of the mix such as:

- Merchandise assortment.
- Location.
- Price.
- Visual merchandising.
- Store atmosphere/ambience.
- Customer service.
- Advertising.
- Promotions.
- Personal selling.

Positioning can be the result of interaction between the four main areas of the retailing marketing mix;

(a) Trading style/format strategy,
(b) Merchandise strategy,
(c) Customer service,
(d) Customer communications strategy.

Implementation and Control

Effective implementation requires that appropriate resources be allocated to required tasks, which requires budgeting in respect of specific elements of the retailing mix, personnel and so forth. Effective implementation also requires scheduling and coordination of retailing activities. It requires the translation of retailing strategies into tactics. Functional strategies led to the establishment of long term objectives that must be translated into day-to-day operational decisions. For instance, when to advertise, what media to use, and the length of promotion campaigns are tactical decisions influenced by the competitive environment and the communication strategy.

Challenges and Opportunities in Retail Marketing

The Indian retail revolution has garnered such unprecedented attention that it now seems to be the hottest sector to be present in. Retailing has seen such a transformation over the past decade that its very definition has undergone a sea-change. No longer can a manufacturer rely on sales to take place by ensuring mere availability of his product. Today, retailing is about so much more than mere merchandising. It's about casting customers in a story, reflecting their desires and aspirations, and forging long-lasting relationships. As the Indian consumer evolves she/he expects more and more each time she/he steps into a store. Retail today has changed from selling a product or a service to selling a hope, an aspiration and above all an experience that a consumer would like to repeat.

For manufacturers and service providers the emerging opportunities in urban markets seem to lie in capturing and delivering better value to the customers through retail. For instance, in Chennai CavinKare's LimeLite, Marico's Kaya Skin Clinic and Apollo Hospital's Apollo Pharmacies are examples, to name a few, where manufacturers/ service providers combine their own manufactured products and services with those of others to generate value hitherto unknown. The last mile connect seems to be increasingly lively and experiential.

Also, manufacturers and service providers face an exploding rural market yet only marginally tapped due to difficulties in rural retailing. Only innovative concepts and models may survive the test of time and investments.

Manufacturers and service providers will increasingly face a host of specialist retailers, who are characterised by use of modern management techniques, backed with seemingly unlimited financial resources. Organised retail appears inevitable. Retailing in India is currently estimated to be a US$ 200 billion industry, of which organised retailing makes up a paltry 3 per cent or US$ 6.4 billion. By 2010, organized retail is projected to reach US$ 23 billion. For retail industry in India, things have never looked better and brighter. Challenges to the manufacturers and service providers would abound when market power shifts to organized retail.

Organized retail too faces innumerable opportunities and challenges. The multitude of 'mom & pop' or the convenience stores are gearing up to face the organized retail by offering increased and personalized customer service. Organized retail faces challenges also in terms of product categories that it can profitably offer. Scale of organised retail impels use of IT and sophisticated techniques to manage the supply chain and customers. For the organized retail, resources in these areas seem scarce. To conclude, every player in the arena, be it the manufacturer/service provider or the organized retailer, faces opportunities and challenges.

Management Game 2

Merchandising

The teams should plan overseas venture with the same product. Select the right country or more than one country. Define your method of selecting the country. Prepare your plan for overseas venture giving the thoughts to the 4 Ps. Do you have a global product or will it need to be modified to suit the host countries.

Discuss the methods of understanding the international business and competitive environment of selected countries.

Management Game 3

Teams should plan to define the ways of finding the customer purchase process along with dealing with the different methods of customer communication like, personal communication, advertising, promotion, publicity and public relations. The teams should organize systematic understanding of buyers behaviour patterns related to the product, who are the deciders of the product and brand selection and who pay for the purchase.

Discuss the customer motivation methods as the teams try to locate the different types of customers.

CHAPTER

8

Motivating Retail—Critical Success Factors

Aims and Outcomes

Retail salespersons need to acquire selling skills, as essentially they are responsible for the success of retail marketing. The chapter gives a detailed and comprehensive account of successful sales techniques.

The following can be considered the critical success factors for retail trade.

Enter into the exciting wondrous and at times languorous world of retail. The retail tells a story in proper likable ambience to the customers. The sales team members become the co-star members of the story. The story relates the benefits that can accrue to the customers as they buy from the retail outlet.

1. The retailers must know their clients (convert the customers into clients by personalising the interaction with them, starting by calling them by their names).
2. The retailers must know their own team members, like their expertise, skills and inclinations in their area of work.
3. The retailers must coordinate all the service activities that have the greatest influence on the clients.
4. The service provided to the clients needs to be unique and distinctive in nature, like offering soft drink on arrival in the store on a hot day or coffee on a cold day.
5. The retailers must deliver the promise made to their clients on quality, quantity, and service with each sale.
6. The retailers must place their efforts on achievement of their goals and not fritter away their energy in fruitless tasks.
7. The retailers must keep innovating their store's activities, including displays, service and merchandise.

8. The retailers must know their competitive stores thoroughly, including their product range, pricing policies, promotion and advertising efforts.
9. The retailers must plan for profit making, be it from high volume business or through quality service and product and skimming prices.
10. The retailers need to learn to market with all out efforts only.
11. The store managers' job is to keep measuring the effectiveness of selling efforts, quality and quantity of product, service provided to the clients on a regular basis.

The retail leader should know the answer to the question, "Why I am in this business" and should ask his team "What is our USP". How do they deliver the goods? When the leader gets the team's answers to these questions he should place the best three answers on stores notice board and then compare these with customer's research on the same.

Retail business has to start looking from strategic angle to ensure the growth and well-being of the business as follows:

(a) Business analysis to cover the retailer's vision, mission, goals and objectives
(b) Understanding management options
(c) Selection of goods or services

Next the firm's objectives need to be defined, as sales, profit, customer satisfaction and delight and image building. The retailer needs to select the market segment it wants to cater to, is it all and sundry passing by the store, or is it focused towards a definite locality and does it require to differentiate its strategy for overlapping market segments.

Retailers have to keep an eye on controlable variables like inventory levels, pricing plans and remain proactive to meet contingent environmental changes like marriages, festivities. Retailers need to plan daily operations like display of goods, display boards as they meet the changes in retail situations. Retailers keep control of the activities through periodic evaluation and budgetary controls.

Retailers must prepare their organisational chart with duties, responsibilities and commensurate authority for different set of people engaged in the stores operation.

The following list gives an idea of the types of products sold in retail stores:

(a) Consumer durables like cars, white goods, hardware, jewellery
(b) FMCG products like petrol, cosmetics, eatable items, drugs
(c) Service products like healthcare, laundries,
(d) Entertainment services like movie halls, theatres, clubs
(e) Repair stations like car repair, white goods repair, watch repair
(f) Hotel services like hotels, motels, and camps.

Retailers have sales and profit as main objectives. Sales growth, stability and market share are the main bases of sales objective. Profit arises out of selling price; which normally is fixed and from efficient operations where running costs are kept under control. Firms need to invest in land building, interiors and aesthetics before going full steam in business.

In Australia perfume retailing has become a big business.

Case Study-Perfume Stores Australia

- **Unique Scents Perfume Warehouse Direct**—Wholesale Perfumes available for purchase online. All the latest and classic fragrances are available for immediate purchase and delivery. All items are in stock and ready to ship.
- **Perfume Station** in Brighton Le Sands, NSW, sells designer brands perfumes and aftershaves at heavily discounted prices, averaging 42% off everything while duty free stores are averaging 30% off!

Discount Stores International

- **StrawberryNET.com**: You can buy virtually all internationally known brands of **perfumes, cosmetics and skincare products** at heavily discounted prices. Based in Hong Kong, see prices in the currency of your choice, delivers worldwide. Major brands available at all times on StrawberryNET include: Anna Sui, Aveda, Borghese, Biotherm, Britney Spears, Bvlgari, Cellex C, Chanel, Christian Dior, Clarins, Clinique, Darphin, Decleor, Elizabeth Arden, Estee Lauder, Givenchy, Glycel, Guerlain, Guinot, Gucci, Helena Rubenstein, Kanebo, Kinerase, La Prairie, La Mer, Lancaster, Lancome, Lierac, MAC, Max Factor, Monteil, Nina Ricci, Orlane, Payot, Revlon, Shiseido, Sisley, SK II, Squina, Swissline, Ultima, Valmont, Versace, YSL plus many more.
- Free shipping anywhere in the world
- Complimentary gift wrapping on all orders
- An additional 5% discount for purchases of 3 or more products
- Over 20,000 product lines from more than 2,700 brand names.

The retailers are concentrating on providing optimized service benefits to the customers for easiest buying process.

Retailers must maintain excellent relationship with suppliers. They can go to the extent of getting Just in Time supplies provided the suppier's location and transport arrangements are suited to JIT. Firms need to have good labour relations as well for being able to provide good service to the customers. Firms must adhere to the laws of the land and follow the government rules meant for retail trade.

Consumer acceptance and response comes from proper positioning in the marketplace. Is it meant for high class or middle or low segment? Is it a discount store or speciality store like a drug store or fashion boutique?

Firms can get into niche markets by providing exclusive range of products like fashion garments, designer furnishings to cater to selected customers. For such stores the competition in the conventonal form does not worry too much.

High price, high service stores are upmarket retailers. They offer a wide range of brands and products. Traditional departmental stores carry electronic goods and product lines and have sales staff to help the customers. Discount stores carry a lot of product lines and offer self-service to the customers.

Retailers need to consider the following areas in strategic planning:

1. Location, ingress and egress, parking facility
2. Products, brands and services being offered

3. Promotion plans
4. Pricing strategy

Retailers planning volume business need to locate near residential areas with high leve of population. They should plan a variety of medium level products and plan mass advertising. Pricing need to be penetrating to be effective.

Niche marketing location should be near a small population base with brand selection as required by the segment customers. Direct mail, pamphlets form the ideal promotion strategy.

All encompassing marketing would need a location close to large population area, with separate types of goods and services to cater to each of the segments in the market. Message too needs different approaches to be directed to each segment. Skimming, penetrating and even medium pricing strategy is required to cover the different segments.

While retailers have no control on factors like consumer behaviour, competition, technology, changes in economic conditions seasonality of demand and legal restrictions, they can decide on areas like, location, merchandising and pricing and customer communication.

Location destination for retail outlets are subject to numerous considerations, including possible retail traffic, cost of the site. Badly located stores face business losses due to low levl of retail traffic. It is important to realise the ideal or near ideal location that can be assessed with the following parameters:

1. Consumer's socio-economic factors
2. Consumer's demographic factors
3. Advertising and promotion possibilities: If customers live in the vicinity, then press adevertising is not required and pamphlets, banners can do the job.
4. If the store belongs to a chain then it is advisable to know if competition can set up stores in the neighbourhood. Chain store open outlets to cover the entire geographic consumer area.
5. Transport arrangements—buses, taxis in the area
6. Suppliers location
7. Legal restrictions
8. Overlap of web marketing in the designated geographic area
9. Possibility of home delivery

Retailers need to find the frequency of shoppers from different geographic areas surrounding the store visit the store. The purchase made by them in rupees on an average need to be seen. Retailers need to know the number of credit card holders and their purchase averages.

For a new store retailers need to do a trend analysis to project the sales in the location. It requires knowledge of the following:

(i) Population of target market area
(ii) Car/two wheelers registrations in the area
(iii) New housing complexes coming up in the area
(iv) Mass transport system

(v) Highways, sidewalks
(vi) Time and distance consumers will travel to come to the store to be found out through a market survey
(vii) Attractive factors of the site—metro station nearby, taxi stand, bus terminus, park for picnics

Computer assistance can be taken to assess new store location. Potential sales can be estimated with reference to other similar stores in the area as an analog model. Regression model with a series of equations for calculating stores expected sales can be drawn up taking certain independent variables like population size, average income, number of households, neighbourhood competition, traffic situation, transport system. Other model will take into account the strength of the locational pull caused by the proximity of the store with the housing area. Being objective such systematic analyses tell the true picture of retail traffic the store will get.

Summarizing, it can be said that the following factors will determine the retail business success in a given location:

(a) Population size, density, age distribution, education spread, houseowners and the renters percentages
(b) For the store, availability of managers, labour force, trainees
(c) Supply point: distance from the source, delivery cost, time required for replenishment of stocks from major suppliers
(d) Media available
(e) Growth and diversification possibility
(f) Number and size of competition—their strengths and weaknesses
(g) Taxes, licencing and local body's approvals

Once the sales start, the analysis base shifts to the number of invoices made in a day, week, month. Credit given to customers and recovery time of dues need to be analysed to understand the average number of days outstandings remain and the loss accrued due to the interest on the same. If credit cards are accepted, then the retailers need to check the payment period and frauds, if any.

Ideally the retail outlet site should be selected on the following basis:

(a) Rental costs are low
(b) There is no competition
(c) There is flexibility in brand selection, product category needs
(d) Better roads, traffic management
(e) Easy parking
(f) Multibrand products possible
(g) Advertising expenses are reasonable
(h) Yard lighting, security, ground maintenance are shared with other outlets.

Most cities have shopping centres with shops rented to retailers. Their success comes from the following:

1. One stop shopping family expedition
2. Shopkeepers sharing common costs
3. Good product and brand base
4. Good ambience
5. Strong population in the area
6. Easy access in individual stores
7. Longer shop open periods
8. Eateries, cinema complexes
9. Children's amusement area

Shopping centres or malls as they are also being called provide competitive goods and in-house competition for the retailers for the benefit of the consumer. At times these centres are used by couples for dating in air-conditioned atmosphere. However, these very couples become shoppers in time.

For long-term growth these centres need periodic investment in renovation, expansion, if possible besides a new look to rejuvenate them for fighting competition from the newer centres that keep coming in the vicinity. Changes in goods selection is essential to keep pace with the changing lifestyle of the population. Certain malls offer low rent temporary shacks to retailers interested in selling from them items of seasonal interest.

Delhi is witnessing the phenomenon of mega malls that cover huge areas with retail space for major shopping plazas like the Shoppers Stop, Spencers, Big Bazaar, food courts, cinema complexes. Such mega malls need a lot of space, besides site needs to be selected on the basis of land and construction costs, visibility from afar on the approach roads.

Pedestrian traffic on the approach road needs to be counted by age, gender and time division. Shopping lists, money used up per shopping visit and stores actually visited are other areas that need to be known through spot surveys.

Vehicular traffic need to be counted with cars, two wheelers moving on the street, parked at different time zones will confirm the if the traffic is just moving on the road or visiting the mall. Is the traffic home bound or has it made special trip for shopping? These are the areas of concern to the mall retailers and their answer can be found through traffic survey.

These malls need to have homogeneous retail outlets like, supermarkets, drug stores, departmental stores, apparel stores, boutiques besides the food courts and cinema complexes.

Retail Operations

Profit planning is an essential task of retail operations. A P&L Statement provides information on the revenue, expenditure and gross, net profit for a given period, usually an year, although companies do make monthly trial balance statements too. These need to include the following:

1. Net sales
2. Cost of goods sold

3. Gross profit
4. Operating expenses – including, salaries, advertising, supplies shipping, insurance, maintenanance
5. Taxes
6. Net profit after taxes

Retailers need to manage its assets and control liabilities. Assets are items owned with money value. Current assets are those items like cash, inventory that can be converted into cash easily.

The retailer is judged with the help of the ratios given below:

Net profit margin: It is calculated by dividing the net profit after taxes by net sales

Asset turnover is calculated by dividing the net sales by total assets

Return on assets is calculated by multiplying net profit margin with asset turnover

Financial leverage = total asset divided by net worth

Quick ratio is cash plus accounts receivable divided by total current liability

Current ratio is total current assets divided by total current liability

Account payable to net sales = account payable divided by annual net sales

Budgeting

1. Retailers need to have fine-tuned budgeting procedure as given below:
2. Expenses along with expected results, with rolling plan for costs as they may keep varying
3. Resources allocation
4. Department-wise expenditure
5. Futuristic view rather than remain reactive
6. Comparing with historicals, best in the industry or industry averages

Budgeting should take into account the capital investments, operating expenses, fixed costs and variable costs.

CHAPTER

9

Merchandising and Inventory Planning for Retail

Aims and Outcomes

Retail trade needs to invest in inventory in areas that make the biggest contribution to gross profit—while meeting customer expectations. Retail inventories are the most important area of retail management. A retail store is as good as its inventories.

Visual Merchandising

Merchandising involves acquiring the required goods, placing them with due prominence on the designated shelf, setting price for the goods that helps the retailer in reaching the goal that has been set. In large stores thousands of items are kept for sale. Retailers often try to keep complementary products that assist in each other's sales like, TV sets, DVD players. Merchandising or buying becomes a vital part of stores operation as the success of stores depends mainly on the products sold there.

Buying organization in a retail business could have a merchandising or purchase manager, with the requisite staff of buyers, local go-fors who run errands of making spot local purchases in emergency situations.

The stores managers are responsible for all the aspects of its operation including purchasing, inventory, displays and sales.

Stores keep certain regular sale items and an assortment of seasonal or trendy products. Innovations in merchandising takes the following route:

Researching the market segment to find if it is traditional or uninnovative in making purchases. New items and continuity depends on the initial thrust of sales and its PLC.

Trends of fashion products must be assessed to ensure their success. The store's brand equity; its image must be reflected in its product and brand range.

Competitive product range often plays a significant role in choice of the merchandise on offer. At times repeated requests by the target segment can force a store to stock a particular brand. Inventory turnover is a healthy sign of retail success and therefore dead items and products incongruous with the store's image need to be deleted from its list

Retailers have to consider their competitors, segment customers requirements, image intensifier products, and products suited to stores location. Profitability, brand strengths and customer service standards are other key success factors for the store. Mostly the retail believes that they are aware of their customers needs towards the benefits they seek from the product and many times they are wrong. It is best to have continuous surveys organized to keep updated on this vital issue. For example, washing powder sellers believe that it is sold for the whiteness of clothes washed by it. The fact could reveal that the powder sells because it does not damage the skin of washing person's hands.

Large stores sell national brands while local retailers could well be selling local brands. Certain large stores develop their own brands and these are sold in consonance with the retailer's brand image.

Large stores keep several brands of one product, known as product category. These categories help the stores in improving better salespersons productivity since the salesperson can offer a variety of brands from where the buyer can choose his favourite brand. Retail outlets having several brands in each category must take the following into account:

Category display should reflect the customer choice in priority.

Category selection should be defined with time they get sold, available space and product utility.

Category salesperson, however must encourage the buyers to look beyond the category once they have made the purchase so that other products and category products too get sold. Category managers should not have a one-sided view of selling their product only.

Category management remains a dynamic, fluid type of decision-making process that overviews the marketing of the entire brand sales within the category.

Category management needs to create consumer value by designing display of several brands from the category. It should not just be for retailer and multi-manufacturer relationship where the retailer tries to please all the different manufacturers by giving each of them shelf space without thinking about the buyers.

Category plans need to be based on trading area demand and preference scenario.

The best way to organize category sales is to have a market survey prior to setting up the sales of different brands of the category.

While the manufacturer is interested in gaining business from the retail sales catchment area the retailer's interest is to increase store's sales and profitability from the different brands of the category.

Category brand sales comparison is made by taking the floor space occupied by the brands and yearly sales. Area-wise profits, return on investment and inventory turnover give the retailer planning tools for each category and their brands.

Manufacturers think that the retailers have become partners in business as the last point of sale in the distribution channel chain. Manufacturers need to provide marketing training and promotional inputs to the retailers in their own interest as the competition is sure to exploit the situation in the absence of such efforts. The retailer, manufacturer partnership requires timely product demand, demand projections to be given by the retailer to the manufacturers.

Manufacturers' task is to gather data about consumer behaviour and provide the input to the retailer. Manufacturers should have clearly defined support plans for the retailers without any ambiguity and these need to be transparent. Manufacturers would normally initiate those plans that favour their brands. Management software is now available for enhancing these interactions between the manufacturers and the retailers.

Retailers' interaction with the goods suppliers is given below:

Manufacturers produce and supply goods, can provide shipping, credit, insurance to the retailers

Wholesalers buy from the manufacturers, can do unbulking, repacking, credit, shipping, storing before dispatch to the retailer.

Agents and brokers do not stock the goods. They only obtain supply order from the retailers and pass them on to the manufacturers for supply for which they get commission.

Purchasing the merchandise requires the following steps:

1. Information about the needs of products and services of the target segment customers
2. Selecting the products to be purchased
3. Locating and interacting with the suppliers, who could be the manufacturers or the distributors, evaluating their products, negotiating and placing the order
4. Receiving, stocking, inventory updating
5. Reordering on minimum stock level
6. Retesting customer preference

When the retailers purchase directly from manufacturers they get, mostly fresh stocks, may get transport facility and credit. Large departmental stores or shoping malls offer retail space or counters to manufacturers desirous of having their own presense in the mall. This adds to the range of products, service to the customers, authenticity of goods for the customers.

Wholesalers carry wide range of products while some can offer credit and transportation as well.

Retailers must take into account the following before selecting their suppliers:

1. Reliability of supplies in quantity, quality and time frame.
2. Exclusivity of supplies
3. Offer of transport of goods, insurance, speedy complaint redressal, credit.
4. Providing service if the product requires it, or training retail staff in service, selling the products
5. Adequacy of profit margins, is their an MRP, if yes level of commission offered. If there is no MRP, then the markup possibilities
6. Local advertisement to be carried out by the supplier, or jointly with the retailer

7. Level of investment retailer has to make in dealing with the supplier and the risk of stock outs and inferior quality of prodct and related service

Retail business can get risks from thefts from employees, shoppers during working hours and also when the store is closed. Therefore, adequate security arrangements, including keeping security guards, electronic securities systems have become a must in the present scenario.

First it is good to know the types of retail outlets available in the country:

1. General merchants shops—local area shops
2. Single brand shops—like Bata, Usha
3. Multi-brand shops
4. Supermarkets
5. Multiplexes
6. Shopping malls

The inventory levels for these shops depend on the following:

1. Variety of goods
2. Different brands for each product
3. Segment of market the shops deal in
4. Volume of business expected
5. Delivery time for getting inventory replenishments
6. Inventory costs

Variety of goods: Retail stores take the demand and supply route for deciding the variety of goods they need to store. For example, a grocery store may find demand of gift items coming from its customers and open a counter for the same. In most shopping areas, there are more than one retail store and each store has to have a niche market segment or sub-segment that it needs to cater to. The shop's façade itself speaks of its clientele. If the shop is upmarket then its product range will be exclusively for its affluent customers, who expect the best product and the price remains a non-debatable point. Following is a partial list of goods sold in retail shops:

1. Food items, cooked variety and raw
2. Cosmetics
3. Toiletries
4. Pots and pans
5. Gift items
6. Medicines

There are exclusive shops for hardware items, paints, sanitary fittings, furniture, petrol and diesel (also known as petrol pumps). Each retail outlet has to decide about the range that sells, products that could be complimentary or even supplementary.

Complimentary products are among others, tubes and tyres; soft furnishings, curtains; TV sets and music systems.

Supplementary products are, among others, shoes and socks and laces, food add-on, like pickles, jams, butter.

Retail Visual Merchandising

Merchandising plays an important role in retail business.

Imagine a retail outlet selling petroleum products. Such retail outlets are also known as petrol pumps. The pumps are so designed that they attract the motorists' attention from quite a distance because of the following reasons:

There is a large enough sign on the edge of the road with the company's logo, proclaiming from a distance that the company's retail outlet is located at the place.

One-company buildings are of same type and design all over the country with it outside colour scheme and façade.

Outer signage of the pumps giving information about their product range is also same.

The actual location of petrol or diesel pumps inside the compound may differ due to the site, but they provide for easy ingress and egress to the motoring public.

The salesroom interior, point of purchase advertising is of same design placed at same locations. Tyres, batteries and accessories sold are also placed and displayed in similar fashion. Colour schemes of the exteriors and interiors are selected for their aesthetic appeals and durability. These also help in persistence of visual exposure of the visitors that triggers memories of happy visits to the outlets.

Furthermore, the colour scheme, similarity of real estate usage gives a continuity of visage to the motorists that, with the help of stored mental memory helps them in easy brand recall and identification.

Summarizing, the perfect multi-retail outlet company like an oil company should plan to have outlet clones all over for easy recognition by the motorists, starting from the outer colour schemes, to signage that draw the driver's attention on the road. McDonald restaurant chain is a typical example of proper merchandising.

Merchandising and Retail Marketing

Retail marketing needs to deliver a comprehensive array of store-level support services that help grocery retailers maximize sales through highly innovative merchandising and marketing strategies.

Expertise in Category Management (Category Management can be defined as management of one line of products, the best example is from Lever Brothers where there are category managers from soaps and the brand managers of different soap brands report to the Soap Category Manager.) is no longer a luxury in the grocery industry. It is now a necessity. Category management services help grocer customers—the channel members, address fierce competition and consumers by enhancing existing merchandising practices with superior consumer insight. Aesthetics, colour schemes, easy access to product for viewing, browsing or feeling become important parameters for merchandisers.

Category management provides grocers with the consumer category and competitive information they need to become or remain market leaders. Retail merchandising enhances consumer value, drives store profits and expands business opportunities.

Today's consumers are sophisticated, knowledgeable and highly fragmented. Product suppliers and retailers both are chasing consumers with extraordinary arrays of new products and categories and new store formats. Category management programme helps grocers determine the reasons behind purchasing behaviour, enhancing their ability to retain loyal shoppers and capture new ones. Today, a large number of retailers participate in the category management programme.

Category (like soaps, shampoos, cigarettes could belong to one category) management programme is a two-way partnership between its suppliers and retailers to manage product categories as strategic business units, turn consumers into satisfied customers and more effectively drive retail sales profitably.

Retail comprehensive programme is helping retailers meet their category management goals. In fact, retailers are obtaining results that equal or exceed industry averages for rupee-sales and unit-sales increases. Through the category management process, retailers help themselves as follows:

- Friendly item mix results in better management of retail inventory assets and improved speed-to-shelf for new items to achieve those important first-time sales.
- Create shelf layouts that increase consumer purchases while reducing retail out-of-stocks.
- Produce effective retail promotions that efficiently allocate promotion funds to drive sales and enhance profitability.
- Strategically price items to heighten consumer-perceived value while maintaining gross profit at retail.
- Create specific store strategies to address alternative-format competition and store layout recommendations to capture today's busy consumers.

Strategic pricing is widely used by retailers across the country to give them a competitive pricing edge. They integrate store data, base area pricing, competitive pricing and pricing best practices to improve sales and gross margin for the retailer. The result is better competitive positioning of the retailer versus the competition.

Grocery retailers today are increasingly losing market share to mass merchandisers, particularly in key centre-store product categories such as paper products and laundry detergents. As an extension of category management capabilities, retailers develop tested, effective merchandising strategies to counteract this trend and reclaim sales in centre-store categories.

Applying the principles of category management to key product categories, works with grocery retailers to assess which categories are most vulnerable to attack by mass merchants. Then comes the need to develop customized pricing and merchandising strategies to recapture lost categories and defend those that are potentially vulnerable.

According to industry research, a well-executed centre-store strategy can improve the average market basket, the store's Product Range. Today, more independent grocers, as well corporate retail stores, rely on centre-store strategy.

Retailer selling companies support grocery retailers with a comprehensive set of creative, advertising and promotional services that help build customer awareness, traffic, loyalty and store sales. The goal of advertising and sales promotion group is to be the most effective marketing communications resource—and the most cost efficient—for our affiliated retailers, regardless of store size or format. They focus on developing sound marketing plans around defined goals to achieve measurable results.

New retailing approaches have emerged as old formats have vanished. We have the Home Shopping Network and Internet shopping. Twenty-five years ago the major retail firms and formats were just a dream in an entrepreneur's head. Today retailers use state-of-the-art computers and communication technologies to respond quickly to changing consumer demand. Changes in the retail industry have brought about many new and varied career opportunities worldwide for college graduates interested in this highly competitive, exciting and profitable field.

Career-Opportunities

Retailers undertake a wide variety of activities. They raise capital from financial institutions; purchase goods and services; develop accounting and management information systems to control operations; manage warehouses and distribution systems; design and develop new products; predict and act upon fashion trends; and undertake activities such as advertising, promotion, sales force management and market research. Retail firms worldwide offer opportunities for people with a wide variety of skills and education.

Graduates of the retail merchandising programme hold positions such as buyers, store managers, visual merchandise directors, regional managers, store owners, interior merchandisers and fashion coordinators. Many stores limit their management positions to employees who have completed a four-year degree. Often, recruiters consider the degree a minimum requirement for a management and/or buying career.

Positions available in the apparel and textiles retail field are diverse; therefore, this option provides you with an educational background, which can fit into both short- and long-range career goals. The course of study includes classes on buying and merchandising, global retailing, retail market management, merchandise promotion, financial management and control, fashion economics, human behaviour related to apparel selection decisions and the analysis of textile and apparel products using textile testing equipment.

Students choose to focus on the area of textile product or interior merchandising. The textile product merchandising focus includes courses such as sewn product manufacturing and analysis, history of fashion, product development, dress and human behaviour. The interior merchandising focus includes courses such as history of interiors, design process and interior graphics; knowledge needed to enter retail interior careers.

A minor in business administration provides a general business background, which prepares students for in-depth work in the retail-merchandising field of study. Overall good grades are required to take business administration courses. A strong general education curriculum assists students in learning critical thinking skills. Computer technology is an intrinsic aspect of the program.

A creative display can draw the customer in, promote a slow-moving product, announce a sale, or welcome a season. Some stores located in a mall or other structure may lack windows, but don't despair. There are many places throughout the store to build beautiful displays.

The supply chain for the retail industry is extremely complex with rapid inventory cycles. In order to efficiently make it through inventory without waste, retail labelling technology must be flexible enough to support more than just bar coding alone.

Bar coding and text is effective at the checkout stand with a scanner, but is completely useless in the actual inventory location and decision cycles. Products in demand that are in stock regularly get mixed up in a mass of similar inventory, resulting in unsold products and diminishing revenue.

From using colours to discriminate sizes on clothing tags, to using colours to differentiate pharmaceutical drug types, colour-coding simply makes it quick and easy to locate the item you or your customers are looking for without using a scanner or having to read a single line of text.

It is important to create high-end graphic packaging and merchandising products that are not only attractive, but also communicate the brand message to consumers.

1. The company can plan a unique collection of printing and structural design capabilities that are unrivaled in the packaging industry. The company can also consider award-winning graphic artists, dedicated customer service, and a full line of package designs, and contract packaging services, it is easy to see why many of the most successful consumer goods manufacturers plan their packaging and display needs with care.
2. Point-of-Purchase Displays
3. Corrugated Retail Packaging
4. Paperboard Folding Cartons
5. Pack 'N' Stack
6. Point-of-Sale Materials
7. Contract Packaging

The mobile retail display unit can be specifically designed to cater for companies wanting to target passing trade in shopping malls, public areas or similar retail environments.

With the ability to tailor the retail display unit to suit an individual company's corporate identity and colour scheme, the retail merchandising unit needs to be unique and versatile.

There are variable levels of security from locking glass doors to alarmed roller shutters:

1. A choice of either downlights or spotlights
2. Full or part glass showcase and/or with slat wall with shelves and fittings

Range of expertise in stores management should cover the gamut from marketing and advertising plan development, to grand opening and event marketing solutions, to website development as follows:

- Retail strategy products
- New store format strategy
- New market strategy
- Media planning
- Creative strategy development
- Marketing planning
- Advertising production
- Point-of-sale material development
- Marketing communications training
- In-store marketing communications
- Communications and media relations support
- Website development and management

Catching-Consumers

Consumers are sophisticated, knowledgeable and a highly fragmented lot. Product suppliers and retailers alike are chasing consumers with superior array of new products and categories and new store formats. Category management helps grocers determine the reasons behind purchasing behaviour, enhancing their ability to retain core buyers and capture new ones. Category management programme is a two-way partnership between suppliers and retailers to manage product categories as strategic business units, to turn consumers into satisfied customers and effectively steer retail sales.

Comprehensive programme is made for helping retailers meet their category management goals. In fact, retailers are realizing results that equal or exceed industry averages for sales increases. Through the category management process, the following help can be provided:

1. Build a consumer-friendly product mix depending on the stores' clientele resulting in better management of retail inventory assets and improved speed-to-shelf for new items to gather the important first-time sales.
2. Better point of purchase advertising formats, including old world items like danglers, posters, to modern-day robotic guides, in-house CCTV for spot product advertising.
3. Unique window displays with robotic mannequins, eye-catching colour backgrounds, and running colourful fountains.
4. Total store display solutions, including store shelves, display units
5. Brand and logo selection, displays to build corporate brand identity
6. Retail graphic displays, including store floor graphics
7. Store front signage
8. Product package design to suit the store shelves
9. Environment signage
10. Plan shelf layouts that increase consumer purchases while reducing retail out-of-stocks.
11. Organize effective retail promotions that efficiently allocate promotion funds to drive sales and enhance profitability.
12. Arrange to price items to heighten consumer-perceived value while maintaining gross profit at retail.

13. Plan store specific strategies to address alternative format competition and store layout recommendations to capture busy consumers.
14. Plan children's activity corner to enable elders shop with ease

Students studying apparel and textiles can make themselves marketable for a variety of careers in retailing fields by following the retail merchandising curriculum. Retail merchandising is such a part of everyday life people often take it for granted, but it is one of the fastest changing, most dynamic industries in the world today.

New retailing approaches have emerged as old formats have vanished. Sears catalogue is gone but in its place are category specialists retail merchandising unit, which clearly demonstrates its ability to create diverse retail display solutions using the modular system.

The mobile retail display unit is specifically designed to cater for companies wanting to target passing trade in shopping malls, public areas or similar retail environments.

Basic Design

First, retailers need to select a theme for the display. All display items should enhance that theme. If an item doesn't fit, save it for another display.

Popular themes include holiday celebrations, tropical islands and romance. Display items can come from many different sources, even those outside the pool and spa industry. One of most effective displays included yard signs, sarongs, beach bags, glitter sunscreen, cheese spreaders and patio torches.

Use of colour is helpful in attracting customers toward the products on display. To avoid a busy-looking display, it is best to achieve unified coloration throughout. This doesn't mean every item has to be the same colour; instead, pick out a few colours from the merchandise that can be used to accentuate the main chosen shade.

Creating the Mood

After choosing the concept for the display, you need to develop an action plan to pull it all together with the following basic checklist for display:

* Inventory: You should plan to have enough merchandise on hand to restock the display at least twice. If you sell the centrepiece (the main item) right away, and don't have another to replace it, your display will be rendered ineffectual in an instant.
* Location: Where do you want this display to be placed? Keep in mind, all stores have dead spots where merchandise may flounder. Make sure you dedicate the best space in your showroom for products with the chance for highest profit. Remember, most stores keep candies, chocolates at low level for young children to be able to see them without any effort and then ask the parents to buy the same.
* Space: Determine the approximate floor or counter space the display will need. Spa fragrances may not need the same amount of space as pool-cleaning equipment. Planning ahead will keep the area from looking too crowded or bare. You don't want people tripping over your display!

* Placement: Decide if the display should be free-standing, on a fixture or wall mounted. Each type has special appeal. An interesting gimmick used is "suspending the product from the ceiling with the help of invisible strong threads".
* Fixtures: Are they appropriate and adequate for the theme? Barbecues look great on natural wood, but not so great on industrial-looking metal shelves. It is better to price everything on the display, including the fixtures and accessories. You would be amazed at what will sell.
* Timing: Are the products seasonal? A patriotically themed display might be used not only on the National days like 15th August, 26th January, 2nd October but a few days before and after the day. These displays should be removed to give way to the displays from the next theme.
* Rotation: Sometimes just moving a display by a quarter-turn will make customers take notice of the product. Before giving up on a display that has not produced sales, move it to another spot in the store. You may be surprised to see your sales soar.
* Freshen: Keep displays well stocked and clean. A sparsely stocked, dirty display is as appealing as yesterday's eggshells. Would they sell?

Remember, not every display will be a masterpiece, so don't become attached to even the best one. If, after following the above plan, you encounter poor sales results, be flexible enough to tear it apart and start over with a new one. If you have a pre-planned display always, you'll have road blocks in the path of sales.

Inventory Planning

Inventory planning is a critical component to replenishment of stocks. Strategy inventory planning can be deployed to implement distribution resource planning, vendor managed inventory, efficient consumer response management system or just-in-time inventory management techniques through balancing cash flow objectives and customer service needs. Comprehensive simulation facilities are used to compare both the financial and service impacts of any policy changes. The following need to be considered in this regard:

1. Managing safety stocks
2. Inventory minimums and maximums
3. Inventory turnarounds
4. Replenishment frequency
5. Order size
6. Seasonal build or manufacturing plans

Inventory planning should help the retailers in the following manner:

- Make effective inventory decisions via real-time sales simulations and quantitative decision support
- Exploit inventory investment through in-depth inventory management techniques
- Meet or exceed customer service level objectives through synchronization of stock levels with forecast accuracy.

- Inventory plans help the company to invest in inventory in areas that make the biggest contribution to gross profit—while meeting customer expectations. Inventory planning calculates time-phased safety stocks and replenishment quantities for each item at each location, synchronizing demand patterns, forecasts and inventory throughout your demand and supply chains.
- Inventory planning is critical to replenishment of stocks. Strategy inventory planning can be deployed to implement distribution resource planning, vendor managed inventory, efficient consumer response or just-in-time inventory management techniques through balancing financial objectives and customer service priorities. Comprehensive simulation facilities are used to compare both the financial and service impacts of any policy changes
- Whether you are managing safety stock, inventory minimums and maximums, inventory turnarounds, replenishment frequency and order size, seasonal build or manufacturing plans, inventory planning enhances collaboration at every level of the business.

Inventory planning helps you in the following areas:

- Make effective inventory decisions via real-time simulation and decision support
- Exploit inventory investment through depth in inventory management techniques
- Meet or exceed customer service level objectives through synchronization with forecast accuracy

Material Planning has the following external factors that need to be taken into account:

- National economy—GNP, GDP. Per capita Income: Interest rates have a direct bearing on sale of most products, other than essential food products. Hence, sales forecasts of finished goods need to take them into account.
- Price trends: With increase in competition, prices take a beating and at times price wars start. Companies can avoid getting into such price wars by creating better brand equity, merchandising and supply chain management.
- Credit policy: It is well known that a credit buyer tends to buy more. As marketers it is useful to take advantage of this human trait of character.
- Taxes—direct, indirect: Since taxes are paid at the time of purchase the money gets blocked. Just in time purchase plans are, therefore, a great help in reducing current assets and keeping more working capital available for other activities.
- Foreign Exchange Regulations: Since FERA got changed to FEMA the users of foreign currency find themselves in more friendly FE regime, with little interference from the government and the suspicion that all businessmen are cheats have been finally lifted.
- Import policy: With liberalized import policy exporters are finding it much easier to import their needs of foreign items required in manufacturing the export products.
- International market: With global economy companies need to assert their presence in the international markets.

- Business cycle: Product life cycle, seasonality of product demand and production time need to conform to the market situation and only then can companies adhere to the "order fulfilment" plans.

Material planning has the following internal factors that need to be considered:

- Objectives
- Technology
- Demand-supply
- Lead time for supplies
- Rejection rates
- Working capital
- Inventory plans
- Storage facilities
- Distance from source
- Information data
- Delegation of power
- Communication system
- Stocking policy of management
- Buyer-seller relationship
- Financial position
- Company's brand equity

There are following three methods of material planning:

- For direct materials
- For indirect materials
- ABC analysis

Methods for high value A type materials are as follows:

- Bill of materials explosion charts
- Material requirement planning
- Inventory control

For B and C type material of low value materials method is given below:

- Inventory control

For indirect materials the methods are given below:

- Past consumption analysis
- Exponential smoothening
- Inventory control

Material for inventory is calculated as given below:

- Bill of materials
- Bought out items

- Raw materials for in-house made parts
- Quantity per unit manufacture – Q
- Total Requirement – Q × production quantity + adjustment for rejection rate
- When final product is complex – several subassemblies have common parts
- High lead time
- Long manufacturing cycle
- Known demand of costly products
- Gross requirement of finished products – age analysis of pending orders
- Time bound sales forecast
- Net requirement – gross minus FGS inventory
- Master production schedule
- Explode bill of materials for gross requirements
- Different products to make in a given time
- For each assembly structured BOM – gross requirements
- Screen B and C items
- Net requirement of items
- Adjust rejection rate
- Aggregate requirement – order quantity
- Place orders
- Follow upon orders placed
- Past consumption analysis technique of indirect materials – tools, oils
- Moving average method
- Recent demand
- Trend of demand
- Seasonal variations and not random variations

Statistical Method of Demand

- Trend of past sales – old data + rolling average for a constant number of periods
- Discard old figures as new ones come in
- Selection of period important – larger period better smoothening effect

Needs of inventory management is given below:

- Anticipated normal demand
- Bulk purchase discounts
- Coping with emergency shortages
- Production process needs – cooling time
- Wastages
- Minus point over ordering

Inventory Costs

- Ordering costs – administrative costs transportation costs
- Stock costs – capital, insurance, security, going bad, rents
- Stock-out costs – cost of loss of production

Inventory Control

- Lead time
- Economic order quantity – EOQ
- Economic batch quantity – EBQ
- Safety stock
- Maximum stock
- Reorder level
- Reorder quantity
- Periodic review system – review and replenish

Basic Inventory Model

- Assumes demand is constant
- Ordering cost is constant and independent of quantity
- Only one type of stock item
- EOQ = Square root of 2×D×C1divided by Ch
- EOQ = 2×D×C1/ch
- D-annual demand
- C1-order cost
- Ch-holding cost per item
- Number of orders per year = D/EOQ
- Length of cycle in days = number of days in year/number of orders in year
- Average inventory level = EOQ/2

Adopted Model

- Stock subject to gradual replenishment
- Economic batch quantity EBQ = 2×DC1/Ch×(1-D/R)
- D-annual demand
- C1-setup cost per cycle
- Ch-holding cost per item
- R-annual production rate

CHAPTER

10

Retail Pricing Strategies

Aims and Outcomes

The exchange value called price of a product is influenced by competitive forces, its own brand equity, company's goals and demand patterns. Value of a product is perceived worth of the product in the buyers' opinion and it reflects the exchange value between manufacturer and the consumer. Price fixation takes the following into account:

1. Cost to make
2. Product demand and supply situation
3. Company's goals
4. Business environment
5. Product brand image

In retail trade retailers tend to keep fixed prices with no room for bargaining. They offer the MRP–Maximum Retail Price fixed by the manufacturers. However, due to severe competition in retail trade they try two methods for meeting competitive forces as given below:

Let the customer bargain even on MRP. This, however, is risky because no matter what is the ultimate price paid the customer always feels cheated. Perhaps he did not bargain enough.

Some retailers keep low price with no extra or frills being provided that target the price conscious customers who buy on the basis of lower price only these retailers work on high turnover basis with low margins of profit.

Middle-class buyers prefer average pricing with good well laid out store and good service. Moderate profits better quality products and satisfied customers are the important facets of such retailers. They keep getting pushed by the discount stores offering low prices. It is only the superior service which keeps them going with as loyal band of customers.

Upmarket buyers are not too much concerned about the price as long as they get superior service at the stores. They cater to the elitist class even if the actual buyer coming from such families is their domestic servant only.

Retail pricing is affected by the following factors:

1. Cost to manufacture
2. Brand equity
3. Government taxes
4. Current and potential competitors

Retailer can decide their pricing formula by remaining consistent in their price fixation plan. They convey a strong message to the buyers that they can come to the shop and not get cheated by bargains that do not tell the real story and keeps the buyer in utter confusion if after all he has been deceived. Seasonal pricing is one option taken by most retailers which allows them keep their stocks moving even in dull seasons. High level of customer service given free contributes to a strict pricing regime. However, penetrating prices can be used to keep potential competitors from entering the market.

Price-quality parity and association lets retailers keep skimming prices that get tagged with the product superior quality. Such prices meet the prestige value attached to the product in buyers conscious or sub-conscious mind.

Retailers have to opt for price stability, flexibility in pricing, bargain pricing and customer based pricing, where price gets dovetailed as per the customer's previous credentials as a buyer. Bata company uses odd value pricing like 199 rupee to create a level of misconception about the price being lower than it actually is.

The retailers keep a separate bargain counter where the products sold are subject to customer bargaining. This helps them to have fixed prices for most of their products sold. Mostly the odd sizes, unsold goods and a few good products are kept there to entice customers to the bargain counters are kept.

In the pre-industrial revolution era, the tribe cantered political entities believed in barter system as means of commerce in which two tribes swapped their produce as per the value each had for each other's products.

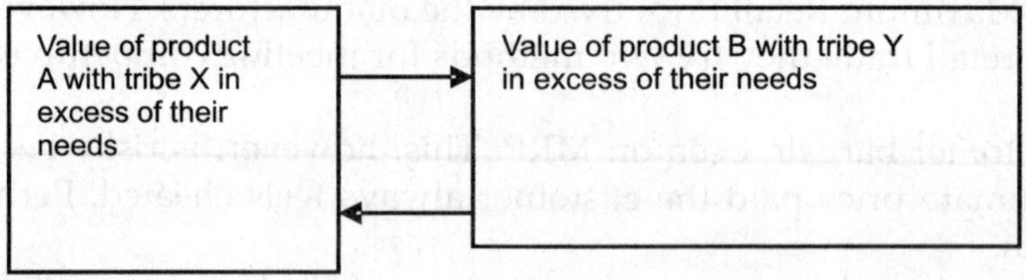

For example, if tribe X has excess of cotton and tribe Y has excess of wheat they would exchange the products to satisfy their respective needs.

Then started the industrial revolution with mass production techniques. The result was search for emerging markets for the products, which were in far flung in area. Need for money was felt and it gave commerce the much-needed fillip. Now people could buy and sell products as per their requirements of a larger variety of things.

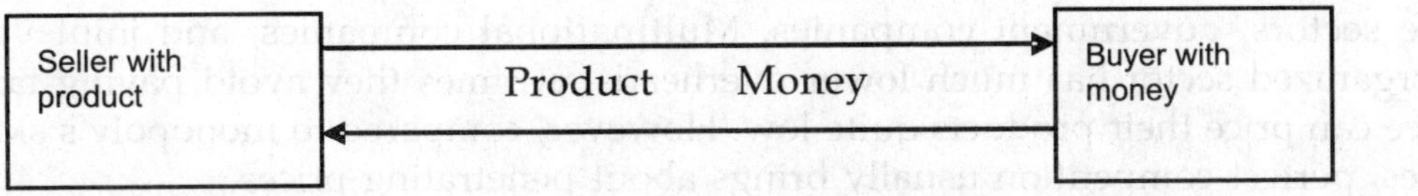

Till that time there were only a few manufacturers of a product and competition was not known as a business reality. With industrial revolution came the affluence in the society and demand for most products started increasing. With increase in demand came competition. Today, we see the competition as a multi-headed dragon swallowing up lesser products or brands or poorly managed firms.

Product pricing in highly competitive world has assumed unprecedented importance in the management of markets for firms' profitability.

Following are the elements considered while prices are fixed:

- Production cost
- Profit plans
- Brand image or equity
- Seasonality of business
- Market segment
- Competition
- Product life cycle stage
- Guarantee/warranty offered
- Payment methods and terms
- Discounts/special offers
- Range of products with the firm
- Product launches
- Product value and utility for the customers

There are usually three types of market situations and each gives pricing opportunities in different ways:

1. Monopoly market
2. Oligopoly market
3. Perfect competition

In case of monopoly, there is only one supplier of the product and in such cases the firm has the following options-

1. Charge premium price or keep skimming price
2. Keep cost plus, pricing

In oligopoly situations, there are just a few suppliers, say four to five. In such cases, customer's purchasing power governs the price. In some cases, the firms join hands to form price cartels with a view of keeping prices high of all the firms. In many countries, including India, cartel formation is considered illegal.

Perfect competition means having a large number of suppliers of the product. These could be of same type and size or could belong to different categories like the small-scale unorganized sector or large-scale organized sector. In between there are medium scale sectors, government companies, Multinational companies, and joint ventures. Unorganized sector has much lower overheads, at times they avoid paying taxes and hence can price their products quite low. However, compared to monopoly's skimming prices, perfect competition usually brings about penetrating prices.

Hence, the first price formula could be shown as follows:

Selling price = *a f* (manufacturing cost + profit), where *a* is the effect of competition on price and *f* denotes function.

With competition becoming severe, its role in pricing has increased which can be shown as given below:

Selling price = *b f* (competition), where *b* represents the manufacturing cost and *f* denotes function.

Let us consider products made for industry, i.e., business-to-business sale product. In most of these cases the price is negotiated between the seller and the buyer. For products for mass consumption, with mass production techniques, costs can be brought down and lower price can be the result. Products for mass consumption are becoming brand managed and customers brand conscious. Firms put higher prices on their products than competition and still keep their market share for the following reasons:

- Better brand equity
- Better distribution network
- Loyal customers
- Complete range of products
- Better service to customers
- Differentiated product
- Better delivery periods
- Better payment terms
- Comprehensive longer guarantee and warranty
- Better value for money
- Better sales team
- Tailor-made products or customization of products

It must be clearly understood that the customers don't pay for the product alone. They pay for the value or the benefit the product is going to provide them. It is the customer's perception of product's value to them, which justifies the price.

Price and product quality gets firmly established in the minds of the customers and many times, lowering of prices to increase market share becomes counterproductive as the customers feel that there has been a lowering of quality in the product which has caused the price reduction.

The price, which is fixed for a new product, is based on the following:

- Price of competitive product, if any
- Cost of manufacture
- Market segment for the product
- Product position in the marketplace
- Hierarchy of distribution network, it determines the total sales commission to be paid to the channel members
- Product itself, its uniqueness as compared to competition

As soon as competition forces its way in the market the firm has to decide to have one of the following price methods:

For top quality product: Skimming price or top price, this will place the product in the elitist market segment and generate good profits.

For top quality product: Medium price, this will give good, value for money to the customers and place the product in select market.

For top quality product: Low price or penetrating price, which would place the product for the lower end of the segment and increase firm's market share, it will act as entry barrier for new players.

For medium quality product: Top or skimming price would provide extra profits, as also it will invite competition.

For medium quality product: Medium price will give the customers value for money and place the product in select market segment.

For medium quality product: Low or penetrating price would place the product in lower end of the segment, give value for money and increase market share and profitability and increase barriers for new entrants.

For low quality product: Top or skimming price would work only during monopoly regime, otherwise, it will lower market share and invite competition.

For low quality product: Medium price will place the product in select market segment and invite competition.

For low quality product: Low or penetrating price would place the product in lower end of the market segment, increase market share and become price barrier for entry of new players.

Hence, looking at the quality of the product, its position in the life cycle, and market share, pricing strategy has to be evolved by the firm. Firms must understand the price-demand pattern for the product based on the selected market segment/s. The demand and price ratio varies with products; in some the demand remains inelastic irrespective of price while for some products even a slight change in product price changes the demand pattern drastically. The change in demand also depends on the market segment being catered to, by the product. It can be seen that the demand of high end products like Mercedes does not change with increase or decrease of price.

Mercedes car, air travel first class, five star hotel rooms and some of the essential items of daily needs like food, the demand remains near constant with price changes as given below:

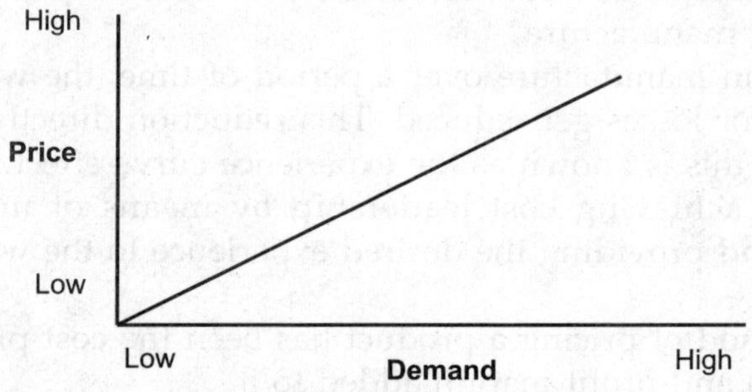

For products like consumer durables refrigerators, ovens, fans the price is a major factor in purchase decisions.

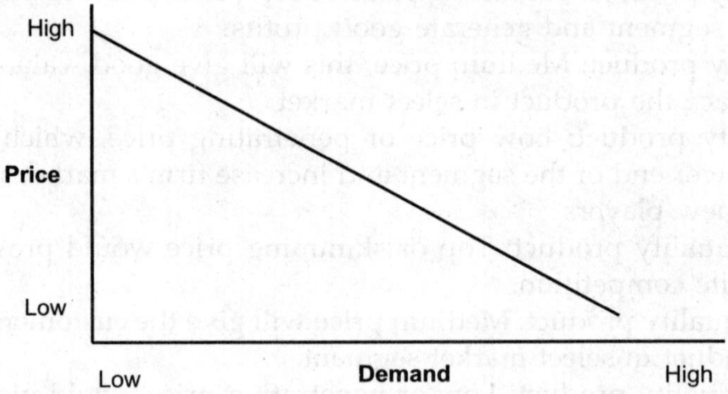

For products, which can show unique features, have not many known substitutes, have low maintenance costs are less *price* sensitive.

As cost of manufacture does affect the final price let us discuss of what the cost is made of. There are fixed costs, the overheads and variable costs, which constitute the total manufacturing cost. Fixed costs remain unchanged with the volume of production, like the interest the firm pays the salaries, power, and telephone and rental bills. In fact, even if there is no manufacture these payments have to be made. Variable costs depend on the volume of production like the cost of material, labour. (Total cost = fixed cost + variable cost).

Suppose for manufacturing 5,000 computers, the fixed cost is rupees 30 million and variable cost rupees 20 million then the total cost would be as given below:

Total cost for 5,000 computers = (30 + 20) = 50 million rupees

Fixed cost works out to rupees 6,000 and variable cost rupees 4,000 per computer.

Fixed cost per computer = 3000,0000/5,000 = Rs. 6,000

Variable cost per computer = 2000,0000/5,000 = Rs. 4,000

Total cost per computer = Rs. 6,000 + 4,000 = Rs. 10,000

Let us see what happens when the firm doubles the production to 10,000

The fixed cost gets reduced as now the total fixed cost is divided by10,000 as follows:

Fixed cost = Rs. 3000,0000/10,000 = Rs. 3,000

The fixed cost therefore gets reduced as the production increases. This is known as economies of scale of manufacture.

With experience in manufacture over a period of time, the workers improve their skills and human error losses get reduced. This reduction directly reflects in lowering of variable costs and this is known as the experience curve effect.

Firms strive for achieving cost leadership by means of manufacturing as per economies of scale and providing the desired experience to the workers.

Pricing formulae –

The original method of pricing a product has been the cost plus method in which, the total cost is taken and profit margin added to it.

Suppose the unit variable cost of manufacturing a bicycle = Rs. 300
Fixed cost = Rs. 3000,000
Sales planned = 100,000
Total unit cost = variable cost + fixed cost/sales = Rs. 300 + 3,000 000/100000
= Rs. 330

If the sellers wants a ten per cent mark up then the selling price of the bicycle would be as follows:

unit cost/ 1- mark-up or, Rs. 330/ 1- 0.1 = 330/ 0.9 = Rs. 367 per bicycle

Too high pricing is in danger of having no sales as also inviting new competition, while too low a price may give sales volumes, but no profit at all. Hence, pricing needs careful planning. Sellers want that they should, even in most severe competitive conditions should not lose money at least on regular basis.

They look for getting a minimum of breakeven sales volume:

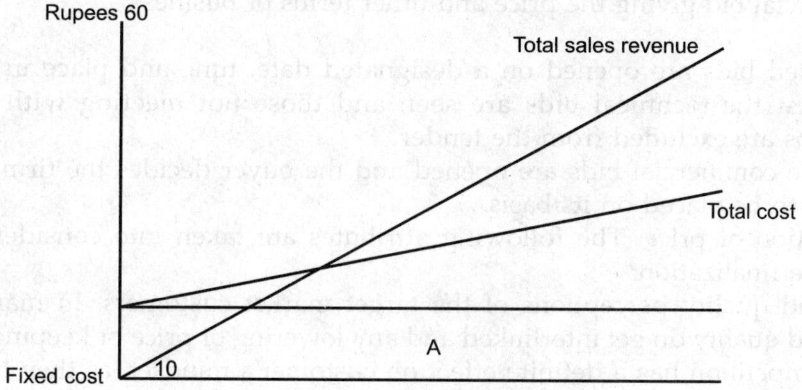

Sales in units (1000)

A is the break-even point where the seller gets, at least the costs, both fixed and variable and that is the minimum the firm would like to sell in the first instance.

Today, the pricing has become more a function of fighting competition than ever before. It is, besides competitors, the customers who are guiding factors in price fixation. The customers view a product and its price on the following parameters:

- Brand name of the product/brand equity
- Product quality as perceived by the customer
- Uniqueness of the product
- Ease of availability of the product
- The product range: Is it a single product offering from the firm or is it a product range
- Ease of usage of the product
- Availability of after-sales service: Speed and quality of service
- Product price in totality: Including price of consumables, loss due to downtime and price of accessories

Firms resort to penetrating pricing in order to increase their market share. Following the leader, other competitors also bring down the prices. Hence, the advantage of lower price is only short lived, which brings the original market share out of the firms back, but for minor changes. It, however, leaves a lasting dent on the profit picture of the firm. This factor has been, at least in oligopoly conditions, responsible for formation of price cartels, formal, if allowed by the government or informal if not allowed by the government. These cartels help firms to keep skimming or higher prices for their product, without losing business to competition. Besides the government regulations, the other danger of cartels is the distinct possibility of more competitors joining the race.

In case of government customers, mostly, sealed tenders are invited from the manufacturers/sellers of the product. In tender business, the firms have, normally to send two different offers as follows:

1. Technical bid giving the product's technical specifications, capabilities and conformance to the specifications needed by the buyer
2. Commercial bid giving the price and other terms of business

The sealed bids are opened on a designated date, time and place in front of the bidders. First the technical bids are seen and those not meeting with the desired specifications are excluded from the tender.

Next, the commercial bids are opened and the buyer decides the firm/s on which the order is to be placed on its basis.

Finalization of price: The following attributes are taken into consideration at the time of price finalization:

- Price and quality perceptions of the target market customers. In many products, price and quality do get interlinked and any lowering of price or keeping price lower than competition has a definite effect on customer's mindset, as they believe lower price could mean lesser quality product too.
- Brand equity
- Advertising penetration and effect on the customers
- Price of other products of the firm in relative terms of their importance to the customers.
- International prices could depend on the relative balance of payment situation with a particular country, currency exchange rates and tariffs. (It would be of interest to the students to know that during the existence of the USSR, India's trade with it was known as rupee trade, as both the countries were short of hard currency, the dollars. Needless to add that the USSR had no need of our rupee and we had none of their money, it was in true sense a barter arrangement where each country could sell to the other some useful but mostly useless items to the other country).
- It could also be in two parts, one barter and the other could be cash payment

Summarizing, it can be said that the firms need to have information on competition and the customer's psychology before the price can be fixed correctly. As the markets are dynamic entities, pricing mechanism also has to be kept in readiness for changes as per market needs and firms own objectives.

As most consumer and several industrial products are sold through distribution channels, their price must take into account the margins to be offered to the channel members or their possible mark-ups, if they are given one price by the manufacturer and asked to add their profits or mark-up on to the price. Hence the retail price could be made up of the following:

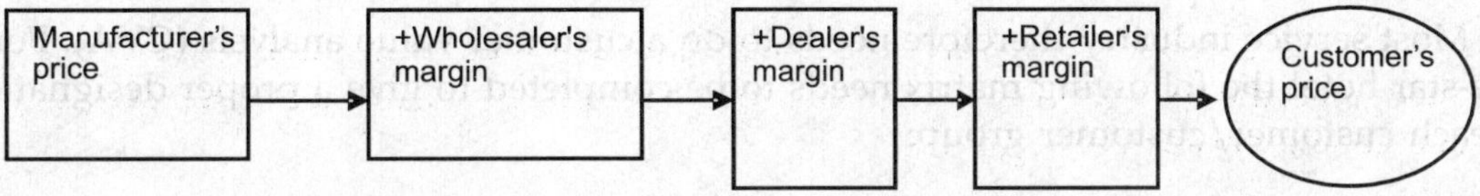

When the firm offers its price to the customer as maximum retail price, it includes the margin of the channel members, which could be as shown above or different. Besides, the firm's offer, cash discounts if the channel members pay cash. Discounts on offer could be the following:

- Cash discount on cash purchases
- Turnover discounts given on the basis of the channel member achieving a given and accepted turnover in product sale.
- Inventory clearing discount is given when the firm has large inventory and the discount acts as incentive for the dealer to buy more.
- Quantity discount is offered for purchase of a minimum specified quantity.
- Advertising subsidy is actually the money given as share of common advertising by the firm and the channel member.
- Off-season discount for buying the product when it is not needed like buying woollens during summers and air-conditioners during winters. (In fact, for air-conditioners there is, at times a premium during summer.)
- Prizes for super achievers among the channel members are offered to those dealers who have at the end of the year done remarkably well. It could be a gift or a free trip to some exotic location at the firm's expense.

Price changes occur due to special circumstances also. At times, firms want to generate extra cash and they offload product at a much lower price, even at a loss. In exhibitions, *melas* special prices are offered to exploit the buying mood of the people visiting these places. Cash discount to the channel members can be extended further to the customer/user, which would ultimately reduce stocks in the distribution channel, and the firms can then have additional sales.

A major cost related incentive offered these days is low cost finance to the buyer, who can buy the product on borrowed money and pay to the financier in instalments. Cars, houses and several consumer durables are being sold in large quantities, which have affected the sale of second-hand goods in India. Extra help can be provided by way of extended payment terms making buying easy and with no worry for making payments.

Service marketing offers different types of challenges to the sellers. For example, a five-star hotel may get two types of customers as follows:

- One person who comes alone, stays for a day in one year and spends about Rs. 5000

- Another person comes three times in a month, brings three to four colleagues with him and spends about Rs. 500 000 per annum.
- It is said that the customer is the king. Can we say that the second customer is definitely the king? What About the first one? Is he only a prince? Maybe he will become a king in time.

Most service industry therefore needs to do a customer value analysis (CVA). For a five-star hotel the following matrix needs to be completed to give a proper designation to each customer/customer group:

	Room type/ ordinary Deluxe/suite	Health club usage	Restaurant/ bar usage	Business centre usage
Tourist solo				
Tourists in groups				
Small businessman				
Senior executives				
MNC executives				

Each customer is rated between 1-5 and then only the hotel can decide about the true value of a particular customer to it.

Coming to pricing the following elements go into hotel room pricing

- CVA
- Competitive pricing
- Cost to sell the room
- Seasonality and
- Location of the hotel

Retail trade pricing is based on the bar code system. It was introduced in the sale of books on the basis of each book's universal ISBN, which relates to the price through the bar code. Some examples of bar codes are given below:

Book Industry

A basic requirement for selling publications through booksellers, wholesalers, and distributors, is the unique ISBN for each book. Once publishers receive their ISBN, they assign individual number to each of their publications. In order for booksellers to automatically capture an ISBN, it must be converted into a scan-able bar code. The bar code is of choice in the book industry worldwide, because it allows for encoding of ISBN.

Large book retailers, as well as many wholesalers require that the books they handle be marked with the bar code. With this machine-readable code on the book, the retailer can scan the symbol and easily electronically identify the book by its ISBN. When a retail clerk scans the bar code at the point of sale, the bar code identifies the book so that the price and other information about the book can be retrieved from the bookseller's database. The computer then automatically reports the price to the cash register and the book buyer pays the correct price for the book.

The corresponding bar code symbol in use in every other country aside from the United States is the European Article Number (EAN). Every EAN begins with a 2 or 3 digit prefix, which indicates the country of origin. EANs for companies registered in France, for example, might begin with the prefix 34; Japan's prefix is 49. Since the book industry produces so many products, it has been designated as a country unto itself and has been assigned its own EAN prefix. That prefix is 978 and it signifies book-land, that wonderful, fictitious country where all books come from.

An EAN which begins with the book-land prefix 978 is called a book-land EAN code and is used on books and book related products internationally. The Book-land symbol is the bar code of choice in the book industry, because it allows for encoding of ISBN's (the numbers publishers use to identify their products). Since an ISBN is unique to one particular title (or product), the corresponding book-land EAN symbol is a title-specific marking which is unique for that title. For example, if a title is available in hard cover, soft cover and as an e-book, three unique ISBN book-land EAN bar codes are required.

The book-land EAN is a 13-digit code. As of January 2007, the barcode data exactly matches the ISBN-13 data. To convert a 10-digit ISBN to the book-land EAN, begin with the book-land Prefix 978. The next 9 digits are the first 9 digits of the ISBN, with the hyphens deleted. The 13th digit is the check digit, calculated mathematically using the preceding 12-digits (Bar Code Graphics automatically calculates the EAN check digit when producing pre-press bar code artwork or when printing bar code labels). For example, the ISBN 0-123456-47-9 becomes book-land EAN 9 780123 45647 2. In this example, as in most cases, the ISBN check digit and the EAN check digit differ. Occasionally the two are the same.

Two Bar Codes in One

The book-land EAN bar code is actually two bar codes side by side. The larger bar code to the left is the EAN derived from the ISBN. The smaller bar code to the right is a 5-digit add-on where various information might be encoded. Most often, the add-on is used to encode the retail price of the publication. A Book-land EAN code which has the price encoded in the add-on is called an EAN-5. It gets its name from the first digit of the add-on, which is the currency indicator. Five is the designation for U.S. dollars. An add-on of 51095, then, encodes the price $10.95. A book priced at $3.00 would have the add-on 50300. For books with prices above $99.00, there are specific coding guidelines.

The larger book retailers prefer the use of EAN/5. When the publisher chooses not to include the price, however, the add-on is 90000 (EAN/9), which is a null code indicating that there is no data encoded. Scanners in bookstores in the U.S. cannot read the book-land EAN code without it's 5-digit add-on. Thus, the use of either the EAN/5 or the EAN/9 is required. There has been a dramatic increase in the usage of book-land EAN symbols, since companies are investing millions of dollars in computer systems and scanning equipment to take advantage of automatic data collection. The foundation of these systems is contingent on bar code print quality. When symbols cannot be read or decoded incorrectly, the efficiency of these systems is brought to a halt. Consequently, many retailers and wholesalers are severely penalizing consumer goods manufacturers who furnish substandard symbols.

U.P.C.—The Other Bar Code

The book industry uses the Book-land EAN code because it can render the ISBN into a machine readable symbol (bar code). This causes problems, however, when books are sold in retail outlets other than book stores. Supermarkets, drug stores, departmental stores and other retailers often sell books, but are not properly equipped to scan the Book-land EAN symbols. A publisher selling to a non-book retailer might well be asked to provide books marked with the Universal Product Code (UPC).

The Book Industry Study Group has articulated clear guidelines about how publishers should do this. Only in the case of mass-marketed, rack-sized paperback books should a book have two different bar codes printed on its covers. In that case, the UPC should appear on the back cover (Cover 4) and the Book-land EAN code is printed on the inside front cover (Cover 2). In all other instances, books should be marked with only one bar code, either EAN for the bookstores, or UPC for non-book retailers.

A small number of publishers accomplish this by actually printing two different runs of a book: one printed with an EAN on the back cover, the other with the UPC. This represents too costly a solution for most publications. The proper way to handle the EAN/UPC problem is to print one bar code on the back cover and then label over the printed bar code with its opposite symbol when necessary. For example, a book which is sold mostly in bookstores will have the Book-land EAN code printed on its cover. When that book is sold to non-book retailers, the publisher will need to cover the EAN code with an adhesive label with the UPC printed on it. Printing two different bar codes on the same cover of any book merely invites confusion among those who scan the bar codes and should be avoided in every instance.

Following are the relevant product codes for ease of product identification, price:

BAR CODE—A printed code consisting of a series of vertical bars that vary in width. Bar codes are capable of being "read" and decoded by bar code scanners. Bar codes are used to identify retail sales items, identification cards, library books and other products. They are also utilized to manage work in progress, to track documents and for many other automated identification applications.

BAR CODE PRINTER—A printer used to produce bar codes on labels, tags and other paper materials. A bar code printer can be a simple dot-matrix report printer or a sophisticated, dedicated device that uses thermal printing technology.

BAR CODE SCANNER—A bar code scanner reads bar codes. Bar code scanners are generally classified as wands, hand-held, projection/vertical or in-counter scanners.

BAR CODE VERIFIER—Bar code verifiers are designed to measure and ensure traditional print quality. Bar codes are normally analyzed for wide to narrow ratio, print contrast, bar growth or loss and quiet zone dimensions and formats.

CASH DRAWER–A cash drawer holds paper money and currency and can either be an integrated component of a complete register or a separate peripheral device. As a separate component, a cash drawer is operated and electronically opened by a printer or directly from a computer.

CREDIT CARD AUTHORIZATION–The process in which a credit card is accepted, read and approved for a sales transaction. Credit card authorization is normally accomplished by reading a credit card through a credit card reader that is integrated into a register or stand-alone reading device. Generally, pertinent credit information is transmitted via a modem and telephone line to a credit card "clearing house". The clearing house (authorization source) communicates with the credit card's bank for approval and the appropriate debit amount of the sale.

CREDIT CARD READER (Magnetic Stripe Reader) –A device that reads the magnetic stripe on a credit card for account information to automatically be processed for a transaction. A credit card reader is either integrated into a register, attached onto a register as a separate component or is part of a stand-alone terminal dedicated for the sole function of processing credit card transactions.

MULTI-USER–Multi-user systems consist of two or more computers that are connected together and that share data and peripherals. A multi-user system includes a host computer (file server) and one or more stations. All stations share the same hard disk and may share other devices such as printers.

POS (Point-of-Sale) –Term normally used to describe cash register systems that record transactions or the area of "checkout" in a retail store.

PROJECTION SCANNER–A type of bar code reader that is normally placed vertically, and that projects laser beams horizontally to scan bar codes. Often used when high performance and speed to reading bar codes is critical.

SIGNATURE CAPTURE–A peripheral device that electronically captures an individual's signature for customer identification and transaction applications.

SMART CARD–A smart card contains a "chip" with memory and is typically used to hold customer account information and a "balance" of money similar to a checking account. The card is inserted into a device that can read and write to it updating information appropriately.

WAND–A pen-shaped bar code scanner that emits a beam from the end or tip of the wand. Wands are older, bar code reading technology but inexpensive and still widely used where speed and performance are not crucial.

WEDGE–A wedge decodes "read" data (i.e., bar codes, credit cards) and communicates that information through a keyboard port on a computer. The keyboard plugs into the wedge and the wedge device plugs into the computer where the keyboard was. Sophisticated wedges can accept a few different peripheral devices. Also See Decode.

Consumer research conducted with university students on 17 different campuses revealed that nine out of ten students cited college stores as their primary retail destination for academic course materials.

Discount stores like Wal-Mart, and general bookstores like Borders, rated second. Only 6 per cent of the students surveyed visited discount stores to purchase textbooks.

Internet sites offering textbooks and course materials rated a distant third and despite aggressive advertising campaigns targeting students in recent years, only about 4 per cent of students frequent them.

Students in the survey reported spending $454 annually for their textbooks and course materials. Seventeen percent of students in the study expected to spend more this year on textbooks than they have in the past.

Given below is the state of retail industry in the USA.

Tasks for the Students

What are the main considerations the firms have while fixing prices of their product? In case the competitors have a lower price of a comparable product, what are the options the firms have to counter it.

Management Game 5

Markets are ever-changing places that reflect the changing business and competitive environments. The teams need to ascertain the sales budgets, expense budgets to match the sales planned. The teams should decide about the type of Market Information System they want to have and place their formats for the same giving updating periodicity.

Discuss the need for controls while playing to reach the maximum profitable sales.

Please discuss if the organizational structure can have any bearing on its success as a marketing firm. If yes, what are the options available today for making the structures more customer-friendly?

Discuss the most appropriate structure for your retail outlet company giving reasons thereof.

CHAPTER

11

Retail Economics Worldwide and Competitive Advantage on e-Retailing

Aims and Outcomes

Retailing is as old as the hills. Over time its importance in the economics of the countries have assumed great significance. After manufacturing, trading starts. While wholesale merchants have their role to play the distribution channel ends with the retailer and thereby begins a life long relationship between buyers and the sellers. Retail has transformed over the last few decades and its impact on country's economy is felt by the buyers, sellers and financiers. In the last two decades service industry has taken the centre stage with its needs of finance, human resource and retailing. Banks and other financial institutions are vying with each other for grabbing the slice of retail trade which is becoming larger day by day.

Chanda Kochhar, ED, ICICI Bank says, 'With a jump in the Indian economy from a manufacturing sector, that never really took off, to a nascent service sector. Banking as a whole is undergoing a change. A larger option for the consumer is getting translated into a larger demand for financial products and customisation of services is fast becoming the norm than a competitive advantage. With the retail banking sector expected to grow at a rate of 30%, players are focussing more and more on the retail and are waking up to the potential of this sector of banking. At the same time, the banking sector as a whole is seeing structural changes in regulatory frameworks and securitization and stringent norms means the faster one adapts to these changing dynamics, the faster is one expected to gain the advantage.

India is poised to become the world's fourth largest economy in the span of two decades. Economic prosperity is providing many in this populous nation with real purchasing power; it simply is an opportunity that cannot be overlooked by global banks.

Despite its appeal, India remains a developing economy. Thus, global banks seeking a presence or expansion in India must craft a business strategy that considers the country's attendant challenges: long-established competitors; rudimentary infrastructure; dynamic political environment; restrictive regulations; and developing country operational risks.

These challenges should be weighed against the potential gains from entering the marketplace, as well as the likely cost of doing nothing. Extensive research conducted by the IBM Institute for Business Value pinpointed four of the most promising product areas for global banks entering the Indian market: housing loans, automobile loans, small and medium enterprise (SME) banking and personal financial services. However, recognizing the growth opportunities is only the beginning. Global banks targeting India as a source of new growth will have to do much more than just "show up" — success will lie in the details of execution.

With one of the most under-penetrated retail lending markets in Asia-Pacific, India offers great potential. India's mortgage debt in 2002 totalled only 2 per cent of gross domestic product (GDP), compared to 7 per cent of Thailand's GDP, 8 per cent of GDP in China and much higher proportions in other parts of the region: Malaysia (28 per cent), South Korea (30 per cent) and Hong Kong (52 per cent)[2]. While India remains characterized by extreme wealth and poverty, a middle class is beginning to emerge, with absolute demand for products and services on the rise. To seize this opportunity, new market entrants must exploit specific market niches and leverage best-in-class capabilities while addressing the unique challenges of the Indian banking environment.

During the last decade, India has emerged as one of the biggest and fastest growing economies in the world. The strengthening economy in India has been fuelled by the convergence of several key influences: liberalization policies of the government, growth of key economic sectors, development of an English-speaking, well-educated workforce and the emergence of a middle-class population.

The Indian players are bullish on the retail business and this is not totally unfounded. There are two main reasons behind this. Firstly, it is now undeniable that the face of the Indian consumer is changing. This is reflected in a change in the urban household income pattern. The direct fallout of such a change will be the consumption patterns and hence the banking habits of Indians, which will now be skewed towards retail products. At the same time, India compares pretty poorly with the other economies of the world that are now becoming comparable in terms of spending patterns with the opening up of our economy. For instance, while the total outstanding retail loans in Taiwan is around 41% of GDP, the figure in India stands at less than 5%. The comparison with the West is even more staggering. Another comparison that is natural when comparing retail sectors is the use of credit cards. Here also, the potential lies in the fact that of all the consumer expenditure in India in 2001, less than 1% was through plastic, the corresponding US figure standing at 18%.

The fact that the statistics reveals a huge potential also brings with it a threat that is true for any sector of a country that is opening up. Just how competitive are our banks? Is the threat of getting drubbed by foreign competition real? To analyze this, one needs to get into the shoes of the foreign banks. In other words, how do they see us? Are we good takeover targets?

Going by international standards, a large portion of the Indian population is simply not "bankable"-taking profitability into consideration. On the other hand, the financial services market is highly over-leveraged in India. Competition is fierce, particularly from local private banks such as HDFC and ICICI, in the business of home, car and consumer loans. There, precisely lie the pitfalls of such explosive growth. All banks are targeting the fluffiest segment, i.e. the upwardly mobile urban salaried class. Although the players are spreading their operations into segments like self-employed and the semi-urban rich, it is an open secret that the big city Indian yuppies form the most profitable segment. Over-dependence on this segment is bound to bring in inflexibility in the business.

The Indian economy is one of the fastest growing in the world. Simultaneously, India is experiencing exponential domestic growth for retail products and services due to the burgeoning middle class, which consists of 300 million consumers.

Many people still equate India with offshoring and the IT services of Infosys TCS, and Wipro, while those remain dominant, over the past few years Indian companies have vaulted new sectors to prominence on the global stage including technology, manufacturing, pharmaceutical, infrastructure, energy, consumer retail, telecom, financial services, media, and hospitality. India has developed a global brand that reflects its best-of-breed ability in not only IT but many other industries as well.

Private equity and venture investment have tripled in 2006 to $7.5 billion, and exit opportunities for venture and private equity-backed startups are only expanding as the Bombay Stock Exchange rises and merger and acquisition activity grows.

Of course, investing in India comes at a cost and with associated risks. India's infrastructure is in need of massive investment. While power reliability, living conditions, and road congestion are improving, they are still nowhere near the levels that businesses enjoy in the U.S. The country's bureaucratic mindset runs deep, from the government to the lowliest street vendor, making seemingly simple tasks take much longer. India's tax and legal systems present an entirely different set of issues for foreign investors. Legal reviews can last for several months, knotted with structures and concepts unfamiliar to U.S. investors. Tax laws and corporate structures are also important to understand. Even the Indian accounting system differs from that of the U.S., requiring reorientation and reconciliation.

When you add the cultural differences in dealing with entrepreneurs in India, the time-zone difference, and the distance to get there, running a successful investing venture in India is no simple feat. And it is impossible to run a venture remotely over the long run; a local presence is ultimately required.

But even with these hurdles, India has never looked more attractive for investment. India's GDP is growing at between 8 and 9 per cent annually. India's GDP growth is fuelling the expansion of its middle class. Further, there is an enormous availability of well-educated human capital. Of India's 1.1 billion people, half are under 25 and 65% are of working age. The stock market has grown 278% from 2002 to 2006. Goldman Sachs believes India will be the world's third largest economy by 2050—and larger than Japan by 2030—if growth continues at its current pace.

Companies from all industries in India have gone public and grown into global leaders, proving that start-ups can indeed move to the next level. There's Reliance Industries in the consumer/retail sector, Infosys in IT services, Bharti in telecom, and Ranbaxy in pharmaceuticals, to name a few. Tata Motors caters to Europe's small-car market as well as India's domestic market.

In India, the revenue necessary to take companies public is lower, similar to U.S. IPO criteria. Valuations are sane, and the stock market is as hot as any global investor could hope.

Most firms concentrate from the beginning on the essentials like manufacturing, marketing and finance with little understanding of the role of retailing in economic development and planning of the connected areas.

To understand the economics of retail in detail independent thinking and research is required instead of large standardized conventional research. Innovative methodologies are required for the unique sector of the industry and business. Independent research has provided the core knowledge base for what has come to be called "Economics of Retail."

Analyses of the economics of retail and service using time-tested, industry standard approaches need to suit the needs and circumstances of each country and community. These include trade area and demographic analyses, consumer and business surveys, retail prospect understanding, retail need analysis, reuse of traditional retail centres, and economic and financial impact analysis.

More importantly, the economic surveys monitor the ever-evolving retail industry. It is known where market forces are heading and what retailers are doing in response, what other communities are doing, providing with knowledge of best and worst practices.

Retail focus has brought about major impacts to the communities it serves. It is possible to manage the impacts for adding on to the benefits while curbing the problem areas. The system of understanding and analyzing retail business helps in creating a reservoir of skills and tools for the purpose.

As communities around the nation have begun asking for independent economic impact analyses for large retail developments, the very first such study in the USA was conducted for the town of Homer, Alaska.

In addition, the analytical tools at the disposal have allowed the study of a number of related issues as given below:

1. The effect of minimum wage increase
2. The comparative benefits of competing firms
3. The economic output associated with a distribution centre
4. The impact of utility rate increases on different classes of users—Mean Time Between Purchase (MTBP)

The retail industry is undergoing a sea change, says Duncan Angove, and Oracle wants to help retailers lead the transformation. Angove, former chief strategy officer at Retek, has spent a career providing retail solutions and now serves as general manager of the recently formed Oracle Global Retail Business Unit. Oracle acquired Retek, a provider of retail operations software, in April 2005, and added inventory optimization software maker Profit-Logic, in July 2005, to create an offering unique in the industry: a standards-based application solution from a single vendor.

Factors such as globalization and multi-channel selling contribute to retail's present-day challenges. These two factors affect the following areas most:

First, the supply chain, an isolated logistics function, now a core competency for retailers.

Second is increased product portfolio, a term for taking more productivity out of existing stores, even as retail square footage per capita increases. Perfect examples in India would be the Bata retail outlets and Usha shops that have an ever increasing array of goods in same top location shops that have been in existence since generations. Despite the fact that retail is changing, not every retailer is at the same point in the transformation. Many retailers are trying to adopt the standard IT services, for cleaning up their infrastructure and connecting different systems. These companies look to IT not just for innovative retail solutions, but as a suitable IT partner.

The IT industry plans to transform the economics of retailing through the combination of technologies from a large number of IT solution providers, merchandising, supply chain, store management, and point-of-sale solutions form the IT base for customers among the newly formed solutions covering the entire retail enterprise.

IT software provides another piece of the retail problem. It creates retail profit optimization software that helps retailers profitably manage merchandise through effective markdown, assortment, and allocation. These areas have been managed by aesthetics and retailers' experience says Scott Friend, cofounder and former president of Profit-Logic, USA, now vice president of marketing and science with Oracle Retail. "Profit-Logic brings a science-based approach to merchandising, resulting in a dramatic impact on retailers' financial results. The newly renamed Oracle Retail Price Optimization and Oracle Retail Assortment Execution solutions can assess the billions of potential combinations a retailer needs to consider, every item, every size, every price, every colour, every store, and do so in a retailer-friendly way.

The idea is to leverage the strength of Oracle products. "Oracle already had a stable platform for retail that includes Oracle E-Business Suite. We have built on that core strength with a set of highly innovative offerings." Oracle says.

Future Plans

Oracle's new retail unit, and Oracle's integration of financial services software provider i-flex serve as a model for Oracle's growth. It is a combination of organic investments coupled with good strategic, selective acquisitions.

Oracle Retail announced an aggressive road map for integrating its technologies into the Oracle stack at a town hall meeting on August 4, 2005. "We're intimately involved in Oracle Fusion and the Oracle Customer Data Hub."

Organizationally, it means giving vertical divisions freedom. "We've kept retail as an autonomous business unit so we can retain focus and consistency for our industry and customers, while leveraging the power of Oracle's global organization, this maintains and nurtures the deep domain expertise, continuity with customers, and industry focus of the acquired companies."

It also found that the local businesses generated slightly more sales per square foot compared to the chains ($263 versus $243). Because chains funnel more of this revenue out of the local economy, the study concluded that, for every square foot of space occupied by a chain, the local economic impact is $105, compared to $179 for every square foot occupied by an independent business.

Three times as much money stays in the local economy when you buy goods and services from locally owned businesses instead of large chain stores, according to this analysis, which tracked the revenue and expenditures of eight locally owned businesses. The survey found that the businesses, had combined sales of $5.7 million in 2002, spent 44.6 per cent of their revenue within the surrounding two counties. Another 8.7 per cent was spent elsewhere in the state of Maine. The four largest components of this local spending were: wages and benefits paid to local employees; goods and services purchased from other local businesses; profits that accrued to local owners; and taxes paid to local and state government. Using a variety of sources, the analysis estimates that a national big box retailer operating in Mid-coast Maine returns just 14.1 per cent of its revenue to the local economy, mostly in the form of payroll. The rest leaves the state, flowing to out-of-state suppliers or back to corporate headquarters. The survey also found that the local businesses contributed more to charity than national chains.

This study examines the local economic impact of two locally owned businesses in Austin, Texas—Waterloo Records and Book People—and compares this with the economic return the community would receive from a Borders Books store. The study finds that spending $100 at Borders creates $13 worth of local economic activity, while spending $100 at the local stores generates $45 in local economic activity. The difference is attributed to three factors: a higher local payroll at the independent stores (because, unlike Borders, none of their operations are carried out an out-of-town headquarters office); the local stores purchased more goods and services locally; and the local stores retained a much larger share of their profits within the local economy.

Analyzing national data, the study found that the opening of a Wal-Mart store reduces country-level retail employment by 150 jobs. Because Wal-Mart stores employ an average of 360 workers, this suggests that for every new retail job created by Wal-Mart, 1.4 jobs are lost as existing businesses downsize or close. The study also found that the arrival of a Wal-Mart store reduces total countywide retail payroll by an average of about $1.2 million. This study improves substantially on previous studies by convincingly accounting for the situation of the location and timing of Wal-Mart's entry into a particular local market. That is, Wal-Mart presumably does not locate stores randomly. When expanding into a particular region, it may, for example, opt to build in towns experiencing greater job growth. Unless this location selection bias is accounted for, one might compare job growth in towns that gained Wal-Mart stores versus those that did not and erroneously conclude that Wal-Mart caused an expansion in employment. The authors of this study have devised a persuasive method of accounting for this bias. They also argue that the method developed by Basker to account for this bias is flawed and therefore the conclusion that Wal-Mart has a small positive impact on retail employment is not reliable.

Often cited and misrepresented by Wal-Mart supporters, this study examines the impact of the arrival of a Wal-Mart store on retail and wholesale employment. It looks at 1,749 counties that added a Wal-Mart between 1977 and 1998. It finds that Wal-Mart's arrival boosts retail employment by 100 jobs in the first year, far less than the 200-400 jobs the company says its stores create, because its arrival causes existing retailers to downsize and lay-off employees. Over the next four years, there is a loss of 40-60 additional retail jobs as more competing retailers downsize and close. The study also finds that Wal-Mart's arrival leads to a decline of approximately 20 local wholesale jobs in the first five years, and an additional 10 wholesale jobs over the long run (six or more years after Wal-Mart's arrival). (Wal-Mart handles its own distribution and does not rely on wholesalers.) This works out to a net gain of just 10-30 retail and wholesale jobs, and the study does not examine whether these jobs are part-time or whether they pay more or less than the jobs eliminated by Wal-Mart. The study also found that, within five years of Wal-Mart's arrival, the counties had lost an average of four small retail businesses, one midsized store, and one large store. It does not estimate declines in revenue to retailers that survive. Basker looked at the effect of Wal-Mart on retail employment in neighbouring communities, but found that the confidence intervals were too large (meaning the results showed wide variation) to draw any conclusion about Wal-Mart's impact. (Her initial working paper, published in 2002, reported an average decline of 30 retail jobs in surrounding communities, but, after correcting an error, she determined the confidence intervals were too large to produce a precise result).

These studies examine the effect of big-box chains, particularly Wal-Mart, on wages and benefits for retail employees.

Retailers face several problems that threaten their ability to perform with profits. Over-saturation of the market in the west including USA, rising operating costs and a dynamic economy hamper retail operations and stress on ther stratagies retailers need to keep evolving. Customers expectations are at an all time high while e-tailing has taken away a lot of shoppers, retailers cannot aford to slip up on any count. Shoppers traffic and the difference between buyers and browsers is becoming extremely important.

Retailers need to have data on foot traffic as an acurate yardstick of percieved sales in the future. If the foot traffic is going down then in the next year or so even the sales will go down. If the retailers are having regular sales with foot traffic going down without their knowledge they are likely to be caught unawares when sales start declining. Each entrant in the shop is a potential buyer. However, accuracy in sales potential is important for forecasting the sales. Traffic monitoring is, therefore, essential for cost-effective management and understanding the following areas:

Conversion rate between buyers and browsers:

- Labour utilization
- Advertising promotional plans

- Peak selling time
- Merchandising visuals
- Opportunities and challenges
- New concepts for the store
- Stocks and types of merchandise
- Location of the store analysis

Store conversion rate is the ratio of traffic as compared to sales. It is the most important indicator of retail performance.

Till 2004 consumers were cautious about spending money. Most countries surveyed remain negative about the current economic outlook, except Ireland and the United Kingdom. French, Dutch, Belgian and Italian consumers are particularly negative about their country's economic environment. In the meantime, mixed feelings prevail in Europe about the economic outlook for 2005. Overall, a small majority of Europeans surveyed are positive about the future, led by the Irish who are by far the most optimistic: 85% expect a more positive economic outlook and nearly 50% expect household income growth. Since anticipated household income is the main driver for Christmas spending throughout Europe, the year-end shopping may be impacted.

Consumers across the countries surveyed wait until the last minute to decide where to shop in order to benefit from larger discounts, which they expect to be as high as 20%. They will shop around more than last year in order to get the best prices. Close to 85% of shoppers will use the internet to research products, stores and compare prices, although only 58% will actually buy their goods over the Internet.

For adults, clothing enjoys a return to the top five, with DVDs, CDs and books high on lists of both gifts consumers want and what they are likely to actually receive. Cosmetics and fragrances will be among the best sellers, as well as gift certificates, fourth on the wish lists for adults across Europe.

Regulatory change in electricity moves slowly, in part because of human dislike of change and aversion to risk. Convincing people that regulatory change is worth undertaking would be a lot simpler if we could demonstrate the possible outcomes of a change, and thereby that such change need not be disastrous and could even create value and opportunity for many people. But electricity networks are so complex, and so expensive to construct, that real-world experiments are very costly and unlikely to occur. It's not like opening a new restaurant and seeing if consumers perceive value in the offerings of food, wine, service, and environment. In this context, the methodology of experimental economics is incredibly useful and can help us place bounds on what may occur if we implement fuller retail electricity deregulation. Experimental economics simulates environments having different rules, with real economic agents facing real choices, and with the potential to earn real money payoffs. Because rules influence incentives and therefore shape outcomes, rules and the institutions that create and enforce them matter, including regulatory institutions. Experimental economics can inform us about the relationships between different rules and institutions and different outcomes.

The perception is that workers in the trade sector have safe jobs as compared with jobs in the heavy, smoke stack industries, construction, and mining, which serves to undermine the need or demand for safety training or use of safety personal protective equipment.

Workers in retail trade are increasingly contract, temporary, and part-time workers with low levels of education; all of which have been used as rationales for not providing sufficient safety and health training for jobs in the trade sector.

Retail Trade

Retail trade, or the sale of merchandise for personal consumption, accounts for over 50% of consumer spending. The value of retail sales has grown in nominal terms (not adjusted for inflation) by over 7% in three of the past four years, and is expected to grow by 6.5% in 2001 to $4.8 billion. Even after adjusting for inflation, retail sales grew by at least 3.3% in each year since 1996 and are expected to grow by 5.0% in 2001. These growth rates are consistent with national trends.

Working London

This working paper provides employment projections for London as a whole and for twelve key London sectors. London's total employment growth is projected to be 194,000 between 2002 and 2007. The best performing sectors are 'other sectors', 'hotels, bars and restaurants' and 'business services'. The worst performing London sectors are 'manufacturing' and 'construction'.

World City, World Knowledge: The economic contribution of London's higher education sector.

There are over 340,000 students in London, studying at 41 higher education institutions. The latest GLA Economics report examines how higher education contributes to the London and UK economies. It also estimates the value of investment in higher education in terms of the human capital it generates.

Spending Time: London's Leisure Economy

A new report from Economics on how the way we choose to spend our spare time drives London's economy. The report explores the importance of leisure to the economy and looks specifically at eating out, drinking, entertaining, gambling sport and visiting attractions. Londoners spend about £150 a month on leisure, and the sector is worth £9.5 billion.

What is driving business investment in London Consumer spending has been driving growth in London's economy over the past two years, while business investment has fallen. Data from the British Chamber of Commerce is used to explore why businesses decide to invest in London success.

Transforming the Economics of Retail: The Four Imperatives for Retail Success. Oracle recently completed a research study on its many retailing customers, comparing numerous metrics with industry averages and benchmarks. These customers had more than $500 million in annual revenues.

Electronic retailing means buying and selling of goods and services across the Internet. An e-commerce site can be as simple as a catalogue page with a phone number, or it can range all the way to a real time credit and processing site where customer can purchase downloadable goods and receive them on the spot.

E-Business is the creation of new, and the redesigning of existing value chains and business processes through the application of information technology. Naturally, e-business is more than e-commerce. It expands the scope of e-commerce to transform the company and the industry itself.

E-commerce site building requires the following:

Custom-built shopping bag

Shopping bag is like a retail shop with displays of products, catalogues, prices. The customer enters the website and selects the product he wants to buy. Later he is given the invoice of the bought products, which can be paid by the credit card to complete the sale.

Payment gateway service provider.

A bank or an authorized company takes care of accepting the credit card and process it on line. The payment software is combined well with the website for securing the transaction and authorized for the task by certification authority.

Strategy for the Net

Firms promoting brands worldwide have realized the immense possibilities of the net. Web user are increasing almost hundred per cent each year, and net economy is doubling every nine months. The Internet does not just provide the vehicle for brand building, but also for creating economic value for the firm and sales transactions are on the up as the marketplace, the shopping mall is slowing but surely giving way to shopping superhighway, net marts.

The main advantage in the cyber marts is the lowering of transaction costs; no paper work, no displays, inventories no distribution costs and yet the customer can use the net twenty four hours in a day for quick response from the sellers. The differences between the normal sales and cyber sales are listed below:

- Information to customers
- Purchase procedure
- Product delivery
- Buyer seller negotiations

While cyber sales deal with the customer's differently, from the customers' viewpoint, they are not in a position to touch, feel the product. (In India it is inconceivable that ladies can buy saris just by seeing their designs on the computer monitor). With no showrooms, no physical product, how should the firm build customer loyalty, especially when the net possesses, any number of similar sites. Hence, the 4 Ps of marketing are replaced by product, superimposed by promotion and sales outlet.

Net users buy product on the net, not because of the firm's advertising efforts, but because of happy experience with the product. Firms need to offer customer additional benefits on line. A health drink seller, like Bourn Vita seller would need to talk about Total Health Package on the net, like age-related diet programmes, gym equipment, yoga, aerobic. Car seller should talk about the road maps of different parts of the country, car accessories, and car stereo systems. A credit card seller needs to provide much more information than just about the card. Information, which he can provide can be on travel, vacation destinations, restaurants, shopping malls, all of those accepting the card.

Firms offering even below par products can just rent server space, and generate some brand awareness programme, to become a competitor. Major brands, which remain indifferent to the net, can really lose business to such upstarts.

Several technologies are available for developing a website; firms could go to consultants and dedicated websites meant for giving instructions on creating websites. The brand firm wants to place on the website must have the following qualities:

- Distinguishing features
- Brand awareness as a distinguished brand among the target market segment.
- Product benefits for the customers; using the Maslow's hierarchy of needs helps in segregating the benefits in a logical manner.
- Product should never oversell itself by promising more than what it can do for the customers.
- Product promise should be delivered time and again
- Reinforce brand positioning in the market

Website provides non-stop buying round the clock, without even a sabbatical (holiday). Following points should be kept in consideration while building a website:

- Attractive opening page, to create browsers interest
- Relevant and interesting contents, with the customers' benefits highlighted.
- Regular and frequent updates to bind the browser to the site
- A box giving the latest products from the firm
- Bookmark for easy return to the site
- Web page should be error free, easy to read and if there are any links, they should be easily accessible, graphics should be easy downloads without taking too much time and web space.
- A well-developed website conveys the excellence of the brand being sold through it.

Website design should always take a holistic view of the entire matter on different pages of the site, with easy entry points from any of the pages as the browsers can enter from any point of the website. Firms' signature or equivalent should be available on each page for easy identification of the site by the web browser. Graphics should take as little download time as possible and should in the cache memory to avoid downloading each time the site is visited. The firm's strategy should be the governing factor for the design of the site. As here are multiple technologies in the market, the site should be designed for multiple browsers. The site should be seen on any monitor. Links on each page help the viewer to find what they are looking for. Too many links could be confusing and would defeat the very purpose for which the links have been provided. Firms would do well to advertise their website addresses, email addresses in other media, like print.

The most important element of the success of the web sales is the quick response, which the firm must provide to its customers. As the website is open round the clock, and with different time zones around the world, firms providing 24 hours service would win the business.

Security has become the biggest waterloo of web sellers as customers are increasing becoming wary of the Spam (sending unsolicited mail) and hacking, which goes on the net and misuse of credit card numbers is not uncommon. Secure server words have calming influence on the customers and in reality more needs to be done to safeguard the interests of the web customers. Visitors on the web should be consulted first before sending information on sale, new product launches.

Now, firms like Oracle are offering total packages for e-business tailor made for individual firm's requirements. These include the following areas of management:

- Marketing
- Sales
- Order processing
- Order fulfilment
- Manufacturing
- Services
- Human resource management
- Finance
- Accounts
- Projects

Considering the above the progress of e-commerce appears to be certain and it will grow quite rapidly. Both the buyers and sellers, once the trust in e-business is built, would benefit; they would save on time, money and manpower in doing the transactions with each other.

e-Retailing

It may surprise many today if a prophet says that in the next twenty years or even earlier, the big supermarkets will disappear from most parts of the world, substituted by virtual stores. The phenomenon had started even in the last decade of the 20th century in the west. In France, the phone customers were provided with a computer like gadget MINITEL, on which the customers could make purchases, buy air tickets, do hotel bookings and a lot more. The data and resource base has since undergone major changes with information available for umpteen products, with clear laid down simple procedures for purchasing the products in India hurdle in the way of electronic commerce was the digital secure signatures. Once that has been sorted out the way for e-commerce has been cleared. E-commerce covers the following activities:

- Fax correspondence

- E-mail transactions
- Smart cards and digital money
- Internet on-line businesses, where the product, its price and other terms of business like payment, delivery terms, and guarantees are available to the customers and they can place on-line orders.
- With digitized data, the customer can view the product advertising video clips, data, text and sound in digital bits, which are reconverted for customer benefit on the computer.

The main components of the virtual markets are the following:

- Information: Combining the text, data, sound, graphics and video into BITS, which can be sent from one place to the other at high speeds.
- Communication: Connecting the places for business through networking which connects the sellers, buyers, and vendors. These networks are formed through telephone connections, where one computer can send and receive data from another directly. Within an organization such connections are known as Intranets and when the connections are made with outside organizations the networking is called extranet. However, when several users get connected on networks these are called Internet connections.
- On the Internet firms selling products can organize their own websites like virtual showrooms and buyers can log on to these websites to get the information about the product, terms of business and also place purchase order on the sellers on-line.

Internet purchase has been prevalent in the sale of the following so far:

- Computer software
- Airline tickets
- Music CDs and VCDs.
- Food items, both raw and from the restaurants
- Flowers, clothing
- Banking
- Shares
- Electronics

The list is a growing one as more firms find web marketing easy and economical firms open their websites providing information on the products and terms of business and solicit business. There are several Internet service providers like, Satyam online, Mantra on line, and NOW network of the world, which charge the Internet user a small amount. Internet is worlds connect of websites.

In India, population of computers is low, rendering the use of Internet minimal. However, in metro cities, the youth, who are computer savvy, are continuously browsing on the net. They see the product displays, but more often than not, ignore the overtures of sellers of the products. Of late, websites like Bazee.com are becoming popular with the young people, and some of them are doing business through the site. It is hoped that as in the west computer population in homes will increase, more people will spend time on the Internet and get the sellers messages leading to purchase of products shown on the net. Use of Internet for stock transfers, investments and banking is yet to take roots in India.

Besides on-line shopping, the Internet browser gets a lot of information on competitive products, which helps him to take buying decisions. Buyers can ask for more information on the net, can get customized products by giving their own design to the sellers. The Internet has provided the buyer with greater power today to get what he wants from the sellers it is the customer who dictates the product specifications, buying terms as against the sellers' terms of the conventional selling process and hence it is totally customer driven.

Internet buying is, therefore, providing the buyers the information they need and not the plethora of information directed on them by the salesmen. As the websites remain open all the time, the buyer can decide the interaction at the time of day or night at his convenience. Shopping trips, bargaining, emotional appeals by the salesmen are eliminated in Internet buying. The sellers get greater adaptability in altering their products, prices, their selling costs decrease as they do not need sales staff, distribution channels, infrastructures, the sellers can estimate the number of interested buyers who log on to their websites. However, for products like silks, customer would still like to feel it with his hands rather than accept what the seller depicts on his website. It may be possible to buy on-line after the first purchase has been made from a real store of the product shown on the website. The other disconcerting problem of website buying is that it takes away the joys which shoppers feel on a day out, reserved for doing the town, shopping, window shopping and generally enjoying themselves in the coffee house too. It is hoped that in the near future, people will go out only for the theatre and restaurants and not for buying products.

Firms need to project their image and for that purpose they open their own website in which they give the firm's brochure to establish their credentials as a company of repute. They add the product website in which they can show the product give its specifications, usages, present customers' testimonials and in some cases product demonstrations. Website designing has become a major software activity. Firms want their websites to be interesting enough for the web browsers to visit them, informative enough for them to keep visiting them. Websites today have text, graphics, video clips, sound and demos of the product. Besides seller's websites there are advertising websites all over the Internet. Special offers, discount vouchers, airline-cum-hotel tickets are usually advertised on the net. People surfing the net have the choice of seeing the advertisement or skipping it. Even the email addresses are being used to post the advertising material or sales offer on people's email addresses. However, the email provider normally has to take the permission of the address holder if the advertising material can be offered to them or not. Every email address holder gets a lot of junk email, advertising a variety of products, which he normally deletes even without reading it.

It is believed that in the future at least fifty per cent of consumer durables and eighty per cent of industrial goods will be bought on the web.

Presently, however, the customer is only surfing the websites with no intention of buying on-line. The surfers are mostly up-market people who may consider buying branded products on-line. The web is surfeit with information confusing the persons on the net. There need to be a search engine which would preclude some sites from coming in view to enable the surfer use the net more usefully. The other problems are of Internet security and unethical use of the net by unscrupulous people.

Internet Auctions

While the Internet auctions have been going on in the world for a few years now, in India they are of recent origin. Bazee.com as an auction website is gradually gaining popularity. People, firms start web auctions for selling their wares in their locality little realizing they are unwittingly becoming part of a global network. The sales on the auction keep multiplying, because of ease of purchase. The only basic requisite for putting the product is that it should be a genuine product and it should perform as per its promise. In India, the latest are the airlines getting into the auction mode. First they started the auction of consumer products; today they are ready to auction air tickets as well. Firms selling from their shops have increased their on-line sales. What was sold from a shop in a month could be sold in an hour on the net. Such is the reach and the power of web selling through auctions. The economics of auction on the net is quite simple. With no overheads, no channel commissions and grand stores, the cost to sell are really low. The customer knows the product's retail price and while bidding keeps that in mind.

The seven-year-old business has come up so fast that it is already doing $15 billion worth of transactions. On-line auctions are changing the face of American business. People are moonlighting for selling on the net and even quitting their jobs for the purpose. Traditional retail stores are getting into the act to sell on the net auction to augment the store sales. The much-maligned middleman is taking his final bow in some cases, thereby reducing marketing expenses and making the products cost-effective.

There are bad cyber sellers too, and in order to safeguard their interests, the customers must follow the guidelines given below:

- Locate those auction sites which guarantee the transaction with insurance policy in case of default by either the seller or the buyer
- Check the antecedents of the sellers
- Check the policies and rules governing the auction as the normal retail sales rules do not apply in the net sales

If paying in advance is a problem, locate an agency, which handles such transactions; the customer gets the product and at the same time the seller gets paid for it.

Task for the Students

Discuss the advantages and the disadvantages of Internet business and where do the web auctions fit in?

Management Game

Plan to introduce a new product in the selected market segment using the product launch strategies. Can the teams try to enter more than one segment, if yes, decide the method of doing the same, do they need more than one retail outlet or the existing one will suffice?

Discuss the plans for products for different stages of the PLC for the leaders and the followers. Price, promotion and product differentiation need to be given the required emphasis.

Discuss the various marketing mix factors and how they relate to their product. What are basic advantages of making strategies around these factors? Pick up three factors of your choice and formulate the product strategy taking these into account.

Discuss the factors that are appropriate to the following product groups in retail business.

- FMCG
- Consumer Durables
- Service

CHAPTER

12

Purchase, Stores, Inventory and Logistics in Retail Management (Materials Management)

Aims and Outcomes

Materials management has become one of the core functional areas in today's business. In retail business the importance of product selection, inventory and related logistics can never be overemphasized. From the days of first half of the last century when the task was restricted to only purchasing from well-known vendors, today, starting from finalization of product specifications that needs to be purchased, to vendor section, negotiations with different vendors right up to logistic support to acquiring the products, including making payments for the purchases made, all come under the broad spectrum of Materials Management. Students will learn materials management from the retail viewpoint.

Activities of a modern materials department of a company can be defined as follows:

1. Selection of goods to be procured.
2. Arranging detailed specifications of the product including aesthetics, packaging and display-ability.
3. Organizing finance for making timely payments as it helps in price negotiations.
4. Selecting the right personnel for manning the department.
5. Logistics support, both inbound and outbound logistics, inbound is meant to organize the input products movement from the vendors to the company, while outbound helps in prompt and timely delivery to the customers' premises.
6. In the last ten years, companies have resorted to outsourcing a number of activities and it has become one of the important tasks of the Materials Manager to establish, organize and monitor the outsourcing operations of the company.

7. Materials department gets involved in controlling production or procurement costs of saleable goods.

Materials department's main objective, however, remains "continuity of supplies". Earlier this was done by keeping heavy stocks of products with several vendors for each purchase product. This entailed blockage of money in heavy inventories and unnecessary dealing with large vendor group with compounded problems linked with each vendor. In fact, most companies considered vendors as vicious adjuncts to the activities but which could not be avoided or wished away. Vendors were kept at a distance as people below the dignity of the buyers. However, over a period of time vendors are being recognized as vital partners for the well-being of the companies, and today their value has been fully recognized. Vendor selection, development and Vendor Relation Management on the lines of Customer Relationship Management has become a critical success factor for the companies.

Purchase price is an important determinant of the company's bottom line. Purchase department plays an important role in price negotiations creating unmeasurable assets. Price covers the quality, reliability, service, guaranty, warranty associated with the product. Price negotiations take the following into account:

1. Price
2. Discounts, including cash discounts, quantity discounts, turnover discounts.
3. Credit terms
4. Installation and commissioning charges
5. Post-warranty annual maintenance contracts
6. Guaranty and warranty terms

Materials department of a retail company is associated with the following functions:

1. Materials planning based on expected sales-at times bulk purchase are made to get the supplies at bulk, lower rates and these are unbulked, put in small containers before retail sale.
2. Buying/purchasing action takes into account the following:
   (a) Selection of suppliers
   (b) Negotiations for price and terms of business
   (c) Order placement
   (d) Follow-up for delays in supplies
   (e) Receipt and inspection
   (f) Record keeping
   (g) Supplier Relationship Management.
3. Logistics—Transportation and warehousing: The area is now extensively covered under Supply Chain Management that oversees the entire gamut of product procurement exercise.
4. Market demand: Finished goods demand is reflected in company's production plans and in case of retail outlets it gets quantified in "Sales Turnover" of the products. For example, if on January 1, the stock of a product is 100 units and at the end of the year on the 31st December too it remains at 100 units, the retail needs to evaluate

how many times the numbers have been turned over. Suppose the inventory has been replenished twenty times with 100 units at each stage the sales turnover is twenty and yearly sales 2000 of the product.

5. Forecasting: While companies use Marketing Research for forecasting the sales of products it is important that a close study is made of the general and competitive business environment factors are taken into account before accurate forecast can be made that would avert positions of stock-outs or of inventory surfeits.

The basic concept of materials management in a retail situation covers the following areas:

- Long-term sustainable flow of quality and quantity of each product being sold
- Involves vendor selection, logistics support, secure supply, contingency plans
- ABC Analysis of products
- Need of financial outlays and commitments

Inventory

Basic concepts of inventory are given below:

1. Product availability on demand
2. Product procurement without loss of time spent in negotiations, transportation, making payments.
3. Safety stocks are needed to cover fluctuations as given below:
   a. Supply time from vendors is expected to be fixed. Therefore, equal amount of safety stocks need to be kept for all the products
   b. Safety stock based on minimum sales taking into account of cost of "stock-outs"
   c. Safety stock based on customer service with no probability of stock-outs per replenishment cycle.
   d. Safety stock based on minimizing total cost of stock outs per year.

Activities profile-inventory management covers the following areas:

1. Selection of vendors
2. Inbound logistics
3. ABC Analyses of goods
4. JIT Purchasing
5. Testing of goods, including keeping records of rejects, claiming refunds or replacements for the same. Statistical quality control can be resorted to in case of low value bulk purchase items.

Storage: Before the products go onto the outlet shelves for customer display they are required to be stored in specified places as per manufacturers recommendations, like temperature controlled areas, moisture controlled areas with enough elbow room for movement of goods needed for outlet shelves. Storage can be arranged in the following manner:

1. First come first out
2. In bins, stacks, pellets, shelves or on ground (for bulk items)

3. Store area to have galleries for movement of trolleys, fork-lifts, hand cards. Overhead cranes, fresh air or air-conditioning depending on the type of goods stored.

Selected vendors need to be evaluated to re-establish their fitness to stay as vendors. The vendor performance measurement is done in the following manner:
1. Vendors' competency for making quality and quantity supplies
2. Commitment for making the supplies
3. Cash resources and firm's stability
4. Total cost of purchase including reject cost, recycle costs
5. Control system for resources of the vendors
6. Quality assurance plans
7. Consistency of supply, quality and service

Simple Vendor Rating System

Price, quality of products, adherence to delivery schedules, technology levels, technology upgrades, (with in-house R&D), cost reduction efforts without compromising on quality, flexibility in supply on buyer's requests and success ratios.

It is useful to define performance measurement yardstick for each of the above stated factors. For example:

Quality can be equated to the ratio of products rejected with products received as given below:

Quality = product quantity rejected X divided by number of products received Y multiplied by 100.

$$Q = X/Y \times 100$$

The simple Rating System Matrix is given below:

Factor	Performance measurement	Performance data	Performance
Success ratio	Order placed/ enquires sent × 100	Order placed = 7 Enquires sent = 10	7/10 × 100 = 70
Delivery	On time delivery/ total deliveries × 100	= 8 = 10	8/10 ×100 = 80
Quality	No. of OK products/total products × 100	900./1000	900 × 100/1000 = 90
Average supplier performance	70 + 80 + 90/3		= 80

Weightage Rating System

Weightage rating system takes the following areas into account:

1. Scale for rating
2. Factors for measuring vendor performance
3. Measuring method for each factor
4. Weightage to be given to each factor
5. Data collection
6. Calculation of total weightage points

Weightage Rating System matrix is given below:

Factor	Weightage	Measuring method	Performance data	Weighted performance
Quality	0.4	Accepted/ total ×	40/50	40/50 × 100 × 0.4 = 32
Cost	0.3	Standard cost/ Vendor cost	Standard cost 12/unit Vendor cost 10/unit	12/10 × 100 × 0.3 = 36
Delivery	0.2	On time/ total delivery	8/10	8/10 × 0.2 × 0.2 = 16
Service	0.1	Fair/good/best 50, 70, 100%	Good	70 × 0.1 = 7
Total	32 + 36 + 16 + 7			= 91

Vendor performance is rated at 91.

Economic Order Quantity

Retail outlets need to have sufficient inventory of products they sell. It is, therefore, essential that goods are replenished before they run out of stock. Extra stocks create problems of storing them as well as of blocking money. Retailers need to maintain minimum, maximum stock level plan along with identifying their reordering level depending on difficulty associated with product purchase—is it to be imported, are there only a few suppliers for it? The following assumptions are made in this regard:

1. Product demand is constant and uniform
2. Vendors are ready to supply product continuously and infinitum
3. There are no shortage envisaged in product supplies
4. Product cost, ordering cost, inventory carrying cost remain constant

EOQ—Economic Order Quantity can be worked out as follows:
S-annual requirement
A-ordering cost per order
I-inventory carrying cost per unit per year

i–inventory carrying cost per rupee per year
C–cost per unit of product
Q–purchase lot size-optimum
TC–total annual cost

Inventory carrying cost = Average inventory × I / 2 = Q × I /2
Annual ordering cost = Number of orders S/Q × A =S × A/Q
Total cost TC = S × A/Q + Q × I/2

EOQ calculation on the following assumptions is given below-
For S = 10,000 units
Ordering cost = Rs. 100
Unit cost of the product = Rs. 10
Holding cost per year = 20% per year
Holding cost per unit per year = 0.20 × 10 = Rs. 2

Q = under-root of 2A × S/I = under-root 2 × 10,000 × 100/2 = 1000 units

EOQ can be calculated with the assumptions given below as follows for finite input rate for product supplies:

1. Demand rate constant and uniform
2. No shortages
3. Unit cost, ordering cost, inventory carrying cost are constant
   S–annual number required of the product for sale
   Q–lot size per order
   TC–total annual cost including ordering and inventory carrying cost
   P–monthly sale rate
   I–inventory carrying cost

$$TC = S/Q \times A + I \times Q/2\ (1 - S/P)$$
$$Q = \text{square root of } 2 \times A \times S/\ I\ (1\text{-}S/P)$$

Annual Demand = 10,000 units
Annual holding cost per unit Rs. 2
Q = square root of 2 × A x S / I
Q = square root of 2 × 200 × 10,000/ 2
Q = 2000 units

Retailers need to keep safety stocks for meeting emergency situations as given below:

1. Equal safety factor for all products
2. Safety stocks based on minimum sales and cost of stock-outs
3. Safety stocks based on customer service with no stock-out probability per replenishment cycle
4. Safety stock based on minimizing total cost of stock-outs per year

Computer-based Purchase Management System

Purchase Management System is a modular, procurement software solution. Purchase Management System, purchasing software automates the entire purchasing cycle for goods and services, resulting in greater efficiencies in time and money savings.

Because the purchasing software is modular, customers can start with the modules they need now and add more as their companies' needs change. Purchase order software helps customers make cost effective as well as informed decisions. Purchase Management System e-procurement software contains detailed reports that keep managers informed throughout the supply chain management process. Purchase Management System procurement software solution manages the purchasing process in a purely paperless mode.

1. Electronic requisitions
2. Budget control
3. On-line authorizations
4. Receiving & Expediting
5. Request for Quotations
6. Inventory Control
7. Bid Analysis
8. Warehouse Management
9. Vendor Management
10. Asset Management
11. Vendor Catalogs
12. Invoice Processing
13. Procurement
14. Accounts Payable Interface

Purchase Management System, procurement software solutions also offer companies buying clout. When businesses consolidate their vendors and negotiate better pricing due to larger volumes, savings are realized. Purchase Management System, purchasing management software solution will house your approved catalogues and keep records with regard to items ordered and the frequency of items ordered. It will also keep track of item inventory and track spending against budgets for time periods you designate. Purchase Management System e-procurement software will reduce unnecessary spending, eliminate common errors, do away with double entries, eliminate approval hierarchy bottlenecks and automate the purchasing workflow.

Purchasing is a strategic function in any company, and Purchase Management System, procurement software solution can help companies meet their financial and business objectives.

Purchase Order Maintenance

As part of the periodic financial reporting process, there is a semi-annual review of outstanding purchase orders in FIS. The review is intended to identify purchase orders:

- Which are no longer required because:

- the items ordered are no longer required
- the vendor is unable to supply the ordered items
- Where goods have been received, but no invoice receipt document has been processed; rather the supplier invoice has been paid by other means.

Departmental Responsibility

This same review should be an ongoing, frequent process at the departmental level, and is encouraged for the following reasons:

- Outstanding purchase orders are "reservations" against budget dollars and tie up departmental budgets. In the case where a GR document has been processed, but the invoice has been paid using the "certified" method, budget dollars have been "used" twice for the same transaction; once for the PO reserve and once for the payment of the invoice.
- There would be reduced instances of insufficient funds messages if commitments tied up in obsolete purchase orders are cancelled.

The following sections cover an overview of the accounting process and the periodic purchase order:

Overview of Accounting Process

This provides an overview of the purchase order process from an accounting perspective.

- **Purchase Order Variance:** Please find recent PO review memos to Business Officers and Financial Officers, which provide deadlines for the review and clean-up of purchase orders, contact information.

Purchase management manages your purchasing cycle from purchase order entry through receipt of goods and the processing of supplier's invoices. You can streamline purchase order processing and automatically generate accurate landed costs. It provides you with close control over orders and on-board shipments and helps you to monitor delivery dates.

You can define import costing formulae by product and/or product group, combining maximum flexibility with minimum maintenance overhead.

These can include freight, insurance and whatever else you require to calculate the true cost of stocking each item.

The Suggested Orders facility automatically generates purchase orders which can be amended on-screen before releasing them. The Shipment Control feature allows you to track by shipment and container, with multiple ETAs, and provides a three-way reconciliation between purchase order quantity, invoice quantity and receipt quantity.

Purchase Order and Payment Management Challenges

Overcoming the challenges that face companies in managing international procurement is critical in optimizing the physical and financial supply chains. As the primary document in what, when, and how goods are shipped and paid for, each step in the international fulfilment and payment lifecycle must be synchronized with the Purchase Order (PO). Purchase Order Management business challenges include:

- Poor communication of POs and change orders to trading partners
- Difficulty in tracking PO events such as vendor order acknowledgements
- Inefficient and error-prone processes for creating import Letters of Credit (LC), LC amendments, and other international payment instruments
- Reconciling order, invoice, shipment and other payment terms
- Difficulty in tracking POs to relevant payment instruments
- Time consuming process in linking Letters of Credit to PO and Payment/Maturity Advice

Solution

Purchase Order Management solution includes:

Electronic Integration: Send PO files automatically from an existing order system. If multiple systems exist, consolidate PO Management by integration through the system. Multiple file formats and secure transmission protocols provide a wide range of flexible and secure integration options.

Electronic Distribution: Automatically route POs and Change Orders to selected overseas vendors. PO's are available via the web or through electronic integration to the vendor's system. POs can also be manually downloaded in multiple data formats.

PO creating Letters of Credit: Receipt of PO data can automatically trigger creation of an Import Letter of Credit. Receipt of Change Order data can automatically trigger creation of an LC Amendment. PO data and Change Order information automatically propagates to the Letter of Credit ensuring that the Letter of Credit stays in synch with Purchase Order data and eliminates unnecessary errors that lead to payment or shipment delays.

Receive LC and LC Amendment Status Updates Electronically: Receive status updates regarding LC creation and LC Amendments electronically and link to them to the relevant POs. Also link Document Examination notices such as Discrepancy Notifications and Exam Rejections electronically to LCs and POs.

Receive LC and LC Amendment Documents Electronically: Receive documents electronically as messages and link them to the relevant POs.

Online PO Acknowledgement: Vendors acknowledge Purchase Orders and Change Orders online and input key production, quantity, and delivery dates. Receive alerts for vendor promise or ship dates that do not meet PO requirements.

Vendor Collaboration: Deliver POs to vendors electronically and electronically alert them to new POs or Change Orders. Enable vendor collaboration through web-based access to POs and change orders and online collaboration and dispute management tools.

Receive Payment Advice Electronically: Received Payment and Maturity Advice notifications electronically and link them automatically to LCs and the relevant POs.

Web Based Architecture: Provides access from anywhere that has an Internet connection. All applications are standards based and designed to be highly scaleable. An advanced security model enables data access and collaboration across organizations and entities. An XML based integration model supports seamless inbound and outbound data sharing with third party applications.

Reconciliation: Reconciliation and synchronization between PO data and other documents like Invoice, Packing List etc.

Report Management: Detailed reporting is available and can be customized to each client's needs.

Solution Benefits

In addition to the financial and operational impact summarized in the graph the Purchase Order Management Solution delivers other clear benefits. Additional benefits include:

Reduce manpower required for Purchase Order communication by electronically creating and distributing Purchase Orders and Change Orders.

Reduce the manual effort to create and update Import Letters of Credit by integrating POs directly with financial partners' LC systems.

Reduce effort in tracking POs vs. LC and Change Orders vs. LC Amendments status updates.

Reduce effort required in tracking Payment and Maturity Advice and liquidation notices against Letters of Credit and linking POs to LC processes.

Reduce supply chain cycle times and improve vendor management by requiring and tracking vendor acknowledgements for promise dates, promise quantities, ship dates and other important information.

Maximize return on investment with existing technology solutions by integrating with a state-of-the-art web-based platform.

Purchase Plan and Process

Purchase department on receipt of a purchase requisition, needs to organize the following activities:

1. Vendor selection
2. Order placement
3. Follow up for timely supplies
4. Vendor relationship management
5. Receipt of products, testing and storing for sending to the retail outlet when needed.
6. Maintaining records of rejects, claiming refunds or credit against such rejects
7. Maintaining inventory records

When a purchase requisition is received by the purchase department it gets it vetted by the technical department to obtain correct product specifications, unless it is standard, often purchased product. Next a list of possible vendors is made as follows:

1. Market surveys
2. Sending out enquires to select vendors
3. Negotiations with selected vendors on price and business terms
4. Selection of vendors
5. Experience with the vendor

Surveys are conducted by going through catalogues supplied by vendors on their own volition. Besides trade registers, publications, directories are good sources of vendor information. At times exhibitions provide opportunities for buyer seller meets and such places provide good sources of vendors. However, company's own records should be looked into for vendor lists.

Enquiry Stage

Preliminary enquiry gets the retailer an effective method of getting information through "Request for Information". The request for information should cover the following are from the vendor's front:

1. Name, offices, top management personnel, phone, fax, e-mail ID, mobile numbers of key persons
2. Business type-proprietorship, partnership, private limited, public limited, cooperative
3. Size of operations, expansion plans, if any
4. Core competencies
5. Technical equipment in place
6. Technology, expertise, R&D facilities
7. Experience in business
8. Sales and P&L in the last five years
9. Bank report
10. List of existing customers and their certificates , if possible
11. Product mix
12. Quality plan, ISO, TQM, BIS
13. Process capabilities
14. History

Once enough data has been collected the next step is to physically visit the vendor's plant or manufacturing facilities. Following areas need to be covered during such a visit:

1. Understand the available technology, is it the latest or not?
2. Do they have state-of-the-art manufacturing equipment?
3. Do they have the latest manufacturing processes?
4. Production control, Quality Assurance Plans, TQM, Cost controls
5. Technical and management personnel, their skill levels
6. Inventory control plans, RM, Components, parts
7. Industrial Relations
8. Morale and energy levels
9. Housekeeping

A study of the above mentioned areas will provide sufficient information to decide in favour or against the vendor.

The next stage is of analysing the data collected as follows:

1. Critical success factors of the vendor

2. Weightage to each factor on a 1 to 5 scale
3. Sum total of all vendor factor ratings

Vendor Rating example is given below:

Factor	Weightage	Supplier 1	Supplier 2	Supplier 3
Technical Expertise	30	4 × 30 = 120	5 × 30 = 150	5 × 30 = 150
Capacity	25	4 × 25 = 100	4 × 25 = 100	4 × 25 = 100
Control Systems	20	3 × 20 = 60	4 × 20 = 80	5 × 20 = 100
Financial Stability	25	4 × 25 = 100	3 × 25 = 75	4 × 25 = 100
Total Reliability	100	380	405	450

Retailers have to decide from where they have to buy the product i.e., wholesalers, dealers or directly from manufacturers. Small stand-alone retailers are perforce buying from the other middlemen like distributors or dealers. Only large retailers or retail chains get the option of buying from manufacturers directly.

Retailers need to go directly to the manufacturers if they are buying large volumes and the product being purchased needs technical support. Manufacturers offer better prices as they do not have to give commission to other middlemen. Products with complicated formation that needs local assembly should be purchased from the manufacturer directly.

Retailers should buy from distributors for low volume purchases and for the following reasons:

1. If they have small warehouse
2. They are buying several products
3. To save on transport costs associated with "smalls" in transportation
4. To get faster replenishments and keep low inventory
5. For getting faster responses to their queries, replacement of defectives

Retailer's next decision is for buying from local vendor or from national distributors. Following would give them answer for making such a decision:

By from local vendor for "Just in Time" suppliers

National distributor would be able to provide better technical support, if required, offer low prices because of "Economies of Scale" they get when buying in bulk. They would also help the retailer in times of scarcity or shortage of the product.

Retailers need to decide if they want to buy a product only from one vendor or from multiple vendors. The following matrix gives them guidelines in this connection:

S No	Multiple vendor purchase	Single vendor purchase
1	Assurance of supply in case of any problem with one vendor	Easy to coordinate
2	Better price control	Volume buying leverage to make the vendor's favoured customer
3	For large volume purchases	JIT possible
4	For handling increased demand	Vendor can invest in latest technology and offer lower cost

Retailers earn profits as they buy products at a discounted price and sell it at Maximum Retail Price, MRP, or at a price where they add a profit margin on their buying price, known as "Cost Plus" price. Therefore, the buying price becomes extremely important as the retailer's profit is solely dependent on it. Retailers who buy large volumes have the bargaining power as can be seen from below:

Grocers: The stand-alone shops are not big buyers and they depend on the demographics of the area they cater to. Rich buyers do not bargain and in such a neighbourhood a retailer can charge the MRP. Grocers earn profits from their volume sales. In poorer areas customers bargain reducing the profit margins when the retailers earn low profits again based on their sales. New retail chains like Subhiksha sell at low prices as they earn profits from high volume purchase prices and high volume of sales. Plus with heavy advertising they draw customers to their shops, with lower prices retain them and make them loyal customers.

Retail store chains: These are also stand-alone shops of one owner, brand. They earn profits from volume sales at multiple outlets and centralized purchases in bulk at low prices.

Shopping malls: These have mushroomed in metro cities and are now spreading across the country. Malls are meant to provide a shopping experience for the family and friends, a reason for outings. Customers or even loiterers hang around in the malls, for the following reasons:

1. Ambience –air-conditioned, clean air
2. Multiple shops for different products
3. Choice of brands
4. Selection of eating joints
5. Multiple movie halls
6. Shopping for a variety of products under one roof.

Retailers need to negotiate with their vendors on prices and other business terms as follows:

Prices are directly connected to volume of purchase, payment terms as a cash buyer can ask for and get "cash discount". A credit buyer has to pay a little more. Bargaining power also depends on number of vendors for the product, lesser their number greater the bargaining power with vendors. A multiple product vendor would have the bargaining power. Likewise, a multiple product buyer will also have the bargaining power.

Delivery period is considered the essence of any sales contract. Retailers' ideal vendor would be the one who can supply JIT-Just in Time for sale. Harrods of London boast of being able to supply anything from a pin to an elephant, and as the story goes they did sell an elephant to a buyer on a day's notice. Naturally they do not stock elephants in their inventory.

Payment terms can vary from advance payment, documents through bank, which gives the retailer time to pay only when the product is received. Letter of credit, usance bills with delayed payment facility are other prevalent payment terms that can be negotiated with the vendors.

Product guaranty and warranty terms draw the customers into buying the products and are offered by the manufacturers. Retailers only extend these terms to their buyers on back-to-back basis, and the guaranty and warranty service is provided by the manufactures or their authorised persons.

Product quality, acceptance norms, percentage of rejections acceptable (especially for low price high volume products like nails, nuts and bolts.) form the other areas of negotiations for the retailers.

Experience Stage

In this stage the retailer sees in practice the working norms, behaviour patterns, product quality, vendors service and its adherence to the terms of sales contract as well as of normal business ethics.

Retailer-Vendor relations are built on trust, on fairness in dealings where it is a win-win situation for both. As retailers plan to have a small vendor base that can cater to their entire product needs, the following happens-

1. Purchase volumes increase
2. Retailer and vendor become mutually dependent
3. They can go for long-term purchase contract
4. The bargaining power gets balanced between the two

Retailers can place several types of purchase orders on the vendors as given below:

1. Cash
2. Against tenders received from vendors
3. Blanket orders for regular supplies of products till further notice
4. Rate contract orders are placed against pre-negotiated prices by some central authority—it is common form with the government buyers who use DGS&D to do the negotiations with different vendors
5. Open ended orders that remain valid till further notice
6. Annual orders placed for supply during one year on preplanned schedules
7. Rolling orders that get renewed each time they expire
8. Stock-less orders, where inventory is maintained by the vendors close to the retail buyers that is meant for the customer only.

Inventory Planning Basics

Retailers need to use the inventory management system to understand when and how much to buy products for retailing. Inventory helps in minimizing operating costs and keeps stock over for bridging the time between demand and supply. Inventory blocks capital and costs the retailers in the following manner:

1. Stock costs of money tied
2. Ordering costs
3. Shortage or stock out costs and excess stock costs.

As the market is a dynamic entity, product demand can never be known with certainty. However, with known probability and some uncertainty can be minimized.

Inventory Functions

1. Stocks for bulk demand: Seasonal or for special occasions
2. Stocks in transit
3. Excess stock of products: With demand taking a dip due to changing customer tastes
4. Display stocks of shop windows, shop shelves
5. Stocks to replace daily sales

Modern-day retail outlets have computer billing systems that are connected to the central computer for updating product inventory. Bar codes on product packages are scanned for price and for inventory correction. With updated product inventories of different products the central computer provides shortage lists for product reordering with the vendors. Inventory of retail outlets is essential for covering up for seasonal demands, balancing supply and demand, time needed for stock replenishments.

Small inventories require frequent placement of small volume orders where quantity discounts are lost, transport charges go up and stock-outs become commonplace. Inventory costs include the following:

1. Inventory purchase cost includes order processing costs, cost of sending the order to the vendor, cost of transportation, testing cost of products received from vendors and costs of statistical controls, computer usage.
2. Inventory carrying costs include store space cost, working capital locking costs, cost of insurance, shelf-life spoilage cost, cost of obsolescence.
3. Product stock-outs costs create economic liability along with loss of customer for the retailers.

Retailers need to organise ABC analysis of the product kept in their stores. Known as Always Better Control requires retailers to scan the inventory of top products first and then of the others. Products are categorised as follows:

(a) Products that are of high value, difficult to buy come in this category, like imported products.
(b) Products are with average costs not so difficult to buy
(c) Products are low cost with no problems in buying.

Products can also be classified as given below:

V-Vital: Stock-out of such products would be disastrous to retailer's reputation

E-Essential: Stock-out will bring loss of sales and profits

D-Desirable: Stock-outs will bring substitute products to the fore and may send die-hard customer of the products away to competition.

For in-depth understanding of products needed for retail a combination matrix of ABC and VED can be made as given below:

Product value/ Criticality	Vital	Essential	Desirable
High	Most significant	Most specific in need by customers	Most desired
Average	Average significance	Average specific	Average desirable
Low	Low on significance	Low in significance	Low in desirability

Inventory Planning helps in improved customer service, reducing inventory costs and enhancing retail outlet efficiency.

Products needed for sale at the retail outlet reach the retailers in the following manner:

Vendor manufacturer's warehouse – regional warehouse – distribution centre – retainer's warehouse.

Retailers need to understand if JIT-Just in Time inventory model will be suitable for them. JIT involves the following:

1. Zero inventories with retailers
2. Inventory only on customer demand with top level customer service
3. Low lead time of getting products
4. Efficient transport flow

JIT has the following plus points:

1. Lowest possible inventory levels
2. Storage space reduction
3. Lead time reduction for customer satisfaction
4. Elimination of waiting time, handling time of products
5. Greater motivation of employees.

Minus points of JIT are given below:

1. High risk of stock-outs and loss of sales and customers
2. Need close coordination with vendors
3. Does not take into account demand surges
4. Need of top quality products with no deviations

JIT need the following for becoming a success for retailers:

1. Organize a number of top flight vendors on long-term basis
2. Have more local vendors for reducing lead time, replacement time for defectives as far as possible
3. Quality conscious vendors only
4. Online data for real time updates
5. Highly organized transporters for specified and accurate delivery schedules
6. Highly motivated personnel trained in JIT culture

Logistics

After the goods have been manufactured they need to be placed at the most convenient locations, retail outlets, to make buying the goods easy for the buyers. The actual transportation, storage and inventory management are part of background or secondary activities. Yet one look at them would make you realize that these are extremely important activities. The firm may have the most suitable product for the customers, but if they cannot find the same easily the value of the product diminishes drastically. Logistics can be defined in this context as follows:

"Planning, operating and managing with the help of modern information system, the movement of goods from manufacturers to the buyers, in shortest possible time and in the most economical manner."

Michael Porter, the Management Guru has drawn up a Value Chain given below, which summarizes these activities in a matrix. The value mentioned is the value the chain adds to the goods for the customers!

The activities of any firm can be divided into two groups:

1. Primary Activities
2. Secondary Activities

Michael Porters Value Chain Analysis is given below:

Customers — Suppliers

Firm's Infrastructure

Human Resource Management

Technology

Information System

In-bound logistics	Operations/ Production	Service Marketing	Out-bound logistics

As can be seen, the Porter's Analysis helps in understanding the various functional areas of a firm. On the left hand there are suppliers who provide the raw materials and components, which are converted into finished product through the operations or production process. On the right side are the customers, the ultimate destination of the finished products of the firm. And the value part of the value chain is the value the firms provide through the entire process to the customers.

It is important to understand that unless the firm/vendor is adding value to the customers/retailers through the conversion or production process the firm can never sustain itself in the market.

In this chapter, we are dealing with mainly the out-bound logistics.

The area of outbound logistics starts with the distribution system of the firm and can be divided as follows:

1. Distribution network—Wholesalers and retailers
2. The customers
3. Finished goods stores
4. Demand forecasting and management
5. Inventory management
6. Final packaging
7. Order processing
8. Transportation
9. Generation of information
10. Billing, in some cases

Distribution network of any firm depends on the range of products, existing pattern in the trade; customer needs as also practicality of the network. Retailers need to understand the distribution chain that ends with them. The following gives the distribution channels currently in vogue:

1. Sole distributor
2. Area distributor
3. Stockists
4. Agents, Commission Agents
5. Dealers
6. Franchisees
7. Own shops
8. Retailers
9. Tele-marketing
10. Tele-shopping
11. Internet shopping

Movement of goods from the manufacturers or sellers takes place on receipt of orders from the customers (the distribution channel members are customers for the seller). Next steps are as follows:

1. Final packing of the product, if required
2. Arranging for the transport carrier
3. Making dispatch documents, delivery notes, packing lists
4. Actual loading on the carrier
5. Transit insurance, if required
6. Inventory update

It is important to look at the customer/retailer's instructions carefully and adhere to them meticulously. In case some instructions cannot be met with, these must be clarified and modified by communicating with the customers. Any oversight in the matter could cause major problems at the time of getting payments from the customers.

As can be seen from below, expenses on transport are substantial when the costing of the product is done (the figures are arbitrary only to give an idea).

Selling price of Rs. 100 is made up of the following costs:

Cost of money	16
Raw materials	24
Transportation up to the customer	28
Manufacturing or conversion	8
Overheads/ profits	24

Cost Distribution on Selling Price

As can be seen, while most CEOs lay stress on cost reduction in manufacturing expenses, the real place is in transportation. For in-land transport, the following vehicles are used:

1. Railways: goods trains, passenger trains
2. Trucks
3. Air cargo service
4. River boats

Within town areas, small tempos, hand or bullock carts, cycle carts are used.

Since the movement of goods involves mostly more than one organization it calls for coordinated efforts between the vendor, the retailer or individual and the carrier. The term, which encompasses the entire operation, is logistics. The value of logistics can be increased by the following:

1. Integration of product movement, information system and cash flow.
2. Coordinated responsibility of both internal and external efforts
3. Efficient and effective methods of logistics
4. Strengths and cooperation of external customers

Transportation for out-bound logistics calls for the following decisions:

1. Transport company's choice
2. Mode selection
3. Freight considerations

Warehousing has the following areas of activities:

1. Receiving, unloading the goods
2. Inspection of the goods
3. Receiving the orders from customers for dispatch
4. Repacking, if needed
5. Billing, if required
6. Shipment or transportation
7. Inventory records management

Decision-making in logistics depends on a good planned information system. The information process flow is as given in figure.

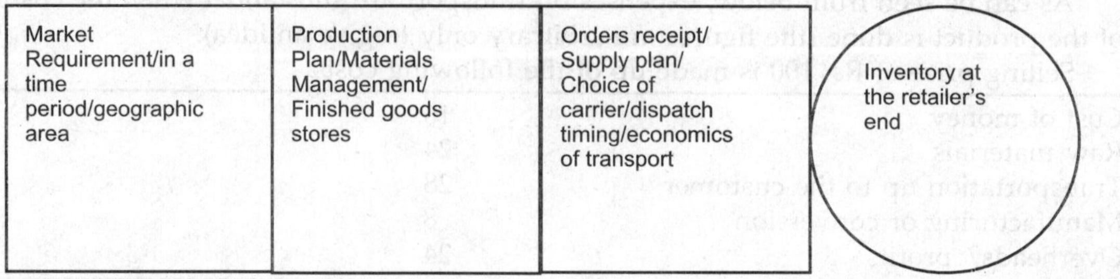

Logistics Planning

With computerized inventory management, faster communication systems, the firms/ vendors can ensure that their retailers have the product just when they need the same, reducing their inventory and cash blocking burden. One important method of gaining competitive advantage is quick response, which the vendors can provide to the market demands.

It is a well-known saying that, *it is the early bird, which gets the worm*. Similarly, in the marketplace the vendor that can place its product at the retail outlets before others gets the customers attention and becomes the market leader. With prudent decisions it can keep the leadership position for a long time as per its plans.

Logistics, including transportation can be used judiciously to provide the market with products at the most appropriate time. The Japanese have given the world an approach to the situation known as "Just in Time". This adds to the competitive advantage to the vendor's armoury.

Many firms spend a lot of money on new product launches. These are followed by major promotional plans. Imagine a situation when, after all the expenses have been incurred, the market is devoid of the product. The firm is likely to lose a lot of money in the process.

With the emergence of e-commerce, while the entire transaction may take less time, the actual receipt of goods by the customer must match with the speed to the possible extent.

In the global marketplace, where most firms find themselves in India, outsourcing of finished goods is becoming a common phenomenon. It calls for a thorough knowledge of logistics, which the firm can plan internationally. International shipments, air cargos, ships and in some cases road transport are the usual means of transport and each one has its own set of advantages and problems. Payment terms, banking regulations currency fluctuations and delivery date sanctity become important criteria for decision-making.

Going back in time, till 1960s, the business scenario in India was quite different from what it is today. Competition was practically non-existent, there was great emphasis on government or Public Sector, and lots of benefits were given to the small-scale sector. Core products like telecom, defence, and power were exclusively meant for the government agencies. In fact, it would not be an exaggeration to say that the private sector was looked at by the government with suspicion. The business was regulated and controlled through licence and permits, which were doled out to the private sector ready to make heavy investments with great reluctance. With little or no competition the firms entrenched in business was making money even with indifferent product quality.

The supply chain, of that period would look as given below:

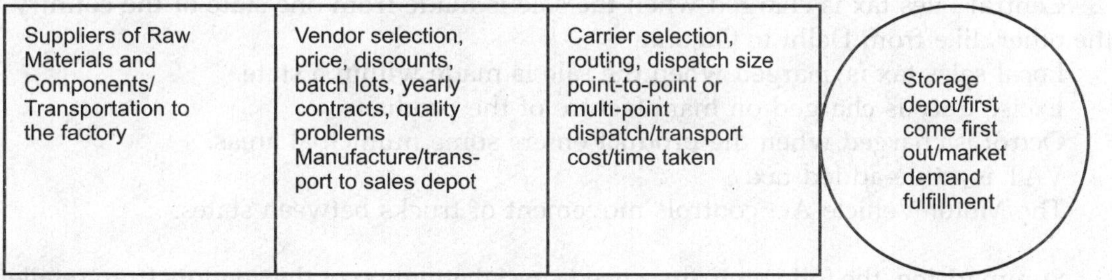

Products are pushed on to the channel members to build push pressure. Firm's own finished goods stores are stocked to service the market demand. In case of consumer goods, the dispatches are made to the first line customers, the distributors. For small towns, the distributors are unable to take full truckloads. In such situations, point to multi-point supply is made to more than one destination, serving several distributors.

Firms finished storage depots have the following tasks to perform:

1. Unloading goods from the trucks
2. Stacking in the depot
3. Inventory management
4. Repacking or unbulking if required
5. Transport to the channel members
6. Transit insurance, if required

Logistics costs have been calculated and they vary from 7% to 35% depending on the product and the market.

Logistics movement has a bearing on the profitability of the firm as also on its cash flow. Hence, the decisions on the following need special consideration:

1. Factory site
2. Geographic markets
3. Sources of main raw materials and components
4. Factory owned depots locations
5. Transport facilities
6. Inventory Management
7. Packaging
8. Material handling equipment

Besides, the government role is important in logistics planning due to the following reasons:

1. Taxation on sales—local and central
2. Excise duty
3. Octroi and entry tax
4. VAT
5. Motor Vehicles Act

Central sales tax is charged when the sale is made from one state of the country to the other, like from Delhi to Gujarat.

Local sales tax is charged when the sale is made within a state.

Excise duty is charged on manufacture of the products.

Octroi is charged when the product enters some municipal areas.

VAT is value-added tax.

The Motor Vehicle Act controls movement of trucks between states.

Summarising, the following areas need special attention of the vendors from retailer's viewpoint to give them critical competitive advantage in the market as a common ground for stand-alone retailer, to retail chains to shopping malls.

- Performance measurement of vendors
- Forecasting of demand for different products
- Order quantity: For the orders placed by retailers on different vendors
- Inventory control and replenishment design
- Inventory deployment from retailer's warehouse to the sales outlet
- Inventory management system
- Supply management
- Transport and distribution
- Warehousing operations
- Implementation of logistics systems
- Logistics organisation design

Success of retail trade depend on the support it receives from a variety of organizations, operations and its ability to not only satisfy its customers but to delight them.

Study of Inventory Control in Garment Industry

Store Layout, Design and Visual Merchandising

Store design objectives

- Consistent with retailer's image and strategy
- Positive influence on customer satisfaction and purchase behaviour
- Cost effective
- Flexible
- Meets needs of disabled

Layouts of Stores

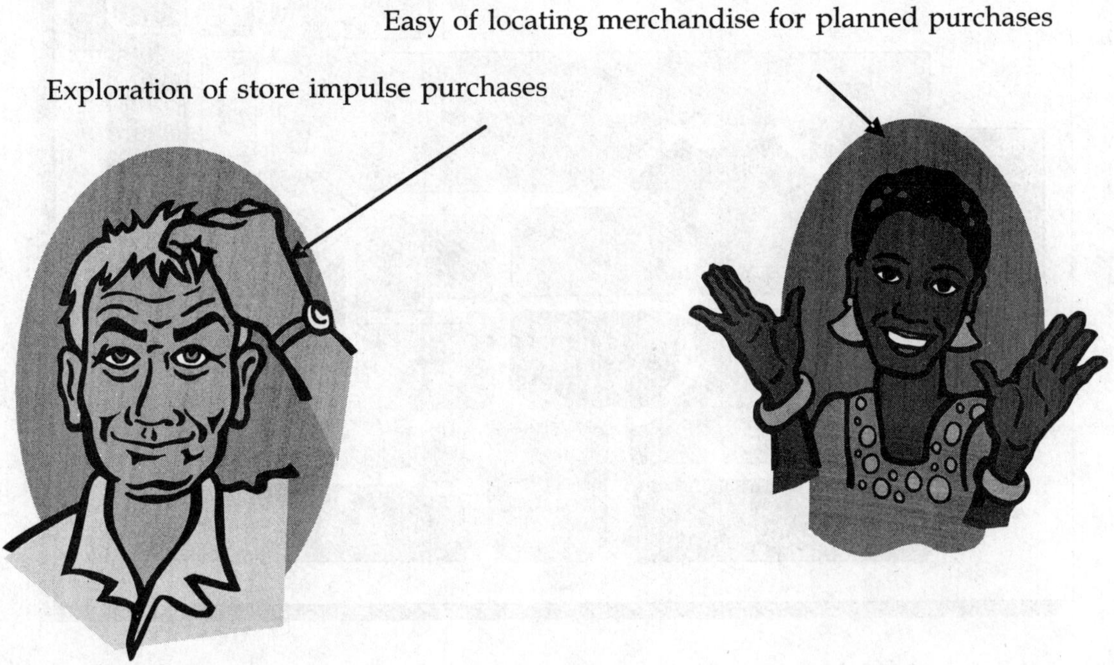

Types of stores layouts
- Free Form

Grid

Long gondolas in repetitive pattern.
- Easy to locate merchandise
- Does not encourage customers to explore store

Limited site lines to merchandise
- Allows more merchandise to be displayed
- Cost efficient

Used in grocery, discount, and drug stores.

Racetrack

Loop with a major aisle that has access to departments and store's multiple entrances.
- Draws customers around the store.
- Provides different site lines and encourage exploration, impulse buying
- Used in departmental stores

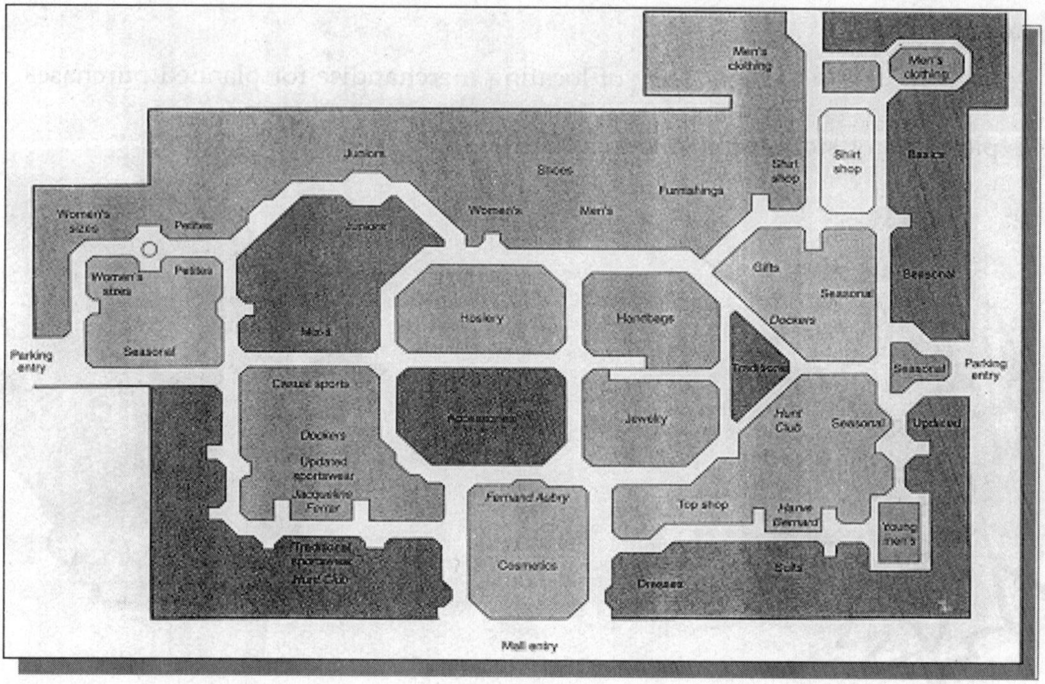

Example of racetrack layout

Free form-boutique layout

Fixtures and aisles arranged asymmetrically.

- Pleasant relaxing ambience doesn't come cheap – small store experience
- Inefficient use of space
- More susceptible to shoplifting – salespeople cannot view adjacent spaces.
- Used in specialty stores and upscale department stores

Layout

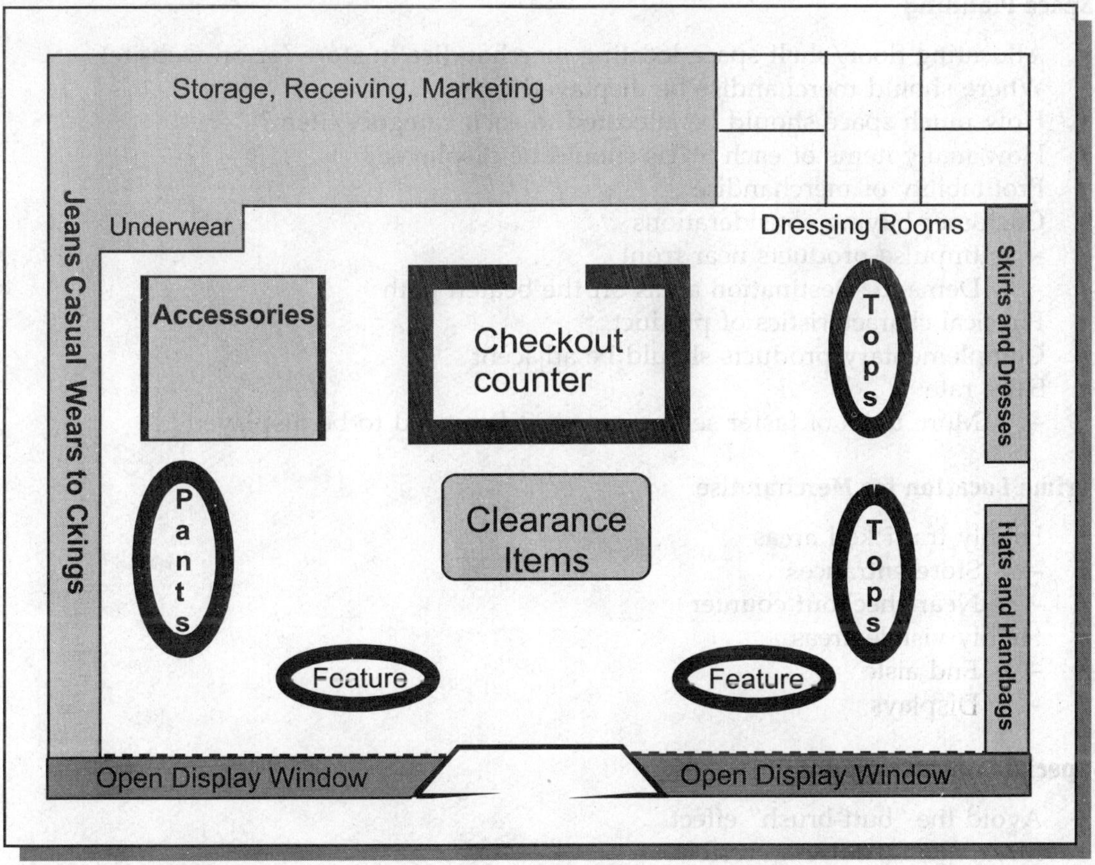

Feature areas

- End caps
- Promotional aisle
- Freestanding fixtures
- Point-of-sale areas
- Walls

Designing a web page—lessons from store designs

- Simplicity matters
- Getting around
- Prioritize
- Design layout based on what you want to accomplish

  Follow the standards of the industry leaders

Space Planning

- Allocating floor/shelf space locating merchandise in store (or on website)
- Where should merchandise be displayed?
- How much space should be allocated to each category/item?
- How many items of each SKUs should be displayed?
- Profitability of merchandise
- Customer buying considerations
  - Impulse products near front
  - Demand/Destination areas off the beaten path
- Physical characteristics of product.
- Complementary products should be adjacent
- Sales rate
  - More units of faster selling merchandise need to be displayed

Prime Location for Merchandise

- Highly trafficked areas
  - Store entrances
  - Near checkout counter
- Highly visible areas
  - End aisle
  - Displays

Special Considerations

- Avoid the "butt-brush" effect.
- Make merchandise accessible.
- Allow a transition zone.

Evaluating Space Productivity

Productivity ratios are output/input

- Sales per square foot
- Sales per linear foot
- Gross or contribution margin per square foot

Merchandise Presentation Techniques

- Idea-oriented Presentation
- Style/Item Presentation
- Colour Organization
- Price Lining
- Vertical Merchandising
- Tonnage Merchandising
- Frontal Presentation

Types of apparel displays

Gondola type

Straight rack

Rounders

Four-track display

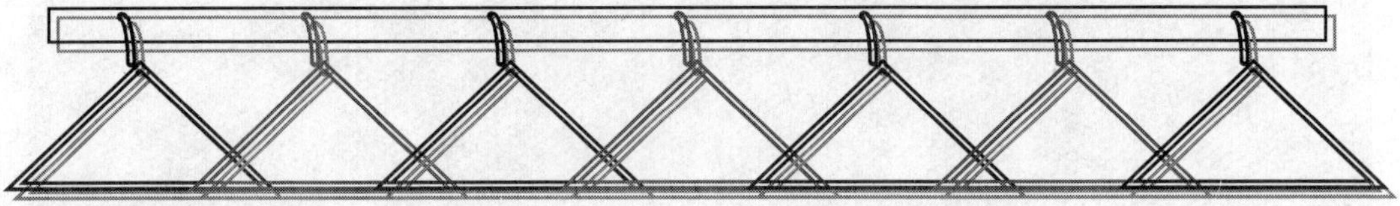

Single line garment display

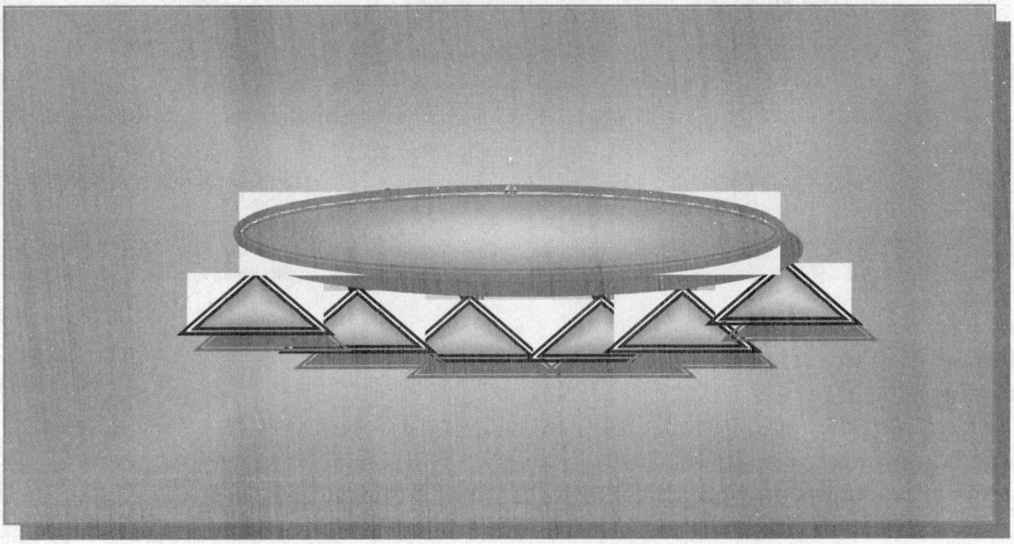

Round rack garment display

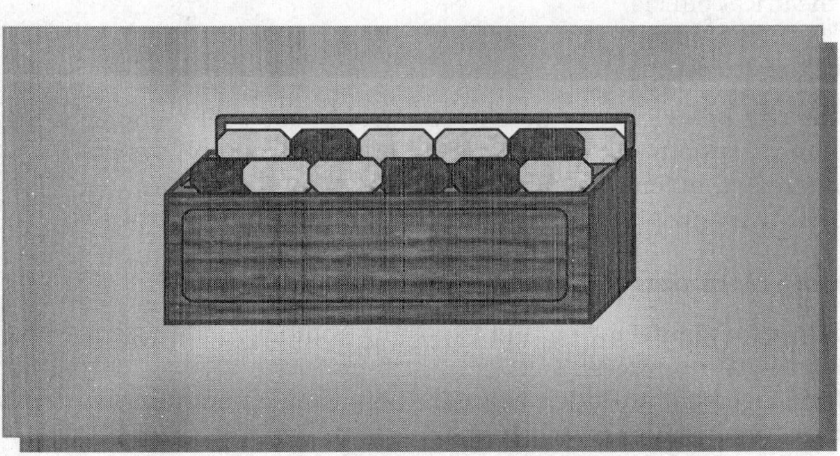

Pack display

Four-way
T shaped display
Gondola

Visible communication signs

- Coordinate signs and graphics with the store's image.
- Inform the customer.
- Use signs and graphics as props.
- Keep signs and graphics fresh.
- Limit the copy of signs.
- Use appropriate typefaces on signs
- Create theatrical effects.

Objectives of the Project

- To get the real knowledge of inventory cotrol in garment manufacturing.
- To structure a systematic and automated inventory control system.
- Make automated inventory counting and valuation procedure.
- Reduce the loss and problems of company in inventory control.

Limitations and constraints to the project

- Small garment manufacturing and exporting company
- Lack of financial resources.
- Lack of management attitude towards investments on adoption of new technology
- Centralized organizational structure
- Absence of clearly defined organizational hierarchy.
- Research methodology for problem identification

Problem Identification

In the organization first we have to try to identify the key problem to the organisation on which we can work and give our best to solve the problem.

Data Collection

Data required for the problem identification uses informal questionnaire method.
Sample size: Three who are in management of the company.

Questionnaire

- What is the problem you are facing presently in your company?
- Are you incurring any loss for that?
- How you are carraying the business with the problem?
- What kind of solution you find beneficial for you?
- Have tried before to solve the problem by some new way?

Analysis of data and getting the key point

After questionning informally to the management of the company and analyzing the data you have come to the conclusion that the company is facing problem in inventory control. There is no proper systematic way of counting the inventory, i.e., finished products, raw material and work in progress. At the end of the month they don't have the data on the total inventory of the company and the valuation of that. They have to stop sometimes their production for manual stock counting and putting them in computerized manner and saving the record. So the company has to face some loss for that. Management wants a systematic computerized updating of the inventory and which will able to solve the problem of inventory control.

Alternative options to solve the problem

The company is presently doing inventory control manually. To make it more systematic and always up-to-date record company need a computerized process. The manual process has some demerits which can be removed by computerized system. For that company has three options in hand.

A. Buying customized software from any software company according to their need
B. They can appoint any software engineer to design their own software
C. They can work with already existing inventory management software in the market

Evaluation of Alternative Wayouts

(I) Customized software

Benefits

- It is made by the software engineers of the software company to whom the order has been given. These engineers have professional experience of many years and they are experts of making customized software according to need.

- As the software will be made especially for the company so it must be perfect for the company.
- The software company will give the training needed for the new software.
- For any kind of problem the software company will help.

Constraints and Problems:

- Buying customized software is much expensive which the company doesn't want to spend.
- It will also take the time of the management as they have to guide on the software designing considering all points plus or minus.
- It will take time to adopt new software by the company.

(II) Appointing programmer for designing the software

Benefits

- The company can develop software under their inspection and constant interaction with the developer.
- The software will be cheaper than the customized software bought from the software company.

Constraints and Problems:

- It will take valuable time of the management.
- As it is made by the company's appointed programmer so it may not be perfect at the first time.
- Software becomes perfect after repeated using, checking, and developing new features. So it is time consuming.
- It will increase the expenditure of the company as they have to pay high salary to a skilled programmer.
- Again it will also take time of adopting and properly utilizing the new software.

(III) Already Existing Software:

Benefits

- It will be very less expensive as they are already in the market and there is much competition in the IT market also.
- These software are tested and upgraded regularly so there no problem can happen.
- Company is already working with such software like TALLY 7.2. So it is not difficult to them to work in that.
- For any problem with the software the software company who has developed it gives necessary help.

Constraints and Problems:

- These kinds of software are developed in a generalized form. As this software is not customized so the company must plan properly to utilize them according to their company and its processes.
- They also need some time to design and utilize the software according to their needs.

Choosing the Right Alternative

All the alternatives for solving the inventory control problem and several aspects of them were discussed with the management of the company and then we choose the third alternative i.e. working with already existing software of the market. We selected **Tally 7.2** as inventory control software. The reasons which were considered for selecting it are given below.

Reasons for selecting the Tally 7.2

- It is already being used and tested as an inventory controlling software in various companies. The software is already very successful in its job and solving the problem.
- The company though has not done inventory control by this software but they are already using this software Tally 7.2 for maintaining their accounts.
- Tally is a cheaper software than other customized software. It is a renowned one.
- It is not very tough to train the existing employees about tally 7.2. There are many courses provided by private institutes at a lesser expense.

Management Game

Teams need to select a number of products that have synergy in purchasing and marketing. Select the package needed for promoting the product group.

Discuss the modalities of selecting new products starting from idea generation to MR to commercial feasibility and viability.

It is said that products become brands with the help of advertising and sales promotion. The teams should take their pick of the variety of sales promotion plans available or think of some new innovative promotion technique for their product to always remain proactive to the market needs, situations and environmental changes.

Discuss the way other products including your competitors in retail trade are promoting their products and with what success.

CHAPTER

13

Strategies for Retail Advertising, Promotion and PR

Aims and Outcomes

The students need to know the various methods of communicating with their customers and the chapter provides them the insight of customer communication through advertising, promotion and PR.

Retailers need to communicate to their target markets to inform about the products they sell and to influence their behaviour for the products and they use the following techniques for the purpose:

1. Advertising
2. Sales promotion
3. Publicity
4. Public relations
5. Personal selling or direct marketing like Eureka Forbes does.

The retailer uses the above in different permutations and combinations to plan its persuasion strategy. These help in stimulating product demand to fulfil retailers' short-term and long-term goals that are in line with his overall business strategy.

Advertising campaigns are planned to achieve certain communication objectives in a given time frame in line with overall product, pricing and distribution policies of the company. The role of advertising in today's severe competitive environment is to differentiate the product from other products in the market. Advertising campaign becomes successful once such differentiation becomes evident. Customers go through stages of information processing before they take the purchase decision, like awareness of the product, learning about its benefits, formation of an attitude towards the product, and actual purchase action followed by post-purchase experience about the product. Advertising is used to build company's image according to the perception of the company in the public mind.

Retail advertisement is predominantly organised in the following manner:

Point of Purchase–POP Advertising using the following:

1. Danglers: These are hanging at strategic locations carrying the required message about the products placed on nearby shelves.
2. Streamers: These are like buntings that convey the advertising messages across the stores' area.
3. Posters: These are placed strategically on the store walls where the opportunity to see is the best.
4. In-house closed circuit TV giving AD films related to store's activities, new products, brands available with their locations.
5. Leaflets: These are placed on certain shelf tops from where these can be picked up by the prospective buyers.
6. Product's attractive packages can become advertising objects with the sheer attractiveness of the package.
7. Signages giving directions: These inform the location of certain product shelves, indirectly advertising the same.
8. Visual merchandising or window dressing: Stores place manniquines in shop windows to attract passersby who may not otherwise give the store a glance.

Promotion

Promotion tries to generate immediate consumer response with respect to company's overall marketing strategy. As advertising builds long-term customer awareness and attitudes, promotional plans are meant to have a short-term influence on the customers. Promotional plans can become counterproductive on the long-term perspective as when the promotion is withdrawn the sales may start dipping as at that time a competitor could start his own promotion plan.

Promotion can help build brand equity and awareness both for long-term and short-term gains. However, promotion does help in improving sales in the short term. Promotion can be a better method as compared to price reduction since price reduction becomes a long-term loss in revenue while promotional plans can be withdrawn once the target for which they were made has been achieved. Promotion plans can force customers to buy without delay when there is an extra advantage given for a short period as "buy the TV today and get a Walkman free and the offer is only for today."

Retail promotion is conducted usually on behalf of the manufacturer or the wholesalers from whom the product has been purchased for sale by the retailer to the customers. Since the money involved in promotion could be huge, it is either carried out by the manufacturer or jointly with their retailers sharing the financial burden, as both get the benefit of higher sales. The manufacturers can arrange for the customer promotion with the retailer becoming the hub of promotion plans. Manufacturer could organise the promotion jointly along with either the wholesaler or alone for the retailer. (If the retailer sells a fixed quantity extra, that is in addition to their average sales during the period, he gets extra discount, or gets a free holiday package to go to an exotic location like Thailand with family). These are known as dealer promotion as against the customer promotion.

After understanding retail advertising, it is important to see the entire gamut of advertising because retail business can use all the different forms of advertising depending on the size of retail operations.

Advertising often grips people's minds, their psyche, in a way that a make-belief world, a virtual world, gets created. So, what exactly is advertising? Who wants it, for whom is it created and how? These and several such questions need to be answered. How the advertiser can hit the bullseye of consumer psyche every time!

Advertising Management today has become an important area of business and that is why, even common man, lay persons are quite aware of the subject. However, for a professional, it is essential that not only the subject is learnt thoroughly but even subtle nuances are understood so that the person becomes comfortable with it. With practice expertise can be gained to strengthen the skills. Advertising is a fast moving, glamorous discipline and yet without proper concepts it can become quite banal.

Kotler says a satisfied customer does the best advertising!

Students of advertising management should learn the steps needed for making an effective advertising campaign. Sales promotion, public relations and publicity are the other methods used for increasing sales, brand awareness and related customer loyalty.

Advertising planning starts with setting sales objectives as also, advertising goals like improving the **top of the mind** recall. Next, advertising budget has to be formulated that takes into account, the stage of the product in the product life cycle, market share, competitor share of the market, frequency of advertising effort and the cost of alternative product (cost of product switching). The students must become familiar with the various media available with their costs to help them select the best possible media for the campaign. They need to know the media reach, impact, and frequency. Besides they should know the major media available, specific media for the campaign, geographical media coverage. Next, they should learn the methods of message generation, evaluation and selection of the message along with the social acceptability of the message. Lastly, the advertising effectiveness measurement must be planned in relation to the objectives selected for the campaign.

It must be clearly understood that there is a direct relationship between customer awareness level of the product and customer readiness for product trial. It can be seen that when the advertising frequency is increased it creates better product awareness that leads to larger trials by the customers. Stores normally organise yearly or periodic sales for boosting their turnover besides for getting rid of slow moving articles in their inventory.

Advertising Defined

Advertising texts have given a few definitions of advertising. With the thrust of media variants, i.e., several new media being available, the definition can now be modified. First we take the most popular definition, which is as follows:

> AMA (American Marketing Association), defines advertising as –
>
> Any paid form of non-personal presentation and promotion of ideas, goods and services of an identified sponsor

*The communication is non-personal, as nobody has personally conveyed it. What we witness in retail shops when the salesman talks to us to sell a product is that he is personally communicating with us and hence by definition it is not advertising.

*The presentation is for promoting the ideas, goods and services to create awareness and assist in selling the product

*A known person or firm does advertising. This becomes essential to avoid wrong messages being advertised, or sometimes the message becoming useless, as the potential buyer would not know to whom to approach for buying the product, idea or service advertised if the advertiser is unknown.

Advertising can be considered the soul of marketing in today's world of complex and severe competition. Or it can be a substitute elder brother who helps in taking purchase decisions.

Advertisement for target audience: It is important that the people who are likely buyers see the advertisement message. Hence, advertisers cater to different market segments with the help of separate media as also target-specific message. Advertisement for Toyota car would not have any takers in a slum cluster; advertisement for low cost clothing material would be of no use to the wealthy elite. Store marketers would do well to understand the local culture of how they use their time to create advertising campaigns most suited to them.

> The differences need to cover the following areas:
>
> 1. Print advertising to restrict itself to local press, pamphlets, hoardings like the wall paintings, audio-visual vans, local cinema, outdoor media like camels, elephants, balloons and product displays, merchandising.
> 2. Language used should be easily understood by the local population.
> 3. Timing should be just before the festive and bonus seasons.
> 4. The art should be simple, easily understood by the retail customers, the masses.

Consumer advertising deals with the actual buyers and users from the market segment and therefore uses a language and a medium best seen by the target segment. Market segment of the stores would have the rich families, upper middle level, and the middle-class families.

Geographic area coverage of media assists in focusing on the target segment where the firm believes there is maximum business potential. Retail trade usually calls for a smaller geographic coverage unless it is part of retail chain of stores. A firm with retail chain of stores, wanting to distribute its products on all India bases would have to look at national press, magazines with national circulation and readership, and national TV, including satellite and cable TV channels.

Similarly, firms with intenational retail chains wanting to do business internationally would select the right media; satellite TV, Internet or national press of the defined countries where the firms want to do business. Wal-Mart, in collaboration with Bharti Telecom, is the latest possible international entrant into India's retail horizon.

Hence, it can be surmised that advertising plays multifaceted roles in business. Not only it informs the target segment of customers but persuades them too to buy the product or service offered by the advertiser.

Since the communication is non-personal, the one drawback remains as no immediate and direct reaction or response is available to the sponsor of the advertising.

Personal Selling

In case of consumer goods, personal selling effort is 20% and advertising backup support is 80%. Since retail is for consumer goods the role of advertising to persuade the customers is considerable.

In case of industrial products personal selling is 80% and advertising support is 20%.

	Personal selling	Advertising
Consumer products	20%	80%
Industrial products	80%	20

Advertising Mix Factors

Advertising is one of the marketing mix factors. Let us analyze advertising mix factors. There are six sides to advertising in totality. They are given below:

1. Advertiser
2. Advertising Agency
3. Media
4. PR Consultants
5. Ancillary Services
6. Freelance Services

Advertisers can be categorized as profit making organizations, the retailers included, and non-profit making organizations. The first category consists of the following:

Government and government bodies including public sector companies. The government advertises for purchasing through tenders, selling surpluses, recruitment through Public Service Commissions.

Manufacturers advertise when they want to sell direct to consumer like power, industrial raw materials. They advertise to buy from the market what raw materials components they need to manufacture their finished products.

1. Service providers like travel agents, hotels, airlines, advertise to sell their services,
2. Importers advertise to sell their goods to the target segment.
3. Distributors, retailers and other members of distribution channel advertise to sell their products. Since their area of operation is limited their advertising is also confined to the geographic area they serve.

4. Mail order suppliers advertise so that their catalogues are purchased by their target segment, which could result in their getting orders by mail. Burlington's and *Reader's Digest* are examples of mail order suppliers.

The second category of advertisers are non-governmental organizations, like family planning groups, destitute children help groups, de-addiction centres.

From the earlier days of hand painted posters, media has come up with cable and satellite TV revolution. Joining the bandwagon is Internet and computer designing of advertisements.

Broadly media are characterized as follows:

For retailers the ideal advertising media should include the following:

1. Press: Local press for the local markets
2. Electronic: Indian urban markets and even the periphery areas are getting the Radio throughout the day, while TV coverage is amounts to 40 per cent (and increasing) of the radio coverage.
3. Computer, Internet: Computers and internet race has started only now.
4. Outdoor: Hoardings like wall paintings are quite popular in India.
5. Point of purchase: Shops keep only robust wall hangings, danglers. They need to look attractive to the customer's sensibility. Besides, posters on the walls, signages, CCTVs are the other media used by retail trade.
6. Direct Mail: With low level of education in several areas, instead of direct mail more effective option would be audio-visual advertising. Retailers do send advertising mail to a selection of prospective customers in their market coverage areas.
7. Miscellaneous, like balloons in the sky, camels and elephants with visual banners can be more useful. These are used during exhibitions, melas where retailers too participate.

Press, more especially newspaper, provides greater flexibility, timeliness, good local coverage, good acceptance by the readers and high degree of believability. Press has, however, low shelf life, and production quality is usually suspect and only a small but the right target audience. Local press, pamphlets in Hindi or in local language would be useful.

Television, on the other hand, although not very popular in retail stores is used by retail chains, multiplexes, malls, combines both audio and visual imagery with colour and motion, causes greater grip on the customer's psyche, has high reach. However, TV advertising costs are high with less time for the customer to see it with a lot of congestion, especially prime time, in a highly erratic viewership situation. With low power coverage and long outages TV viewing, although much looked for, becomes a rarity, a dream only. However, with better power situation, TV in the long run is going to be the media for the masses.

> Cable TV Network is ideally suited for retail shops. A new trend has emerged of having a stream carrying advertising message as a bottom space cover in specified popular channels.

Radio provides for mass exposure with high geographic and demographic coverage to low cost. However, it gives only audio exposure and like TV gives only for fleeting moments. Radio has a much bigger population cover of the country and to that extent is well suited as a media. Retailers can use the popular FM Radio channels as the teenagers listen to the channel as a craze. Retail promotion can be advertised on FM Radio as it covers the right geographic area and population.

Magazines can be used for selective high density geographic and demographic coverage, are associate with prestige, lifestyle and related credibility. It can have good high quality advertising long life on the shelf of the target audience and several people read each copy. However, all the magazine readers may not be in the target customer group of the retailers.

Outdoor advertising is cost-effective, has high focused repeat exposure. Its use is limited to the passersby of the route of the advertising and it limits creativity as well.

Press relates to newspapers, dailies, English, Hindi and regional language papers, magazines, in different languages, targeting various segments, cultural, religious, sports, fashion, films, wildlife, the list is a long one. The advertiser has to look for the right paper, magazines which are read by the target segment to ensure OTS (opportunity to see). Many top executives have virtually no time to watch television and hence they get the news and other information from newspapers and business magazines. Marketers of products meant for this market segment should therefore use newspapers and magazines to reach the target segment effectively. Expensive cars, laptop computers, and expensive dress materials could fall in the category.

Electronic media relates to television, radio, video cassettes. Television as a media for advertising has made the biggest impact on almost all the segments of customers. Satellite and cable TV have invaded practically all homes. Viewership of TV has increased manifold and terms like couch potato have been invented for people who are constantly viewing the TV. This fact has opened up advertising vistas for majority of the products. The advertiser has only to understand the programme one-segment views and then he can plan to place his advertisement during that particular programme. Similarly, FM channel of the radio has become popular in Metro towns with a large teenage following. Products meant for teens can be advertised on FM with great certainty of success. Tele-marketing and Tele-shopping are making strides as the latest media. Products are sold through telephones in one case while in the other; TV is used for demonstrating the working of the product and orders solicited.

Computer and Internet: The medium of communication of computers and the Internet are relatively new in India but they are making great strides in advertising and marketing world.

Hence, in the present day context it is important to understand these to succeed. With online e-commerce, banking, and purchasing it is expected that people with buying power will be more hooked to computers then ever before. It is important to note that information technology is the future of communication with computers and telecommunications joining hands to provide the safest, fastest and low cost reliable communication. Advertisers need to understand the medium and take full advantage of the same.

Outdoor: Relates to hoardings, billboards, neon signs, bus panels, kiosks, balloons and the like. Advertisers use these as reminder advertisements as well as product launch ads too.

Direct Mail: Several marketers resort to sending technical literature by post to prospective customers, including *Reader's Digest*, Burlington.

Point of Purchase Advertising: It has been updated with technological advances. Retail shops were content earlier with posters, danglers and products innovative packaging. Today, multimedia has provided with interactive computer screens where the customers can get any information about the shop including availability of product, stocks prices. Many shops keep continuous TV programmes with animation, cartoons and product-advertisements.

Teleshopping is becoming popular but gradually, as the Indian shopper wants to see and feel the touch of the product before buying it. Additionally, shopping expeditions become fun time outings for the family and it would be difficult to replace them by **television-on screen-shops**.

Telemarketing uses the telephone line to tell the prospective customers about the services the marketer is providing and is, at times a good approach to elicit right response from the customer.

Miscellaneous Advertising Media

We have all seen big balloons in the sky carrying advertising messages, advertisements on bus panels, yellow pages, directories, and rail and air tickets, even on matchboxes. We have also witnessed advertisements on camels and elephants especially designed for fairs. Human imagination can only limit to the extent people will locate an existing unutilized medium or discover or invent one for the purpose.

India had witnessed lowering of prices of newspapers from rupees four to rupees one and a half. This drastic reduction had been possible because of heavy advertising revenue the newspapers get. In order to get a good share of advertising, the press depends on its circulation figures—higher the circulation more the advertising revenue. And yet, in view of heavy competition the newspapers face, they resort to selling and advertising their space too. Let us see how it is done.

- Rate cards: These are mailed or given to advertising agencies and advertisers to make them aware of advertising costs for advertising in the paper.
- Direct mail with copies of successful campaigns and promotional folders
- Maps of geographic areas covered with its demographic details
- Availability of research material
- Copies of special numbers and advance programme of special issues
- For TV Channels: Information about TV programmes of interest like films, chat shows
- Outdoor-hoarding positions availability and number of vehicles passing through that place

Media Planning

The questions to be answered are the following:

- Whom are we trying to reach?
- Where are they located?
- The best time for them to see the advertisements?

To answer the first question we have to know the exact market segment. Since all the people in the vicinity of the store could be prospective buyers, some are more inclined to buy. These marketers segregate through demographic, psychographics social class and lifestyle categories. It is believed that people in one segment would behave in similar manner and would have same type of needs and preferences. Rich people with trendy lifestyle will be reading magazines like *Vogue, Cosmopolitan,* while those not in that class will not be reading these magazines. This helps in focusing on the segment directly interested in your product. Residential areas near the stores have the best possible customer groups living for these stores. If the area is of middle and lower-middle class persons, then the media selection should consider the likes of the people living there like the soap operas of the TV channels. Women oriented products can be advertised during the showing of these soaps. If the neighbouring area is of elitist class, then magazines of the elite class, certain news channels are more suited as advertising media.

With several languages spoken in the country, there are newspapers, magazines for each language and they are the best media to reach the people of the area using a particular language. Products used by metro towns can be advertised in English as it is the language that most people understand.

Television as a media has a wide reach today and telecasting is available in several languages. If price is not a major deterrent then TV as a media is most effective.

In order to find the answer to the question "what to advertise and when?" it is best to see the creative advertisement. If the Ad is pictorial full of exquisite colours then glossy magazines are the right print media. If a lot of demonstration is to be shown, use TV.

Magazines have their definite readership and language flavour. What will go well in *India Today* will look out of place in a movie magazine.

Readership surveys of magazines tell us the following:

- Percentage of men and women readers
- Percentage of age group in each case, for example what percentage of women readers in the age group of 25 to 34 read *Femina's* every issue
- Percentage of income groups reading a magazine, for example what percentage of men in the income group of Rs. 25,000 pm read *India Today's* each issue
- Percentage of education segment, for example, what percentage of graduates read each issue of *Business India*

In the same way information is available with respect to marital status of the readers, number of children they have, what religion they practice.

Given below is the advertising volume in the USA in the year 1980:

Media	Million $	%	Media	Million $	%
Newspaper total	15615	28.5	TV Total	11330	20.7
National	2335	4.3	Network	5105	9.3
Local	13280	24.2	Spot	3260	6.0
Mags. total	3225	5.9	Local	2965	5.4
Weekly	1440	2.6	Radio total	3690	6.7
Women's	795	1.5	Network	185	0.3
Monthly	990	1.8	local	2755	5.0
Farm publications	135	0.3	Direct mail	7655	14
Outdoor	610	1.1	National total	30435	55.6
Business publications	1695	3.1	Local	24316	44.6
Misc.	10795	19.7	Grand total	54750	100

Media Status

- Newspapers: Good for information, news, entertainment and local activities
- Reading public is adults mainly elderly, better educated and comfortably off

Wide Market Coverage

Consumer Magazines: Good for current social and cultural events, mostly local, glossy but quality not uniform in every magazine. Reading public is athletes, cooks, housewives, hobbyists and investing public. Circulation in large and medium size towns.

Specific Magazines: Good for special needs, like women magazines, film based, health, cooking, business, sports and cultural/social magazines. They are for the trendy public and they increase their awareness of the social and cultural environments.

Radio is a media of the masses, highly varied in content, from news to classical music to art and film music. The media covers entire country and with FM it is becoming popular again amongst the youth as it provides clear voiced music of all variety. Especially popular in villages where colour TV is not yet available. Can be used as a media for the masses and for the youth with FM. Radio does not provide international exposure in a way TV does with satellite channels.

Television is most visible and covering large part of the country including the remote villages. Great impact due to audio-visual effect can use it to give LIVE demonstrations. Viewers are from the entire market including all segments, the whole family (timing may differ for parents and children). Advertising costs are high. Uncertain about reaching the desired segment as TV remote is used to blank advertisements most of the time.

Outdoor advertising has high visibility in a limited way, for the people on the road. It distracts drivers and hence is being banned by some states including Delhi. Gives brand awareness and broad product view.

Direct Mail: Selective and personal, becoming popular, the mailer controls the persons who will get to read the mail but has no control on their responses.

Cable TV uses the superimposing technique, mostly not acceptable to the channel owners. Low cost and local advertising is possible. Viewers find it an irritant as they watch their favourite programme. These are ideally suited for retail advertising.

Yellow Pages: Mass media, with phone owners, limited usage. Can be used by retailers extensively, especially for dedicated product sellers.

New media on the cards: In France phone service has provided small computers Minitel to their subscribers, from which they can contact, banks, shops, and travel services among other services. Computers, at home have software, which superimposes, advertisements with any matter you may be browsing on the Internet. You see the advertisements on the bottom of the computer screen, in supermarkets; big screens show views of their selling area and products telling the viewers where in the mart they can find a particular product. This is an extension of the Point of Purchase (POP), which has remained in vogue for a time.

In order to make the music albums popular, singers and others in the music world have started resorting to showing music videos with vibrant motion/colours and action which attracts the young mind. Music videos are short films which have specialized directors actors dancers and the crew.

Situation: Music videos are good entertainer's ads. They also advertise the music albums. Discuss if you rate them as advertisements or as entertainment. If they are a bit of both, discuss their role as advertisement. Do the music videos follow the telecasting norms of decency in India? Do you think in this way, subtle advertising of music albums through music videos is side tracking the real advertising time?

Solutions: Divide the class into groups of five persons, who will form an advertising agency. Each group will do the following:

- Give a name to their agency
- Allot portfolios among themselves as given below-

1. CEO
2. Account director
3. Creative director
4. Copy writer
5. Media planner

Next, jointly they meet a firm and take a brief for planning its advertising for the next year. (Select a retail firm where one member has easy access to the top brass. In case it is not possible, ask your professor to give you a hypothetical firm's brief.)

- After getting the brief, find out the target market segment. Most likely, the client will give you ample information on this subject.
- Next, the media planner should suggest the right media for reaching the target segment. This is discussed and finalized after taking client's approval.
- Keeping the media in view, the creative persons should work out an advertising layout. CEO and others then test the layout through advertising research in the market segment and modify the layout if needed.
- Find out the current rates of media purchasing and finalize the budget. It should be in line with the budget idea given by the client.
- Prepare their individual portfolio of such total retail advertising plan and keep with them. These will come handy when the students go out for job interviews.

As a corollary, find out who are the members of other market segments who will be exposed to the advertisements and discuss if a demand which cannot be met is being created by the advertisement. If yes, is it ethical? Especially for countries like India.

Now add one more member to the team, and he should play-act the role of advertising manager of the client's firm... now, arrange a meeting of your team with the advertising manager and discuss the campaign with him. (If possible do it with the real advertiser's man) prepare for the meeting, anticipate the question he is going to ask and your answers to them. One member should be asked to minute the meeting.

At the end of the meeting, please analyze the entire episode with the help of your professor and locate the improvement opportunities in your presentation.

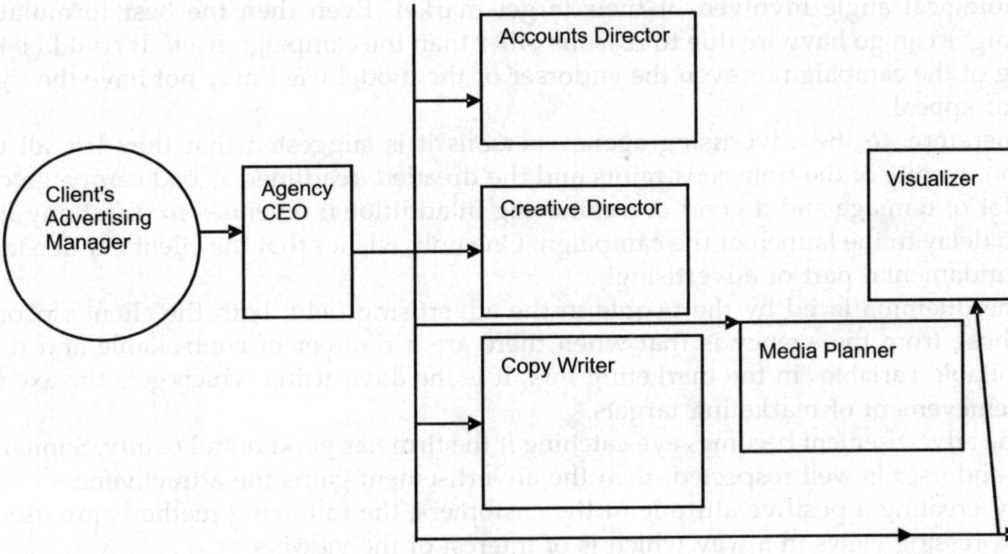

Once the team has been formed it can be used to do many such tasks. A well made campaign is a reward to the students itself.

Bob Jones, the Advertising Pundit from the UK, says, *"Of course advertisers want accountability, but it must often be measured in a more modest and intangible way than we would like. I am afraid that we will have to accept that much advertising can repay fully over long periods of time and its payback is impossible to monitor with any degree of precision."*

We find that millions of rupees are spent on advertising everyday. Firms spend up to 30% of their profit after-tax on advertising. What is the method in the paradoxical situation? We will try to analyze the same in this chapter.

Are the products made by us needed or used by any one? If yes then who are they, when and how they buy and what they are willing to pay for it? An advertising agency needs to understand answers to these questions in great degree of accuracy.

Successful campaigns are the result of this knowledge and how the agency uses it to a large degree. Besides they should know the market changes occurring on a continuous basis and be good at communicating. An excellent copywriter using good correct language may not be able to cause even a ripple if the copy is high flouting and going above the intelligence level of the target market. The mindset of the people, the slang, the use, and the imagery acceptable or valued by them will create the right impact. What matters most to the copywriter in a product may have little interest to his audience. The lifestyle of advertising people, with good salaries may be totally at variance with the customer group. As film actors sometimes live in the slum areas to get a feel of the place and the mindset of the dwellers there, it will be a good idea for the agency people to at least investigate the target market segment persons in depth with an open mind.

Making of an advertising campaign is a team task and that is where the team members who may be experts in their own field of activity must teach one person the psychological angle involved of their target market. Even then the best formulated campaigns can go haywire due to reasons other than the campaign itself. It could be the timing of the campaign or even the endorser or the model used may not have the right kind of appeal.

Therefore, to the advertising agency persons it is suggested that they use all the caution in spite of the time constraints and the dreaded deadlines. A bad campaign can do a lot of damage and a good one can bring in additional revenues to offset any loss due to delay in the launch of the campaign. One only wishes that the clients understand this fundamental part of advertising!

The dilemma faced by the people in the advertising field, both the client's people and those from the agency is that when there are a number of controllable and non-controllable variables in the marketing mix, it is the advertising which gets the axe for non-achievement of marketing targets.

The advertisement becomes eye-catching if the firm has good brand equity. Similarly, if the endorser is well respected, then the advertisement gains the attractiveness.

For creating a positive attitude of the customers, the following methods are used:

- Expressing views in a way which is of interest of the viewers
- Enhancing customer's ego by praising him for taking the right decisions
- Making statements that can be verified by the viewers, through logical reasoning.
- Giving the benefits the customers will derive from the products. At times living the conclusion to be drawn to the viewers to arouse their curiosity. The cream makes skin smooth and glowing, have you tried it?
- Giving the competitive benefits with stress on the positive side of your product and not so positive of the competitors. The comparison highlights the product as the right choice. These days' competitive advertisements have become the vogue. Care must be taken to give the right picture, the truth and nothing but the truth, because otherwise you may be dragged into courts by the competitors.
- Emotions play a vital role in purchase made by people, although most will not agree to this statement. For a prettier you! Get the man of your choice—use xxyy cosmetics
- Do you know what will happen when you are no more? Save for your loved ones, insure with us–LIC
- What life you want to give to your grand children? Vote for a pollution free world – grow more trees!

- Today your friendly neighbour may kill you—an advertisement against drunken driving

Now that you have got your customers to buy your products how are you going to retain them? The onslaught of competitive forces is never ending.

Raising your brand equity through is one way of doing it. Next, the risk associated with the change need to be stressed, "Change your car's engine oil and lower the time of overhaul."

"The substitute toothpastes cause tooth decay, are you willing to risk it?" or, "you did try to change once and it led to disaster. Please make sane decisions now."

> The customers can be immunized against the virus of competitive product by putting your own product on its rightful pedestal.
>
> Another method is to keep stating what the competition is saying and then one by one refuting all their claims, logically.

Continuous sales promotional plans are other methods albeit they can be copied sooner than later.

You sell pure fruit juices. Competition claims that no fruit juice can have a shelf life to be able to sell in the entire country. Talk about it and then give proof of your several filling and juice extracting facilities around the country.

You have to sell the metro rail to the local public. So far, personal transport has been in use, as other public transport like the bus has been over-crowded and the people do not want to go near it. Talk about the cost saving, rising petrol costs, and reducing pollution levels, making roads safe for children.

In most advertising there are four factors, which need to be considered together.

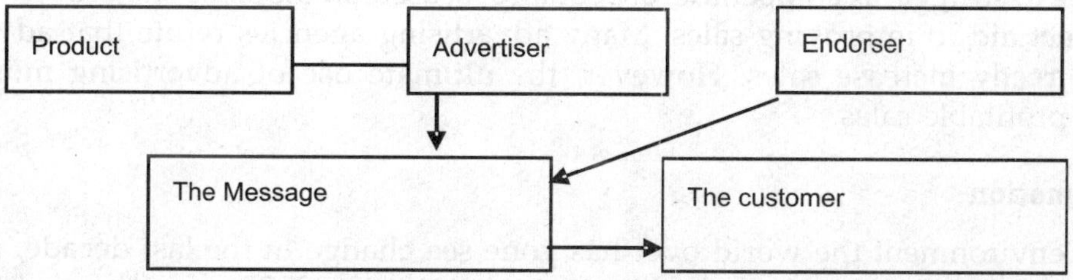

Person belonging to a group with similar attitudes should make endorsement. Furthermore he should stand the customers self-scrutiny test. He should be imaging the self-testing of the customer. He or she should be likeable and attractive. If the product qualities are nebulous in nature and cannot be verified easily then endorsements will be more useful. The customers should know endorsers as worthy of their acceptance. Endorser should take care to project his image as that of an outsider! He should talk like an expert, endorse the firms product only, and not competitors, should give a long time endorsement.

Objectives of Advertising

Given below are some of the objectives of advertising:

1. Sales as objective
2. Communication
3. Prompt direct action: This is the major objective in retail where a customer comes to buy and advertisement offering a promotional plan can have the desired effect
4. Encourage customer to ask for information
5. Giving message of need and its satisfaction
6. Product's success stories to reinforce product/brand loyalty
7. The benefit story
8. Attitude change
9. Reassurances
10. New retail outlet promotion

Besides, the purposes of advertising are as follows:

1. Launch of a new product
2. Modification in products
3. Changes in price
4. New packing or, promotional plans, e.g. buy one get one free
5. Educating the customers for proper usage of the product
6. To retrieve lost sales, e.g. due to strike in the factory
7. Reminder ads and for maintaining sales
8. To recruit staff

Sales as objective: Business today is for continuous improvement in the bottom line. Profit remains the prime motive and to achieve a reasonable return on investment firms have to struggle as competitors are equally focused on the same subject. Advertising is a distinct aid to improving sales. Many advertising agencies refute that advertising should directly increase sales. However, the ultimate use of advertising must be to improve profitable sales.

Sales Promotion

Business environment the world over has gone sea change in the last decade, more so because of the political upheavals, like disintegration of USSR, opening up of China, turmoil in far-east economies. Let us understand the business environment, as it exists in India today:

1. Severe international competition
2. Large middle and upper middle consumer class
3. Changes in money supply and interest rates

These factors have led to an era of continuous sales promotion. It is therefore important to learn what sales promotion is and how it can be made effective.

With the number of products increasing in each group the customer is the main beneficiary. However, he is also a bit confused as each advertiser is telling the benefit story to him. The need to give that extra benefit to clinch the order leads to promotion.

Consumers need extra stimulus to buy the product. The dealers or retailers need that extra benefit to stock and push the product these promotional activities must be advertised to be of any value in increasing market share.

In sales promotion the marketers are giving something extra. This is in lieu of price reduction. Price reduction, unlike promotion gets to be an extended expense; while promotional expenses can be withdrawn any time you feel you have achieved your objectives.

Sales promotion provides extra incentive, an offer of direct inducements that enhance the basic value of a product for a limited time to stimulate immediate distributor commitment, sales force effectiveness and consumer purchasing.

Coke and Pepsi advertise in order to promote sales as well to encourage retail trade.

Customer promotion can be undertaken as follows:

- Test our new product or re-buy. Added incentives make people give new products a try.
- Be loyal to us, we are there to look after you through our promotional plans
- Buy more—Pepsi says, "yeh dil mange more" —the heart wants more.
- Buy our entire range—for this purpose sometimes products are bundled together.
- Promotion increases sales immediately. It helps in advertising and other marketing efforts like personal selling. Just as it is important to advertise the promotions so that the customer gets to know about it. Lack of advertising for the target market will render the promotion campaign unrewarding and the objectives will not be met.

Trade promotion helps in the following manner:

- Get better retailers
- Better shelf space at the retail stores
- Superior merchandising
- Increase stocks and sales push
- Training the sales personnel of retailers
- Better product knowledge (as a spin off)
- Improvement in retailer's responses in future

Sales promotion can take upto 70 of total marketing budget and hence it is a major factor, which needs constant nurturing. The main reasons for the shift towards promotion are as follows:

- Immediate results: With focus on meeting target sales promotion provides quick response technique.
- Measuring effectiveness: As the results are quick to achieve, promotional plan results can be seen early.
- Retailers have acquired a status they never had, as through computerized information base they know their customers, their buying powers and habits best. Therefore, promotion plans with retailers at the hub, can be most effective.

- Increased competition and plethora of products make you vie for customer's money. Advertising may not provide the motivation needed for making customers buy your products.
- Buyer's loyalty is limited and can be enhanced with active participation of retailers. Since your competitors are doing exactly the same, you have to be on the constant look out for better and more rewarding promotional plans for both your customers and retailers.

There are various ways of product promotion.
Buy one, get one free
Buy now, pay later

Many firms offer discount coupons as incentive to buy at a lower price. When the customer goes to redeem the coupon a good salesman can sell a lot of the company products. At least the customer would have tried your product and may be, he will like it so much that he buys it again.

Special low cost packs are offered as promotion to encourage trial. Similarly, some firms give money-back offers where in the unlikely event of the customer not liking the product he can get the money back. Experience shows that hardly anyone ever comes to return the product for cash, unless the product is defective.

Contests are also used as sales promotions. If your product package has a gift written on it you get it, Colgate offers, millions of rupees, besides other goodies like computers.

Hotels and airlines offer high usage, discounts, and frequent flyers free tickets as promotion plans.

Trade promotion plans offer the following to retailers:

- Display incentives for better merchandising and shelf use
- Short-term discounts for inventory control and sales push
- Turnover discounts are given for achieving sales targets
- Assistance in running sales contests among retailers/salespersons
- Cooperative advertising with the retailers where advertising expense is shared on mutually agreed basis.

Sales promotion is an offer of direct money saving to the customer without diluting products brand equity (as can happen in case of price reductions). Consumer sales promotion encourages new product sales, increase usage of existing products, helps sales of entire range of products and adds to selling efforts. Retail promotion helps in building inventories with the distribution network and indirectly acts as a sales push in the market as no one can keep large inventories for long.

Depending on product and trade practices firms send dealers on trips to foreign countries on achieving the targets. Some firms offer cars and other consumer goods as incentive to achieve the sales as planned. Promotion programmes are known to increase sales and market share, which lasts as long as competition does not retaliate. Hence, it is wise to closely observe competitive activities, and being proactive rather than reacting to losing situations.

Public Relations (PR)

Focus is on defining PR, common objectives of PR, the PR process, and the target public for PR, the PR message. PR can be and usually is an effective form of creating positive marketing climate for the firm and thus becomes part of marketing communication methods.

Marketing PR can be organized through publications that carry company's annual reports, articles. Besides events like press conferences, seminars, trade shows are used to reach the target public. Sponsoring of a variety of events in shopping malls, cultural events, contests help in marketing PR. News items about the company on television, radio or TV and the press are some other tools used for marketing PR.

Marketing PR achieves greater credibility of the public, as it has no bias of the company's own advertising. It can help generate excitement and product expectation in the market before the product launch and the related advertisements. It creates an acceptance base amongst the customers who become loyal and also help in increasing sales by recommending it to others. It makes influencers more tuned to the product and the company.

What we see on TV as advertisements for eggs, milk is not direct marketing/ advertising if you do not find any sponsor. Drink more milk, eat eggs everyday are meant to create awareness among the public and hence can be called PR campaigns. Unfortunately, the task of PR is not appreciated by most of the persons and it tends to become a thankless job. In election campaigns, after the candidate has finished talking and gone his secretary remains to answer the questions regarding how the speech should be interpreted for improving the candidate's image. After the corporate Chairman has given an expose of the firm's plans, its elaboration and explanation is done by the PR persons. Press releases are part of the PR job. In case of any catastrophe the PR has to explain how the firm is coping with it and the damage control measures it is going to take. The famous oil spill in the ocean had the oil company's PR people on their toes. It may be added that in such crises even the CEO takes the role of PR. Retail PR is tuned to customer and prospective customers service by providing the desired information and facilitating their movement in the store.

Public relations cover all the communications of the firm except the marketing/ advertising and personal selling communications.

Public relations can be defined as, "the process of understanding public attitudes on relevant issues, interpreting these attitudes for management, and then working either to go with the organizational polices and practices with those attitudes or to modify the attitudes themselves." Retail shops, shopping malls, chain stores and speciality shops all need to get a good rapport with their customers. Therefore, each member of the retail team must become a good PR person for the store.

Publicity is only one aspect of PR job, which covers the making of press releases given regarding the firm's activities and plans. Besides PR is a useful tool in creating positive attitude.

The sale of retail products in the target market segment depends on the following:

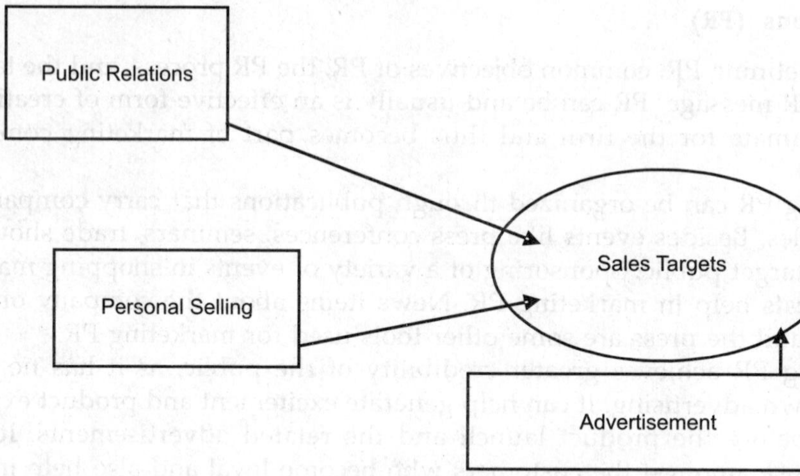

Public relations task in marketing activities is subtle. Nonetheless, it is equally important, as through PR, the firm is able to build custom/ customer base not as a hard sell exercise, but with gaining customer support. This is done with great finesse and yet with bringing customers on the right side of the retail shop. *You like us you buy from us.*

The main features of PR are as follows:

- When the firms arrange PR activities they do not have total control on the message being sent. It becomes the prerogative of the editors of the media and they can surely use their right. In personal selling or in marketing/ advertising the firm talks all good things about the product. In case of PR the media men can express their likes and dislikes in their reports and not just what the firm wants them to do.
- PR is addressed to several different classes of people, the customers being one of them. The message goes to the firm's stakeholders, the buyers, the sellers, the investors, banks, the government, local bodies, trade associations and social activists like the environment protection groups. It pays to keep these people on the firm's right side.
- PR does not have any direct media cost as the PR message goes in the form of media editorial. No media space or time needs to be purchased for PR.
- PR besides assisting in improving sales also does a number of pre-planned tasks like improving investor's interest in the firm. Labour relations and activities connected with labour welfare get publicity through PR.
- The most visible role of PR is seen during annual general meetings of the shareholders of the firms. The entire programme is managed by the PR department of the firms.

The PR Base

Firms have plans for marketing, advertising with properly laid down objectives. Same way they have plans and objectives for PR activities. While marketing objectives could be increasing market share, enlarging geographic base or even training of their sales persons, PR objectives can be stated as follows:

Two-way communication between firm's management and its public, as can be seen from the chart given below:

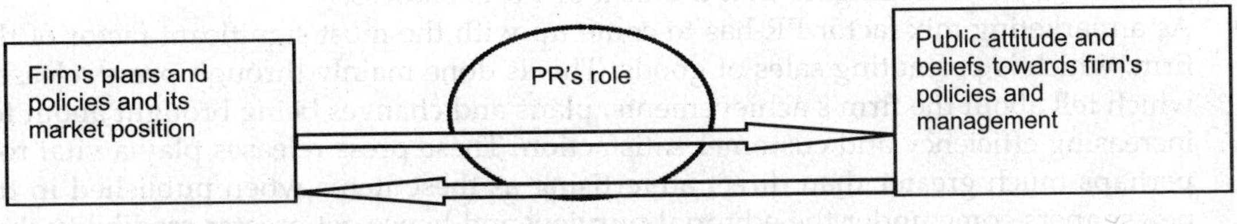

PR department, therefore is not just the custodian of firm's information base, but it also plays a dynamic role in highlighting the public opinion about the store as it tends to modify it in its favour.

An example of the effect of PR activities or lack of them will clarify the point for the students.

It was in 1960s that the Bangalore based excellent public sector firm Hindustan Aeronautics Ltd. had been manufacturing small aircraft used to spray insecticides in the vast expanse of agricultural land. Some of these aircraft crash-landed due to some technical problem and such a good firm went into disrepute. It took a lot of PR work to bring it back as a major technology driven firm in the Indian mindset.

As against this, about the same time an American firm operating in India came to know that its Aviation Turbo Fuel (ATF) has got a tiny trace of extra moisture than specified. The firm promptly downgraded the ATF as kerosene oil and gave prominent PR advertisements in this regard thus taking a mileage from an otherwise sure disastrous situation for the firm. The high image of the firm in the public mind carried the day for the firm.

For this purpose it becomes the foremost task of the PR department of any firm to keep its eyes and ears close to the ground and plan proactive interaction rather than trying to retrieve lost ground on any account. It is always better to remain above suspicion rather than keep organising only "firefighting job" all the time.

- PR has to coordinate between public opinion and firm's plans and policies. This would help even at the last minute for taking corrective action if needed. Most firms are aware of the strong sentiments of the public towards environment and pollution control. Stores need to stock only eco-friendly products. As the firms take measures in the direction of becoming non-polluting, they should also keep the public informed about their actions in this regard. Plans and policies are not enough as the people want to know the action firms are taking. Firms need to address themselves with other socially relevant issues like stopping the use of plastic bags and adopting green areas of the town for maintenance. The firms are corporate citizens of the country and it is imperative that they behave as such. It is equally important to let the public know that you are a responsible corporate citizen and this is achieved through PR.
- As new competitive firms start operating they can, with a little effort develop a good image. Even if your firm's image has been good so far, where does it stand in competition today? The best way to answer the question is to have a survey conducted and after that take corrective measures as required.

With the advent of several reputed TV brands like AIWA, SONY, THOMSON and LG, firms like Videocon and BPL would have taken a bigger beating but for their good image. Hence, you can imagine that the task of PR is endless.

- As a marketing mix factor PR has to come up with the most significant factor of the firm, which is promoting sales of goods. This is done mainly through press releases, which tell about the firm's achievements, plans and changes being brought about for increasing efficiency and customer satisfaction. These press releases play a vital role perhaps much greater than direct advertising as these items when published in the newspapers come under the editorial purview and hence get greater credibility than advertising. The only danger is of editorial pencil that may remove even the punch lines and make the whole thing drab.
- Firms gain good mileage through their brand equity. With high brand equity firms can charge higher prices and still sell in large quantities. It is the name sells in most cases. Name provides for guarantee of quality. For the people for whom price is of no consequence, brand is what they buy. Even price conscious people buy good brand product for value for money and product life thus rendering them economical to the buyers.
- Damage control is a major responsibility of PR. This task is usually needed to be performed once in a long while it is of great importance as not handling it properly could lead to greater disaster. Natural calamities like floods, earthquakes cause problems for firms, but how the firms deal with the problems and what becomes the people's perception about it is of importance to the firms. Then there are man-made problems like the Bhopal gas leak. Smaller hazards keep on plaguing the firms and only good PR can nullify the negative effects of these on the firm's image and as a rub off on the firm's sales and profits. **It is the reputation of the firm, its goodwill which is at stake!**

Marketing research for the effect of communication sent by the firms to the public is important as the perceptions of the message sent could be different with the sender firm and the receiver. Understanding the nature of public acceptance will help PR manager to tailor the next message according to the corrections required.

As we have seen objectives PRs is different from that of advertising. PR has to project the public view of the firm in the first instant. PR managers are in constant contact with the public, the opinion leaders, the government and the customers. These contacts provide with knowledge of the attitudes of people as the PR person has to be alert to catch even stray phrase of significance to the firm.

One problem which many firms feel that they are being perceived as laid back firms Philips had this image till eighties in the 20th century. With dynamically pursuing the task of changing the image their PR department did bring about a turn around in the public mind.

When the readers read any article from the editors it has a different effect on them then seeing the advertisements.

Earlier the success of PR campaign was measured by the column centimetre space it could get in the favoured media. Bigger the space, better the PR. It does not however tell you the effect of the space gained has had on the public mindset the ultimate test, as in the case of advertising comes from the increase in sales figures and change for the better in the customer's attitude towards your product. For understanding the attitude changes, adverting research type research is required to be done.

Unlike advertising research where the target segment is the group of customers likely to purchase your product, in case of PR, the public means investors, stockholders, customers and suppliers towards whom the PR effort is directed.

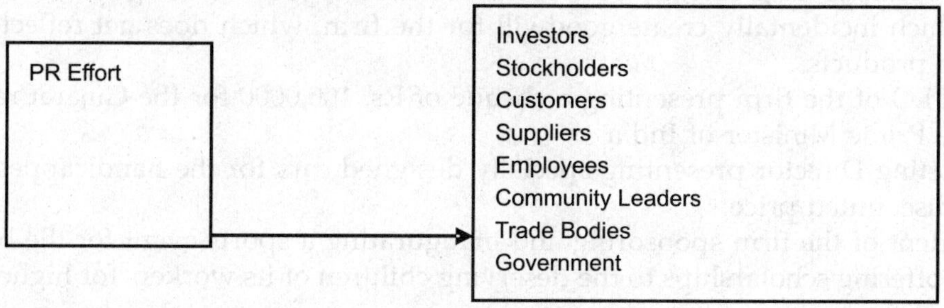

Public relations manager's job is to have a firm grip of the media available for transmitting the message to the public. Understanding media thus is an important aspect of his job. In this case, PR manager approaches the media editors, correspondents with information about the firm, its activities and plans. This is an useful information, which makes the media and the PR interdependent.

These days a lot of advertising uses direct attack on competition, which if not refuted can create misinformation among the customers. Between two competitive toothpaste brands the difference of opinion came regarding the time one of them kept the mouth of the user fresh for ten hours said one firm and soon the competitor said fifteen hours. A PR job would have sufficed by telling through editorial comments about the true nature of the toothpaste.

With plethora of non-banking financial institutions, to gain advantage one such firm advertised the norms public should use to assess the firms. The advertisement had a reverse effect as many persons read it out of context and felt that that particular NBFC is not good. It took a lot of effort as also their PR team's rapport with the press, which helped them in retrieving the situation and giving their side of the story as a press release.

PR too depends on endorsements to an extent!

If the firm says in the advertisement that their Matiz car is the best in its range, public may or may not accept the statement. The thinking becomes "any way it is their advertisement and who will ever say any thing bad about their product." However if Murad Ali Baig says the same thing or the editor of *Motoring Times* says it, the public is surely going to believe it.

Marketing efforts too get a boost with the help of marketing PR activities.

A technical short film shows how the car engine gets corroded because of friction between cylinder walls and the piston rings. Next it shows good brand of lubricating oil being used halves the corrosion. And then the film shows the firms brand being used totally removing any possibility of corrosion. The film does a subtle job of marketing PR as the visuals leave a lasting impression on the viewers about the efficacy of the oil.

PR helps in image building. Every firm wants to be known as a good corporate citizen. When the public is shown a movie that highlights the efforts taken by the firm in removing pollutants from its effluents going in the river, it endorses the public opinion about the firm as a good corporate citizen. Such films help mould the opinion when negative opinions have already been formed. Following scenes will give other examples of PR, which incidentally create goodwill for the firm, which does get reflected in the sale of its products.

- The CEO of the firm presenting a cheque of Rs. 100,0000 for the Gujarat relief fund to the Prime Minister of India.
- Marketing Director presenting specially designed cars for the handicapped persons at a discounted price.
- President of the firm sponsoring and inaugurating a sports event for the blind.
- Firm offering scholarships to the deserving children of its workers for higher studies.

Such events if not given right publicity would go unheard of and unsung. It becomes the major task of the PR department to ensure that the good deed does rub off on the cash register of the firm bringing in extra profitable sales.

It is said that, **a company is known by the men it keeps**. And how? Good, happy, hardworking employees do provide a good general backdrop in the public mind. Firms go out of their way these days to keep their employees happy. Perquisites like good housing, medical aid for the family, sports activities, and children's education are a must for this purpose. PR's job is to focus the public attention on the theme of happy workmen. The firm automatically gets a boost as a good firm, as only a good employer can be good firm. And who wants to do business with a firm which is not good. A good example of personnel PR is the advertisement of Tata Steels, in which happy employees are shown involved in various activities. In the end the advertisement says, **"We also make steel."**

Management Game

Teams should plan to give their products new brand names to create brand value. Plan methods of enhancing the value. The team should plan to have their own outlets for their products and then plan to popularize the brands in the segment selected.

Discuss broadly the usefulness of brand value in sustained competitive advantage.

CHAPTER

14

Marketing Research

Aims and Outcomes

Market scenario, especially in retail is both complex and chaotic due to major competitors now operating in the country, in most products, and for this reason the managers cannot just depend on their experience or their gut feeling for taking marketing decisions. Marketing research has therefore become an important tool used by the marketers to understand the marketing opportunities, marketing problems as well as for making marketing strategies. The students will learn the different ways of conducting the research for the retail company's benefit.

For the students of Retail Marketing it is important to understand the theory and practical applications of market research. Retail research is carried out in several ways, mainly as given below:

1. Personal interviews of shoppers, at the entry or exit point with the help of a questionnaire which should be necessarily short with easy direct multiple choice questions that can be answered in a short time, say, in ten to fifteen minutes.
2. Focus groups for deciding the type of shopping mall, products to be sold can be decided.

Information in retail trade needs to flow from the manufacturer who supplies the goods to the retailer and then information has to be gathered from the customer. Retailer in turn, supplies information both to the supplier of goods and to the customer. The information need to both is assessed through surveys, feedback and direct dialogue.

The consumer provides information both to the supplier of goods and to retailer through purchase surveys, credit card data, feedback forms. This information should form the basis of improved service to the customer.

The information can be gathered at the retail outlets through consumer surveys, including reactions of buyers on new product launches, perceived product benefits by the consumers and focuses on brand loyalty equations and reasoning. At times retailers act on half baked or inadequate information that can cause real problems as given below:

Intuitive planning can cause unnecessary shifts in pricing policies where no change is required. Marketing strategies based on intuition are mostly ill formed and they miss the target by a margin. Organizing sale through price reduction during lean season may not work since the buyers do not make purchases due to heavy workloads on them. Festive time is the right time for such activities.

Maintaining status quo in strategic planning—when people believe that what succeeded before will work well even now is an erroneous assumption since during the passage of time competition may have changed, shifted gears or area demographics may have changed.

Several people believe that a success story even from competitors can be replicated with equal success without understanding the unwritten, between the lines message that had carried the day for competition.

Taking decision based on the advice of just a few individuals could lead to disastrous results. It could create either a overstock situation or stock-outs—both causing huge losses.

People take for granted that success brings opportunities for expansion, diversification. However, unless the market is ascertained with the help of research such decisions could harm the company.

Companies need to be sure of consumer behaviour on the strategic issues that are going to affect them as giving surprises could prove to be costly and counterproductive.

Summarizing, retailers need to gather the required information, and decisions can follow their analysis.

Retail Information System–RIS

RIS help in seizing opportunities that come the retailers way. The information base created is company specific, organised and focused. RIS works for the company in the following manner:

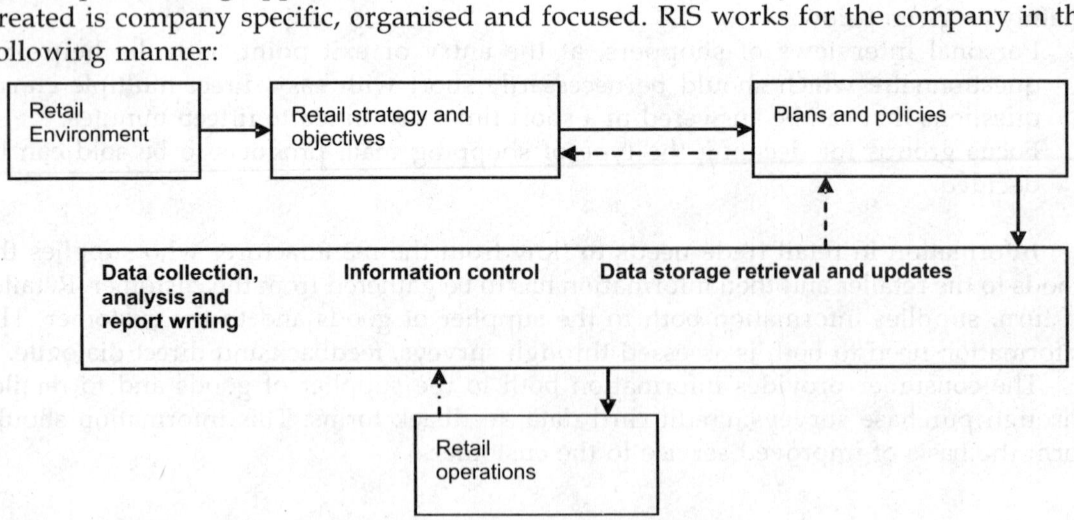

The RIS provides the insight into market situations leading to strategic planning. It is important to understand the role of RIS in making strategic decisions as can be seen from the following:

1. RIS has to make management decision in proactive mode rather than in reactions towards given situations.
2. The cost of RIS is a subject of debate. Ideally it should be about one per cent of the sales turnover.
3. RIS has become technology driven with computer network doing the job of correlating the information received from trade associations, surveys etc.
4. Retailers have to decide about the volume of RIS required by them for decision-making and strategic planning.
5. The RIS data needs to be distributed amongst the persons who can use it in the organization.
6. The RIS data should be stored in a manner where easy retrieval is possible.
7. One important source of data is the Universal Product Code besides the electronic data interchange.

It is however, important to provide the students an insight into the vital aspect of Market Research (MR) in easy to understand language without the clutter of MR jargon. With a view to making reading interesting, several examples have been included. MR is associated with primary research for most beginners. MR starts with secondary research, which can be conducted by looking at an immense amount of data already available somewhere and we need to locate it. Secondary data can provide valuable information regarding market size historically and future growth patterns. Once the secondary data is obtained and interpreted the researcher can decide to go for primary reseach for in-depth information requirements.

Qualitative research is an integral part of MR. It helps in product development, design and modifications. Retailers can use it in locating the right market segment for the products, as qualitative research directs us towards the customer's mindset.

Introduction to Market Research

Before the student starts learning Market Research, it may be useful to have a recap of Marketing Mix Factors. Marketing has become an all-pervasive discipline, in as much that no business, industry can remain untouched by marketing. In good old days, when there were only a handful of manufacturers of a product, competition was limited or just not there, marketing as we understand it today was a luxury only as it was not required. Manufacturers made the products and sold it in the market. The stress was on sales. In India even up to sixties, in the 20th century, manufacturers were confident of selling their products at a profit without the fear of somebody undercutting them as there was enough business for all. Competition increased, especially after India liberalized its economy, and the floodgates of international players were opened. Now, the competition has become a vital force which the business has to reckon with.

With increased competition, firms need to play their cards according to the competition and market condition. Hence, the need to systematically understand competition and market conditions and of Market Research!

Let us take an example. When you want to buy an expensive thing like motorcycle, how would you decide to go about it? Most likely you will take some of these steps:

- Check out on the different brands available by visiting motorcycle dealers.
- Compare the prices, specifications like HP, after sales service, and dealer's attitude towards customers.
- Ask your relations, friends, colleagues who own bikes about their experience, views about different bikes.
- Look for the advertisements in different media like newspapers, magazines, TV to get as much information you can get about competitive bikes.
- See your budget and then take a decision based on the gathered facts.

Similarly, as a seller it is important to know what the product the buyer wants, where he wants it, what price he is ready to pay for the product, how would he like to pay for it, by credit card, cash, cheque, or by some hire-purchase arrangement? Getting the answers of these questions is the task before MR.

Let us examine what constitutes marketing in the 21st century. To start with let us again understand the Marketing-Mix factors as given below:

1. Market Research (including market survey, and analysis), as will be seen is used for virtually all other Marketing Mix factors.
2. Product
3. Brand
4. Packaging
5. Trademark
6. Logo
7. Label
8. Price
9. Placement or simply, distribution
10. Promotion or sales promotion
11. Advertising
12. Credit and its control
13. Personal selling
14. Training of marketing personnel of the firm and retailers

Items 3 to 7 are directly related to the product.

As already stated Market Research (MR) can be undertaken for any of the above stated factors. Besides, MR is conducted to get the total market potential, its possible growth and strengths and weaknesses of competition in respect to the marketing mix factors.

Starting with the **product,** MR can be conducted to get information or trends in the following areas:

- Is there a demand for the product in the vicinity?

- If yes, in which market segment?
- What is the level of demand?
- Is there a demand in peripheral segments, geographic areas? If yes then what is its level?
- Is the product acceptable to the market as it is, or any modification would be necessary?
- Are the product package, brand, trademark, label and logo eye-catching enough?
- Is the package size acceptable?

MR can be conducted to ascertain the market acceptability of **price** vis-à-vis competitive product and its price. It may be important to know the hidden costs of competition, like extra, for immediate delivery, and lower discount levels for the distribution channels. Most retailers of competitive products try to play one against the other by implying that your competitor is paying higher discounts while the case may be just the reverse. Retailers need to get a fair deal in terms of commission from their principles.

In pricing it is of utmost importance to find out the **real** competitive price and also to know if the products under comparison are having similar if not the same specifications, or are we comparing apples with oranges?

Higher prices, as we know can be charged by firms for better product, immediate delivery, better brand name (higher brand equity). Yet, to be sure of the right price to be charged for your product it is best to conduct MR and be sure that you are making reasonable profits and not losing money by undercutting on price.

Advertising and promotion need to be planned carefully, as a lot of money is going into these heads. Naturally a wise marketer would like to consider the best way to promote and advertise his or her product. Due to the special significance of Advertising Research, it will be discussed at length later on.

Market Research can be compared to the army spy network, which gathers information about the enemy so that strategies can be made to defeat the enemy.

MR ultimately builds a data bank or creates an Information System for the firm to remain proactive in the marketplace and acquire and maintain its position. Since the market, competition and customer needs are ever changing in today's business, it is important to have a dynamic, continuous MR in the organization.

Here, we can differentiate MR and Market Information System (MIS) as follows:

- MR is mainly for finding solutions while MIS is also needed to prevent problems from occurring.
- While both are continuous processes, MR is usually conducted on the basis of problem solution in the area of marketing.
- MR provides external information while MIS is mostly for internal data.

People sometimes confuse Market Research with Marketing Research. Let us see how marketing guru Richard D. Crips defines them:

Marketing research is the systematic, objective and exhaustive research, for the study of the facts relevant to any problem in the field of marketing.

Market research is restricted to the study of actual and potential buyers, their location, their actual and potential value of purchases and their motives and habits.

Let us examine the process involved in conducting MR.

Significant elements of MR process can be shown as follows:

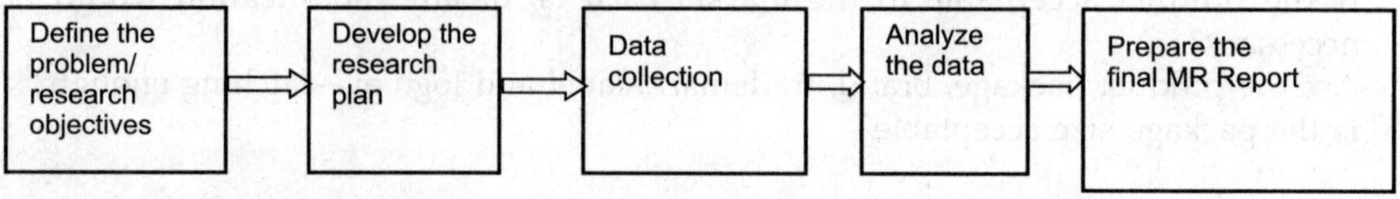

Marketing Research Objectives

From the viewpoint of Marketing Manager, the most useful role of MR is in the area of market demand and supply, in ever changing, mostly growing market and increasing competition. Shopping malls have several single brand manufacturer's showrooms and they need to get wise to competitive strengths in the mall.

It is important to define MR objectives as the starting point of MR. The accuracy of the objective definition would be the key factor in the accuracy of MR findings. Main objectives of MR are as follows:

- Demand projection for the product in a given area for an acceptable period like one year. This takes into account the historical demand of past years, market dynamics and changing business environment
- Competitive activities, product differentiation, entry barriers.
- Competitive market share
- Brand positions
- Competitive prices vis-à-vis brand equity
- Advertising and promotional strengths of competition.

The next range of MR objectives are in the area of customers' needs, as given below:

- What product benefits customers are seeking
- Product usage with different customer groups, light or heavy usage
- Top of the mind recall
- Price and quality perceptions
- Purchase decision procedures, who are the persons involved in it.
- Reasons for brand preferences

Let us see the types of MR being conducted.

- Exploratory research is conducted to confirm thoughts and ideas. Since these are conducted in small areas, they are low in cost and they take less time.
- Statistical research deals with frequency of events like the purchase action. Such research provides inputs for analysis, as the variables for the research are pre-decided, as how often car batteries are changed in Maruti cars, time, and brand of batteries being the variables
- Casual research is conducted on case to case basis, like effect of price changes on the product sales

Primary MR or Market Survey is conducted by collecting data or information directly from the consumers. Before launching on a full-scale survey which entails heavy expenditure, it is advisable to conduct a sample survey where the survey is conducted in a limited area to test the methods used. Both Qualitative and Quantitative information can be gathered through market surveys.

The survey can be conduced in several ways as follows:

- **Observation method** can be used to find out the number of shoppers who stop to look at and deliberate purchasing a product. Cameras and other signal gathering devices can be used for gathering such information
- Personal interviews: In this method you with your team meet a number of users personally, ask them questions as per a predetermined questionnaire and get first hand information from them. The information collected is then used to extrapolate for the entire customer group to get the real answers. These surveys are time consuming and expensive, but more accurate.
- Mail surveys are conducted by sending the questionnaire to a number of customers with request for filling them and returning to the surveyor. The method is not expensive, but it may not give accurate results, as the rate of getting replies from the customers is poor. Also the information which comes in may be skewed as people when replying to such questionnaires, tend to give inflated figure.
- Telephone surveys are conducted as a low cost easy method of gathering information. The problem in such surveys is the fact that people replying to telephone may not be the right persons.

Marketing Research Methods

There are two basic methods of doing Marketing Research:

1. Primary research
2. Secondary research

As normally secondary research is done first, we will discuss it first. Sources of secondary data are as follows:

- Firm's internal source, include, P/L statements, inventory levels, sales visit reports, previous MR reports
- Incoming staff members who may be coming from competitive firms
- Government publications and notifications, like from directorate of audio visual publicity, research organizations.
- Trade publications: Each trade has its own journals which carry information about the historical business and projections. Magazines on Computers, IT, Electronics, Cinema, TV, Agriculture, Science and Technology, Dress designing, Interior Decoration, practically every possible area of business are in the market.
- Competitor's balance sheets
- Publications of industry associations like FICCI, CII, ASSOCHEM.
- All India Management Association journal
- Trade and business newspapers and magazines like *Financial Times, Business Today, Business India.*

- Internet
- Market research organizations, like ORG-Marg, who sell MR Reports at a price.
- Sales statistics of product's dealers
- Publications of Reserve Bank of India, financial institutions like, IFCI, IDBI, ICICI, UTI.
- Foreign Government Data, International publications: These help in the area of international business as also at the introductory stage of products as they can tell about the rate of product penetration in other countries as a benchmark for India. Of course, other economic parameters, which may be differentiating the countries, will have to be kept in mind.

Secondary data as the name itself suggests, is the data for which somebody else has done the job of collecting the information as primary data.

At this stage it may be a good idea for the students to get some secondary market survey data, by gathering information from libraries, where old newspapers, magazines and other publications are available. (You may also list down as many secondary sources as possible from where you can get the data). Please collect information about any one of the following:

- Mid-size car price variation in the last three years
- Washing powders, introduction of several new brands in the last three years
- New distribution systems in the area of consumer durables

To get an idea about the objectives let us take Surf Excel as the product. You can find out the following from your respondents (persons you are going to talk about the product).

1. Reasons why housewives prefer the product.
2. What types of housewives are likely to use the product?
3. In a given area how many would be using the product?
4. How many more would use it if cheaper package is used to sell to another segment at a lower rate?
5. Besides package and price what are other factors, which help the buyer to decide in favour of the product?

Once the objectives are well defined, it is important to go to get the source of data.

Focus group research is conducted by inviting some ten persons from the market segment of the product, to get to know from them their views about the product, its price, channels of distribution. The expert conductor of the meeting will ask them, "What do you think about the quality of Surf Excel"?

With free and easy dialogue, and without the burden of family presence, persons come out and give their frank opinions.

Questionnaire method can be used for collecting information in the case of Surf Excel. It consists of relevant questions, which the respondents can easily answer. It is the most common and effective way of getting the answers as it means direct contact with the user and gets the replies to the problems baffling the marketer.

Questionnaire consists of questions, which are closed type, where options are provided and the respondent has to just give his choice from among the options.

The questions can be asked in the following manner:

- Yes/No type –Did you personally select the product? Yes/no
- Multiple choice: Who helped you in the selection? brother/sister/uncle/ friend
- Answers are given on a five point scale:

1. I like the Surf Excel very much
2. I like it all right
3. I barely like it
4. I do not like it
5. I do not like it at all.

The first part of the questionnaire consists of demographic information about the respondent. A sample is given below:

Name

Address Phone/fax/e-mail

Age- below 25/25-40/41-60/60+

Income level/pm below Rs. 5000/5001-15000/15001-30000/30001-50000/50001-80000/80001 +

Family size: below 3/3-5/6-9

People find it easier to give a range for age, income rather than giving accurate figures, as it could be less embarrassing.

Questionnaires should be carefully developed, tested through a sample test, modified as required and then used for gathering information.

Questions can, at times, influence the answers. Hence, to make them totally objective, they should be carefully prepared.

Close ended questions, like giving answer choices guide the respondent into the area with which the researcher is familiar.

Open-ended questions get the respondents to use their own words and individualistic replies come from such questions. Such questions are useful in exploratory type of MR. However, if time is an important factor, it is better to ask close questions, which can be answered in less time.

Open-ended question could be "What is your opinion about Surf Excel as a detergent powder?"

Or, "what is the first name which comes to your mind when you think of detergents?"

Or, the interviewer shows the respondent, an extra clean used shirt and asks, "What does the shirt remind you of?"

Or. The interviewer shows the respondent a picture of Surf Excel and asks, "What can it do for you?"

Questions should be as simple as possible, direct, to the point, with no possibility of any ambiguity.

The questions should follow a pattern, a logical sequence.

It is time that the students prepare a questionnaire for conducting MR for any one of the following products:

- A car
- Cosmetics
- Readymade garments

The student can select a brand and build the questionnaire around that brand.

Testing the questionnaire needs to be done next. For the purpose a small sample is adequate. It should be from the market segment for which the product is meant. If any question is found to be difficult, or objectionable it should be modified or removed. A mix of 20-25 respondents should be normally sufficient for the test purposes.

A sample questionnaire is given below:

Sir/Madam,

This is a survey of households with respect to small cars purchase. We request you to kindly help in filling the questionnaire giving your ideas, as we attach great value to your judgment in this regard. We thank you in anticipation of your cooperation.

1. Do you have a small car? yes/no
2. If yes, please tell its model and make.
3. If no, then please go to the last question.
4. Buying the small car, what were you looking for?
5. What is your opinion on the features of small cars listed below:

Features	A	B	C	D	E
Design					
Availability of colours					
Horsepower					
Speeds possible					
Seats and sitting comfort					
AC/Stereo					
Safety aspects					
Service facilities					
Luggage space					

(Since this is only a sample, many questions have been left out)

A EXTREMELY IMPORTANT, *B* IMPORTANT, *C* SOMEWHAT REQUIRED, *D* MAY BE REQUIRED *E* NOT NEEDED AT ALL

6. How do you rate the price of your car, is it, high, medium, low for the car? Did you get value for money?
7. Did you make outright purchase or took the hire/purchase option? If you bought the car under H/P, which company offered the loan?
8. Who all helped you in deciding about the car? Rate the following as per their importance:
    - Wife/husband
    - Sons/daughters

- Other relatives
- Neighbors
- Colleagues

9. Did you see any advertisement of the car prior to purchase and if yes, did it help in decision-making?
10. Some statements are given below. Please give your opinion on the same:

Statement	Yes/Yes	Yes/	Yes/No	No	No/No
Small cars are family cars					
Status symbols					
Good for town run					
Roads not suitable for small cars					

11. About yourself please:
    - Name: (optional)
    - Age: below 25/26-35/36-50/51 and above
    - Education level: undergraduate level/ graduate/postgraduate/doctorate
    - Family income pm: less than 7,000/7,001-10,000/10,001-15,000/15,001-30,000/ 30,001-60,000/60,001 and above
    - Purchase decision process: who all are involved in the family?

Thanks for your valuable time!

The students should make a questionnaire with the above sample only as a guideline.

Second sample of a questionnaire, for a furniture maker as follows:

Questionnaire

1. When did you last change your main furniture?
   (i) Less than one year back
   (ii) 1-3 years
   (iii) more than three years
2. What type of furniture did you buy?
   (i) Wooden
   (ii) Wrought iron
   (iii) Sunmica top
   (iv) Combination
3. What style of furniture did you buy?
   (i) Continental type
   (ii) Indian style
   (iii) Ethnic
4. Which member of the family went with you to select the furniture—wife/husband, brother/sister/father/mother/others/friend/ or did you go alone
5. Why did you select this type of furniture?
6. Did you consult any interior decorator? If yes, then whom?

7. Who were consulted-

Consultation with	Type of furniture	Style of furniture
Self Brothers/sisters		
Wife/husband		
Advertisements		
Interior decorator		
Dealer of furniture		

8. What were the essential features you sought in the furniture?

Factors	Most Essential	Essential	Desirable	Not important	Least important
Durability					
Finish					
Range of colours					
Matching sets					
Price					

9. Please give your particulars as follows:
   (i) Name
   (ii) Age (give a range as suggested earlier)
   (iii) Income –(give a range)
   (iv) Occupation

Thanks!

Now it is time to understand, what we are going to survey? Who are our target audience? Defining the market segment, the right geographic area, gives us the parameters, along which we have to organize the survey. We call it the universe or the population, for the purpose of the MR. the universe, or the total population for Surf Excel would be the entire middle and high-income group of a town.

Organizing a Market Survey for the ENTIRE universe can, and usually is, a time-consuming, expensive process. It may take so much time meeting and asking questions from a million people, that by the time the results appear the product itself may become obsolete. Therefore, the survey is done on the basis of a sample of the universe, which is made using well-established techniques.

Sample Size

The larger number of people to be interviewed, the better or more reliable the result. However, in practice, it is better to cover a much smaller sample, may be one per cent of the universe to get reasonably good results, in lesser time and money. It really depends on how the sample gets selected.

Sample Selection

There can be two ways of selecting a sample:

1. Probability Sample: It ensures that each of the members of the universe have equal chance or probability of being selected for the survey. It helps in understanding the levels errors on account of the sample selected. There are three ways of probability sampling:
   (i) Simple random sample: Every member has an equal opportunity of being in the survey
   (ii) Stratified random survey: The population/universe is divided into mutually exclusive groups such as, age, income and then random samples are taken from each group.
   (iii) Cluster sample: The population is divided as per geographic divisions, like for example, Delhi could be divided into, north, south, east west and central zones and sample taken from each zone on random basis.
2. Non-probability sample: As the cost and time involved in probability sample surveys is quite high, MR people use non-probability sample. This can be done in three ways:
   (i) Convenience sample: The research person selects the persons most easily met for the MR.
   (ii) Judgment sample: Researcher uses his judgment about the sample, which would provide the most accurate answers.
   (iii) Quota sample: The researcher meets with a set of persons in each category.

As an example, in sampling methods, if one person is not available then no one else takes his place except in quota sample method where the researcher has to find out another person in the same category and meet him.

At times even with proper sampling errors creep into the collected data. The reasons of such errors are given below:

- A portion of population may have been omitted.
- People not included in the sample may differ widely from those interviewed.
- Substitute interviewees may not be right ones if you are not able to meet the person in the sample.
- The respondents find questionnaire difficult.
- Respondents may not have enough information on the subject or they may not like to reveal it for some reason.
- Some questions in the questionnaire may have a bias or slant towards one answer.
- Interviewer may not be fully qualified to take up the job of getting respondents opinion.

The researcher must take these into account when analyzing the collected data.

When systematically the sample is drawn, it helps as, data collection becomes lower in cost, and it is easy to control.

Planning Samples

Let us plan a sample for EPABX of large size say which cater to 1000 lines. Who would be interested in the EPABX?

1. Industrial units, MNCs, large Indian firms, public sector companies
2. Government departments and offices
3. R&D Labs in private and government sector
4. Banks, Indian and foreign, Financial institutions
5. Universities and educational institutions like IITs and IIMS.

As a starting point let us get list of all the organizations in the population group with a turnover of Rs. 50 crores.

Pick up 100% of organizations with turnover of Rs. 500 crores.

Select 20 units from the organizations with turnover of more than Rs. 100 crores but less than Rs. 500 crores

Select 15 units with turnover of less than Rs. 100 crores

Pick up all the government departments and their head offices.

Likewise select some units from each of the other categories.

To sum up the sampling technique for EPABX 1000 can be as follows:

- Defining the population
- Sampling unit would be the firms and offices having population needing about 800 phones.
- Sample size could be 400.

Task for the Students

Please develop a questionnaire for the organizations for the EPABX Survey.

As per Philip Kotler the marketing guru their are characteristics of a good Market Research as follows:

1. Scientific method: Effective MR, is conducted on scientific lines, with formulation of hypothesis, theory, testing and results
2. Creativity: A teenage clothing firm gave video cameras to several young persons, who were asked to film the discos restaurants where the teenagers went most of the time.
3. Multiple-methods: To increase credibility, marketing people use several methods together.
4. Value and cost of information: Marketing persons have to find out the cost to value ratio of the MR. For example, if the MR is to find the extra sale on decreasing the price to some extent, and it is found that the cost of research outweighs the profit benefit, such MR should not be undertaken. For example, if the increase in sales is likely to bring extra profits of Rupees ten lacs, and the research is going to cost twelve lacs, it is not worthwhile to conduct the MR.
5. MR Managers must take a close look at the assumptions made by the marketing personnel, as they may be lop-sided.
6. MR should not use the survey, to sell the product.

Managers because of the following reasons are sparsely using marketing Research:

- When marketing team has a problem with some options and Market Research does not pinpoint towards a solution it makes MR of not much use. Only with a **well-defined problem** can the MR provide the right answers.
- When MR personnel are not fully qualified to do the job, they will not be able to get the right answers.
- MR takes time to be complete in all respects to give valuable market insight. When time is not enough MR may not give correct results.
- Market research reports sometimes give only indications, trends and not concrete facts, which is not appreciated by the marketing team.

Students should plan Market Research objectives in view of the above and develop a questionnaire for the same.

Example

Given below is an imaginary discussion between the Managing Director and Marketing Manager of a television manufacturing company, who are scanning the Indian TV market to enter the same after achieving big success in the western markets like Europe and the USA.

MM, "We have seen the growth of Indian's TV market. In the last three years it has been growing at a steady rate of five per cent, which is much better than the growth of negative two per cent in the developed world. However, as you, a number of MNCs are in the field like, Thomson, Sony, AIWA, Samsung, LG, and a number of Japanese firms are well entrenched through selling kits for assembly in India, such as Toshiba. Now we have to plan our strategy for entering this growing yet difficult market. What are your ideas on the matter?"

MD, "I believe there is still big room for players like us who believe in their product and customized service which no one can provide. You should be trying for at least seven per cent market share in the second year of our operation."

MM, "I would like to organize a market survey to know what the market wants and who would buy our rather higher priced products."

MD, "By all means get your market information updated, keep me informed and let us plan our marketing strategies based on your information."

Following is the brief the MM gave to the market research agency.

Our information on Indian TV Market is as follows:

In 1986, the market was of 4 million TV sets in the country. More than 75% of these sets were b/w versions. Colour TV came to India as late as 1982. Only after the liberalization of economy, in 1991, the demand started to grow rapidly. By 2000 AD, 6 million colour sets were being planned for sale. The growth of manufacturers has been rapid too.

The growth and competition has brought several changes in the product offerings. Multi-channel, remote operated, several firms are making Colour TVs. Innovations like flat square screens, Picture-in-picture, ambience light adjusters, virtually automatic TV sets, with memory, data bank of information are in the market, some features may be yet trying to find their feet in the market, due to concepts being new and high costs.

You have to find out which of the features plus, Internet access TV, would find a reasonable demand in the market. We want to put the best features in our sets and get 7% market share in second year of our operation.

Please organize MR, and send your recommendations within a period of three month, covering north Indian markets.

The MR report says:

- TV manufacturers, are coming out with latest innovations and they try to educate the buyers about the same. Most of the time the customers are unaware of the benefits the innovations provide and may have a little reluctance for purchasing such difficult to use products.
- The buyers commonly understand picture and sound quality.
- Price, warranty, after sales service, play an important role in purchase decisions.
- Psychological aspects such as, looks, foreign collaboration, brand equity too have their value.

Since the price of TV sets is quite high, TV purchase is a high involvement purchase. Opinions of other users, friends, neighbours, colleagues, and sometimes the TV dealers are sought. With some twenty brands and each brand having four to six models, the task of decision-making is rather onerous one.

The following features of colour TVs were tested of a scale of one to five in several areas in the northern India and the results obtained are given along side:

Feature	Mean score	Position
Picture quality	5	1
Sound quality	5	2
After sales service	4.9	3
Price	4.2	4
Brand equity	3.8	5
Appearance	3.3	6
Foreign collaboration	3	7
Picture in picture	3	8
Internet capable	3	9
Dealers location	2.8	10
Friends recommendations	2.8	11

As can be seen the customers place a good deal of importance on picture and sound quality, followed by after sales service and price. Distinct features do play a role in purchase decisions, but it seems that their relative importance is less due to the latent fear in the minds of buyers that they may be paying high price for features they may not be able to use due to their being too high tech. Hence, the conclusion can be drawn that while new features will bring more business as they would certainly differentiate the products, a lot of concept selling as also, training in the usage would be required, before the benefits can be cashed in.

Advertising for creating and enhancing brand equity is a must, as brand plays a major decisive role in purchase actions of the customers.

Areas like built-in stabilizers are not in consideration at all as most TV has the feature. Same way remote-control feature has become common and hence it ceases to be a differentiating point.

Advertising too has become the done thing and at best, it is a negative factor. In other words, less or no advertising would mean poor quality marketing effort.

> **Market Research should be avoided** if enough **time** cannot be given for the research. Also, if **budget** does not permit thorough enquiry or **information** possible is not going to be sufficient, MR can be avoided. If marketing people want to get the research done only for having their **decisions endorsed** it need not be undertaken. Also if the cost or research outweighs possible savings, it should be avoided.

However, marketing people can get valuable inputs from MR, like demand forecasting, product specifications, advertising and promotion plans endorsement, locating new markets, market segments, finalizing distribution channels for optimizing their effectiveness, MR can also help in making strategic plans for the firm.

The MR process can be shown in graphic form as given below:

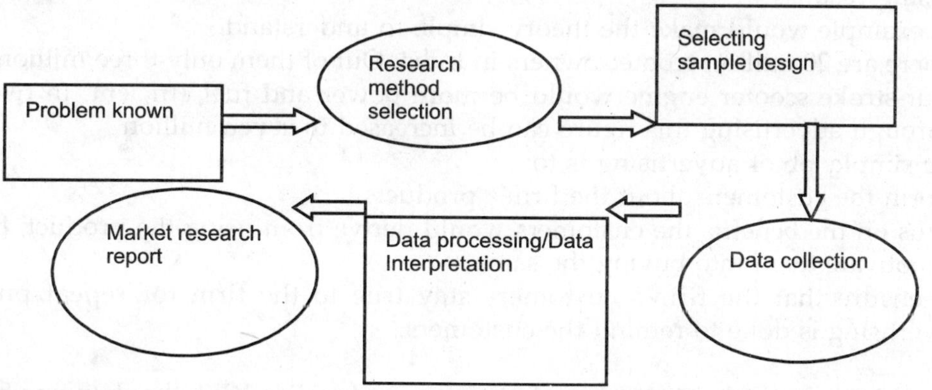

For instance, if management problem is of poor market image, or low brand equity, MR would find out "what is the exact brand equity of the firm with the target market segment."

If the management wants to know if the advertising budget is adequate or not, MR would try to find out, "the effectiveness of advertising."

And if the marketing team wants to know the customers of the product, the MR would find out "the target customers of the segment."

If sales are stuck in recession, MR would "find out the price elasticity of the product in the selected segment."

For new product development, MR would find out if new product needs to be developed and if yes, with what specifications."

Data Processing and Analysis

In data analysis, it is important to understand that based on application the scale of measurement is made. For instance, when you apply, classification of sex, geographic area, or social class, when objects are either identical or different, **nominal scale** is used.

If ranking or preferences, class standing are the applications, then objects could be smaller or larger, **rank order scale is used.**

For altitude measurements, temperature scales, when intervals between adjoining ranks are equal, **interval** scale is used.

For sales, income, units made, **ratio** scale is used.

Advertising Research and DAGMAR

We have seen that in order to be focused on firm's overall goals, marketing department has to play a vital role as the revenue earnings of the firms are mainly from selling of products. Hence, once the firm's goals have been formulated the marketing and advertising people set their own goals and objectives.

Colley found that a relationship between advertising and marketing goals should be considered and his theory says, that advertising efforts can bring results, which can be measured. DAGMAR's full form is, "Defining advertising goals for measured advertising results."

An example would make the theory simple to understand.

"There are 20 million scooter owners in India. Out of them only three million accept that four-stroke scooter engine would be more power and fuel efficient. In two years time through advertising this figure can be increased to seven million"

The simple job of advertising is to:

1. Inform the customers about the firm's products
2. Focus on the benefits the customers would derive from using the product, in order to motivate them into buying the same.
3. To ensure that the firm's customers stay true to the firm for repeat purchase, advertising is done to remind the customers.

The objectives of advertising have been discussed earlier. With the changing business environment, product life cycle shifts the objectives keep moving too. The DAGMAR theory needs constant updating and vigilance to be of real value.

Hence, DAGMAR becomes effective only when there is continuous advertising research is conducted as per requirement.

Advertising Research

In the context of retail management advertising research is being extensively used by, both advertisers and advertising agencies, to pretest the campaign, evaluate the media's effectiveness, understanding the market segment best suited for the firm's products. Pretesting is undertaken with the help of people residing in the neighbourhood of the store, besides by using the visitors as sample for knowing the effect the advertising campaign will have on the target audience.

Most firms arrange for market research for obtaining market segment's viewpoints and preferences about products in their category. These researches tell about product acceptance levels, brand awareness, top of the mind recall, as also modifications needed in the products. A significant part of market research is advertising research, which concentrates on the type of advertising campaign, would be most suitable for the product, the ideal time for the product launch, limitations of the product. Advertising research tries to correct any aberrations in the selected market segment for the product.

Advertising research tells the advertisers about the type of creativity, the language including slang and dialect would stimulate the segment.

Take the example of an air compressor advertisement. It talked about the ozone layer depletion and need for having clean air. It also hinted at the specific design of the compressor without talking about its usage. Technical managers seeing the advertisement thought that it is some sort of air cleaner for the homes especially when they saw a pretty girl waving in the advertisement. After the research findings it became clear and another campaign was launched giving technical details with photographs of the compressor section by section, which attracted the attention of technical people and asked for more information about the product.

It will be difficult to find an advertisement of a perfume, which gives its chemical formula. Instead, the advertisement would be talking about love, and euphoria created by the perfume. The advertisements are the result of the research conducted which says that in personal care products people are interested in what it would do to them. It is said that nobody buys a product. They buy the performance promised or given by the product.

Media research is conducted to establish the suitability of a particular medium. Some advertisements have a dotted line cutout telling the readers to cut it and post to the advertiser for additional information, free sample or a demonstration of the product. The number of prints of the media is compared to the cut-out responses to know about its readership and correctness of the media for the target segment.

Research on the advertising copy is done with the help of primary research, when individual customers are contacted to get their reactions to the advertisement. It confirms the acceptance level of the campaign and can be used to determine the frequency of the insertions in the media.

Advertising research helps in making advertising campaigns more powerful thereby they are able to perform better the task of meeting advertising objectives.

Advertising costs are high. To make the best impact research ensures that advertisement is creatively acceptable, in the right media with correct frequency and for the chosen market segment.

The current Nescafe advertisement starts with a woman enjoying a mug full of the brew. The research had shown that women enjoy coffee during a lull in their work, be it household chores or office work. Later in the advertisement some men are also shown as it would be too risky to ignore a major customer group, in fact fifty per cent of the population.

Advertising research results thus show the advertiser how to place correct advertisements at the correct places and at the most appropriate times making them both effective and efficient. Retail advertising research carries out several jobs simultaneously as given below:

1. The correct media for the target audience
2. Copy and art suitable
3. Timing most appropriate

How is the research is conducted? Let us understand in some detail.

- Testing research methods is done by having a **Preliminary Research (PR).** It calls for a small sample size and it only validates the reasons, objectives and creativity of the campaign.
- After PR, advertisers are interested in finding out the likes and dislikes of the customers, reasons for the same. Research is conducted by doing primary survey, by **interviewing** customer groups. Such a research is similar to the market research, as information needed is akin to the one required in market research.
- Advertising research can also be conducted by **observation.** Researchers stand near shopping malls and observe the shoppers, their likes and dislikes, their behaviour pattern. Such a researcher has to note down his observations without prejudice, objectively, otherwise the decisions would be entirely lopsided.

It may be useful to note that watching/observing customers in shops for collecting data without their knowledge may not be purely ethical. Also, asking questions may look like selling gimmicks rather than advertising or market research.

To find out why people buy from a shop, the research would ask questions as follows:

1. Do you buy here for its location, products, brands, its food, and ambience?
2. Because it comes within your budget?
3. Do you find service a favourable factor here?
4. Is the staff cordial enough?
5. Does the shop provide extra care and benefits to regular customers?
6. How is the communication system?
7. Does it have prompt service and does it have a good enough range of brands?

The next type of research can be termed IDEA-RESEARCH where attempt is made to understand how some changes in an advertising campaign would affect the result as far as the advertising objectives are concerned. For example, would increase in advertising size improve its acceptance, or its frequency improves ***top of the mind recall.***

Define research objective, list out problems for which answers have to be found:

Has the market acceptance increased for the new Maruti 800 car? Or does the new detergent help in catching the mood of the housewife better with its non-caustic chemical formula, easy on the hands? While framing the questions it is advisable to make them short and unambiguous, to ensure right response. For getting response on relative likes and dislikes it is correct to give just five options,

(a) like the product greatly, will surely buy it from this store
(b) like it and may buy it,
(c) the product is just like others, may or may not buy it

(d) do not like it and it is unlikely that I buy it
(e) the product is bad and I will never buy it.

Care should be taken on the following areas while planning the research:

- Time and money spent should be commensurate with the objective of the research. For example, if the benefit to be obtained from the research amounts to rupees two million, it would not be prudent to spend two and a half million on the research. In the same way if the research is going to take one year in fashion industry, the very purpose of the research would be defeated.
- Research results would, at best give indicators for decision-making not perfect answers.
- Going through the exact methods to be used by the field researchers in detail would make you more aware of the nitty-gritty and less vulnerable to problems, which can occur due to subjectivity of the researchers.
- Be specific what has to be done rather then leave it to the field people who may come up with unnecessary, redundant data. It may look good that you are in the know of several facts, but you should understand the cost and time implications. It is better to get just enough information.
- Research budget need careful analysis. It may be apt to spend some amount of money when the decision to be based on the research is for large sums of money and it includes avoidance or limiting risk for the firm. Naturally for simple problems, many times previous experience is the best guideline for decision-making and no research needs to be conducted.
- Getting the research done for your book rack or your shelf only is not a good idea. Unless you are sure that people who are going to use the research findings it may be only an exercise in futility. Remember that people generally do not want to change their ways just because of some research findings.
- Many times the firm may already have the data called for, or available with another source, e.g. some research organizations like ORG-Marg.

Secondary research data is available from a variety of sources, including the firm's own records. Trade publications, and government publications and from research firms like ORG-MARG.

Secondary data is valuable information and its analysis can give the right direction for marketing and advertising. Firstly, it takes less time and effort. Plus it could prove to useful if it is not out dated.

Finding the Right Sample Size

Imagine sending teams to contact the entire population. Even a single metro town like Delhi has 16 million population. It would be a exercise in futility, because, by the time the research report comes out the problem or the situation, which triggered the research, would have disappeared. Hence, only a carefully chosen sample is used for being met for getting the data.

These are just a few samples.

How do you rate the following retailers in Delhi?

- Ansal plaza
- Pacific mall
- Subhiksha
- EDM
- Ebony

The way I look is important to me

- Strongly agree
- Agree
- Normal
- Disagree
- Strongly disagree

Surveys, observations and experiments with the help of questionnaires, checklists and plans help in completing the advertising surveys. Then comes the important aspect of analysis and report writing.

Research, as stated must be used or else the time and money is a total waste. Research results enable firms in reassessing their goals on the basis of new opportunities, in confirming the target segment and creating a useful message for the segment.

Advertising results can be measured by simple brand recall tests with the target segment. These can be aided or unaided recalls.

"Which is the best toothpaste in the market?"

"Which blue and red bottle drink gives most satisfaction?"

Research confirms the strong views held by the firm. If there is major divergence then a re-look is required at the objectives, sample and methods adopted in the research. A very apt example of how the research could go wrong is given below:

A firm planned to start manufacture of Fax machines in India in 1980s. The task of finding out the demand and product acceptance levels was given to an outside research agency by the firm. The result was flattering in as much that 80% respondents were looking forward to buying a fax machine. When the note was sent to the Department of Telecommunications, Government of India, it came back saying that the telecom network was not efficient enough to make fax a success. (It was only in late eighties that digital electronic exchanges, fibre optic cables made the telecom network good enough for fax to operate).

The research should make you aware of consumer's behaviour towards competitive product.

> Advertising research is a part of marketing research, confined to development of advertising plan, creative work, market segment and the best possible media, which would cater to the segment. The research should increase the effectiveness and efficiency of the advertising campaign. Data collection is done from primary sources as also secondary, already available sources. In primary data collection it is important to select the sample correctly. The research steps are:

1. Setting up goals for the research,
2. Finding the sources of secondary information/data.
3. Analyzing secondary data
4. Planning sample for primary research
5. Data collection
6. Data analysis and report writing

Marketing Conscience

In the race of achieving the sales targets, the firm's retail salespersons, at times forget that selling must be carried out within the legal and ethical framework of the government and the society in which we live. Profit making leads to satisfying the stockholders of the firm and the other stakeholders. However, profiteering, as different from profit making, does not satisfy anyone except the greed of the person indulging in the same. With competitive forces keeping price in check, the methods available to the dubious marketer are, supply of substandard goods, spurious material; even food items and life saving drugs are not excluded from such activities.

The sellers, therefore, have to abide by certain rules and regulations. Some contraventions are legal and punishable, others could be ethical or moral and from these too the customer must be protected. Following is a basic list of the do's and don'ts for the seller:

Do's for the retailer

- Supply goods as per specifications given by the seller
- Keep quality of goods and service uniformly good
- Supply products in correct weights, volumes, before its expiry date.
- Announce the product price on the container/package
- Announce the ingredients of the product where necessary
- Supply only the product ordered, not its substitute
- Provide proper training in correct usage of the product.

Don'ts for the retailer

- Do not adulterate the goods to be sold
- Do not supply inferior quality goods
- Do not exaggerate product's virtues, do not oversell
- Do not give incorrect delivery date
- Do not use puffery in advertisements by giving false information of the product
- Do not refuse to give service, which is part of the product sale.

Any business, which starts with in some way cheating the customer, is not likely to succeed in the long run. Short-term benefit could also prove costly as violation of country's laws can lead the retailer in serious trouble.

Consumer or the buyer needs protection from unscrupulous retailers, and this need has given rise to the consumerism or the consumer movement, which provides the information about the rights of consumers and also ways of redress to the victims of unfair practices of the sellers.

All along the book has emphasized the fact that the customer is the king. He must be treated with kindness, dignity and must never be ignored. The seller while dealing with customers must keep his benefits paramount. However, the ideal situation is never there and hence there is a need for consumer protection against the unscrupulous sellers. Ideal situation imagines the following:

- The consumer is well aware of his own requirements.
- The retailer knows the needs and tries hard to fulfil them with his product and services.
- The retailers are all the time communicating with the buyers, telling them about the products. Their benefits service, which go with the products and terms of business.
- The products purchased by the buyers meet their needs and expectations.

Consumerism

However, the ground reality is quite different from the above stated premises. Consumerism has become a force today to combat retailers' dubious plans and the task undertaken by it is given below:

- Informing consumers of their right of getting a product of good quality of acceptable price.
- Helping in fighting against the seller in getting the redress in case of buyer feeling cheated.
- Focusing on existing laws meant to protect the consumers and telling the government the need of more such laws.
- Forming consumer groups in each city to fight against the malpractices of some sellers.

In India, the consumer is facing the problem of self-created shortages by the sellers, who can then increase the price, hoard products forcing the consumers to buy the offered product without recourse to fair treatment. Ignorance of the laws and long drawn out legal proceedings deter the wronged consumer, who just bears the brunt of the malpractices of the seller.

The above-stated malaise can be considered a mirror of the times, we live in. However, the marketing fraternity must take the cudgels on behalf of the consumers to protect their own market from these fly by night operators, who are there only to make quick money and then decamp. The regular sellers owe it to themselves as also to the society they cater to, as also the society they are very much part of.

While discussing the need for fair practices one can hardly forget the story of a seller of dubious medicines who was enjoying his newly created wealth with a gala party with friends, wine and music when his servant came running to inform that his own son was dying after taking the medicine from his own firm. The business, the society, the government are all part of us, the citizens of India and should never be taken apart. The social responsibility of the business, the ethics involved are part of our heritage and a rolling consumer movement, like the juggernaut, gathering momentum can bring back the sanity in our business dealings. For this purpose, the consumers have to be made fully aware of their rights, the way they can get redress without cumbersome legal procedures. It is therefore the duty of those in power to ensure that there is proper legislation in this regard.

Consumer Rights

The consumers have the rights on the issue of protection against dubious sellers as given below:

- Right to know – The product in detail, its quality, purity, size, weight, package, brand, and its price before the purchase is made. For many products in India it has become mandatory for the sellers to provide the information on the product package or label if possible. Food products, medicines, toys for children must follow the norms strictly. How the local application medicines need to be used must be given on the container.
- Right to have safety – Products, which are substandard, (electrical goods which give shock), unhygienic food products, can cause unimaginable damage and the consumers have a right to get the correct products.
- Information on consumer protection and the rights of the consumers must be made known to all the consumers through widespread advertising.
- The consumer also must have the right to select the most appropriate product amongst those in the market. Advertising gives this right well in its own way.
- The consumers have the right of getting redress in case the seller has cheated them. If the product carries a guaranty, then the seller must replace or repair the defective piece, otherwise the seller must compensate the buyer for selling him the bad product, or product not exactly like the one promised or advertised. In case excessive price has been charged then the seller must refund the extra amount charged.
- The government of India has passed the Social Welfare Legislation for consumer protection, with ample safeguards against consumer exploitation. Special courts have been instituted in states to deal with consumer cases. These consumer courts deal with only the consumer cases and hence can be quite fast in passing judgment.
- The government of India has also created a commission to check monopoly business and unfair trade practices under the Monopolies and Restrictive Trade Practices Act (MRTPA). Under this Act price consortium are not allowed as these give advantage to the sellers.

The objectives of a retail outlet firm can now be redefined as follows:

The firm has to meet its obligations towards its stake holders including, buyers, sellers, vendors, employees, employers, trade bodies, the government and public at large. For this purpose, the firm must ensure proper utilization of its financial, manpower, technological, and human resources. The firm must offer value for money products to its customers. It must standardize its operations on fair trade practices. It must treat its employees with consideration of a genuine friend. It must also conform to the national objective of increasing exports. Profit as an objective cannot be denied as only with adequate profit comes survival and growth besides the firms need to satisfy its stakeholders can be met only by making profits. Besides, the firm should actively espouse the social causes like literacy, healthcare to the extent it can. (Many firms have opened hospitals for its employees, also used by the general public living in the area.)

Firms have run their operations in socially and ethically acceptable manner, as given below:

- Fair price for the products
- Correct weight, volume of the product sold
- Pay taxes to the government
- Should ensure that products sold are not adulterated in any manner
- Not sell contraband goods
- Give weight, volume, price, ingredients on the package of the products
- Make supportable claims in advertising campaigns
- Hoarding of goods to create artificial shortages should never be done
- Firms should never pay bribe to get orders
- Firms should assist the customers in proper usage of the product, if required, by training the customer in the proper use of the product.

Tasks for the students: Discuss the role of marketing considering the firms, legal, moral and ethical obligations to the consumer.

Marketing Game

Discuss the need for control points for marketing teams, how they can be formalized for different types of products, channels.

Company studies: These topics involve field interviews and correspondence combined with documentary sources.

1. A marketing audit. Design a marketing audit that a company can use to determine where it is in the stages of development of the corporation and what it should do with the information.
2. Reports analyzing the marketing strategies of companies.
3. Product management. Under what circumstances have companies integrated their domestic and foreign product planning and management? What factors have led to this integration? What are the explicit and hidden costs and benefits?

CHAPTER

15

Consumer Behaviour and Market Segmentation

"We are all consumers and we behave in the marketplace in different manner, sometimes logically and at other times irrationally. Study of consumer behaviour helps to predict with a high degree of accuracy how a particular person will behave under certain circumstances. This gives rise to more scientific approach to business communication".

Aims and Outcomes

Students need to learn that retailers have to understand the needs of the customers, their buying habits. Demographics of the area, lifestyles often define the needs and desires of the buyers, besides the business environment and retailers' actions often dictate the buyer behaviour.

Ostrow and Smith have defined Consumer Behavior as actions of consumers in the marketplace and underlying motives for those actions. The study of consumer behaviour is the study to understand how consumers spend time, money and effort on consumption related items. It includes what they buy, why they buy, when they buy, where they buy, how often they buy and how often they use it?

> Philip Kotler has designed a consumer behaviour model, which offers the variety of stimulus present for consumer for their decision-making for purchase action.

Model of Consumer Behavior

Market stimuli	Other stimuli	Buyer Characteristics	Buyer Decision Process	Buyer Decisions
Product	Economic	Cultural	Problem Recognition	Product choice
Price	Technological	Social	Information Search	Brand choice
Placement	Political	Personal	Evaluating Alternatives	Dealer's choice
Promotion	Cultural	Psychological	Purchase Decisions	Purchase timings

Market stimulants: The main marketing mix factors, famous four Ps, Product, Price, Placement and Promotion can provide stimulus to buyers. It can be seen how can a particular product just by being in the market makes us buy the product. Listed below are influencing factors.

Social Factors

Reference groups: They are the community leaders, religious gurus, professors, councillors and others.

Family includes, parents, children, grandparents, siblings, uncles and aunts.

Roles and Structures: Role of head of the household, the breadwinner, in the family which could be a new one, just husband-wife, or with small children, teenage kids, or grown up children who have left the household.

Age and Stage in life cycle: With better medical facilities the average age of Indians has increased. There is a large group of senior citizens. With lower rate of child mortality the population of teens and preteens has increased manifold giving rise to multitude needs and products to satisfy the same.

Occupation and economic circumstances: Standard of living of people differs because of size of regular income as also on the occupation. A white collared worker would like to project an image of a well-dressed person as against a small businessman, who would not be bothered with appearance.

Lifestyle and Psychographics are used to understand the mindset of people and for measuring and categorizing lifestyle.

Good Resource People—With financial backing.

Actualizers: Those who have achieved their desires, who have become **somebody** i.e. gained recognition.

Fulfilled are the satisfied people

Achievers are the people who have targeted their dreams and fulfilled them.

Experienced are those who have gone through the struggle and come out successfully.

Low resource people—With low finance

Believers are optimists who feel their time will come soon.

Strivers are hopeful about their future.

Makers are busy people who are into nitty-gritty of making a success.
Strugglers-are not so optimistic about their future.

Personality and Self-concept

People have physiological needs like food, clothing, shelter and psychological needs like need of love, esteem and self-actualization. Maslow has propounded that people's needs follow a hierarchy in terms of importance of the needs and their place in the person's life.

Maslow's hierarchy of needs

Self Actualization-A

Esteem B

Safety D

Physiological needs E

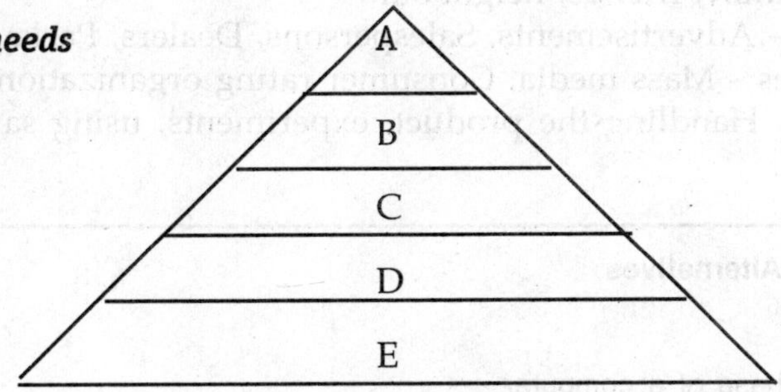

Perception: Select, organize, and interpret information to obtain a meaningful understanding for selecting and deciding in favour of a product.

Attitudes and Beliefs–Attitudes are a person's evaluation of emotional feelings and tendencies for action towards some object or an idea.

Buying roles can be described as follows:

1. Initiator is the person who puts forward the idea of obtaining a certain product
2. Influencer is the one who gives his opinion about the suitability of the product
3. Decider is the one who has the authority to decide whether the product should be purchased or not
4. Buyer is the person who places the order
5. User is the one who puts the product tom use

Thus, we can develop **Complete Buyer Behaviour** as given below:

- Believe in the product
- Develop attitudes
- Make thoughtful choice

Habitual Buying Behaviour

Major difference in brands	High involvement	Low involvement
	Complex buying behaviour	Variety seeking buying behaviour
Less difference in brands	Dissonance reducing buying behaviour	Habitual buying behaviour

Stages of buying decision process

1. Problem recognition is defined by obvious or inherent need of the consumer.
2. Information search
3. Evaluation of alternatives
4. Purchase decision
5. Post purchase behaviour

Sources of Information

Personal - Family, friends, neighbours

Commercial - Advertisements, Salespersons, Dealers, Packages, Displays

Public Sources - Mass media, Consumer rating organizations,

Experiment - Handling the product, experiments, using samples of products like shampoo sachets.

Evaluation of Alternatives

A caselet

Problem: Purchase of a computer

Identify decision criteria is as follows:

1. Price
2. Manufacture/Model
3. Support
4. Repair record
5. Warranties
6. Reliability

Weightage to criteria allotted by consumer

Price 70, Manufacture/Model 60, Support 40, Repair record 75, Warranties 50, Reliability 70

Alternate choices–Wipro, LG, HCL, Compaq, IBM, Local Assembly

Now for each of these six computers, put weight, e.g.

Wipro–Price 30, manufacture/model 50, support 40, repair record 60, warranty 40, reliability 60

As can be seen, price weightage is inversely proportional to price. In other words, higher the price, lower the weightage.

Select the one where the numbers add up to the highest. Then implement the decision, make the purchase.

Post-purchase behaviour comes from satisfaction, use and disposal after use.

Retailers need to know the demographics of the buyers in terms of gender, age, population growth rate, life expectancy, literacy, language spoken, income and size of the family, mobility, place of residence. These factors affect people's buying in retail shops and retailer's response. The demographic factors can be considered as follows:

- Household income and its discretionary element
- Population movement
- Ratio of genders
- Profession—white collared or blue collared workers
- Education level
- Religion and ethnic groups

Lifestyle of the consumers are influenced by the area, demographics and have pronounced effect on retail purchases as given below.

Group culture defines beliefs, norms and customs prevalent in the society.

Social class differentiates people on account of income, occupation.

Opinion leaders provide the vital push to make the decision.

Family status, nuclear, joint, only couples give the decision methodology in families.

Besides discretionary income, people need time for going to the retail outlets for browsing before making purchases. Buyers time division between work, travel and home leaves the extra left for making purchases. The location of store and householder's residential areas determine the extra time availability.

Risks and perceived risks of making purchases are given below:

1. New retailer, new product
2. Buyers' budget
3. Past experience
4. Available alternatives
5. Lifestyle visibility of the product
6. Information availability on product
7. Shopping time
8. Need urgency
9. Price

Retailers need to prepare a lifestyle profiler for their geographic area customers before they build their strategy.

Social status confirms if the customers are from lower, middle or upper class of the society that would be responsible for Mean Time Between Purchase—MTBP, besides it would define likely brands they would buy.

Culture signifies the values, norms, customs and beliefs the potential customer possesses.

The buyers decide to buy new brands or stick to the old ones. They may try to get more information on new brands or ultimately decide not to buy the product at all.

The retailers must understand the customer's viewpoint on the following:

1. The distance customers can travel to come to the shop to buy
2. Is the location convenient for the buyers
3. Preferred time or hours for shopping by the customers

4. Brand selection, type and level of service expected by the buyers
5. Importance of price in the segment market
6. Complaint redressal needs and related time factor
7. Is-home dlivery important to the buyers

Normal purchase is done at the places given below:

1. Primary shoppers:
   - Departmental stores
   - Self-service stores
   - Discount stores
   - Factory outlets
2. Weekly purchase is done as follows:
   - Supermarkets
   - Convenience stores
   - Discount stores
   - Neighbourhood retail
3. Travellers buy at the following locations:
   - Shopping centres
   - Airport
   - Hotel stores

Ethics in Marketing: Marketers are required to sell products which give value for money to the customers. Non-standard products, defective goods, prices which give wrong impression to the buyers (hidden charges like transport, taxes duties not mentioned in the beginning) short packing are some areas of unethical practices. Such deals can give only short-term small benefits and in the long run even if the law does not catch up, the customers eschew purchasing such goods and dealing with such marketers. In the bargain even good products of the marketer are discarded. A few examples will make the subject better understood by the students:

- Food items mixed with unhygienic products like non-food grade preservatives.
- Fake branded products
- Products like video and audio tapes which are pirated
- Quoting different prices to customers for standard products, unless quantity discounts are being offered.
- Advertising five-star hotel when it does not have even three-star facilities
- Advertising contraband goods like liquor, drugs
- Cheating in annual sales where the prices are jacked up from original; then the discounted price still remains almost as original.

Incorrect or misleading advertising should be firmly avoided. It can cause untold harm including legal action, which has become one of the deterrents of such advertisements now.

Motivation is the inner urge which propels people to act. Seeing and smelling food people get motivated to eat while they may not be even hungry. *Graphically it can be shown as given below:*

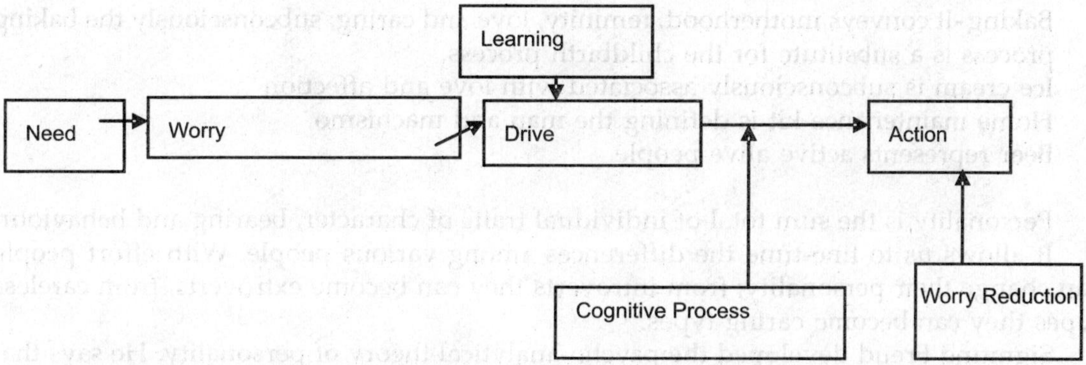

When the need is felt and till the time it is not fulfilled, the person suffers from anxiety and worry which forces him to understand the nature of the need and its fulfilment propelling him to purchase action, which reduces his worry.

(From *Consumer Behaviour* by Schiffman and Kanuk)

People have two types of needs, physiological, i.e., requirements of their bodies and psychological needs of the mind. Food, water, clothing and shelter are the primary physiological needs, and needs of power, self- esteem, affection, love are the secondary ones. House may be the primary need but a bungalow where you can entertain guests becomes psychological need.

Behaviour is oriented towards achieving personal goals. People have general types of goals and then they have product oriented goals. *We will travel to the hills once I purchase my Ford IKON CAR* becomes a product and action oriented goal. We can see that everyone has rational and emotional motivations, with purely objective or subjective criteria.

Changing nature of goals and needs-When a particular goal or need cannot be fulfilled, a substitute goal emerges. Similarly, after fulfilment a new goal or need arises. In any case needs can never be fully satisfied. When a person becomes Vice President of a firm, he changes his goal to becoming the President. Product updates, newer technologies help the firms to use this **urge** as a springboard for launching innovative products.

Once the basic needs are fulfilled, people want to achieve higher goals. After getting a good house to live people would like to be community leaders.

As the saying goes, "Nothing succeeds like success", success gives extra fillip to people for going to higher level goals. Failure, on the other hand make people redefine their goals, by either lowering the standard or taking a different road altogether.

Goal substitution occurs on non-attainment of goal. If you cannot buy Honda City car, buy a Maruti 800. Some people go into a dream world devoid of reality.

Non-achievement causes people to go into depression, which can result in behavioural changes like sulking and going into a shell, anger, rationalization of failure which is bad as it makes a person complacent and frustrated.

Motivational Research is conducted as a psycho-analysis of consumer's mind to understand, sometimes not so apparent reasons for his motives. The subconscious mind works for reasons of its own. Some product personalities types have been profiled as a result of motivational research as follows:

- Baking–It conveys motherhood, feminity, love and caring; subconsciously the baking process is a substitute for the childbirth process.
- Ice cream is subconsciously associated with love and affection
- Home maintenance kit is defining the man and machismo.
- Beer represents active alive people

Personality is the sum total of individual traits of character, bearing and behaviour.

It allows us to fine-tune the differences among various people. With effort people can change their personality; from introverts they can become extroverts, from careless types they can become caring types.

Sigmund Freud developed the psycho-analytical theory of personality. He says that human personality consists of three overlapping areas—Id, super ego and ego

Id is the primitive animal-like instinct, which drives person's hunger, thrust and sex urges. Lots of advertising is based on using this animal force to advantage, and that is why female form is used to attract the males and vice versa.

Super ego is the mind's control on Id, the animal instincts, so that people can live within social norms.

Ego is the balancing force between id and super ego helping people to keep to the right path between id's drive and societal norms.

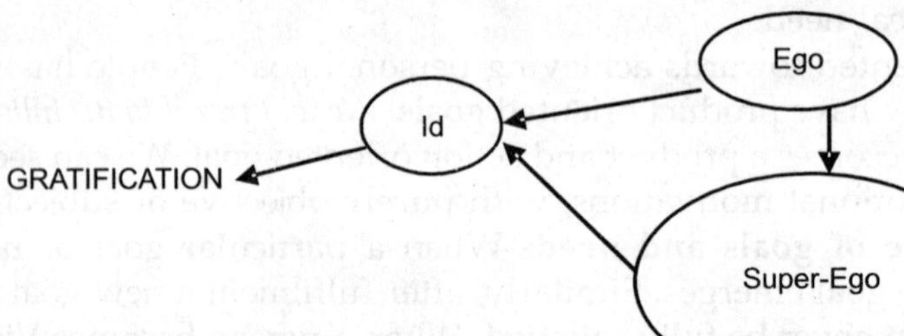

Freudian theory and brand/product personality: Some products are best represented by a celebrity, like Shah Rukh Khan can be called Mr. SANTRO, the car he is successfully advertising. He can also be named as Shah Rukh **Mayur** Khan when he personifies Mayur Suitings. Customers tend to associate the brands with the brand personality. Hence, marketers need to use a personality who can be fully identified with the product. Hrhitik Roshan is promoting Coke, and yet as there have been many coke promoters, it is difficult to name Hrhitik as Mr. Coke.

Personality Theory of Post Freud People: Unlike Freud, other social scientists felt that motives cannot be confined to basic and sexual instincts. Social interaction and lifestyle too gives motivation to people to act.

There are four types of personalities as follows:

1. Thinking and sensing types are rational, logical, objective and fast decision-makers
2. Feeling and sensing types believe in their ownselves, are subjective and they consult others in decision-making
3. Thinking and intuiting types take broad view, look for wider range of options and take decisions for long range of time.
4. Feeling and intuiting types take broad view, are people oriented, take subjective decisions for long-time zones
5. Most often, especially for consumer goods price and quality of a product get associated with each other and reduction in price can create doubts about the reduction in quality of the product. Similarly, product, country, quality and price are perceived by the customers.

Price and Quality Relationship: This takes into account that each product has some service attached to it.

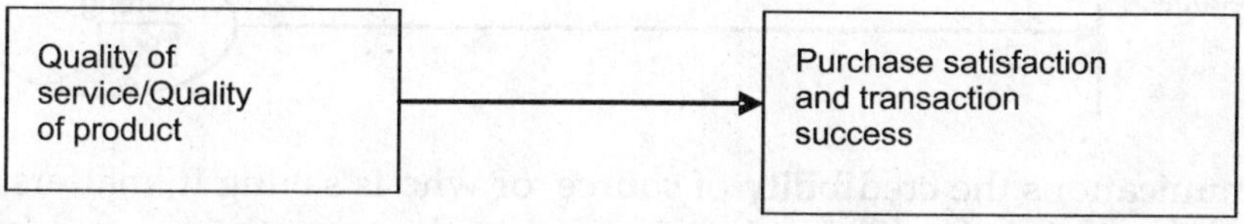

There are different types of consumers with unique personalities. There are consumers ready to experiment and they buy products in the introductory stage of product life cycle. Computer notepads, palmtop computers find a good market among this type of personality, who is always ready to innovate and experiment.

Dogmatic types have rigid behaviour pattern. When this type buys a new product it is contrary to their belief. Therefore, they have to be on the defensive and are uncomfortable with such purchases. They can be persuaded by authoritative dramatic and dynamic advertisements, which help them overcome their basic negative attitude.

Open-minded consumers take to new products easily.

Social "typesets"–self centred persons look for answers within themselves while extroverts are ready and at times eager to find out what their peers and seniors have to say, (**who says what** becomes important and a significant purchase decision tool).

Stimulation levels are important guides for consumer behavior study. Some consumers lead a sedate life and minimum level of curiosity arousal is enough for them to become interested in the product. There are hard core consumers who look for being shaken out of their slumber and for them heavy dosage of stimulation is needed. These persons can practically psyche themselves into getting into the purchase mood.

Attitudes are predisposition levels people have towards a product or an idea. These positive or negative attitudes are based on, earlier experience, odd remark heard from a known or even unknown person, from persons like salesmen connected to the product, the environment or mood in which the message about the product was given to the consumer.

Attitudes are normally consistent for a particular product. **If a thing is not liked then just it is not to be purchased**. Housewives may not even think of purchasing a twin drum washing machine. At times attitudes change for reasons like, "let us economize" or non-availability of favourite brand in the shop visited and imminence of need. "Let us buy Godrej soap as Lux is not in stock." Such decisions for FMCG purchases are taken easily as the cost of replacement is not heavy, unlike a consumer durable product like a car or TV which cannot be purchased everyday.

Communication Process is planned taking into account the target market segment and the mindset of the people of the segment.

One communication model is given below.

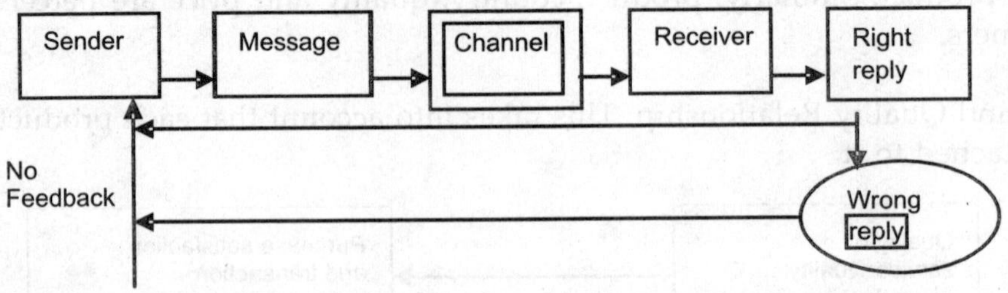

In communications the credibility of source, or who is saying it, matters a lot. Firm's brand equity can authenticate what is being put in the advertisements. Most firms use endorsers to talk about their products which make the target segment believe in the product. Wrong endorsers can cause harm to the product or can have no impact rendering the advertisement useless. A top heroine endorsing washing powder may not have any impact as people know that she does not wash her clothes at all. When she endorses a beauty cream people believe her.

Sender or source's credibility is important as it defines how or how much the receiver is going to believe it. **"Let us take it with a pinch of salt."** Such negative impressions come with unreliable senders of information. Use of endorsers becomes necessary in such cases. Source or sender has its own need for sending the message. How right is that need? For example, many retail firms resort to having **yearly sale** of their products. People want to know if it is a genuine sale, and if yes why the firm is selling good products at heavily discounted prices? Is it that they have odd size unsold products, heavy inventory as their export order got cancelled, or, is it that the discounted prices are in fact the same as original. The firm increased the prices first and then declared the sale. Increase of prices was of 20% and discount offered is 17%. Such types of sales lose their impact in no time.

The receivers understand the message on the basis of earlier experience and mindset. Mrs. Mohan purchased a set of kitchen knives on mail order as advertised in a firm's brochure, only to find the knives not sharp enough and of bad quality. Mrs. Mohan will be least inclined to buy any thing on the basis of a catalogues. Demographic and social grouping effect people's understanding of any message. A young man may interpret a young girl's invitation to her dance recital while it may be only for having a sizable audience.

Personal involvement is the key factor on the interest the customer is going to have in understanding and correctly interpreting the message. Sachin Tendulkar will like to go through the exact specifications of the cricket bat, while a non-playing cricket TV commentator may just take no notice of the bat.

Moods of persons at the time they are receiving the message govern how well they will receive and accept the message. Watching a tragic sob story movie on TV would make people less willing to accept the positive aspects of a product. It calls for proper selection of media, sitcoms, news bulletins, and movie based programmes are viewed on TV with a happy frame of mind, generally.

In order to monitor customer response to a message and its media pre-testing is done where the advertisement is shown to a select group of the market segment to gauge their reaction and get their feedback. In case of poor response, corrections in message and media can be made.

After the advertisement has been released, post-testing is done to find out how effectively the advertisement has met its objectives.

Persuasion strategy: For proper impact of the message, selection of the market segment to be catered to, creativity of the advertisement and objectives associated with the communication are key elements of strategy Some examples are given below:

- Housewife, family income Rs. 20,000 pm, urbanite, graduate would be reading, Famina, Cosmopolitan, Star Dust magazines, watching afternoon soap operas like, Saans, Santa Barbara, Dynasty
- College students family income Rs. 40,000 pm would be reading sports , motorcycle and car magazines, listening to FM Radio.
- Achievers, family income Rs. 80,000 pm, would be reading business magazines like Business India, Business Today, financial newspapers and watching news on Star TV.
- Senior citizens family income Rs. 20,000 pm would be reading health and investment magazines, watching travel related TV programmes for enjoying vicarious adventure and thrills.
- Computer addicts would be surfing the Internet and the best media for communicating to them about software updates would be the web.
- There is always cross-over in segments. For instance, for a person with monthly income of Rs. 10,000 a woollen suit worth Rs. 5,000 may be out of reach. However, he may buy it at least for his marriage.

Persuasion comes in the form of personal influence of some person who **counts.** In daily life, we communicate with other persons in social political or business situations. A good communicator listens more then he/she speaks. When in doubt, we seek advice, or sometimes we get advice totally unasked for. In both cases, it is stored in the brain from where it can be restored at the time of purchase decision making. We normally go to people whom we consider more knowledgeable than us. These people are the **opinion leaders**. Buying a set of golf clubs it is best to ask the golf champion, rather then a lay man. For cameras and films, the professional photographer, not the camera salesperson would be the best bet.

Opinion leaders being experts on their subjects can be trusted to give correct opinion on their subject of specialization. Marketers, on the other hand would invariably give only the positive aspects of their products.

Several times customers seek only information, and sometimes they ask for advice. Can we trace which of the following statements of opinion leaders is information and which is advice.

1. Which is the best gent's shoe for formal wear? "In my view, Bata is still the best".
2. How to use the vacuum cleaner? "I use it once a week to clean the carpet, the curtains, the floors and the ceiling. You could do the same".
3. Where to take my Maruti for servicing in Delhi? "There is no better place then Competent Motors, my dear".
4. Where can I get a gift for my girl/boyfriend? "Try Giggles in CP and you will not go wrong".

As can be seen opinion-leaders are mostly "product" specific. You will not ask your milkman where to buy computer software. In case of doubt, people take second or even third opinion until they are satisfied by the opinion. People with set ideas, often stop after they have got an opinion which agrees to their own thinking. Such subjective opinions can be misleading resulting in wrong decisions.

Advertisers extend the theory of opinion leadership in advertising by using the **leaders as product endorsers.**

Self-image is the some total of a person as he thinks about himself and it is a guiding factor in purchase decision along with wisdom of opinion leaders. "What type of person am I? The image I project to outsiders, how people view my personality" make for the self-image. There are several types of self-image:

- How people view themselves
- How they want others to view them,
- How they would like to be seen in the future

Self-image and products purchased has an interesting connection, as an industrialist buys Mercedes to project the self-image of a successful person. Actors and actresses want to look good and attractive to their fans and their clothes, makeup is meant to focus on that image. Marketers take advantage by using this concept while communicating to them.

Consumer Perception is the consumer's view of the things including messages and stimuli seen/focused on him. These perceptions are given or acquired by visual stimulus, like seeing pictures of products in advertisements, hearing about the products from friends and looking the retail shops, point of purchase (POP), VISUAL Impact.

To heighten the impact advertisers use sensational gimmicks including adventure sports, pretty women as sex objects to make the impact. The level of minimum stimulation which can attract is called the **threshold level**. For two different stimulus the minimum difference which becomes noticeable is known asd JND, **Just Noticeable Difference**.

Weber has given the law which stipulates that, "an additional stimulus equal to JND must be added for majority of people to perceive a difference between the resulting stimulus and the initial stimulus."

Car polish makers add some ingredients in the product which keeps the lustre for a week as compared to competitive product where the shine lasts for four days. The danger in making it better to the extent that the shine lasts for a month or even a fortnight would increase the gap between purchases. Marketers and advertisers use the JND to good use in their **product development and advertising strategy**.

Subliminal perception considers even below the JND stimulus as psychologists have found that even such stimulus leaves an impression on the subconscious level and while it remains dormant it may manifest itself at the right time when product purchase is being considered. Years before a friend had said that the best TV set is from Sony and today finalizing the purchase it comes as bolt from the blue and the decision is made in it's favour.

Hence, the decision process is based on the complex nature of human insight, which the marketers find ways to stimulate and bring to surface in their favour.

Marketing and communicating to the target market segment of new innovative product calls for sustained efforts of advertising, personal selling and word of mouth appreciation of product for a period of time.

The **innovative or the new product** is seen by the firm as new to it and the firm becomes buoyant about it. The firm ignores the fact the product may not be new to the market as competitors may already have introduced the same.

Furthermore the prospective customer may not be as enthusiastic about the product as the retailer wants him to be. This happens when the product is launched without proper test marketing and research.

Product innovation takes into account the features which are unique to the product. One refrigerator manufacturer is claiming novel door cooling system, not available in other refrigerators.

Market based new product, which the market considers as new. When Airtel company introduced cellular phones in Delhi, they were new to the market, and consumers took it as such.

Consumer based new products are the ones which the consumers find totally new.

The new product development can be on a continuous basis or on one-off base. Telephone industry has had both types of innovations as can be seen from the following table:

Discontinuous development	Dynamic continuous development	Continuous development
Telephone	Answering machine, voice mail	Auto-dialling facility, memory phones
Pager	Nationwide paging, two-way paging, sports scores	Message displays, alarm clocks
Fax	Fax modem, mobile fax	Speed dial, delayed dispatches

Consumers look for **relative advantages** in each product. Also the expense of making change and product's compatibility with other products with the consumer too plays an important role in buying new products. For example, the modem, and printer should be able to work with the computer before they are purchased.

Consumer behaviour and firm's responses find that firms do take care of how the consumer will behave.

1. ITC Agro introduced their branded Atta, HEALTH WORLD first in the South India, as their study showed that south Indians are more quality conscious than North Indians in the matter of a product like Atta, in spite of the fact that the Atta consumption in the north is nine times more than in the south. Once the brand gets established in the south, they will move to the north as well with region specific brands and tastes to suit different palates.
2. Dwarka Men's Wear offering cool cotton trousers and shirts, chose the month of March 2000 to launch the product just before the onset of summer. They have successfully marketed their product in the West Asia and European markets.
3. Targeting their cell phones for the youth of the country, Ericsson has introduced FM Radio in the phones which come in a range of right colours to capture the fancy of the youth. Others had to follow suit.

Example

Umasons P. Ltd. had spare capacity for manufacturing Teflon because of change in government policy. They decided to coat aluminium pans and introduce Non-Stick Cooking Pans in the market. Non-stick quality would help the housewives in preparing food with less oil for the cholesterol patients. For others also food with less oil would be more health giving. It will use less gas/electricity in cooking. Benefits customers would derive were as follows:

- Food with less oil
- Use of less gas
- Easy cleaning of the pan
- Dosas and paranthas easy to make on the pan.

The firms found that in spite of the benefits the customers were not finding it the right thing to buy. Being a new concept as a product customers were generally uncomfortable with anything new. Besides it costs about four times than the usual pans. Also the housewives had lingering suspicion that the coating could be toxic and bad for health. The firm arranged to meet with housewife groups in clubs at kitty parties and at retail shops.

A big change in consumer behaviour and attitude towards the product was needed as unless the customers were fully convinced about the benefits of the product, it was doomed for failure. The firms were faced with other problems as well as follows:

- It was a small firm with limited advertising budget.
- As there was no competitive product the entire burden of concept selling fell on their shoulders (later firms benefited from their efforts).

- Frying pan was not a popular cooking vessel in the country.
- Maid servants often rubbed the Teflon coating out considering it as accumulated dirt.

The road to business was finally found in exporting the pans. In 1970, Nirlep exported 70% of its production to Britain, Poland and Malaysia. In 1974, they got an award for exporting from the Engineering Export Promotion Council.

In the domestic market the firms patience paid as in about eight years the product got established.

The change in attitude was the result of firm's communications targeted towards the working women who were growing in numbers and it was found to be a convenience product by the housewives.

In 1986, the housewives realized the following about the product:

- Nirlep cooking was healthy with less oil
- It was low cost with less oil and gas consumption
- It was a convenient and versatile product

The perception of the pan as a western cooking vessel had been gradually altered. With the metropolitan lifestyle it was best received in Mumbai and Kolkata first. Later on some dissatisfaction remained as the coating had low durability and pan's handle was weak. The firm changed the design and built its brand equity with heavy advertising campaigns which laid stress on health foods, ease of cooking and economy and the durability aspect of the pan. The Nirlep pan had arrived!

FIRST NON-STICK FRYING PAN FROM NIRLEP, OF COURSE!

Questions

1. Describe the Maslow's hierarchy of needs. How can you relate the needs with consumer behaviour?
2. Is it necessary to segment the market? If yes then give four important criteria with which the segmentation is done.
3. Discuss the user based segmentation with examples.
4. How does the innovative product penetration take place in the market? What pitfalls it has to surmount?
5. It is important to understand the socio-cultural ethos of your market segment discuss.

Use the knowledge gained:

Pick four products, washing powder, ready-made garments, cars, and washing machines. Describe the market segment in each case giving examples from your town.

Consumer Behaviour—positivism and interpretism

Positivism—prediction of consumer action–quantitative-consumer rational, weigh alternatives.

Interpretism-understanding consumer practises—is subjective, each usage experience is unique, and research findings can be subjective. Cannot be generalized.

Attitudes, how they are formed

- Direct experience
- Influence of family and friends
- Direct marketing
- Exposure to advertisements
- Personality factor

Attitudes - four functions

- Utilitarian function: Brand utility
- Ego-defensive function: Product enhances self-concept
- Value expressive function: Consumer values, life style are reflected
- Knowledge function: Fulfilling need to know
- Also, there can be a combination of several functions.

Resolving conflicting attitudes:

- Tasty vs healthy food
- Quality vs price
- Sturdy vs elegant
- The family
- Economics
- Emotional support
- Lifestyle
- Family socialization—manners, values goals

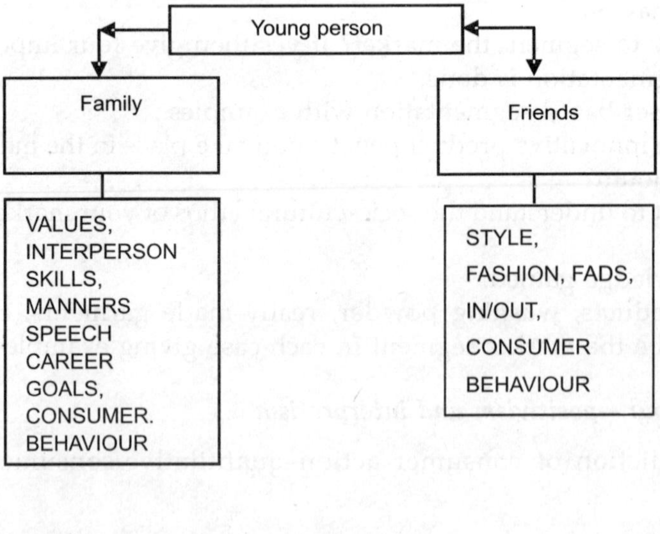

Family Consumer Roles

- husband/wife
- children
- teens
- family life cycle
- bachelor
- honeymooners
- Parent's-young children
- parent's-teenage children *Parents with children away from home * dissolution

Feeling and Emotions

These can be measured on a scale. Let us try out a skin cream and get reactions of women after they have used the cream on a scale as follows:

A-Like it very much—B-like it—C-nothing special—D-do not like—E-do not like it at all.

The survey can be done on the following parameters:

Skin felt	A	B	C	D	E
Relaxed					
Beautiful					
Tight					
Smooth					
Supple					
Clean					
Refreshed					
Oily					
Pampered					

Designing persuasive communication

- Proper market segmentation
- If product transcendent segmentation: Umbrella messaging for all audience
- Good PR
- Media plan: Consumer profile to match with media audience profile
- Each medium is effective for some products, audiences and advertising objectives
- WWW
- Overlapping audience

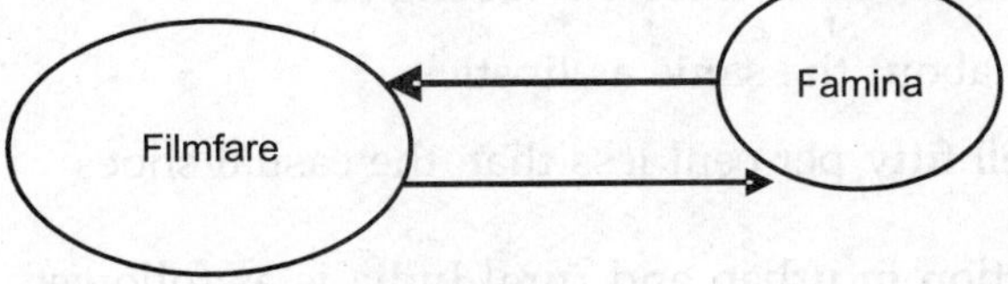

Some customers read *Filmfare* other read *Femina* and yet others read both
In advertising copy, it is important to think of the following:

- Copy appeal
- Copy length
- Endorsements
- Visuals
- Time limit offers
- Free trial offers
- Pricing

1. Information search—Personal—family, friends, neighbours, acquaintances, Commercial—Advertising, Salesmen, dealers, packaging, displays, Public source—Consumer rating organizations, Experiential—handling, examining, using the product.
2. Evaluation of alternatives with weightage given on parameters decided by you, cameras—size, weight, auto-focus, zoom, speed, price, Hotels—location, cleanliness, atmosphere and price.
3. Purchase decision—There can be a situation where after deciding to buy you delay or even cancel the purchase. Sometimes if people close to you have a negative attitude towards the product you may not buy it. Secondly, there may be a change in situation.

Post-purchase decisions

You could be satisfied by the product.

If you are not satisfied then you could try to reverse the purchase action or sell the product.

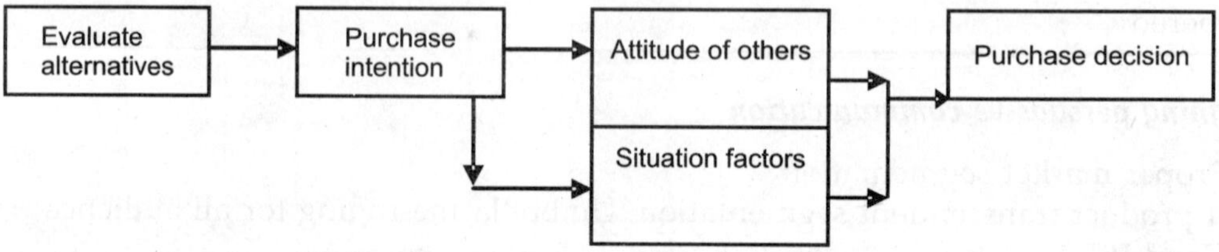

Let us discuss Indian buyers' purchases of some common FMCG products.

- Washing powder sells about 30% less than washing soap cakes.
- Toilet soap sells about fifty per cent of washing soap cakes.
- Electric bulbs sell six times than the tubelights.
- Nail polish sells about the same as lipstick.
- Leather shoes sell fifty per cent less than the casual shoes

Product penetration in urban and rural India is as follows:

S. No.	Products	Urban%	Rural%	Total%
1.	Tooth care	90	50	60
2.	Washing powders	100	90	98
3.	Tea	90	70	80
4.	Milk powder	9	3	5
5.	Butter	10	2	4
6.	Salt	100	95	97
7.	Chocolates	10	2	4
8.	Ice cream	25	10	14
9.	Shampoo	25	9	13
10.	Hair oil	90	85	87
11.	Wrist watches	45	20	28
12.	Talcum powder	45	25	30
13.	Lipsticks	22	12	15
14.	Nail polish	40	30	32

India's population in crores

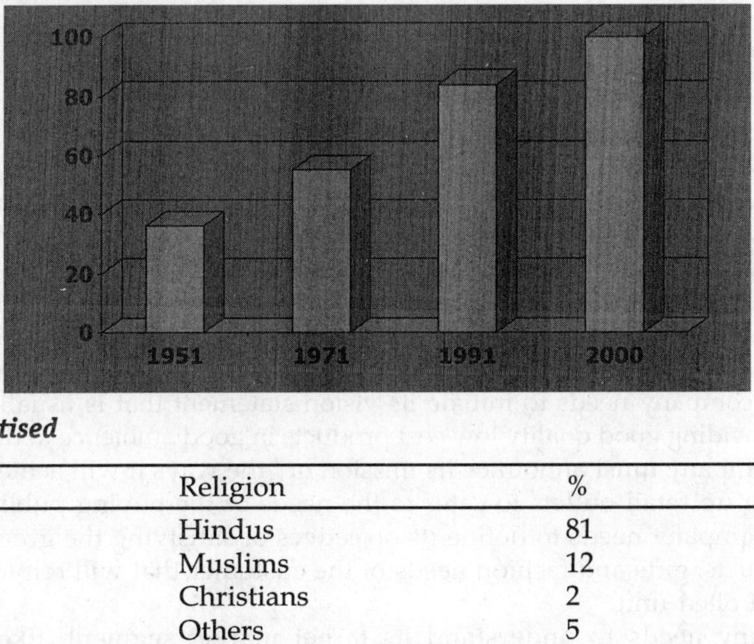

Religions practised

S. No.	Religion	%
1.	Hindus	81
2.	Muslims	12
3.	Christians	2
4.	Others	5

Adult Population Dispersion

	All India	Urban
Males	52 %	53%
Females	48 %	47%

CHAPTER

16

Comprehensive Retail Strategy

Aims and Outcomes

Retail has gained high degree of importance the world over and retailers need to understand the strategy that will help them to remain successful in spite of major thrusts from competition.

It is necessary to define firm's goals and objectives, the direction it needs to take. This requires careful and yet speedy planning where the top management is involved with making plans, policies, procedures and objectives that cover the entire organisation. The middle management is involved in the action plans, team tasks which need to have result orientation. Besides, the managers at different levels must create control points to ensure smooth flow of avtivities in direction conducive for goal achievement.

Firstly, the company needs to initiate its vision statement that is usually altruistic in nature like, "providing good quality low cost products in good ambience to the customers."

Next the company must announce its mission of "the ways it will achieve its vision" like, "by setting up retail outlets to cater to the needs of the buying public.

The retail company needs to define its objectives of satisfying the grocery, clothing, electronic products, gifts and fashion needs of the customer that will reinforce the retail teams as a well oiled unit.

The company needs to understand its target market segment, like, youngsters between ages of 18 and years men and women who are looking for having fun as they make the purchases.

The company must give a distinctive thrust to its strategy like "we provide specific fashion garment not available in other stores." It can plan its vertical integration with designing, manufacturing, merchandising and retailing its products. Customer relationship building and improving brand image are other two distinct objectives for the retail company.

Companies must plan their employee policy, including recruitment, training, career planning and keeping employees motivated to reduce employees attrition levels.

Companies have to study the opportunities available with research and assessment of sales potential in the market, competitive forces and their strengths and weaknesses.

Buying strategy with selection of brands, single or multiple is essential for the outlets success. Retailers' strategies will be fulfilled once the sales and profit targets have been met and costs have remained under control. Each brand needs store space for profit generation. The need is to understand if the space allotted is justified for the brand's profit picture.

Retailers have to think of finding levels of trade-offs like providing self-service counters to save on staff in upmarket area or providing service with a downmarket customer group. Both could be counterproductive in the long run.

Retail performance need to be benchmarked with the following criteria:

1. Total sales
2. Average sales per store/counter
3. Sales of each type goods or category
4. Sales per square metre of floor space
5. Gross margin and its return on investment
6. Operating income
7. Inventory turnover
8. Markdown percentages
9. Employees turnover
10. Financial ratios
11. Profitability

Ideally the comparison needs to be made with the following:

1. Company's historical figures
2. Industry average
3. Industry's best figures

Service retailers use the customers feedback by knowing their assessment on reliability of service, staff helpful attitude, assurance of service quality, individual attention to them, availability of modern equipment for providing the service like computers for billing.

Companies have to analyze the customer's mindset about their view on retail profits, costs and sales. They need to have customer profile of both the customers and the prospects. The business model needs to address the best prospect base, their demographics, relationship building mechanism, and the best methods of brining customer delight. Next, the plan implementation must receive top priority otherwise the best of the plans are likely to fail.

Retailers must organize both financal and non-financial audit to minimise shocks that are inherent in large operations that can tend to become impersonal.

Marketing

The marketing strengths of a retail opeation are the most important single factor for its success. Outlets selling the entire produce at a reasonable profit, increasing sales of the same product portfolio, selling at a higher price or successfully developing new products and selling them too profitably would not face serious problems. Evaluating the marketing strengths of the retailers, the following areas are examined:

- Marketing environment: Markets, customers, brand equity, competition levels, economic trends, money supply position in the market, legal issues, and social developments, causes and problems besetting the market like huge population movements, new major competitors coming in.
- Marketing action: Products, pricing, advertising and promotion, and personal selling, publicity.

The real questions to be asked during audit are summarized below:

- Customer's primary and secondary levels of satisfaction derived from the product; the idea of product as sold by the firm and the customer's viewpoint about what product he is purchasing. For example, retailer sells soap as a personal hygiene product while buyers may be buying the soap for the daylong fragrance it may be providing.
- Outlet's special skills as compared to competition in marketing, could be in visual merchandising, purchasing.
- Marketing problems and opportunities the firm is facing today and may have to face in the future.

Environmental Threats and Opportunities

In the dynamics of country's economics, firms must understand that the changing conditions will make some markets more amenable than the others. Firms need to have constant vigil in the following areas:

- Law and politics: Government regulations can change product emphasis in the market; a recent example being the stopping of sales of cars not conforming to the Euro emission norms. Other examples are, Government of India disinvestments in some prominent firms, their Voluntary Retirement Scheme, the famous VRS, price regulation of some commodities and at times deregulation of prices. These affect the business of some firm or the other.
- Competition: Competitive action needs continuous attention, especially if the market is an oligopoly one. Remaining proactive on competitive product launches, new pricing, advertising and promotion would help the firm in retaining their market share and in even increasing it.
- Suppliers: Oligopoly supply firms tend to have the edge and they keep changing the prices (always to the higher side), and other terms of business to their advantage. Firms, which have diversified vertically, are at a distinct advantage over others. It is therefore necessary for firms to keep a constant vigil on supply scene and always keep more than one supplier for vital raw materials.

- Demographics: Population composition is changing; there is a large teenage group, a large population of senior citizens and migration of workers from villages to towns is a continuous phenomenon. These all, present business opportunities.
- Alternative products are available with better technology (electric shavers became popular for a while in the 1970-1980 period)
- Understanding the product location in its life cycle is important to understand the behaviour of competitors who could be market leaders or market laggards. The firms have their own priorities with regard to placing the product in a particular segment. Competitive information can lead the firm to a vigilant proactive decision in terms of its own products business plan.
- Understanding the consumer: Consumer needs, their buying patterns and habits, purchase decision triggers, and the answers to the five W and one H questions is required—what do they buy, why do they buy, where do they buy it from, when do they buy, what price they pay, and finally how do they buy. In the normal circumstances, when the firm is making a profit and selling its entire produce these questions become irrelevant. It is only when new technology or competitive product swamps the market, the firm does not know what hit it. Maslow's hierarchy of needs and the Freudian theory of desires must be addressed to plan market policies. A car is just not a means of transportation alone; it could reflect the owner's status. Mercedes is bought more as a status symbol than for any other purpose. Firms do better if they understand consumer behavior in their selected market segments for the product.

Market Segmentation

In the first half of the 20th century the firms stress used to be on production and whatever was produced was sold, competition was either not there or it was just not enough, with market for all the players in the field. With severe competition from international players, each selling multiple brands and models, it would be futile for firms to sell in the mass market. The segment variety needs different selling techniques, advertising messages and what works for one segment may not work for the other. Product, price promotion and placement all need different strategies for different segments. Segmentation is done on the following lines:

Demographic Variables

- Age
- Sex
- Family size
- Children's ages
- Occupation
- Income
- Education
- Religion
- Social status

Geographic variables

- Country
  - Climate
  - City size
- State
- Population density
  - Country's main religions

Psychographics variables	**Product usage variables**
• Lifestyle	• Heavy users
• Personality	• Light users
• Product loyalty	
• Product awareness	

Strategic audit should trace the firm's growth and standing in the marketplace, which can be done on the following parameters:

- Market growth-
  (i) Same product increased sales through penetrating prices and increased efforts of the marketing team,
  (ii) Same product sales increase in extension of geographic areas
  (iii) New or improved product in the same geographic area.
- Acquisitions involve investments of available funds of cash rich firms in product or business diversification by acquiring other firms, business. Diversification can be vertical or horizontal depending on whether the firm has bought into its supplier or a product with which it has some synergy.
- Distribution channels: Ability of selection of the type of distribution network as also the actual dealers of the product to cover the geographic segments is of vital importance for the success of the firm, especially for consumer goods. It is the last link in the chain connecting the manufacturer to the consumer and the only one which gets the buyer's money in exchange of goods supplied.
- Pricing policy is governed by the following considerations:
  (a) Elasticity of demand does the price change affect the product demand or not; the firm if they are marketing in multiple segments must be fully aware of the demand changes in each segment on variation of price.
  (b) Government price regulations: In some products the government has its own price mechanism, especially in the food and drugs, and the firms must take this into consideration while fixing the price.
  (c) Competitors: Price becomes a function of competitive pricing, unless the firm can claim a higher price based on their better brand equity.
  (d) Pricing and promotions: Short-term extra benefits are given to customers, which reduce the profits for the firm, but gain additional market share. Such increases are mostly short-lived as they invite competitive reaction nullifying the increase in the market share. At times the commission given to the channel members change as the firm expects the channel members to pass on the benefits to the customers, putting a smoke screen before competitors, giving the impression that they are not involved in any price war on their own.
  (e) Price and quality: For premium quality goods high prices can be kept with high brand equity, for low quality goods keeping high prices could be the means of getting quick profits before competition catches on. Keeping low prices of high quality products would mean generic product, high growth market and firms wanting to improve its market share. Low quality low price would be for bargains and discounts often to unload extra inventory.

(f) Product strategy: It should take the product's brand equity, stage of its life cycle, competitive products, production capacity or product availability (heavy advertising and promotion will fall flat if the product is not available, unless the firm is trying to create artificial scarcity to increase demand.

(g) Advertising and promotion: Creating product awareness, leading to interest in owning it can be generated through intelligent use of advertising, which does not oversell the product and remains in the realm of plausibility. Besides, personal selling, publicity and promotion have definite roles to play in market communications. The audit judges the efficacy of these communications with the market segment.

(h) Level of brand equity.

Financial Analysis

The audit must take into account the fact that financial analysis is the starting point of the audit, as also of management decision-making process. Considering the entire picture is a massive tasks; the audit should take only the most relevant figures, accept the limitations of the study and then only give the recommendations.

Income and Balance Sheet

The balance sheet is the mirror image of the firm as it reflects its strengths and weaknesses, at a given point of time, usually at the end of the financial year of the firm, which is 31st March for most Indian firms. From the audit viewpoint monthly trial balance, which may even be unaudited by the firm's statutory auditors, would suffice. The balance sheet gives the firm's resources, its debt and equity base, its assets and liabilities. It tells about the financial health of the firm. The audit could define and also design the resource needs of the firm and its justifiable allocation.

Business Audit Checklist

The checklist covers the essential points of any business plan or strategic audit. All the points are not relevant for every firm. Certain points are for start up firms, others for on going firms. Certain points are for service industries as compared to product firms. There is a separate list for firms offering equity to the market.

The check would be found useful in the following areas:

- Preparing a comprehensive business plan by presenting the required relevant information on the format as per the checklist
- As a questionnaire while interviewing firm's employees to gather information to prepare documents needed for strategic audit
- For evaluating the business plan or the firm's strategies as it provides specific points for evaluation. It is not required that the checklist format is adhered to completely but the evaluators would find it appropriate to stick to the checklist to the extent possible

Summary Checklist

1. Brief statements on the firm
2. Activities
3. Management
4. Performance
5. Special features of products or service
6. Market growth
7. Financial projections
8. Amount of money needed now
9. Form in which the money is needed, equity debt or both
10. Purpose of the funds needed
11. Is the proposal made by the firm so far understood by the evaluator?
12. Is it interesting enough?
13. Will it stimulate investments?
14. Background of the firm in the business
15. Business intending to enter
16. Products / services
17. Prospective customers
18. Physical area of operations
19. History of the firm; when was it formed?
20. Product selection methods
21. Business development process and roles played by the CEO and other top managers in it.
22. Present plans of business expansion – sales
23. Profits
24. Return on investments
25. Information on setbacks and losses
26. Type and extent of losses and plans for avoiding recurrences
27. Information missed out in the questions so far
28. Current status and prospects of the industry
29. Main competitors
30. Competitors' performance
31. Competitors' profit and loss
32. Competitors' forecast for the year regarding sales and planned profits
33. New entrants and exiting firms with reasons for both
34. Major trends affecting business
35. Economic trends
36. Social trends
37. Technological trends
38. Regulatory trends
39. Features and advantages of products and services, what is sold, customer benefits, drawbacks and business opportunities
40. Description of products in demand, what needs they will satisfy

41. Diagrams, pictures, sketches
42. Distinctive features as compared to competition
43. Advantages—feature-wise
44. Disadvantages—feature-wise
45. Proprietary position
46. Patents
47. Trade secrets
48. Other proprietary features
49. Product early launch and its advantages
50. Potential
51. Extension of product line
52. Development of related products and services
53. Market Research & Analysis—will market support the sales target?
54. Customers
55. Who are the buyers?
56. Where do they buy the products
57. Why do they buy the products
58. When do they buy the products
59. Is there seasonality in business
60. Rank by customer value
61. Price
62. Quality
63. Service
64. Personal contacts
65. Political pressure
66. Master list of customers and prospective customers
67. Reason of the customers interest in the product
68. Customers dropped or having no interest now.
69. And reasons thereof (of no interest)
70. Plans for overcoming the negative reactions
71. Market size and trends
72. Size of the market segment
73. Numbers of product on demand
74. Demand in rupees
75. Source of information
76. Information from the dealers, sales team, customers
77. Next three years demand projection, factors affecting the demand
78. Industry trends
79. Technological developments
80. New or changing customer needs
81. Review the previous trends
82. Differences between past and present trends
83. If there is no change in trends identify the reasons thereof
84. Competition

85. Competitive products and services
86. Strengths
87. Weaknesses
88. Data for competitive analysis
89. Product comparison with the competitors
90. Price
91. Performance
92. Service
93. Warranties
94. Other features
95. Tables used or not
96. Competitors' management strengths
97. Marketing strengths
98. Operational strengths
99. Financial strengths
100. Recent trends in market share
101. Sales
102. Profitability
103. If competition has failed why the firm can succeed
104. Why customers buy from more than 2 or 3 competitors
105. Strategy for taking customers from competitors
106. Estimated market share and sales
107. Major customers ready to buy from the firm
108. Extent of commitment in numbers and rupees
109. Estimated market share in numbers and rupees
110. Market share in the next two years and by quarter
111. Last two years sales
112. Correlation with assessment of customers

Marketing Plan Checklist

1. How does the firm plan to achieve the sales target
   (a) Sales and service policies
   (b) Pricing policy
   (c) Distribution plan
   (d) Advertising and promotion plan
   (e) What is to be done, when and by whom
   (f) Public relations plans

Capital and Working Capital

(a) Debt equity ratio
(b) Capital base
(c) Promoters capital
(d) Detailed project report

(e) Overheads
(f) Profit planning
(g) Profit and loss forecast for the next 3 years
(h) Three years cash flow projections
(i) ROI, Profit on sales percentage
(j) Cash flow with price increase and decrease
(k) Ability to attract finance from the market and financial institutions

Management Team

(a) Key personnel education experience and training
(b) Staff in different departments
(c) Organizational structure
(d) Duties, authorities and responsibilities of the key people
(e) Role of consultants
(f) Profit, productivity, reduction in operating costs; living within the budget benchmarking the performance of key people
(g) Plans for training
(h) Persons showing leadership qualities
(i) Management compensation packets, stock options
(j) Employee turnover,
(k) Board of Directors, their background
(l) Management check points, controls, PERT, bar charts

Public Issue Offering Checklist

(a) Needed finance as per detailed project report
(b) Cash flow plans
(c) Money needed for the next three years
(d) Equity plan
(e) Loans plan
(f) Promoter's share holding value and percentage
(g) Capitalization plans
(h) Deployment of funds
(i) Working capital needs

Case Studies

CASE STUDY

0

Understanding Case Studies

Case studies help to relate to the practical aspects of the theories. In fact, the students can analyze the information given, find alternative solutions, assess the best option and then give their recommendations on the case. It would be the task for the teacher or the guide, to steer the students on the right path enabling them to arrive at the best recommendations. However, it is believed that there are no perfect answers to the case studies, the case studies are judged by the clarity of analysis and forcefulness and unambiguity of the recommendations. The following method is suggested for arriving at the recommendation stage:

- Read the case cursorily in the first stage
- Study any figures or tables provided in the case.
- Analyze the figures
- Study the case in detail again
- Use the tools available for analyzing the case
- Write down rough report
- Discuss the rough report with your guide
- Make final report on the basis of the discussions

Final report should have the following elements in it:

- Title page
- Acknowledgements page where you express your gratitude to those who helped you in the case analysis
- Table of contents with page numbers
- Executive summary of the recommendations on the case
- Brief information on the case
- Tools you are planning to use in the case study

- Case analysis
- Recommendations (with possible expected results, if possible) and conclusions
- Glossary of important words used
- Bibliography of written matter used in the case study, if applicable

The students must understand that while solving case studies there is no absolutely right or wrong answer. The areas to look for are the following:

- The student has understood the case, its problem areas well.
- The student is using the right tools in solving the case.
- The student has analyzed the figures and tables given in the case (if any).
- The student has presented his recommendations in a forthright unambiguous manner.
- The recommendations need not be many, but they should be hard hitting and direct.
- The recommendations must arise out of the case analysis, the tools used. Any major deviation, which is not explicitly mentioned in the case, must be stated clearly with reasons for the same.

CASE STUDY 1

Pharma Retailing

Pharmaceutical retail market in India comes up to US$6 billion. At the moment it is consolidating and priming itself for severe competitive challenges. The change is starting at the small chemist shops spread around in towns, cities and metros, offering prescription medicines and over the counter drugs, like painkillers, antibiotics. The country is poised for free medical check-ups, faster turnaround in hospitals, low cost diagnostics in stand-alone and hospital labs. All these are ready to stimulate pharma retail networks.

A few corporates who have already forayed into this segment include Dr. Morepen (with Lifespring and soon to be launched Tango), Medicine Shoppe, Apollo Pharmacies, 98.4 from Global Healthline Pvt. Ltd., and the recently launched CRS Health from SAK Industries. Zydus Cadila and Cipla too are rumoured to have plans for this segment. In the south, RPG group's Health & Glow is already in this category, though it is not a pure play pharma retailer but more in the health and beauty care business.

In fact, recent surveys show that healthcare now ranks third on the Indian consumer's spending list, higher than apparel or entertainment. And it is not only rising disposable income among the Indian middle and upper classes or growing awareness about health, which is responsible for this phenomena. Points out R.B. Smarta, Managing Director, Interlink Healthcare Consultancy, "Expenditure on healthcare is bound to increase, particularly due to changing lifestyles. For instance, while consumption of packaged food products are increasing, consumption of grains is going down. Such shifts in lifestyle means getting into different nutritional deficiencies tomorrow."

Says Gautam Thadani, Director of Global Healthline Ltd. (GHPL), promoters of 98.4 (which was launched last month), "Spurious and fake drugs is a problem these days. Consumers can be assured of buying genuine products at these stores, without worrying about issues such as expiry of drugs and billing, and so on."

In addition, apart from providing an upscale shopping ambience at no extra cost, most of these branded outlets are providing value-added services as well.

"We are planning to introduce value-added services for the consumer such as home delivery, prescription records, and reminder services. In addition, our health stores consist of a state-of-the-art pharmacy, a special diabetic care section, self-diagnostic equipment, natural foods, babycare products, skincare, toiletries, among other things," says Rahul Chadha, Managing Director of SAK Consumer Retail Services.

If only Maharashtra is considered, drugs are going to be retailed at ten per cent discount. Its 32,000 stores are gearing up for a major retail boom period. As the chemists fight competition with large MNCs, the customer is going to benefit in the following manner:

1. Discounted pricing of drugs
2. Free medical check-ups
3. Concessional rates on drug testing reports
4. Tie-ups with labs and hospitals in the city
5. Empanelment of pathologists, doctors and top managers with the retailers
6. Home delivery of medicines

The above change in scenario has become possible due to the following reasons:

1. Low cost retail chemists like Subhiksha, Apollo, Medicine Shoppe
2. Ambani Brothers investment in pharma retail chains. They have been talking to the All India Organization of Chemists and Druggists
3. Retail giants entry into pharma retailing

Subhiksha has launched its pharmacy products at 10 per cent discount. Other chemists are going to follow suit. They are planning membership cards and other concessions along with other value added services to their customers.

US based Medicine Shoppe International, the largest franchiser of independent community pharmacies in the US is planning for competitive moves in India. Medicine Shoppe says, "get ready for a tough fight nine out of ten major drugs will require special storage and transportation as they will belong to biotech genre. Most existing pharmacists in India would not be able to meet these stringent requirements. At that time our reach and strength will be realized."

Though corporations are putting in major investments in this segment, it would be some time before they actually manage to displace the position of the neighbourhood chemist, due to the sheer reach and size of the latter. However, they are hoping that a higher degree of attached credibility combined with value-added services that are being provided would attract consumers to these novel outlets.

Another advantage is that when a consumer usually visits a chemist with a prescription for a medicine, it tends to be unavailable and a substitute is offered in turn (the brand which brings in higher margins for the chemist). This situation can be avoided at a branded store.

Meanwhile, though analysts agree that branded outlets will catch on in tune with international trends, these would coexist hand-in-hand and not result in the phasing out of the chemists, primarily because such outlets would cater largely to the upper and middle-end of the population.

For those entering pharmacy retailing, it may be a great opportunity but profits may come only after being in the business for years, that is, because the government controls prices and profit margins on medicines and price based competition is getting tougher by the day.

However, there are challenges on the way ahead. For one, retail still does not enjoy an industry status. There are still not many players in the organised retail sector, lack of skilled workforce coupled with the fact that there are few takers for jobs in retailing makes it difficult to manage retail operations. Companies are tackling this by investing heavily in training programmes.

Meanwhile, even though it does appear that corporate India is gearing up to provide a new buying experience to the Indian consumer, much would, however, depend on how well the concept is implemented in India.

Task for the Students

Find out strategies the existing chemists would need to protect their market share in India.

CASE STUDY

2

Reliance Retailing

Reliance is gearing up to revolutionize the retailing industry in India. They are aggressively working on introducing a pan-India network of retail outlets in multiple formats, world-class shopping environment, state-of-the-art technology, a seamless supply chain infrastructure, a host of unique value-added services and above all, unmatched customer experience.

Reliance industries, which opened nine retail outlets in the NCR on Monday, is aiming at opening 6,000 outlets in 784 cities and towns by 2010-11. CEO of reliance retail Raghu Pillai said by 2010-11, company's revenue would be Rs. one lakh crore.

The company has earmarked an investment of Rs. 25,000 crore to create a pan-India retail network that would connect farmers to end consumers without involving any middle man. As per the plan, the company will have a cold storage to store the vegetables and dairy products.

Reliance Industries Ltd. will make an equity investment of up to Rs 10,000 crore, "over time," in a new company, Reliance Retail Ltd. that will manage the group's new retail initiative."

Reliance Retail Ltd. (RRL) will be a wholly owned subsidiary of Reliance Industries, except for a holding in it through employee stock options.

Its retail outlets will sell food, groceries, apparel and footwear, lifestyle and home improvement products, electronic goods and farm implements and inputs. They will also offer products and services in energy, travel, health and entertainment. In addition to this, partnerships would be developed to bring the best of global luxury brands to India as well.

At the district level towns, the procurement centres will have food processing facilities where seasonal fruit and vegetables will be processed to enhance their shelf-life. For example, surplus tomato produced in a region will be aggregated at one point and would be processed. The vegetables and fruits collected at the procurement centre would be aggregated at the district level to supply them to the big cities as per the requirements and process the rest. This will push up farmers' income as they would get better price of their seasonal products.

Conceptually, Reliance is creating a virtuous circle of prosperity by bringing farmers, small shopkeepers and consumers in a win-win partnership, said Mr Ambani, who called this new business of Reliance a "defining point in its history."

Reliance Retail mentor Kamal Nanawati said "The venture would not help end customers in getting fresh products at affordable price but would also help farmers to earn more."

The company is developing a huge logistic network to maintain supply chain. President of agri and food business, Sanjiv Asthana said, a part of the logistic network would be developed in house and rest would be out sourced. In fact, to make optimum use of the network, the company is planning to sell the products not only to the end customers but also to the cornerstores. "In Hyderabad, the company has already started selling farm products to vendors and the experiment is working well", said Pillai.

In the large cities and towns, the products would be sold through Reliance retail outlets. At present, the company has opened 49 outlets in cities like Hyderabad and NCR. Nanavati said by December 2007, the company will have 1000 stores in 35 cities. In fact by April 2007, he said in NCR, the company will have 100 retail outlets—50 in Delhi and 50 in the NCR. By the year end, the number will go up to 250 stores in the NCR.

The tremendous talent shortage in the retail sector has forced retail giants who are taking their first step in the country to look towards the gulf to headhunt for talent. According to market sources, the country's biggest and newest entrant, Reliance Retail, has asked its HR team to camp in Dubai and do a sort of 'gate interviews' of sales, marketing, purchase, merchandising staff of huge hypermarkets such as Carrefour, Lulu and Lifestyle stores.

The mega investment plan announced by RIL comes at a time when global retail majors are waiting in the wings to gain an Indian entry.

It would also bring a new level of competition to the existing players who do not have the financial strength of Reliance.

Despite its ability to deploy huge resources, industry observers say that it will not be a cakewalk for Reliance as many players have already established an early lead, including Pantaloon Retail, RPG group, Shoppers' Stop, Lifestyle and Trent.

Why big corporations like Reliance are being allowed to eat up every small and medium retail business? On one hand government seems firm on its decision to not allow foreign retailers like Wal-Mart to come to India to safeguard India's small markets but on the other hand it is allowing these giant Indian corporations to threaten the industry. Why not to encourage many small organized retailers to grow and flourish instead of allowing one single greedy giant corporation to be wealthier? Is this move by Reliance to help India growing or to fill their bank accounts with more money? Would a small organized retailer be able to stand and survive in front of Reliance? Should this greed and aggression be allowed by Indian government? Will it not result in throwing these small but ambitious retailers out of business? Can somebody answer these questions?

Task for the Students

Discuss the strategy adopted by Reliance in retail and suggest improvements in the same.

Discuss the relevance of large companies like Reliance getting into retail. Who will be the beneficieries, the company, customers or the government?

CASE STUDY

3

FMCG Retail

Retail has taken a leap to join the league of information technology and financial services sectors in the employment outlook survey made by an independent agency. TeamLease India, a staffing solutions company, had in its survey indicated the highest index points of 95 for hiring by the retail, media and FMCG sectors followed by IT with 94 and financial services 91. In the survey for the quarter October to December, all sectors are expected to increase their hiring, the main drivers being the services and FMCG sectors. The survey covered 490 companies across the following eight cities—Delhi, Mumbai, Kolkata, Hyderabad, Bengaluru, Chennai, Pune and Ahmedabad. Bengaluru projects the highest Business Outlook Index point, followed by Mumbai and Delhi, in the next three months with a major contribution from retail, media, FMCG, infrastructure and financial services.

The survey also suggests that against the national average of 80 index points, Mumbai with 98, Delhi 93 and Bengaluru 84 had the largest employment base indicating that most of the companies would be hiring in these cities. Chennai, Ahmedabad and Pune trailed these cities. Even cities such as Kolkata with index points below the national average reflect larger hiring activities. Bulk of the recruitment will be at the junior level at 86 per cent. Hiring trends across functions project marketing as the highest performer at 31 per cent followed by IT 18 per cent, production 17 per cent, finance and others (customer service, quality assurance and maintenance) 11 per cent, administration 8 per cent and human resource 4 per cent. The emergence of modern trade (or organised retail) is currently the biggest challenge facing FMCG manufacturers, who could see increasing pressure on sales margins as a result.

The Rs. 52,000 crore Indian FMCG market is predominantly driven by the traditional retail format, which accounts for 97 per cent of the category sales. Modern trade has made some strides; it accounted for 6 per cent of the FMCG sales in urban India in 2004, compared with 2 per cent in 2003. While the emergence of modern trade could hurt margins, dealing with the traditional format is not cost-effective either. Super-stockists, who cater to smaller towns, are offered higher margins than normal stockists.

Since, Delhi and its suburbs have so far seen the growth of 100 bigger and smaller malls, roughly 600 new malls are coming up in other metropolis and large townships in which less than 35% of retail business is going to be transacted. The paper reveals that over 1000 malls are in the pipelines for smaller townships in which the retail sector is projected to grow at over 60% because of ample availability of land and increased purchasing power of the folks living in those areas because of increased economic activities. Naturally, the large players will prefer to go there and put up their shops by sourcing their supplies from the places convenient to them, further states the paper. Some of the key areas in which retail boom will prevail in towns beyond metros and even large cities will include food items, FMCG products, grocery, sportswear, outerwear, tailored clothing, eyewear, watches, footwear and accessories and the like.

It also highlights, pointing out that even in the case of non-agricultural products such as apparel, FMCG and general merchandise, the situation is far from ideal. The key cause for inefficiency is the poor integration between the retailer and supplier. None of the retailers, in view of ASSOCHAM has so far an automated system for information exchange with their suppliers.

In developed countries, retailers practise Vendor Management Inventory (VMI) systems, where the supplier has access to the point of sales data of the retailer and plans automatic replenishments responding to the stocks available at the retailer. On the other hand, best practice retailers globally have implemented techniques like milk runs—having continuous orders to suppliers as the inventory depletes and doing multiple small lot shipments from the supplier to stores. Such efficient replenishment practises are today practised in the Indian auto and auto component industry. So retailers in India can leverage such expertise available to implement a better retail supply chain.

Non-uniform sales tax laws in India further result in higher distribution costs for retailers since the latter need to maintain infrastructure for state level procurement and distribution rather than a more efficient regional/national model. Is VAT the right answer, students need to learn.

As one of the world's largest fishing tackle companies, Pure Fishing has millions of customers around the globe. The company fell hook, line and sinker for a Linux-based value network solution that IBM Partners Distributed Systems Services, Inc., (DSS) and eOneGroup are designing to help it better serve these customers as an on-demand business.

What's more, the on-demand solution could translate into millions of dollars in new opportunity for Pure Fishing.

In order to deliver the multifaceted solution Pure Fishing needed, eOneGroup was brought onto the scene. The ISV is a winner of the IBM PartnerWorld Beacon Award in the category of "Hot Linux Solutions" for 2004.

Together, the Business Partners are delivering an extranet that will empower Pure Fishing's customer service and field sales with wide-ranging, self-service capabilities, including order entry and inquiry, shipment tracking, and account inquiry. The extranet will automate once manual business processes. The solution will also serve as the platform for SAP integration for Internet, extranet, and Intranet functionality. The multiphase solution has created an on-demand operating environment for Pure Fishing. It is built upon eOneGroup's eOneCommerce offering and IBM Integrated Platform Express, a complete e-business infrastructure which is part of IBM's Express portfolio of solutions for mid-market. This Express offering includes WebSphere Application Server Express, and IBM xSeries with Linux.

Headquartered in central Spain, Grupo SIRO is one of the country's largest food manufacturers. With 1,000 employees, it had sales of approximately $125 million in 2003.

At issue were Grupo SIRO's outdated processes for connecting staff members with the company's enterprisewide software applications. Not only did these multiple applications require individual, they also were not available over the Internet.

The company's previous environment consisted of numerous applications running on an IBM iSeries server, including DB2 Universal Database and a mission-critical CRM program. To provide faster access, Grupo SIRO began looking for a way to integrate its various solutions into one common Intranet portal with single sign-on capability. Requirements included support for open standards, as well as advanced collaboration features and scalability.

To help build its new portal, Grupo SIRO turned to IBM Business Partner Aitana. Working with Aitana, Grupo SIRO created a solution based on IBM WebSphere Portal Express Plus for Multiplatforms.

For high availability, the new portal solution is based on an IBM xSeries 225 server running SuSE Linux Enterprise Server 9.0. The system provides maximum reliability at a competitive price point, while Linux helps keep licensing costs down.

Call it a twist in the retail as new entrants keep it too basic. New retail players are simply jumping on to the 'Fresh' bandwagon, and painting the town red and green in concert. Before experiential differentiators and brand personalities kick in, the retail revolution is banking on the old 'fresh' theme, and primary colours to foster mass appeal. Reliance, Heritage Foods and ITC, all rushing to book consumer mind space, have ended up making a chorus instead of separate clarion call. They're all shouting Fresh! So it's Reliance Fresh and ITC Choupal Fresh, for instance. And former Andhra Pradesh CM Chandrababu Naidu's family owned, Heritage Foods has named its stores as Fresh@ !

And if they're all getting 'fresh', they're going red and green too, when it comes to their colour code. With some differences: like Subhiksha has used the same colours but it hasn't called itself 'Fresh' as well! So striking colours hasn't really shown much diversity as the nascent modern retail infrastructure in India grapples with a whole lot of branding issues while seeking to be right up there with the Wal-Marts and Tescos of the western world. Call it flawed branding creativity but these companies unanimously argue that 'Fresh' as a concept is inseparable from food retailing. It simply cannot be replaced with any other word. When it comes to colours too, they believe red and green mirror the values their stores represent—red for vibrancy and green for, what else, freshness.

Point taken. But is it necessary to hammer home 'Fresh' in every brand? An early entrant in the organised retail space, Subhiksha, which also uses red and green, begs to differ. The Chennai-based chain has positioned itself on the convenience and discount plank instead of freshness to attract footfalls. "We believe freshness is given in the Indian context since Indians are used to buying fresh food and the supply chain is rather short. So we have positioned ourselves in terms of price and convenience," says Subhiksha MD R. Subramanian.

Brand experts have a caveat on that. "The issue of lack of distinctiveness in terms of branding is something that needs to be tackled from inception because it is harder to breakdown and rebuild a brand afresh," says Technopak VP, consumer insights division, Preeti Reddy. "Defining a brand at the start would influence everything including retail design and help these brands differentiate themselves. If any brand does not position itself consciously it may end up getting positioned by default."

That's where a brand with an enormous equity and recall, Reliance, has a clear edge, besides its deep pockets. The mother brand rubs off on new venture. Even Reliance Retail chief executive (customer ops) Venugopal Komanduri agrees that it is not colours or the store name that really matters. "All these come under the big brand umbrella 'Reliance' and that's what gives us all the credibility and recall value," he points out. Moreover, a retail store is differentiated from others not merely by brand alone, but by ambience and services too, he adds. Analysts also point out that colour schemes hardly determine purchase decisions on the shop floor. "Consumers have function in mind when they buy, rather than form, and so people relate to service and other "real' parameters to judge the brand in the market," says Delhi-based ad agency A's art director Prasad Raghavan.

The retailers on the other hand, say it is early days and the contours of differentiation will emerge. They argue that common brand codes may lead to confusion among customers for FMCG, but that's not true of a retail store. "Brand-building of our stores is centred on quality products, pricing and ambience. As long as customers can differentiate their experience in various retail stores, they will not have any problem in recalling our brand of stores," explains ITC chief executive (agri) S. Sivakumar. The company, incidentally, has not gone for the red-green norm, but has chosen green and white as its colours for its retail stores.

Agrees Subramanian of Subhiksha, "Colour schemes may confuse consumers in the long run, but separate formats are bound to differentiate in terms of value and delivery."

Brand-comm CEO Ramanujam Sridhar, feels that in the long run, similar positioning and colour schemes may act in concert to queer the pitch. "Probably, many of these companies are looking to break into the market and are hence not paying too much attention to branding. I'm in favour of a colour that's dominant so that consumers associate with it and over time, it becomes the brand's property."

Moreover, marked colour differentiation alongside resonating USPs create strong retail brand identities. "The players should be more focused on branding as it is the face of their identity. Since (organised) retail in India is still in its infancy, big retailers focus largely on logistics like supply chain and manpower," says India Retail Forum director RS R.

Reliance is gearing up to revolutionize the retailing industry in India. Towards this end, we are aggressively working on introducing a pan-India network of retail outlets in multiple formats. A world class shopping environment, state-of-the-art technology, a seamless supply chain infrastructure, a host of unique value-added services and above all, unmatched customer experience, is what this initiative is all about. The retail initiative of Reliance will be without a parallel in size and spread and make India proud. Ensuring better returns to Indian farmers and manufacturers and greater value for the Indian consumer, both in quality and quantity, will be an integral feature of this project. By creating value at all levels, we will actively endeavour to contribute to India's growth.

The project will boast of a seamless supply chain infrastructure, unprecedented even by world standards. Through multiple formats and a wide range of categories, Reliance is aiming to touch almost every Indian customer and supplier.

Mumbai: The Retailers Association of India (RAI) along with ECR India has launched the Win-Win 2006 initiative for the FMCG (Fast Moving Consumer Goods) sector to standardise quality and ensure efficient supply chain management in the modern retail trade. The initiative is a mandate by 12 leading Indian retailers under the umbrella of RAI to their suppliers to use barcodes with internationally accepted GS1 (earlier EAN) product identification standards for all FMCG supplies.

Retailers will not accept supplies from the FMCG suppliers without the GS1 barcodes. Among the signatories to the mandate are Pantaloons, Piramyd, Shoppers' Stop, Dollar Store, Spar International, Subhiksha Trading, Apna Bazaar, HAIKO, Great Wholesale Club, Food World Supermarkets, Dmart and HyperCity Retail, Spencer's Retail, Reliance Petro Marketing, Odyssey Bookstores, Shoprite and Sangam Direct.

Annual Fee

All suppliers will have to pay GS1 an annual fee of Rs. 5,000, but larger suppliers will pay a one-time fee of Rs. 20,000, while small-scale suppliers will pay Rs. 5000. "There is no doubt that suppliers will willingly pay the amount once they realise the benefits of the access to information they can enjoy. Today, there is a lag of up to two weeks to get the right information about inventory and goods movement," Gibson Vedamani, CEO, RAI, told *The Hindu*.

Bar-coding started 30 years ago in the developed world to ensure 100 per cent accuracy of data capture at high volumes and high speeds. Besides, it provides real time information on availability of stock and allows for reconciliation of daily sales and cash collections. The modern retail trade operates on thin margins—even large global retailers operate on 1-2 per cent margins—and, thus, every part of the business process is important with supply chain being critical and its efficiency being a differentiating factor.

The deadline is to ensure that the fringe 25 per cent suppliers, not conforming to industry standards, fall in line. "We have informed all retailers and brand owners about the initiative and are spreading awareness about its importance. Till date, there was no uniformity in systems and several in the modern retail trade have their own barcodes," said Mr. Vedamani.

"It is important that the retail trade in India is geared up to accept international norms especially when the foreign direct investment is opened up. Globally, GS1 is the de facto standard in retailing," said Ravi Mathur, Chief Executive, GS1 India.

The Government has in the past successfully enforced exporters to conform to global standards. According to Mr. Vedamani, even Indian book publishers have complied with the ISDN standards—a GS1 coding system.

"The Ministry of Commerce and Industry and the Ministry of Consumer Affairs should enforce it right across the retail industry. With this, price changes cannot be easily affected, audits are easier and inventory follow-up is much simpler."

Indian enterprises, especially in the FMCG and retail sectors, are increasingly looking at SCM solutions to improve their business and operations processes.

In an age of intense competition, supply chain efficiency and adaptability are not just requirements for success. They are necessities for survival. This is especially true for India's emerging and promising retail market? Logistical challenges, constantly changing consumer tastes, evolution of retail formats, high cost and availability of real estate typify the growth characteristics of the market. Effective supply chain management holds the key to push breakthrough growth in a crowded marketplace and better customer responsiveness.

High consumption patterns driven by disposable incomes, lifestyle shifts and availability of a wide range of brands are dictating the high growth of different retail formats in India. No wonder, Indian retail players are under tremendous pressure to make the supply chain of retail more efficient in order to deliver quality, selection and service to consumers. Retail customers such as Barista, Caffee Day, Hariyali, Pantaloon Retail India and Vishal Megamart, have chosen SAP solutions to enhance their critical business processes. These processes include global sourcing, distribution, transportation and logistics, product innovation, inventory visibility, financial transparency, compliance and point-of-sales data management. "As we continue to grow our presence through the region, we needed a single, enterprise-wide IT platform to manage our increasingly complex operations," says Chinar Deshpande, CEO, Pantaloon Retail (India) Ltd.

The supply chain management (SCM) market in India, albeit in a nascent stage, has relevance to both service and manufacturing organizations. According to Gartner, annual revenue from licences for supply chain management software in the Asia Pacific region will reach $129.8 million in 2005 and $184.7 million in 2009. The CAGR for 2004 to 2009 is forecast to be 8%. Closer home, some of the verticals that have gone in for SCM solutions include e-manufacturing, automotive, FMCG, retail, oil and gas. Manufacturing and automotive sectors have been the leaders in adopting SCM solutions in India. Be it auto giant Mahindra & Mahindra, Korean consumer electronics giant LG Electronics or FMCG major Hindustan Lever, the adoption of SCM solutions has resulted in reduced inventory and judicious optimisation of the entire supply and distribution chain. In future, FMCG and retail sectors are likely to see an increase in SCM adoption, says Gartner.

Typically, supply chain management is the practice of coordinating the flow of goods, services, information and finances as they move from raw materials to parts supplier to manufacturer to wholesaler to retailer to consumer. The extended supply chain for a given company may also include secondary vendors to their immediate vendors, and the customers of their immediate customers. This process includes order generation, order taking, information feedback and the efficient and timely delivery of goods and services. "Supply chain is a complex network, which needs lot of monitoring and administration due to its complex nature," says SSA Global India country manager Alok Tandon.

"SCM solutions help your organization transform a linear supply chain into an adaptive supply chain network, in which communities of customer-centric, demand-driven companies share knowledge, intelligently adapt to changing market conditions, and proactively respond to shorter, less predictable life cycles," says Peter Zencke, SAP AG executive board member. "The design and operation of an effective supply chain are fundamental to the successful operation of enterprises," he adds.

SCM includes the activities of supplier management, purchasing, materials management, manufacturing management, warehousing, materials handling, transportation, and physical distribution and customer service. A number of innovative approaches and best practices are required for balancing the objectives of the partners of the supply chain and the requirements of customers, as there are many conflicting goals such as high customer service, low inventory, low unit cost, etc.

Through continued spending on research and development, or through acquisition, major players like SAP, Oracle and SSA Global—as well as ERP vendors that specialize in the mid-market and specific industries—are making significant inroads in the SCM arena. According to Mr. Zencke, there is growing preference for supply chain solution that integrates collaboration, planning, execution, and coordination of the entire supply chain network—empowering enterprises to:

- Synchronise supply to demand? Balance push and pull network-planning processes. Replenish inventory and execute production based on actual demand.
- Sense and respond with an adaptive supply chain network. Drive distribution, transportation, and logistics processes that are integrated with real-time planning processes.
- Provide network-wide visibility, collaboration, and analytics. Monitor and analyze an enterprise's extended supply chain.

The bottom line: Indian enterprises are moving up the value chain and looking at SCM solutions to improve their business and operations processes.

Today's competitive environment requires supply chains to be agile and adaptive. According to R. Seshadhri, executive director of Take Solutions, a Singapore-based SCM firm with operations in India, Bahrain, Sri Lanka, Malaysia and USA, "there are best practices that are followed by the more successful firms and others try to emulate them. Given the dynamics of the current global business scene, the best practices themselves undergo revision.

Some of the best practices in vogue include:

- **Look beyond the organization:** Supply chain decisions are now influenced by what is happening at the vendor, the customer and the service provider, thus transcending organizational boundaries. An immediate benefit that arises is that there is no sub-optimization? What benefits the organisation does not become a burden to its partners.
- **Product visibility across the chain:** A great deal of effort is now being made to ensure end-to-end product visibility on an almost real-time basis. While visibility earlier on meant discrete visibility at the end of an activity (say shipping, order execution, dispatch) there is now a requirement to generate information real-time for effective inventory planning.
- **Outsourcing:** Going by the principles of core competence, many businesses are working to shed all activities that are better done by third party logistics providers/ contract manufacturers/BPOs. Manufacturing outsourcing is now happening in many FMCG/consumer durable industries where the manufacturing processes are not complicated.
- **Integration of vendors:** Another trend that is emerging especially in the automobile sector is the requirement of manufacturers to expect their Tier I suppliers to provide assemblies instead of discrete parts. This way, there is a large reduction in the vendors that the firms deal with as also making the manufacturing process less complicated with smaller number of parts entering the factory.
- **Integration of service providers:** A large number of service providers handle many of the outsourced functions especially related to transportation and warehousing. This leads to a huge effort on coordination both with regards to day-to-day transactions and contract management. Some of the larger companies are now trying to move to one or at best two service providers for the warehousing/transportation functions.

According to Seshadhri, each business needs to identify its own set of priorities in their processes and set benchmarks to excel. A good starting point is the firm's own backyard.

By the turn of the 20th century, the face of the Indian retailing industry had changed significantly. The retailing industry, which, until the early 1990s, was dominated by the unorganised sector, witnessed a rapid growth in the organised sector with the entry of corporate groups such as Tata, RPG, ITC and Bennett Coleman & Company into the retailing market.

With the liberalization and growth of the Indian economy since the early 1990s, the Indian customer witnessed an increasing exposure to new domestic and foreign products through different media, such as television and the Internet. Apart from this, social changes such as increase in the number of nuclear families and the growing number of working couples resulting in increased spending power also contributed to the increase in the Indian consumers' personal consumption.

These changes had a positive impact, leading to the rapid growth in the retailing industry. Increased availability of retail space, rapid urbanization, and qualified manpower also boosted the growth of the organized retailing sector.

Food retailing was a key area that saw some action at the national level, with players like Foodworld and Subhiksha, establishing stores all over India. While supermarket and departmental chains replaced traditional grocery and general store formats, introduction of fast foods (McDonalds), packaged foods (MTR, Namma MTR), vending machines and specialty beverage parlours (Nescafe, Tata Tea, Café Coffee and Barista) brought about significant changes in the eating habits of Indian consumers.

However, it was the non-food sector that saw tremendous action, with the introduction of new product segments. These segments mainly comprised lifestyle/apparel/fashion/accessories (e.g. Shoppers' Stop, Westside, Lifestyle, Pantaloons, Reebok), books/music (Landmark and Crosswords), drugs and pharmacy and beauty (Health & Glow, CavinKare and Shahnaz Husain). The emergence of new segments also resulted in new store formats, including hypermarts, large supermarkets (3,500-5,000 sq. ft), mini supermarkets (1,000-2,000 sq. ft), convenience stores (750-1000 sq. ft) and discount/shopping/grocer.

According to reports, organised retailing, which accounted for about 6% of the total retail industry in 1999, was expected to increase to about 20% by 2005. In October 2003, the total organised retail market in India was valued at about Rs. 200 bn and was estimated to grow eightfold in the next decade.

The Indian FMCG industry was also witnessing significant changes through the 1990s. Many leading FMCG players such as Hindustan Lever Ltd. (HLL) and Proctor & Gamble India Ltd. (P&G), have been facing severe problems on account of increased competition from small and regional players and from slow growth across its various product categories. As a result, many of these companies were forced to revamp their product, marketing, distribution and customer service strategies to strengthen their position in the market.

The realization of the customer's growing awareness and the need to meet changing requirements and preferences on account of changing lifestyles also contributed to the formulation of customer-centric strategies. HLL led the way in revolutionizing the product, market, distribution and service formats of the FMCG industry by focusing on rural markets, direct distribution, creating new product, distribution and service formats such as Sangam, Ayush Ayurvedic Center and Lakme Salons.

From shampoos to skin creams, they're flying off the shop-shelves. Fast moving consumer goods (FMCG) firms have been doing fairly good business for about a year now as consumers found they had had enough of televisions and music systems and were willing to pay more for their toiletries.

But few expected such a sharp rebound. AC Nielsen's retail sales audit numbers for August 2006, confirm that growth is robust—sales growth y-o-y hit 24 per cent—about a year back it was barely in double digits.

Of course, AC Nielsen's FMCG retail sales audit figures from July 2006 are based on a larger panel size that has led to better coverage of rural sales. As a result, the sales and market share data have undergone a change and are more reflective of the current market scenario.

But, the trend is reflected in the September quarter numbers too and the industry's relieved. Not so long ago, in July 2005 most firms were unable to pass on even basic cost increases and growth had plunged to under 3 per cent y-o-y. That's changing for many.

Ironically, the BSE FMCG index has underperformed the Sensex over the last three months since August after outperforming the broad market between February and July. The culprits: Hindustan Lever and ITC. Since mid-May, HLL underperformed by about 19 per cent with the Street anxious about how it would manage input costs.

However, Sivasubramanian K.N., senior portfolio manager-equity, Franklin Templeton Mutual Fund, believes that the outlook for the sector is promising.

Says he: "The cyclical recovery appears to be underway with a combination of increasing incomes, improved marketing and innovation and better price-value equation."

Sivasubramanian adds that growth will depend on two structural drivers—increasing penetration and consumption in rural areas and changing aspirational values of the urban markets. Both factors seem to be at work already.

For the sector as a whole, the volumes in the September quarter are estimated to have grown at around 15 per cent y-o-y compared with 12 per cent in the June quarter.

While ITC was a star performer showing a revenue growth of 32 per cent y-o-y, HLL managed just under 14 per cent y-o-y for continuing businesses, while Colgate turned in a top line growth of 15 per cent y-o-y.

Britannia and Marico did better at 24 per cent and 26 per cent respectively, while Nestle too didn't disappoint at 16 per cent. With the economy in fine fettle and disposable incomes rising, consumers in urban India are clearly buying.

And rural demand is kicking in. Confirms Sunil Duggal, CEO, Dabur India, "Rural demand is much stronger this year and many of our SKUs (stock-keeping units), which cater to the rural population such as shampoo sachets, are doing much better. Thus, rural demand is now catching up with urban demand."

Observes Sanjay Sinha, head-equities at SBI Mutual Fund, "From what we understand, the rural market is growing at around 11-12 per cent while both together (urban and rural) are growing at around 8 per cent."

This is reflecting in the the AC Nielsen August numbers, which show that all the top-12 categories have grown in double-digits while two-thirds of the companies have seen a growth of over 20 per cent y-o-y.

The increasing presence of large format retail stores in the metros, has also spurred sales, according to Milind Sarwate, CFO, Marico.

While sales through modern trade still form a very small percentage of overall sales, the growth through these larger stores—on the low base—is today much higher at around 20 per cent, than that through traditional grocery outlets.

While companies admit that margins on sales to organized retail are slightly lower, they realize that modern retail encourages growth because the interaction between a consumer and a product is far greater in the modern stores.

Says Sarwate, "Modern trade allows increasing visibility of good brands and encourages trials of new categories, and customers who are satisfied with a new product will make repeat purchases."

Clearly, the opportunity to make products more visible by creating special units or doing special promotions is leading to increased throughput. Going ahead, it could be a key factor in driving growth FMCG space because it's a good way to capture the wallet share of the consumer.

Observes Duggal, "Sales through this channel are growing three times as fast as through the regular channels. We expect exponential growth through modern trade from now on."

The recent price hikes announced by FMCG majors indicate that they are able to pass on the increased input costs. HLL has taken one of the biggest price increases in recent times covering nearly 30 per cent of its domestic FMCG portfolio.

It has raised prices by 2-20 per cent on products such as soaps, Lux and Lifebuoy, laundry care—Surf and Wheel, skin and oral care, Pepsodent and the weighted average price hike across all categories would be about 1.5 per cent. At Dabur, the increase has been 3-4 per cent on an average over the last nine months.

The HLL management indicated after the results that it had taken a judicious increase in prices and would continue to do so to cover raw material costs, in other key categories, such as skincare and shampoos.

The others are not far behind. Says Hoshedar K Press, executive director and president, Godrej Consumer Products (GCPL), "We have started raising prices in a staggered manner as we supply fresh stocks to dealers and on an average the increase would be between 6-8 per cent for soaps. For hair colour though, we are not upping prices yet."

At Marico, Sarwate says Parachute has been selling at the same price for about 20 months now but prices of Saffola are up.

Observes Sivasubramanian, "The recent price hikes reflect the continued cyclical turnaround that the sector is witnessing. Revenue growth has been encouraging in recent times on increased demand and appropriate product positioning, and these price hikes should help companies experience higher margins through better price realization."

Indeed, consumer down-trading (buying cheaper products in the same category) seems to have almost come to an end and money which was being diverted to aspirational products is now coming back to household and personal care products.

Observes Press, "It's true that down-trading is being reversed and I feel that even if prices go up, it would not impact demand because the environment is favourable."

Agrees Duggal, "Price hikes have been necessitated by raw material cost increases but we don't expect that to affect demand." Godrej's Press believes that the soaps category could continue to grow at 15 per cent over the next couple of years.

Companies such as Marico managed to improve margins by about 485 basis points to 16 per cent in the quarter while HLL's OPM was higher by 50 basis points at 13.1 per cent. Thanks to the changing product mix, away from cigarettes, ITC's OPM lost around 400 basis points.

Not everyone managed to tide over the cost inflation though: Britannia's operating profit margin crashed to just over 5 per cent from 14 per cent in Q2 FY06. In a highly competitive environment, Britannia was not able to pass on the higher input costs. Nestle too saw margins dip 80 basis points y-o-y to 19.7 per cent.

Industry watchers believe that with volumes kicking in, companies will look to increasing market share and while they may take price increases, it is likely to be limited to the extent of cost inflation in inputs.

Explains Duggal, "Few firms are likely to risk losing market share in a growing market and will keep a close watch on their competitors' price lists."

However, what they are more likely to do is to improve the product mix and try to push higher value-added products, which would pull in better margins. That way even if volumes were to remain stagnant or taper off somewhat, the improved product mix would cushion margins.

In fact, D. Sundaram, director, finance, HLL, mentioned after the results that gross margins had improved in the September quarter thanks to a better product mix.

For instance, two high-end ranges were introduced in Ponds, and in laundry wash a new variant of Surf was launched. Duggal, however, believes that with rural demand being so robust, companies would also try to offer new price points at the lower end. "Companies are unlikely to use pricing as a tool to enhance margins," he observes. Says Templeton's Sivasubramanian, "The mass market can contribute to a major chunk of volumes in the future as consumption of goods increases and many companies are realising the importance of creating a good mix of volumes."

SBI Mutual's Sinha feels that should there be a softening of input costs, companies will also not roll-back prices which will help boost margins.

Sumeet Budhraja who tracks FMCG at Edelweiss believes that while stocks may not be cheap, there could be a 15-20 per cent upside from current levels, over the next three to four quarters.

"The inference from our interaction with managements is that the growth momentum is sustainable and that together with some price hikes, it should help margins sustain or move up by about 50 basis points," says Budhraja.

Sinha, however, feels that much of the upsides, stemming from good volumes, are already factored into the prices. "A re-rating of the sector will happen only if there are signals that margins are expanding," he observes, adding that "the stocks are now a defensive play and evenly valued."

Adds Sivasubramanian, "On a relative basis, valuations appear to be reasonable compared to the broad markets and as earnings visibility improves further, we could witness increased interest in the sector that offers an exposure to the consumption boom in India over the coming decades."

On a weekday, the DLF Mega Mall—located in the IT and ITES hub of Gurgaon on the outskirts of Delhi—bears a deserted look. Of the few operating shops in this large mall, most have nary a customer. The same goes for several other retail outlets and many of the other malls in the vicinity.

True, a retail chain like Future Group's Big Bazaar may be clocking heady sales (growing at 100% year-on-year), but the dozen-odd shops operating in its proximity wear a deserted look, giving a somewhat hollow ring to the much-talked-about retail boom in the country.

In what seems like a quirk of circumstance, malls have sprung up all over urban India in anticipation of a consumption boom that may itself prove to be eventually truant.

Move to Mulund (West), a suburban locality of India's financial nerve, Mumbai. Rajesh Parashar, a resident of the area has the option of shopping at Big Bazaar, Apna Bazaar, Subhiksha, Spinach, Shoprite, Food land or at the local Sai Supermarket, all of which are within a two-kilometre radius of his residence.

This is paralleled by the developments happening in the Delhi suburb of Ghaziabad, where the upcoming Shipra Mall at Indirapuram already has Big Bazaar operating out of its lower-ground floor, while Reliance is slated to open shop on the third floor. Customer footfalls, however, are more in the projections of the occupiers of the mall than real.

All this retail activity, and more, and the sheer gargantuan size of the investments planned, beg the question—does the consumer's wallet have enough money in it for everyone?

"Only time will tell," is KPMG's executive director, Deepankar Sanwalka's laconic answer. To a great extent the success or the failure of malls will hinge on the consumer population of the area. "If the spending power of consumers is high in a locality, it could sustain two-to-three large players." Not so, elsewhere, he adds poignantly.

The significance of these remarks sinks in gradually. With planned investments of $22 billion over the next five years—excluding what might be brought in by new global and large local players henceforth—the retail sector is expected to grow 40% to $427 billion by 2011.

Organised retail, which is 3% of the whole currently, is in turn pegged to grow to $64 billion by 2015. And one consequence of all those investments will be the fact that India's present two square-feet per capita retailing space will rise 15-20% by 2010.

To be viable, the huge investments made in the sector by India Inc would have to be responded to by a corresponding massive surge in footfalls. And for that to happen, a lot of links would have to fall in place.

Between the drawing board and the emerging market realities, the realisation dawns that a lot of things can go wrong with India's much-heralded retail revolution. The more visible among these loose ends: vexingly high real estate prices, the loosely-knit distribution networks in India's hinterland, the near-absence of any modern supply chain logistics, shortage of skilled personnel, and a regulatory system that resembles a patchy quilt more than anything else.

Then there is the nature of the business itself. Retailing is a low-margin, high-volume, commodity business where profitability gets strained as competition intensifies. And if wrong choices are made regarding the location or the formatting of the store, woe betide the retailer. The catches are many and to make it big, a retailer would have to negotiate all the tricky turns most of the time.

The big players are sanguine, however. "There is enough room for six-to-eight players," says Reliance group chairman Mukesh Ambani, who recently kicked off the first Reliance Fresh outlet in Hyderabad. There are reasons for his optimism: the country's preponderantly young working population, disposable incomes that are expected to increase at an average 8.5% per annum till 2015, and a steadily climbing per capita income (from $460 in 2002, it rose to $620 in 2005).

In fact, it is the expectation of a large working and earning population that has attracted most global retailers to the country. But most analysts agree that the Indian retail market could at best support 10 large players with revenues in excess of $2 billion each by 2015.

Given the number of players getting into the fray today, this clearly means a winnowing out of the weaker retail players. What's more, that time could be sooner rather than later, maybe just three or four years down the line.

That's not so surprising, industry insiders even say, pointing out that a large number of the new entrants may not be committed to retailing in the long term. While some almost certainly are looking to act as silent partners for foreign players, others may be more willing to look at an exit option a few years down the line.

Says Hemant Kalbag, principal, AT Kearney: "I see consolidation happening in the next five years. That's when the shakeout will happen and the successful retailers will look acquiring less profitable ones."

But that's still in the future. As of now, the retail turf is set for some frenetic activity. Reliance has drawn up a Rs. 25,000 crore (Rs. 250 billion) retail plan that would see its outlets dotting 784 cities and small towns by 2010.

Already it has 17 stores in Hyderabad alone (the number will go up to 40 by end of the above period). More recently, Sunil Bharti Mittal made news when he announced an alliance with the world's biggest retail chain Wal-Mart, for a supply chain and cash-and-carry venture, besides a franchise agreement for retail.

Seen as a coup of sorts, this could exert pressure on other retailers in the country to explore similar collaborative opportunities.

Between them the likes of Reliance, the AV Birla Group, the Tatas, the Godrejs, the Bhartis, the Mahindras, the ITC Group and the Wadias—and a horde of others—will be sinking in close to Rs. 1 lakh crore (Rs. 1 trillion) in the business of retail over the next five years.

In their crosshairs, are a host of retail-related activities such as cold chains, retail supply logistics, warehousing, sourcing and merchandising management. All of which are seen as absolutely essential if the front-end retail business is to take off on a meaningful scale across the country.

The players have hit the ground running. Reliance is hiring overseas talent to improve its management capabilities—it has roped in Peter Bracher from Asda Wal-Mart as special adviser for Reliance Fresh stores and Kevin Pleass from Tesco, UK, to help with store design and construction—even as the AV Birla group is on a talent hunt ahead of its Rs 15,000 crore retail rollouts.

Retail icon Kishore Biyani is also stepping on the gas; he has announced plans to roll out 225 Big Bazaar stores and hundreds of other outlets in other formats in the next four years.

The Tata group too earlier this year expanded its footprint (beyond the formats rolled out by group company Trent of Westside fame) by entering the durables segment, in a tie-up with Australian retailer Woolworths, with the launch of its Croma store.

"We plan to have a national presence with 30 stores by March 2008 and double it to 60 by March 2009, with a capital of Rs. 400 crore (Rs. 4 billion)," says R.K. Krishna Kumar, Director, Tata Sons, who is spearheading Tata's retail venture.

He adds that the company zeroed in on the segment given the findings of an internal study, which revealed that only 0.5% of Indians own air-conditioners, just 1% own computers, 3.5% washing machines and 11.7% telephones. Other players like the Dubai-based Landmark group, with its Lifestyle and Max branded outlets, are also keen to expand into the grocery segment.

Reports indicate the company is in talks for a tie-up with Carrefour. Then there are players like the K. Raheja group's Shopper's Stop and the Rajan Raheja-controlled Globus that are expanding their reach in the apparel and accessories segments. Others like ITC (a big player in its own right), the Godrej group, Century Textiles and Raymond as well as mid-size players like Vishal Megamart, Subhiksha and Sabka Bazaar are busy increasing their footprint.

Taking a cue from the global leaders (whose eyes are also on India), India Inc's retailers are thinking big. Reliance Retail, for instance, has chalked out a plan to roll out about 5,500 stores of all kinds in 800 cities, 85 logistics centres and 1,600 farm supply hubs. A.V. Birla Group is looking at pumping in Rs. 15,000-20,000 crore (Rs. 150-200 billion) —with an initial investment of Rs. 5,000 crore (Rs. 50 billion) in the next few years.

Similarly, Bharti is expected to invest Rs. 6,000 crore (Rs. 60 billion) in the initial phase. Biyani's Pantaloons is not far behind. The group plans to increase its total retail space to 30 million sq.ft. from the current 3.2 million sq.ft. and take its turnover to Rs. 2,500 crore (Rs. 25 billion) by June 2010.

By global scales, the numbers are not out of the ordinary. The Bentonville, Arkansas, based Wal-Mart—the big brother of retailers—operates 6,640 stores and wholesale clubs in 14 countries, while its counterpart in Europe (it is based out of UK) Tesco runs 2,600 stores across 13 countries.

The others have chains of comparable sizes and reach. To keep their stores stocked with their myriad products, the global retailers have sophisticated procurement strategies in place that hinge on sourcing products globally based on prices, quality and timely delivery.

Not to mention deployment of cutting-edge technologies that enable real-time inventory tracking and ordering mechanisms. "Tesco, for instance, can sell jeans cheaper as bulk buying can help it source the same from its global suppliers at far less than this," says KPMG's Sanwalka. Thus, globally, retail is a business involving massive scales and deep pockets.

Moving up the evolutionary ladder won't be easy for India's retailers. Especially given the large number of potential spoilers. Availability of quality retail space will be a key determinant for the growth of the sector. With most Indian cities undergoing rapid urbanisation, spiralling rental costs has most retailers worried already.

Hitherto, most retailers have preferred to go in for long-term leases. But with real estate prices in most top tier cities hitting the roof, lease rental increases are making business unviable for organized retail.

According to PricewaterhouseCoopers (PwC), the current average lease rentals across some of the top cities range from Rs 88 per sq feet per month to as high as Rs. 120 per sq.ft per month. On an average, lease rentals account for 7-8% of the revenue and 40-45% of the non-material cost for retailers. Unless these prices stabilise, most retail businesses could end up taking much longer than originally planned to break-even.

Not surprisingly then, within hours of making his deal with Wal-Mart public, Sunil Mittal, the chairman of Bharti Group, said his top priority would be real estate acquisition, whether through leasing or buying.

To that end, the newly-formed combine is roping in DLF, Emaar, MGF and Ansals to act as partners and developers. Such an arrangement could prove to be a win-win solution: while it will ensure quick roll-outs and lower capex, it could also improve asset utilisation of the developments. At the other end, players like Reliance could set up hypermarkets in their own SEZs to meet the needs of local residents.

Another way out of this problem, as some astute retailers have found out, is to become an anchor tenant. According to PwC estimates, an anchor tenant typically commands a discount of 30-45% on lease rentals and is responsible for attracting footfalls into a mall.

Retail biggies like Pantaloon Retail, Shopper's Stop and McDonald's have been quick to endorse this strategy. For instance, Pantaloons has signed up with 100 of the 300-odd malls that will be developed over the next three years. This, points out PwC, will enable the retailer to leverage its first-mover advantage on a pan-India basis.

Pantaloon Retail currently has 3.2 million sq.ft spread across several formats and is expected to have 10 million sq.ft of space in the country by 2010. Again, in Tier-II cities, where lease rentals are 40-50% lower than those in top tier cities, Pantaloons has been quick to establish its presence.

The retailer's real estate fund, Kshitij 1, which has a corpus of $80 million at its disposal, is understood to have invested in projects in cities like Ahmedabad, Baroda and Surat. Pantaloons expects to have nearly 400,000 sq.ft of retail space in these destinations by 2008.

The other determinant of success here is the location—if the outlet is not easily accessible by a large section of consumers due to distance or other issues, viability could come in question.

Here the neighbourhood format has an edge. Sanwalka of KPMG is of the view that smaller stores of 1,500-2,500 square feet (as against 150,000 square feet hypermarkets) in neighbourhoods might do better in India. The verdict is still out on that one, and we won't know till one fails.

Adds KPMG's associate director Kaushika Madhavan, "All new entrants are planning rapid expansion and such a scale of ramp-up requires scalable processes and systems, which retailers are yet to develop. So we would witness mistakes being made as Indian retail evolves. Ability to learn from mistakes will be a critical success factor." And here deep pockets will help.

While Biyani already has a successful retail model in place and Bharti will look to cut corners with some help from Wal-Mart, players like Reliance and the A.V. Birla group would have to go through a longer learning curve.

Grapevine has it that soon after the Bharti-Wal-Mart MoU, Reliance Retail's A-team went into a huddle to discuss its response. The fact that the world's biggest retailer will be pitted against them has not been lost on them: now, Reliance has to worry about Wal-Mart's strength in the make-or-break area of supply-chain management.

This will no doubt be factored into the retailer's own mammoth Rs. 6,000-crore drive to set up its own logistics, complete with its own airstrips and a fleet of transport aircraft dedicated to airlifting supplies to key markets.

Indeed, the key imperative facing retailers in India is that of creating robust, scalable supply chains that would facilitate their rapid spread across the country. "India is a fragmented country and an absence of a strong infrastructure and logistics system makes it all the more challenging to reach consumers," says N.V. Sivakumar of PwC.

A vital logistical link in most retailers' plans happens to be the cold chain. And many of them like Reliance Retail and Future Group are reported to be investing Rs. 6,000 crore and Rs. 400-500 crore (Rs. 4-5 billion), respectively, on setting up logistics.

Another big player in the segment will be the Bharti Group. Overhauling this part of the supply chain will be key to the success of any retail venture in food and groceries segment. Currently in India, the wastage levels for perishables are as high as 40% because of a large number of intermediaries as well as loss during transportation as well as through lack of storage.

Says KPMG's Madhavan: "The fact is that most retailers in India still don't have a stronghold on operations—be it merchandising, supply chain management or procurement."

Clearly, while the players can build on the experience of industry leaders in other markets while developing their supply chain, the Indian market may require them to improvise frequently.

Foreign retailers have shown that managing operations innovatively can provide a significant competitive advantage to retailers. Wal-Mart, for instance, leverages IT to track supply chain processes like cross-docking very effectively. Similarly, Tesco requires lean production techniques of its suppliers and has high-reliability delivery systems in place such as 'milk-runs'.

Most analysts agree that retailers would have put in place global operational metrics. One way to measure efficient operations is the inventory turns ratio. A comparison of the US and India is revealing. Where, in the US, the retail sector has an average inventory turns ratio of about 18 (some retailers like 7-Eleven score over 50), most Indian retailers range between four and 10, says KPMG.

The other key metric—stock availability—is telling too: Where global retailers achieve more than 95% availability of all stock-keeping units on the retail shelves, their Indian counterparts cut a rather poor figure at 5-15%.

There are other areas that retailers would have to master—such as reaping economies in procurement and transportation, bulk storage, trend forecasting to minimize inventory levels—before they can truly claim to have arrived.

Early entrants such as Shoppers' Stop and RPG Group are acutely aware of this truth: both took years to bring their supply-chain models to the present efficiency levels. Even a player like the Dubai-based Landmark Group—which has been operating in India for eight years now—insists it still needs to bring their ERP solution system up to speed.

Others may face new, unexpected problems. Scalability is what the likes of Kabir Lumba, Executive Director, Lifestyle International, is banking on for growth. The group, which currently runs 12 stores, plans to open 45 more stores at a cost of Rs. 450 crore (Rs. 4.50 billion) over three years. Lifestyle's stores attract 40,000 customers every day, and are projected to close fiscal 2006-07 with a sales turnover of Rs. 500 crore.

Again, when it comes to technology adoption and usage, there's a yawning gap between the Indian retailers and those in the west.

According to a recent survey conducted among the country's top retailers by KPMG, while retailers like Wal-Mart and Metro have started using RFID technology (offering high inventory visibility), retailers in India are still to take to bar coding. As systems grow in size and complexity, retailers would have set aside increasing amounts as IT spend.

The challenge posed by the global retailers is clearly formidable. But local retailers' more intimate understanding of their customer base will help them survive.

Besides, even the world's largest retailers have slipped when it comes to the emerging markets—Wal-Mart was forced to rework its model in Mexico and a similar thing happened to Carrefour in China, where it had to revise its strategy. Also, Wal-Mart's track record in markets such as South Korea and Germany has been nothing to write home about.

The other big issue for retailers is people. Analysts agree that the manpower shortage will get acute as retail spreads beyond the metros. Says Sanjiv Goenka, Chairman, RPG Group: "The biggest challenge for us and, for that matter, any retailer will be getting trained personnel."

With Wal-Mart's advent in the US, the relationship of manufacturers with consumers was drastically altered in the latter's favour. While the results in the case of India's retailers may not be necessarily as dramatic, some major changes would definitely be in order.

Strategic sourcing tie-ups between retailer and manufacturer will be the main drivers in this respect. A few weeks after Reliance rolled out its retail plan, one of the first things it did was to negotiate with leading FMCG companies, including Dabur India and Nestle India, for a direct retail account for the products they sold at its outlets. Earlier this year, Pantaloons did a similar exercise and sought 5% higher margins for products sold at its Big Bazaar and Food Bazaar outlets.

Says Atul Joshi, head of the no-frills chain Subhiksha's northern operations: "For an FMCG manufacturer, the cost of dealing with us (modern retail) is negligible. We were the first direct retail account with HLL about seven years ago." The no-frills chain assures 8-10% discount to consumers on all products it stocks.

While retailers like Reliance, Pantaloons or Subhiksha may be bringing a change, the fact is that ordering or sourcing by retailers is still tactical than strategic, points out a KPMG study. Not many retailers have long-term agreements with suppliers.

Also, traditionally retailers have played a passive role in this relationship. In contrast, Wal-Mart actively partners with manufacturers who supply it products to ensure that consumers are offered prices at the lowest prices possible. In fact, it was precisely the retailer's legendary aggression in bargaining that partly drove the massive wave of restructuring of the US industry.

Indian retailers have their work cut out in this regard, but it is far from clear whether they would be able to emulate this dimension of Wal-Mart's success story.

More likely, the retail chains coming up will be less combative in their approach towards manufacturers. "We will have to have a collaborative approach. But the threat from retail to packaged goods industry will prompt companies to invest a lot in R&D," says Adi Godrej, chairman, Godrej Industries.

The statement's import is not lost—private labels have a big potential as promotional costs are low for retailers and the margins fat (as much as 60% against 35% for others). Also, these non-branded products can be offered at far lower price points, generating volume sales.

Organised retailers in India are trying out a variety of formats, ranging from discount stores to supermarket to hypermarkets to specialty chains. However, of late, most players appear to be gravitating towards the hypermarket format.

Retailers ranging from Pantaloons to RPG to Piramals or the Tatas are working towards exploiting this model, perceived by consumers as more value-enhancing. But in the long run, what is most likely to succeed is a more balanced multi-format strategy.

This helps retailers adapt to the very different shopping patterns that can exist within the country and even within regions. Here again, merely copying global trends will not help. In a research conducted by KPMG International in developed markets, it was found that single-format players generated higher shareholder value than multi-format ones.

Some feel a combination of cash-and-carry and neighbourhood stores, as in a hub-and-spokes model can be a good bet. Says one retail analyst, nascent markets like India need a lot of room for experimentation on part of the retailers. Ergo, there are no cut-and-dried solutions when it comes to fixing on the right retail format.

Finally, while in the first flush of the retail boom, the elimination of traditional intermediaries may bring windfall gains (as well as bring welcome and much-needed relief to the producers), this source will increasingly dry out as competition intensifies and margins come under pressure a few years down the line.

What would set the survivors apart from those who are forced to sell out (or go belly-up) will be differentiators like location, value-added services (convenience), private labels and customer loyalty programmes, other than price. The last, a result of retailer-manufacturer tie-ups, state-of-the-art supply chain infrastructure, global sourcing and scale will be a key factor. And, if experience in other markets is anything to go by, an uncanny ability to read shifting trends.

Task for the Students

The students need to make a comparative study of retail in India and the West. How can Indian retail learn from the western counterparts?

CASE STUDY

4

HDFC Bank

HDFC Bank began operations in 1995 with a simple mission: to be a **"World-class Indian Bank"**—their story in their own words follows:

We realized that only a single-minded focus on product quality and service excellence would help us get there. Today, we are proud to say that we are well on our way towards that goal.

It is extremely gratifying that our efforts towards providing customer convenience have been appreciated both nationally and internationally as can be seen from the following:

2006	
Business Today	Best Bank in India.
Forbes Magazine	One of Asia Pacific's Best 50 companies.
Businessworld	Best listed Bank of India.
The Asset Magazine's Triple A Country Awards	Best Domestic Bank.
Asiamoney Awards	Best Local Cash Management Bank in Large and Medium segments.
Euromoney Awards	"Best Bank" in India.
2005	
Asiamoney Awards	Best Domestic Commercial Bank
Asiamoney Awards	Best Cash Management Bank - India.
The Asian Banker Excellence	Retail Banking Risk Management Award in India.
Hong Kong-based Finance Asia magazine	Best Bank India
Economic Times Awards	"Company of the Year" Award for Corporate Excellence.

Asiamoney also named the bank:

- Best Local Cash Management Bank in India 2004 - US$11-100m
- Best Local Cash Management Bank in India 2004 - >US$501m
- Best Local Cash Management Bank in India 1989-2004 (poll of polls)
- Best Overall Domestic Trade Finance Services in India 2004
- Most Improved company for Best Management Practices in India 2004

The *Business Today*-KPMG Survey published in the leading Indian business magazine Business Today has named HDFC Bank "Best Bank in India" for the third consecutive year in 2005.

The *Asset* magazine named HDFC Bank "Best Cash Management Bank" and "Best Trade Finance Bank" in India, in 2006.

HDFC Bank named the "Most Customer Responsive Company—Banking and Financial Services in *The Economic Times*—Avaya Global Connect Customer Responsiveness Awards 2005"

HDFC Bank has been named Best Domestic Bank in India in The Asset Triple A Country Awards 2005.

HDFC Bank has been named Best Domestic Bank in India Region in The Asset Triple A Country Awards 2004 and 2003.

In 2004, HDFC Bank was selected by *BusinessWorld* as "One of India's Most Respected Companies" as part of The *Business World* Most Respected Company Awards 2004.

In 2004, Forbes Global again named us in its listing of Best Under a Billion, 100 Best Smaller Size Enterprises in Asia/Pacific and Europe, in its November 1, 2004 issue.

In 2004, HDFC Bank won the award for "Operational Excellence in Retail Financial Services" —India as part of the Asian Banker Awards 2003.

In 2003, Forbes Global named us in its ranking of "Best Under a Billion, 200 Best Small Companies for 2003".

Leading business newspaper '*The Financial Express*' named HDFC Bank the "Best New Private Sector Bank 2003" in the FE-Ernst & Young Best Banks Survey 2003.

Leading Personal Finance Magazine in India *Outlook Money* named HDFC Bank the "Best Bank in the Private Sector" for the year 2003.

Leading Indian business magazine *Business Today* in a survey rated us "Best Bank in India" 2003, and "Best Private Sector Bank" in India in 1999.

NASSCOM and economictimes.com have named us the 'Best IT User in Banking' at the IT Users Awards 2003.

There have been some other proud moments as well

London-based *Euromoney* magazine gave us the award for "Best Bank - India" in 1999, "Best Domestic Bank" in India in 2000, and "Best Bank in India" in 2001 and 2002.

- *Asiamoney* magazine has named us "Best Commercial Bank in India 2002".
- For our use of information technology, we have been recognized as a "Computerworld Honors Laureate" and awarded the 21st Century Achievement Award in 2002 for Finance, Insurance & Real Estate category by Computerworld, Inc., USA.

- Our technology initiative has been included as a case study in their online global archives. The *Economic Times* has conferred on us The Economic Times Awards for Corporate Excellence as the Emerging Company of the Year 2000-01.
- Leading Indian business magazine *Business India* named us "India's Best Bank" in 2000.
- In the year 2000, leading financial magazine *Forbes Global* named us in its list of "The 300 Best Small Companies" in the world and as one of the "20 for 2001" best small companies in the world.

We are aware that all these awards are mere milestones in the continuing, never-ending journey of providing excellent service to our customers. We are confident, however, that with your feedback and support, we will be able to maintain and improve our services.

Task for the Students

Students need to study the working of the bank through the net and their Annual Report and analyze how the bank has been doing well even during the western meltdown. Has the nationalisation of the banks in India helped the banks, especially HDFC Bank?

CASE STUDY

5

TESCO

The following gives a clear idea of how the retail store operates.

- Loans
- Credit cards
- Car insurance
- Life insurance
- Personal finance
- Club cards
- Baby club
- Wine club
- Groceries

Tescodiets.ie

Join Ireland's largest online diet community as well as getting expert advice for only •3.99 per week.

Six easy steps to shopping online

Getting around www.Tesco.ie couldn't be easier, all it takes is six easy steps.

Buy and fly!

Free •200 Holiday Voucher when you register to have your Clubcard Points converted into buy and fly points. For other information, the students must look the net and other secondary sources.

Task for the Students

Discuss the salient features of the online outlet and suggest how they can improve their services.

CASE STUDY 6

Westside Store

The Tatas having realized the importance of retailing in India planned to open 20 departmental stores under its brand name 'Westside' by the year 2004 all over the country, according to Noel Tata, managing director of Trent Ltd. a Tata enterprise. Speaking at the launch of the store, Tata told reporters that the company has already opened 'Westside' departmental stores in Mumbai, Hyderabad, Pune, Chennai, Bengaluru, Kolkata and New Delhi and added that more important cities would be brought into the network. It offers a shopping experience for a variety of products for men and women, kid's wear, household accessories, cosmetics, perfumes and other fashion accessories, he said.

Westside—A Unit of Trent Ltd

High quality, latest in-style products, international shopping experience and value for money pricing that's what you get at Trent Ltd's Westside stores, starting with one store at Bangalore in April '98, Westside is already a part of the city's landscape in Mumbai, Hyderabad, Pune and Chennai, Delhi. Westside is arguably the fastest growing retail chain in India.

Westside is one of a kind with its own brand of merchandise, which is both trendy and often customized. Everything you find at Westside is exclusively designed for Westside. The range is changed frequently with new arrivals every week. Every time you visit you are likely to find something different. Boasting of a variety of designs and styles, the merchandise at the Westside stores are an exciting mix with a range extending from stylised clothes and accessories for men, women and children to well-coordinated table linens, artefacts, home accessories and furnishings. Add to it the plush interiors, sprawling space, prime locations, a lovely coffee shop, Café West by Taj and ever-helpful personnel, and you have the ultimate in retail ambience. It is shopping experience redefined.

Westside stores have the following departments—Men's wear, Women's wear, Lingerie, Kidswear, Household Accessories, Cosmetics, Perfumes and other accessories. Each of Westside's departments offers a complete range.

For women there are Western casual, Western formals and very classy Ethnic wear with a look unique of Westside. In Western wear again the range has great depth spanning from basic lines to very trendy casual wear. Unlike a lot of stores, the range at Westside caters to a wide age group and takes into the account the differing tastes and requirements. The range does not end with clothes but extends right into accessories. The store has a great range of Handbags, jewellery, scarves and other accessories.

Kids also have huge range to select from. Catering to a wide age band-starting from infants to early teens the garments sport a look that is hip, trendy and very international.

In Men's wear the range extends from formal to casual to sporty. Also there is a wide price range starting from value and extending into premium.

The household section boasts of the most contemporary around. Every item here is exclusive and unique. The merchandise is well coordinated and customers can mix and match and put it together their way. The range is extensive starting from colourful towels and bathroom sets to bed linen, table linen, and crockery down to bric a brac for the household. There is also a wonderful gift section with the trendiest of collection.

The Westside stores are open on 365 days. Most of the stores offer exclusive parking. So shopping becomes that much more convenient.

So the next time you want to feel really good about shopping, striking that fine balance between style and price, you know where to head!

High quality, latest in-style products, international shopping experience and value for money pricing-that's what you get at Trent Ltd's Westside Stores, Starting with one store at Bengaluru in April'98, Westside is already a part of the city's landscape in Mumbai, Hyderabad, Pune and Chennai. Westside is arguably the fastest growing retail chain in India.

Business Studies Profile: Westside Stores

This document is part of AcademicDB, a database of over 15,000 UK university essays and coursework documents written by UK university students covering all subject areas.

Given below is a short sample of the document with all formatting removed:

Westside Stores—A History of Westside: Style, affordable prices, and quality, these are the factors that have shaped Westside's success story in the retail fashion stores business. Launched in 1998 in B, the Westside chain has, ever since, been setting the standards for other fashion retailers to follow. The Westside story really began in 1997, when the Tatas sold Lakme, their cosmetics business, to Hindustan Lever and acquired the Britain-based Littlewoods retail chain. A new entity called Trent Limited emerged from this move and Littlewoods was renamed Westside. Today, Westside has seven outlets, one each in Bangaluru, Hyderabad, Chennai, Mumbai, Pune, New Delhi and Kolkata. Profile of Trent: Trent Limited was incorporated in 1952 as Lakme Limited. A leading player in the cosmetics and toiletries segments, Lakme divested its business to FMCG giant Hindustan Lever Limited in 1998.

Investors with an appetite for high risk can consider exposure to the stock of Trent. The stock has been re-rated considerably in the past month, following its foray into the rapidly-growing hypermarket format (a combination of a department store and a supermarket that offers a wide variety of products such as apparels, groceries and consumer durables at low prices).

Trent now trades at 40 times its trailing earnings per share. The stock has been accorded a lower multiple in the past compared to Pantaloons—the only other listed play in the retailing sector. This is because while Pantaloons grew at a scorching pace on the back of its expansion frenzy.

Trent followed a more conservative growth strategy, which tempered earnings growth. Also, Pantaloons' experiment with other retail formats has paid off, further boosting the stock. But Trent's foray into mass-market retailing (hypermarket format) is likely to fast-track its earnings growth. The company plans to open 25-30 such outlets over the next six years, with two/three likely to be set up over the next one year. This is besides furthering its apparel retailing chain, Westside. The aggressive plan is one of the factors for the recent re-rating of the stock. Trent also promises to bring a more distinct model to the retailing format, as private labels would account for 90 per cent of the products sold. The strategy of focussing on private labels has already paid off for its Westside departmental stores.

Venturing into this format would mean playing the volumes game, which would make safeguarding margins challenging.

While the use of private labels would help maintain margins, the lower operating margins may not provide much of a cushion if revenues were to take a hit. Profits would depend primarily on revenue growth.

As stores are added, the company would benefit from economies of scale, and efficient supply-chain management and a substantial portion of the revenues from additional stores would improve the bottom line. Trent is sitting on a cash pile and marginal debt, which puts it on a sound footing to expand in the near term.

Over the long term, however, it may have to resort to either higher debt or an expansion of the equity base, which may temper earnings growth.

Hypermarkets to Drive Growth

With 16 Westside stores, Trent is among the top apparel retailers. It plans to take this number to 19 next year. The growing popularity of retail formats that target the middle-class has, however, prompted Trent to pursue the hypermarket format more intently.

In October, it set up its first "Star India Bazaar" hypermarket in Ahmedabad, in October, and, by the end of this fiscal, plans to open two such stores in Mumbai and Bengaluru, where Giant and Big Bazaar, are already present. Trent would be taking Giant and Big Bazaar stores—the two hypermarket formats of the RPG Group and Pantaloons respectively—head on. Unlike the competition, Star India Bazaar sells a majority of its products under private labels, which earn higher margins.

Trent hopes to leverage these margins in pricing its products more aggressively and also offers better discounts on some of the branded items it showcases. If this pays off,

Trent would be better placed than its competitors to drive up volumes. And, at the same time, in a better position to maintain at least margins at the same level as its competitors.

Trent's ability to garner market share for its private labels, particularly in segments where branded players dominate, such as consumer durables, would also be crucial to the success of its venture.

Customer Driven Excellence

A strategic concept that places emphasis on maximizing value for customers, enhancing referrals, and anticipating future customer desires.

Organizational and Personal Learning

Emphasizes not only process improvement but also the need to invest in employee development to enhance motivation, value, and innovation.

Valuing Employees and Partners

Challenges include demonstrating leader commitment to employees, providing recognition beyond normal compensation, opportunities for growth and development, sharing knowledge to help employees contribute, and creating an environment to encourage risk taking.

Agility

Emphasizes faster, flexible, customized service and shorter cycle times for new and improved products and services.

Focus on the Future

Emphasizes future orientation to achieve sustainable growth and market leadership, including e-commerce and developing employee capability and innovation.

Managing for Innovation

Emphasizes the need to make meaningful change to improve products, programs, processes, and value for stakeholders.

Management by Fact

Emphasizes measures and analysis aligned to strategy to focus work, decision making, and operational improvement.

Social Responsibility

Emphasizes the need to ensure that product/programme/service designs meet public responsibilities and good citizenship, including compliance, but also treating as an opportunity for improvement the challenge of "going beyong compliance."

Focus on Results and Creating Value

Emphasizes the need to create and balance value for all stakeholders. Organizations often use a balanced score card to focus and communicate.

Systems Perspective

Emphasizes systems perspective to managing; integrates core values, criteria, scoring guidelines; synthesis of all management system elements; alignment linking strategy, processes, and resources throughout the organization.

Core Values and Concepts

The criteria are built on a foundation of eleven core values and concepts. These values and concepts are embedded beliefs and behaviours found in high-performing organizations. The eleven core values create a basis for action and feedback because they establish a foundation for the criteria that integrates key performance and operational requirements within a result-oriented framework.

Visionary Leadership

Create a customer focus and clear values, balance needs of all stakeholders, and promote innovation, creativity, and empowerment.

Loyalty Club Members/Sweepstakes Participants - CLUBWEST INDIA consists of active shoppers who have made purchases at the prestigious Westside Department Stores across India and have signed up for the Clubwest Loyalty Club Programme. It also consists of individuals who have participated in the sweepstakes gathered from various in-store promotions of Westside. Westside Stores, a Tata enterprise, is arguably the fastest growing retail chain in India. In a crowded Indian market, Westside is one of a kind with its own brand of merchandise that is both trendy and individualistic. It offers a wide range of high quality, latest in-style products as well as provides an international shopping experience. Westside Stores have the following departments—Men's Wear, Women's Wear, Lingerie, Kid's Wear, Household Accessories, Cosmetics, Perfumes, Gift Shop, Toys, Handbags and Other Accessories. Departments are selectable. Unlike other stores, Westside caters to practically all age groups, starting from 18 years up to 60+ years. It always takes into account the differing tastes and requirements of these customers, majority of whom are males. Minimum average order value is Rs. 1000. Clubwest is the extraordinary rewards programme designed exclusively for Westside regulars. It was launched in May 2001 and is the fastest growing retail Loyalty Programme in India. It has an existing member base of approximately 80,000 active customers and is growing everyday. Clubwest is point-based and consists of a two-tier programme— Clubwest Classic & Clubwest Gold (depending on the amount of purchases made). Membership is valid for two years and members enjoy the benefits across all Westside Stores. They receive regular mailings including announcements of special promotions on women, men and children's apparel, home furnishings and other distinctive Westside merchandise and contests. Members are elite, well-educated and affluent consumers who can afford to buy Westside exclusive merchandise. This list is 100% sourced through retail. The list owner mails the list six to eight times a year hence data is regularly cleaned and updated. The file is 95% deliverable. Telephone numbers are also available and are 90%–95% accurate. This list is recommended for publishers (B-B and Consumer) tapping affluent individuals, lotteries, insurance companies and airlines, to name a few. The promotional sweepstakes database is also available for rental or outright purchase. It has been collected as part of the various in-store promotions of Westside. Currently available is the October 2001 Diwali sweeps promotion base (approximately 67,000 records) consisting of customers who made a minimum purchase of Rs. 2,000 (approximately US$40+) and have participated in a sweepstakes promotion for a chance to join several draws and win prizes. The following fields are available—Title, Full Name, Mailing Address, Pin Code and Telephone Number. Diwali and Christmas database is available.

TRENT Ltd, Ms Simone Tata's venture into retailing with the Westside chain after she bid goodbye to Lakme, is set to expand its operations and will add at least two stores to the existing in (2005-06).

The company will also expand the hypermarket business it kicked off in October in Ahmedabad, said Ms Tata, Chairman, Trent Ltd.

At the sidelines of an exhibition on the Tata Group here on Tuesday, Ms Tata said the company is all set to take its hypermarket to Bengaluru and Mumbai. "We will make significant investments in growing this business," she said.

Trent Ltd. recently forayed into mass market retailing with Star India Bazaar, which sells household items, grocery, food and beverages, health and beauty products and electronic items targeted at the budget buyer through discounted prices.

Ms Tata said the company would launch two more Westside stores in Mumbai and Delhi. It also plans to open a store in Vadodara in the next fiscal. "It is fun to be in the retailing business when there is so much action happening all around you," Ms. Tata, who earlier steered the group's Lakme cosmetics business, said she has no plans to return to the beauty business. Shoppers at Westside may soon get to splurge on brands other than the in-house Trent stock. The company recently started stocking a limited selection of outside brands on an 'experimental basis' in its Kolkata and Delhi stores to gauge consumer response. Ms. Tata said any decision to extend the experiment to other outlets would depend on this response.

Task for the Students

Analyze the case with the help of SWOT, discuss its critical success factors. Check out their loyalty programmes through CLUBWEST.

CASE STUDY

7

Complete Retail Plan

Considering the importance of retail this case study is devoted totally to retail marketing. How the marketing team of a manufacturing unit can transform non or profit making retailers into dynamic businesses? As the students study the case they will get involved into the nitty gritty of retail trade and how firms can profit from the same. In easy to understand steps the reader is taken to the intricate mindsets of the retailers and how they can be motivated into making profits.

It may look obvious to students that the retailers must be keen on making and increasing the profits and yet several anomalies are found. Hence, this exercise would greatly benefit the students and others handling retail trade. The case is divided into the following areas:

- Objectives of the case
- Benefits from the case
- Retail philosophies and concepts
- Development of retailers for success
- Gathering retail data
- Evaluating the data
- Locating opportunities
- Prioritizing the opportunities
- Plans for retail improvement
- Select best approach
- Improvement factors
- Business model
- Retail assist
- Personalities

The next area to be covered is business communication for the retail trade:

- Communications towards retail trade
- Retail viewpoint
- Retailer's motivation
- Retail trade communication plans
- Calling on the retailer
- Objectives of the call
- Retailers benefits from the call
- Retailer needs
- Retailer resistance
- Retailer oriented communication
- Adding impact to the communication
- Follow-up action needed

Now let us discuss how the retailer's organization can be analyzed to enable the marketing team tailor make the plan for individual dealer for maximum impact and profitable results both for the retailer and the firm.

Objectives of CPR:

- Firms philosophy and concepts for the retrial trade
- Marketing team's confidence building
- Help in increasing retail sales
- To make the marketing team more efficient in the job, who will have better job satisfaction, increased recognition in the firm, better retail support
- The retailers will benefit with bigger profits, better management and enhanced customer visibility
- The firm will benefit with better profits, satisfied retailers with an edge on competition and happy marketing team

The firm's philosophy and concepts (as generally accepted) are given below:

- To make increasing profits and to grow
- Increase market share and improve brand equity
- Supply quality products, advertise and promote its products, get retailers' cooperation in the same for achieving retail goals
- Support the marketing team in doing an excellent job

Improving Retail Performance is essential to the firm as the sale and financial gains are made here only. Firms spend a lot of money in developing the retail outlets, advertising the same, providing service for retail customers and training their sales and service staff. Retailers help in firm's brand building efforts too through their word of mouth publicity. The retailer, on his part must benefit with improved returns on his investments to ensure he is not tempted to invest elsewhere. The retailer should earn enough from selling the firm's product to keep him totally involved in it. He emerges as a successful businessman in the area.

The marketing team's benefits come from increasing number of retailers looking for help from the team. The team gets time to devote to marginal retailers with undeveloped potential. The team's success ensures rewarding career growth for its members.

Retail reluctance for change comes from the following factors:

- Owner busy with day-to-day working of the outlet
- He does not have the finance needed for the change
- He feels changes are too sophisticated for his customers
- He feels his own team will not accept the changes.

Firm's marketing team is not just for getting the orders from the retailers, but for helping the retailer in building the trade, sales and profits, providing a permanent bridge of relationship with the firm for trust and confidence. The marketing team needs to become the retailers' professional counsellor and for doing it well the team needs to act as follows:

- Understand the retailers' growth potential
- Define the retail sales and profit goals
- Calculate the retail expenses
- Establish the retail business expansion plans

At this stage it is required to define the retailer's **Improvement Opportunities** (improvement opportunities are just the **Problem Areas** thus known as no retailer would like to be told that he is having problems, while every one accepts that they all have opportunities for improvement).

- Not meeting the sales targets
- Not getting profits as possible
- High on expenses
- Stilted growth plans
- Staff with low morale

As Retailer Counsellor (RC), the job would entail helping the retailer set up long range programme to meet his targets, suggesting merchandising, service and sales techniques; help plan control on expenses and for arranging low cost finance.

For the task, the RC needs to have:

A positive frame of mind, with the following attributes:

- Belief that the retailer can make profitable business with the firm's products
- Ability to understand the retailers viewpoint and see his problems
- Vision for locating retailers improvement opportunities
- Ability to provide training and other resources needed
- Belief in himself that he can solve the retailers' problems
- Open to suggestions from the retailers
- Desire for self-improvement
- Zeal for achievement

RC also needs the following:

1. Knowledge of the retail trade; ability to analyze the retailers' situation and financial results, which would help in locating opportunities
2. Developing plans for using the resources properly for improving performance
3. Ability to get retailers acceptance for the plans

The RC must therefore be aware of the motivating factors of the retailer, existing practices followed by him and methods of improving the same. Besides he must develop skills for analysis, evaluation, planning, communications and motivating the retailers into accepting his plan. He should know how retailers' resistance could be converted into action. Besides for long-term relationship, there has to be long term RC counseling to the retailer. RC should be able to persuade the retailer into things like extending outlet hours, arranging better displays, play house for kids of the shoppers.

Defining Improvement Opportunities: Retailers are normally not aware of the opportunities existing and hence cannot analyze to find out the areas where improvements are possible, or may be he is too preoccupied with his work to find time for the purpose. To be really useful the improvement opportunities must be definable, big enough for the efforts to be made, and realistic for improvements. RC must ensure improvement in performance takes place to keep his own credibility with the retailer as also with his own firm. For this purpose, the RC must gather relevant facts, evaluate them and then only define improvement opportunities. For example, if the outlet is not having enough parking place and many, say fifty per day, as per actual count, customers go back because of this fact then, building underground parking facility could be the answer, with the provision of valet parking. If the small children, say thirty families with children, do not let the shoppers buy in peace, then a children's park, or play area could be the answer.

Let us discuss why facts are important. Because:

- Retailer tends to accept the hard facts only
- Retailer would also agree to the improvements suggested if they are based on facts.
- Facts are timer savers, as from well-accepted facts wrong calculations, trail and error methods are avoided, and the retailers' confidence in the plan is fortified.
- If several facts have come to light, RC should concentrate only on important facts only to ensure retailer's interest and immediate improvement impact. And the effort comes to fruition quickly.

Let us see what could be the important facts for a retail outlet. They are given below:

- Retail gross profit for the firm's products
- Quantity of major product sold per annum, decline or increase taking market growth in to account
- Labour cost
- Other expenses like power, rentals, entertainment
- Worker morale

These factors can be found out by looking at the retailer's monthly/yearly balance sheet, talking to the owner, his staff and his customers. It is better to find out the facts from more than one source to achieve accuracy. These results can then be compared with some yardsticks as given below:

- Firm's objectives
- Retailer's historical figures
- Retailer's objectives
- Competitive performances

It can be applied as follows:

Result yardstick	Results	Difference
Firm's plan		
10,000 refrigerators per annum	9200	800
Retailers plan		
11,000 refrigerators per annum	9200	2200
10 lacs/monthly gross profit	8.2 lacs	1.8 lacs

These can also be expressed in ratios as given below:

- Labour cost as per cent of gross profit
- Other expenses as per cent of gross profit
- Rentals as per cent of gross profit
- Total operating expenses as per cent of gross profit
- Retailers' net profit as per cent of gross profit

These figures provide the guidelines for identifying the improvement opportunities (weaknesses), which figures exceed and which fall short of standards of the firm. It is worthwhile going into details of the opportunities, which would enable the RC in diagnosing the real problems/weaknesses. Vague ideas can lead the RC into avoidable traps of irrationally simple approach to some complicated problems. At times observing the following can be a real eye opener:

- Outlet's exterior—entry and exit points, parking areas
- Outlet's façade
- Salespersons attitude towards the customers and towards each other
- Economic standard of the area being serviced by the outlet
- Competitors' outlets in the vicinity
- Mystery shoppers experiences (to be sent by the RC)
- Credit provided by the outlet and credit outstanding with age analysis

Task for the Students

Discuss the entire coverage of Retail Counsellors work and his contribution in the development of retail business for sellers. Retailers are mostly multibrand suppliers. Therefore, manufacturers need to handle their retailers in a manner that enthuses them into selling the manufacturer's products. Students can be asked to make role plays out of the case study.

CASE STUDY 8

Carrefour

Carrefour could be the next high profile alliance in the Indian retail space. The world's second largest retailer Carrefour is close to tying up with the Nusli Wadia group to set up its operations in the country.

The Wadia group has interests in a range of industries—from textiles to aviation. The development comes on the heels of Sunil Mittal's Bharti Enterprises preferring US-based Wal-Mart over Tesco for its retail venture.

Carrefour, like many foreign retailers, has been looking to enter India for some time. It was earlier in talks with Dubai-based Landmark group, owners of Lifestyle departmental stores, and even Bharti Enterprises.

A source in the Wadia camp confirmed that Carrefour has approached the group for a retail initiative. However, what structure the arrangement will finally take could not be ascertained. When contacted, a Wadia group spokesperson declined to comment.

The group's flagship company Bombay Dyeing & Manufacturing Company already has a presence in home furnishing and apparel retail.

Its food company Britannia Industries recently acquired Cafe Coffee Day's 50% stake in Daily Bread—a Bangalore-based high-end food retailer. The deal signalled the Wadia group's foray into the food retailing business.

Europe's leading retailer—$74 billion Carrefour operates more than 11,000 hypermarkets, supermarkets, hard discount and convenience stores in 30 countries and has 4,30,000 employees. Carrefour already has a sourcing office in New Delhi, which it uses to procure textiles and garments worth $300-400 million from India for its global operations.

Over the last couple of years, Bombay Dyeing has been working at re-engineering itself from being just a textile and apparel player to include real estate.

The Wadia group had recently closed down its textile mills—located in Central Mumbai – and is developing an integrated complex that could possibly be home to its retail forays.

The real estate business headed by Nusli Wadia's eldest son Ness Wadia is also looking after the retail initiative. The younger Wadia has plans to bring in international lifestyle brands into the country. This is expected to give the group's retailing plans a fillip.

Grocery Stock Up

Carrefour, Singapore's first ever hypermarket, is also most savvy shoppers' first shopping choice for stocking up on groceries. Everything you'd expect is neatly and conveniently displayed.

Gourmet World

Carrefour's French origins have much to do with its constant stocks of gastronomic indulgences. The Reflets de France house brands delivers a host of regional French gourmet delights.

Healthy Eating

Health is our most valuable asset. We at Carrefour believe that eating healthily can and should be a delicious experience. For a healthy eating, do check out.

Healthy Living

Making a commitment to wellness means committing to an active lifestyle and paying heed to that old adage of 'prevention is better than cure'. Carrefour stocks everything under the sun.

Lucky Charm Winner

Every dollar spent at Carrefour gives you one chance to win! Triple chances when you charge your purchases to POSB Everyday Credit Card.

Task for the Students

Discuss the USP of the company and how it is going to be accepted by the Indian buyers.

CASE STUDY 9

Marks & Spencer Department store

Marks & Spencer Direct, the catalogue and Internet selling division of Marks & Spencer, brings the best of the UK's leading department store to shoppers throughout the UK, including the Channel Islands, Northern Ireland, the West Country, Wales and the Highlands and Islands of Scotland.

For those UK shoppers already familiar with the Marks & Spencer departmental stores, yet possibly too busy to fully enjoy the Marks & Spencer shopping experience, the Marks & Spencer website and the sensational Marks & Spencer catalogues offer a perfect alternative, with the best of Marks & Spencer shopping just a couple of clicks away!

For a wide range of UK electrical products, Comet UK offers a great choice, at very competitive prices.

Marks & Spencer is one of the UK's leading retailers of clothing, foods, homeware and financial services, serving 10 million customers a week in over 300 UK stores. **Marks & Spencer** also trades in 30 countries worldwide, and has a Group turnover in excess of £8 billion. [Source: **www.marks-and-spencer.com**]. Marks & Spencer are always a force to be reckoned with when it comes to British retail, and **Marks & Spencer lingerie** is some of the finest (1 in 3 British women wear Marks & Spencer lingerie)—the latest Marks & Spencer lingerie collection is *Truly You*—a design that sets even higher standards of desirability.

Marks & Spencer Clothes Catalogue: Shop for Clothes Bargains @ Marks & Spencer UK.

Marks & Spencer has possibly the largest range of *quality*, UK merchandise available online with discounts and bargains. Marks & Spencer prices are most reasonable. The best price and quality—for UK shopping by far Marks & Spencer has years of experience with UK retail—the Marks & Spencer online shopping experience is testament to that.

The Marks & Spencer website is just so easy to navigate, and to purchase goods. It really is a pleasure to shop online at Marks & Spencer. Cutlery, Elegance Bone China, Glasses, Maxim Porcelain, Party Tableware, Picnicware, Platinum Fine Porcelain, Reflection Porcelain, Serving Dishes, Table Accessories, Table Decorations, Table Linen, Table Sets, Tea & Coffee, World Cuisine and more are all available at Marks & Spencer **Marks & Spencer** is the leading UK retailer of quality fashion products, unique furniture, glassware. Marks & Spencer has a massive range of products, ranging from furniture & clothes to sportswear, wine, **Marks and Spencer lingerie** and much more. Browse through thousands of Marks & Spencer fashion ideas for you, your family and home all at low, low prices. Shopping online at Marks & Spencer UK is so easy!

Marks & Spencer online shop has a fantastic range of products—here's just a sample: Chandeliers, Ceiling Lights, Floor Lamps, Pendant Lights, Shades, Table Lamps, Uplighter Shades, Wall Lights, Cutlery, Elegance Bone China, Glasses, Maxim Porcelain, Party Tableware, Picnicware, Platinum Fine Porcelain, Reflection Porcelain, Serving Dishes, Table Accessories.

Mothercare UK Stores: Mothercare stores are located both out of town and on high streets. Mothercare larger stores carry the full 'destination' range of merchandise across all product areas: home and travel, toys and clothing for the pre-school child. Mothercare's high street stores provide a range of clothing for mums-to-be, babies and pre-school children, together with home and travel products and toys tailored to the local market.

Mothercare Direct: Mothercare Direct comprises the direct mail order catalogue and mothercare.com, the shopping and information website. These direct channels extend the reach of the Mothercare brand and provide customers with a convenient way to shop and to access a wealth of information for mums-to-be and parents of young children on a range of topics, including pregnancy and childcare.

Plasma Televisions from Panasonic, Plasma TV Discounts from Pioneer, Plasma TV deals from Samsung, Philips plasma televisions, Best Plasma Television Price from Daewoo ... At **Comet** "Plasma TV" is just another name for "bargain".

Widescreen televisions and Projection TV and LCD television deals at **Comet** cannot be beaten. Best prices all round!

Widescreen HDTV Monitors, TV/DVD Combo, LCD Drop Down TV, Real Flat TV, LCD HDTV—all at **Comet Online**!

The **Marks & Spencer UK Store** is well known for its quality products and extensive range of affordable fashions and unique range of Marks & Spencer furniture:

Marks & Spencer store has one of the best selections of luxury lingerie and fashionable clothes of any UK online department store.

The Marks & Spencer Online Store has an outstanding collection of **unique** products and the best prices!

At Marks & Spencer Online, as in any Marks & Spencer store, you'll find a strong commitment to great prices throughout

The Marks & Spencer Direct team has an equally strong commitment to making your Marks & Spencer shopping experience fun—and also very affordable!

At **Marks & Spencer UK Website**, as with any Marks & Spencer transaction, whether in-store or via the Marks & Spencer Catalogue, you'll find well-trained staff committed to quality service.

The enviable reputation of **Marks & Spencer** has been established over many decades, and is built upon the well-founded principles of respecting one's customers and offering value for money. Marks & Spencer brand-name which is recognized throughout the UK, and also far beyond. When you buy from **Marks & Spencer Website** you won't be disappointed!

Marks & Spencer Online: At Marks & Spencer Direct You'll Get The Best Selection of Internet Shopping *and always* The Best Prices!

Marks & Spencer—Everyone's Favourite UK Department Store: **Marks & Spencer.com** offers an exciting selection of Flowers, Gifts, Fashion, Lingerie, Home and Health and Electronics products to buy, at prices second to none. The same great range you find in Marks & Spencer stores you'll also find at Marks & Spencer Online and more! Marks & Spencer offers an excellent Website together with exemplary customer service. One thing you can be sure of when you shop online at Marks & Spencer—you won't be disappointed!

Here are just some of the departments you'll find at **Marks & Spencer website**: Clothing and Jewellery, Gardening, Fitness Equipment Store, Marks & Spencer Furniture, Computers & Gaming, Gifts and Flowers, **Marks & Spencer** Nursery Store, Toys and Games, Sports and Leisure, Home Electronics, Marks & Spencer Fashion for Women, Fashion for Men … You'll also find the wonderful range of *per una* at **Marks & Spencer** website. Marks & Spencer and George Davies launched **per una dué** in May 2004, building on the strong success of the Marks & Spencer **per una** clothing brand, which launched in 2001.

Marks & Spencer have phenomenal online furniture department. **Marks & Spencer** have furniture for everyone's taste—Bathroom Suites, Beds, Bookcases, Cabinets, Chairs, Chests of Drawers, Coffee Tables, Console Tables, Desks, Dining Tables, Entertainment Units, Mattresses, Screens, Shelves, Sideboards, Side Tables, Sofas, Trunks, Wardrobes. If it's affordable, quality furniture you're after, then you must be looking for **Marks & Spencer**.

Marks & Spencer Home Decor: The Best Quality Furniture and Home Decor are at Marks & Spencer UK!

Task for the Students

Do a SWOT Analysis of the company and make a marketing plan for improving the company's brand loyalty further.

CASE STUDY

10

Changes in the Oil Industry Retailing

Late 1990s and Beyond

The oil industry in India changed dramatically throughout the 1990s and into the new millennium. Reform in the downstream hydrocarbon sector – the sector in which Indian Oil was the market leader – began as early in 1991 and continued throughout the decade. In 1997, the government announced that the Administered Pricing Mechanism (APM) would be dismantled.

To prepare for the increased competition that deregulation would bring, Indian Oil added a seventh refinery to its holdings in 1998 when the Panipat facility was commissioned. The company also looked to strengthen its industry position by forming joint ventures. In 1993, the firm teamed up with Balmer Lawrie & Co. and NYCO SA of France to create Avi-Oil India Ltd., a manufacturer of oil products used by defence and civil aviation firms. One year later, Indo Mobil Ltd. was formed in a 50-50 joint venture with Exxon Mobil. The new company imported and blended Mobil brand lubricants for marketing in India, Nepal, and Bhutan. In addition, Indian Oil was involved in the formation of ten major ventures from 1996 through 2000.

Indian Oil also entered the public arena as the government divested nearly 10 per cent of the company. In 2000, Indian Oil and ONGC traded a 10 per cent equity stake in each other in a strategic alliance that would better position the two after the APM dismantling, which was scheduled for 2002. According to a 1999 *Hindu* article, Indian Oil Corporation's strategy at this time was "to become a diversified, integrated global energy corporation." The article went on to claim that "while maintaining its leadership in oil refining, marketing and pipeline transportation, it aims for higher growth through integration and diversification. For this, it is harnessing new business opportunities in petrochemicals, power, lube marketing, exploration and production ... and fuel management in this country and abroad."

In early 2002, Indian Oil acquired IBP, a state-owned petroleum marketing company. The firm also purchased a 26 per cent stake in financially troubled Haldia Petrochemicals Ltd. In April of that year, Indian Oil's monopoly over crude imports ended as deregulation of the petroleum industry went into effect. As a result, the company faced increased competition from large international firms as well as new domestic entrants to the market. During the first 45 days of deregulation, Indian Oil lost Rs. 7.25 billion, a signal that the India's largest oil refiner would indeed face challenges as a result of the changes.

Nevertheless, Indian Oil management believed that the deregulation would bring lucrative opportunities to the company and would eventually allow it to become one of the top 100 companies on the Fortune 500—in 2001 the company was ranked 209. With demand for petroleum products in India projected to grow from 148 million metric tons in 2006 to 368 million metric tons by 2025, Indian Oil believed it was well positioned for future growth and prosperity.

Principal Subsidiaries: Indo Mobil Ltd. (50%); Avi-Oil Ltd. (25%); Indian Oiltanking Ltd. (25%); Petronet India Ltd. (16%); Petronet VK Ltd. (26%); Petronet CTM Ltd. (26%); Petronet CIPL Ltd. (12.5%); IndianOil Petronas Ltd. (50%); IndianOil Panipat Power Consortium Ltd. (26%); IndianOil TCG Petrochem Ltd. (50%); Librizol India Pvt. Ltd. (50%).

Principal Competitors: Bharat Petroleum Corporation Ltd.; Hindustan Petroleum Corporation Ltd.; Royal Dutch/Shell Group of Companies.

Bharat Petroleum

Bharat Petroleum's efforts have all along been to build a superior understanding of customer needs and relentlessly work towards fulfilling these needs. Bharat Petroleum is consciously working towards providing added value to customers, both in fuel and non-fuel areas. Initiatives, some of them pioneering efforts, have been introduced based on need gaps articulated by consumers during focus group discussions and extensive market research.

Recognizing that the basic need of the customer is pure quality and correct quantity of fuels. As one of the major initiatives in this direction, Bharat Petroleum has triggered a virtual movement at select retail outlets (petrol pumps) to guarantee pure quality and correct quantity to its customers. This 'Enhanced Fuel Proposition' movement, which is the sign of a new revolution, has been gaining nationwide momentum after its initial launch at a few centres. Retail outlets enrolled in the movement display the **'Pure for Sure'** signage very prominently at the outlet.

Bharat Petroleum's efforts began with remodelling and upgrading retail outlets to world-class standards back in 1996. Retail outlets have been equipped with state-of-the-art modern infrastructure, including the **Multi Product Dispensers** to pre-set price and quantity of fuel and Electronic Air Gauges facilitating precise inflation of tyres. Attractive canopies are suitably designed to provide shelter and adequate lighting of the forecourt at most retail outlets.

On the non-fuel front, Bharat Petroleum has introduced the Errand Mall concept successfully at select markets. Called the **'In & Out'**, these malls offer the customer a broad range of facilities and brands to choose from. ATM's, cybercafe, laundry, photo studio, music, fast food, greeting cards, courier services, bill payments, movies/ entertainment tickets, etc. have made Bharat Petroleum's retail outlets a happening place and indeed an rewarding experience for motorists.

To make life more convenient and rewarding for customers, Bharat Petroleum has introduced the **'Petro Card™'** for individual customers and the **'SmartFleet Card'** for fleet owners. Using the Petro Card entitles the customer to PetroMiles under the PetroBonus rewards programme.

Bharat Petroleum has also pioneered the concept of convenience stores at select petrol pumps that operate under the name **'Bazaar'**. These Bazaars provide a wide range of convenience items and fast foods to customers in a clean, air-conditioned and friendly environment.

Retail Woes

Reliance retail outlets have clocked sales per month of about 410 kilolitres per petrol pump, whereas the corresponding figure for PSU outlets is 140 kilolitres.

Govt feels state-owned companies may have to review their retail plans. **The four** PSUs IBP, Indian Oil Corp, Hindustan Petroleum, and Bharat Petroleum are chalking out ambitious retail plans to counter threat from private sector.

Competition is hotting up for state-owned oil marketing companies (OMCs) with the private sector retail petrol outlets clocking much higher monthly sales on an average vis-à-vis the public sector ones.

Owing to this, there is a thinking within the Government that state-owned companies may have to take a closer look at their retail plans, particularly the practice of going in for a cluster approach where a number of PSU outlets are located in close proximity and thus cutting into each others' sales.

According to estimates, while Reliance Industries Ltd's retail outlets have notched sales per month of about 410 kilolitres per petrol pump, the average sale (petrol and diesel) of the state-owned companies are said be about 140 kilolitres.

Concerned over the declining sales at petrol pumps of the OMCs across the country, the Ministry of Petroleum and Natural Gas is planning to ask companies to go slow on their expansion plans for retail outlets. An official told *Business Line* that these companies—IBP, Indian Oil Corp (Indian Oil), Hindustan Petroleum, and Bharat Petroleum—need to take a relook at their retail plans, but admitted that no formal communication has been sent as yet.

However, the companies should themselves see the trend and review their plans, the official added.

A Parliamentary Consultative Committee has also expressed concern, he said, adding that the Committee has been critical of the retail performance of the state-owned companies compared to the private retailer RIL. Reacting to this, OMCs sources said measures were being taken to avoid such situations. The four oil companies, which are taking a hit on their bottom line for selling petroleum products below the cost price, are chalking out ambitious plans on the retail front.

The companies have made aggressive plans to ramp up their retail networks.

Indian Oil (including IBP) the most dominant player in the market with 50 per cent share of outlets, plans to put up 2,000 more petrol pumps, including 1,000 in rural areas.

This would take their total to almost 17,000, up from 15,000 at present.

Indian Oil is also rolling out several new initiatives to increase its per tonne throughput. These include upgrading of outlets, expanding the reach of branded fuels to more areas and creating more synergy between Indian Oil and IBP in the market place.

The OMCs say that it is not fair to compare sales with RIL, which has around 1,200 outlets.

"It is like the aviation sector where private players have eaten into the business of Indian Airlines, the domestic carrier, but that does not mean it should divert business," the sources pointed out.

Related Stories: Reliance to focus on marketing products through its own outlets Govt. not to change norms for petroleum retail business Reliance rolls out food outlets to fuel petrol sales on highways, Signs pact with US hospitality service provider ONGC plans more retail prototypes Shell India opens retail station in Chennai.

Reliance Industries Ltd. (RIL) has invited franchisees for managing its proposed petroleum retail outlets.

The company, which is setting up a countrywide retail network has fixed a minimum Rs. 25 lakh capital investment requirement for each franchisee.

RIL expects to start its retail outlets in the next fiscal year. Reliance will have both company-owned and franchisee-managed outlets. Earlier, the company had floated tenders for acquiring lands for setting up own retail outlets.

According to sources, although Reliance is looking at strategic sites across the country, the immediate focus will be on sites in "high consumption areas," where product can be reached easily from RIL's 27-million-tonne Jamnagar refinery.

The company has specified that applicants owning lands would be given preference.

"High margins, proximity to a feeding station and larger consumption, would ideally be the three criteria for selecting the locations," the source said.

Although the company has not set a formal deadline for putting in place the entire retail network, sources said around 1,500 retail outlets are expected to be set up by April 2004.

In August last year, Reliance had called for responses from landowners to buy sites for retail outlets. The process of examining these offers is still going on, company officials said.

RIL has the Government approval to set up 5,000 retail outlets across the country. In April 2002, Reliance, along with Oil and Natural Gas Corporation Ltd, Essar Oil and Numaligarh Refineries Ltd., was granted permission to set up a retail network as part of sector decontrol.

Hughes, a leading global provider of broadband satellite services, networks and products for businesses, governments and consumers, announced that it has signed a definitive agreement to connect 1000 retail outlets of Reliance Industries across the country. This deployment will be complete by October 2005. The deal valued at Rs. 8

crores involves Hughes installing a technology backbone for all of Reliance petroleum outlets in a phased manner, connecting 3000 outlets by 2006.

Reliance will deploy the DiRECWAY 7700 platform, a two-way satellite broadband solution. Reliance will be the first customer to use this in India that will run all its applications on a single infrastructure. These applications include tank monitoring, sales management, credit access, back office applications, POS services and value-added services like WiFi access, multicasting, package delivery and internet access. Hughes will build, manage and provide on ground support for all these services.

"Oil & Gas is one of the strongest market segments for Hughes worldwide. I am confident that with our experience and understanding of this industry, we will be able to deliver on Reliance's vision of superior customer experience," said Partho Banerjee, President, Hughes India.

Hughes will enable turnkey networking solutions encompassing network design, Data Center services, security infrastructure, VPN services, systems integration, facility management of network components and a 24×7 network management services for the connected outlets.

Hughes works with BPCL, HPCL and Essar Oil in the Indian market. Worldwide, Hughes has connected over 50,000 oil retail outlets via satellite allowing them to offer techno differentiators to their customers. These include clients like Exxon Mobil, BP-Amoco, Chevron, Shell and SK Gas.

Petrol bunks are no longer fuel dispensing outlets only. Sporting all new look, retailer-friendly approach, they now outsmart the best of the retail chains in the country offering laundry, courier, photo, medicines, flowers, fresh fruits, insurance, fast food, ticket booking service, telephone & net surfing facility, letter box, convenient banking service, pollution checking points and what have you. **ReachoutHyderabad.com** examines the changing face of all new look, customer-friendly modern gas filling stations.

Time was when petrol bunks served little purpose other than dispensing fuel. They are now stopped being merely just that some time ago.

Times have changed. They have also changed along with time. And are still changing. Gone are the days of old and not so impressive gas stations. The all new look petrol pumps are in things now. Most of 185 odd retail outlets in twin cities have received lavish face-lift. The same old pumps now look more spacious, have a brighter look. In fact, they have even become an accepted feature of cityscape. The retail-friendly pumps are on the increase all over the country. The demand for shelf space in these fuel filling stations is also on the increase.

And now lot of these retail petrol outlets provide convenience shopping and other services which were not heard before. They don't stop at conventional things. They added whole variety of stores and services. The range of services offered at these outlets is mind-boggling. It is beyond bright illumination and provision of modernised dispensing units. There is much more in store for the consumers. A range of value-added services have been introduced, all beneath one roof.

On the operations side, computer have added to the new look of the petrol pumps. Gone are the days where a person had to file the daily transactions, check the cash, tally the accounts and then close the petrol pumps at the stroke of midnight to leave home with the thought of next day's dreaded morning. A drastic change which has taken the city by storm is the petrol machines that have invoked a new look with computers invading this area also. Now one can get print out of the bill for the said amount and the quantity mentioned in liters.

This makes the customers know the exact quantity of petrol that has to be filled in, getting over the perennial problem of foregoing small change which most of the times the attendants at the pumps pocket for themselves.

The traditional archaic pumps have now been replaced by more advanced EMP petrol pumps. Christened as the 'multi-purpose dispenser', the digital equipment presets itself according to the payment by customers and fills the tank with petrol, diesel or unleaded petrol corrected to millilitres. This not only ensures accuracy, but also saves a lot of time for customers and avoids misconceptions and arguments.

Apart from sporting new look and equipping with latest equipment, now petrol pumps house a wide variety of value added and service centres which include departmental stores, coffee shops/pubs/kiosks, cyber cafes, laundry service, pizzas, courier, drugs, pollution check, ticketing, music shops, auto LPG stations, auto service centres, kerosene distribution, photo shop, pay by card, telephone directories distribution, ATM counters, round-the-clock drug and general stores and what have you.

To add to these services is the latest announcement of the Bengaluru based (already present in Hyderabad), coffee chain Cafe Coffe Day's tie-up with Bharat Petroleum Corporation Ltd. (BPCL) to open Cafe Coffee Day outlets in select In & Out BPCL Petrol Pumps including twin cities. Cafe Coffe Day has already set up nine cafes at BPCL outlets—three each in Mumbai, Delhi and Bengaluru.

The outlets, according to Mr. Naresh Malhotra, Director, Café Coffee Day, will be stand-alone café's or kiosks/coffee counters within Bharat Petroleum's chain of convenience centres In & Out which are located within the petrol pump.

Mr. S. Ramesh, General Manager (Brand Management), Bharat Petroleum says, their alliance with Café Coffee Day is a reiteration of their commitment for providing value-added products and services to their customers in a convenient manner through innovative means. The Café Coffee Day proposition which is being offered at select In & Out stores and also at select retail outlets is a further step towards offering products and service levels of the highest quality to customers along with an element of fun and excitement.

Coffee Shops apart, BPCL came out with a photo-shop earlier. To this effect it had tied-up with Kodak. Some petrol pumps have web-enabled kiosks to be used for booking tickets for favourite movies, musical concerts, entertainment shows besides cricket matches.

That is not all. These filling stations have become abode for unconventional shops and services. It is told that a 'Surf Laundry Service' is on the anvil at one of the outlets of BPCL, where consumers could avail of dry-cleaning and mending of garments. Said to have been piloted in Mumbai, the concept involves dropping the garments at the In & Out Stores and picking it later. The laundry would offer a regular 48-hour service, an express 24-hour service and a lightning 8-hour service.

Slowly but steadily, petrol pumps have become a convenience retailing propositions for many oil companies. Even Cyber Cafes are attached to some of the petrol outlets. These are already a common site when we go to fill petrol at some of the Indian Oil Corporation (IOC) pumps. DishnetDSL said to have been the first to open Internet Hub at an IOC outlet. But according to some news reports published earlier, Cyber Cafes are just one aspect of the Retail Visual Identity improvement programmes of the OIC as it was also establishing pharmacies, Conveno Stores, fast food and pizza joints, besides Servo Lube Shops. Also talked about other services are automatic car wash and self-mixing multi-nozzle pumps. Of course, not to mention the auto LPG stations.

Domino's Pizza has tied up with the Indian Oil Corporation (IOC) to set up drive-in-drive-out Pizza outlets at its petrol pumps.

Not to forget the pollution generated by over 12 lakh registered vehicles that ply every day on city roads. Using pumps, the Government of Andhra Pradesh plans to put a full stop to pollution hazard. It is believed to have made serious efforts in concert with NGOs, Forum for Better Hyderabad, associations of transporters and others to reduce air pollution levels in the twin cities.

Already some state governments are contemplating distributing kerosene to public through pumps following increase in alleged irregularities such as adulteration and faulty measurement and delayed distribution in Public Distribution System outlets. To put an end to such unhealthy practices, Karnataka is one government which thought about the idea in the past.

Several advertising agencies have tied up with petrol pumps as they serve as an excellent place for effective outdoor advertising medium.

Following the cue to tap the potential of petrol pumps is another company Apollo Pharmacy, which is said to be in the process of setting up of round-the-clock drug and general stores with petroleum major, Indian Oil Corporation. It is said to be setting up 500 such shops in Mumbai alone. The shops are not only planning to sell medicines but are also planning to offer services such as medicare, testing and insurance.

Along with these new trends and changes taking place all over the petrol pumps, we have heard of All Women's Petrol pumps in Bengaluru city making big news recently. With encouraging results coming by hiring all women at petrol pumps and decreasing customer complaints, more and more pumps are to jump at the new idea soon.

The reasons for such a drastic facelift may be partly to prepare for the competition (which may pose a threat once Reliance launches its services) and outshine competition. Or may be to offer more facilities and value added services. Whatever may be the reasons, one thing is certain, the age old petrol pumps in our neighbourhood certainly have come a long way.

You can soon buy your train tickets from petrol pumps.

In line with its aim to increase the points where tickets can be bought, Indian Railway Catering and Tourism Corporation (IRCTC) entered into an agreement with BPCL to make available e-tickets at BPCL retail petrol outlets.

BPCL also plans to sell e-tickets at its liquefied petroleum gas distributor locations.

At these outlets, people can even book tickets for various tour packages arranged by IRCTC.

By January end, the service will be available at 38 'In & Out' outlets of Bharat Petroleum Corporation Ltd. (BPCL) in Delhi, Chennai, Hyderabad, Kolkata, Bengaluru, Pune and Mumbai.

By March, 100 BPCL outlets are likely to be covered.

The number of such ticket selling petrol outlets may further increase as IRCTC is also in talks with other oil marketing companies to make available train tickets at their outlets.

For booking sleeper and second-class tickets, users would have to pay a service charge.

Bookings for up to six passengers can be done in each ticket. Payments can be made using credit cards and debit cards also.

However, the total booking charges may come down as the IRCTC Managing Director, Dr P.K. Goel, today said that IRCTC is contemplating reducing booking amount per ticket.

The memorandum of understanding for setting up e-ticketing facilities at BPCL outlets throughout the country was signed by Dr Goel and the BPCL Executive Director (Retail), Mr Sanjay Krishnamurti, here today.

Mr. Krishnamurti added that the out of the extra charges collected by BPCL per ticket, 70 per cent would go to the dealer whereas 30 per cent would go to BPCL.

Tiruchi: The Indian Oil Corporation's tap-off facility at Vazhavanthankottai is set to supply petrol mixed with five per cent ethanol to retail outlets in Tiruchi and peripheral districts soon. The era of 'green' transport fuel provides high hopes to sugar industry in the region.

Two tanks, each with 120 kilolitre storage capacity, are to store ethanol that will be procured from sugar mills, as in Brazil, pioneer of 'gasohol' concept.

IOC officials, citing the benefits for macro economy, are certain that more areas can be brought under sugar cane cultivation once the scheme takes off, thanks to sustenance of assured income for farmers. Large-scale cultivation of sugar cane is undertaken in the neighbouring Karur and Perambalur districts. More areas in Tiruchi district too can be brought under sugar cane cultivation in future.

While the economics of sugar industry will witness an upswing by producing ethanol from molasses, an important byproduct, the environment will also be saved of substantial dosage of hydrocarbon, carbon monoxide and dioxide emissions.

Ethanol, when mixed with petrol, supplies extra oxygen for complete combustion. The blended fuel is already in use in other states and in those areas served by the IOC's facilities in Tuticorin and Coimbatore, according to C.M. Chandrakantan, Chief Terminal Manager, Tiruchi Tap-Off, Vazhavanthankottai.

Since the country imports nearly 70 per cent of its petroleum requirements, ethanol, a renewable source of energy available indigenously, is easily an import substitution.

As early as in September 12, 2002, the Centre issued a notification for mandatory supply of five per cent ethanol-blended petrol to nine states, including Tamil Nadu, and in four Union Territories.

The demand for ethanol is bound to grow since the country is looking forward to raising the extent of ethanol blending to 15 per cent, in phases.

India's Fortune Global 500 company—Indian Oil and the leader in the organized retail business—the Future Group (formerly known as Pantaloon Retail Limited), today signed a Memorandum of Cooperation (MoC) for setting up petrol stations at Future Group Malls and for establishing Food Bazaars at Indian Oil petrol stations. The MoC was signed by Shri G.C. Daga, Director (Marketing), Indian Oil and by Shri Kishore Biyani, Group CEO, Future Group in the presence of senior officials from the respective companies. Mumbai, 7th November, 2006.

"Indian Oil is a pioneer in petroleum retailing in India and we were the first to launch colour coded fascia, coordinated lighting, multi-product digital dispensing pumps, modern signages, auto car wash, Convenio stores, digital air towers etc. way back in the mid-90s. Today, with automated facilities, loyalty cards, branded fuels and exclusive retail formats for urban, highway and rural segments, we continue to set new standards in the petroleum retail business in the country." The tie-up with Future Group will help in the growth of our retail forays, said Shri G.C. Daga, Director (Marketing), Indian Oil.

Commenting on the tie-up Mr. Kishore Biyani said that "the MoC with Indian Oil will provide a new and added impetus to the growth of their retail business plans, as it would provide newer footprints into virgin markets particularly in the semi-urban and highway segments where Indian Oil has huge presence. The synergy in retail vision that exists between Indian Oil and Future Group will only strengthen this tie-up, to achieve more" he said.

The MoC envisages the setting up Indian Oil petrol stations at select malls, hypermarkets and supermarkets of the Future Group (comprising of retail formats Big Bazaar, Food Bazaar, Fashion Station, Pantaloons, Central). Also the hugely successful Food Bazaar stores will also be set up at select Indian Oil Retail outlets while Future Group will operate the large format stores, the smaller stores will be operated by Indian Oil dealers who will source merchandise from Food Bazaar. Both Indian Oil and Future Group will also participate in Loyalty Programmes and undertake joint marketing efforts to promote their business models including sharing of customer database/research and analysis.

When you drive into a petrol pump some months down the road, you'll probably insert a smart card into a device and punch in the amount of petrol you want to buy.

The software behind the card will check your bank account to see whether you can pay for the petrol before the petrol station is instructed to release the petrol.

What is more, you'll get a combined bill for everything you buy, including whatever you buy at the adjacent oil company-owned store (today you have to pay separately for this).

Thanks again to software, the chances of your petrol being adulterated will be slim. You'll also perhaps be able to zip through a petrol station in double quick time.

Faced with impending international competition, India's state-owned and private oil companies are embarking upon an unprecedented automation drive at petrol outlets and supply chains (real-time monitoring of every step of the supply process).

Last month, the state-owned Hindustan Petroleum Corporation Ltd. invited global tenders to automate 500 petrol stations by year end.

Says a senior HPCL official: "We have already drawn up a detailed plan in consultation with international petroleum consultants." IOC too wants to automate 250 petrol stations in the first phase (up to 1,000 stations by year end) and plans on spending Rs. 200 crore (Rs. 2 billion) on this.

Says a senior IOC official, "Costs are not a constraint, as we have to gear up for competition from private oil companies such as Reliance, Essar and Shell."

The 250 stations will sport the Chairman's Club (IOC calls the entire project 'Operation Everest').

Reliance Industries has tied up with the Ogden, Utah (US)-based Flying J, an integrated petroleum company, to automate its retail outlets.

"Flying J has expertise in setting up fuel stops along national highways. Reliance will draw on this expertise to cater to the needs of long-distance truckers in India," adds an industry source.

Reliance apparently is looking at 'real time monitoring of stocks from the refinery to customers' vehicles.'

It is considering automating all its retail outlets, whether a small one in the city or big service stations on a city's outskirts or stations on the national highways.

IBP too says it is exploring the possibility of automating its stations. Raj Agnihotri, president of the US-based ProcessBiz Technologies Inc, says IBP is talking to his company on this.

In March 2002, IOC had 7,870 retail outlets, HPCL had 4,729 service stations and Bharat Petroleum Corporation Ltd. had 4,711 retail outlets.

While only a small percentage of these will be automated initially, it nevertheless represents a huge business opportunity—Rs. 1,000 crore (Rs. 10 billion) market, according to Agnihotri.

Sensing the opportunity, the Netherlands-based Petroplus International is pitching to sell unmanned filling stations under the Tango brand to the oil companies.

So far, ProcessBiz Technologies has automated three petrol stations in Mumbai: IOC's Top Gear on Warden Road, another IOC petrol station at Napean Sea Road and HPCL's Bandra petrol pump, which will go live in two months. IOC has, in fact, issued smart cards at one of its outlets.

IOC officials say they have already received a "very positive" response from its pilot projects, for which it has roped in McKinsey & Co, the consultancy firm. IOC has also launched dealer awareness programmes to train dealers in automation.

The oil companies, however, say the three outlets are only partially automated. Automation involves much more than the petrol pumps—it also involves back office operations. Automating these will benefit the oil companies hugely. They'll get real-time data on retail sales and can better manage their inventory levels (for example, they'll be able to know whether petrol levels are low at a station) and they'll be able to reconcile stocks and sales.

Secondly, they'll be able to check adulteration—if a tanker delivers petrol at a certain time and two hours later the level of petrol in the station is much higher, they'll know that the petrol has been adulterated.

Thirdly, as Agnihotri points out, automation will help the oil companies later if there are price wars—they'll know which petroleum products' sales are moving slowly and will be able to offer discounts on it.

Still, automation is unlikely to usher in unmanned petrol stations. The state-owned oil companies won't be able to sack petrol station attendants, though they have the option of making their outlets self-service ones at night.

Private oil companies like Reliance can open unmanned stations, since they don't have the legacy of employees. But even Reliance won't plump for unmanned stations.

A Slick Affair

- HPCL and IOC to automate 500 and 1,000 stations, respectively, by the year-end.
- Automation will help oil companies get real-time data on retail sales and manage inventory levels better.
- Move will also curb adulteration.

ATM's in ROs

ATMs—Automatic Teller Machines of various leading banks have been provided at select Bharat Petroleum Retail Outlets (petrol pumps) for the convenience of the customer. The convenience of the ATM is that it removes the restriction of timings of the traditional banking system. In an emergency, especially at night when the good old bank is closed, the ATMs become a boon.

Our petrol pumps are ideal locations from the customer convenience point of view. With various networks emerging amongst the banks in future, a cardholder will be able to draw cash from the ATM of any bank. Bharat Petroleum has started this initiative with two banks and now has ATMs of over 13 banks on its sites.

Lubricant Top-ups

Lubricant fills & top-up

Getting the oil changed for a vehicle is no longer time consuming. One can drive into one of Bharat Petroleum's modern petrol stations that have the latest equipment, which just sucks out all the used oil and automatically fill the engine with fresh Automol Gold Engine oil - All this in just 14 minutes.

Also, attendants at Bharat Petroleum petrol stations gladly carry out lubricant top-ups as per customer requirements. Do drive into any of Bharat Petroleum's petrol stations to check out this service.

Air, Water & Washroom

While free air, water and washroom are mandatory requirements, Bharat Petroleum has extended it beyond the mandatory need by providing automatic air gauges at its new generation outlets.

Credit Cards & Debit Cards

Bharat Petroleum pioneered the concept of a co-branded credit card. Today, over 1,500 Bharat Petroleum Petrol Pumps accept Debit & Credit cards that have either a MasterCard or Visa logo on them. In addition to this, selective petrol pumps offer a waiver of the fuel surchage on HDFC Bank Debit Cards, SBI Debit Cards, Standard Chartered Bank Credit Cards, Standard Chartered Bank SmartFill Debit Cards and HSBC Credit Cards.

Shell commences retailing petrol and diesel in India **New Delhi:** Royal Dutch/Shell has opened its first petrol station in India in Bengaluru. According to Vikram Mehta, chairman, Shell India, the company has a licence to set up 2,000 outlets across the country.

He said Shell's retail network would be set up in phases and the first stage would involve an expenditure of Rs. 250 crore. The company plans to import liquefied natural gas for its proposed 5 million metric tpa LNG import terminal at Hazira in western India in the first quarter of 2005. The Hazira terminal would have a capacity to import 2.5 million tonnes of liquefied natural gas every year. The regassified LNG would be sold to major power producers, fertilizer and ceramics industries located along the coast of the western states of Gujarat and Maharashtra that are easily accessible from Shell's LNG import terminal.

Since India's oil sector was deregulated in April 2002, Shell obtained a licence to build 2,000 oil gasoline stations in the country. All those wanting to enter the country's $15-billion per annum oil retail market have had to meet government requirements, including a minimum Rs. 20 billion rupee ($435 million) investment in the country's petroleum sector.

Till now, state-run oil companies had a near monopoly in India's oil retail business, expanding at more than five per cent a year. Reliance Energy Ltd., India' largest private oil refiner, began retailing petrol and diesel earlier this year.

Shell, will be the first multinational to begin fuel retailing in India after the opening up of the sector.

Essar Oil (EOL) has commissioned its first petrol and diesel retail outlet in Gujarat in its hometown of Jamnagar. The opening ceremony was attended by a large number of Government Officials, VIPs and Promoter Director Mr. Anshuman Ruia.

Mr. Chetan Nakhva of Astha Petroleum is the franchisee of the retail outlet. This outlet is to basically test marketing exercise that Essar Oil has undertaken before it freezes on the types of services and convenience to be provided to the customers. This outlet is part of the company's plans to set up 1700 retail outlets by the time its refinery comes into production in 2005.

EOL plans to open over 300 retail outlets in the State of Gujarat by 2005. EOL has already appointed 150 dealers in Gujarat.

It may be recalled that Essar had soft launched their first retail outlet at the historical town of Devrukh, in the district of Ratnagiri in Maharashtra last month. However, the significant aspect is that this is indeed a historic occasion where an Indian private sector oil company has set up the first private retail outlet in the country, after 102 years. The first outlet in India was opened in 1901 by a multinational oil company. In the 70s the first public sector oil company opened their outlets.

Competitive Pricing & Quality Products

The basic approach of Essar Oil is to deliver petroleum products at a competitive cost from a consolidated retail outlet that ultimately would have all the hydrocarbon products such as diesel, petrol, LPG, kerosene, lubricants, etc. for the convenience of the consumers. Retailing of petroleum products is no different from retailing of consumer products. The only major difference is in the product—one being liquid which is dispensing in bulk. "Packaging" in terms of the quality and service at the outlet is as important as the packing and appearance of a consumer product. The quality of diesel is as per international specifications and has a much higher cetane number than the local standards. This helps the truckers get better mileage. Further, fuel is clean and has no gummy residues which helps in reducing maintenance cost and keeping the engine clean.

Trained Manpower; Complete Infrastructure

Every employee of the retail outlet undergoes extensive training in customer service before they are deputed in the retail outlet.

The outlet has four dispensing units—of which three for HSD and one for petrol. This outlet is equipped with high-speed dispensing units. A full tank for a truck can be filled up within one minute. This will help to avoid conjunction and waiting.

Local Employment

Over 300 retail outlets are planned in the State of Gujarat which will provide employment both direct and indirect to at least 30,000 families. Essar plans to set up outlets in backward areas, rural areas and places where no outlets exist.

The distribution network planned by Essar Oil is to induct new dealers into the business and give multiple outlets to each dealer. This will enable the dealers to run retail outlets professionally and profitably despite offering competitive price to the consumers.

The logo of Essar Oil is similar to the logo of Essar parent group except that it has been encased in an owl shaped flying saucer device with speed line below. The colours used are red that stands for energy, white for purity and green for Essar's concern for the environment.

Essar Oil has started marketing large quantities of diesel in bulk to actual users such as cement plants, state transport corporations, power generation plants and other bulk users very successfully. All the customers are very appreciative of the quality of HSD, which is being supplied by Essar, setting new international standards of quality.

Essar Oil is implementing a 12 mmtpa refinery at Jamnagar. On completion, it is expected to produce 55 lakh tonnes of diesel and 22 lakh tonnes of petrol annually besides other petroleum products like LPG, kerosene and Naptha.

Essar Oil is part of Rs. 17000 cr. Essar Group having interests in steel, shipping, oil & gas, telecom and constructions.

The leader in India with over 7,500 petrol/diesel outlets spread throughout the country, and an additional 1,500 of subsidiary company, IBP Co. Ltd., Indian Oil commands about 45% market share in the petroleum retail segment in India.

Visual Identity: Indian Oil has been continuously anticipating customer needs in urban areas for better, cleaner and well-designed petrol/diesel outlets. A focused visual identity and modernization programme to improve customer service has been undertaken under 'Retail Visual Identity' programme to reorient the design and standards of our petrol and diesel outlets viz. colour-coded canopies, multi-product dispensing pumps, concrete driveways, digital air towers, cybercafes, automated teller machines, auto-car washes, etc.

Q&Q Concept: Indian Oil's retail marketing initiatives are oriented around two vital concepts – Quality and Quantity. Under this concept, products can be tested for correct quality & quantity before making the purchase.

Top Gear: "Top Gear" in Mumbai is an example of a state-of-the-art petrol/diesel outlet with multiple associated facilities. It is tailor-made to provide 'fill-and-fly' service to the Mumbai motorists who battle 'time' in their daily lives. With facilities like multi-product dispensing pumps, auto carwash, Convenio store, SERVO shop, digital air tower, ATM, customer lounge, art gallery, computerized online billing system, help desk, Cybercafe, etc. Top Gear symbolizes the cutting edge of petroleum retail marketing. Several more 'Top Gear' outlets are being planned in major cities in India.

Jubilee Outlets: The ever-changing trends in highway traffic and the increase in the number of automobiles plying on trunk routes set Indian Oil to commission a new range of facilities to meet the demands of this vital segment of our business. In 1997, Indian Oil commissioned the country's first Jubilee Retail Outlet in Ongole, Andhra Pradesh, in what was a revolutionary step in petroleum retail marketing. The Jubilee Retail Outlet concept, introduced on the occasion of the Golden Jubilee celebrations of India's independence, is a pioneering effort in petroleum retailing in India.

Each Jubilee outlet, built on a sprawling four acre area, has facilities like fuel islands, Convenio store, parking lots, cafeteria for motorists, dhabas for truckers, dormitories for tourists, playground, bank extension counter, post-office, pharmacy, first-aid facilities, STD/ISD facilities, etc. Today, Indian Oil has as many as 80 Jubilee outlets spread across the country.

Cashless Transactions: For customer convenience, Indian Oil at its petrol/diesel outlets introduced cashless transactions through co-brand credit cards like Indian Oil—Citi card. In 2002, Indian Oil introduced the PowerPlus Fleet card in association with Sundaram Finance. Very recently, a co-branded debit card (MyShoppe) has been introduced, through which customers will pay only at the time of buying goods, including fuel, and also collect bonus points, which can be redeemed at Indian Oil petrol/diesel outlets.

Indian Oil's tie-ups for services at petrol/diesel outlets: The Corporation has also tied up with reputed agencies like Akbarallys' for Convenio stores, with Dominos and Kamats for food courts, with ICICI Bank, Centurion Bank, etc. for ATMs to provide a pleasing retail experience to the motorists. In all these, our effort is to facilitate easier and cashless transactions so that the customers spend 'Quality Time' at our outlets.

Indian Oil's retail tie-up with private partners:

- Citibank for co-branded credit cards
- ICICI Bank, Centurion Bank and Bank of Punjab for ATMs
- Apollo Hospitals for pharmacy/Convenio stores
- Akbarallys for Convenio stores
- MTNL for telephone bill payments in Mumbai/Delhi
- Dishnet DSL for cybercafes
- JK Tyres for digital air towers
- Dominos for pizza takeaway outlets

About Pantaloon Retail (India) Limited

Pantaloon Retail (India) Limited is a leading retailer with a turnover of over Rs. 2,018.76 crore for the financial year 2005-06. Headquartered in Mumbai, the company operates through primarily the Lifestyle and Value formats through multiple delivery mechanisms and lines of business—some of them being, fashion, food, general merchandise, home, leisure and entertainment, financial services, communications and wellness. The company has stores in 30 cities across the country, constituting 3.5 million square feet of retail space. The company caters to the lifestyle segment through its 22 Pantaloons Stores and 3 Central Malls, as well as its other concepts. In Value retailing it is present through 33 Big Bazaar hypermarkets, 52 Food Bazaars and 5 Fashion Stations, and other delivery formats.

About Indian Oil

Indian Oil is the largest commercial enterprise in the country and is the highest ranked Fortune Global 500 Company in India with global rankings of 153. With 32,000 sales points, dominant refining capacity and the largest pipeline network in the country, Indian Oil has diversified into petrochemicals and upstream exploration besides gas marketing and globalization of its marketing operations. Indian Oil owns SERVO, the largest lubricant brand in the country with a staggering range of over 500 grades and 1500 formulations and which is marketed in Middle East, South-East Asia and South Asian regions. Indian Oils Indane LPG brand is one of the largest packed LPG brands in the world. In branded fuels, XtraPremium Petrol and XtraMile Diesel are already leaders in their respective categories. The Indian Oil Group of companies consists of the merged entity of IBP, stand-alone refineries CPCL, BRPL besides overseas entities Indian Oil Mauritius Ltd. and Lanka IOC Pvt. Ltd.

Tasks for the Students

Discuss the competitive strategies of different players in the oil industry, both in the government and private sector.

CASE STUDY 11

Wal-Mart

Wal-mart wants to be a welcome and positive community partner. They want to explore ongoing commitments to being a better neighbour here. They know what's needed in own backyards, they do most of their giving @ 90% at the local level. They believe community membership is a privilege. Find out how listening and learning are leading to a better Wal-Mart and a better world.

Given below is the Wal-Mart story in its own language.

They try to help wherever possible in those locations affected and believe in using their resources to help make a positive difference in people's lives. The Wal-Mart Foundation is a not-for-profit organization dedicated to giving and doing whatever they can to help improve the quality of life for their customers, address environmental issues and promote education.

The students need to understand the Wal-Mart supply chain and see how they are taking their first steps towards sustainability now, with an eye on the future of the planet, they will come to know the company better.

Their motto—Take care, Listen, Connect: Helping Families During Military Deployment. Our associates around the world are committed to supporting their local communities. They post video clips about company culture, community involvement and more. They help students and kids to become responsible towards the environment by reducing waste.

Task for the Students

Wal-Mart takes good care of its stakeholders. Discuss.

CASE STUDY

12

Subhiksha

SUBHIKSHA's Slogan

Bachat Mera Adhikar! Subhiksha Mera Abhiman—is meant to strike at the heart of middle-class Indians, who are looking for solace amidst rising prices of items of daily needs.

When R. Subramanian became an entrepreneur and started a retail chain called Subhiksha, there were not many entrepreneurs in India. In his family too, there were no entrepreneurs.

After obtaining an engineering degree from the Indian Institute of Technology, Madras, he decided to join Indian Institute of Management, Ahmedabad as he was sure about one thing—that he would not go abroad. As a consequence Subhiksha, the Chennai based, a decade old, no frills, food, grocery, pharma and telecom, discount retail chain is gearing up to spread its wings around the country to fully exploit the market potential.

Ten years after Subhiksha was set up, the retail chain had around 500 outlets all over India which Subramanian wanted to double by 2007-end. Subhiksha's story is given in their own words.

We looked at all sorts of names; and finally we chose the Sanskrit word Subhiksha *(prosperity)* because it reflects the Indian ethos and it is a word that can be understood all over India. What we were trying to do was different from the western model; our model is truly Indian. Our theme was, why pay more when you can get it for less at Subhiksha?

The rapidly expanding chain, claims to be the biggest chain in the country, is following the carpet bombing strategy for its expansion, wherein, to create maximum impact, it simultaneously launches a cluster of stores in a given geograp.

We are already India's largest retail chain store with 500-plus stores. We plan to have 1,000-plus stores by the end of this year.

India is a large country and there are still opportunities to avail of. At the moment, the thought of opening stores outside India is not tempting because there are enough opportunities in India. We may look at overseas markets too...Maybe later, after we open 2,000 or 2,500 or 3,000 stores in India.

Subhiksha, pioneered a unique form of retailing. Subhiksha's establishing a no-frills stores that does not provide air-conditioning, dazzling lighting, or a touch and feel experience to its customers.

Subhiksha has also been in step with technological advancements. The **E-Shop** facility helps customers to order their goods on the net.

If you have to stand out in the crowd and draw customers, you need to give value to the customer. That's where this concept proves useful. At Subhiksha, we provide value to the shopper. You have the feel of an Indian shop but you get added value like high-speed transaction, lesser price, free home deliveries, etc. We have not spent money on developing frills like ambience at the shop. All the same we keep the place clean and hygienic. We want to cater to the middle-class segment, who constitute the majority of shoppers.

We are not perfect. There are certainly things that people complain about us. One common complaint is unavailability of products. This happens due to different reasons and we are constantly striving to fulfil customer expectations in this regard. Another complaint is the crowd at our stores. The crowds are even bigger at festival season.

People did not seem to care what kind of a shop they bought their groceries from and whether it was air-conditioned or not.

Among other things, we found that customers were conscious of the distance of the store from their house, availability, quality and price of branded groceries

Lowest prices on everything.

It doesn't get lower than us, and IMRB international has proven this. The Indian Market Research Bureau has now come up with facts that prove that Subhiksha has the lowest prices ever! Lower prices ever! Lower than any self service store, and shockingly lower than your neighbourhood Kirana store. The survey conducted in 5 cities, Delhi, Bengaluru, Chennai, Ahemedabad, Hyderabad showed that prices at Subhkisha are a solid 6-10% lower than usual, for all your favourite brands! Read the papers, see the signs, it's out there… Subhiksha has the lowest prices, and if missing our point, you are going to end up spending a lot of money.

City	ON MRP (%)	Vs Other Supermarkets (%)	Vs Kirana (%)
Bengaluru	8.7	11.8	6.8
Delhi	14.6	6.4	9.6
Hyderabad	8.1	7.0	6.0
Ahmedabad	12.2	9.2	8.5
Chennai	13.8	6.0	6.7

Cheaper than bazaar prices on all 365 days of the year only at Subhiksha. Savings everyday on everything is a fact that you already know about Subhiksha. All your favourite brands and groceries at the lowest prices.

Why larger stores cannot be cheaper? And Subhiksha can be!

Because of the following reasons.

1. Larger stores are located in busy streets or good locations
   These areas usually have high property rates and the stores have to pay large sums of money as rentals.
2. Large stores have large spaces
   Needless to say, most large supermarkets provide ample playing space for your children, wide aisles for you to do your morning and evening walk in and of course enough space to put up film sets. We are sure you know that large spaces cost large money as well. And how do you think these stores recover their high costs? Simple- by charging you.
3. High operating cost
   Most such stores have air-conditioners which as we all know cause electricity bills to rise phenomenally. How can they offer discounts?
4. Large number of smiling staff
   How many times have you noticed the sweetly smiling staff at these supermarkets? Given that they have very little else to do, they stand and smile at you. And guess who is paying for their simle? Consumer of course.
5. No large volumes
   Most large supermarkets have few other stores in their chain. Their overall volumes are therefore relatively small. Don't get misled by their false claims. With their volumes they cannot possibly get big discounts and therefore, have to rely on buying from the local wholesale markets or middlemen. Thus, their prices are always higher.
6. Huge amount of stock
   To impress you they also keep a huge amount of stock. So many times that they themselves can't accurately keep stock of. Haven't you always wondered who picks up half of those things anyway? This of course means that their inventory costs are high as well.

And then somebody has to pay the price for double paid ads in newspapers too!

Most consumers who buy there once or twice realize that these stores just cannot offer genuinely low prices. What they do is just a sham. It is better to safeguard your hard earned money by putting it to better use than spending needlessly more at such places.

Can Mr. Retailers sustain in India. Major concerns are as follows.

1. Loss prevention and shrinkage management would be a critical area with the rapid growth of the retail networks.
2. Cost of financing is higher in India. Thus, in business where margins are low working capital management, efficient logistics & cost management becomes 'the key' operational parameter.

3. In operations management by leveraging technology, retailers in India are at a nascent stage. This would be one area of opportunity for winners of the future.
4. Paucity of trained retail personnel both at the store as well as managerial level and thus knowledge retention will prove critical.
5. In India supply chain and customer relations followed by merchandising, facilities management and vendor development are areas which have significant gaps that need to be addressed.
6. Management Accounting Systems are not dynamic enough to support better decision making and efficient management of the members of the organization.

Task for the Students

Subhiksha stores are a step ahead of small shops but do not offer any shopping frills. Considering the dynamic changes in the retailing industry, do you think that Subhiksha's Single Rating System business model is sustainable? Give reasons to support your stand along with a SWOT analysis.

CASE STUDY

13

Kinetic Honda Case

Before Kinetic Honda 100 cc scooter was introduced in the Indian market, all the other scooters looked almost alike. Kinetic was a differentiated scooter, because of its sleek looks, aerodynamic styling and its manufacturers felt these attributes were enough to outsell other scooters in the market like Bajaj, LML. However, the scooter sales did not pick up the envisaged volumes in the market.

In April 1986, the position was as follows:

- Kinetic Honda had sold 11,000 scooters with 2.1 % of market share.
- Bajaj Auto lead with 3,80,000 scooters sold with 73% market share.
- LML sold 1,09,000 scooters with market share of 21%

Kinetic had launched their scooter with unique features:

1. Electronic start
2. Automatic gear shift
3. Automatic choke
4. Built-in turning indicators
5. Wind tested streamlines design
6. Plastic bright colours

The market survey conducted by the marketers indicated that the reasons for poor market acceptance were as given below:

- Unfamiliar design
- Was considered lightweight and therefore flimsy
- Power of the scooter at 100 cc was considered less strong than Bajaj's 150 cc scooter
- Electronic was also looked at with suspicion as it was taken only as a ladies scooter.

To correct the misconceptions the marketers, had to physically demonstrate to the buyers:

1. Scooters body was metallic and not that of plastic
2. In 1988, several scooter including, Bajaj Super 150 cc, LML, Kinetic Honda Vespa 150 were put on a gruelling 20,000 km test run

Kinetic Honda was adjudged the best scooter in that test.

Massive Advertising campaign was launched with facts of the test and sales increased.

Main objectives of advertising are, to increase profitable sales, improve market share and the brand image. Brand image builds brand equity, which in turn brings brand loyalty.

Kinetic Honda won three more rallies and reached the high Khardungla pass.

Kinetic Honda got established as a premium product for a customer who is a social somebody with age group 25-40 years, income of Rs. 15000 pm.

Customers of Kinetic Honda are different from the customers of Bajaj and LML as they are upward mobile, quality conscious, not willing to settle for less than the best. Market share has improved to 11%.

NOW THEY SAY THE FUTURE BELONGS TO US!

CASE STUDY 14

Shoppers' Stop

Investors with a long-term horizon and modest return expectations in the near-term can consider investment in the Shoppers' Stop stock, which offers a quality exposure to the retail sector.

With a strong focus on lifestyle retailing (apparel, accessories, footwear, furnishing, and so on), Shoppers' Stop is best placed to capitalize on the surge in discretionary spending among the listed players.

An option to buy out a 51 per cent stake in "Hypercity," the hypermarket (large stores that sell a wide range of products from food to apparel and consumer durables at low prices) venture of its promoter group, K. Raheja Corp, provides an opportunity to the retailer to participate in that high growth segment as well, once past the teething problems.

Valuations

In its first year as a listed player, Shoppers' Stop has surprised both with its impressive performance and its transparency/governance. At current levels, valuations factor in an annual growth rate of about 35 per cent over the next five years. Such growth rates do not appear unattainable for the retailer, at least over the next three years, even as it continues to roll out new stores. Significant growth could come in after 2008, if it decides to invest in the hypermarket venture. Most of its newly-opened stores are also likely to turn profitable by then, which would have a favourable impact on earnings growth.

Shares of Shoppers' Stop Ltd. soared on the bourses on the day of its listing today. The stock, which made its debut on the BSE and the NSE, started trade at Rs. 335.50. It rose to an intra-day high of Rs. 419.80, up by over 76 per cent from its allotment price of Rs. 238.

Though the stock was expected to have a strong opening, the strength of trade today did take the market by surprise. Several brokers attributed this to the lack of quality stocks in the retail segment. Pantaloons and Trent are the two other listed companies in the sector and both have had a significant runup in the last 8-10 months. The sector is poised for growth and this interest is reflected in the stock, said an analyst.

Shoppers' Stop had entered the capital market with its maiden public offering of 69 lakh equity shares of Rs. 10 each with a price band of Rs. 210 and Rs. 250 a equity share. The issue opened for bids on April 28 and closed on May 4.

"We are committed to create a world-class organization and are focussed on creating India's No.1 retail chain. As part of our aggressive growth plans, we opened two new stores recently—one in Pune and the 18th store of the company in Juhu, Mumbai. We will work tirelessly towards creating value for our existing as well as new investors which totals to more than 56,000," the CEO and MD of Shoppers' Stop, Mr. B.S. Nagesh, was quoted in a company press release.

This marriage can never take place! Not so long ago, this would have been the normal refrain from any status conscious Indian parent whose child was planning to marry someone from the retail industry. This was because the retail industry had a very 'low image'. Most retail outlets were 'mom and pop' outlets with a family person behind the cash counter and a few 'not-so-smart' boys milling in the outlet waiting for the customers. Most retail outlets were the epitome of 'customer unfriendliness, shoddy product display and a singular lack of variety or brand names to choose from'.

Not so any longer. Today, a career in the retail industry is on par with other careers. Products of prestigious business schools, who once shunned the industry, are eager to get into the thick of action. Retail marketing has become a specialized course in many business schools. Retail outlets have become 'family outing' experience, with entire families spending many hours browsing through shelves displaying alluring products. Clearly, the retail revolution has hit the country.

The credit for this change of heart can be laid at the doorstep of a man who, with his handsome looks and boyish face, could have easily become a leading hero of the Kannada film industry. This man is none other than, **B.S. Nagesh, chief executive officer of the Shoppers' Stop** chain of departmental stores. Nagesh entered the retail industry at a time when the concept of 'organized departmental stores' was considered a non-starter in this country. Prior to his entry there were some attempts made by others in the past, to set up departmental stores of the type one encountered abroad. They all died a premature death and perpetuated the myth that 'foreign style' departmental stores would never succeed in India. One can never hazard a guess as to why the previous attempts failed and why Shoppers' Stop took off the way it did. Was it the fact that the country just became ready for the retail concept? Were the previous attempts badly organized? Was there a big gap between customer expectations and its fulfilment? Or, was Nagesh just *plain lucky*? It could be a combination of all these factors. But attributing the last factor to Nagesh's success would be doing a great disservice to the man.

Born in Bengaluru forty-one years ago, Nagesh has spent his early years in Gorakhpur, where his father, who was working with the Railways, was posted. He did his schooling in Bareilly and acquired a degree in management from BHU, Varanasi after finishing college from Gorakhpur.

After getting the management degree, he worked with Blow Plast Ltd. and Orson Electronics, before joining Carona Ltd., where his thirst for retail was ignited. At Carona, which was the country's second largest footwear company, he was the youngest manager in the hierarchy and had over 100 stores assigned to him. Though he was in trade sales, he really moved the retail way by encouraging secondary sales to pump up primary trade sales. This saw the man stand behind many a counter at the retail level, which helped convince the secondary tier that his involvement was genuine–thus, boosting primary sales.

After having handled over a hundred retail stores of 500 and odd sq. ft. each, he had a burning desire to set up and run a huge departmental store of 50,000 sq. ft. He got the opportunity to realize his dream when a head hunter called him, presumably on the reference of his mentor, Mr. Rajiv Sahai, currently a senior executive with a leading entertainment company—and to whom he had mentioned his desire. The head hunter took him to a real estate tycoon based in Mumbai. This tycoon had a huge property lying vacant and had the intention of making commercial use of this property. For some reason this tycoon believed that a huge retail departmental store at this property would be the way out. The tycoon was none other than Mr. G.L. Raheja, the country's undisputed king of real estate. This belief led Mr. Raheja to meet Nagesh. And, the rest is history.

True to his nature, Nagesh refuses to take sole credit for building Shoppers' Stop into what it is today. While the arclights for the success are on him, he is very clear that the credit for the same is to be shared with two groups:

- first the promoters of Shoppers' Stop and Mr. G.L. Raheja, in particular, for having reposed their total faith in him and his team and allowing them to make mistakes; and,
- his team, which has stuck by him during the critical phase of growth to make the store a thrilling shopping experience.

Starting off with the group as a general manager, Nagesh walked the length and breadth of the existing retail stores in the country, virtually taking in every inch of their stores. His toughest act was to get the right people into the company. For retail, as it existed then, was way below the status ladder for boys and girls to take on as careers. He still remembers the time he had to book a whole wedding hall and invite the parents of prospective candidates to tell them about the project. He had to convince them that if they could send their children aboard planes to be stewards and stewardesses, send them to five star hotels to be front office personnel, there was no reason for them to feel belittled by their children manning the counters at a superstore like Shoppers' Stop. Obviously, his charm worked. He did manage to recruit the right people and today, nearly 65% of the front end sales staff are graduates. This is way above the global benchmark where most of the front-end sales staff are just high school qualified.

He has gone a long way since then. The company is now a 850-people organization with plans to become a 30-store organization in five years time. Already the company has a store in all the prominent locations of Mumbai, Bengaluru, Hyderabad, New Delhi and Jaipur. He has been adequately rewarded for this stupendous growth by being promoted to chief executive officer. If imitation is the best form of flattery, then Nagesh can justifiably feel very flattered. Many an industrial group are following Shoppers' Stop's footsteps into the retail arena and the industry is seeing a lot of action in terms of investment and people.

Not only that, the very people who kept him waiting for hours on end outside their offices, are the ones to come to his office to do business with him. The very associations, who denied him entry to trade fairs, are falling head over heels to get him to be the chief guest at their functions.

So what is in store for him in the future? Despite the success, he believes there is a lot more to be done. He has great plans to make Shoppers' Stop a global player in the retail industry. He was already working towards that end and has made the right moves in that direction.

He is ensuring that the group does its bit towards the very society that has allowed it grow and succeed. He plans to take the group into education for children and do it professionally in the same manner as he has done for Shoppers' Stop. He also plans to set up a training institute for retail management, and hopes that this will become the foremost of such institutes in the country.

As he rests briefly after a successful divestment of nearly 14% of the equity in favour of strategic investors who had queued up at his doorstep, he reflects on the unfinished agenda ahead of him. Now that the pressures of daily operation have eased a trifle, Nagesh finds time for his family of wife, Shailaja – who is a teacher by profession – and two daughters Pooja (13) and Pallavi (7). Though he does not openly say so, the expressions on his face, when he speaks of them, clearly shows that but for their stoic acceptance of his long hours away from home, at work, he would not have achieved this success. Now he hopes that he would be able to give them more of his time, and indulge in a little for himself too. He is a very keen sportsman and a badminton player, who had to give it all up in the pursuit of success at Shoppers' Stop. He hopes he will be able to play a few games once in a way.

But is this all going to reduce the pace at which the man has kept himself going? One look at his energetic frame makes one wonder whether he will. But then, with all the plans that he has for the future, the old saying may well hold true: "...... and I have miles to go before I sleep!!".

She's a shopper as well as an observer of what consumers buy. As a consumer, she swears by Giorgio Armani for clothes and Prada for bags. "As a customer, I go for understated and subdued designs. It's getting harder to get them day by day as every brand is becoming loud and big in their quest to talk to customers," she confesses.

And when she is not shopping for herself, Radha Chadha keenly observes the increasing consumption of luxury brands by the masses. "In 1997, when I moved to Hong Kong, everyone from secretaries to accountants came with Prada shopping bags. It was fascinating to see the demand for the luxury brands," she says.

All that and a whole lot of other observations have been encapsulated in a book, *The Cult of Luxury Brand*, which she has co-authored with Paul Husband. The consumption of luxury brands, according to Chadha, is growing because of the socio-economic changes sweeping across Asia.

"Now it's respectable to make money and show it. In my generation, it wasn't so—people used to cringe at the thought of ostentatious display of wealth," she says, adding that in India, too, the trend is evident, though it still has some catching up to do compared to markets like China.

Chadha believes India is in phase two of the evolutionary stage, where Indian consumers have the money, and their craving for luxury goods is now getting satiated. "The retail platform needed to showcase luxury brands is getting established across the country."

Chadha says that markets like China and Japan are currently going through a phenomenon called 'Luxeplosion'—the explosion of luxury products. "Japan is going through it now, and China will overtake it in a decade," she explains. The explosion, she says, is a contradiction, one which keeps the premium image but is no longer exclusive to a select few.

"Luxury goods are ensuring that they are available to the masses. There are entry-level price points for consumers to experience," she says. The Indian market, according to her, is a clean slate to write the rules for luxury brands.

"In Asian markets, there are no rules and consumers have the money. So it's not just the western brands that can create the market, but even Asian brands can attempt to do it. It's a question of who moves first," she says.

Bengaluru: Shoppers' Stop is planning to enter the luxury retail segment with large format properties retailing a range of products from many of well-known luxury brands.

Sources close to the K Raheja Group company said Shoppers' Stop has already signed up properties in Bengaluru, Delhi and Mumbai for this format. In Bengaluru, a deal is said to have been signed with the Prestige Group and the UB Group for the 1.2 lakh sq. ft. retail space in city centre UB City.

Susil Dungarwal, head of Prestige Group's mall business, said he could not comment on the matter. Shoppers' Stop managing director B.S. Nagesh said the company was in talks for the UB City space but nothing had been finalized. UK departmental store chain Debenhams was also negotiating for that space, through its Indian franchisee Planet Retail Holdings. But that appears to have fallen through.

Shoppers' Stops new luxury retail concept will, as per sources, showcase more than 40 global luxury brands, including Louis Vitton, Gucci, Zegna, Hugo Boss, YSL, Mont Blanc and Christian Dior. Each store will be spread across 1.2 lakh to 1.5 lakh sq. ft. The company will invest Rs. 100 crore into this model in the first year, sources said.

Shoppers' Stop already has speciality retail formats like Home Stop, Crossword (books and music) and Hypercity. It has entered into licensing agreements with international brands like Mothercare and MAC, and is said to be in talks with Spanish fashion brand Zara.

Mumbai: Shoppers' Stop Ltd. (SSL), a leading retail chain, is entering the capital market with an initial public offer of 69.46 lakh equity shares of Rs. 10 each. The company has fixed a price band of Rs. 210-250. The issue opens on April 27 and closes on May 3.

The company will use the proceeds of the issue to finance its expansion plans, including setting up of 11 more stores over the next two years in Bengaluru, Delhi, Noida, Mumbai, Pune and Hyderabad. A part of the proceeds will be used for renovation and expansion of existing stores. The cost of setting up the 11 stores is Rs. 110-120 crores and the renovation of three existing stores around Rs. 15 crore.

SSL is a pioneer in setting up nation-wide chain of large format departmental stores in India and has been promoted by K. Raheja Corp Group, one of the leading groups in the business of real estate development and hotels in India. The retail chain has grown from a single store in Mumbai with an area of 2,800 sq. ft to 16 locations across India occupying an aggregate area of 750,000 sq. ft.

The promoter group shareholding will come down to 67 per cent post-issue from almost 80 per cent. In 2003-04, SSL's gross retail sales were Rs. 395.30 crore with the operating profit at Rs. 24.60 crores and net profit Rs. 12 crores.

New Delhi: India's never-ending appetite for entertainment has found a new extension in cyberspace. Close to 66% of metropolitan Indian netizens are now indulging in various forms of online entertainment, ranging from games to downloading music or videos, while financial activities on the Net or even shopping appear to have been relegated to the margins, according to a report by Forrester Research.

However, in pure percentage terms, India trails neighbouring China where 89% of the urban online consumers indulge in entertainment activities on the net.

The Forrester report, The Asian Way: One PC Per Three Generations, notes that in the case of metropolitan China, Hong Kong, and metropolitan India, entertainment activities were much more prevalent than online shopping.

"With 89% of urban Chinese online consumers, 80% of Hong Kong consumers, and 66% of urban Indian online consumers engaging in entertainment activities online, marketers can find consumers on game, music, and video sites," Forrester said. As the action hots up in cyberspace, marketers too are taking stock of the new medium and responding with separate Internet strategies. "India is a robust market growing at around 7.4% compared to a paltry 2.4% growth in the US. Blogs, gaming and other forms of entertainment are a big opportunity for branding for Indian marketers," says Harish Bijoor, a marketing consultant.

Mass brands such as Motorola, Pepsi (Bluebillion), and even FMCG behemoth like Hindustan Lever Limited (Sunsilk Gang of Girls) have been quick to adapt to the Internet. "Our choice of media is changing as our communication is directed to the youth. That is where the internet plays a huge part," says Lloyd Mathias, marketing director, Motorola India.

According to Forrester, the percentage of urban online consumers in India, who are engaged in financial actvities including bidding or selling in online auctions, checking stock quotes, trading stock, paying bills, checking bank accounts and making bank transfers, was less than 10%, and those indulging in online shopping even lesser (less than 5%).

South Koreans also show a preference for online entertainment, with 73% of online consumers seeking fun activities online. By comparison, 54% of South Koreans engage in financial activities online and 62% in online shopping. Online Aussies, on the other hand, preferred financial activities to entertainment 88% versus 74%, while also showing tremendous engagement with online shopping at 69%. Japan was almost as invested in online finance as it is in entertainment and shopping.

Shoppers' Stop deployed various technologies for the roll-out of HyperCITY, a one-of-its-kind hypermarket. From a technology standpoint, the challenge was to deploy technologies that had never been used in India before. Further, the company wanted to have common applications across all retail formats.

HyperCITY was a completely new retail format that the Shoppers' Stop group had embarked on in order to diversify and capitalize the immense retail potential for hypermarkets. The group started selecting the technologies for this venture around August 2004. The technology selection involved acquiring several pieces of software and hardware.

Says Unni Krishnan T M, Customer Care Associate & CTO, Solutions & Technology Team, "We first focussed on closing the enterprise software applications like merchandising, advanced replenishment, Point-of-Sale—PoS. Then we started focussing on hardware, where we tried to look at what is available in the local market and then searched across the global to find technology that will provide us the strategy differentiator. Thus, we sourced technology from this point, the group took a strategic call to have a common application across all retail formats after an extensive evaluation. The company is among the early adopters to use the IBM i550 performance server in the industry, on which the JDA-MMS and PoS application resides. In order to optimize the hardware cost, four enterprise applications and six retail formats are running on a single server.

The K. Raheja Corporation group of companies laid the foundation of Shoppers' Stop on October 27, 1991. One of India's biggest hospitality and real estate entities, the Group entered the lifestyle segment with Shoppers' Stop.

A Challenging Task

Shoppers' Stop having been successful in lifestyle and books retail formats, subsequently decided to branch out into the hypermarket format. The initiative was challenging in itself because the use of state of the art technology was never used in the Indian retailing segment before. The company had to implement a set of technologies from scratch. In addition, the selection and deployment of technologies had to bring in efficiencies, productivity and justify RoI requirements.

"Some of our biggest challenges involved sourcing this technology and building it in India. This has never been done before in India, hence, we had to develop the entire solution on our own. In many instances, we had to provide guidance to the manufacturer or developers of the technology in building the solution," says Unni Krishnan.

He explains further, "Our key focus area was to cater to the A & B target market segment with a hypermarket format. Today, HyperCITY-Malad store is the most successful hypermarket format in India. We went all out to bring technology that has previously never existed in India or never used in large numbers. The entire shopping experience for the customer is unique and highly satisfying; they don't have to face indefinite and long queues. The check out process is a breeze."

It is noteworthy that the store achieved one million customer entries in 90 days creating a turnover of Rs. 1 crore in a day mark and now Rs. 2 crore in a weekend.

Shoppers' Stop is a leader in the Indian retail sector and one of the pioneers in setting up large format departmental stores in India. It has a national presence, with over 7 lakh square feet of retail space with stores in Mumbai (7), Delhi, Bengaluru (3), Hyderabad, Jaipur, Pune (2), Kolkata (2), Gurgaon, Chennai and Ghaziabad. The chain stocks over 200 international and Indian brands.

From its inception, Shoppers' Stop has progressed from being a single brand shop to becoming a fashion and lifestyle store for the family.

It is the only Indian member of IGDS (Intercontinental Group of Departmental stores) along with 29 other global retailers. Shoppers' Stop has been awarded Super Brand status 2003/2004 by an independent Superbrands Council comprising the most eminent professionals from marketing and advertising out of a national list of 711 brands across 98 categories.

Technologies and Products Implementation

This merchandising management system runs on the IBM i550 server on top of DB2. The application is run centrally and accessed by stores over leased lines, VPN, RF links or broadband connections.

Products/Technologies	Purpose
JDA-WinDSS (Windows Distributed Store System)	
JDA E3	This replenishment system runs on the IBM i550 server atop DB2. E3 is managed and run centrally at Shoppers' Stop's corporate office.
I-scan	Self-scanning shopping cart.
360° bio-optic	Scanners for security purpose.
Networking	Wireless for PoS, price checking and stock taking.
Handhelds	Stock taking and price checking.
Next-gen Replenishment and Scanning	

The key technology deployed in HyperCITY is JDA E3-an auto replenishment application that helps to replenish stock back to the shelf at a rapid pace. The technology helps in generating purchase orders with right economic order characteristic (EoQ), min-max quantity rules, order lead times, inventory carrying cost and so on. E3 enables the next-generation in precision replenishment. Another interesting technology deployed is the I-Scan (Symbol Technologies, New York) that allows the customer to scan the merchandise as they pick the products off-the-shelf, thus saving them significant amount of shopping time. Once the shopping is completed, they can handover the device to the customer service desk and can cash-out quickly.

"For I-Scan, even today companies like Microsoft are still experimenting and exploring such technologies. Symbol Technologies themselves were surprised as to how we were ingenious and innovative in our effort. They originally never expected this hardware to be used in this manner," says Unni Krishnan.

I-Scan also has small bar code scanner. From a RoI perspective, the company has used platform technology concept to apply a single hardware for many users. I-Scan has four-plus applications like inventory scanner, price check, self-check, self-check-out PoS and warehousing receiving.

Implementation in a Nutshell	
Company	Shopper's Stop
Solution	Roll-out of HyperCITY using technologies like JDA-MMS, JDA-WinDSS, JDA E3 and I-Scan.
Commencement of project	Jan. 2005
Completion of project	May 2006
Investments made	Rs. 4 to 5 crore
Challenges	Use of state-of-the-art technology was never used in the Indian retailing space before and to make customer shopping experience unique and interesting.

Major benefits	The store achieved one million customer footfalls within 90 days of the project implementation. In terms of the RoI, HyperCITY has crossed Rs. 2 crore on a single day of trading; the Rs. 1 crore per day mark was hit several times. A million transactions have been processed in the first three months.

Jury View

The implementation is unique and they are the first to implement it in the Indian market. It is commendable that a company takes the risk of experimenting with new things,

- Shoppers' Stop has done a fabulous job but there is always room for improvement. Whatever they did resulted in value addition for its customers resulting in good business for the company. In terms of strategy, they were perfect. In terms of operations, there is some room for improvement. Jury members focussed on innovation and uniqueness of the project. We did not go into the nitty-gritties of operations. There might be more things to add to the project in the future. Shoppers' Stop is amongst the first companies in India to have a hypermarket with above 35 PoS machines in a single store. Customer who walks into the store benefits from a fast cash-out process.
- The company's initiative is focused on customers, saving them a significant amount of shopping time by scanning the merchandise as they pick products off the shelf. This is the first reason for Shoppers' Stop to win and the technology deployed, which is the I-Scan (Symbol Technologies, New York) is perhaps the second reason.

Fast Cash-out Process

Shoppers' Stop becomes the first company to set up a hypermarket in India with more than 35 Point of Sale (PoS) machines in a single store. Customers benefit from a speedy cash-out experience. For this, the company invested in advanced 360 degree scanners (Metrologic USA), using the same technology as TESCO. The model used by the company is Metrologic's latest bioptic scanner with high throughput and a slim profile for seated and space constrained checkout environments. The company's receipt printing devices had been extensively tested to ensure fast speed (20 seconds to print 60 items).

Future Plans

The company will be rolling out E3 to its other retail formats namely, Crossword and Shoppers' Stop. The I-scan technology is being leveraged for fresh applications at Shoppers' Stop. On the heels of a successful deployment of this technology at HyperCITY, the company is exploring other technologies from Symbol Technologies.

Task for the Students

Organize a SWOT Analysis of the company and give your recommendations for its improvement.

CASE STUDY

15

Bata Factory Store

Bata Factory Store is a new Bata sales formula, addressed to the family, to offer the customer choice, practicality, service and real savings with respect to normal market prices.

This Means

- On an area of more than 1,000 m², the stores present a collection of 10,000 different models of footwear, a large sports department, a play area for the children, casual clothing, luggage and accessories;
- The assortment is arranged to supplement the Bata collection with end of season products and special offers;
- Store layout and internal communications are very carefully studied, to give the customer the utmost support in choosing from this vast assortment.

Strong Points

Large sales area.

Wide assortment

10,000 pairs of footwear in the men's, women's, children's and sports categories together with a wide selection of clothing, luggage, bags and accessories.

Large sports department with the best international brands.

Real savings with respect to normal retail prices.

Department selling end of season and sample products at below-cost rates.

BATA India Ltd. is endeavouring to transform itself "from a manufacturing company to a market-driven company". The idea behind the exercise is to garner a larger share of the domestic footwear market in the organized sector, according to Mr A.L. Mudaliar, Chairman of Bata India.

Mr. Mudaliar told shareholders at the company's 68th AGM held that Bata India's future and profitability were dependent upon growth in sales volumes. Marketing efforts would be stepped up especially in semi-urban and rural areas. He was confident that customers would "feel the need to visit Bata shops as the growing preference was to move towards branded products".

Quality would be accorded top priority and "no shoe shall leave the factory without the quality stamp". Retail stores would be upgraded even as wholesale depots would be set up in smaller towns and semi-urban areas. A technical knowhow and services agreement has been signed with Bata of Toronto to enable the Indian outfit "to draw on the international experience".

Media campaigns would be aimed at conveying to customers the "value of Bata products". Celebrity endorsements would be resorted to as and when needed. In fact, promotion of the mass-volume, low-priced Sundrop range—endorsed by filmstar Rani Mukherjee—had been a great success with sales in that particular shoe category going up by over 500 per cent.

Open to imports from China: The priority, according to him, was to fully utilize the installed capacity at its factories. Outsourcing would be resorted if it worked out cheaper. It was also open to the idea of importing shoes—mostly from China—if it worked out cheaper, when compared with local manufacturing costs. "We shall import shoes, if good shoes are available cheap". In fact, test marketing of imported Chinese shoes has already proved to be successful.

While retail sales went up by five per cent in 2000, the company had to reckon with some setback in the wholesale business "which had been restricted as a means to recover customer outstandings."

In 2000, Bata India recorded an income of Rs. 761.29 crore, down from Rs. 774.62 crore the previous year. The profit before tax stood at Rs. 25.3 crore, substantially down from Rs. 48.08 crore in 1999. The profit after tax was Rs. 15.59 crore against Rs. 30.45 crore in 1999. A dividend of Rs. 1.50 per share of Rs. 10 has been declared for 2000. It thus maintained the dividend rate of 1999.

The company was founded in 1894 in Zlín (then Austro-Hungarian Empire, today the Czech Republic) by Tomáš Bat'a (pron. toh-mahsh bah-tyah) whose family had been cobblers for generations. A large order from the army, military shoes and rising demand for them, during World War I started rapid growth and small manufacture turned into modern industrial concern, one of the first mass producers of shoes.

Tomáš Bat'a was recognised for his social conscience, establishing housing, cinemas and advancement programmes for his employees. The phrase "work collectively, live individually" is one of his sayings. Bat'a recognized the potential of large-scale production, and was often called the "Henry Ford of Eastern Europe." He saw technology as a means of progress, and wanted to make shoes as cheaply as possible so that the greatest number of people could access them.

In 1932, Tomáš Bat'a died in a plane crash at the Zlín airport (attempting to take-off under bad weather conditions) and his half-brother Jan Antonín Bat'a became head of the company.

At the time of Tomáš' death, the Bat'a company employed 16,560 people, maintained 1,645 shops and 25 enterprises. Most of what Tomáš had built was centralized in Bohemia-Moravia (15,770 employees, 1,500 shops, 25 enterprises) and Slovakia (250 employees and 2 enterprises). The total international contribution to the Bat'a organization at the time of Tomas' death consisted of 20 international enterprises, 132 shops, and 790 employees.

Jan Antonín Bat'a

Under Jan Antonín Bat'a the company grew quickly, continued its expansion throughout Europe, North America, Asia, and North Africa. Zlín accommodated the largest part of the company, with manufacturing and headquarters.

Apart from shoes, Bat'a also diversified into other areas (tyres, toys, plastic fibres, etc.).

Thirties and Forties

Jan Bat'a expanded the Bohemian and Moravian part of the business, more than doubling its size to 38,000 employees, 2,200 shops, and 70 enterprises. In Slovakia, he grew the business from 250 employees to 12,340 and 8 enterprises.

In the face of a worldwide depression, Jan Bat'a (through his vision and skill) expanded the company more than sixfold its original size throughout Czechoslovakia and the world. From the time of his brother's death in 1932 to 1942, he grew the Bat'a organization to 105,770 employees.

During the 30's imports from Czechoslovakia ultimately became too expensive due to the economic crisis in Europe at the time. Jan Antonín also established subsidiaries in several foreign countries (for example, in Brazil, Britain and Canada).

Bata-villes

Company policy was to set up villages around the factories for the workers and to supply schools and welfare.

These villages include Batadorp in the Netherlands, Bat'ovany (present-day Partizánske) and Svit in Slovakia, Bat'ov (nowadays Bahòák, part of Otrokovice) in the Czech Republic, Borovo-Bata (nowadays Borovo Naselje, part of Vukovar in Croatia then in Kingdom of Yugoslavia), Bataville in Lorraine, East of France, Batawa in Canada, East Tilbury in Essex, England, Batapur in Pakistan and Batanagar and Bataganj in India.

The company which established itself in India in 1931 started manufacturing shoes there, in Batanagar, in 1936.

In 1922, the first Bata shop abroad opened in the Netherlands, in 1933, construction began on the Bata shoe factory in Best, in the Dutch province of Brabant, at the intersection of the railway tracks leading to Eindhoven and the Wilhelmina Canal located nearby. There was an abundance of inexpensive and hard-working labourers in the Brabant countryside.

The British "Bata-villes" in East Tilbury and Maryport inspired the documentary "Bata-ville: We Are Not Afraid of the Future".

During the War

After Germany occupied the rest of pre-war Czechoslovakia (15 March 1939) Jan Antonín Bat'a, who left the country with his family after a brief time in jail after the Nazi occupation, tried to save as much as possible, subduing to the plans of Germans as well as supporting financially the exile government led by Edvard Beneš.

An episode: A Bat'a-owned Lockheed plane was flown out of Czechoslovakia 2 days before the Nazi occupation. The plane made it to Britain where it was dismantled and shipped to Canada.

Foreign factories were separated from mother company and ownership of plants in Czech lands was transferred to one member of the family.

Jan Antonín Bat'a stayed in the Americas from 1939-1940, but as America entered the war, he felt it would be safer for his co-workers and their families back in occupied Czechoslovakia if he left the United States.

At the moment he left the protection of the United States, the British placed him on the "black list." It is believed that the communist influence on the Beneš' exile government was behind this. The official reason for this was Mr. Bat'a's inability to pay a demand by the British government amounting to 2,50,000 pounds sterling (a huge sum of money at the time). The United Kingdom insisted on the huge bail due to the fact that Mr. Bat'a was the owner of largest industrial concern in occupied Czechoslovakia, located in enemy territory and employing more than 40,000 Czechs and Slovaks.

During the war, Jan Bat'a helped hundreds of Jewish families to escape from Czechoslovakia, sending them all over the world throughout the Bat'a organization and beyond the Nazi's reach. During the war, among other patriotic deeds, Jan Bat'a devised a plan to save more than 1,00,000 of his countrymen from Nazi concentration camps by setting up plans for a Czech/Slovak infrastructure buildout plan for a highway and aqueduct system. This frustrated the Nazi decrees that took unemployed Czechs and Slovaks to concentration camps in Germany and elsewhere. The road and aqueduct system envisioned by Mr. Bat'a was based on his book entitled, "Building a nation of 40,000,000" (circa 1938).

During the war Jan Bat'a was also the largest contributor to the Czech cause prior to Munich and after. Even though he disagreed with the pro-Soviet politics of Edvard Beneš and Jan Masaryk, he gave monetary support to them during the war. More than 250 pilots were trained by Jan Bat'a's organization in preparation for the German invasion, many of whom served as pilots or airmen in the RAF.

AFTER THE WAR

Communist Czechoslovakia

After the war Jan Antonín Bat'a attempted (unsuccessfully) to purge his name of the accusations against him.

Members of the family started to sue one another over ownership of the company; mutual hatred among branches of the family lasted for decades.

In 1945, the company was nationalized as a part of large-scale nationalization programme in Czechoslovakia.

In spite of incredible odds and a political climate that had put the machinery in motion to nationalize all large businesses, Jan Bat'a fought against the 64 crimes that the communists had accused him of. And in fact, the jury at the time, composed mostly of socialists and communists found Jan A. Bat'a innocent of all 64 charges. The verdict enraged the communist judge, who immediately added two new charges, declared Jan Bat'a guilty, then used the guilty finding as a reason to confiscate all Bat'a properties in Czechoslovakia and sentenced Mr. Bat'a to 15 years of hard labour in absentia.

After the communist party took all power (1948) it tried to suppress all memory of Tomáš and Jan A. Bat'a. Bat'as were portrayed as ruthless capitalists, exploiting workers in pursuit of higher profit. The company was renamed to *Svit* and Zlín to *Gottwaldov* (after the leader of communist party). The Svit factory concentrated on the domestic market. During the following decades its ability to compete and its technological infrastructure declined due to under-investment and weak management.

Bat'a Shoes' Former Headquarters in North York in 2007

Bata Shoes' former headquarters in North York is a historic building dating to the 1960s designed by architect John Parkin. It was scheduled to be demolished after 2005 and replaced by an Islamic cultural centre after being denied historical status. The Bata family and the company have founded Bata Shoe Museum in Toronto, supported Trent University, where the *Thomas J. Bata Library* bears Bata's name and Tomáš Bat'a University in Zlín.

The organizations abroad became *Bata Shoe Company* and were led by Thomas J. Bat'a (Tomáš Bat'a Junior), son of Tomáš Bat'a. In 1960, the headquarters were moved to Toronto, Canada and the company grew significantly. Since 2002, it is led by Thomas G. Bat'a, grandson of Tomáš Bat'a.

Present

After the global economic changes in 1990s the company closed almost all its manufacturing factories in developed countries (USA, France, United Kingdom) this caused the elimination of thousands of jobs and it stayed only in retail business there. In developing countries still run manufacturing, for example in Zimbabwe's third city of Gweru, it is the biggest shoe manufacturer in Southern Africa outside of South Africa.

The company is currently headquartered in Lausanne, Switzerland, with 4 business units:

- **Bata Europe**, Lausanne
- **Bata Asia Pacific-Africa**, Singapore
- **Bata Latin America**, Mexico
- **Bata North America**, Toronto

Current shoe brands are:

- **Bata** (Bat'a in former Czechoslovakia)

- **Bata Premium** (handcrafted dress shoes)
- **Bata Industrial** (safety footwear)
- **Bubblegummers** (children's)
- **Power** (sports shoes and boots)
- **Marie Claire** (women's)

According to Bata, in 2007 the company serves 1 million customers per day, employs over 40,000 people, operates 4,600 retail stores, manages a retail presence in over 50 countries and runs 40 production facilities across 26 countries [low cost labour].

Czechoslovakia After 1989

After the "Velvet Revolution" in November 1989, Thomas J. Bat'a arrived as soon as December 1989. He was warmly welcomed by the population remembering his father and uncle.

The Czechoslovak government offered him investments into the ailing Svit. Since companies "nationalized" before 1948 were not returned to original owners, the state went on to own Svit and "privatized" it during voucher privatization. Its low ability to compete in the free market led to decline and in 2000 Svit went bankrupt.

Nowadays, **Bat'a a.s.** (the official name of the Czech subsidiary) is mainly a trading business. Apart from shoe stores, it also runs a small production facility in Dolní Nìmèí, a shoe museum in Zlín and Bat'a Foundation (*Nadace Tomáše Bati*), which supports cultural and educational projects. The main street in Zlín and its university are both named after Tomáš Bat'a.

Bata Primary School in Gweru, Zimbabwe

It was built in 1955 and now counts 16 classrooms from Grade 1 to 7 with 26 qualified teachers attending to 884 students per year. It is a fully fleshed Grade 1 School which is wholly run and supported by the Zimbabwe Bata Shoe Company according to the statutory requirements of the Ministry of Education, Sports and Culture.

The results of school at the Grade 7 national examination for the last 10 years average 98.9% pass rate, which makes it one of the best schools among 600 schools nationwide. This is a clear testimony to the effectiveness of the education provided.

The curriculum includes all subjects as per government requirements as well as extracurricular activities such as drama and debate, rugby, swimming, or music, for example. The school also undertakes educational tour to places of educational value in an attempt to marry theory with practice. The school takes advantage of the nationwide location of the Bata shops in that through the retail management, Bata personnel in visited areas arrange and prepare for the school visits.

CASE STUDY

16

Maruti Retail

In a bid to increase its sales from rural India, the country's largest car maker, Maruti Udyog Ltd., is offering over 2.1 million functionaries in panchayats (local self-governing bodies in villages) its cars at special discounts.

The offer, titled 'Mera Sapna—Meri Maruti', retails the Maruti 800, the Alto and the Omni at a cash discount of Rs. 5,000, Rs. 4,000 and Rs. 3,000, respectively, to panchayat functionaries, who are considered to be influential figures in rural India.

These discounts are in addition to other sops like zero insurance already available in rural markets. The scheme has been launched in Haryana and will go all-India in a few months.

The car maker is also considering offering exclusive after sales service and convenient payment options.

To combat hardening interest rates on car loans, Maruti has tied up a retail finance pact with 14,000 branches of 196 regional rural banks as well as Mahindra Finance and Magma Leasing for first-time buyers in rural markets. These loans will cost 7-8 per cent.

In the first phase, Maruti has identified 2,00,000 representatives of the Zilla Parishad and the Panchayat Samiti to sell the cars. The target is to sell 15,000 units in the next few months.

MUL executives claim the initial impact of the drive has been felt in the 10 per cent increase in sales of the Maruti 800 in April this year. Sales of the Maruti 800 slid for the past 11 months, but the company reversed the trend and sold 6,324 units in April this year.

Rural markets accounted for over 35 per cent of MUL's total domestic sales of 6,35,629 vehicles in 2006-07. The sharp rise in interest rates would soon end the party for the country's car makers, the prophets of doom said. It seemed their predictions would turn out to be true when the industry reported single-digit growth in May, after a dream run of three years. But in June, the numbers once again were robust.

Maruti Udyog Ltd. the country's largest car maker, reported a growth of over 25 per cent in sales, up from 9.9 per cent in May. **Jagdish Khattar**, the company's managing director, spoke to *Business Standard* on survival strategies in a tough market. Excerpts:

What Do the June Numbers Suggest?

For the rest of the industry, the growth has come largely from new products in the first three months of this financial year. If you take them out, there has been flat growth. I have never drawn any conclusions from the performance of a new product in the first month. You need to watch it after the first few months when it stabilizes.

If you look at the Maruti numbers, the new models have not contributed much. But we have grown far more than our competitors.

The reason why this happened is that we have strengthened our network and increased manpower. We have made the operations of our dealers more robust and their confidence is high. Insurance and used cars have given them new revenue streams. They are not dependent on the sale of cars alone.

If your new models did not contribute much, where did the growth come from?

Through the dealers, we have sent 1,500 sales executives in rural areas. We have sold over 3,400 cars to members of village panchayats in the last six-eight months.

There are 2.1 million panchayat members and 2,00,000 block pramukhs in the country. It is a huge market. We are networking with regional rural banks for this initiative. Ninety- six of them have branches in 14,000 villages.

So How is it Working?

So far, we have had 21,000 enquiries. Though not all of these will get converted into sales, the initiative is gathering momentum. Once you make the initial penetration in these small towns, future sales become easier.

In the rural areas, the quality of roads has improved quite a lot which, in turn, has improved the possibility of owning a car. We still sell 50-60 per cent in the top 20 cities. But the growth is much higher in other centres.

I tell my people not to look at just the market share for the number of cars sold—they should also look at the opportunity share. There are 60 million two-wheelers on the road. How many of these can we convert to cars? What can we do to see that they can afford to buy our products? For this, we need to keep our costs and services reasonable. Our strategy is to expand the market. We don't wait for the customer to come to our showrooms.

Some time towards the end of May, I told all company employees that the market seemed headed for a soft landing. The option before us was to either reduce the production at the shop floor or get aggressive at the marketplace. We chose the latter option. I told the employees, how about each one of them selling at least one car for the company?

So far, they have got 7,656 referrals, resulting in the sale of 1,937 cars. This helps in another way: these employees also get an idea of what the consumer thinks.

The period from May 15 to June 15 was an inauspicious period for new purchases, according to the Hindu calendar. But we did not slow down our production and built-up our stock. This really helped us when we shut the plant for a week for routine maintenance.

What Difference Did it Make to Your June Sale Numbers?

Between the sales brought in by the employees and our retail initiative, we will get incremental 10 per cent volumes. That will make the difference between 15 per cent growth and 25 per cent growth. The markets are tough. The interest rates are high. Our marketing spend is much higher.

Such initiatives have really helped us in the past. Two years back, we had a special scheme for teachers where we visited 30,000 schools across the country and sold 13,000 cars. We have a scheme for government employees called 'Wheels of India', where we have sold 58,000 cars in the last two years. There is a scheme for insurance companies called 'Premium Wheels', which has helped us sell 9,000 cars. We have sold 2,500 cars in our offer for employees of the railways, the 'First Class' offer.

What Has Been the Impact of Rising Interest Rates?

We have seen a 10 per cent drop in the financing of cars in the last two months.

How Does One Cope with this Situation?

Some manufacturers are subsidizing the additional burden resulting from the higher interest rates. We are giving cash discounts because we feel the customer likes it this way. The bulk of the burden falls on us, though the dealers share a part of it. Our job is to ensure that the profitability of our dealers is maintained at all times.

What IRR Do they Generate?

Our dealers are doing better than those of others.

Till Recently, Maruti was known as an Efficient Producer of only Small Cars? What Does the Success of the SX4 Mean?

The success of the Swift and now the SX4 means that we have made the transition from a small car company to a complete car maker. We will soon have three global products in our portfolio: the Swift, SX4 and Grand Vitara. It will be smaller than what we had launched earlier. So the pricing also will be different. We are producing at 100 per cent capacity, even at our new plant at Manesar where we make the Swift and the SX4.

But How will the Success in the Mid-sized Segment Impact Your Future Strategy?

Nothing is going to change in the market within the next one year. Some distortions will take place when a new model is launched, but India will by and large remain a compact car market. India is fast emerging as a manufacturing hub for small cars. Everybody is talking of making small cars here for their global needs.

Are the Price Points being Talked about by Some Companies for their Small Cars Possible?

Let us see. Good people are thinking along these lines. Anyway, it will be a tremendous boost for the vendors.

The Small Car from Tata Motors Will Come First. How Will that Impact You?

The small car will be purchased by those who cannot afford our car. At the moment, the gap between a two-wheeler and our cheapest car is around Rs. 150,000. With the Rs. 100,000 car, the gap between us and the next alternative will go down.

Maruti Udyog Limited is a publicly listed company in India. It is a leading four-wheeler automobile manufacturer in South Asia. Suzuki Motor Corporation of Japan has the controlling stake in the company. It was the first company in India to mass-produce and sell more than a million cars. It is largely credited for having brought in an automobile revolution to India. To this day it is the market leader in India in its segment.

Profile

The old logo of Maruti Udyog Limited later the logo of Suzuki Motor Corp. was also added to it.

Maruti Udyog Ltd is one of India's leading automobile manufacturers and the market leader in the car segment, both in terms of volume of vehicles sold and revenue earned. Until recently, 18.28% of the company was owned by the Indian government, and 54.2% by Suzuki of Japan. The Indian government held an initial public offering of 25% of the company in June of 2003. As of May 10, 2007, Govt. of India sold its complete share to other financial institutions. With this, Govt. of India no longer has any stake in Maruti Udyog.

Maruti Udyog Limited (MUL) was established in February 1981, though the actual production commenced in 1983. Through 2004, Maruti has produced over 5 million vehicles. **Marutis** are sold in India and various several other countries, depending upon export orders. Cars similar to Marutis (but not manufactured by Maruti Udyog) are sold by Suzuki in Pakistan and other South Asian countries.

The company annually exports more than 30,000 cars and has an extremely large domestic market in India selling over 500,000 cars annually. Maruti 800, till 2004, was the India's largest selling compact car ever since it was launched in 1983. More than a million units of this car have been sold worldwide so far. Currently, Maruti Alto tops the sales charts.

Due to the large number of Maruti 800s sold in the Indian market, the term "Maruti" is commonly used to refer to this compact car model. Till recently the term "Maruti", in popular Indian culture, was associated to the Maruti 800 model.

History

Around 1970, Sanjay Gandhi, political advisor and younger son to the then Prime

Minister of India, Indira Gandhi, envisioned the manufacture of an indigenous, cost-effective, low maintenance compact car for the Indian middle class. Indira Gandhi's cabinet passed a unanimous resolution for the development and production of a "People's Car". Sanjay Gandhi's company was christened Maruti Limited. The name of the car was chosen as "Maruti", after a Hindu deity named Marut.

At that time Hindustan Motors' Ambassador was the chief car, and a new entrant from Premier Automobiles, the Premier Padmini which was slowly gaining a part of the market share dominated by the Ambassador. For the next ten years, the Indian car market had stagnated at a volume of 30,000 to 40,000 cars for the decade ending 1983.

Sanjay Gandhi was awarded the exclusive contract and licence to design, develop and manufacture the "People's Car". This exclusive rights of production generated some criticism in certain quarters, which was directly targeted at Indira Gandhi. Over the next few years, the company was sidelined due to the Bangladesh Liberation War and emergency.

In the early days under the powerful patronage of Sanjay Gandhi, the company was provided with free land, tax breaks and funds. Till the end of 1970s, the company had not started the production and a prototype test model was met with criticism and skepticism. The company went into liquidation in 1977. The media perceived it to be another area of growing corruption. Maruti started to recover only after the death of Sanjay Gandhi, when Suzuki Motors joined the Government of India as a joint venture partner with 50% share.

After his death, Indira Gandhi decided that the project should not be allowed to die. Maruti entered into this collaboration with Suzuki Motors. The collaboration heralded a revolution in the Indian car industry by producing the Maruti 800. The car went on sale on December 14, 1983. It created a record by taking 13 months time to go from design to rolling out cars from a production line. By the year 1993 the company had sold up to 1,96,820 cars, mostly by selling its chief product the Maruti 800s. By March 1994, it produced one million vehicles, becoming the first Indian company to cross this milestone. It reached the two million mark in October, 1997 and rolled out its 4 millionth vehicle, an Alto-LX, on April 19, 2003.

Impact of Maruti Udyog

The introduction of the Maruti 800 in 1983, marked the beginning of a revolution in the Indian automobile industry. Maruti Udyog brought in the latest technology then available, more fuel-efficient cars, and brought down the price of cars in India. This led to the creation of a huge market for all car segments as the Indian middle class grew in size. This in turn brought in more players to this segment. A number of auxiliary car parts making units were setup as most car manufacturers realized it was more cost effective to make their car parts in India rather than import them. Maruti's most major influence was in helping the component industry in the country because of its emphasis on localization and indigenization. As in the beginning that sector hadn't grown much, Maruti had to start a dozen joint ventures with Indian entrepreneurs. It got them foreign collaborations, that led to collaborations for other manufacturers so that over a period of time the whole component industry was able to upgrade itself and improve its quality. Leading to a major existing export potential in vehicle components. It also brought in better methods of financing that allowed more people, who given their income levels could not afford to buy a car on their own. It still remains the leader not only in terms of market share but also in customer satisfaction surveys—it has consistently topped J.D. Power quality surveys, including 2005.

Partner for the Joint Venture

Pressure started mounting on Indira and Sanjay Gandhi to share the details of the progress on the Maruti Project. Since country's resources were made available by mother to her son's pet project. A delegation of Indian technocrats was assigned to hunt a collaborator for the project. Initial rounds of discussion were held with the giants of the automobile industry in Japan including Toyota, Nissan and Honda. Suzuki Motor Corporation was at that time a small player in the four-wheeler automobile sector and had major share in the two-wheeler segment. Suzuki's bid was considered negligible.

In the initial rounds of discussion the giants had their bosses present and in the later rounds related to the technical discussions executives of these automobile giants were present. Osamu Suzuki, Chairman and CEO of the company ensured that he was present in all the rounds of discussion. Osamu in an article writes that it subtly massaged their (Indian delegation) egos and also convinced them about the sincerity of Suzuki's bid. In the initial days, Suzuki took all steps to ensure the government about its sincerity on the project. Suzuki in return received a lot of help from the government in such matters as import clearances for manufacturing equipment (against the wishes of the Indian machine tool industry then and its own socialistic ideology), land purchase at government prices for setting up the factory at Gurgaon and reduced or removal of excise tariffs. This helped Suzuki conscientiously nurse Maruti through its infancy to become one of its flagship ventures.

Joint Venture Related Issues

Relationship between the Government of India, under the United Front (India) coalition and Suzuki Motor Corporation over the joint venture was a point of heated debate in the Indian media till Suzuki Motor Corporation gained the controlling stake. This highly profitable joint venture that had a near monopolistic trade in the Indian automobile market and the nature of the partnership built up till then was the underlying reason for most issues. The success of the joint venture led Suzuki to increase its equity from 26% to 40% in 1987, and further to 50% in 1992. In 1982 both the venture partners had entered into an agreement to nominate their candidate for the post of Managing Director and every Managing Director will have a tenure of five years.

Initially R.C. Bhargava, was the managing director of the company since the inception of the joint venture. Till today, he is regarded as instrumental for the success of Maruti Udyog. Joining in 1982, he held several key positions in the company before heading the company as Managing Director. Currently he is on the Board of Directors. After completing his five-year tenure, Mr. Bhargava later assumed the office of Part-Time

Chairman. The Government nominated Mr. S.S.L.N. Bhaskarudu as the Managing Director on August 27, 1997. Mr. Bhaskarudu had joined Maruti in 1983 after spending 21 years in the Public Sector Undertaking Bharat Heavy Electricals Limited as General Manager. Later in 1987 he was promoted as Chief General Manager, 1998 as Director, Productions and Projects, 1989 Director, Materials and in 1993 as Joint Managing Director.

The Suzuki Motor corporation didn't attend the Annual General Meeting of the Board with the reason of it being called on a short notice. Later Suzuki Motor Corporation went on record to state that Mr. Bhaskarudu was "incompetent" and wanted some one else. However, the Ministry of Industries, Government of India refuted the charges. Media stated from the Maruti sources that Bhaskarudu was interested to indigenize most of components for the models including gearboxes especially for Maruti 800. Suzuki also felt that Bhaskarudu was a proxy for the Government and would not let it increase its stake in the venture. If Maruti would have been able to indigenize gearboxes then Maruti would have been able to manufacture all the models without the technical assistance from Suzuki. Till today, the issue of localization of gearboxes is highlighted in the press.

The relation strained when Suzuki Motor Corporation moved to Delhi High Court to bring a stay order against the appointment of Mr. Bhaskarudu. The then Industries Minister, Murasoli Maran had even offered Suzuki to exit from the venture if they are not interested.

Bhaskarudu's appointment without consulting us violates the spirit of the 1982 pact, which commits the partners to consultations on all major decisions including key appointments.

— Osamu Suzuki, *Chairman, Suzuki Motor Corporation in a press statement over the appointment of Mr. S.S.L.N. Bhaskarudu as the Manging Director.*

The issue was resolved in an out-of-court settlement and both the parties agreed that R S S L N Bhaskarudu would serve up to December 31, 1999, and from January 1, 2000, Jagdish Khattar, Executive Director of Maruti Udyog Limited would assume charges as the Managing Director. Many politicians believed, and had stated in Parliament that the Suzuki Motor Corporation is unwilling to localize manufacturing and reduce imports. This remains true, even today the gearboxes are still imported from Japan and are assembled at the Gurgaon facility.

Disinvestment and Public Listing

The National Democratic Alliance Government headed by Atal Behari Vajpayee passed the resolution on December 22, 2003 to dilute its stake in the venture. Maruti was not a special case, but it was the policy of the government to reduce the public debt by offloading its stake in many public sector companies and joint ventures. The preparations had began much earlier. The Suzuki Motor Corporation suggested the government to offload its stake in the Capital Market. Some believed this was a ploy to gain control of the company at cheap price due to the unhealthy conditions of the capital market.

The red herring prospectus was filed with the Securities and Exchange Board of India on May 2, 2003. The Union Government made an offer of 7.22 crore shares representing 25 per cent of the fully diluted equity state of the Maruti Post offer. After the dilution, the government's stake was reduced to 20.8 and the Suzuki Motor Corporation's stake increased to 54.2 per cent. The remaining equity belonged to institutional and individual investors. As the offer was oversubscribed by the general public, the Government raised the size of the Initial Public Offering by 10 per cent. Investors had submitted bids ranging from Indian rupees 115 to 360 per share. As per Bombay Stock Exchange data, about 69% or 5.83 crore (58.3 million) bids received were for Rs. 120 per share.

The company has 28,89,10,060 shares, As on February 15, 2006 the government stake reduced to 18.28% and the Suzuki Motor Corporation has a stake of 54.21%. As on May 10, 2007 the government sold its complete stake to financial institutions. Currently 71.06% of the equity is held by foreign investors including Suzuki Motor Corporation.

Industrial Relations

For most of its history, Maruti Udyog had relatively few problems with its labour force. Its emphasis of a Japanese work culture and the modern manufacturing process, first instituted in Japan in the 1970s, was accepted by the workforce of the company without any difficulty. But with the change in management in 1997, when it became predominantly government controlled for a while, and the conflict between the United Front Government and Suzuki may have been the cause of unrest among employees. A major row broke out in September 2000 when employees of Maruti Udyog Ltd (MUL) went on an indefinite strike, demanding among other things, revision of the incentive scheme offered and implementation of a pension scheme. Employees struck work for six hours in October 2000, irked over the suspension of nine employees, going on a six-hour tools-down strike at its Gurgaon plant, demanding revision of the incentive-linked pay and threatened to fast to death if the suspended employees were not reinstated. About this time, the NDA government, following a disinvestments policy, proposed to sell part of its stake in Maruti in a public offering. The staff union opposed this sell-off plan on the grounds that the company will lose a major business advantage of being subsidized by the Government.

The standoff with the management continued to December with a proposal by the management to end the two-month long agitation rejected with a demand for reinstatement of 92 dismissed workers, with four MUL employees going on a fast-unto-death. In December the company's shareholders met in New Delhi in an AGM that lasted 30 minutes. At the same time around 1500 plant workers from the MUL's Gurgaon facility were agitating outside the company's corporate office demanding commencement of production linked incentives, a better pension scheme and other benefits. The management has refused to pass on the benefits citing increased competition and lower margins.

The largest selling car from Maruti's stable, **Maruti 800**

In the order they were launched:

- Maruti 800: Launched 1983. Largest selling car in India, till 2004.
- Maruti Omni: Launched 1984.
- Maruti Gypsy: Launched 1985.
- Maruti 1000: Launched 1990
- Maruti Zen: Launched 1993 with a facelift in 2003. Production ended in 2006.
- Maruti Esteem: Launched 1994
- Maruti Wagon-R: Launched 1999 Modified 2006
- Maruti Baleno: Launched 1999. Production ended late 2006/early 2007.
- Maruti Alto: Launched 2000. Currently the largest selling car in India
- Maruti Grand Vitara: Launched 2003
- Maruti Grand Vitara XL-7
- Maruti Versa: Launched 2004
- Maruti Swift: Launched 2005
- Maruti Zen Estilo Launched in 2006
- Maruti Swift Diesel Launched in 2007
- Maruti Suzuki SX4 Launched in May 2007
- Maruti Grand Vitara Sports Utility Vehicle Launched in July 2007

Authorized Service Stations

Maruti is one of the companies in India which has unparalleled service network. To ensure the vehicles sold by them are serviced properly Maruti had 1545 listed authorized service stations and 30 Express Service Stations on 30 highways across India.

Service is a major revenue generator of the company. Most of the service stations are managed on franchise basis, where Maruti trains the local staff. Other automobile companies have not been able to match this benchmark set by Maruti. The Express Service stations help many stranded vehicles on the highways by sending across their repair man to the vehicle.

Maruti Insurance

Launched in 2002 Maruti provides vehicle insurance to its customers with the help of the National Insurance Company, Bajaj Allianz, New India Assurance and Royal Sundaram. The service was set up with the inception of two subsidiaries Maruti Insurance Distributors Services Pvt. Ltd. and Maruti Insurance Brokers Pvt. Limited.

This service started as a benefit or value addition to customers and was able to ramp up easily. By December 2005 they were able to sell more than two million insurance policies since its inception.

Maruti Finance

To promote its bottom line growth, Maruti launched Maruti Finance in January 2002. Prior to the start of this service Maruti had started two joint ventures Citicorp Maruti and Maruti Countrywide with Citi Group and GE Countrywide respectively to assist its client in securing loan. Maruti tied up with ABN Amro Bank, HDFC Bank, ICICI

Limited, Kotak Mahindra, Standard Chartered Bank, and Sundaram to start this venture including its strategic partners in car finance. Again the company entered into a strategic partnership with SBI in March 2003 Since March 2003, Maruti has sold over 12,000 vehicles through SBI-Maruti Finance. SBI-Maruti Finance is currently available in 166 cities across India.

"Maruti Finance marks the coming together of the biggest players in the car finance business. They are the benchmarks in quality and efficiency. Combined with Maruti volumes and networked dealerships, this will enable Maruti Finance to offer superior service and competitive rates in the marketplace".

– **Jagdish Khattar**, *Managing Director of Maruti Udyog Limited in a press conference announcing the launch of Maruti Finance on January 7, 2002.*

Citicorp Maruti Finance Limited is a joint venture between Citicorp Finance India and Maruti Udyog Limited its primary business stated by the company is "hire-purchase financing of Maruti vehicles". Citi Finance India Limited is a wholly owned subsidiary of Citibank Overseas Investment Corporation, Delaware, which in turn is a 100% wholly owned subsidiary of Citibank N.A. Citi Finance India Limited holds 74% of the stake and Maruti Udyog holds the remaining 26%. GE Capital, HDFC and Maruti Udyog Limited came together in 1995 to form Maruti Countrywide. Maruti claims that its finance programme offers most competitive interest rates to its customers, which are lower by 0.25% to 0.5% from the market rates.

Maruti True Value

Maruti True Value is a service offered by Maruti Udyog to its customers. It is a market place for used Maruti vehicles. One can buy, sell or exchange used Maruti vehicles with the help of this service in India.

N2N Fleet Management

N2N is the short form of **End to End Fleet Management** and provides lease and fleet management solution to corporates. Its impressive list of clients who have signed up of this service include Gas Authority of India Ltd., DuPont, Reckitt Benckiser, Sona Steering, Doordarshan, Singer India, National Stock Exchange and Transworld. This fleet management service includes end-to-end solutions across the vehicle's life, which includes leasing, maintenance, convenience services and Remarketing.

Accessories

Many of the auto component companies other than Maruti Udyog started to offer components and accessories that were compatible. This caused a serious threat and loss of revenue to Maruti. Maruti started a new initiative under the brand name **Maruti Genuine Accessories** to offer accessories like alloy wheels, body cover, carpets, door visors, fog lamps, stereosystems, seat covers and other car care products. These products are sold through dealer outlets and authorized service stations throughout India.

Maruti Driving School

As part of its corporate social responsibility, Maruti Udyog launched the Maruti Driving School in Delhi. Later the services were extended to other citites of India as well. These schools are modelled on international standards, where learners go through classroom and practical sessions. Many international practices like road behaviour and attitudes are also taught in these schools. Before driving actual vehicles participants are trained on simulators.

"We are very concerned about mounting deaths on Indian roads. These can be brought down if government, industry and the voluntary sector work together in an integrated manner. But we felt that Maruti should first do something in this regard and hence this initiative of Maruti Driving Schools."

— **Jagdish Khattar**, *at the launch ceremony of Maruti Driving School, Bengaluru*

Exports

Maruti Exports Limited is the subsidiary of Maruti Udyog Limited with its major focus on exports and it does not operate in the domestic Indian market. The first commercial consignment of 480 cars were sent to Hungary. By sending a consignment of 571 cars to the same country Maruti crossed the benchmark of 3,00,000 cars. Since its inception export was one of the aspects government was keen to encourage. Every political party expected Maruti to earn foreign currency.

Angola, Benin, Djibouti, Ethiopia, Europe, Kenya, Morocco, Sri Lanka, Uganda, Chile, Guatemala, Costa Rica and El Salvador are some of the markets served by Maruti Exports.

Key Competitors

- Tata Motors
- Hyundai India
- Ford India
- FIAT India
- General Motors India
- Honda India

Task for the Students

Organize a SWOT Analysis. What lessons new consumer durable companies can take from Maruti?

Index